More praise for *Becoming Ella*

"*Becoming Ella Fitzgerald* is a treasure—a comprehensive, deeply researched, and documented biography that finally gives Ella the complexity and depth that she deserves. Placing Fitzgerald in the intersection of race and gender at mid-twentieth century and overturning often repeated half-truths about her life and career, Judith Tick highlights the beauty and artistry of Fitzgerald's voice and the full range of her genre-crossing career. *Becoming Ella Fitzgerald* is essential reading for anyone interested in Ella, jazz, or American popular culture."

—Ingrid Monson, author of *Freedom Sounds: Civil Rights Call Out to Jazz and Africa*

"Today the searchable digital archive has remapped the horizons of biography, rendering once-definitive works incomplete and ready for revision. Judith Tick's plunge into Ella Fitzgerald has disinterred veins of uncharted documentation, particularly in the Black and trade press, unseen by previous researchers. She exposes speculation, fills fissures with fact, and finds a fresh feminist heroine of transformative authority."

—John McDonough, senior contributor, *Down Beat*

"More than a decade in the making, Judith Tick's *Becoming Ella Fitzgerald* is a biography truly worthy of the 'First Lady of Song.' Combining groundbreaking research, new details on her beloved recordings, and compelling insights into her offstage persona, Tick has produced a work that will be a touchstone for Fitzgerald's legion of fans, past, present, and future." **—Ricky Riccardi, Grammy-winning author of *What a Wonderful World* and *Heart Full of Rhythm***

"Judith Tick's much-needed updated biography uses new research and keen musicology, and brings forth a revealing and fully convincing portrait of Lady Ella as visionary, social activist, and still-modern singer."

—John Szwed, author of *Billie Holiday: The Musician and the Myth*

BECOMING
ELLA
FITZGERALD

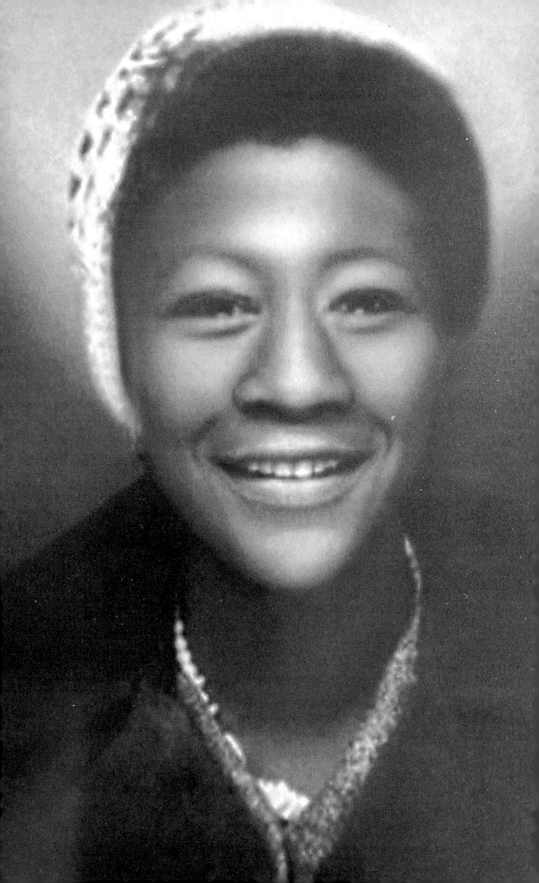

BECOMING ELLA FITZGERALD

The Jazz Singer Who Transformed American Song

JUDITH TICK

W. W. NORTON & COMPANY
Celebrating a Century of Independent Publishing

To Stephen and our daughters, Allison and Erica, and our grandchildren, Liv, Aria, and Ella; and to the extended Ella Fitzgerald family of Jim Blackman and Tad Hershorn.

CONTENTS

INTRODUCTION

When my mother, Miriam Tick, was eighty-eight years old, she told me about her silver slippers. As a teenager, she wore them when she and her cousin Irving went dancing at the Roseland Ballroom in Boston. (She cried when she mentioned him because he was killed in the war in 1944.) Silver slippers announced to boys who might ask her to dance that they had to keep up. Sometimes she went to the Spanish Gables dance hall in Revere Beach, a town a few miles north from her home: "I heard Chick Webb there, even before Ella. He was great." She said their names like they lived next door. She was born in 1918 and Ella was born in 1917, so they belonged to the same generation.

My mother told me this story in 2007, knowing that I was planning to write a book about Ella Fitzgerald's musical odyssey. She died the following year, five years before I signed a book contract. I received this story as an unexpected and touching confirmation of her devotion to Ella Fitzgerald, which had filled our home with her music.

Thirty-three rpm LP albums were stacked upright like books on the shelf below the hi-fi record player that sat on the console in our living room, where popular music reigned supreme. And Ella Fitzgerald was always front and center. Indeed, when my father died in 2004, my brother delivered an alphabetical eulogy that included the words "E is for Ella." In

1956, when I was thirteen, I memorized the double LP *Ella Fitzgerald Sings the Cole Porter Song Book*. At the time, I had no way of knowing that this seminal album would be the first of eight similarly assembled Fitzgerald *Song Book* collections, each one curated with sophisticated cultural values, including the long verses to ballads and rediscovered esoteric gems. While I was just another listener, inhaling the lofty beauty of Fitzgerald's voice, I was also a teenager who adored the radical songs she sang with their aspirational lines of bravado. "As Dorothy Parker once said to her boyfriend, 'fare thee well,'" Ella blithely sings in "Just One of Those Things." I quickly found a favorite line in Porter's comic subversive "Let's Do It" verse: "People say in Boston even beans do it."

Then in 1960 I brought my piano-vocal selections book of Cole Porter songs to Smith College, a single-sex institution in western Massachusetts where I was simultaneously introduced to the complexities of music and feminism. In a former working-class Victorian rooming house turned into a dormitory for twenty-five white girls, many times after dinner we gathered around the upright parlor piano and sang Porter's ballads and novelty songs. I heard Ella's thrilling pure vinyl voice in my ears when we sang the line "Every time we say goodbye, I die a little." I played the accompaniment at the piano in a tempo worthy of high tragedy. I did not know the phrase *torch song*. When we'd exhausted the Porter canon, we'd move on to George and Ira Gershwin, or Rodgers and Hart, or Irving Berlin, our choices no doubt influenced by the other *Song Books* that Fitzgerald had recorded by that time.

My fond girlhood memories of Ella Fitzgerald would inspire a more personal—and decidedly ambitious—pursuit in 2010, when I read an interview with Fitzgerald in which she explained how those *Song Books* I used to listen to—recorded two decades into what was already a thriving career—had marked a significant transformation in her artistry.

> In the Fifties I started singing with a different kind of style . . . picking out songwriters and singing their songs. Cole Porter was the first. It was like beginning all over again. People who never heard me suddenly heard songs which surprised them because they didn't

think I could sing them. People always figure you could only do one thing. It was like another education.[1]

Those consequential *Song Books* represented a before-and-after demarcation in the long and colorful arc of Ella Fitzgerald's career. They suggested the ideas of "becoming" and "transformation" as potential themes for a book. For twenty years or so before they were recorded (roughly from 1935 to 1955), Fitzgerald had established herself as a quintessential jazz singer.

She had started out as an impoverished young girl from Yonkers, who would later describe her boots as camouflage for her skinny legs. She achieved recognition through an amateur night contest at the Apollo Theatre at age seventeen and then in February 1935 got a real job through a week-long engagement at the Harlem Opera House. After being signed by Chick Webb, who initially said, "I don't want no *girl* singer," she began to transform the role of "girl singer" into a position of leadership. Her success at the microphone transformed not only her career but also the status of other female vocalists throughout the music business.

Before Fitzgerald, girl singers were typically relegated to a single chorus of a song; following Ella's example, the "canaries"—as the girls were called—flew higher, especially after Fitzgerald's swinging rendition of a classic children's nursery rhyme, "A-Tisket A-Tasket," became a global hit in 1938. Yet management dressed her up in schoolgirl clothes, boxing her into an image that overstated her innocence and compromised the achievements of a budding artist and innovator. Nevertheless, Fitzgerald's drive to break new musical ground won the day as she programmed more adult fare into her act: after Webb died in 1939, she became the official conductor of the orchestra. In 1940 she said, "I used to sing nothing but jittery stuff but now everybody likes me to sing sweet songs, so I give 'em a little of each."[2]

Fitzgerald's sweet and jittery musical transformations kept coming. In the mid-1940s she swerved into improvisational bebop as her personal avenue for change, digging deeper into scat and inventing complex fantasias on single tunes almost at will. Her phonographic memory allowed her to become a one-woman jam session. "That's what gave us females permission to dig in and do some improvising ourselves," said Betty Carter, a sister improviser. "It was no longer a man's world."[3] She treasured her stylistic breadth. "What is the Ella Fitzgerald style today?" *Ebony* magazine asked in 1949.[4] In the 1950s, touring as a member of the popular Jazz at the Philharmonic (JATP) ensemble, Ella joined a troupe of soloists, seizing the stage and announcing her arrival as a vocalist of astonishing agility. As keyboard legend Oscar Peterson recalled in his 2002 memoir, in the joint finales of a JATP concert, competing with the horns, she gave no concessions, she played "rough": at one of these performances, tenor saxophonist Lester Young turned to Peterson and said, "You stay out there long enough and Lady Fitz will lay waste to your ass!"[5]

And yet her soaring popularity notwithstanding, it was with those *Song Books* that Ella surpassed even herself, performing an artistic feat that would have been remarkable if attained by any artist, let alone a Black woman. She transformed the culture of an entire repertoire, deftly infusing with swing the sophisticated show tunes from the golden age of Broadway musicals from the 1920s and '30s—shows that had left their mark on the Great White Way, an apt nickname for a cultural institution that had routinely excluded Black artists from its stages. Through those eight *Song Book* albums, Fitzgerald dominated a category of standards, recording more than 250 of them.[6] What lent the *Song Books* special authority was the way they enabled Fitzgerald to ignite a double transformation: by reinventing herself as a singer, she transformed a vintage repertoire; and by modernizing it, she laid the foundational stones for what would soon be known as the Great American Songbook. One transformation begat another.

In the wake of her *Song Books* breakthrough, Ella enjoyed worldwide acclaim—not just as a popular singer whose appeal easily crossed geographical and cultural borders, but also as a classical artist who provided a creative paradigmatic model for others, especially for the female singers populating the field, and even more especially for African American artists.

This brings me to the title of this book, *Becoming Ella Fitzgerald*. Over the course of my research, my purpose underwent its own transformation. When I initially conceived the title *Becoming Ella*, I thought that the *Song Books* had vaulted Fitzgerald into that rare sorority of single-named artists. But that premise changed when I realized that, prior to the *Song Books*, she had already been "Ella" among Black Americans and the jazz world. Between 1933 and 1950, she performed mainly but not exclusively for Black audiences in ballrooms and then in Black theaters (in "colored show business," as it was widely known during the Jim Crow era), then moved into jazz clubs catering mostly (but not exclusively) to white audiences in the latter part of that era. The same model of diversity applied in her post–*Song Book* decades. In the 1960s, she continued her artistic evolution as she perfected the hybrid idiom of jazz-pop, experimenting with adaptations of soul while also deliberately engaging with a new generation of songwriters whose work she believed deserved the appellation "standards." She insisted on reaching out to younger audiences, her lifeline to relevance. "I'm not going to be left behind," she said throughout the decades. "If you don't learn new songs, you're lost. I want to stay with it. And staying with it means communicating with the teenagers. I want them to understand me and like me."[7] Across her entire career, the artist was *always* "becoming Ella Fitzgerald."

Though her trajectory made her a "mixed singer," as she once described herself, she flourished in collaboration with the great jazz instrumentalists of her era. In this stretch of her career, in the late 1960s Fitzgerald reached a peak of excellence touring with Duke Ellington, pushing many of his lesser-known songs into the jazz playbook. (Her stature as the foremost interpreter of Ellington's vocal repertoire is only now, in the twenty-first century, being fully appreciated.) When age changed her voice in the 1970s, her decades of cumulative interpretive wisdom allowed her to adapt and innovate through new collaborations, particularly with Count Basie and the guitarist Joe Pass.

Becoming Ella Fitzgerald thus chronicles a continuum of self-invention and resistance to a "category," to use Duke Ellington's favorite term.

She embraced hybridity. Diversity became her core identity, and surprise the wings of her imagination. Over a remarkably long career of sixty years or so, she fearlessly explored many different styles of American song through the lens of African American jazz. She treated jazz as process, not confined to this idiom or that genre. And through her own transformative quests as an artist, she changed the trajectory of American vocal jazz in this century.

★ ★ ★

A BIOGRAPHY REFLECTS its moment in time, and in writing this one, I pose questions and emphasize certain time periods, from the vantage point of the early twenty-first century, guided by my own scholarly priorities. Since I did not write this book during Fitzgerald's lifetime, I did not encounter the frustrating "lack of access" problem that previous biographers faced—either from Ella Fitzgerald herself, or from the business policies of her "office" in Los Angeles, or from friends who were thwarted from their own interviews. Instead, I was able to take advantage of modern resources in an effort to craft new scholarship on Fitzgerald, shining a light primarily on three neglected aspects of her life and work.

My focus on the early part of her career emerged as a response to a new era of documentation through new technology of both recorded sound and print. The digitization of newspapers in the United States and in some European countries as well has made accounts of her successes and failures outside New York accessible. Although subjected to many paywall restrictions, newspapers from France, Germany, and Denmark yielded new interviews with Fitzgerald. Regional newspapers in the United States broadened my understanding of the nature of her reception at home. I was especially fortunate to have access to the extensive coverage that Fitzgerald's career received for a national Black readership through widely circulated African American newspapers. Among these important newspapers and journals were the *Pittsburgh Courier* and the *Chicago Defender*, both of which enjoyed national circulation; both were digitized around 2010. Their extensive coverage of entertainment provided a rich fount of new information about Fitzgerald's evolution in the 1930s and '40s. These sources serve as the foundation for the first three sections of this book.

Of course, part of the editorial mission of the Black press was to document racism in its full ignominy. As a white American, such racism was a part of my history and my present; the civil rights revolution took place in my lifetime. As a music historian, I also knew how the history of American song reflected the mores of each era, promoting them but also confounding them as well. Sometimes the documents of everyday life captured painful truths and astonishing assumptions. In 2004 I read the diary of a Southern white woman in 1858, who wrote, "One of my friends owned a real African princess. She must have been over a hundred when I knew her. . . . We dearly loved her songs, which were African ones, thrown into rough English by herself."[8] Then followed decades of racist song and stereotypes familiar to American music historians. One hundred years later, in 1958, here was Ella Fitzgerald, the "First Lady of Song," accepting a Grammy Award. Offering a rich counterpoint to the sunnier mainstream coverage of her recording activities at Decca, the Black press offered an overview of the cruel prejudice Fitzgerald had endured during tours outside the urban North. To those carefully tracking her ascension as a star, she was a community asset—a "race woman" as a symbol of excellence, one of the "heroines of our history," in the words of Coretta Scott King in 1988.[9]

Black newspapers put within my scholarly grasp a way to begin to fill a void in the literature about Fitzgerald's career. Lacking lived experience within a Black community, I took advantage of the access these new sources gave me to a world unknown to most white Americans at the time—the reportage of everyday life along with pride in excellence and in honors and benchmarks of achievement as sources of hope that sustained "keeping on." Newspaper interviews with Fitzgerald, previously largely hidden from view, offered new insights into her early life in Yonkers and her thoughts at the start of her career. These precious resources helped shape my view of Ella's ambitions, bringing into focus, among other things, her role in the Black community during these years. Those interviews in the Black press enabled me to let Ella speak for herself.

In writing this biography, I also relied on my own career as a second-wave feminist music historian who contributed to the development of women's history in Western classical music and in American musical life. I had provided entries in new encyclopedias willing to cede space to topics about women in the wake of the women's movement of the 1970s and '80s. I had been engaged in chronicling the prejudice and discrimination that had burdened the creative autonomy of white women in nineteenth-century United States: socialized into dilettante roles through learning music as an "accomplishment"; discouraged from serious training; excluded from orchestras; crippled in access to instrumental education by the false "masculine" or "feminine" designations of certain instruments; ambition stigmatized as "showing off." Perceiving and chronicling these themes were already part of my toolbox as a historian.[10] Therefore I gravitated toward "Jane Crow," a term popularized by the Black civil rights lawyer and feminist activist Pauli Murray, who in 1964 wrote, "Negro women, historically, have carried the dual burden of Jim Crow and Jane Crow." Murray, whose work would influence Supreme Court justice Ruth Bader Ginsburg, used this formulation to describe the dual burden of sex discrimination and racial prejudice. She was building on a still-emerging history of Black women in the United States, from which I benefited as well.

I took one piece of this perspective to address Fitzgerald's experience. As a female African American jazz singer, Fitzgerald was all too familiar with both Jim and Jane. Columns and interviews by early Black female reporters and journalists amplify the picture of Fitzgerald's appeal to women in particular who were invested in her success. In her historic 1937 interview with Lillian Johnson, Fitzgerald, then just twenty years old, summarized her then-greatest challenge: the "public likes beauty" but "when a girl comes up and she looks like me, she just can't get a chance."[11] Over her lifetime, she challenged those conventions through different strategies, variously embracing glamour and telling self-deprecating jokes onstage, accepting that her phrase "I'm just me" was more than enough.

My second focus is on Fitzgerald's private life. Through archival genealogical research and interviews with relatives, friends, and close associates, I assembled new factual documentation regarding her nuclear and extended family. A new death date for her mother resolved some of the discrepancies in Fitzgerald's own accounts of her life. New information about her stepfather, Antonio Correy, and her half-sister Frances Correy explains the many young children who lived with her in the 1960s and '70s. Fitzgerald's role as "Auntie" helped ameliorate the absence of a steady partner in her later years. While she experienced ambivalence about her career, she did not change her habits of touring and living on the road. In tempering the image of her as a lonely, unhappily bereft single woman, I cite her personal selection of songs, and on occasion, even her changes in lyrics to reflect the woman inside the singer. She was honest enough to include the Burt Bacharach–Hal David ballad "A House Is Not a Home" to her repertoire, both onstage and in recordings, even at times adding her own words "without a man." Offstage, she accepted her unmarried state as a product of her nomadic lifestyle, along with the solitude and sometimes loneliness that fit her own sense of privacy. Besides, there were all those children making noise in her mansion.

Like many who knew Fitzgerald, Oscar Peterson gestured to the psychological barriers she erected between herself and the public, calling her "innately shy and insecure, a very private person who remained somewhat enigmatic even to her closest friends." And yet Peterson knew her as a musician far better than most. He offered remarkable insight into her competitiveness, power, and "imperturbable musical confidence" and the way she used her robust professional personality to prop up the less anchored woman inside.[12] In that vein, I developed a perspective on Fitzgerald's improvisations linking musical practice with lived experience. Through new scholarship from jazz experts, I learned how Ella forged personal connections by "talking" to other musicians onstage—whether they were physically there or not—that is, by quoting them in her improvisations. Hearing them, feeling their presence, and speaking to them as connoisseurs while pleasing the amateurs with obvious shout-outs to popular songs were all part of a calculated language through which she remained connected to her beloved community of "musicians," as she called the instrumentalists she so admired, and whose superior stature in the hierarchy of jazz she accepted.[13] Her practice of transforming her conversations into brilliant, often playful competitive dialogues began early in her career and continued to the end, displayed in live recordings.

I also have questioned the prevailing stereotype of Fitzgerald as an artist who ceded control of her artistic practices to Norman Granz, the producer and manager who brilliantly guided the second half of her career. They forged a historic partnership to be sure. I do not doubt the veracity of musicians who called him a Svengali, a puppet-master pulling the strings of his acolyte. She rarely challenged him in public. Yet my approach to his influence is more skeptical. In Fitzgerald's lifetime, when he was asked "How articulate is she about her music, her relationship, herself?" he was quoted as replying "Not at all."[14] I'd argue that another real response to that question is "More than Granz was willing to grant"—and through both her words and her music, I show how Fitzgerald, in fact, established her own agency. "He instilled in me confidence," she told a columnist for the *Pittsburgh Courier* in 1962.[15] And that confidence transformed her artistry beyond Granz's reach.

The third aspect of Fitzgerald's legacy that I explore in depth is the intellectual context of her reception as an artist. Although for decades critics have taken for granted that vocal jazz was expendable in jazz history, I welcomed the change of perspective I encountered from younger music and cultural historians in the early twenty-first century.[16] I was surprised to discover the extent to which Fitzgerald's stature as a jazz singer had been the subject of considerable controversy during her lifetime. Even as she earned accolades from jazz critics from the mid-1930s through the mid-1950s, thereafter she became the focal point of aesthetic debates about her artistry.

In 1961 Fitzgerald said, "I've heard where music critics say I'm not just a jazz singer anymore. But we all try to grow and improve. What is jazz, anyhow? I don't know. To me jazz is music."[17] Critics charged her with indifference to the lyrics she sang, a lack of emotional intelligence, a glib virtuosity, and a penchant for commercial opportunism. They noted the overplayed clichés leveled at Fitzgerald in discussions of her artistry—about her "innocence," her "natural" ability (as opposed to learned craft), and her "little-girl" persona onstage.[18] In my assessment, these debates are by-products of the void left by the still-undocumented history of vocal jazz and its acknowledged second-class status within jazz history.

This void demanded my attention. As a music scholar and a feminist, I felt personally challenged to fill it, to look at the ways patterns of gender bias in earlier American music were echoed in post-1950s jazz. This has enabled me to question the reductive oppositions between popular singing and jazz singing, between Billie Holiday and Ella, and between art and entertainment. The ebb and flow of commentary around Fitzgerald's music-making has a "fascinating rhythm" of its own, to quote her admirer Ira Gershwin, leading me to include many reviews of records and live dates in this book. The "conversations" between Fitzgerald and her listeners via recording, and the experience of seeing her onstage, tell a story all their own.

★ ★ ★

AROUND 2015 ELLA FITZGERALD'S SON, Ray Brown, Jr., said to me, "My mother was all about the audience." At first, the comment seemed a stock phrase, one that could be attributed to any performer, whether a Las Vegas headliner or street-corner busker. And yet the more I wrapped myself in the life and music of this peerless artist—her grit and grace, her raw power and refined elegance, her commercial savvy and artistic genius—the more I returned to her son's words. From her first performance to her last, Ella Fitzgerald had a pact with her audience. As she aged, she refined that pact into a mission to use music for social harmony, to turn an audience into a family, and to create a community. "When Ella sings, when she moves on stage, it's like learning how to live," wrote a journalist in San Juan, Puerto Rico, in 1973.[19] That was the point, as Ella Fitzgerald said in 1985, when she was sixty-eight. Explaining herself to another reporter, she fused the artist and the woman. "I want to make you feel happy," she said. "I want you to feel that you're enjoying what I am doing. I want you to feel love, just like you were loving a person, not just because [I'm] a singer."[20]

Her onetime road manager painted for me a scene he routinely encountered. Pacing nervously backstage, twisting her signature handkerchief, waiting to go on and sing before a crowd ranging anywhere from 300 to 12,000, Ella would review her setlist. *Are there enough offerings on the menu to satisfy everyone? Am I going to forget someone's favorite song? Are all the seats filled?* And then after the show, new questions would arise. *Did they like me? Did you see that person in the balcony who fell asleep? Was I okay? If not, whose fault was it?* No matter. There would be another day, another concert, another hall, another city, another country, another continent—another audience with whom she could perfect her genius.

BECOMING
ELLA
FITZGERALD

Chapter 1

YOUNG ELLA

(1917-1932)

O
n June 27, 1992, in Hampton Roads, a small city located within the expansive tidal coast of ocean, ports, and beaches in south-eastern Virginia, 8,332 people sat in the air-conditioned Hampton Coliseum on a Saturday night to hear seventy-five-year-old Ella Fitzgerald give one of the last concerts of her six-decade-long career.[1] Because she had been born in Newport News, about eight miles away, she was billed as the honorary headliner of the Hampton Jazz Festival's twenty-fifth anniversary concert. What had begun as a local event, honoring the centennial of the Hampton Institute, a historically Black college, in 1968, had left its mark on the region in the decades since. In June 1992 Ray Charles and Aretha Franklin came and went on the Friday night.[2] Then on that hot humid Saturday morning, people began lining up for tickets to see Ella. "One Fitzgerald fan brought a huge basket of yellow flowers and asked they be delivered backstage," paying tribute to the whimsical novelty song that had made her a star fifty-four years earlier.[3]

Now, courtesy of the screens projecting her image above the stage, even folks in the upper reaches of the arena could see the frail elderly woman make her way to the stool. There she sat for an hour delivering her set; partially sighted, she had asked that no flash cameras be used because they disturbed her fragile eyes.[4] "She proceeded to sing as if she was eighteen," said the festival organizer, John Scott. A newspaper reviewer wrote, "Ella Fitzgerald got the most robust applause of the weekend."[5]

At the festival, people from Newport News pressed their claims of having special ties to Fitzgerald. Denizens of her old neighborhood gave her a plaque listing her accomplishments.[6] She had few memories of her early years, finding a diplomatic way to stay "admirably honest," a reporter wrote.[7] Earlier that year she had told an interviewer, "I know nothing of Newport News."[8] Now she softened that statement through a family reference. "I'm just so proud to have passed through Virginia. I was a little bitty baby here. My mother was the real representative here, and so I'd like to accept this [honor] for her. If she was alive, she'd be so so proud."[9]

★★★

Ella spent the first three and perhaps four years of her life in Newport News, the early years that few of us remember but that matter so

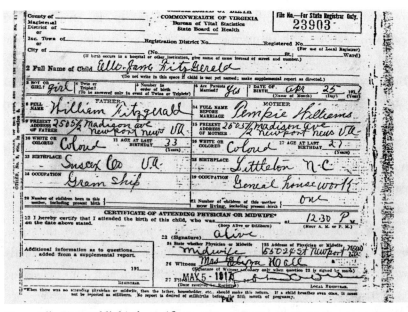

Fig. 1. Ella Fitzgerald's birth certificate. *Office of Vital Records, Virginia Department of Health.*

much. Born on April 25, 1917, she was delivered at home by a midwife to Tempie Williams, age twenty-one, and William Fitzgerald, thirty-three.[10] Both parents came of age between 1890 and 1920, in the nadir of African American history, when white supremacy reasserted its power politically through disenfranchisement of Black voters, socially through segregation, and economically through racialized capitalism. Ella's parents were on the move in the Great Migration of African Americans leaving the rural South. Tempie was born in Littleton, North Carolina, on June 10, 1895.[11] (See Fig. 1.) The scant documentary evidence for William Fitzgerald places him in Sussex County, a land of peanut and tobacco plantations in south-central Virginia. Exactly when they arrived in Newport News is not known, but they fit the trend of urbanization at the turn of the century, leaving rural life for cities with industry, not necessarily heading north right away. Newport News boasted itself as a place that "combines the highest traditions and historical associations of the 'Old South' of song and story with the industrial development and progress that characterizes the 'New South.'"[12]

After the United States entered World War I on April 6, 1917, work was plentiful and prosperity peaked. The government designated Newport News as a "port of embarkation" for thousands of soldiers and sailors who were shipped overseas. William worked as a longshoreman, a job classified as "skilled labor," for the H. B. Stevedore Company, driving a "transfer wagon," hauling grain to store in the massive silos that dotted the nearby landscape.[13] The city's Shipbuilding and Dry Dock Company was touted by its president, Homer Ferguson, as "the largest employer of skilled Negro labor in the world," and it promised equal pay for equal work at a time when that was unheard of.[14] As for Tempie Fitzgerald, she most likely benefited from the wartime boom as well. She entered the rank and file of Southern Black women workers who typically entered a household to become "help" between ten and sixteen years of age, then remained there for the rest of their lives.[15] The going pay rate was typically six or seven dollars per week. As Ella's birth certificate confirms, Tempie did "general housework." She "worked out" rather than "in place" (to use common expressions of the time), meaning she lived in her own home, not in someone else's.

By happenstance, a local historian and writer for the Newport News *Daily Press*, Park Rouse, Jr., had some contact with Tempie Fitzgerald's employers. Many years later, writing in a column, he offered anecdotes with credible detail: "Nearly every family had a black cook, who came and went by the street cars which ran along Virginia Avenue to Hilton [the upper-class neighborhood]. Mrs. George Walker Pierce's cook brought to work her small daughter, Ella, who played outdoors with my brother Dashiell in his preschool years. Who could have guessed that girl would grow up to be Ella Fitzgerald?"[16] In another column, he wrote that Ella "played sometimes with other neighborhood white children [including Rouse's brother], but she was conscious of the color barrier, which was then strong."[17] While we do not know exactly what Rouse meant, he was evoking the world into which she was born, through a theme so common that it became the subject of a popular "coon song," marketing racist slurs and stereotypes in blackface minstrel fare: "Now honey, yo' stay in yo' own back yard, / Doan min' what dem white chiles do."[18]

At the end of each day, Tempie took her daughter home to their own world. Black settlement in Newport News had already produced "a splendid colored section with excellent houses, well arranged, and a very self-respecting population," in Ferguson's words.[19] Ella's family, however, lived in the "close-packed shanty area of Eighteenth Street and Jefferson Avenue."[20] Still, their flat at 2505½ Madison Avenue near 25th Street put them near the main business and social thoroughfare.[21] They would have had easy access to businesses, including two Black-owned banks and a theater that was a stop on a vaudeville circuit recently organized by an enterprising Black businessman. Ma Rainey came to town in 1916.[22] Other kinds of music-making, like the Newport News Brass Band, abounded for the thousands of troops in town.[23] Nathaniel Dett, the idealistic conductor of the Hampton Institute choir, gave many concerts featuring his mixed repertoire of European classics along with spirituals.[24]

After the Armistice of November 1918, Newport News's economy went into a recession. Its population had grown from about 20,000

in 1910 to 35,000 in 1920, and during the war boom, population pro-
jections had climbed to over 100,000, but over the next two years
the shipyard's workforce shrank from about 14,000 to 2,200.[25] The
Daily Press ran a story in 1921 about the surplus of servants.[26] Providing education and health care for Black people sank lower in the
town's priorities. A municipal report in 1919 stated that only two of
the city's eight schools were reserved for Black children. Beyond that,
they would have no access to education until 1924, when the first high
school was built.[27]

In the 1920 Census, Tempie and William were still together, Ella was
two and a half years old, and they were all labeled "mulatto" (mixed
race). At some point after that, Ella's parents separated. No further trace
of William Fitzgerald remains in her family history. He left only his
name to his daughter, who later said she did not remember him and did
not even know if he was alive. Only a fleeting memory offers the detail
that William had played the guitar.[28]

★★★

TEMPIE FITZGERALD FOUND A NEW MAN to share her life: Antonio Correia Borges, a Portuguese immigrant from the island colony of Cabo
Verde. He was roughly her age, described as "black" when he arrived in
Bridgeport, Connecticut, in 1917 by ship. A year later he registered with
that city's draft board, suggesting that he had become a citizen.[29] He and
Tempie met in Newport News, and sometime between 1921 and 1923,
they headed north for Yonkers, New York, where he had relatives and
friends in the Portuguese immigrant community. What a change for
Tempie, a Southern woman: she left a large Black community of about
14,000, or 40 percent of the population of about 35,000, to move to a
city where a tiny minority of African Americans made up only about 2
percent or 2,000 people or so, in city numbering around 100,000.[30] How
would this family find their place in such an environment?

Ella Fitzgerald spent her formative years through 1934 or so living
in Yonkers, sometimes succeeding and at other times being undone

by the city's many contradictions. Yonkers had two distinct sides. One was a trolley-car suburb of Manhattan, with an upper-middle class of white professionals who owned single-family homes and "commuted" to work about forty years before that term entered social conversation. This side of Yonkers, on the east bank of the Hudson River, was prosperous. Hilly tree-studded terrain sloped down to the shoreline, providing vantage points from which to watch sunsets along the New Jersey Palisades on the other bank.

Ella's family, like most of the Black population, lived on the other side of Yonkers, a highly industrialized section, which since the mid-1800s had been drawing on immigrant labor (mainly Irish, German, and Italian) to service its factories and port shipping. That trend had only accelerated in the early 1900s during the "great wave" of European migration between 1880 and World War I. From 1900 to 1910, Yonkers's population doubled as immigrants from Poland, Hungary, and Portugal settled in the poorest section, close to the Hudson River and the railroad tracks. The better jobs were reserved for those immigrants, who were on their way to assimilating as "white" people, while the Black population settled for the worst-paying, least-skilled jobs in a "split labor market" controlled by racial restrictions.[31] Antonio Correa Borges, who was probably still learning English, was a "laborer," a ditch digger, and as his stepdaughter said, a man who "tried to be a chauffeur at night."[32] Tempie became the reliable breadwinner. Both in Yonkers and in neighboring New Rochelle, she worked in commercial laundries, a burgeoning industry. As an extension of "women's work" within the home, commercial laundries typically hired women, especially Black women, because they paid them less. In an economy that exploited American female workers and Black female workers in particular, Tempie stood at the "cusp of a new era, the onset of an era for the 'New Negro woman,'" in the words of the historian Paula Giddings, "making gains in controlling their own lives and in their roles as wives and mothers."[33]

Ella grew up in the poorest section of the city along with the immigrant populace on a crowded street with brick tenements, cold-water flats, and decrepit wooden buildings that looked like they might collapse on a windy day. As the land leveled out near the river, the "School-Street area was known as 'Bottom,' . . . the *red light* district of Yonkers, where there were numerous bars and barber shops, sprinkled with gambling, hustlers and prostitution."[34] Ella's family lived at 27 Clinton Street; by 1927 they moved to 72 School Street, a large apartment complex occupied by Black families in a tough neighborhood.[35] In both Clinton and School streets, petty criminals and rowdies got arrested, their offenses publicized in the police dockets in local newspapers. The streets were occupied by "disorderly" houses, or brothels and gambling holes.[36] Ella would later recall, "For a while I worked as a lookout for the best-looking house on the street—what do they call them now—sporting houses. I'd watch and knock on the door to let the girls know if the police were coming. Oh yes, I had a very interesting young life."[37]

In Yonkers she heard many languages spoken around her by "Hungarians, blacks, Spanish, and Italian, everybody. We went to school together, slept together, and mothers babysat for each other." She developed a sense of security from having other trustworthy parents around and neighborhood ties. Watching her mother love other people's children[38] instilled in her a reluctance to generalize about cultural difference later in life, when she sang for audiences who did not speak English. When asked about her "down-to-earth" attitude, she said, "I have my upbringing to thank for that. Nobody was better than anyone else."[39] She laughed as she told an interviewer, "I learned to talk with my hands. *Capice?*" In 1989, when friends from her old neighborhood were interviewed, they supported her perspective, talking about how "we were all poor in that neighborhood. . . . But we all got on."[40]

Tempie and Antonio worked hard to build a solid family life. Antonio Correia Borges became known as Tony Correy or Corey or Corri. While the couple did not officially marry, Tempie also became Correy, and they named their child, born in 1925, Thelma Frances Correy. Ella remained a Fitzgerald on census data and on school documents. Seven years older than Thelma Frances, she grew up feeling responsible for her sister. The family struggled, she said; they ate horse meat on occasion.[41]

He tried to transmit his heritage to her, but she resisted. "I was raised by a Portuguese stepfather," she said in 1987. "He wanted to send me to a Portuguese school. He tried to teach me Portuguese himself, but all I wanted to do was play, and he got disgusted with me." The Yonkers Portuguese Cultural Club, founded in 1928, hosted events with Portuguese dance music. She remembered the indigenous *cuíca*, a drum, and fiddles played with catgut. She later regretted her rebellious indifference.[42] Perhaps her affinity for Brazilian timbres, which surfaced with the rise of bossa nova in the 1960s, had its roots in this early exposure.

An African American neighbor in the apartment building on School Street said she had known Tempie "very well." Mrs. Correy "would come home from work and she would stop and talk with us all. She was a very nice lady who used to work very hard. She came home, cooked her dinners, and kept her house, and would mind her own business."[43] Her daughter later wrote, "My mother made a living as a cook and at one time she was a foreman in a laundry. But it was decent and respectable. I'm proud of my mother. She always provided when she had to. She did her duty."[44] And so did her daughter, who made "providing" for her family the moral core of her responsibility.

These values were reinforced in Yonkers's community of African American "strivers," or those pursuing self-reliance in the face of systemic racism. In the 1920s and '30s, as two local historians wrote, "most of us had middle class ideals. *Middle class* was understood as a cultural phenomenon in the Black community. Many people had a striving mentality. Even though we worked in white folks' kitchens and our fathers were laborers, there was a cultural striving that would separate us from other people."[45] The Black press chronicled strivers' lives in Yonkers and Westchester County, with local correspondents for the *New York Age* and the *New York Amsterdam News*. Such acknowledgment supported the "politics of respectability," a major theme for Black women in the early twentieth century, one that helped shape Tempie Fitzgerald and the way she reared her daughter.[46]

When Ella was thirteen, she went to a surprise party for a ten-year-old girl on School Street, where "a most delightful time was had by these youngsters"—an item that was deemed newsworthy enough that the squib from the *New York Age* was reprinted in the *Chicago Defender.*[47] In Fitzgerald's adult years, her co-workers and friends sometimes made fun of her sense of propriety, her aversion to obscenity, and the importance she attached to good manners. These traits had roots in the politicized etiquette that bolstered pride and stiffened resistance. In a society where Black women were routinely called only by their first names, not Miss or Mrs., and where the term *lady* was reserved for white women, Fitzgerald later said, "it used to bother me when people I didn't know came up and called me 'Ella.' It seemed to me they should say, 'Miss Fitzgerald,' but somehow they never do."[48]

★★★

IN 1924 TEMPIE CORREY enrolled her seven-and-a-half-year-old daughter in Public School 10. The girl made a strong impression on two of her teachers, who pinpointed her "marked characteristics" with insight: her first-grade teacher at P.S. 10 labeled her "self-reliant." Her third-grade teacher called her "ambitious," hardly a conventional description for a nine-year-old girl.[49]

Others recognized her ambition as well. How could they miss it? Friends from School Street who later shared precious memories said, "She always knew she was going to be somebody someday because she kept on saying, 'I want to do something. I want to make something of myself. Someday you're going to see me in the headlines. I'm going to be famous.' We'd all laugh, Oh yeah, sure!"[50] There were prophetic signs: when she was ten or so, she found a way to turn a schoolyard into a stage and her friends into an audience:

It would be at lunch-time or in the morning when we were outside the building. She would be standing up against the wall, and she would be popping and shaking and swaying, dancing to herself. She wasn't anybody then, just one of the kids from school. She would just be out there, and we'd just hang around watching her. She just smiled all the time, just shaking her shoulders and singing. She had dangling earrings, those big hoops, and broken-down shoes.[51]

All this helps explain why a striving mother gave her daughter piano lessons. In a 1992 interview, Fitzgerald recalled that the results were disappointing. Fascinated by her teacher's piano technique, "with big hands, who could stretch," she "would be so thrilled by him that by the time he got through playing, it would be time for me to go home!" Ella said, "I knew one song and played it over and over." What it was, she never said. Then came the bemused memory of her mother's rebuke: "I work too hard to let you go there and you come back and you don't know *nothin'*!"[52] Fitzgerald would later describe her skill level as "playing a little."[53]

She may have learned to read music through these lessons and perhaps in school as well. The official Yonkers Schools records list a missed year due to illness, and her record stops after the sixth grade. But other sources, including Ella herself, establish that she attended Benjamin Franklin Junior High School for two years or so, taking one music course worth a half-credit. She learned rudimentary solfège, or her do-re-mi's, a form of ear training linking pitches with scale syllables that she would use for the rest of her life. One of her accompanists, Tommy Flanagan, would later remark that "she has a method of reading music that is really uncanny."[54]

Maybe if she had earned a full credit, she would have let herself be called a musician more easily. As it was, regret and self-effacement mingle in this short exchange from an interview in 1983, with Leonard Feather, a notable music critic from her generation who became a confidant.

LF: You *are* a musician.
EF: Well, I never studied.
LF: No, you taught yourself to read music, right?
EF: Well, I had to do that to get that half credit in school. . . . In Yon-

kers, well you know, I mean I had to learn it [music]. Either you take art—at the time you either had to take art or you had to take music. Well, I know I was no artist—that's one thing.

LF: Can you read a little sheet music though?

EF: Yes, I'm fortunate that way.[55]

At home, Tempie Correy influenced her daughter's musical life. In Ella's words, she had "a very beautiful classical voice. And she liked a lot of classical music. She used to sing real high."[56] In fact, she used to play more classical music in the house. Perhaps this was one source of the comic imitations of operatic vocalizing that Ella used later in her career.

By 1930 the Fitzgerald family owned both a radio and a phonograph, at a time when few Black families could afford such luxuries.[57] As she recalled, "My mother had [records by] not Bessie Smith, Mamie Smith, so all we used to hear in the house was Mamie Smith and Connie Boswell, and the Mills Brothers had just come out, and they had just played at the RKO Theater in Yonkers.[58] So those were the records that she was playing, you know. And I tried to sing like Connie Boswell."[59] "Anything the Boswell Sisters sang my mother liked and she would sing it."[60] In 1920 Mamie Smith became the first Black woman to make a record, and her "Crazy Blues" launched an extraordinary era for Black blueswomen. But by 1930 Smith's heyday was over: her urban style sounded old-fashioned compared to the roots style of Bessie Smith, the decade's dominant figure. Yet Tempie Correy stayed a fan.

The Mills Brothers, a Black vocal quartet, were innovators in popular singing, renegotiating the relationship between words and music, singing their arrangements with surgical precision. On their hit record "Tiger Rag" (labeled with the disclaimer that "no musical instrument or mechanical devices were used on this recording other than guitar"), they imitated a tuba, trumpet, and trombone. Equally innovative were the Boswell Sisters, a white vocal trio. Born and raised in New Orleans, they retained a Southern lilt and boldly deconstructed lyrics to introduce daring harmonies and novelty swing, with enough jazz to make some assume they were Black.[61] As Connie Boswell later said,

"We didn't sing everything straight, the way other groups did. After the first chorus, we'd start singing the tune a little different—you, with a beat, the way jazz musicians would."[62] Both the Mills Brothers and the Boswell Sisters were prophetic choices for Fitzgerald's evolution as an artist because they treated the voice as a human instrument. The freedom flowing from this perspective would spark Fitzgerald's own innovative approach to vocal jazz.

American popular music dominated Fitzgerald's young girlhood and early adolescence. Two songs stand out as harbingers of her future: show tunes from Broadway and Hollywood (what would be called the Great American Songbook) that became famous as Black music or through the white adoption of Black styles. Friends from School Street remember Ella impersonating Louis Armstrong's version of the Fats Waller tune "Ain't Misbehavin'."[63] Armstrong had picked it up from the revue *Hot Chocolates*, when it moved downtown from Harlem on to Broadway and he played in the pit band. Fitzgerald, by listening to "Ain't Misbehavin'," assimilated his trademark swoops, blurred syllables, and theatrically "shocking" scat.[64] It was the beginning of her lifelong engagement with the music of this supremely influential artist.

The second song from these early years is one Fitzgerald recalled as significant, in a TV interview in 1986. Smiling at the memory, she talked about how it came to her: "I got in a couple of school plays. And there was a song called 'Sing You Sinners.'" The novelty song was just so right for her. Introduced in the Hollywood film *Honey* (1930), "Sing You Sinners" was a satirical song-and-dance takeoff on rural Black church practices. Improvisation is built into its opening verse, and the hit version as a pop song delivered by a white dance band imitated a Black preacher's raspy tone.[65] "I used to try and growl that 'Sing You Sinners,'" she recalled. "And the kids liked me. And they said, 'Oh, she sounds good.'" And she growled the title right there on television.[66]

Mel Heimer, another Yonkers resident, wrote about his memories of Fitzgerald in the 1950s as an entertainment feature writer for King Features Syndicate. "I was a couple of years older, and we were in separate schools and now and then news would drift around that there was this girl singer who really had it, see."[67]

Sometimes Fitzgerald's mother would slap her into humility:

> And I'll never forget, I got a little big head, and one day somebody spoke to me in the street, and I turned my head up, and I thought I was great, and my mother *slapped* me, and she says, "If a man is lying in the gutter and he speak to you, you say hello! Don't you ever do that again!" So that was one of my *first* lessons: to remember to always speak to anybody anywhere. Because someday that might be the very person who could be in a position to help *you*.[68]

The incident either inculcated or reinforced a latent personality trait that others would note—the "fear of being considered bigheaded," as a friendly jazz critic wrote later.[69] That lesson became her lifetime challenge as she negotiated the boundaries between self-esteem and egotism.[70]

★★★

IN HER ADOLESCENT YEARS, Fitzgerald was also making a name for herself as a dancer. Members of the Gulliver family, her neighbors on School Street and longtime residents of Yonkers, remembered that "she was crazy about dancing," as Annette Gulliver Miller put it. Charles Gulliver said, "She was some dancer, oh yeah! She was a terrific dancer!"[71] The word *dancer* covered a lot of territory in the early 1930s. Dancing ranged from the social dancing associated with big ballrooms to the professional dancing featured in vaudeville theaters, especially tap dancing, at which Black artists excelled, and even to individualistic eccentric solo dancing, seen in nightclubs and variety theaters. Ella explored all these forms in her youth and adolescence.

As a girl on School Street, most often when Fitzgerald talked about dancing, she meant social dancing. In the late 1920s, the Lindy Hop arrived in Harlem and revolutionized the meaning of a couple on a dance floor. As the dance historian Constance Valis Hill has written, "Jazz music through the first half of the twentieth century always had its social dance counterpart."[72] The Lindy Hop turned Charles Gulliver and Ella Fitzgerald into addicts. "We'd learn all the latest dances," Charles recounted. "We used to go down to one of the dance halls in New York a lot called the Savoy. . . . Then Ella and I, we'd be out there on the street corner just practicing different steps, and people would stand there and watch us."[73] Ella said, "They thought that young, skinny me could really do 'mean steps.'"[74] She and Charles continued to visit the Savoy Ballroom through their junior high school years. Charles recalled, "If I ever learned a new step, she would want to know what it was. And she'd keep on trying till she got it."[75]

Social dancing was one thing; dancing onstage alone was quite another. Charles described his friend as "just a plain person. She was more like a tomboy, and she was a girl, a girl because she used to pal around with a lot of boys. . . . Now, never bother too much with girls."[76] She was a "plain person who wasn't beautiful by a long shot, you know." But Ella thought of herself differently, using dance to express her sexuality. She knew how to "shim-sham-shimmy" and "belly-roll" so that her friends teased her and called her "Snake Hips," a nickname most often associated with Earl "Snakehips" Tucker, whose career was launched in the Broadway revue *Blackbirds of 1928* and who worked at the Cotton Club with Duke Ellington in his elaborate revues.[77] "Every streetcorner urchin tried to ape the eccentricities of this elastic performer," wrote Ralph Matthews in the early 1930s.[78] Tucker took an act that could have been consigned to burlesque houses and dignified it as art.

Fitzgerald's youthful desire to be a dancer became a staple of her later interviews. In her teenage years, the possibility was real to her: many young African American women aspired to dancing as a gateway to freedom, an alternative to lives of laundry and domestic service. From the many hopefuls who filled chorus lines on Harlem stages, exceptional stars emerged, among them Florence Mills, Fredi Washington, and Lena Horne, along with sister acts like the tap-dancing Whitman Sisters, "one of the longest-running, highest-paid, and most popular companies on the Black vaudeville circuit."[79] Even in the male-dominated field of tap dancing, "African American women were out there too, laying down steps like it was nobody's business."[80] So why not Ella? A photograph taken of her around this time shows a beaming girl with braids and a wide guileless smile. "Everyone in Yonkers thought I was a good little dancer," she said, "so that became my ambition."[81]

Chapter 2

AMATEUR NIGHTS

(1933-1935)

Whatever Ella's ambitions might have been in her early years, she soon ran up against a collapsing economy in a city that offered little security to its working poor. Yonkers prided itself on its attempts to surmount the Depression. In 1930 it had an unemployment rate of a mere 3 percent; in 1931, as things got worse, the best the city could do was organize a "relief committee composed of prominent citizens who advocated sending out teams to every neighborhood in the city to request small contributions." But that did little, for in 1932, "large numbers of people who have never before asked for help" were asking for it.[1] Whether Ella and her family were among them is not known, but that year also inflicted an unexpected blow on the family. On October 10, 1932, a few miles east of Yonkers, Ella's mother was hurt in a serious automobile accident.[2] Tony Correy was teaching Ella's cousin to drive in a car with four young children onboard. He escaped, but Tempie suffered serious injuries, sidelining her as the family's primary breadwinner. The accident would remain a traumatic memory for Ella, who fifty years later recounted her mother's heroic actions: "To save the little boy from hitting the front, my mother grabbed him, and hit her head. She got fifty-four stitches in her head. They didn't have all the medicines they have now, and it didn't heal. I was fifteen, going on sixteen."[3] Her mother lived, but we know little else about her health or if and when she went back to work.

Within the semiautonomous African American community of Yonkers, Ella kept her dreams of a musical career alive by performing in social clubs that ran entertainments and dances, often as benefits. (Social life was segregated.) Yonkers had so many Black social clubs that around 1933 eight of them formed a "federation," adopting striving names like Ivy Social Gaiety Girls, Exclusive Girls, Regular Fellows, and Les Courtisans Douze.[4] Even their routine meetings were reported in the social pages of the *New York Age* and the *New York Amsterdam News*.

Ella Fitzgerald's first known public performance took place in that milieu when she was fifteen. On January 19, 1933, the Yonkers Federation of Negro Clubs sponsored a "charity entertainment and dance" for the "aid of the Negro unemployed" at the Women's Institute.[5] Featuring theatrical stars imported from Harlem, the event drew around five hundred people. Even the white press took note, describing Fitzgerald as a "singer," among many locals, perhaps for the first time in print.[6] The top performers Ella would have seen there included Buck and Bubbles, a singer-dancer act with the great John W. Bubbles (né Sublett), dubbed the "Father of Rhythm Tap," and the vocalist Adelaide Hall.[7] Well-known for her wordless refined vocalizing on Duke Ellington's composition "Creole Love Call," Hall had made her career in the 1927 Broadway revue *Blackbirds*; maybe that evening Hall sang a hit from that show, "I Can't Give You Anything But Love," a song Ella would go on to sing many times. Around the time of the benefit, Hall was performing at the Harlem Opera House, billed as "the crooning blackbird."[8]

Little is known about this watershed moment in Fitzgerald's development except for a poignant recollection by Tommy Seay, Jr., the talented young president of the Yonkers Federation of Negro Clubs who doubled as the local correspondent for the *New York Age*.[9] His portrait of young Ella as a would-be belly dancer challenges the conventional image of the young Fitzgerald as a shy novice; he described her instead as a girl who believed in her own seductiveness, showing off her "snake-hips" moves.

Ella Fitzgerald, a short-haired brownskin gal, was just a few years ago singin' and dancin' anywhere and at any time she felt so inclined. This reporter first saw her and just faintly heard her at a benefit dance given by the local Federation. Handicapped by the lack of a mike, Ella with plenty of abdominal activity, attired in a scanty costume of Black and white, drew more than her share of applause on the occasion. She has always been just a happy-go-lucky kid . . . a real gypsy of song.[10]

Another mention of Fitzgerald in social club activities came two months later, when her name appeared in a *New York Age* squib about a modest event at the Twentieth-Century Club in Tarrytown, a smaller suburb upriver. The notice read simply, "Miss Ella Fitzgerald . . . rendered a song and dance number which was well received."[11]

The "gypsy of song" was trying to make money any way she could, in the desperate times for her family that followed the October automobile accident. But one disaster led to another: while skipping school and hustling for small change on Yonkers street corners, she was arrested for truancy. On April 10, 1933, she appeared in children's court in Westchester County, where she was labeled "ungovernable" and unwilling to "obey the just and lawful commands of her mother." Ella had hit bottom. Despite having her mother and stepfather at home, she was sentenced to five years at the New York State Training School for Girls in Hudson, about one hundred miles north of Yonkers.[12] While awaiting transfer to Hudson, she was briefly remanded to the Riverdale Colored Orphan Asylum; she arrived at Hudson by April 18.[13]

The Training School for Girls, a formidable institution with a long history, occupied a large campus dotted with some nineteen two-story "cottages," each housing twenty-five to thirty girls.[14] It had a decent reputation in the early 1930s, with an educational curriculum that included the arts, including music.[15] She received some decent instruction there, as was confirmed by a random encounter decades later. On June 30, 1957, Fitzgerald had just opened the summer season at the Berkshire

Music Barn in Lenox, Massachusetts, when two women from the Hudson area approached her backstage.[16] "Do you remember when you were in school in Hudson?" Taken by surprise, Fitzgerald volunteered some remarkable information that she never again repeated:

> I sure do. . . . I loved singing and even played the piano a little. Harmony was my tough problem, but there was a wonderful woman at the Hudson Training School who helped me out. We worked together for hours until we had real, wonderful harmony. It was really Helen Pitcher who started me out and gave me my first taste for success.[17]

This rich experience of singing was a bright spot amid Fitzgerald's unacknowledged suffering at Hudson. In the 1960s, the school would ask Ella to return as a distinguished alumna, but as the superintendent explained, "She hated the place. She had been held in the basement of one of the cottages once and all but tortured. She was damned if she was going to come back." Racial segregation prevented young Ella from joining the school's choir. How could a white girl be expected to stand next to her? Instead, at least once, "she sang her heart out" in a choir at the Hudson Zion AME Church, as recalled by a woman lucky enough to hear her.[18]

By the spring of 1934, Fitzgerald was back in Yonkers. How she managed her early release remains unclear in the absence of any surviving records.[19] In the late 1930s, publicists would describe her as a "runaway." But her reform school incarceration likely inspired her public and private philanthropy for the next sixty years, as she frequently gave benefit performances and donations to help needy children and working mothers.

Returning to her family and to freedom, looking for musical action, Fitzgerald sought out jazz. In Yonkers around May 17, 1934, she performed for the Regular Fellows' Club in its "first annual reception and minstrel show" at the Women's Institute.[20] She floated between Yonkers and Harlem. The pianist Red Richards recalled meeting Ella when he was hired to play solo stride piano for dancers at Harlem rent parties, which were held by tenants in private apartments. "I first met Ella [Fitz-gerald] at one of these parties. She was sixteen years old and we used to go to house parties together," recalled Richards. "She came from Yonkers and used to stay with a fellow and his sister on 128th between Convent and Eighth Avenue." She must have been hearing a lot of stride piano, judging from Richards's account of his own taste for Fats Waller and James P. Johnson—"they were my favorite piano players."[21] She too liked Fats Waller and his insouciant irony, his relaxed way of swinging a tune—all approaches she would go on to emulate in her interpretations of Tin Pan Alley material.

Fitzgerald visited Harlem theaters to hear the jazz musicians play the stage acts between film screenings. In her seventies she would describe these encounters, making light of her poverty and self-consciousness:

> I used to go to a theater on 148th Street all the time. I'll never forget. My legs were so skinny, I used to wear boots so nobody could see the bottom of my legs. They would see me coming, and they'd say, "Oh, here's that little chick with them boots on." If it was summer, winter, spring, here come those boots. There she is again.[22]

But later that year, tragedy struck the family. On October 10, 1934, Tempie Correy, age thirty-nine, died suddenly from a cerebral embo-lism, according to her death certificate. She was buried in Oakland Cemetery in Yonkers under the name "Fitzcorry," honoring both hus-bands.[23] (See Fig. 2.) Tony became a single parent of two adolescent girls: Ella, seventeen, and her half-sister Frances, eleven. In the aftermath, Ella's childhood friend Charles Gulliver spoke of friction with her step-father. "He wasn't taking good care of her," he said, and once after she came home late from a dance, she was grounded "for quite a while."[24]

Other clouds hang over this period in Fitzgerald's life. Rumors of abuse circulated within Fitzgerald's extended family and among Yon-kers friends interviewed in the 1980s.[25] At some point Ella told her cousin Georgiana Williams, who was four years older, that a relative or

Fig. 2. Tombstone for Tempie Fitzcorry, Ella Fitzgerald's mother, at the Oakland Cemetery, Yonkers, New York. *Photo courtesy of Chris McKay.*

someone in her extended family had molested her, and the story persisted in family lore.[26] She survived that trauma partly through effective repression, in the opinion of a close friend. "Ella had a mind like a windshield wiper," purging what she did not want to remember. She did not like to be touched—a trait sometimes linked to the psychological effects of child abuse.[27] Give her a child to hug, that was one thing. An arm around the shoulder from an adult outside the family was quite another.

After her mother's death, Ella turned to her aunt Virginia Williams, who was Tempie's sister-in-law, and her cousin Georgie. "My mother ran with Georgie," said Ella's son, Ray Brown, Jr., describing their lifelong bond.[28] She did not turn her back on her Yonkers family; she crossed paths with her stepfather when she came back to Yonkers to visit Frances, who lived with him and his second wife, Lucy Barnes. But Virginia Williams became her second mother.[29] She "reared me," Ella said later. Roughly the same age as Tempie, Virginia Williams had been part of Fitzgerald's extended family in Newport News, where she worked as a "housekeeper" while raising her own two children—her daughter, Georgie (b. 1913), and her son, Leon (b. 1918).[30]

Exactly when Virginia moved to New York is not known; in 1930 the Williams family lived in the "Valley," a stretch of flat land from 130th to 151st Street, with some of Central Harlem's worst slums. A few blocks from their tenement apartment at 317 West 145th Street was the "Lung Block," so called for the rampant tuberculosis there, at a time when that disease was the leading cause of death among African Americans.[31] Around 215,000 people—almost the equivalent of Wyoming's population in the 1930s—were crowded into Central Harlem's three square miles.[32]

★★★

LIVING BETWEEN A DREAM AND A PLAN, Ella began to build her future even as the fabled jazz age, when "Harlem was in vogue," yielded to the grimness of the Great Depression. The repeal of Prohibition shut down many Harlem clubs, and in the mid-1930s such venues as the Cotton Club and Connie's Inn—exclusive clubs that did not admit Black customers—followed their customer base downtown. Harlem was overloaded with redundant musicians and dancers who were generally excluded from opportunities in radio and film. One unexpected consequence was a surge in Black show business, geared to a local population eager to spend money in theaters catering to their tastes. While white critics were writing obituaries for vaudeville, especially after the Palace Theatre downtown abandoned stage shows for films in 1933, Black variety entertainment flourished in a separate cultural milieu through entrepreneurial adaptation and new social relationships between white business and a Black public. The slogan "colored shows for colored audiences" captured the trajectory of the change.[33] The two theaters on 125th Street, then a predominantly white neighborhood, yielded to political pressure from the Black community and hired more Black staff. The Apollo promoted itself as the first Harlem theater to employ an all-colored crew, including stagehands, service staff, and cashier.[34]

In 1934 the top Harlem theaters included the Lafayette Theatre at 132nd Street and Seventh Avenue, the Harlem Opera House at 211 West 125th Street, and the Apollo, which had just taken over a former burlesque house at 253 West 125th Street. All three joined together to offer an amazing prize: a week's booking for their well-advertised "Negro acts and revues."[35] Competing for audiences in tough times, the white owners of these theaters resorted to marathon presentations on a bill with feature movies and stage shows, a format known sometimes as a "vaude-pic date" or a "presentation" show. One night a week they tagged on an amateur contest, and as such contests were proliferating in Harlem, Ella Fitzgerald went looking for an audience.

In 1934 the names coming through these theaters included future famous stars across the spectrum of music, theater, and dance: the important bandleaders Benny Carter, Earl Hines, and Fletcher Henderson; the dance acts Whitman Sisters, Snakehips Tucker, Pops and Louie, and Buck and Bubbles; the singers Billie Holiday, Adelaide Hall, and Emma Moten; and the comics Dewey "Pigmeat" Markham and Jackie "Moms" Mabley. To their performances were added a line of chorines, or dancing girls. Anyone who won first prize in such a contest achieved a significant accomplishment, securing press attention and future work opportunities.

The Apollo had the foresight to understand and cultivate local audiences and the challenges of racial integration.[36] Shirley Sussman Greenes, daughter of the Apollo manager, Morris Sussman, recalled the amateur contests:

> It was a great big struggle. . . . The whole purpose was to have black and white sit together and watch a show. The black people were sort of drawn into it when Harlem amateur hour started, and they began to come to the Apollo and be a little more comfortable. When amateur hour came in and entertainers of all colors came in to do it, black people started to come down, and that's when it became a major success.[37]

On November 7, 1934, the Apollo enjoyed a major triumph: a radio wire hookup for the program *Harlem Amateur Hour*. A few candidates were selected from open auditions on Monday, and the show was scheduled for Wednesday night after the feature film and the 10:30 p.m. stage show. Carried by more than twenty stations on the American Broadcasting System, usually from midnight to 1:00 a.m., the program over the next two years would reach cities as far away as Scranton, Pennsylvania, Davenport, Iowa, and Los Angeles.[38] To avoid a dreary recital of mediocrity, the theater management peppered the lineup with professionals like the tap dancer Bill "Bojangles" Robinson and the bandleader Duke Ellington.[39] Ralph Cooper, a local showman-celebrity serving as master of ceremonies, sustained the flow with wit, while the stagehand Porto Rico, in costumes worthy of a medieval jester, dramatized the exits of collapsing acts with a cap pistol.

Over the course of 1934, *Harlem Amateur Hour* gained a distinctive source of notoriety: its audience. The Apollo management spurred viewers into exhibitionism, giving them noisemakers on entering and encouraging "wild pandemonium" at signs of a performer's failure as well as success. In *Variety*'s words, "when one does go over, the approval sweeps the entire house with the microphone gathering all the added enthusiasm."[40] The critical sophistication of the Apollo audience turned it into a superior court, issuing verdicts that could make or break a career. Francis "Doll" Thomas, a veteran Apollo stagehand, said:

> The Apollo happened to have one of those peculiar types of audiences that appreciated a performer's talent and ability. Here, they heard colored performers sing. They saw colored people dancin'. They saw a line of colored girls that were beautiful and talented, so naturally they appreciated it, that's all. You appreciate what your people can do.[41]

Ella had to muster courage and confidence to apply to the amateur contest. Late in her life, she credited her mother for entering her name.[42] Other times she told the story as if it were a children's fairy tale, changing some details over the years: "One day two girlfriends and I made a bet—a dare. We all wanted to get on the stage, and we drew straws to see which of us would go on the amateur hour."[43] Still another time she said her girlfriends "believed I had talent. They gave me encouragement when I needed it. They *forced* me to do it."[44] She said her friends were as "stage-struck" as she was.[45] It sounded so random, especially considering her success in Yonkers club evenings. But this was Harlem and the big-time Apollo. A postcard arrived for her with a date for a Monday night audition. She asked Tommy Seay to lend her money for carfare to get there.[46]

The audition occurred on November 21, 1934, on the third broadcast of the *Harlem Amateur Hour*. Years later, in the *New York Age*, Tommy Seay recalled the scene among Ella's home crowd in Yonkers: "Do you remember when Ella Fitzgerald took her first audition and we all listened in?"[47] An ad for the Apollo that evening reveals the marathon of acts that preceded her. First came the feature detective film *Charlie Chan in London*, then a stage show including a striptease fan dancer, a "soubrette" singer from musical comedy, the tap dancer Bill Bailey, and the future comic legend Dewey "Pigmeat" Markham. Always on hand were the overworked chorines, the Famous 16 Apollo Rockettes.

For the next twenty-five years, Fitzgerald would have little choice about what she recorded, but the song she chose for her audition represented her unencumbered taste at that crucial moment. She planned to sing "Judy," a rhythm song that had lighthearted lyrics and a danceable tempo. It was perfect for her, a song-and-dance girl who could maybe do a few "mean steps" while singing its quirky lyrics. It had been composed in 1927 by Hoagy Carmichael as an instrumental tune; he described it as "so weird, so modern in style," perhaps because it had a relaxed swing, compared to frenetic Charleston tempos. "Judy" got lyrics in 1934 intended for a male not a female singer: "If she seems a saint, but you find that she ain't, that's Judy."[48] Carmichael thought the words would be too "racy" for radio, but Ella, at seventeen, must have liked the song's aura of adolescent rebelliousness. So did thirteen-year-old Judy Garland, who adopted it for her stage name.[49]

What happened next was so unexpected that it filled Fitzgerald with stage fright, turning her legs and feet to stone. The act that preceded was the Edwards Sisters, a dancing group management had slipped in to spark the evening, most likely.[50] They were good, so good that "I knew I could not follow them," Ella recalled. Triggered, she realized she would have to fall back on her other, lesser talent (in her eyes): singing.

The emcee Ralph Cooper later described the moment in his memoir:

> One youngster I was convinced would win in a walk was almost run off her first minute out there. . . . She came out onstage all jumpy and unnerved. . . . When she started to sing, she was off-key, and her voice sounded like a hoarse croak. I could feel the audience start to rumble. They didn't boo immediately, but I could feel the blood rising. So I stopped Ella in the opening verse and said, "Folks, hold on now. This young lady's got a gift she'd like to share with us tonight. She's just having a little trouble getting it out of its wrapper. Let's give her a second chance."[51]

Another eyewitness, Shirley Sussman Greenes, recalled that Fitzgerald "was a nervous wreck. Ralph Cooper had heard her sing and he knew she was wonderful. Well, she was getting booed off because she was nervous. And he went out and asked the audience if they would give her another chance because she was so good, and he spoke to her for a little bit and calmed her down."[52] Norma Miller, a Harlem resident and professional dancer around Ella's age, amplified: "We booed Ella Fitzgerald 'cause she came on stage looking like 'Who? You gotta be kidding.' And then she starts to sing, 'When his eyes say yes, and you're wrong in your guess, that's Judy, my Judy.' Honey, we heard a voice, and like I said before, she shut us up so fast, you could hear a rat piss on cotton."[53]

Ella shocked herself, it seems, judging from the many times she recalled her decision to relegate her dancing to the background, sometimes with ruefulness, sometimes with self-irony. The phrase "I wanted to be a dancer" turned into a cliché as the press repeated and highlighted it. How could she have so underestimated the uniqueness of her vocal gift? "I thought my singing was pretty much hollering," she said in 1957.[54]

But the real breakthrough that evening transcended the issue of song versus dance. Fitzgerald's contest-winning performance is worthy of the term *epiphany*, not only evoking revelation but also explaining the priority, even a sense of obligation, that she placed on her relationship with her audience, "her fans," as she often called them. When asked about this late in her career, she turned the hush and the cheers and the noise into an expression of love rather than mere success: "I think it was forgetting myself, and getting up there before a mike. Those bright lights on stage really show you up. You can't hide . . . but it was the turning point in my life. Once up there, I felt the acceptance, and love from the audience—I knew I wanted to sing before people the rest of my life."[55]

Fitzgerald's Apollo victory was supposed to earn her a week's booking, but the managers reneged, and in the fiercely competitive and exploitative world of Black theater in Harlem, Fitzgerald had little recourse. As she explained in 1937, "They told me the same thing they tell all the other amateurs who win prizes and don't get them. Sometimes they make you see that audience picked you for some reason or other, you're really not good enough for the stage yet."[56] In fact, they deferred, honoring the prize a few months later, at the Harlem Opera House.

On the night of her Apollo triumph, the music director was twenty-seven-year-old Benny Carter, leading his own band.[57] Acknowledged today as a jazz master of the big band era, Carter was also widely respected as a saxophonist and arranger in Fletcher Henderson's Roseland Orchestra. Carter was bowled over by Ella, saying later that he realized "she was a singer who was born to happen."[58] He arranged a private audition for his friend John Hammond, a scion of Vanderbilt wealth who was a fervent jazz advocate; at twenty-four he was already an influential figure in the music business. The year before, in 1933, Hammond had "discovered" Billie Holiday, arranging for her recording debut with Benny Goodman, and he had helped Bessie Smith record for the Okeh label, paying her fee himself.[59]

In 1967 fifty-six-year-old Carter reminded fifty-year-old Fitzgerald of the audition:

> I arranged to have you sing a few numbers with the band so John
> could hear you. Right? We all went down to the theater in John's
> old Ford with the rumble seat. When we got in the car, I told you
> to sit in front with John, and you were afraid to sit with him. So
> you and your cousin [Georgiana Williams] sat in the rumble seat,
> right? . . . When we got down to the theater, you sang.[60]

Hammond, upon hearing her, said she lacked "uniqueness," and Carter said, "John was totally unimpressed."[61]

One reason may have been the material Fitzgerald chose: songs by writers Hammond scorned that had been popularized by singers he considered irrelevant. In November 1934, the very month of Fitzgerald's Apollo victory, Hammond publicly dismissed Tin Pan Alley songs, including those by George Gershwin and Irving Berlin. He further lamented that Hoagy Carmichael, Fats Waller, and Harold Arlen "had gone Broadway," however "ingratiating and charming" their songs.[62] What chance did Ella Fitzgerald have with Carmichael's "Judy" or any of the other songs in her audition repertoire, which included items on *Billboard*'s hit charts: "Believe It Beloved," a Fats Waller song; "The Object of My Affection," an anomalous smash hit by Pinky Tomlin, a little-known songwriter from Oklahoma; and "Lost in a Fog," a ballad by Dorothy Fields and Jimmy McHugh, veterans of the Cotton Club theatrical revues, the counterpart of Broadway in Harlem.[63] Apart from Bessie Smith, Mildred Bailey, and Billie Holiday, Hammond considered everyone else, in Teddy Wilson's words, "women singers you could flush down the toilet."[64]

When the bandleader Fletcher Henderson heard her, he also reacted unfavorably. Fitzgerald later said, "I guess they weren't too impressed when I sang for Fletcher, because he said, 'Don't call me, I'll call you!' "[65] In this case, his reaction likely had little to do with her song choices. The thirty-nine-year-old bandleader had a history of ambivalence toward vocalists; in the mid-1920s he allowed even Louis Armstrong few opportunities to sing as a member of the Henderson band.[66] Further, Henderson was "high on looks at the time," recalled the trumpeter Irving "Mouse" Randolph.[67] It was a moment missed, to be sure. Although Henderson was no longer conducting at the Roseland Ballroom downtown, in the fall of 1934 he had signed a contract with a new label, Decca Records, and was working in Harlem theaters. In a few months, John Hammond would connect Henderson as an arranger with the white bandleader Benny Goodman; the partnership would help spark Goodman's success and his leadership in the emerging style known as swing.

★★★

AFTER THE *HARLEM AMATEUR HOUR*, Fitzgerald's auditions in amateur contests have a sketchy history. At an unsuccessful audition at the Lafayette Theatre, her song choice "Lost in a Fog" proved too sophisticated for the piano player, who "couldn't get the chords right," even though many popular singers had recorded the song.[68]

But the resilient Fitzgerald "kept right on."[69] The up-and-coming bandleader Willie Bryant was working a nightly fifteen-minute radio spot billed as the NBC Radio Orchestra. In February 1935, when he was booked into the Harlem Opera House, he received a note from Fitzgerald written in her perfect Palmer method penmanship: "Dear Mr. Bryant: I would like to go on your amateur program if possible. Will you step outside and speak to me? Ella Fitzgerald." He apparently sloughed it off, only to write about the incident with regret a few years later.[70]

Fitzgerald's career finally got the boost it needed when she appeared at the Harlem Opera House for the week starting on February 15, 1935. Her week-long prize from the Apollo contest was likely transferred to this co-managed theater.[71] Professionally, this booking was the crucial turning point for her, far more consequential than the Apollo tryout. Her week at the Harlem Opera House was a vaude-pic date with an extensive lineup of dancers and musicians, headlined by Tiny Bradshaw, a twenty-seven-year-old vocalist with a recently formed fourteen-piece band.[72] Bradshaw had been recording scat vocals for Decca in his hard, raspy voice, taking manic tempos on tunes like "Darktown Strutters' Ball" and finding success on a recent tour with the Mills Brothers. Just as the Apollo contest had fabulist elements clinging to the few facts of the occasion, here too Fitzgerald made her success seem magical. In Bradshaw she found a friend, recalling how first "Tiny and the chorus girls all kicked in to buy me a gown."[73] Then he made sure everyone heard her, in a scene worthy of a fairy godfather. In her words, "Everyone had their coats on and was ready to leave when Tiny introduced me. He said, 'Ladies and gentlemen, here's the young girl that's been winning all the contests,' and they all came back and took off their coats and sat down again."[74] Then "they all cheered at the end of my songs." On the scene that evening, Harlem comedian Timmie Rogers recalled, "She didn't know that she could sing that well. She stopped the show cold. They made her take an encore."[75]

For the first time, Fitzgerald's voice was celebrated in print. Ted Yates, a theatrical columnist and New York correspondent for the *Baltimore Afro-American*, the most widely circulated Black newspaper on the East Coast, began his prescient review with a tribute: "Ella Fitzgerald can learn here that I am the first to congratulate her. The lass with a remarkable voice—one of those Boswell swaying voices—has been signed to vo-de-o-wah-wah with Tiny Bradshaw. I like her when she sings 'The Object of My Affection.' "[76] This song, one of the biggest hits of the year, recently recorded by the Boswell Sisters, was another adolescent anthem with flippant lyrics—"You can do what you want and say what you want, / and I don't care." Its buoyant, airy rhythms suited Fitzgerald's song-and-dance background. Perhaps she even executed a few steps onstage. That perfect word *swaying* suggests the swing and lilt that were essential to the Boswells' appeal, and Yates's scat phrase *vo-de-o-wah-wah* summoned their instrumental timbres and improvisational feel. Tempie Fitzgerald's enthusiasm for the Boswells in the early 1930s had its impact. Ella had learned "Believe It Beloved" and "Judy" as well as "The Object of My Affection" from listening to Connie Boswell sing them on the radio.[77] "Something about her sound and timing appealed to me," she recalled; "she didn't sound like all the others. I know that Connie Boswell was doing things that no one else was doing. Just check the recordings made at the time and hear for yourself."[78] Her idol had a way of accenting particular words through dynamics and rhythmic phrasing that made a line sparkle. Fitzgerald would refine that approach and make it an essential element of her style.

"The Object of My Affection" also tapped into Fitzgerald's sense of playfulness and her often-understated wit in dealing with a racialized culture. In an era when the 1930 U.S. Census eliminated *mulatto* from its race categories, fictionalizing a binary Black and white populace, Fitzgerald's choices for her auditions, songs drawn from urban popular music, confounded the idea that "blackness" and "whiteness" belonged to separate spheres of musical practice. Later she recalled that after delivering the song's opening line ("The object of my affection can change my complexion / From white to rosy red") in a Black theater, "the audience freaked out laughing."[79] They understood and appreciated the sly irony of her choice. Clever girl. In 1968, in a rare funky performance of the song, she substituted the words "from brown to rosy red," getting a knowing laugh from the audience.[80]

★★★

"ELLA FITZGERALD SHOULD BE HEARD FROM," read the one-line prophecy in the *New York Amsterdam News* review of the Harlem Opera House show.[81] But how? Starting on February 22, Tiny Bradshaw was replaced by Cab Calloway and his Cotton Club Revue.[82] Fitzgerald probably returned to her usual spots on 125th Street, busking along with the rest of the street musicians, orators, preachers, and dancers who populated that Harlem thoroughfare. Opportunity arrived sideways. Following Calloway, a new show was announced for March 1 featuring Chick Webb, a virtuoso drummer and bandleader who was acclaimed in Harlem for his residencies at the Savoy Ballroom. It was quite a bill, including Mamie Smith, who had "not appeared in New York in a long time," according to publicity.[83]

Bardu Ali, Webb's front man and master of ceremonies, had heard Ella during her week with Tiny Bradshaw and was as thrilled as Benny Carter had been a few months earlier. The son of a Bengali immigrant father and an African American mother, Ali had been in show business since the 1920s and had linked up with Webb not long before.[84] He later cherished the memory of this prophetic moment: "We had just played the first opening day show at the old Harlem Opera House Theatre and I was the last one to leave the stage. I spotted a little skinny girl, standing in the shadows of the wings. I had heard her singing the night before on this same stage with Tiny Bradshaw's band. It had been amateur night and she won first prize."[85]

It could not have happened quite that way, as her appearances with Bradshaw had come and gone the week before, and her amateur night victory had been even earlier. Nonetheless, the spirit of the experience was intact. Ali continued, "I'll never forget what she was wearing: brown, low-cut boys' shoes and a raggedy dress with some cat fur around the collar." He watched her charisma, how she glowed onstage, how she established a magical bond with her audience, and how it propelled her into action. Webb *had* to listen to her. In Ali's words, he said, "Say, little girl, I told Mr. Webb about how nice you sang last night and he'd like to hear you." As he told his enabling lie, he did not anticipate how hard it would be to make that actually happen.

Chapter 3

INTO CHICK WEBB'S ORBIT

(1935)

"Don't forget when I started out, Chick Webb didn't want me. And John Trueheart. Him and Bardu are the ones who took me to Chick. You know, he didn't want no girl singer. He didn't want to hear me. And that was funny. So Bardu sneaked me into his dressing room and said 'listen to her.' And he [Chick] said, 'I don't want no *girl* singer.' And he [Bardu] said, 'Man, just listen to her.'"[1] That was how, about fifty years later, Ella Fitzgerald remembered her so-called audition. It was "funny" only in an ironic way and after the fact, considering the subsequent history of Chick and Ella. The stubborn Chick finally listened, maybe because he respected the musicianship of his best friend, the guitarist John Trueheart; or maybe because this kid was already in the room and it would have been too awkward to throw her out. So on March 6, 1935, he gave Ella Fitzgerald two minutes of his time.

Chick Webb was thirty years old and on his way to becoming a legendary "rhythm man" or virtuoso drummer. He pioneered the rhythmic push and the beat, or what musicians call "time," that shaped big band swing and helped make social dance music an art form within jazz.[2] Born in Baltimore in 1905 into the working-class poor, he was, in the words of Teddy McRae, the tenor saxophonist who joined the band in 1936, "a self-made drummer. . . . He'd tell his story where he used to beat on tin cans and things in Baltimore."[3] Webb's life in the 1930s was a rags-to-riches story: hustling as a newspaper boy and scraping up money to buy his first set of drums.[4] In his childhood, he contracted spinal tuberculosis, a classic disease of Black poverty; the metastatic condition left him a hunchback with a stunted height of maybe four and a half feet and shortened his life expectancy. His disability, which he ignored, would give him a skewed celebrity as the "midget" drummer and conductor.

In 1924, after gaining some professional experience in Baltimore, Webb made the obligatory move to New York. By 1927 he had laid the foundation for his career as the leader of his own group. In February, Chick Webb and His Harlem Stompers played the Savoy Ballroom for the first time, one year after it opened.[5] Once the management installed wire remotes, the ballroom became a center for hot dance music, and in the late 1920s Webb's orchestra reached a national audience on some of these broadcasts.[6]

Webb's style of "hot" music—that is to say, African American music—got its racialized branding early on. In December 1927 a booking at the Rose Danceland earned him his first known mention in the white music trade press: *Variety*'s main critic, Abel Green, labeled his music "colored-man's jazz." It deserved better than this venue, "the wooziest of creep joints," because "the ultra-type of jazz Webb plays is just too bad," that is, good. The term *ultra* meant ultra-modern or modernist in American classical circles as well. We don't know what Green heard because Webb had yet to make a recording, but some white bandleaders came up to hear him, among them reportedly Paul Whiteman.[7]

In the early 1930s, Webb constructed his career tenaciously, gig by gig, out of opportunities he found in Harlem's intense musical and cultural life. As the music historian Christi Jay Wells emphasizes, Webb played dance music in any style, from tangos to waltzes, not just the latest trends. He had to be versatile to handle the diversity of events that gave him a living: social club dates, benefits, debutante dances, ballrooms, and vaudeville theaters like the Lafayette, the Harlem Opera House, and the Apollo.[8] As his reputation grew, so did his bookings at the Savoy Ballroom, where his ability to inspire its dancers earned him a passionate fan base.

Slowly Webb formed a trusting business partnership with Moe Gale, one of the two white founders of the Savoy Ballroom in 1926. A second-generation American born in 1899, Gale was the son of Polish-Jewish immigrants. He grew up on the Lower East Side of New York and entered his father's luggage business, a niche occupation for many Jewish émigrés who arrived in the Great Wave from Eastern Europe in the early 1900s. The Gale family's success in that world gave Moe the capital to invest in arguably another Jewish niche industry, the music business.[9] Leveraging the visibility of the Savoy Ballroom, Gale built a small empire in Harlem by handling African American talent in the late 1920s and early '30s. Industry racism provided opportunities for white entrepreneurs who were willing to take risks and operate on the margins. In 1931 Gale founded Savoy Enterprises, "a 'booking company' for colored orchestras and entertainers."[10] In 1934–35 he formed the Gale Agency, a separate but parallel management company that took on African American entertainers excluded from big corporate firms like the Musical Corporation of America (MCA).

In 1934 Moe Gale signed Chick as his first client. Gale's public relations strategy was to have his publicists issue a steady flow of press releases and feed them as "news" to columnists of Black-owned newspapers. In the Black media world, that kept Webb's name in circulation. He had little trouble placing his barrage of sometimes dubious reportage in newspapers, as his Savoy ads brought them revenue. At the same time, Gale recognized the importance of radio and had established an office in the RKO Building in midtown Manhattan, where the radio network NBC had its operations. Gale's contacts there helped Webb gain crucial on-air access. In 1934 Gale arranged for Webb to be one of the 111 bands in the NBC lineup of typically fifteen-minute dance slots. Gale's press release claimed it was "the first time that a Race orchestra has ever been signed for a net-work studio sustaining program," even if it meant playing for nothing, without the commercial sponsorship that many white bands had.[11]

On the advice of Gale, Webb also signed with Decca Records, a label that was launched in April 1934. The bravura optimism of its cofounder, Jack Kapp, then about thirty-four years old, defied the gloomy mood prevailing in the recording industry, which had crashed along with the stock market; sales fell from 100 million units in 1929 to around 4 million in 1933. Kapp had turned the Brunswick label into a viable operation; taking much of that roster with him, he priced his shellac 78 rpm records at thirty-five cents apiece or three for a dollar, at a time when Victor, Brunswick, and Columbia were charging seventy-five cents each.[12] He would soon be seen as a savior of the business.

In some ways, Chick Webb faced an uphill battle at Decca. He was allotted two studio dates, yielding eight tunes released in late 1934, in contrast to the fifty tracks the Dorsey Brothers Orchestra got that year. Slotted as an African American dance band, Webb had as his Decca mates Fletcher Henderson, Noble Sissle and His International Orchestra, Claude Hopkins, Tiny Bradshaw, and the Jimmie Lunceford Orchestra. Lunceford, the "King Syncopator," led the best-known Black dance band in the country, having issued seventeen titles on Decca by the time of Webb's first session with the label in September 1934.

At Decca, Webb made recordings that reflected his own evolution as a musician. By the mid-1930s he had evolved from late 1920s Chicago-style improvisation to a smoother big band sound, indebted to the bandleader Fletcher Henderson. When the twenty-six-year-old tenor saxophonist and composer Edgar Sampson arrived in 1933, Webb's reputation soared: Sampson's brilliant arrangements for a fourteen- or fifteen-piece ensemble typically included three trumpets, one trombone, four or five saxophones, and a rhythm section that included a guitar. Applying contrast and color to every moment, Sampson juggled tunes into exciting riffs, giving the melody sparkle and leaving room as well for Webb's vital introductions and fills. He took surprisingly few solos, but even ten seconds of Webb had enough voltage to kick his band "like no one else," recalled Benny Carter.[13]

On May 18, 1934, Webb recorded Sampson's great version of "Stompin' at the Savoy" on the Columbia label; it received little attention at the time, although Benny Goodman's recording two years later would make it into a motto of the era. In November, at Decca's studios, Webb recorded other classic titles of swing dance music, including "Don't Be That Way" and "Blue Lou," both of them outstanding Sampson arrangements. (Way in the future, Ella Fitzgerald would put some words to "Blue Lou" and sing it.) Music publishers marketed Sampson arrangements among collections of "torrid tunes orchestrated in ultramodern fashion by the top-notch rhythm arrangers of today."[14]

Because it was Webb's instrumentals that made the band's reputation between 1929 and 1934, it is easy to overlook the role of vocal jazz in his output. He did not neglect singers as potential sources of hits. His recordings using five different male vocalists constitute about half of his output. His "chirpers," as they were sometimes called, had a repertoire of white and Black styles at their disposal. Sometimes they growled like Duke Ellington's trumpet players or scatted like Louis Armstrong; other times they crooned like Rudy Vallee in the tenor range or emulated the seemingly natural style of the baritone Bing Crosby. In 1934 Taft Jordan joined Webb's roster, impersonating Louis Armstrong as part of his stock in trade. Webb hired more cultivated voices as well, using the baritone Chuck Richards for ballads, and then in 1934 Charles Linton, a crooner with a tenor voice gracefully reaching into falsetto range. Crooning was in fashion.[15] In 1934 a reporter included Linton in a list of male vocalists who were changing the norm. "No longer do the hoarse and husky voiced singers dominate the air waves," led a story in the *Chicago Defender.* "No longer do singers with the leading name bands swing out with 'gut' songs": fans preferred "sweet singing."[16] By the time Ella showed up on July 6, 1934, Charles Linton had already made his first recording, "If It Ain't Love," a well-known rhythm song by Fats Waller and Andy Razaf.

Why should Chick Webb want a *girl* singer? A second singer would be a drain on his payroll and potentially cause trouble on the road. It irritated him that management was pushing the issue. Yet Gale and company seem to have recognized trends in the dance band world that Webb chose to ignore. There were already precedents for girl singers within dance bands, and their numbers were growing. In the late 1920s the white singer Mildred Bailey had proved to be a formidable asset for Paul Whiteman's influential orchestra. Among Black women, some pioneering artists included June Richmond and Ivie Anderson; in 1931 the latter became, according to *Down Beat*, "the first singer ever to join a colored band as part of the regular organization" when Duke Ellington hired her.[17] In 1932 Anderson ushered Ellington's swing anthem, "It Don't Mean a Thing (If It Ain't Got That Swing)" onto the *Billboard* charts. Perhaps the front office at the Savoy Ballroom recognized a trend when they witnessed Anderson perform with Duke Ellington in October 1934 at the Apollo. White bandleaders also began hiring girl singers in the mid-1930s. Benny Goodman hired Helen Ward in 1934, and Edythe Wright joined Tommy Dorsey's orchestra in 1935.

We need not belabor the obvious point that "girl singers," whose voices were still a novelty on airwaves and on recordings, added "s.a.," as the press often abbreviated sex appeal, to live performances. Of course, male singers did as well, as Chick Webb knew. A female reporter gave out Linton's statistics in February 1935: "about 5 feet nine inches, tall, slender, weighs 150 pounds, has straight black hair, dreamy eyes."[18]

It is hard to know how much Ella Fitzgerald knew about the backstage drama surrounding her spontaneous audition in front of Chick Webb—hopefully not much. It is equally hard to reconcile the differences among various eyewitnesses whose stories sometimes collide.[19] In the end they all deliver the same message: a young girl who possessed extraordinary vocal charisma faced hurdles due to her painfully plain looks. When she sang, the other musicians in the room playing cards fell suddenly quiet that Taft Jordan, Webb's ace trumpeter and a singer, recalled "the first day she sang with us, I was doing a tune called 'Judy'[!]. Bardu Ali brought Ella backstage at the Harlem Opera House for Chick to listen to, and he called up Moe Gale, who . . . came and looked at her. 'Ah, no, Chick,' he said. 'No, No, listen to the voice,' Chick said. 'Don't look at her.' When he listened, Moe Gale said, 'Uh . . . Okay, I'll hire her.' "[20] Charles Linton, claiming priority as her discoverer without any second source supporting him, said he battled Charles Buchanan and even threatened to quit if she were not hired. Exactly when this next conversation occurred is hard to know, but it is evocative nevertheless. In a 1991 interview, the drummer Hal Austin, who was active on the Harlem scene, said that Webb "didn't want her 'cause she was ugly. He said she was too ugly! I don't want that old ugly thing!"[21] Austin reported that another drummer friend, Kaiser Marshall, defended Ella to Webb: "You damn fool, you better take her."[22]

Fitzgerald told the story from her point of view in October 1937 in an interview with Lillian Johnson, a columnist for the *Baltimore Afro-American*. She confirmed that Bardu Ali was the catalyst in an experience that rivals the Apollo amateur contest as a staple in her repertoire. She understated and compressed her description:

> You know how it is. When someone's very busy, . . . there are always so many things to demand his time. Well, I went back, and kept going back every day that week. Finally, it was the last day, and the shows slipped by until it was the last performance. Chick Webb was playing the next day at Yale University and he was hurrying after the show to pack up and leave, but Ardouali [*sic*] kept pleading for just one chance for me, and finally Chick agreed to listen to one song. I sang "Judy" just as I had done on the amateur programs, the band following me. When I was through, the boys told Chick they liked my voice, and they took me to Yale with them. I've been with them ever since.[23]

In the interview, Fitzgerald without much prompting raised the question of her plain looks. When Lillian Johnson asked her: "Do you think there are many youngsters around who really have talent but who don't get a chance to prove it?" Ella answered:

> Well, it's hard to say that there are many, but the public is fickle and likes beauty, and stage-managers try to please the public. Many of these kids [aspiring singers] are good, but if they're not

nice looking, the odds are against them. So, when a girl comes up and she looks like me, she just can't get a chance.

She was honest, diplomatic, and courageous in so few words.

★★★

At Yale University, where white upper-class students adored big band music, Fitzgerald's charisma glowed. During the week that she and Webb were booked into St. Elmo's, a residence hall, Paul Whiteman, "America's King of Jazz," as the *Yale Daily News* called him, played at Yale's junior prom.[24] Mario Bauzá, Webb's trumpet player, later recalled, "Forget about everything. I took this lady with us. An hour later our room was like this. Everybody running there to listen to this lady. All the big orchestras white and black all over the university."[25]

Once they were back in Harlem, before her opening date at the Savoy Ballroom on March 9, Fitzgerald got a makeover. Chick Webb's wife Sally "kind of adopted me," she recalled decades later.[26] According to one of Webb's colleagues, Webb even floated the rumor that he had adopted her.[27] Webb and the Gale Agency scrubbed her past by branding her a virtual Little Orphan Ella who ran away from the Riverdale Home for Colored Children, and Ella did little to contradict the party line. "All around her were the famously groomed Savoy Ballroom hostesses, including Chick Webb's elegant wife, as well as Harlem chorus girls, who forced recognition of the beauty and charm of the colored woman," the "Modern Woman," in the words of Eva Jessye, a professional choral conductor.[28] "Chick and Sally were wonderful to her," recalled Al Feldman, a nineteen-year-old newcomer to the Webb band who soon found himself responsible for Ella's arrangements. Sally Webb, he said, "took her in hand, and bought her clothing and taught her how to dress. Ella was working in a glamorous environment and had to fit in."[29]

Tommy Seay, the Yonkers cultural correspondent for the *New York Age*, recorded his impressions of his friend. "I met her one time there [at the Savoy] some time in 1936: A little taller (the high heels, I guess), hair waved and curled, and evening gown hiding her slender shafts. All dolled up. . . . When the music went round n' round, she became the Ella I used to know." Seay then added one more descriptive about Ella's voice that went beyond Norma Miller's "We heard a voice" or the reporter Ted Yates's "remarkable voice, swaying voice" in this comment: "With the husky soft voice and swaying hips [Ella Fitzgerald was] just a small town girl in her element of song."[30]

In March 1935 Fitzgerald moved into the Braddock Hotel, a seven-story building on Eighth Avenue and 126th Street. There a nearby disaster cut short her first booking. On March 19, rumors surrounding the arrest of a young Puerto Rican teenager caused a crowd to gather on 125th Street. It flashed into a mob.[31] Spreading uptown, the infamous Harlem riot, or "uprising" as some called it, damaged the Savoy Ballroom, which lost all its first-floor windows and shut down for a while. The New York *Daily News* headlined the disaster: "Harlem Race Riot. Police Fire on Mob."[32] A later report from Mayor Fiorello La Guardia's official commission, which included the sociologist E. Franklin Frazier, laid some of the blame on "the terrible unemployment situation among our people in Harlem, together with the lack of relief, discrimination and starvation of the Race people, plus the vicious police hounding and persecution."[33]

In the aftermath, a psychological barrier of fear and alienation among the white population diminished the once-carefree atmosphere of uptown adventures. The Savoy Ballroom reopened and weathered the change because of its mostly Black clientele, its white student crowd, and its reputation as a major tourist attraction. Fitzgerald soon thrived in its musically intense atmosphere.

On April 24, 1935, one day before her eighteenth birthday, she witnessed her first "battle of the bands," as Webb took on a white band, Glen Gray and his Casa Loma Orchestra, at a Monster Benefit for Unemployed Musicians sponsored by Local 802, the New York chapter of the American Federation of Musicians.[34] She probably had never seen Chick Webb in his fierce, competitive state, but the battle format was a feature for Black bands across the country. Duke Ellington said Chick Webb was "battle mad," and he always prepared intensely thorough section rehearsals. Despite the home team advantage, the Casa Loma's manic rendition of a flag-waver tune ("Chinatown, My Chinatown") bested Webb's band. It was sport as much as dance.[35]

On June 17, 1935, the Chick Webb Orchestra went on a "Going Around the World" tour, playing in dance halls, amusement halls, and major Black theaters. There was little geographical logic to the grueling schedule. In June and July, Webb filled ballrooms in Massachusetts, Pennsylvania, Indiana, and New Jersey, then returned to Boston for Labor Day weekend. October brought band battles in Baltimore and Nashville, plus a dance in Newport News.[36] In November they battled Jimmie Noone's Orchestra in Chicago, played a dance in Pittsburgh, and filled theater dates in Philadelphia and Washington, D.C.

Ella was coming into her own as a performer for her lively mix of singing and dancing. In September 1935 she applied for a Social Security card, acknowledging she was in the band to stay, listing her birth year oddly as 1918 and her residence as the Braddock Hotel.[37] Her name grew bigger on advertisements, and reviewers took note. At the Sunset Casino in Atlanta, advance notice for the October 25 performance mentioned "Ella Fitzgerald, that brownskin package of personality who's going to 'truck on down,' that new Savoy novelty step."[38] She projected the moves of carefree youth, swaying from side to side, pointing her fingers to the sky as she strolled across the floor.

By November 1935 she had acquired a small following in Harlem. When the band returned for an engagement at the Apollo on November 8, she got some spotlight coverage in the *New York Amsterdam News*: "the swingy Ella Fitzgerald in scintillating rhythm with unique arrangements on an old favorite, 'You're a Heavenly Thing,' delighted the audience." She was covering material being recorded by other girl singers, particularly Helen Ward, Benny Goodman's increasingly popular vocalist. Once again the song that had proved her stalwart companion from her audition years brought her luck: "Miss Fitzgerald, an outstanding local favorite, came back with 'Judy' which, to my mind, is about the spiciest bit of vocal doings I've come across at recent date."[39]

Fitzgerald was clearly flourishing in a supportive environment. Later interviews with band members, who called her "Sis," describe a warm working relationship that made for easy traveling on the road. A photograph of Ella with Charles Linton suggests their comfortable coexistence.[40] He continued to make a few records, even getting space to sing a whole number rather than one chorus on a ballad. There was room on the bill for two singers until the fall of 1937, when Webb let Linton go.[41] Some of the musicians had issues with their leader bringing up teenage Ella as the proverbial "boss's daughter." In 1937 Ella told Lillian Johnson that Webb "has been unusually kind, taking a fatherly interest and giving advice when it has been most needed, even to seeing that I take care of my money."[42]

She could be so annoying. Ella would get "evil," imagining slights in simple social situations.[43] Al Feldman remembered an incident when Chick Webb insisted, over her objections, that Ella cancel a date and stay for a rehearsal. The bass player Beverly Peer would recall in 1998: "most of the musicians didn't care much for her personality. I don't think she was really nasty, but she was insecure and came off as being nasty."[43] *Who is looking at me?* she would wonder. *Who is talking about me?* Ella reported that "my cousin [Georgie] had told me once that I used to think people were talking about me and then I'd get evil. And she used to tell me, she says, 'you know these same people if they're saying something bad and you smile, you make them feel bad.' So I keep all these little things in my mind. Those are a few of my treasures." Charles Linton recalled a subway ride where she got upset over passengers allegedly staring. Worse, he saw her mete out the treatment to Chick Webb himself. On one occasion, while Webb was beaming at her, she returned his prideful gaze with a look that Linton parsed as "What the hell are you grinning at me for?"[45] Such painful moments recall her words to Lillian Johnson about a girl who "looks like me." If looks were at issue, then no matter what the situation, how could she be sure what hidden message lay behind a gaze?

In the end, what mattered most was the spirit of Chick Webb's musical community. She admired his outstanding musicians, the "Five Horsemen," as the brass players were dubbed; his saxophonists, who took lyrical solos on ballads; his rhythm section; and the boss presiding over the magnificent drum set. Her total engagement in the ensemble comes through in a remarkable recollection from George T. Simon, then a critic for *Metronome* and later an expert on big band history: "I didn't know anything [about her] until I went up there [to the Savoy] and was so knocked out by her, knocked out not only by the way she sang but the spirit and the way she would lead the band by throwing kicks on the side of the bandstand."[46] Fitzgerald would retain these habits vestigially throughout her concert career, snapping her fingers, patting her hips, whipping her head from side to side—as if she were hearing the bite of Sampson's arrangements or one of Webb's drum breaks, and transferring the band's dynamic energy into her body as well as her voice.

★★★

AFTER TOURING FOR MOST OF THE FALL IN 1935, Fitzgerald and the Chick Webb Orchestra settled into a residency at the Savoy Ballroom from January to June 1936. The Savoy was a mecca for musicians, a community center, a wellspring of innovative social dancing, and an institution of "social conscience," to use a phrase from the era. No other singer of her generation had such easy access to the opportunities it offered. On February 21, 1936, she was exposed to left-wing politics in an extraordinary historical moment, when the Webb orchestra played a benefit for the Scottsboro Boys, defendants in an egregious miscarriage of justice. Roy Wilkins of the NAACP (National Association for the Advancement of Colored People) spoke, and the event drew many important musicians including Mildred Bailey, Fletcher Henderson, Duke Ellington, Benny Goodman, and Willie Bryant. Fitzgerald most likely heard Bessie Smith sing, and perhaps Smith heard her as well.[47] The event drew a heavy white attendance of five hundred people but only fifty African Americans, so it was reported.[48] Another "routine" evening at the Savoy stands out as an encounter among towering figures of African American song. In March 1936 Fitzgerald met up with Bessie Smith, again with Mildred Bailey, and with Ethel Waters—the most famous African American actress and singer in the 1920s and '30s—to judge a dance contest.[49]

Fitzgerald held a visible position as Chick Webb's singer, and other important musicians left their impressions of hearing her for the first time at the Savoy Ballroom. Mary Lou Williams, the young pianist-arranger in Andy Kirk's swing band Clouds of Joy, recounted:

> One night, scuffling around Harlem, [Dick] Wilson and I fell in the Savoy. After dancing a couple of rounds, I heard a voice that sent chills up and down my spine (which I never thought could happen). I almost ran to the stand to find out who belonged to the voice, and saw a pleasant-looking brown-skinned girl standing modestly and singing the greatest. I was told her name was Ella Fitzgerald, and that Chick Webb had unearthed her from one of the Apollo's amateur hours.[50]

In the jazz press, Fitzgerald had conquered the heart of *Metronome*'s editor, George T. Simon, who in January 1936 patted himself on the back.

> During the past year or so this column has emitted various touts and raves about various heretofore unknowns. . . . Some of them have fulfilled their promise . . . others haven't. . . . At any rate this column is continuing same policy during the coming year. . . . Here's number one for 1936: Ella Fitzgerald. . . . The seventeen-year-old gal singing up at Harlem's Savoy with Chick Webb's fine band . . . unheralded and practically unknown right now, but what a future . . . a great natural flare for singing . . . extraordinary intonation and figures.

We may add Simon's comment about "intonation" to the lexicon of descriptions of Fitzgerald's voice in these early years. Singing with accurate pitch, being neither sharp nor flat but dead center on, is being "in tune" and produces the sensation of purity of tone. Simon added, "She's one of the best of all femme hot warblers . . . and there's no reason why she shouldn't be just about the best in time to come. . . . Watch her!"[51] In the Black community, Billy Rowe—the recently hired entertainment journalist for the *Pittsburgh Courier*, one of the two most important Black newspapers in the interwar years—included her name in his "Honor Roll of '35."[52] Rowe would reliably chronicle her career for the next fifteen years as an ardent advocate for new talent.[53]

The small-town girl from Yonkers was growing up fast. The British jazz critic Leonard Feather wrote of his "unforgettable evening" with Webb's band, "the perfect swing orchestra," and noticed how Fitzgerald asserted her musicianship: "Then a young Ella Fitzgerald walked onto the bandstand—in the middle of an Edgar Sampson arrangement no less, asked, 'Please, Mr. Webb, may I sing this number?' and captivated the audience utterly."[54] What nerve. Ernani Bernardi, a member of Tommy Dorsey's orchestra, told a complementary tale. In the spring of 1936 he sat on the Savoy's bandstand while the rest of Dorsey's crew listened to Chick's set, and Ella asked "whether I thought that one day she would get to record with an orchestra like Tommy's."[55] What ambition.

Chapter 4

SWING-SONG SINGER

(1935-1936)

Ella Fitzgerald began her recording career on June 12, 1935, shortly after she turned eighteen, at the Decca studio in New York. It could have been another case of "no girl singer" wanted: as she recalled twenty years later, "Chick wanted to record me with Decca [and] they turned me down. But he insisted, and he won."[1] He already believed in her future. Emulating Ella's own taste for Fats Waller (his "Believe It Beloved" was one of his audition songs), Webb assigned her two more songs that Waller had recently recorded: "Love and Kisses" on the first Decca session, then "Rhythm and Romance" on the second session, on October 12. (Waller's version of "Rhythm and Romance" reached *Billboard*'s list for jukebox play that fall.)[2] She recalled:

> I'll never forget it; the record was "Love and Kisses." After we made it, the band was in Philadelphia one night when they wouldn't let me in at some beer garden where I wanted to hear it on the jukebox. So I had some fellow who was over twenty-one go in and put a nickel in while I stood outside and listened to my own voice coming out.[3]

Better fare prevailed on October 12 as she handled an original melody, "I'll Chase the Blues Away," composed by Edgar Sampson, Webb's top arranger. After an instrumental chorus, she delivered the lyrics, then receded for the final chorus, when the soloists strutted their stuff.

Decca gave Webb more studio time the next year, and Fitzgerald was allotted eleven new titles. It would be a mistake to attribute the band's improved standing solely to her voice, and there was no such perception at the time. Instead, her arrival in Chick Webb's band coincided with a new acceptance of his style as a whole. In late 1935 and 1936, the "hot" dance music that Webb and others played was growing in popularity, rivaling the more commercial "sweet" music of the white bands dominating radio such as Guy Lombardo, Glen Gray's Casa Loma Band, and the Dorsey Brothers.

Swing had arrived, and with it came "swinging the songbook," an alliance between jazz and popular songs from Broadway, Hollywood, and Tin Pan Alley.[4] Just as in the early 1900s ragtime could be applied as a style to whatever one chose, so too in the 1930s swing, a rhythmic idiom, turned into a musical style, then into an identity for big dance bands. It expanded into a cultural youth movement, shorthanded in conventional jazz history as the "swing era," running from 1935 to 1946.

The ascendancy of swing among white bands caught the entertainment press by surprise. In *Variety*, the ever-wry Abel Green asked, "So what is swing?" while describing 52nd Street as "the capital of the swing world," where "addicts sit around entranced, in an ultra-modern jazz coma."[5] In the *New York Amsterdam News*, a review of a special radio program that aired on March 12, 1936, opened with "What is 'swing' music?" According to the review, the broadcast showcased "numerous and varied definitions of this new kind of rhythm" through interpretations by a "specially picked orchestra" including Chick Webb.[6]

Many Black musicians considered that they had established the foundations of swing in the late 1920s and early '30s, in what one might call the B ("Before Benny Goodman") Era. Their point was reiterated by the noted writer Albert Murray in the 1970s when he referred to the "so-called Swing Era."[7] Webb insisted on his precedence, at a time when the white bands of Benny Goodman and Artie Shaw were grabbing the headlines, sweeping away their forerunners. Webb tried to set things straight in an interview for the *New York Amsterdam News*. Journalist Roi Ottley, who would have a distinguished career as a cultural historian in the 1940s, wrote that Webb "takes the position that success is no mere 'accident,' but a gradual public awareness of a personality, a talent or a type of music." In the interview, Webb told him:

> When Fletcher Henderson arrived with his unusual rhythms and distinctive orchestrations—he was terrific—the public was ready to receive a departure from the harsh jazz renditions. People flocked to hear his smooth interpretation of popular music. Duke Ellington then followed with a sort of jungle rhythm, which captivated the public. I feel the public has moved away from that type of music to my specialty, which is now known as "swing music." I have been playing this type of music since I organized an orchestra in 1927. Now my type of "stuff" is what people want.[8]

How amazing that the stuff was the "Harlem-Savoy" style?[9] A new generation, flaunting the prerogatives of youth to set fashion, codified the slang of swing music, or jive, for the mainstream. In the mid-1930s, Chick Webb turned into a "hot skin beater," noted for his "lift"—making tired feet dance—and for his "hot torrid" style as opposed to "corny" bands. Ella Fitzgerald was his "crack canary" delivering "swing-songs."[10] She was a "jive singer."[11] She was making friends with the "cats" (swing fans and musicians) and learning to "get off" and "get in the groove" (swing hard) in a ballroom. She was learning how to come in after the "repeat chorus" (the second chorus after the "stock" arrangement, or the standard printed version), hoping someday to also be part of the "sock chorus" (the last chorus of an orchestration).[12]

The ascendancy of swing changed the frame around Fitzgerald's singing. To the lexicon of song types such as blues and torch songs, the "swing song" was added. In general, swing songs were rhythm songs intended as dance music, with lyrics geared to youth and with references to dance in the title, sometimes using slang—familiar hooks in the popular music world. Lyrics with "swing" in their titles multiplied;

for example, "Swing Me a Lullaby" and "You Can Call It Swing" were the A and B sides of a 1936 Decca release by Connie Boswell with the Bob Crosby Orchestra. In tandem with the genre, the term *swing singer* started to proliferate in the general press around 1935, referring more often to women. In the next few years, the designations *swing singer* and *modern swing singing* would be attached to the most important vocalists of the day, including Mildred Bailey, Billie Holiday, Maxine Sullivan, and Martha Raye, as well as to lesser-known figures.[13]

Thus the timing of Fitzgerald's arrival in Chick Webb's band was an extraordinary stroke of luck for two musical soulmates who embodied the vital essence of dance. "As a drummer, Chick had his own ideas about what he wanted to do," wrote Duke Ellington in his memoir. "Some musicians are dancers, and Chick was. You can dance with a lot of things besides your feet. Chick Webb was a dance-drummer who painted pictures of dances with his drums."[14] Just as Webb "lifted" and "kicked his band," so Fitzgerald learned to lift and kick lyrics, choreographing swing by pushing ahead of the beat, emphasizing key words in the melodic line, and embellishing a melody with a flourish or ornament. She gave songs momentum or, as musicians called it, "time," making her voice "dance."

★★★

THESE ARE THE THINGS WE LOOK FOR in Fitzgerald's 1936 Decca recordings: What moved her? When did she break the shackles of the "vocal chorus"? What's worth listening to now? Who noticed? She had to start at the very bottom. A review of "I'll Chase the Blues Away" in *Tempo*, a young publication catering to serious jazz fans, made it all about Webb, "that truly great drummer [who was] unusual for a colored group for there is no evidence of that tendency to overdo everything so familiar in Lunceford and Ellington." The reviewer did not mention Fitzgerald's name.[15]

Things got better fast, with an unexpected boost from outside Decca: the pianist Teddy Wilson recruited her for a special date on the Brunswick label. On March 17, 1936, he tapped her to replace Billie Holiday, who was away in upstate New York on a theater bill with Jimmie Lunceford's band.[16] Two years older than Fitzgerald, Holiday had recorded fifteen songs with Wilson from July 1935 to January 1936, including the now classic "What a Little Moonlight Can Do" and "Twenty-Four Hours a Day." The Wilson sessions on Brunswick established her reputation as an original song stylist.

That top-selling Teddy Wilson entrusted Ella Fitzgerald to maintain the quality of these sessions shows her growing reputation. Having not yet signed an exclusive Decca contract, she was free to join Wilson's octet of fine swing musicians, which included two sidemen from Webb's band.[17] The musicians were perhaps not as stellar as those for Holiday's sessions, but they were solid nevertheless, delivering a vibrant performance of the standard "My Melancholy Baby" and a lesser interpretation of the ballad "All My Life."[18] In a *Metronome* review, George Simon wrote that "All My Life" featured "one of the greatest of Teddy Wilson piano choruses plus a fine vocal by the up and coming Ella Fitzgerald."[19] In "All My Life," one of the most popular songs of 1936, Wilson and Fitzgerald swung the tune into a rhythm ballad that sold well in the "amusement machine" market, or jukeboxes.[20] What record companies put into jukeboxes depended on where they were located. "All My Life" had debuted in a sweet version by the Irish tenor Phil Regan, star of the film *Laughing Irish Eyes*, in which his crooning voice floated in a soft arrangement of harps and strings. Wilson's version headed for Black venues. Covering popular songs written for white audiences in a Black style for jukeboxes was a wise investment because, in John Hammond's words, "suddenly all those black bars had juke boxes."[21] And suddenly "race records," supported by social segregation, had another outlet as a market reality. People voted, one nickel at a time.

Billie Holiday came back to New York and resumed her sessions with Teddy Wilson. While she scored hits with "These Foolish Things (Remind Me of You)" and George Gershwin's "Summertime," from his opera *Porgy and Bess*, Fitzgerald returned to a sleepy session at Decca on April 7, 1936, where she was assigned vocal choruses in "Crying My

Heart Out for You," "Under the Spell of the Blues" (another Edgar Sampson effort), and an edgy ode to marijuana, "When I Get Low I Get High." Such ephemera got virtually no attention from other bands.

Finally, on June 2, 1936, Fitzgerald made an important professional and artistic breakthrough with "Sing Me a Swing Song (And Let Me Dance)," with words and music by Hoagy Carmichael and Stanley Adams. It was her very first song listed on a *Billboard* chart (see Appendix).[22] Fitzgerald sang from beginning to end, her voice youthful, lucid, and "centered," meaning each pitch sounded pure and clear.

The new girl singer and the maestro were beginning to form a musical bond, already explicit in their third studio session. At the end of the song, she cheered, "Ol' Chick Webb is beatin it out / Makes me feel like I want to shout / All the boys are ready to prance," and they did, as Webb offered some all-too-brief, mesmerizing solo work using cowbells. The arranger, young Al Feldman, later known as Van Alexander, wrote that Webb and Fitzgerald's first joint success gave her artistic independence: "She was not looked upon any longer as Chick Webb's band singer."[23] The Webb recording outsold the version recorded six days earlier by Benny Goodman.[24] Now that was a moment—topping the clarinet of Goodman, never mind his vocalist, Helen Ward.

In a *Down Beat* review of Webb's two latest Decca releases, which included "Swing Me a Swing Song," Edgar Greentree wrote, "Probably the most important thing about them is Ella Fitzgerald's vocals on three of the four sides. Possessed of an unusual voice, this young singer is really sensational in every sense of the word. Chick's drumming is also captured well on these platters and the rest of the band is right in there behind their 'guiding light.' "[25]

Webb soon made the shrewd decision to designate Feldman as Fitzgerald's main collaborator. Born in 1915, Feldman grew up in Washington Heights in a solid middle-class Jewish family. His father was a pharmacist, and his mother was a classical pianist who home-schooled him at the piano. Webb's musicians knew of her, for she also gave lessons at some point to Webb's pianist, Tommy Fulford. By his senior year in high school, Feldman had his own seven- or eight-piece dance band,

and soon after graduation in 1933 he joined Local 802, the New York musicians' union.

"I was a lindy-hopper in those days," Feldman recalled. "I would go to the Savoy three, four times a week."[26] As a nineteen-year-old Savoy regular, he got up the nerve to ask Webb if he would consider trying out his arrangements. Webb said, "Sure, bring them next Friday." Moe Gale soon hired Feldman to produce three arrangements per week for seventy-five dollars.[27] He was twenty-one when he first met Ella, "a shy young lady and very humble. I initially thought that she might be a bit cocky and into herself but she wasn't that way at all. She had a gentle way about her, yet she was loaded with unbridled enthusiasm as only a teenager could have. That enthusiasm came across loud and clear in her singing."[28] His high-school classmate Peter Dean, a future music professional, echoed: "Ella was the queen. In the beginning she sang with all that freedom and excitement. . . . We went *nuts* for her."[29]

The next watershed moment was Webb's fall studio session at Decca on October 29, 1936. Fitzgerald sang the novelty song "(If You Can't Sing It) You'll Have to Swing It," known unofficially by its shorter title, "Mr. Paganini," written by veteran Hollywood songsmith Sam Coslow. (The original target of the muddled lyrics was Arturo Toscanini, but Coslow feared offending the famous conductor, instead scapegoating the legendary nineteenth-century violinist Paganini as a proxy "longhair.")[30] Ella's "Mr. Paganini" reached the jukebox charts for a week in mid-December 1936. That month John Hammond added a solid plug in *Down Beat*: "Although the heading reads Chick Webb, the record is all about Ella Fitzgerald and her rise to the top of girl singers. [She] is responsible for this being the biggest selling record in New York—according to a Decca pal of mine—with the first side ['Mr. Paganini'] being the one given the play in the automatic machines."[31]

The song had launched the movie career of swing singer Martha Raye. "I think she sings the craziest," Ella told a radio interviewer thirty years later. Raye had premiered "Mr. Paganini" in the Hollywood film *Rhythm on the Range*, a Bing Crosby vehicle cashing in on the singing cowboy trend. Backed by Louis Prima on trumpet, and Bob Burns on bazooka for a comic touch, Raye parodied the formal stage manners of a classical singer, then ran wild as a rambunctious modern girl, marching in place like a swinging majorette. She even scatted a little with Prima. "That's the way to do it," thought future jazz singer Anita O'Day when she saw the movie.[32] It took a while for Martha Raye to come out with a record of her film song. As Will Friedwald writes, "the megamoguls who ran old Hollywood viewed the other arms of the mass media with suspicion," believing their films would be harmed by recording hits out of context and making them independently available.[33] Thus Fitzgerald's version managed to take advantage of the film without much competition from Raye. With an arrangement by Al Feldman, Fitzgerald refashioned the song, smoothed out the lyrics, replaced the slapstick with swing, and added musical interest to the melody with blue notes and Black inflections. There are even two fleeting breaks of scat singing; a hint of bold chromaticism in the melody; and an early use of the "flatted fifth," the most dissonant interval in common-practice Western harmony.[34] Medieval music theorists called it *diabolus in musica*, "the devil in music"; bebop musicians would claim it as a badge of honor. Fitzgerald dared to use it in 1936.[35] Tapping the comic and ironic elements in her personality, Fitzgerald delivered "Mr. Paganini" with genuine affection and understated charm.

Nobody could have predicted that this film novelty would turn into one of her signature songs, which she would revisit to the delight of audiences in the 1950s and '60s. "Mister Paganinny," she sings, mispronouncing his name then and forever in the many subsequent performances, from Ed Sullivan's *Toast of the Town* TV show in 1948 to sophisticated nightclub dates.[36] It traveled well, particularly in Europe. "Oh my gosh, if I play Italy or France and don't do 'Paganini,' forget it," she later told her critic-friend Leonard Feather.[37]

Fitzgerald had the magic to help Chick Webb transition from a local big shot to a national star. "The only way you could make decent money was if you jumped the fence, like they used to say. You jump the fence and stop looking back."[38] By mixing the repertoire, balancing sweet arrangements with jazz, and including pop hits and novelties as well,

Webb was compensating for years of struggle. Very quickly Webb treated Fitzgerald strategically. Teddy McRae, an outstanding saxophonist and Webb's "straw boss," hired to take care of business matters and advise on repertoire, expressed this point of view in a 1981 interview:

> We were ahead of everybody in getting the material for Ella. We got a lot of material. We did a thing called "Mr. Paganini," they [other bands] don't ever do nothing like "Mr. Paganini," but Ella could do those novelty type of things. She could do them good! And she put a style to them. She had a lot of talent. . . . We'd be rehearsing the arrangements, she'd be listening, you know. "You all ready for me?" And Chick would say, "Okay, Ella, we're ready." She'd come over, and we'll hand her the sheet. She could sight read better than anybody of all the singers. She was real fast. . . . I was thinking to myself, how many songs Ella got in her.[39]

★★★

BEGINNING IN 1936, Fitzgerald built a national fan base through radio broadcasts. Moe Gale had secured contracts for Chick Webb for fifteen-minute broadcasts of "sustaining programs," meaning airtime without commercial sponsorship.[40] A few extant radio logs from late November and December 1936 show that Fitzgerald sang one or two songs, usually chosen from her latest Decca studio sessions, as well as miscellaneous covers of popular hits like "Honeysuckle Rose," which she never recorded on that label.[41]

Then in January 1936 Fitzgerald got her first opportunity to reach a mass audience on *Gems of Color*, a variety show modeled on the vaudeville fare in Harlem's Black theaters. *Gems of Color* debuted on NBC on January 27, 1936, in a prime-time 10:30 slot. On February 19, *Variety* gave it a nod: "Chick Webb, with crack canary Ella Fitzgerald, the Ink Spots, and the Cecil Mack choir, presented on a 'Gems of Color' hour that sent the cats."[42]

Radio programming during the Great Depression was marred by

demeaning stereotypes and entrenched discriminatory practices: most live swing broadcasts showcased white dance bands and vocalists.[44] While Moe Gale was promoting the modern swing of the Savoy Ballroom, he also believed he had to heed the norms for Black entertainment on white radio, whose audiences expected minstrel shows and blackface. So he vacillated and straddled these imperatives. *Metronome* wrote, "While on the subject of the colored boys, don't forget Chick Webb's band . . . getting plenty of deserved build-up three times a week on NBC studio sustainings. . . . [The] band itself is right there, but program is ruined by some smart-alecky white announcer who just doesn't know what it's all about . . . more commercial showmanship pfui."[44] While the critic was talking about the blackface dialect affected by the show's announcer Juano Hernandez, the kind of music Fitzgerald sang on the show was another case in point, including "Darktown Strutters' Ball" and "Shine." She jumped the fence in her own way by receiving what was probably her first review of a live performance outside a recording studio: "The revamped 'Gems of Color' hour hit the ether waves with plenty [of] splash. Chick Webb, with Ella Fitzgerald on vocal, backboned the program while the Ink Spots, and the Cecil Mack Choir alternated. . . . The theme-song 'Shine' allowed Ella Fitzgerald to swing out with her youthful tone and fine phrasing in spite of a tempo that dragged."[45] Charles Isaac Bowen, writing for the Associated Negro Press news service, observed, "Personally, I am fond of hearing Miss Ella Fitzgerald sing 'Shine,' the theme song of the *Gems of Color* program." But the song would later be repudiated as a Jim Crow relic.[46]

Later in 1936 Fitzgerald recorded both "Shine" and "Darktown Strutters' Ball" for Decca, likely echoing the style used on *Gems of Color*. "Darktown Strutters' Ball," from 1917, has regressive blackface built into the title and begins with a carousing "Dixieland" introduction. Fitzgerald then enters with her first vocal chorus. After some instrumental solos, she returns for a final "stop-time" chorus, half-improvising on the tune and half singing it straight. She had little say with the Gale office. For *Gems of Color*, Ella sang other songs that were not mentioned in press accounts. Recordings were supplied to the stations by specially made platters called transcriptions, and Gale had several made for the program, including some surprisingly modern choices such as "You Hit the Spot" by Hollywood composers Mack Gordon and Harry Revel.

★★★

AT THE END OF 1936, the *Metronome* "All Star Band" poll listed Webb and Fitzgerald highest among Black musicians in their respective categories. Webb placed third, behind white drummers Gene Krupa and Ray Bauduc, while among "girl vocalists," Fitzgerald tied with Mildred Bailey for second place behind "pretty Helen Ward," Benny Goodman's singer.[47] The Black newspapers celebrated both as entertainment stars and therefore as models for the race. On April 4, 1936, about a year after Fitzgerald started with Webb, Billy Rowe was beginning his career as a major chronicler of Harlem's entertainment scene.[48] He included her in a list of noteworthy "personalities of the stage" in "the greater colored show world" for his "Harlem Notebook" column in the *Pittsburgh Courier*.[49] To become a "personality of the stage" in only one year meant combining many activities, from touring out-of-state ballrooms and theaters to making records to performing on radio broadcasts. Webb's touring schedule from about June 10, 1936, through November 1 shows that their band bus journeyed from the urbanized Midwest (Akron, Indiana) to smaller cities closer to home (Taunton, Massachusetts, and Portland, Maine).[50]

Despite her success, Fitzgerald had dreams to do more, to "jump the fence" and not "stay in her own backyard" singing second-rate Tin Pan Alley fare. "The material that Ella was assigned had no substance. In fact, a lot of it was pure junk," said Van Alexander—quite a judgment coming from Webb's designated arranger of her songs. "Even Ella was concerned about the material she was asked to perform. She wanted to make a hit record, and she felt that most of the songs she was asked to sing wouldn't help her accomplish that goal. But what she recorded seemed to grab listeners' ears. That's what Chick wanted, so it worked."[51]

Other stakeholders in the music business saw a vacuum and tried to fill it, particularly music publishers making their way to Moe Gale's Radio City office. According to Webb's straw boss and sax player Teddy McRae, "Mills Music, Robbins, Shapiro-Bernstein, you name them—all the top publishers—everybody was trying to get Ella to do the top hit songs." Every publisher hired a sales force to approach dance band conductors, independent singers, and radio program directors with its tunes, enlisting, cajoling, and bribing them to give a tune a whirl on their remote broadcasts. They needed "plugs" and airtime to promote their main product: sheet music, the vocal-piano scores of individual songs with eye-catching covers, priced between twenty-five and thirty-five cents, aimed at amateurs making music on the ubiquitous spinet pianos in the parlor. The major publisher, Jack Robbins, was among the first to court rising bandleaders. "Robbins called me downtown one day," said McRae, "and he'd say, 'Look, you have the best thing in the country. Why do you have her sing those second-rate songs?'" He offered to give Webb songs for his Saturday night Savoy broadcasts: "You have the best thing in the country, I'll give you a deal."[52]

Chapter 5

THE SECOND FEATURE

(1936–1937)

The ace Jack Robbins had big ideas. He promised Webb priority access to "all the top songs from Hollywood" if Ella Fitzgerald would sing them on Savoy radio broadcasts. That was quite an offer, especially considering the improved quality of songs in recent Hollywood film musicals like "Cheek to Cheek" (from Irving Berlin's *Top Hat*, 1935) and Cole Porter's "I've Got You Under My Skin" (from *Born to Dance*, 1936). Robbins's plum offering was Mack Gordon and Harry Revel's "Goodnight My Love," written for *Stowaway*, a musical film due out in December 1936, starring the popular child star Shirley Temple and the actress-singer Alice Faye.[1] "We had the song before anybody had it," said McRae, though Fitzgerald would record it with a different bandleader and reach new heights. McRae explains, " 'Goodnight My Love' became so big that when she did that song, Benny Goodman had to ask Chick, 'Look, will you let Ella do this on my show?' "[2]

Chick Webb agreed and allowed Ella to record the song on November 5. Benny Goodman's career was booming. His new CBS network variety program, *Camel Caravan Hour*, reached a far bigger adult audience than Webb's fifteen-minute radio spots and would surely help spread Webb's name and sell his records. From that moment through most of 1937, collisions between art and commerce plunged Fitzgerald into the middle of legal, professional, and ethical disputes between the two bandleaders and the president of Decca Records. Goodman had asked for Fitzgerald because he needed a substitute for Helen Ward, his regular vocalist since 1934. Roughly the same age as Ella, Ward had first gained recognition on the *Let's Dance* radio show from December 1934 through May 1935. Ward's career trailblazed the uncharted paths for "girl singers" during Goodman's rise to fame and turned her into a major asset, which he resented. As she told Goodman's biographer, Ross Firestone, "Singers were a necessary evil to Benny. The real McCoy he was after came in the instrumentals. But it was an absolute necessity that we play the pop tunes of the day . . . what we called the commercial music of the day."[3] Jazz critics had a similar point of view. In *Down Beat*, the producer, jazz writer, and publicist Helen Oakley, whom Gale would hire to represent Chick Webb, once came to Ward's defense. Under the gender-neutral name of H. M. Oakley, she wrote, "I can't understand why Helen Ward is not more generally appreciated. . . . In this day and age, when a girl vocalist is so often a thing of horror, I would think this miracle should be duly acknowledged."[4] By November 1936 Ward's playful voice, with its slightly metallic edge, had been featured on several Goodman hits that are now considered pop standards, including "Goody Goody" and "These Foolish Things." Rumor had it that Ward was in Hollywood making movies, but in fact she had temporarily left the band to sort out some messy romances, hoping perhaps for a marriage proposal from Goodman.[5]

For Fitzgerald's November 10 debut on *Camel Caravan*, Goodman let his radio audience know that he was presenting a Black singer. Months later, a reporter for the *Baltimore Afro-American* "remembered well the first night that I heard her on the radio—the night that Benny Goodman introduced her on the Camel hour, explaining that he usually went down to Harlem, trying to find talent, and that Ella Fitzgerald was the best thing he's ever seen." "I will always remember this," Fitzgerald told the reporter. "I was so thrilled! We had been playing at the Savoy and Benny Goodman often came in, and came back to talk to us, but when he asked if I'd come up to Radio City and be his guest on the Camel hour, I nearly swooned."[6]

"Goodnight My Love" was an ideal vehicle for Fitzgerald's vocal personality as an ingenue. She sang it in addition to "You Turned the Tables on Me," another Hollywood song that found favor with jazz musicians, and that she would reprise memorably in later decades. The white mainstream press paid scant attention to Fitzgerald's *Camel Caravan* debut, except the syndicated columnist who asked, "And what did you think of Goodman's new swingstress, Ella Fitzgerald, a Negress with an Irish name and a slight Scotch burr? [She had] clean tricks, a swell style." He also suggested that "Miss Ward, now in Hollywood a-muggin for the movies, must have slow-burned at Benny's blazing banner introduction of his new discovery."[7] An African American newspaper, the *California Eagle*, noted the buzz and said Fitzgerald had been "heard to great advantage." The writer added, "Yes, she's sepia," letting readers know that she belonged.[8] It stands as an early comment on Fitzgerald's vocality—her sounding "white" or rather race neutral, delivering lyrics in perfect diction in "General American English," as it was known in the 1930s.

Benny Goodman was indeed smitten with Ella's voice, and before the *Camel Caravan* show, he ushered her into a Victor studio to record a few tunes with his band, which included Gene Krupa, his star drummer, and Vido Musso, the twenty-three-year-old tenor saxophonist Ella was dating.[9] Upon its November 25 release, "Goodnight My Love" quickly found its audience and by the next month was charting for radio plugs and disc sales.[10] Jack Robbins got his reward when his sheet music arrived on the best-seller list even before the December 18 Hollywood film release of *Stowaway*, which drove the song to the top of a nationally known radio show, *Your Hit Parade* (see Appendix).

For Ella Fitzgerald, it was a bittersweet triumph. Decca's president, Jack Kapp, swooned too. What was a Decca singer doing recording for a rival label? Even though Decca had never officially signed her, Kapp insisted that her name be removed from the Victor label. With licensing arrangements in flux, particularly for Black artists, both parties could claim just cause. Record companies still hired most musicians—especially Black musicians—on a per-session, piecework basis, and even exclusive contracts were sometimes skirted with pseudonyms. Although Fitzgerald's records with Teddy Wilson for Brunswick had her name printed on the label, recording with Goodman was another matter. In the Victor archives, an undated, handwritten note on the session history card reads, "The name of Helen [sic] Fitzgerald is not to be used on the disc label," and Ella's masters were "to be destroyed." John Hammond's review in Down Beat noted, "The customers better rush and grab this record, for I hear that it is being withdrawn from the market."[11] Even though the record was pulled, limited copies continued to circulate, and Webb and Fitzgerald broadcast the song from the Savoy.[12] Fitzgerald never forgot the slight, as she recalled near the end of her life: "Remember when I made 'Goodnight My Love' with Benny? It became such a big hit and they killed it! Yeah, they took my name off. They killed it. Used my initials Ella Fields or something. They took my *name* off! So then Decca said that I was supposed to be with them because Chick was with them. So then they killed it. But it was a good song and it *still* is a good song, a good song!"[13] Goodman did not invite Fitzgerald back to any radio show for the next twenty years. Nor did they make another studio record together.

With the Goodman discs, critics sometimes seemed to be hearing Fitzgerald for the first time, realizing that her striking rhythmic elasticity placed her at the forefront of vocal jazz innovation. Hammond's review referred to her "effortless ease and spontaneity that belongs only to great artists. Her rhythmic relaxation is an inspiration to the whole band." It was exactly the quality that Mildred Bailey, another singer Hammond admired, described as the essence of swing for vocalists.[14]

After that, as Mario Bauzá recalled, "everybody wanted that lady, everybody."[15] That included another radio program, one that preserves an even better live performance of "Goodnight My Love." On January 6, 1937, she sang it on a broadcast backed by the jazz violinist Stuff Smith and his all-star ensemble drawn from the bands of Webb and Cab Calloway. She earned an excellent review in the trade press for her "sultry" interpretation.[16] The fifteen-minute show Let's Listen to Lucidin (an over-the-counter eyewash) was a rare commercially sponsored radio spot for an African American musician. By March the show, which hosted Fitzgerald at least four times, fired Smith: "No Air Commercials for Colored: Nix Products with Sepians," read the notice in the *New York Amsterdam News*.[17]

Just when Goodman was integrating his orchestra with Black musicians Lionel Hampton and Teddy Wilson, John Hammond suggested that Ella Fitzgerald "quite possibly" might join Goodman as a permanent vocalist.[18] Behind the scenes, as was confirmed later by Ella herself, Hammond tried to get Goodman to take her on.[19] In public, that remark from a prominent jazz writer and producer preceded a firestorm of speculation in the Black press, overwhelming a young singer barely used to such attention and provoking her own justified pride, yet at the same time throwing her into chaos. She saved clippings in her scrapbook at the time that chronicle a beginning and an end.

On December 5 the *Pittsburgh Courier* published: "Benny Goodman Offers $5,000 for Ella's Contract, But Chick Webb Says 'No Sale.'"[20] Could such an astronomical sum really be plausible? Then came panic—causing even more furor—in which she simply went "AWOL" from conflict. She further preserved that press notice in another scrapbook clipping:

> December 31: Ella Fitzgerald Returns to Chick Webb Again After Run-Away Scare. Sensational Girl Singer Disappeared After Learning Benny Goodman's $5,000 Offer to Buy Her Contract Had Been Turned Down. As mysteriously as she disappeared, the great singing youngster reappeared on the scene and refusing to answer any questions whatsoever, she went about her job which the public has grown to love so well.[21]

While it feels like puffery, such coverage captures aspects of both Ella Fitzgerald's personality and persona: subverting and deflecting press attention would remain a fixture of her career, interpreted in many ways—sometimes, as here, as youthful shyness, other times as introversion, or elitism or neurotic social anxiety, sometimes exaggerated, sometimes accurate. "Excuse me while I disappear," a line from the song "Angel Eyes" written some ten years later, which Fitzgerald sang when she was around thirty-five years old, fits this moment perfectly. She would develop less drastic coping mechanisms as time went on.

At the time, the whole situation around the triangle of Chick, Ella, and Benny Goodman spoke to large cultural issues for Black musicians and for the Black press as well. It is hard to believe how little attention the white press seems to have paid to this scandal. But then Goodman stood in the spotlight to such an extent that he superseded precedents and alternative realities could not compete. As the ethnomusicologist Ingrid Monson has written, Goodman had "the structural advantages of being white in the music industry. The economic success of the white swing bands and the American public's mistaken assumption that Goodman had originated the style led to a greater cultural protectiveness on the part of African American musicians. The discourse about white musicians being primarily imitators who profited excessively from the creativity of African American musicians grew well in this soil."[22] Small wonder then that reactions from journalists in the Black press to the possibility of Fitzgerald leaving Webb generated contradictory responses, including accusations about Webb's selfishness, questions about Fitzgerald's indebtedness, and arguments about separatism as a strategy for survival, as this following sample shows: "Why Chick Webb refused her one big [blurred text] to fame and lasting fortune we don't know. . . . it sounds screwy to us and a dirty break for Ella."[23]

> Benny Goodman (the white swing band man) went to Harlem to find a colored band he would like to pattern his band after. He picked Chick Webb's band. And with the assistance of colored arrangers like Bennie Carter and Edgar Sampson, he developed a good "swing" band. . . . Goodman still wasn't satisfied: he knew, and still knows that colored musicians are superior to white musicians, instrument for instrument . . . and picked up Teddy Wilson . . . and . . . Lionel Hampton. . . . Still not enough! A few days

ago he is said to have offered Chick Webb $5,000 to release Ella Fitzgerald. Yeah, I am still talking about Benny Goodman. To this column, Ella Fitzgerald tops the women's division of the swing singers. Uh, huh, that's why Benny wanted her as a part of his band. . . . But, what if: Other big white bandleaders start raiding our best bands for the best musicians in the world? Picture colored bands without Ace musicians! Picture the best colored bands becoming "farms" or "sandlots" with the big white bandleaders always stepping in to "buy" the best man! Yeah, I admit it would make a very sad picture.[24]

Finally, Chick and Ella had a chance to address the issues publicly. In January 1937 Webb said, Goodman "has been trying to get Ella in the worst way. There is no one offering the kind of money that I would ask for releasing the services of Ella Fitzgerald, star singer with my band. I turned him down because I didn't like his method of approach. He knows me well, but instead of coming to me direct, he went to other individuals and tried to get them to coerce Ella to join his orchestra."[25] It seems likely and in fact later was confirmed by Fitzgerald herself that Webb was referring to John Hammond. Webb was so angry that he refused to let her appear on Goodman's Camel Caravan again. On the other hand, Goodman declined to confirm anything, Instead, interviewed for the same story, he dismissed the rumors of the $5,000 offer as "a lot of poppycock," denying he offered any sum for Ella's contract.[26] In *New York Amsterdam News* on February 13, the reporter Roi Ottley—his career as a best-selling author several years away—interviewed Fitzgerald, whose voice was supposed to be "worth $5,000," and wrote, "I found her to be an unaffected, modest and a thoroughly naïve miss. . . . She still can't really believe that 'this is me.'" "Wistfully" she had stated that she really wanted to be a dancer.[27]

While the controversy faded over the next few months, in October 1937 Fitzgerald had her quiet say in an interview with Lillian Johnson for the *Baltimore Afro-American*. Sounding like a mature artist, speaking with the tact of a diplomat, she said, "Benny Goodman is a good friend and is interested in my work, but he did not make me an offer." The reporter pressed, "Do you think color would keep him from bidding for your services?" Ella replied emphatically, "Oh, no, but you see, I am under contract to Chick Webb, and Benny thinks a great deal of Chick."[28]

The Webb-Goodman affair—a myth with a core of truth—took on a life of its own within the African American community. While Goodman had earned respectful acclaim for hiring Black musicians, no amount of good intentions on the part of one white individual could compensate for structural inequities in the American music business; nor could music cure the racism in American society at large. The community savored the story of faithful Ella, principled Chick, and humbled white maestro as a moment of redress in the balance of power between the races, enhancing Fitzgerald's stature as a heroine. In 1939 journalist Vivian Morris, in Harlem documenting "folkways" for the WPA Federal Writers Project, visited a beauty shop and reported,

> The conversation was about a currently popular star. The fellow who is getting his hair washed says, "Chick Webb sure pulled some 'hep jive' when he signed Ella Fitzgerald up. I hear from good source that Benny Goodman offered gangs of money for her contract. Chick said, 'no can do.'" "Yeh," answers a dreamy eyed girl getting wavy ringlets pressed over her entire head. "I remember Ella when—ain't changed a bit towards little Fifi."[29]

★★★

OVER THE COURSE OF 1937, in dates small and large, people noticed not only Fitzgerald's great onstage gifts but also the chasm between the private person and the public persona. Not for twenty years would she evolve into a performer able to take requests and joke with audiences without fear. In 1937 people's expectations of her as an "entertainer" required of her social skills that she did not have. At a private gala on February 4, 1937, marking the second anniversary of the hugely successful radio show *Make Believe Ballroom*, hosted by the amiable Martin Block—perhaps this was the evening she asked him for the autographed photo for her scrapbook—she was thrust into speaking impromptu alongside bandleaders Benny Goodman and Jimmie Lunceford. It was barely covered in the white press, but the *Pittsburgh Courier* reported:

> It was all very informal and delightful, and it was amusing to see people who face "mikes" almost every day become suddenly shy and retiring when asked to speak. Ella Fitzgerald, Chick Webb's young singing star, was frightened when her turn came. She sidled up to the microphone and in a timid, low-pitched voice said something that was barely audible but sounded like: "I'm very happy to be here." The crowd adored her naivete and applauded sympathetically when the child retreated hurriedly from the microphone.[30]

The "child" showed growing pains at another date that should have been an easy triumph. On February 19, in Yonkers, she appeared at a benefit in her own honor, where she received the keys to the city from Mayor Joseph Loehr. "We're mighty proud of Ella's achievements," the mayor said at the "welcome-home dance" held at the Polish Community Center on Waverly Street in her old neighborhood, organized by the Paradise Boys Club. With a local band behind her, she sang to a crowd of 1,200 to 1,500. But something went awry, and Tommy Seay, her old supporter, wrote, "As to Ella not coming up to expectations, I say: what did you expect? she could not compare to Ethel Waters or Florence Mills."[31]

Descriptions of her voice in this period use language generally reserved for Black female singers. Discussing a ninety-minute variety show, *Billboard*'s music trade writer wrote that "Miss Fitzgerald stopped the show completely and could have sent the house home with the milkman. She has that sob-in-the-throat sultry delivery that grows on one."[32] In the *New York Age* she was "the warm warbler, Ella Fitzgerald, gorgeous in white satin, looking springy and turning 'em out of their seats to roll and rock in the aisles in rhythm with 'Big Boy Blue.' The torrid torcher gets a swell hand per usual."[33] One coy reporter in the *Norfolk Journal* praised the improvement in her dress while criticizing her "Fatty Tissue." She had gained, as she told Lillian Johnson, forty pounds in two years.[34]

But that was a small blip in a solid year of recognition. Throughout 1937 she learned to read audiences, to share trust onstage, and to get along on the road. Amid ballroom bookings of "one-nighters" in the South and Southwest, she performed at big dates at the Apollo (April 9–15) and at Chicago's historic Regal Theater. Black vaudevillians remained a constant presence in her development—audiences loved their comic banter, their impersonations, their freedom. At the Apollo she was billed right after Webb and just above the sketch comedian Dewey "Pigmeat" Markham, known for playing the "Judge" in "Heah comes de judge," a skit he invented in 1928.[35] "To a sweet girl, love from Pigmeat," is his inscription in her scrapbook.[36] Fitzgerald would reference his routines in the 1960s, when Markham became a television personality.[37] On June 18, 1937, Chick and Ella performed at the Regal Theater for the first time, booked into the entertainment surrounding the hugely hyped title match for the heavyweight championship between Joe Louis, the African American fighter and great hero of the race, and James Braddock, his white opponent from England. Their full vaudeville road show came with them, including dance teams Chuck and Chuckles, the Lindy Hoppers, and the courageous comedian Jackie Mabley, who was pioneering the freedom of satire for African American stage women.[38] Before Jackie Mabley became "Moms," her act included impersonations of Louis Armstrong, taking on whatever song he was featuring in his performances. That night at the Regal, a young Ella watched Mabley "steal the show" for her send-up of Armstrong's "Ole Man Mose."[39] The word *clowning* would stigmatize Black performers in coming decades, but it had a long legacy in variety, and it was something Fitzgerald said she did.

In the latter part of 1937, Chick Webb's prominence was rewarded with bookings in white mainstream picture houses, called "white time." Webb's great battle with Benny Goodman on May 11, 1937, thrust him into the spotlight. On the sidelines, Fitzgerald helped Webb win, so said Helen Oakley, the talented publicist who engineered the now legendary battle. "When Ella Fitzgerald made her bow as the

'Queen of Swing Singers,' the hundreds of people linked arms and swayed back and forth in rhythm with the music," wrote Oakley in her *Down Beat* review.[40] She later said that that night "Ella turned the tide" in Chick's favor.[41] The *New York Amsterdam News* ran the headline "Chick-Benny—Oh, Man!" with a now-widespread image of Webb, "from the way he is smiling up at Ella as she 'sends' the crowd, he is solidly scoring a home run. Jack, the jam session was just too hard."[42]

Beginning August 19, 1937, Chick Webb and Ella Fitzgerald played their first booking downtown, at Loew's State Theatre in Times Square. Preceding them were Fats Waller, Paul Whiteman and His Orchestra, and the rising white comedian Red Skelton. Moe Gale placed a huge ad in *Variety*, which ran not one but three reviews, all on the same page—one for the show overall, one for Webb's orchestra, and one for Fitzgerald's "new act," her twelve minutes in the spotlight during the thirty-eight-minute show. "Chick and Ella" had arrived as a team.

Variety shrewdly pointed out the differences between Fitzgerald's uptown and downtown styles: "The buxom Ella Fitzgerald on Broadway in a family vaudfilmer and in Harlem are two different types of singers. On Broadway she's swingy but polite, while in the colored spots she goes Ethel Water-ish in her lyrics, but she's a sock whether classy or lowdown." The writer added, "She's a forte song-seller, sweet but hot, with a wealth of personality," referring not just to swing songs but to her delivery of a ballad, "There's a Lull in My Life."

When they secured a second week-long booking, Billy Rowe gilded Fitzgerald's success: "Miss Fitzgerald to those who know her signifies more than just the top singer of swing songs. . . . To them she is synonymous of a race of people, the struggle of her people which brings joy and pathos so close together."[43]

In the fall of 1937, more bookings in white theaters followed this triumph. One is worth noting for its unintended influence. After a performance at the RKO Palace in Chicago on November 19, 1937, senior drama critic Ashton Stevens presciently evaluated Fitzgerald as an artist. She was "the most exciting find this column has encountered since a quarter century agone, [when] it spread its space for a young woman in a ten-cent South Side colored variety show. Her name was and is Ethel Waters."[44] Indeed, Ethel Waters herself had told Ella in September that her voice was "so refreshing" and "something different."[45]

> For, as the wisensteins of her profession say, she's got something there. She's got not only a singing voice with a peach-like fuzz on it which unfailingly makes dramatic clarity of the words, while at the same time making discreet love to the melody, but she has also a slyly arresting ingenue speaking voice, with which in good time she ought to be able to break your heart in such sheet music as, say "Miss Otis Regrets."[46]

The phrase "peach fuzz" would be used over and over again in years to come. Critics loved the metaphor. It became a Homeric detail in Fitzgerald's life. Stevens saw farther than any trade critic, jazz critic, or Black critic by predicting that she would achieve international stardom—if only she would grow up and stop treating the stage like it was the Savoy.

> It is too easily seen that Miss Fitzgerald lacks poise. Alas and alack! Any experienced cabaret performer could note her ignorance of stage technique. Her featured band number finds her working with her back to the audience, paying more attention to Webb and members of the band than to the front of the house. La Fitzgerald finds it difficult to grasp that a fine performer must develop a stage personality in order to win the whole-hearted plaudits of the audience.[47]

He was describing a singer who belonged to the band rather than one who saw herself as a solo artist. Making that transition would take time.

★★★

THE LIGHT SHINING ON CHICK AND ELLA woke up Jack Kapp. On November 20, 1937, *Billboard* reported that Decca had offered Webb a contract for three more years, dramatically increasing his studio time to forty-eight sides a year and agreeing to four sides for the "Chick Webb Quintet." Fitzgerald signed a contract as well, which "precludes any possibilities of the swing diva being snatched away by another maestro."[48] At the same time, he authorized small-group recordings by "Ella Fitzgerald and the Savoy Eight." By that time, Kapp had been recognized as a catalytic force in the record business, recovering from the Depression's horrific decline and dramatically improving the label's profits.

In early 1937 Kapp summoned the white songwriting team of Sammy Cahn and Saul Chaplin into his office. The newcomers had already proved their worth, having supplied catalytic hits both to Jimmie Lunceford ("Rhythm Is Our Business") and to Andy Kirk's Twelve Clouds of Joy ("Until the Real Thing Comes Along"). Kapp asked if they could do the same for other Decca artists, mentioning, by Cahn's account, his "new artist by the name of Ella Fitzgerald." Between June 1937 and May 1938, Fitzgerald sent three Cahn-Chaplin melodies into the top twenty, with "If You Ever Should Leave" the most successful. As Cahn recalled, "I'll never forget how excited Jack Kapp was when he phoned me to say that Ella's record was well on its way to selling 40,000 copies." Cahn referred to the song as a "heartbreak ballad" sung from "the depths of despair," with lyrics such as "If you ever should leave, why would I want to live / Darling you must believe, won't you try to forgive?" *Metronome*'s George Simon wrote that "it was one of the most exciting things she has done." In fact, she had not quite grown into the lyrics, which Edythe Wright, the vocalist for Tommy Dorsey's orchestra, rendered with more poignancy in her one chorus.

In a further sign of her growing prominence at Decca, Kapp matched her up with the Mills Brothers in another Cahn-Chaplin romantic swing song, "Dedicated to You." It had enough traction to enter the *Billboard* chart. "Rock It for Me," written by the twins Kay and Sue Werner and recorded on November 1, 1937, reached number nineteen the following February. For this swing-song-and-dance number, Al Feldman's expert arrangement supplied colorful dissonant chords in the opener and brash brass riffs between Ella's verses, as she flipped the song into a vaudeville showstopper, half-rapping some of the words, adding blues inflections in other spots, and generally partying her way through.

"Rock It for Me" made a big impression on Bobby Short, the future cabaret artist, who said he "made it my own all through high school."[49] The composer-conductor Leonard Bernstein, a jazz enthusiast, cherished the song from his youth and in 1989 sang it from memory to a surprised interviewer for *Rolling Stone,* to rebut the idea that rock and roll was invented in the 1950s.[50] In 1997 Clora Bryant, a jazz trumpeter and former member of the all-women's orchestra International Sweethearts of Rhythm, invoked "Rock It for Me" as a rejoinder to Elvis Presley's "King of Rock of Roll" title, "because, you see, we were rocking and rolling in the '30s. Ella Fitzgerald had this song out called 'Rock It for Me' in 1938."[51]

One noteworthy development in Fitzgerald's style was the increased prominence of scat singing, beginning in 1936 and accelerating in 1937. Webb's generosity of spirit showed her the way, letting her into the after-hours male domain of jamming, a privilege typically outside the experiences of band vocalists. "We used to have nightly jam sessions in which all the musicians would improvise on their instruments," she told an interviewer about ten years later, in 1947, "so I felt out of place until Chick suggested that I improvise on my voice. After that jam sessions were a lot of fun."[52]

In November 1936 that newfound freedom lit up her recordings with the Savoy Eight, a small group of Webb players backing her on the first releases under her own name. One of the first was a vocal cover of Jimmie Lunceford's "The Organ Grinder's Swing." Keying off Sy Oliver's deeply satirical arrangement of the nursery rhyme, Ella lopes along in cut time (2/2, also called two-step). Al Feldman's arrangement includes some playful dialogues between Ella and tenor saxophone, then trumpet. "Bap yado dooda bop dooda dodedoda dadooday," she sang, as she shifted the power between the vocalist and the men. Despite its negligible sales, Fitzgerald once said it was one of her favorite recordings, and it would get its due in 1955, when Langston Hughes included it in a celebratory recorded anthology, *The Glory of Negro History.*[53] At the time, she was reproached for the space she claimed. In his review for *Tempo* magazine, the journal of the Hot Club jazz crowd, Marshall Stearns regretted the absence of solos for the boys. "There's too much of Ella," he wrote, and she "warbles a corny lick that brings the boys down."[54]

At the end of 1937, Fitzgerald used scatting to swing another pop song into jazz, in her version of "Bei Mir Bist Du Schoen" (pronounced *shayn*) ("To Me You Are Beautiful"), recorded with her Savoy Eight on December 21, 1937. The song was written in 1932 by Jacob Jacobs and Sholom Secunda for the Yiddish musical theater in New York. In November 1937 Sammy Cahn, at Jack Kapp's suggestion, translated the song from Yiddish into English; a version covered by the Andrews Sisters reportedly sold over a quarter-million records and moved at least 200,000 copies of the sheet music.[55] In her version, Fitzgerald uses scat as her melting pot, blending Yiddish idioms into swing. "Y ay ay," she sang, paraphrasing the melody with each chorus, approximating a *schmear* (a Yiddish term for glissando) of a chromatic run at the end.[56]

Her version got some attention when a photo-journalistic essay appeared in a two-year-old magazine, *Life*, matching her name with her face for 1.5 million readers, who most likely had never seen her image.[57] The caption below read: "Natural for 'hot' treatment, Bei Mir's swing apotheosis is sung by Ella Fitzgerald, black swingstress." *Billboard* wrote, "Even if your phono is overstocked with 'Bei Mirs,' you must find place for this Harlem swing-and-scat sing." "Don't miss it," wrote Marshall Stearns.[58]

People had to adjust, ears had to shift to accommodate the innovative singer Webb had hired. Descriptions of her work and that of Webb's band increasingly invoked the damning epithet "commercial."[59] Somehow, in some critics' estimation, Fitzgerald's popularity undermined Webb's authenticity. Were they influenced by implicit bias against female singers, or had Webb truly changed course? George Simon reviewed four Decca sides with vocals (including one with Louis Jordan and a trio with Charles Linton) and concluded, "Chick is going a bit too commercial on these sides and doesn't do his band complete justice."[60] Several months later John Hammond wrote, "At least partly because of Ella Fitzgerald the band is extremely popular these days, but I'm afraid that its musicianship is far below the standards Webb ought to set for himself," and he called Charles Linton "a saccharine male vocalist."[61]

In the meantime, Fitzgerald had room to rise and shine, bringing much-needed attention to the achievements of African American female vocalists along the way. The death of Bessie Smith in 1937 triggered an article about the transition from blues to swing, lamenting the passing of the old style while celebrating the coming of the new. In an early acknowledgment of the distinctive role of women in Black music, St. Clair Bourne wrote, "The high pedestals of public adulation from which Bessie Smith and her contemporaries once ruled supreme are now occupied by Ella Fitzgerald, Billie Haliday [sic], Louise McCaroll, and Ivie Anderson, who have discarded the 'blues' and wield instead the more sophisticated sceptre of 'swing.'"[62] Ella pasted the article into her scrapbook.

The year ended with another milestone in November 1937 when *Down Beat* ran its first ever "Readers Poll." With categories for bands, instrumentalists, and vocalists—but not yet distinguishing male from female—the poll gave Fitzgerald 250 votes more than Mildred Bailey or even Bing Crosby, Decca's biggest star. "Queen Ella," the Black press called her. "Acclaimed by many as the greatest of all singers in the business," wrote George Simon.[63] It boded well for the next big date on Chick Webb's schedule, a big "Battle of the Bands" at the Savoy Ballroom between his band and Count Basie's, which the press was already anticipating.

Fitzgerald intended to follow Chick Webb's advice: "You've got to get there with the bestest and the mostest first."[64] *There* was shorthand for jumping the fence, anticipating trends, sensing innovation, and taking risks. She was ready.

Chapter 6

"TRUCKIN' ON DOWN THE AVENUE"

(1938)

O
n January 16, 1938, in a highly publicized Battle of the Bands at the Savoy Ballroom, Ella Fitzgerald and Billie Holiday competed. "The two voicetresses will do their utmost to help their respective units win the swing battle," read a squib in the *Chicago Defender*.[1] Webb would be defending his title against Count Bill Basie, who had arrived in New York in the fall of 1936 and was hogging the spotlight as the hottest band in town. In March 1937 Basie signed Holiday as his band singer, and they were accumulating great reviews. He seemed supreme even in Webb's own home venue when Billy Rowe raved about Basie's date at the Savoy Ballroom on April 11. Rowe quoted the French music critic Hugues Panassié's opinion that "Count Basie's swing is without equal in the world today."[2] That night Ella was there, and so were Louis Armstrong and Benny Goodman.[3]

Billie Holiday got some great press as well. In May at the Apollo, *Billboard*'s reviewer observed that "Billie Holiday, one of the top hat warblers around, sang 'I Can't Get Started with You' with a drawl and sex and feeling that made you want to listen to her forever."[4] It contrasted starkly with Fitzgerald's notices, which usually emphasized her girlish qualities and "sock singing," along with frequent comments about her weight. In the summer of 1937, Basie played the Savoy while Webb was on the road.

Norma Miller, a jazz dancer and Savoy regular, wrote, "Chick Webb was the best and the quickest, and if anyone disagreed with that, Mr. Webb would tell them in a minute what to do with their opinion."[5] When Helen Oakley, Moe Gale's publicist, got a date scheduled, she set the stage for an exceptional evening. She timed the battle to begin right after Benny Goodman's now-historic, then controversial big band concert at Carnegie Hall. The event drew everybody including Duke Ellington, Goodman, Gene Krupa, Red Norvo, and the "feminine swing contingent" of Ivie Anderson and Mildred Bailey.[6] Even before the battle started, crowds were filling the ballroom.

With so many great players in both bands, the reviews focused on the instrumentalists. Still, Fitzgerald and Holiday both impressed their personalities upon the event. Holiday thrilled her fans with "My Man," her latest hit on the Brunswick label. As a torch song of feminine martyrdom (initially "Mon Homme" in the 1920s), it foreshadowed the fame that repertoire would bring to her reputation in the 1940s. "My Man" allowed her to "characterize," to borrow a term used by Ethel Waters, describing her immersion in lyrics as if they were lines in a play.[7] That evening Holiday hypnotized one listener at a time.

In contrast, Fitzgerald chose her specialty, upbeat swing songs, including her current novelty hit "Bei Mir Bist Du Schoen" and "Loch Lomond," a swing version of a Scottish folk song that had launched Maxine Sullivan's career. (Benny Goodman's singer, Martha Tilton, had scored five encores with that number downtown.) Transporting the audience into community, Fitzgerald "had the whole crowd rocking with her," *Down Beat* reported.[8]

The battle of the bands was lively debated in the Black press, and the consensus registered it a draw. In its aftermath, this wise statement appeared anonymously in the *New York Amsterdam News*: "The final vote of Judge Public will not necessarily show a superiority in ability since the two types of singers vary so differently, but a preference for a singing style."[9]

Behind that facade of generosity, Chick Webb and the boys in his band knew that Basie's band had shown them up, and they blamed Helen Oakley for pushing Webb into the contest. "Oakley had ramped up her efforts to publicize this particular battle, casting it as a gladiator to-the-death contest instead of the fantastic musical event those who attended experienced," in the words of Stephanie Stein Crease, Webb's biographer.

> Oakley defended her actions by saying that she had arranged the battle to teach Chick a lesson. "Chick was concentrating on Ella's share all the time on his sets. She was a wonderful singer, but he wasn't concentrating on the band. . . . And I kept thinking if we could sting them, then maybe they would decide they'd go for it themselves. . . . And of course it was a very touching moment . . . because you couldn't defeat Basie, you couldn't out-swing the Basie band."[10]

Moe Gale recognized discontent within the band and fired Oakley. Her departure from his agency was announced in *Billboard* on March 26, after which she was hired by MCA, which had changed its Jim Crow policies to promote "colored bands," with Count Basie on the client list.[11] This talented young publicist adopted a strategy intended to produce defeat for a client whom she loved—even though she had already used her promotional skills to help Webb a great deal—to teach him an unnecessary lesson, but it is possible that she had a bias against band singers. She would later write, "Singers have done untold harm to bands."[12] She was hardly alone in associating singers with inferior popular songs as opposed to hot instrumentals; popular songs, in her view, led to "commercialism."

While all singers provoked skepticism, female singers received a special kind of disdain. About a month after the battle, Holiday quit Basie's band. Basie's fine trumpeter Harry "Sweets" Edison remembered, "After Billie Holiday left, we didn't really want a singer anyway. The singer was just an ornament on the bandstand in those days, more of an accompaniment to the band. Sing a chorus and sit down!"[13]

★★★

"WHAT SOCIETY DEMANDED OF WOMEN in the 1930s was complex and contradictory," women's history scholar Sara Jane Deutsch has written, "but it did not completely erode the image of confident, competent, public womanhood created in the 1920s."[14] The "historic dissonance" of women in jazz as vocalists in the big band era captures these contradictions.[15] The most prominent female vocalists could and did exemplify the "modern woman," paralleling the empowering competence that was lighting up the screens in Hollywood's screwball comedies. Their stalwart optimism conveyed an emotional resilience that contrasted with the martyrdom of the 1920s white torch singers.

But beyond their star personas, female singers, in the realities of the profession, endured low pay, low professional status, and low musical autonomy. Yet at the time of the Basie-Webb battle, women were entering the field in greater numbers than ever.[16] In the late 1930s they flocked to what seemed like an open field and a glamorous lifestyle. In the words of the historian Donald Bogle, "Almost automatically, the girl-singers stood as symbols of resourceful, knowing women on the move, hip and clever enough to travel on the band's bus with the boys, to play cards with them (and win), and to swap stories."[17] From that perspective, they were comparable to the fast-talking, spunky heroines in the era's movies, which sometimes even depicted vocalists as heroines. In the late 1930s the white singers Edythe Wright and Martha Tilton, employed by powerful bandleaders like Tommy Dorsey and Benny Goodman, were admired figures, indeed minor celebrities, in the American mainstream.

On the negative side, within the music profession itself, female singers could expect tolerance rather than equality. Their entrance into the field in the mid-1930s met with skepticism and indifference; Martha Tilton was not listed on Goodman's Carnegie Hall program but was added at the last minute. But as their professional visibility increased, attitudes toward them evolved into sexism that was accepted as part of the public discourse in jazz. In *Down Beat* and *Metronome*, band singers could casually be referred to as "decorative furniture," and articles with titles like "The Gal Yippers Have No Place in Our Jazz Bands" or "Why Women Musicians Are Inferior" aired reactionary rhetoric with some clout.[18] The singers themselves sometimes responded: a 1938 article in *Variety* reported, "Major peeve is that the chirpers must lend the s.a. [sex appeal] touch to a bunch of horn-tootin' muggs, must wear Poiret creations and Antoine coiffures but have a tough time making ends meet at the $35 to $75 weekly salaries most of 'em get."[19]

Within this framework, the differences in the careers of white and Black singers reflected Jim Crow contradictions. African American singers had more artistic autonomy than vocalists with Benny Goodman or Larry Clinton were typically granted. But white "chirpers," "canaries," "thrushes," and "warblers," as the slang-addicted trade writers labeled them, enjoyed easier access to radio, more location jobs at fancy hotels, and better promotional backup and product endorsements. The musical tradeoff was that they were limited to only a minute or so on a recording, singing the tune relatively straight. Meanwhile the "dusky," "sepia," "colored femmes," while struggling against industry apartheid, tended to have more musical freedom.

At just this moment of focus on their craft, both Billie Holiday and Ella Fitzgerald represented creative brilliance and independence. By the late 1930s, they painted a vibrant cultural portrait for Black female vocalists aspiring to become modern singers.[20] Fitzgerald said, "I idolized Billie and her songs. She was the first really modern singer to my way of thinking. We all wanted to be like her."[21] Fitzgerald later remarked on the illusion of autobiographical authenticity that Holiday communicated and that she understood as a fellow professional: "Billie wasn't like what people say. She was [seen] like that because of her songs, not the other way around."[22] Mario Bauzá once offered, "In those days Billie Holiday was going strong, and I used to tell Ella you have nothing to be afraid of. You got your own."[23] Billie Holiday named Ella Fitzgerald her favorite singer in 1937.[24]

There was room for both of them. Norma Miller said, "Ella and Billie—the best there was for a new kind of singer for Black women. Ella and Billie showing that Black women were not just blues singers."[25] In 1937 Ivie Anderson, billed as a "sophisticated song stylist" by Ellington's management, praised Fitzgerald to such an extent that the reporter who was interviewing her asked in wonderment about professional jealousy. "I can't help it," Anderson replied. "Ella has what white imitators like Connie Boswell and Mildred Bailey have tried for years to get. [Swing.] Ella has it naturally; she's always had it."[26] Maxine Sullivan, a rising star in 1937, said, "Ella and Billie were on a throne."[27]

★★★

ON FEBRUARY 7, 1938, Chick Webb landed his first hotel "location date" with a radio wire hookup at Levaggi's Flamingo Room, a Boston nightclub in the Hotel Gardner near Symphony Hall.[28] Webb's orchestra was the first Black band to play there, and without Helen Oakley's promotion, it would have languished.[29] Posh hotel venues typically had race moats around them, and each new booking for an African American band meant a small advance in an endless struggle. *Metronome* wrote, "The old Beantown is writhing from its first concentrated dose of real, colored swing in many a moon."[30] Both a city and a college town, Boston gave Webb's band a decisive victory. George Frazier, Harvard class of '35, a novice jazz critic, reported that Webb's band drew "far and away the most astonishing business any Boston night-club has been able to boast of in at least two years."[31] Webb gave the college "cats" hot music for dancing and added a "floor show," exploiting Louis Jordan's huge talent. In a vaudeville routine called "Deacon Jones," Jordan satirized a preacher, and as a glitzy finish, the ensemble marched around the room.

A veteran of the vaudeville circuit, the charismatic Jordan had joined the band by October 1936 on alto saxophone, and in 1937 he had shown off his singing skills in a few vocal trios with Ella and Charles Linton. But he was gone by August 1938, mainly for hatching mutinous plots. Mario Bauzá said, "When Louis was planning to form his own band he may have thought it was a secret but to everyone else it was obvious. He and Ella were pretty close at the time and he was definitely trying to corral her in his great plans for a band. But Louis was always for Louis, he was aggressive and always scheming."[32]

Louis Jordan's romantic pursuit of Ella confounded some of Webb's sidemen, one of whom said many years later, "We couldn't understand this at all. Louis was a sharp, good-looking cat and he was making up to Ella. In those days she was quite a gawky girl, who, it must be said, was real plain."[33] Bauzá said he almost got in a fight with Jordan on Ella's account, telling him, "Louis, are you taking advantage of this girl here? I'm like her father. I don't want you to not respect this lady or nothing like that. [Jordan said,] 'No, no, no. I'm a married man.' I said, 'I *know* you are a married man.'"[34] Jordan's wife—the second of five—was the seasoned vaudevillian Ida Fields, who recalled, "Louis was messing around with Ella. He bought her some fingernail scissors. It wasn't what she wanted so she threw them on the floor and he hit her and she hit him right back."[35] By October 1938 Jordan had formed his "jump band" and was standing at the threshold of a remarkable career in Black popular music.

In late February 1938, a reporter from the *Harvard Crimson* interviewed Chick and Ella. Webb attributed his own success largely to Ella, adding, "Breaks count a lot in this game." Ella must have deflected diplomatically. "If Ella Fitzgerald thinks it's great to be famous, however," the reporter wrote,

> she certainly doesn't show it. She talks about Boston, which she says is a "fine city—just like home to me," or about Bessie Smith, whom she calls the "finest blues singer that ever lived," but about herself she has little to say. . . . Asked whether the college "cats" who have been seen flocking around the bandstand every night really know anything about swing, she replied, "I really couldn't say, but they sure do enjoy it."[36]

That they did, enough that a month at Levaggi's turned into three, closing on May 4. Webb benefited from their wire hookups for radio broadcast, leaving the spot only occasionally for other bookings. On March 11 Webb and Fitzgerald returned to the scene of their first gig together, a dance at St. Elmo Hall as part of junior prom weekend at Yale.[37] Then for two weeks at the end of March, he was out of action for surgery at Hudson View Hospital in New York. This hospital stay marked the first of several setbacks. Webb spun the procedure as "only a minor matter" to the *Chicago Defender*, which received "wires and air mail specials" of inquiry. But another account in the jazz press called it a "serious operation."[38]

★★★

In March 1938 Fitzgerald stood at the threshold of a major change in her career, all through the success of a novelty song that astonished the music business, when she asked her arranger Al Feldman, "Did you do anything with that nursery rhyme?" At the Onyx Club on 52nd Street, Maxine Sullivan was drawing big box office with "Loch Lomond." In the words of Milt Gabler, the owner of the Commodore record label, the song "drew the masses because it was a pop hit—not just jazz for jazz lovers. Maxine's success created a market for singers."[39] But Ella felt threatened: "I felt like everyone forgot about me."[40]

When Feldman procrastinated, Fitzgerald pushed: "If you're not gonna be interested in that, I'll ask Edgar Sampson," she told him. Feldman recalled, "She was growing a little testy, something she had never done."[41] On April 1, 1938, Fitzgerald registered the "A-Tisket A-Tasket" lead sheet for copyright, with her handwritten lyrics included. (See Fig. 3.) Feldman stepped up and turned it into a finished arrangement, with the sheet music published by Jack Robbins, crediting both Feldman and Fitzgerald.

Throughout 1938, this unlikely vehicle brought Fitzgerald success of unprecedented magnitude. In August 20 "A-Tisket A-Tasket" arrived as number one on the radio music program *Your Hit Parade*, lodging there for over two months.[42] The song attracted competitive covers from others, including Teddy Wilson, Mildred Bailey with Red Norvo, and Tommy Dorsey. In Dorsey's recording with his small group "The Clambake Seven," made for Victor in 1938, Dorsey's singer Edythe Wright treats the song as a roll call of his musicians, who take feature solos. The spillover continued with Jack Robbins issuing sheet music with various photo inserts of other white bandleaders featuring the tune (including Gene Krupa and Ozzie Nelson). By December a Paris publisher produced sheet music with French and English lyrics; a Danish dance orchestra recorded "Min tiske min taske" in Copenhagen; in Hitler's Germany, a young jazz fan bought her record in Munich. Fitzgerald's devoted first biographer, Jimmy Jungermann, wrote,

Fig. 3. Ella Fitzgerald's manuscript lead sheet for her version of "A-Tisket A-Tasket" before Al Feldman made his arrangement for Chick Webb's band. Her bridge section is filled with blue notes, altering the mood of the original into modern swing. It bears little resemblance to Feldman's deft solution, which has his great riffs at the beginning. Fitzgerald submitted this sheet for copyright on April 1, 1938. *Copyright Office, Library of Congress. Courtesy of Ella Fitzgerald Charitable Foundation.*

"Mit einer Platte war Ella Fitzgerald zum Weltstar geworden." ("With one record Ella Fitzgerald became a world star.")[43]

The history of this musical phenomenon deserves to be chronicled in some detail. By mid-April, Webb was back in Boston to hear the new arrangement that Al Feldman had told him about. When the band ran through "A-Tisket A-Tasket" in rehearsal, Feldman later recalled, a song plugger for Jack Robbins was there. The plugger then phoned Abe Olman, general manager at Decca, suggesting he hear an air check. "I didn't know what we had," said Feldman, "but everybody went crazy the minute they heard the thing."[44]

On May 2, 1938—a date that rivals her debut at the Harlem Opera House as a definitive landmark in her career—Ella brought "A-Tisket A-Tasket" into the Decca studio. But there Chick Webb had to rescue her. "That recording of 'Tasket'—we almost didn't take it," recalled Beverly Peer, Webb's bassist. "Bob Stephens [of Decca] didn't want to take it. Chick started to pack up his drums and forced the issue. If he hadn't bothered, there'd be no 'Tasket.' That was down to Chick."[45] According to Webb's clarinetist, Garvin Bushell, "He's the one that picked 'A-Tisket A-Tasket.' Everybody said, 'I don't want to hear that garbage.'"[46] Others reacted as if she were Mother Goose wheeling a baby carriage into the dressing rooms of scantily clad chorus girls, aiming to paint the walls pink and blue. When Moe Gale showed the song to Frank Schiffman, owner of the Apollo, busy selling sexy chorines as part of his vaude shows, Schiffman exploded: "What the hell kind of a song is that? 'A Tisket, a Tasket!' What the hell are we running, a kindergarten with nursery rhymes? She can't sing it in my theater."[47]

It wasn't just a nursery rhyme but what folklorists call a "play-party song" or a "game song," of a kind that was still played and sung in Ella's generation. "I picked out the melody from the drop-the-handkerchief game I used to play at school," she said.[48] No need to change much to get the opening chorus, as one can hear in a 1939 field recording of African American schoolkids singing the melody in North Carolina: "A-tisket, a-tasket, / a green and yellow basket, / I wrote a letter to my love / and on the way I dropped it. . . . / Someone of you have picked it up / and put it in her pocket, / it was you, it was you, it was you!"[49] Maybe Ella changed the addressee of the letter to "mommy." But it seems likely that Al Feldman expanded the original, making "It was you!" into a goofy dialogue, typical of the era's novelty songs, where the band turns questions about the color of the basket into a musical repartee. She made two crucial changes, as he recalled, replacing "walking" with "truckin'" (in "she was truckin' on down the avenue") and adding "she went peck, peck, peckin'," referring to dance steps popular at the Savoy and inviting listeners to move. Feldman composed a terrific opening riff that swung the game song into dance.

Within the jazz press, critics' commentaries on "A-Tisket A-Tasket" ranged from indifference to unexpected praise, along with the occasional slam. In *Down Beat*, Paul Miller dismissed it as "a screwy novelty lyric, which she sings in pleasing fashion."[50] Marshall Stearns, dean of the United Hot Clubs of America, wondered "why do the best women . . . sound so immature and babyish."[51]

But a few smart ears heard the cleverness. Anita O'Day registered Fitzgerald's "sly little-girl quality."[52] In London, Leonard Feather, writing under the pen name "Rophone" in the influential British magazine *Melody Maker*, wrote, "I doubt whether her personality has ever been more vivid on a record. Technical Tidbit: Note how she deliberately cuts short the last syllable of some phrases for a sort of breathless effect; and the way she can fascinate you by subtleties of phrasing and diction even with the words 'No, no, no, no' repeated three times at the end."[53]

"A Tisket A-Tasket" made Ella Fitzgerald a heroine for families in the Black community, and she often dressed the role, wearing a schoolgirl costume of a white blouse and black skirt onstage. In retrospect, "A-Tisket A-Tasket" offered a fresh representation of Black girlhood, in contrast to the "pickaninny" characters on the *Our Gang* comedy shorts. Teddy McRae recalled,

> She became like a feature attraction with this "Tisket a Tasket" where we played. When we went back on the road, everybody would bring their little girls up, dressed up and sing "Tisket a

Tasket." I know when we get into Savannah, the bus came in and went down and come around and circled the main street of the colored neighborhood. And everybody was standing with their little girls waiting to meet Ella.[54]

On August 18, 1938, Fitzgerald and her song "made the column"—that is to say, they were an item in the nationally syndicated column of the country's most powerful journalist, Walter Winchell. As many as 9 million readers could take in his fabricated account of the song's origins. In Winchell's version, a press agent made up the nursery rhyme gimmick, trying to get a reporter on *The World Telly* to do a series on swing singers.[55] Winchell would continue to pay welcome, quotable attention to Ella Fitzgerald for the next thirty years.

★★★

THE REAL REWARD FOR THE SONG'S SUCCESS happened on August 10, 1938, when Webb and his band opened at the Paramount Theatre, a movie palace seating around 3,400 customers in Times Square. They arrived there after an extensive road trip from late June to early August that had taken the band to Chicago, Detroit, Kansas City, St. Louis, and Louisville.

Landing a date at the Paramount was a coup. The prominent theater presented mainly white bands, including Goodman and Dorsey, so Webb rightly considered the booking a major career triumph. *Down Beat* claimed that Webb was the only Black bandleader to play at the Paramount besides Louis Armstrong and Cab Calloway.[56] Fitzgerald saw her name in lights on the marquee, second to Webb's, but both names were equal in size to those of movie stars Martha Raye, Bob Hope, and Betty Grable in the accompanying feature film, *Give Me a Sailor*.

Gale and Webb lavished attention on the evening's bill, deciding the stage show needed boosting, even though it already included the veteran dance-comedy team Chuck and Chuckles, the popular gospel vocal quartet the Charioteers, and Ella's friends the Lindy Hoppers. The Gale Agency promised guest star nights, one of which had *Courier* columnist

Billy Rowe bringing in Black celebrities while Martin Block handled the white contingent.[57] One night "Pigmeat" Markham and trumpeter Roy Eldridge dropped by, while the novelty jazz duo Slim and Slam presented their hit "Flat Foot Floogie" and participated in "St. Louis Blues," a jam session number that Webb was developing. For the rest of Webb's career, the "St. Louis Blues" finale would end many evenings. But he had been struggling with chronic tuberculosis for a year, and this night when the curtain came down, he had to be carried offstage.

"Chick and Ella Set Attendance Record at the Paramount," headlined Isadora Smith's review in the *Pittsburgh Courier*.[58] Although this headline gave Fitzgerald equal billing, the date belonged to Webb. *Variety* reported that the Paramount "boasted the most surprising result," taking in a "nifty $40,000" for the week.[59] The *Brooklyn Daily Eagle* noted, "The jitterbugs, who are always to be found at the Times Square house, haven't been so enthusiastic about a stage show since they stampeded in the aisles and overran the stage to the rhythms of Benny Goodman."[60] In response, Moe Gale promised Webb a $1,000-per-week salary increase for a rebooking the following January, and he took out a full-page ad in *Variety* featuring a letter of congratulations from Harry Kalchen of the Artists' Booking Agency in the Paramount Building.[61]

Variety's knowledgeable music editor, Abel Green, had been following Webb's work since 1927. His review called the show

> 100% Harlem, and all of it clicky. It's all so consistently effective that it almost verges on being embarrassed with riches, causing the show to run overboard. Ella Fitzgerald, whose "A-Tisket A-Tasket" Decca waxing teed off that nursery ditty into swingo immortality, comes . . . after the others milk the ofays' palms dry, and tallies a neat score on her own. . . . Basically, the show is Webb's. . . . Webb has a drum-solo style all his own, and he merchandizes it solidly, showmanly, and well.[62]

Harlem welcomed the event as a tour de force for African Americans. Billy Rowe, a master of ceremonies at the Paramount, wrote in his column of the "first time that such has happened to a colored columnist or any of our ilk," raising the rhetorical question of whether he could "hold high the tradition that the race has brought to Broadway and through it reach out throughout all the world."[63]

The Paramount date and the sustained fame of "A-Tisket A-Tasket" generated enough publicity to warrant a major feature in the *New York Post* by its new reporter Earl Wilson, who would later become an influential Broadway gossip columnist.

> We've got all the news for you today about that new song, "A Tisket, A Tasket." Ella Fitzgerald, the Negro gal whose voice, somebody said, "has peach fuzz on it," bounced her 170 pounds into a dressing room at the Paramount Theatre yesterday, hauled a pink rayon housecoat tightly round her and pleaded guilty to writing it.

Wilson then described how the song "was driving a lot of people nuts." Interviewing Fitzgerald for the piece, he asked her why she had chosen that song. At first she sidestepped, clowning around with the other band members, but eventually she responded:

> "Aw right, aw right," said Ella, grinning to her ears, "but don't say I STOLE it. Jes' say I borrowed it." Now she dated the song as a game she played in Newport News and at Yonkers, "and that orphanage which some folks say I run away from. . . . We was playing Boston in April, and I says to Al Feldman, our arranger, 'Look here, I got something terrific! They're swinging everything else—why not nursery rhymes.' I had most of the words wrote out, so we sat down and jammed around til we got the tune, and that's the way it was."[64]

Wilson then asked her disingenuously whether she "look[ed] up the words in a library." Her response: "I remembered all them words I put in my song." Then "Ella thought at this point that it would be awfully nice to show everybody her new dance step. She calls it the boogy woogy. It's ducky."

About twenty years later Wilson reread his column and apologized for having been "a bit superior."[65]

★★★

THEIR SUCCESS AT THE PARAMOUNT and with "A-Tisket A-Tasket" brought Webb and Fitzgerald a dramatic blitz of studio sessions that increased their Decca output significantly; they cut twenty-one tracks from May to August. Little of this repertoire had much impact in the jazz world, as Decca aimed straight for the jukeboxes and the high school and collegiate crowd with tunes such as "Gotta Pebble in My Shoe" ("Ouch, I gotta keep dancing all the time") and "Wacky Dust" ("They call it wacky dust, it brings a dancing jag"). "Spinnin' the Webb," the B-side of "Wacky Dust," was an instrumental, but Webb and Fitzgerald shared the copyright attributions so she could share in the profits.

One of Webb's novelty tunes, simply titled "Ella," promoted Fitzgerald's identification with his band. Attributed to Webb and veteran tunesmith Bob Ellsworth, "Ella" features a duet between Fitzgerald and the trumpeter Taft Jordan and has to be marked off as a personal indulgence. In his Louis Armstrong clone mode, Jordan sings, "Now Ella, it's you I'm adoring," and Ella answers, "Then you'll really have to swing it."

Critics who understood their mission as protecting the status and integrity of jazz against commercialization took aim at novelty tunes. Among the most vociferous was Leonard Feather, who wrote in early 1939:

> Presenting the Decline and Fall of William Webb, Esq. This band has now reached a stage where one feels that everything it plays has the express object of pleasing those audiences that have been roped in by the attraction of Ella's personality and are not otherwise interested in jazz. . . . "Got a Pebble in My Shoe" is such an irritating and childish piece of affectation that it embarrasses me to play it. It is directed at the twelve-year-old mind. . . . After hearing this record, I said, "Thank Heaven for Basie."[66]

Courting the jitterbugs—a term introduced by Cab Calloway in 1934, then widely adopted by swing dancers in 1937—was the main strategy behind the Decca sessions. On May 2, 1938, in the same session that produced "A-Tisket A-Tasket," Webb and Fitzgerald recorded "I'm Just a Jitterbug," which the following year would be adopted for an animated cartoon from the Walter Lantz studio.

★★★

WEBB AND HIS ORCHESTRA spent months on the road, especially in the summer, when they toured the South. Dealing with racism and toggling between Black and white audiences were challenges demanding ingenuity and courage. Bardu Ali, recounting a performance in Fort Lauderdale, Florida, captured the fear that was a part of daily life for the entire band:

> So, this one little white guy is dancing around, he says, "Hey, Ella. Sing 'Tisket A-Tasket.' " And Ella, she just ignored him. So finally, he hollered again, so about the third or fourth time he said, "Ella, you black n—— bitch, I ain't gonna ask you no more." So, I said to Ella, "I'm going to sing it myself if you don't sing it."[67]

On September 7, 1938, Webb's orchestra appeared in Atlanta for a midnight concert at the City Auditorium. Columnist I. P. Reynolds of the *Atlanta Daily World*, a Black paper, described a performance that made Benny Goodman's "Paramount riot" sound like a Boy Scout rally. Before the band started,

> the right hand side of the Auditorium fills first, as the left hand side has traditionally belonged to whites. Colored people whooping and hollering as if wild. . . . The hollering increases; it's worse than a Joe Louis fight. . . . Ella Fitzgerald enters and as she goes behind the stage she is given a great ovation. . . . Ella Fitzgerald comes to the mike and sings the Jitter Bug Blues [probably

"I'm Just a Jitterbug"]. Chick makes a grand stand play on the drums. . . . And as Ella Fitzgerald sang, the crowd went wild. We had some time 'till morning.[68]

As this account indicates, Fitzgerald's stage life with Webb was a kind of musical vaudeville, or rather swing vaudeville. Unlike the "girl singer" performing in front of a white swing band, Fitzgerald behaved like a band member, and when she wasn't singing, she was dancing as an adjunct entertainer or cheerleader urging on the crowd. In Macon, Georgia, she told a reviewer, "I'm crazy about dancing and do the shag and lindy-hop whenever I get a chance." In the reviewer's account, "The swing-songstress, comely and buxom, is a bundle of energy, lifting her skirts and trucking while performing before the 'mike.' Even in her seat she is forced to move in time with the wildish tones sent out by the 15 'chicks.' "[69]

For the rest of the year, Webb did solid box office, mainly at Black theaters rather than at ballrooms and dances. For their October 7 to 13 booking at the Earle Theatre in Philadelphia, the *Down Beat* headline ran, "Chick Webb's $25,000 Gate Breaks Benny Goodman's Record."[70] But Webb's health was deteriorating. At the Earle engagement, he reportedly collapsed onstage, and the drummer Bill Beason took his place.[71]

From October 21 to 27, Chick and Ella played the Hippodrome in Baltimore, in what *Variety* described as their "first hometown appearance . . . since hitting the upper brackets." They did good business, attracting "many curious stub-holders"—that is, more than just swing fans—a sign of Ella's newly won fame.[72] Chick Webb went all out for this show, incorporating a grand finale that Ella's old friend Lillian Johnson, a columnist for the *Baltimore Afro-American*, described in detail:

That finale started off with the band lightly muggin' "St. Louis Blues," then Taft Jordan comes in on it for some hot trumpet work. Next Ella comes out and sings two choruses. Then Chuckles does some strokes on his vibraphone to step it up still further, and then his partner, Chuck, and himself strut out with some extra fast footwork. As if that wasn't enough, Whyte's [Whitey's] Lindy Hoppers come on, and the pace gets furiouser and furiouser, what with the whole cast lindyin', truckin', boogie-woogiein', and kangaroo hopping.[73]

Shortly after this engagement, Webb's health collapsed. He entered Johns Hopkins Hospital in late October or early November. A press release acknowledged he had been "ailing for several months."[74] This time when the band moved on, he stayed behind, and it is not clear when he rejoined the arduous November-December itinerary that brought them to Cleveland, Buffalo, Toledo, Chicago, St. Louis, Kansas City, Tulsa, Oklahoma City, Dallas, Galveston, Bunkie (Louisiana), Philadelphia, and West Orange (New Jersey).[75]

"A-Tisket A-Tasket" had been a "provider," helping to balance the profit margins at Decca and to brand the Webb orchestra. In October 1938 the band recorded a sequel, "I Found My Yellow Basket," copyrighted in both Fitzgerald's and Webb's names and arranged by Feldman. Once again the song involved novelty repartee. In January 1939 they brought the tune to the Apollo in New York, and a *Variety* reviewer found, "Tune that secured Miss Fitzgerald prominence, 'A-Tisket,' is properly ignored here, since it's stalemated by now, but she does a sequel to that, 'Found Yellow Basket,' which scores."[76] Elsewhere the music trade press and the Black press panned the record as a disappointment.[77] Its dull arrangement only pointed up the vitality of the original.

Al Feldman marveled, "It's funny how one song can make celebrities out of persons literally overnight and subsequently make anything else they record become minor hits. Such was the case with Chick and Ella."[78] Fitzgerald, as ambitious as she was, still saw her success as a joint effort with Webb. He had saved her breakthrough song in the Decca studios, bringing fame on a scale few could have foreseen. He also gave her what she later called "the only advice I ever needed." She would quote it often:

Honey, in this business, you've always got to get there with the firstest, the mostest, and the newest. . . . Everybody else had been singing swing tunes for so long that I felt like a Johnny Come Lately. So I took a chance and recorded this nursery jingle. Chick's advice wasn't bad.[79]

Chapter 7

CHICK AND ELLA

(1939)

Chick and Ella were a team, and in the winter and spring of 1939, as they rode the crest of its wave, they swung together. "It's all Webb and Fitzgerald here," read the review of their Apollo date on January 13.[1] In the wake of her success with "A-Tisket A-Tasket," she was blooming, and Webb knew she was helping him reach a level of professional success that had eluded him, even helping the band survive his illness. In its January 1939 issue, the music magazine *Bandwagon* announced, "Chick Webb, the skin-beater, is hospital-bound. Ella Fitzgerald will probably front his ork [orchestra] until the dark dynamo recuperates."[2] That he might not live much longer did not figure into anyone's plans, at least in public.

In late January, Chick and Ella reached a professional milestone when they were booked at the Cocoanut Grove, an elegant penthouse night-club at the swank Park Central Hotel in midtown Manhattan. "A double innovation for this hotel because of the band being both costly and a colored combo," reported *Variety*, their financials varying from $1,500 to $2,000 a week.[3] Billy Rowe wrote, "if successful [it] might mean the return to glory of the race bands."[4] A photograph from the Cocoanut Grove shows a coiffured twenty-two-year-old Ella donning the formal garb of a debutante: an elegant, sequined gown and evening gloves. She stands tall at the microphone, floating her voice over a white couple dancing cheek to cheek. Displaying the Cocoanut Grove's quality, the lady is wearing her mink stole on the dance floor.

Fitzgerald's "handling of any tune in any tempo seems so effortless, yet so much better than most of her contemporaries that comparisons are impossible," wrote *Variety*'s anonymous critic in his review of the Cocoanut Grove date.[5] She sang the standards "Heart and Soul" and "St. Louis Blues," the obscure "(Oh! Oh!) What Do You Know About Love," and "F.D.R. Jones," the hit from Harold Rome's topical musical, *Sing Out the News*. She had bested fifteen rivals and landed her version of "F.D.R. Jones" on the charts for three weeks.

But after the four-week trial, Webb's contract at the Cocoanut Grove was not renewed. The reasons are a murky controversy. *Chicago Defender* columnist Al Monroe wrote, "Chick Webb's band laid an egg. . . . Among the criticisms reported by residents of the hotel is that music was too loud."[6] More intrigue soon followed, when the prominent journalist Floyd Snelson invoked race prejudice and snobbery, charging that "certain 'cheap' jealous Nordics" forced the "ouster." He quoted Moe Gale saying, "We'll fight to the finish," but with whom exactly, and over what?[7] How could Webb's orchestra succeed in such a conservative all-white venue, *Billboard* asked, given "the heavy obstacles that Webb or any other colored combo has to overcome in such environs"?[8]

In his superb 1941 essay "The Dance Band Business: A Study in Black and White," Irving Kolodin, a classical music critic and opera expert, used the incident as a case study of "pathological" policies pursued by hotel managers. Judging from his description, Kolodin appears to have attended in person and was aiming his criticisms at the management

who encouraged a kind of exhibitionism which had a disastrous effect on the playing of the musicians. There was so much "Jim Crow" in the air, together with the kind of antics which the white public believes to be inseparable from the colored man's expression of his immortal soul, that the musicians were humiliated, the knowing public repelled, and the engagement a failure.[9]

The minstrel mask was hard to dislodge. The Park Central Hotel would shun Black bands for six more years. When Cab Calloway was booked in 1943, Billy Rowe optimistically hailed a "new opportunity" for sepia bands.[10]

★★★

AFTER THE GLOBAL SUCCESS OF "A-TISKET A-TASKET," Jack Kapp granted Webb and Fitzgerald more studio time than ever. In sixteen months, Ella recorded forty-nine new songs, about half of her total Decca output with Webb; the bandleader benefited as well, as his twenty-six titles "accounted for more records in the last two years of his life than in the all time before," noted the English jazz scholar Stanley Dance.[11] Most important, the quality of the material handed to her improved. Never mind "I Found My Yellow Basket" and "Chew, Chew, Chew Your Bubble Gum": a session on February 17 included "My Heart Belongs to Daddy," her first recording of a Cole Porter song that she loved and would record two more times in the 1950s and '60s. The song was then making the career of Mary Martin on Broadway in Porter's musical *Leave It to Me*. Ella had to record censored lyrics to accommodate radio stations in their most righteous mode. The original text: "If I invite a boy, some night." The Decca version: "When some good scout, invites me out."

Two other songs, "'Tain't What You Do (It's the Way That Cha Do It)" and "Undecided," landed on the charts. "Undecided" warranted the sophisticated treatment Fitzgerald gave it. A currently popular song with clever lyrics by Sid Robin and an instrumental by jazz trumpeter Charlie Shavers, it would soon become a jazz standard. Fitzgerald handled Van Alexander's (the former Al Feldman) arrangement with aplomb, juggling tempos and letting the band rip, capped with a dazzling four-bar flourish by Webb. She also recorded the sophisticated lyrical love song "Don't Worry 'Bout Me" (1939), another future standard. Her treatment of it foreshadowed the ballad singer she would become in future decades. The oldie "Little White Lies" (1930) showed up on April 21, which she would retrieve in later decades as well.

★★★

ANOTHER BIG DATE AT THE PARAMOUNT THEATRE between March 8 and 21, 1939, consigned the Cocoanut Grove scandal to the Webb band's past. Despite the contradictory reviews, the booking confirmed the band's stature. In 1938 Webb's band had ranked thirteenth on Paramount's poll of theatergoers. A year later, with Ella at his side, Webb could fill two weeks at the venue and draw a profit, despite his being paired with the flop film *Never Say Die* with Martha Raye and Bob Hope. Webb included the Lindy Hoppers as part of the show.

As Webb's health declined and his absences lengthened, Fitzgerald assumed a larger role in the band's presentation. Judging from his associates' recollections, Webb carried on at the Paramount with heroic tenacity, then was carried on and off stage by his loyal valet, Joe Saunders. Like the manager at a prizefight, Saunders prepped Webb for the curtain rise when he returned. Nor did the energy of the band diminish. As a big finale, it perfected a vocal jam based on "St. Louis Blues." Fitzgerald joined the raucous conclusion, afterward getting variously praised and reproached for transgressing the boundaries of girl-singer convention. *Billboard*'s critic said she "adds her bit to the whirlwind finish," while *Variety*'s man wrote that she "lingers too long, making not-so-forte impression when she cuts up away from the mike for a final hot stanza with the band."[12]

The roller-coaster continued over the next few months. After the Paramount, Chick and Ella worked the East Coast theater circuit, including the Howard Theatre in Washington, D.C., the Royal in Baltimore, and the Fox in Philadelphia, finding good box office overall. At the Fox date in April, Fitzgerald sang her latest Decca sides and participated in what a reviewer called a "tremendous pot of jam-medley," which by now included both "St. Louis Blues" and "Tutti Frutti," a novelty hit by Slim and Slam—Slim Gaillard on vocals and Slam Stewart on his bowed bass.[13] All this touring occurred in tandem with a serious decline in Webb's health. Webb missed the Howard date, instead entering Johns Hopkins Hospital and explaining his absence to the trade press as a semiannual checkup.[14]

Webb was back for a memorable month-long booking at the Southland Café in Boston from April 21 to May 20. "All of the top bands played there year after year," said Count Basie, who had played there previously. "They also had a very important radio wire in there, and those broadcasts were popular all through New England at that time."[15] *Metronome* noted, "Although Chick Webb and Ella Fitzgerald didn't break any attendance records at Southland, they were a real draw and a place for the jitterbugs to hang out."[16] Air checks from May 4, 1939—Webb's last surviving recordings—show Fitzgerald swinging popular hits, among them "If I Didn't Care" (a hit for the Ink Spots), "A New Moon and an Old Serenade" (a hit for Tommy Dorsey's band), "I Never Knew Heaven Could Speak" (a Hollywood film tune and hit for the Bob Crosby orchestra), and "Chew Chew Chew Chew (Your Bubble Gum)," more kiddie fare recorded for Decca two months earlier, with Fitzgerald credited as cocomposer. Webb's band grabbed the spotlight here with its robust, manic swing—listeners would hardly have known the bandleader was in the last stages of a fatal disease. The band's humor and energy animated a zany, surrealistic arrangement of John Philip Sousa's "Stars and Stripes Forever," and Webb's drum solos in "My Wild Irish Rose" alternate with burlesque tempos in an outrageous romp.

The band returned to familiar territory in New York, with five nights at the Savoy and a week at the Apollo from May 26 to June 1. *Variety* praised the band and Webb's drum skills—despite his needing a substitute for some numbers—but Fitzgerald seemed to carry the weight of the evening. The opening sentence of its review reflects that "Chick and Ella" was sliding into "Ella and Chick": "Apollo has another b.o. [box office] layout this week in Ella Fitzgerald and Chick Webb's band." Webb and Fitzgerald occupied around thirty minutes of a ninety-minute stage show, but the band's performance was seen as her opening act: "The band is on for fully 15 minutes before Miss Fitzgerald appears. The customers at this catching then didn't want to let her go." She sang a mix of tunes, heavy on novelty, with an obscure "rhythmic original" called "Peek-a-Boo" and the "whacky novelty" "Chew Chew Chew Chew (Your Bubble Gum)," along with the popular hits "And the Angels Sing," a number-one hit for Benny Goodman and Martha Tilton, and the poignant "Don't Worry About Me."[17]

Chick and Ella kept on meeting dates in late May and early June, as he refused to yield to pain and fatigue. On May 29 they participated in a mammoth event sponsored by the National Swing Club at the Hippodrome in New York. That was Webb's last public outing.

In the winter and spring of 1939, Webb seems to have recognized he was losing his battle against tuberculosis. And he was anxious about Ella. On one occasion during a Hartford booking around New Year's Day 1939, the reporter who reviewed the show later recalled that "all he did was worry for Ella. Worry about her voice . . . Worry about her future. . . . Worry about her health . . . Worry about everything. . . . His attitude was like a parent of a lone child. Sure that child will fall by the wayside if the parent doesn't watch, tend, care and instruct."[18] That spring Webb tried to promote a romance between Fitzgerald and Heywood Henry, a musician with the Erskine Hawkins Orchestra. Decades later Henry vividly recalled how Webb approved of Ella going around with a college man from Alabama State: "He told others I was the right type of guy because she didn't know nothing about nothing. She didn't know nothing about no man."[19] What would happen to her? Teddy McRae, in Washington, D.C., recalled Webb's last words to him, which fit his paternal heart: "Anything happens to me, take care of Ella. Don't let the guys mess up. Just take care of Ella."[20] Then he entered the hospital. That was on June 9. On June 16, 1939, Chick Webb died of renal tuberculosis at thirty-four.

The band had started its road tour without him, traveling through Virginia, South Carolina, and Georgia. In Montgomery, Alabama, playing a dance at the Colored Elks Auditorium, they heard the news of his death. Instead of applauding, Teddy McRae recalled that "everybody just stood there and looked at us."[21] A local reporter wrote two days later, "The spectators and members of the orchestra were unable to restrain real tears, and Ella Fitzgerald kept on singing the 'hot' numbers that made her famous despite the fact that she was choking with sobs."[22]

Back in Baltimore for the funeral on June 20, Ella fell apart. For comfort, she turned to Teddy McRae, who seemed to carry too heavy a grief to help her:

> Ella was following me around, crying and carrying on. I'd walk down the street; she'd be behind me. I was going down Pennsylvania Avenue. I say, "Go on back to the hotel, don't bother me." We stayed in that little hotel, and she followed me down the street. "Don't leave me, I want to go with you." We'd walk around the streets. The band was just like in a daze, we were just in shock. "Don't leave me." "I want to go." "Where are you going?" "I'm going with you." She was crying. I say, "Ella don't be crying. Everything is going to be all right."[23]

Then he left her on her own to face the most significant loss of her life since the death of her mother five years earlier. Webb's funeral was by all accounts an extraordinary outpouring of love and affection for Baltimore's native son. His mother, sisters, friends, and colleagues filled the Waters AME Church, and ten thousand people lined the streets to bid him farewell. A photo in the *Baltimore Afro-American* showed Ella comforting Webb's wife, Sally. Teddy McRae played his elegy, "The End of a Perfect Day," a classic parlor song from 1910. Ella sang "My Buddy" and "was so far from being the smiling Ella Fitzgerald of the footlights and bandstand that the whole audience was affected," reported the *Baltimore Afro-American*. "Bardu Ali . . . broke into tears, and several of the boys in the band who had been sitting quietly through the services, wept."[24]

★★★

ENTERTAINMENT REPORTERS AND CULTURAL COLUMNISTS in the Black world had followed Chick Webb and the rise of Ella Fitzgerald for years. Upon his death, the press eulogies formed rich narratives around their relationship, focusing mainly on Webb's achievements as a drummer and leader of a major swing band from Harlem. They noted his heroism, embodied in his rise from poverty and his triumph over disability and illness. Some reporters acknowledged Webb's foresight in recognizing the spark of genius in Ella Fitzgerald; in turn, they saw her refusal of Benny Goodman's 1936 offer to join his band as a sign of her filial gratitude and loyalty. On the whole, right through Webb's death, accounts in the Black press did not describe Fitzgerald as overshadowing Webb's career or disrupting his musical mission.

In Lillian Johnson's piece for the *Baltimore Afro-American*, Fitzgerald emerged as a heroine in her own right: "After that appearance at Yale, Ella's place with the band was permanent. Her sweet, baby voice, that somehow reminds one of peach fuzz, was something new and caught on immediately. That voice was to help the band soar to new heights of popularity."[25]

The obituaries in white periodicals varied in tone and focus, depending on their readership, but most adapted the longer obituary released by the Associated Press. It did not name Webb's instrumentals but instead referred to the "Webb-Fitzgerald swing records" as "musts" for record buyers. The AP praised the "hot" music of "the little colored boy who graduated from thumping a butter tub to become Harlem's drumminest maestro" and the "little hunchback king of the skins [who] began beating out his wild tempos 15 years ago."[26] Such praise marginalized Webb by ignoring his influence on mainstream swing, particularly on Benny Goodman and Gene Krupa. While he was alive, Webb had received scant coverage in the *New York Times*, so its one-paragraph obituary reflected hard-won recognition.[27]

In the specialized music trade press, Webb's fate was even more intertwined with Fitzgerald's. "It's ironical that Webb died just a year or so after hitting the big time with his band," *Variety* wrote. "Fairly well known since first coming to New York in 1926, Webb didn't reach the peak of his popularity until then and a great deal of it hinged on his and Ella Fitzgerald's penning of 'A-Tisket A-Tasket' which started a cycle of nursery rhyme swing tunes."[28]

Commentary was more complicated in the jazz press, which automatically demoted vocals to "commercial" status. A *Metronome* editorial credited Webb for his generous spirit: "There was never any trouble when Ella, whom he picked out of a Harlem amateur show, began to soar to fame and when folks began to talk as much (and sometimes more) about her as they did about him. Chick wasn't jealous; he showed that by featuring Ella even more."[29] Other jazz writers regarded Fitzgerald's success as Webb's failure. A voice like peach fuzz did not fit the image of masculine competition among striving instrumentalists. In a 1941 retrospective on Webb's career in *Metronome*, Barry Ulanov praised Fitzgerald's "extraordinary feeling for singing like a good jazzman plays," but he nevertheless painted Webb as a martyred soul: "He'd sacrificed many of his deepest musical convictions to make a success of his band, commercializing way out of his own kind of music, and had taken the family wolf from the doors of his hardworking musicians."[30]

One wonders if Ella Fitzgerald ever read the judgments passed on her role. Judging from clippings in her scrapbook, she paid attention to her reviews in *Metronome* and *Down Beat*. But she likely did not have access to *Melody Maker*, where Leonard Feather published a punitive obituary:

> The discovery of Ella set Chick's band on a commercial path irrevocably; one could even go further and say that ever since [Edgar] Sampson left the band it was never quite the same. It is much better and kinder to think of Chick as a swell artist and fellow who was carried away by something too big for him in the form of Broadway commercialism.[31]

"Language is the most powerful of human weapons," writes the historian David Green, analyzing the rhetoric of politics. It can manipulate human understanding and bring people "to cooperate in their own subjugation. . . . By the same token, understanding of language is the beginning of political independence."[32] So too with aesthetic rhetoric, in which words change meaning over time. The debate over Webb's decline in relation to the arrival of Ella Fitzgerald would continue after his death in memoirs written by his sidemen, in scholarship by cultural and music historians, and in box sets showcasing their intertwined legacy.[33] Whatever the quality of Webb's late arrangements, his career spawned a literature within jazz history partly because of the power of the binary oppositions it embodied: commercial/authentic, female/male, white/Black, singer/player, and sweet/hot, just at the time Fitzgerald was forging bridges between them.[34]

In terms of her artistic evolution, Fitzgerald was fusing jazz and pop into a new style while remaining indebted to both, developing traits that neither possessed separately. That fusion was what made her original, and it emerged through mutual dependency. Webb enabled her to develop her style while immersed in the band rather than out in front of it. His letting her join the band in its after-hours sessions had been crucial for her, which she acknowledged by releasing her classic 1947 vocal jam, "Lady Be Good," as "a memorial to Chick."[35] Crossing the bridge from amateur to artist, she "instrumentalized" her vocality, as it were, not just through obvious scatting but also through her "time" or rhythmic placement of the beat. She too "kicked the band." Harvard student Michael Levin, who would later write for *Down Beat*, listened and heard this quality. In the *Harvard Crimson* he wrote, "Ella's singing is a lot like a good 'dig' tenor sax player: She sings most of her licks ahead of the beat, so that you get a drive effect which packs power in quantity. Result is that she is just about the back-bone of Chick's band."[36] For her that was the true meaning of "Chick and Ella."

Fig. 4. Advertisement for Ella Fitzgerald and Chick Webb Orchestra at the
State Theatre in Hartford, Connecticut, January 1939. Reproduced in Ron
Fritts and Ken Vail, *Ella Fitzgerald: The Chick Webb Years & Beyond 1935–1948*,
Ken Vail's Jazz Itineraries 2 (Lanham, Md.: Scarecrow Press, 2003), 35. *Courtesy of
Rowman & Littlefield Publishing Group, Inc.*

★★★

SOON AFTER CHICK WEBB'S DEATH, questions surfaced in the Black press
about Fitzgerald's future. Headlines, most likely adapted from Moe Gale's
press releases, noted, "Ella May Be New Boss of Chick Webb's Band"
and asked, "Will Ella Fitzgerald Be Same Minus Chick?" and "What
Next for Ella Fitzgerald?"[37] An article in the *Chicago Defender* read,

> Now that Chick is dead, some people are inclined to say that per-
> haps Ella Fitzgerald is sorry she did not accept Benny Goodman's
> offer to sing with his band. . . . Miss Fitzgerald stood by Webb
> because it was he who gave her the start which resulted in her fame

as a swing singer. . . . How do you think she would have felt now, if she had deserted him when he needed her the most? . . . We'd say Ella deserves ORCHIDS.[38]

One gossipy column said she "has been sought by numerous bands of both races," floating Goodman, Shaw, and Sammy Kaye as suitors. "But Ella says Chick Webb made her and she believes his wish is that she remain with the band. 'So with the band that Chick made and that made me, I am sticking,' she told reporters."[39] All sources agreed that rumors of other offers had been put to rest. The few comments Fitzgerald relayed to the press mostly reaffirmed her intent to focus on her career and not get married anytime soon. Seven years later George T. Simon wrote, "How she still raves about Chick! She is still truly grateful to the late little drummer, grateful for his having discovered her, having featured her, having been so completely unselfish about everything."[40]

Fitzgerald may have been content with her decision, but she was also overwhelmed. She trusted Moe Gale and relied on him to decide her future. "My father loved Chick," recalled Richard Gale, and "Ella really loved my father."[41] Fitzgerald's fame was too great to consider dissolving the band, at a time when the music industry was purring and the band business was estimated at $90 million to $100 million a year.[42] "She never skipped a beat, was back the next day," recalled Beverly Peer. "She was thinking about her future. All the musicians were thinking about their future."[43]

Whether Ella or Jack Kapp at Decca had any concerns about her future with the label seems unlikely. "A-Tisket A-Tasket" had made her a world-famous star, and between 1936 and May 1939, sixteen songs from 110 titles had charted either as single records or through jukebox play. Fitzgerald soon proved her worth again on June 29, 1939, when the band assembled for their first recording session without Webb. They set down five vocal numbers under her name, including two novelties and two standards, "Out of Nowhere" and the highlight of the session, "Stairway to the Stars." Beverly Peer recalled, "That was a good seller and things began to move on."[44] A "classic," *Billboard*'s critic wrote.[45] It was a great beginning for the post-Webb era. "Stairway to the Stars" was then owned by Glenn Miller and his vocalist Ray Eberle, and though Fitzgerald's version could not dislodge it, she benefited from a fresh treatment by the master arranger Edgar Sampson, and her own melodic paraphrases gave some lift to the lyrics—a real alternative to Glenn Miller's hit. Sampson had returned to the fold to pitch in, hired by her, according to the *Pittsburgh Courier*.[46]

In the band's first public appearance as a new unit at Loew's State Theatre in New York, Webb remained its reason for being. Advertisements billed them as "Ella Fitzgerald and the Famous Chick Webb Orchestra" and included a statement, "In keeping with the wishes of the late Chick Webb / We continue as a unit / May we be a credit to his name and maintain his standard of music! / Signed Ella Fitzgerald and the Boys in the Band." In the middle of the advertisement was a portrait of Fitzgerald posing stiffly, like a Madame Tussaud wax figure, in a full-length gown with no band in sight.[47]

On opening night, Eddie Cantor made a surprise cameo, pitching the gig as a kind of tribute to Webb: "He was not only my friend but the friend of all America," said the veteran variety entertainer. "He gave us a lot of amusement and a lot of music, and he discovered Ella Fitzgerald, who is deservedly the First Lady of Swing. Out of respect to Chick Webb, all of you should tell all of your friends to come here this week."[48]

The stage show was paired with the feature film *Wuthering Heights*, the now-classic adaptation of Emily Brontë's novel. Fitzgerald, appearing as the closer after forty-five minutes of the band and two variety acts, used her repertoire to express her grief. In addition to "You Showed Me the Way"—which she recorded with Webb in 1937, with both their names on the copyright—she sang "Don't Worry 'Bout Me," from a session on April 21, 1939, giving the outstanding ballad's lyrics an emotional reading. At Loew's State, one review said, she had "a sob in her throat," dedicating her performance to the man "who made it possible for me to be here before you tonight."[49]

Despite Cantor's support, box office results fell flat, and the reviews suggested that the newly constituted band would not find an easy path to acceptance. How could it succeed when its presentation was muddled: was it a memorial concert, a rebirth, or a trial by box office? Without Webb, *Variety* wrote, "some of the boys seemingly have become listless. There's a possibility that this date came too soon after Webb's death and the boys haven't yet recovered from the shock."[50] The Gale Agency shifted its strategy then. In *Variety*'s July 26 issue, a headline read, "Death Reminders Eliminated: Chick Webb Name Dropped—New Drummer in Background—Ella Fitzgerald Now Tops."[51] Then the band stayed home and booked at the Savoy from July 16 through August 26, while the members retooled the arrangements.

Air checks from Savoy broadcasts on July 16, July 20, and August 24 reveal Fitzgerald's eclectic repertoire, showing that the band was still swinging and that she was musically ready to join them as one of them. She could jam with the best of them—and did. On July 20, 1939, Fitzgerald sang "St. Louis Blues." In this little-known side, which first became available in 2000, her innovative genius emerges in a high point of her collaboration with the band.[52] Reviewers had been mentioning her role in the concert's finale for months, and here it proves her stature as a formidable competitive improviser. After the "Latin" opening and Taft Jordan's trumpet solo, joking about the repeated-note melody of the novelty hit "Tutti Frutti," Ella takes a star turn to solo in the spotlight. One expects her to put on *Carmen* airs in the habanera rhythm that W. C. Handy built into the song. Instead, she continues the joke in her long scat chorus, announcing the title "Tutti Frutti," popularized by Slim and Slam. She knew the vocalist Slim Gaillard and the singing bass player Slam Stewart because she and the band had shared a five-day engagement with them on January 2–6, 1939, at the State Theatre in Hartford.[53] She would continue to transform "St. Louis Blues" into a jam tune in the decades ahead.

Swinging the band was one responsibility—leading it was another. The Gales were keeping expenses down, refusing to hire a new leader, expecting the band to adapt. The novelty of her position, they thought, might even be a draw. There had been precedents, starting in the 1920s, of African American "female maestros," including Blanche Calloway, Valaida Snow, and Lil Hardin Armstrong. In the 1930s, writes music historian D. Antoinette Handy, "Black female orchestral leadership and total Black female organizations continued throughout the decade."[54] Leading a hugely successful band would be different from fronting it. Time would tell if the band could truly survive without Webb. There were moments after Webb's death when Fitzgerald felt like quitting. But at this point, as the leader of what had become an institution, quitting was inconceivable for this musical heiress.

Chapter 8

ORCHESTRA LEADER

(1940-1942)

I n the fall of 1939, Fitzgerald's career began anew as she assumed a prominent role in a dynamic environment of big band music, "one of the most profitable active and bullish branches of the amusement industry."[1] For the next two years, until the onset of World War II, big band music would dominate the scene. Only in hindsight does Ella's survival seem obvious. These years saw the meteoric rise of Glenn Miller, a white bandleader whose mesmerizing, innovative blend of horns and reeds made everybody else sound old-fashioned. His "phenomenal success" in 1939 would make him "one of the great legends of American popular cultural history," in the words of the historian Gunther Schuller, and give "sweet music" a new life.[2] How was a singer known for novelties and jive tunes going to keep afloat a band that had been famous for its "Harlem sound"? Fitzgerald did it by growing and changing as an entertainer in these challenging years of transition.

It happened step by step, beginning with her stage routines. In mid-September 1939 the band arrived at the Grand Terrace Café in Chicago for a six-week stay. There Ella presented a more mature stage persona. In the words of *Variety*'s critic, the "smooth jive warbler stopped terping."[3] While the poster ads for the Grand Terrace showed her trucking and shimmying in her schoolgirl outfit, onstage she traded juvenile clothes for a dark floor-length gown.

That didn't change the music much, however. The Grand Terrace Café, a black and tan nightclub, promoted jazz with coast-to-coast wire hookups that brought national exposure to its resident pianist, Earl "Fatha" Hines. Hines had a long run, but when business failed, he went on leave in July 1939; the club shut down, declared itself renewed, and then brought in Ella Fitzgerald's fresh face. In one auspicious notice, *Billboard* reported that Ella was "proving a magnet out front and drawing them in by droves." She was a "vocal stylist, giving her individual interpretations alike to ballads and swingeroos." The Webb band also won praise for keeping the "jitterbugs in the groove" with "unorthodox yet entertaining versions of standards" even without the "predominating drum work which was the life blood of the old Webb band."[4] "Hep hep" and "jive" overshadowed sweet tunes on set lists. An air check from September 21 includes her own composition, "Oh, Boy, I'm in the Groove," along with "Well All Right," with a little quote from "Buffalo Gals" tucked in.[5] The floor show, produced and emceed by Leonard Reed, offered a "dozen brown-skinned shapelies," a

Fig. 5. Advertisement for Ella Fitzgerald and Her Famous Orchestra at the Grand Terrace, Chicago, September 1939. Reproduced in Ron Fritts and Ken Vail, *Ella Fitzgerald: The Chick Webb Years & Beyond 1935–1948*, Ken Vail's Jazz Itineraries 2 (Lanham, Md.: Scarecrow Press, 2003), 46. *Courtesy of Rowman & Littlefield Publishing Group, Inc.*

tenor for sentimental tunes, an eccentric dancer, a pair of expert ballroom dancers, and a tap-dancing duo. Afterward Fitzgerald was "ushered in majestically thru a trumpet-blaring chorus" to sing.[6]

Sometime after Chick's death and the band's arrival in Chicago, Ella Fitzgerald and Leonard Reed became an item. About ten years older than she, Reed was an attractive, well-known figure in Harlem show business. Having started out in the 1920s as a tap dancer with the Whitman Sisters, in the 1930s he produced dance revues for the Apollo and the Cotton Club downtown. A *Chicago Defender* article—headlined "Say Ella Fitzgerald Is Wed to Len Reed: Singer Denies There Has Been Ceremony; Grand Terrace Producer Hints the Wedding Will Be Soon"—reported that some said, "they eloped one morning after the show and had the ceremony performed at Crown Point, Ind. To this Miss Fitzgerald said, 'No, no, no.'"[7]

Fitzgerald's relationship with Reed fit the pattern of her quick romances in the late 1930s. Jo Jones, the great drummer in Count Basie's band, said he "was snoring in her face" in 1937. Reed later recalled he was so "sweet on Ella" that he signed on as her road manager, even though "it was a step down." Then about two months later their connection ended, according to Reed, in a rather unpleasant manner:

> We had pulled into Indianapolis and we were piling out of the car when she turned to me and said like she was a queen, "Pick up those bags." And I said, "Not me." It was in front of a lot of people. It was the *way* she said, "Pick up those bags and bring 'em in." So I said, "Okay," got the bags, set 'em down beside my car, got back in and drove off for Chicago. . . . I didn't see Ella again for a number of years, by which time she was a really big star, so I guess she was just trying out her prima donna act on me there in Indianapolis.[8]

For Ella Fitzgerald and the orchestra, the Grand Terrace Café box office proved disappointing. The owner, Ed Fox, contracted to pay her some $2,000 a week but claimed she left him over $7,000 in the red. Bad draws like the Grand Terrace were balanced by better results, seemingly in less urban areas with more enthusiasm for hard-core swing. In Chattanooga on November 29, some 5,125 dancers and onlookers crowded into Memorial Auditorium for a jitterbug contest, equaling an attendance record set by Cab Calloway. As reported in *Billboard*, "The section reserved for white spectators filled before the dance was well under way and hundreds were turned away."[9]

In December Ella and the band returned to the Savoy Ballroom. For a day, on Christmas Eve, the charismatic Glenn Miller, billed as leading "America's greatest swing band," held sway at the ballroom. But Fitzgerald and her band were back on Christmas Day and stayed in place for about two months delivering familiar Webb classics and her most recent Decca novelties. Baby talk was still selling: "My Wubba Dolly," recorded for Decca on October 12, charted briefly. The song spoofed "Little Rubber Dolly," an early-1930s hit for a western swing band. According to an air check at the Savoy on December 12, the band used a simpler, featherlight arrangement, and Ella laughed and giggled her way through the song, clueing the crowd in on this silly novelty as a big joke.

★★★

AT THE DAWN OF THE 1940s, the Webb band was back on the road, and reports were grim. "A new era of ickey and sweet music is dawning," wrote *Billboard* in February, noting that Swing Street (52nd Street) is "Getting Ready for the Grave as Pop Talent Supplants Jive."[10] Black bands were particularly vulnerable.

Fitzgerald's next residency was at New York's Roseland Ballroom for a month beginning February 26. Air checks reveal that the band pulled together and did solid business. She reprised "Sugar Blues" and "The Starlit Hour," two recent Decca releases, the latter a cover of a Glenn Miller hit. The Gale Agency turned the end of the Roseland gig into an A-list publicity event attended by Miller himself, the Andrews Sisters, Fats Waller, Gene Krupa, Bob Crosby, Louis Armstrong, Duke Ellington, Benny Carter, and Teddy Wilson.[11] Quite a crew.

Then came a volatile spring at the Famous Door, a 52nd Street club.

For her April 16 opening, the Gale Agency confected another celebrity event guaranteeing publicity. Ella greeted Artie Shaw and his new wife, the movie star Lana Turner, and in another part of the room she said hello to Shaw's former girlfriend Betty Grable.[12] On April 23—two days before her twenty-third birthday—the indefatigable Gale publicists drummed up "*Down Beat* Night," presenting her with a trophy for her triumph as "best female singer" in the *Down Beat* poll.[13] But Fitzgerald failed to draw large crowds to the Famous Door, and in the aftermath Gale sued the club owners for not paying them.

Despite this ongoing pattern of success and failure, the band's relative prosperity testified to her perseverance. In March *Billboard* reported on the lucrative big band market in an overview, including the asking prices—not always met—by name bands. Fred Waring was tops at $12,500 per week, followed by Kay Kyser, Glenn Miller, Horace Heidt, Benny Goodman, and Artie Shaw at the $10,000 tier. The $7,500 bracket included Tommy Dorsey and the highest-paid African American band, the Cab Calloway Orchestra. Of the thirty-six bands listed, five were headed by African Americans. Louis Armstrong and Duke Ellington came in at $6,500, then Fitzgerald at $5,000 (matching Webb's previous high-water mark), followed by Jimmie Lunceford at $4,500. The only other female bandleader listed was Ina Ray Hutton, pulling in $3,500.[14]

But acting as the orchestra head was proving to be too much responsibility for her. A former band vocalist rising to a position of public leadership did not translate to leadership within the group. Serious management problems surfaced. The Gales, keeping expenses down, still refused to hire a new leader. A few months prior, in December 1939, Edgar Sampson had already aired the band's troubles, saying "too many people" were trying to lead it, and worse yet, "The boys were more interested in listening to ball games than in coming to rehearsals."[15]

Things came to a head in May 1940. According to Teddy McRae, in late spring "She told me, 'Being out front there, I can't make it. Well, you have to take over the band.' It was too much for her."[16] Finally, Gale considered hiring a new leader-arranger. The leadership issue was tricky, as the "Chick and Ella" pairing still hung over the ensemble.

Gale offered the leadership job to Sy Oliver, who was then working with Tommy Dorsey's band. When Oliver declined, Gale approached Benny Carter, whose career he had been managing since 1939. According to a press account, the new aggregation "would be called 'Ella Fitzgerald and Her Orchestra,' as her position was not to be disturbed, but the tag 'Conducted by Benny Carter' was to be added."[17]

But Carter was not interested in leading the continuation of a ghost band. Further, he couldn't stand the Savoy operations, later saying of Gale and Charles Buchanan, "They thought of us—in management and remuneration—as maybe a cut above the waiters."[18] After these negotiations failed, Carter left Gale to sign with MCA, which promised him a publicity campaign and far better pay. On May 15, 1940, *Down Beat* reported that Teddy McRae would soon "take over the band as front man and director and Ella sticking only as vocalist."[19]

It is not clear how Fitzgerald rallied, but around this time she gave an interview expressing resistance to any change of leadership. If the band failed, she felt it would be her personal as well as professional failure, and that would mean failing Chick Webb too. She ardently expressed her sense of obligation to Bill Nunn, the respected managing editor of the *Pittsburgh Courier,* in a remarkable interview that did what the *Courier* did best—kept up a "constant stream of publicity" to nurture African American talent,[20] one generation after another:

> There is no force on earth strong enough to take the Chick Webb orchestra away from me being there is a breath of life within me. . . . On June 16, 1939, I inherited the Chick Webb Orchestra. At that time, I promised myself that I would always do my best to maintain the standard of musicianship that was Chick's very soul. I intend to keep that promise if I have to scour the entire world to find musicians who believe as I do in the greatness of the late Chick Webb. . . . I have made several moves to protect his name and it is these . . . that started the rumor that I am going to disband my orchestra.[21]

Ella explained her division of responsibility with McRae: "You see, . . . with Teddy helping me I get a chance to go around and find material for myself. In the course of a day, I can listen to at least 20 new tunes from which I must select those I think the public would like to hear me sing. Teddy does the same thing for the band, and at the end of the day we get together and make the final choices." Nunn concluded, "If anybody tells you that Ella is about to break up her orchestra, just don't believe it. It's not true."[22]

To enliven the stage, Gale hired male vocalist Emmett "Babe" Wallace, a handsome song-and-dance man whose career went back to the Cotton Club in the late 1920s. He was soon singing his tune "A Chicken Ain't Nothin' But a Bird," which would be popularized in a September 1940 recording by his co-writer Louis Jordan for the Black pop market. If it kept the jitterbugs happy, that's what counted.[23]

That springtime reorganization staved off the band's marked vulnerability. From one perspective, and in comparison to other big bands that spring, Fitzgerald was holding her own. In March an overview by *Billboard* reported on the lucrative big band market, including the asking prices—not always met—by name bands. Fred Waring was tops at $12,500 per week, followed by Kay Kyser, Glenn Miller, Horace Heidt, Benny Goodman, and Artie Shaw at the $10,000 tier. The $7,500 bracket included Tommy Dorsey and the highest-paid African American band, the Cab Calloway Orchestra. Of the thirty-six bands listed, five were headed by African Americans. Louis Armstrong and Duke Ellington came in at $6,500, then Fitzgerald at $5,000 (matching Webb's previous high-water mark), followed by Jimmie Lunceford at $4,500. The only other female bandleader listed was Ina Ray Hutton, pulling in $3,500.[24] Yet race qualified everything as usual. "The truth is that the public will absorb only a very limited number of Negro bands," wrote Paul Eduard Miller, a respected columnist in *Down Beat*. Miller placed Fitzgerald's band among those whose "financial success, to put it optimistically, is only mediocre," and who were "practically out of the picture so far as the general public is concerned."[25]

★★★

GALE KEPT THEM BUSY with grueling one-nighters on extended road trips in barely adequate buses. "Ella Goes 18,000 Miles Touring 36 States," crowed one press release about the summer tour in 1940. We do not know the precise itinerary, but they hit cities in the South, Southwest, and Pacific Coast.[26] Few road tales from this tour have survived that match the many accounts of troubles and danger traveling in Jim Crow America recounted by contemporary historians. While Earl Hines's comments about his travels in the 1930s routinely dealing with surveillance and danger have famously described his men as virtual "Freedom Riders" (that is, as brave as the Civil Rights activists in the 1950s), Ella Fitzgerald said little about life on the bus.[27] Nevertheless, some stories and interviews offer glimpses of unpredictable random troubles. One story, which made the rounds in the Black press, concerned a near riot at the New Rhythm Club in New Orleans in June 1940 when a crowd of four thousand almost turned into a mob. What was going on here? In the background was the tragic story of over two hundred Black people perishing in a tragic fire at the Rhythm Club in Natchez, Mississippi, two months earlier.[28] Fear combined with enthusiasm surging around Ella led to headlines like "Ella Fitzgerald Exits from New Orleans Dance Tattered and Torn by Frenzied Mob."[29] She left it behind her, so it seems.

In contrast to public perils, life inside was an oasis of boredom. The band's bass player, Beverly Peer, offers vignettes about the way Ella and the gang passed time on the bus and off. He talked about playing games of "tonk," a short, five-card version of gin rummy: "We'd play that for miles and miles on the bus, and Ella would be playing tonk also." Peer also observed that while Ella the musician was extroverted, Ella the young woman "wasn't much of a mingler. She was more in her room. Introvert, I'd call her. She didn't want to be bothered with people."[30] Jim Crow problems also separated Fitzgerald and the musicians, and management that left them to find their own places to stay. "We stayed in black folks' homes, and every musician had to have his own contacts in the South," said Peer. "Ella had her own contacts. We never saw her when we weren't playing or on the bus. On the bus she was 'one of the boys'—she'd sing and dance and scat on the bus. But when we got off the bus, she kept to herself."[31] She needed solitude to recharge, not social pressure or small talk from autograph seekers and curious admirers.

In Portland, Oregon, in July, where the band appeared at the Spanish Ballroom, Fitzgerald gave an unusually colorful interview to the veteran journalist David W. Hazen. In a state where 98 percent of the population was white, Hazen opened by observing, "Life is just one fried chicken after another," then followed with some decent questions and unguarded answers. He asked what voice classification she had—an important consideration for classical singers—and she replied, "I don't know what you would call it." He asked if she was dancing. "Oh, little bit, jitterbug once in a while," came the coy answer. "I can play the piano, but nothing to brag about. Diamond is my birthstone. That's why I wear this ring. Chick Webb gave it to me for Christmas." Noting her soft voice and gentle drawl, Hazen attributed "her languid way" to her Southern roots. He also asked what sorts of songs she liked.

> I used to sing nothing but jittery stuff but now everybody likes me to sing sweet songs, so I give 'em a little of each. I like classic songs, but I don't try to beat Marian Anderson singing them. My favorite songs right now are "Shake Down the Stars" and "Sugar Blues." No, I don't write then, I wish I had. But I have written some songs; the one that went over the best is "Tisket Tasket," which Chick Webb played so much. I also wrote "You Showed Me the Way," "I Found My Yellow Basket," and I just finished one with Joseph Myrow of New York called "'Just One of Those Nights." I spend a lot of time on these songs of mine. When I have a little spare time and can't find no one to play pinochle with, I'll read anything I can get hold of.[32]

Fitzgerald's interest in songwriting deserves further comment, especially considering her election on September 13 to ASCAP, the prestigious performance-rights organization that collected licensing fees for members when their compositions were broadcast or performed live. She would remain a member for the rest of her career.[33] At the time of her election she held at least partial copyright on fifteen songs, of which Decca recorded eight, three made the *Billboard* charts, and three were recorded by other artists.[34] To be sure, some of the tunes were little more than chart bait, including nursery rhyme spinoffs. But the band needed hits, and Fitzgerald maintained a sincere interest in songwriting through the 1960s.

Among her repertoire, Teddy McRae remembered the sweet songs in a touching vignette:

> One night there around 11 or 12 o'clock, she started singing a medley of things, and she had everybody in the ballroom in tears. She was singing her heart out that night. That's one of those nights—I guess she was thinking about Chick. I guess something just hit her. Boy this was about a half-hour, and the ballroom was just as quiet and Ella was going through all these songs. . . . She just tore the place up. . . . The next day they gave her the key to the city.[35]

In the fall of 1940, Fitzgerald was back in New York for week-long dates at the Apollo and the Savoy. Reviews were inconsistent. At the Apollo, where raves were more expected, *Variety*'s reviewer felt Fitzgerald was eclipsed by the band, which had started the year as a "very disorganized bunch" and was now "a well-rehearsed solid crew, playing snappy arrangements that click with little trouble." Her singing, on the other hand, "lacked the life and push it usually has; the impression gathered was that she was vocalling mechanically." Nonetheless she "clicked heavily with the audience on four numbers," including "Woodpecker Song" (a hit for the Andrews Sisters), "Imagination," "I Found My Yellow Basket," and "What Can I Say After I Say I'm Sorry."[36]

Who would have expected what happened next—the emergence of a ballad singer consolidating her gains over the year on the road. It happened at the Club Tropicana at 52nd and Broadway, yet another venture in bringing "colored vaudeville" downtown. Fitzgerald and Her Famous Orchestra launched the venue's opening running three shows a night with various acts, including what *Billboard* described as "a line of eight girls" who were "briefly dressed and dance[d] with abundant flash and rhythm."[37] An unusual account appeared in the *New York Sun*:

> In her work at the Tropicana you'd hardly recognize Miss Fitzgerald as the creator of the swing song "A-Tisket A-Tasket." Although she can and does swing out in the hot tunes, she apparently is willing to let "A-Tisket A-Tasket" remain in the dead and buried past. For that, we, for one, are grateful.
>
> Ella Fitzgerald is a Negro girl who impresses her listeners as a sensitive, sincere, and talented performer. She resorts to no tricks; she just stands up there with her hands behind her back and sings— simply and with a warmth of feeling that is strangely moving. She does a particularly fine job with Gershwin's "Summertime," which tugs at the heartstrings as she sings it. Perhaps the finest critical compliment to her work is that her night club audience listens to her with rapt attention—drinks, food, everything else forgotten.
>
> This is true even in the last show, at 2:30 a.m., when audiences are likely to be noisier and much gayer than earlier in the evening.[38]

Fitzgerald would not record "Summertime" until 1957, but this early description has a dignified aura more typically associated with classical vocal recitals and what Fitzgerald had called "classic songs." Such performances, in light of her own statements about singing "sweet and hot," were keys to the survival of an outdated swing band as well as to her continued growth as an artist.

"Summertime," however, could not save the Tropicana engagement. Fitzgerald left because of poor business, and nobody got paid until Local 802, the powerful New York branch of the musicians' union, exerted pressure on the owners.[39] Gale defected because, he claimed, the club did not arrange for radio remote broadcasts as expected.[40] But Major Robinson in the *Chicago Defender* blamed Fitzgerald:

Failure to draw the capacity crowds expected of her was the reason this week advanced by Broadwayites and "those in the know" for the sudden exiting of Ella Fitzgerald and her swing crew from the Tropicana club. . . . Those who saw her agreed . . . she definitely was lacking of new material. . . . She has lacked hit numbers to keep her in the public's eyesight.

This isn't the first time that Ella has failed to draw huge crowds. Last year she entered the Famous Door but soon left. Many hinted that internal differences with members with the band have hindered her greatly.[41]

At New York's Academy of Music in the vaude-pic format on November 26, business kept on track. "Ella Fitzgerald's ork is capable of sock entertainment, still touting her old image for an audience of 'mostly shoppers and kids of jitterbug age,' with Taft Jordan singing 'Stardust.'" Ella, singing three numbers, "easily walked away with the show."[42]

The year 1940, amid a major economic downturn, brought crises to Black bands. *Billboard*'s lead story of November 23 reported, "Negro Employment Down: Opportunities for Sepia Talent 25 Per Cent Under '37; Passing of Swing Held Partly to Blame." The article pointed to "the growing resentment towards blatant, blary music, which is a feature of many Negro bands," then pivoted to a comprehensive survey of discrimination and prejudice, including segregation in the Broadway theater and exclusion from movies, location jobs, and sponsored radio network shows. Of the twenty-five "full-sized" Black bands touring the country, "only about 10 of them get the choice location jobs." Fitzgerald's band, however, endured and placed just below the top tier: "It is generally conceded that Duke Ellington, Cab Calloway, Louis Armstrong, Count Basie, and Lunceford cop the creamy jobs. Ella Fitzgerald is making gains, doing well currently at the Brunswick in Boston." Her orchestra was the first African American group to play at the Brunswick, enjoying enough business to win a return engagement.[43]

When *Down Beat* recycled the *Billboard* story, it asked, "Are Negro Bands Doomed?" That provoked a response in the Black press. In

"Negro Bands Are Not Doomed," bandleader Lucky Millinder credited Moe Gale for Fitzgerald's continued viability:

> He kept Ella Fitzgerald living when Chick Webb died, something
> no other individual could have done. By living, we mean he kept the
> Fitzgerald name from fading from the picture. When the "name"
> individual of an organization dies, any other name connected with
> it, big or small, invariably starts from the bottom. Such is not the case
> with Ella Fitzgerald. When Chick Webb passed on, the band was
> selling for $1,500 to $1,800 a night. When Ella Fitzgerald took over
> under the aegis of Gale, the organization sold from nine to $1,000
> a night. In the past year, the organization has risen in price from a
> thousand to $1,500 a night again. Who else could have done it?[44]

Moe Gale juggled the usual bookings at the Savoy Ballroom, which
was his private safety net, along with Black theaters and occasional dates
in white time. Millinder's praise of Gale diminished Fitzgerald's self-
sufficiency and vocal charisma, both on live dates and as a recording
artist. Plus Millinder was biased. After declaring bankruptcy in early
1939, he signed with Gale in late 1940, and possibly at Gale's suggestion,
he fronted a new band with Sister Rosetta Tharpe, marketed as a combination following in the footsteps of "Chick and Ella."[45]

Fitzgerald had already outgrown that partnership label. She was reinventing herself as a jazz-pop stylist, moving far beyond the swing singer
Webb had raised. In November *Billboard*'s Sam Honigberg wrote:

> The singularly important change in the outfit fronted by Miss
> Fitzgerald is its departure from the hot swing style to the smoother
> and more listenable brand. Unorthodox arrangements are still fre-
> quent, but they are not as brassy as they used to be, nor as appealing
> to the jitterbug trade as formerly. And Miss Fitzgerald herself has
> deserted the hot rhythm tunes for ballads, and to good advantage.
> She dispenses sentimental ditties with real meaning and flavor and
> a voice that is very easy to take.[46]

Whether she chose this path or had it thrust upon her, Ella sang more ballads than ever before. Fitzgerald's work for Decca in 1940 showed continuous vocal improvement and in repertoire, chart success, and press reception, which sometimes read like divining rods of gifts still under-ground. The label seemed happy with her showing in *Billboard*'s "Top Music Machine Records of 1940." With six Decca studio dates yielding twenty-one issued sides, she charted five times. Several were covers of hits by Glenn Miller. "Imagination" made a considerable impression on the market considering the competition with Glenn Miller.[47] Unlike Miller's singer Bob Eberle, who was restricted to singing the chorus, Fitzgerald sang right from the start. With this ballad, she was developing a voice beyond "peach fuzz," as her vocal maturity enabled her to make relatively limited melodies interesting through paraphrase. In another Miller cover, "Stairway to the Stars," she used a careful vibrato at the ends of phrases for the straight delivery. The lyrics "climb," while the melody does not, but somehow Ella gets momentum into the whole.[48] Both of these Miller classics were favorites of hers, which she would revisit in later decades.

"Five O'Clock Whistle," a novelty song about marital mischief, recorded in September 25 and sporting an arrangement by Edgar Samp-son, was Fitzgerald's biggest commercial success of 1940. Dorothy Kil-gallen, a syndicated columnist at the *New York Journal-American*, awarded it a "gold star" endorsement that carried weight in newspapers across the country.[49] *Down Beat*'s critic preferred Ella's version to Glenn Miller's, and her single outperformed sleeper versions by Duke Ellington (with Ivie Anderson) and Count Basie.[50] Even Leonard Feather (writing under the pseudonym Geoffrey Marne), who had decried her song choices at Decca, succumbed to its charms: "Commercial, cute, and all that, but still good. And I like that simple little coda."[51] That "simple" coda embodies Fitzgerald's remarkable relaxation and creative phrasing that critics were starting to pick up on. Other sleepers got the "conven-tional Miss Ella lift," to quote *Billboard*'s attentive critic in his review of another Glenn Miller cover, "What's the Matter with Me?" in which she met different vocal demands.[52] She hit a solid groove with her first recording of "Sugar Blues," a cover of a song made popular by the white trumpeter and bandleader Clyde McCoy. Among her best works from this period is the song "Taking a Chance on Love," from the Black-cast Broadway musical *Cabin in the Sky* by John La Touche and Vernon Duke. The show opened on October 25, 1940, and Fitzgerald recorded the song two weeks later. Her rendition projected smooth confidence and subtle swing, and other than a short tenor saxophone solo providing contrasting color, the band largely receded to the background.

Fitzgerald was blending swing momentum and melodic relaxation in material ranging from romantic to hip, foretelling a flexible jazz style for popular song. Along with Billie Holiday and other singers, she was bringing the musical language of jazz to songs from Broadway, Tin Pan Alley, and the blues tradition, before any notion of "jazz-pop" had entered common parlance.[53] This process owed little to commercial pressure from her white manager, Moe Gale, or her handlers at Decca. On the contrary, her innovations were rooted in her experiences touring the country, performing mainly for Black audiences.

In 1941 Decca seemed to finally recognize that its jive singer had turned into a major vocalist who could make a hit "crooning" lyrical ballads. She could still sing "Melinda the Mousie," but she was also adding ideas from the world of white bands and white pop singers like Dinah Shore and Frank Sinatra. A recording session on January 8 included "The One I Love Belongs to Somebody Else," competing with the hit version recorded the previous June by Tommy Dorsey and his new vocalist. Sinatra's chorus stood out from the cluttered brilliance of Sy Oliver's arrangement; the ultimate "boy singer" of a later hour had a voice that was "virile with an earthy baritone," as a smitten Gunther Schuller later wrote, unlike the norm of "colorless, lightweight, expressionless male voices—mostly effeminate-sounding crooning tenors."[54] So much was at stake in performing masculinity and femininity in popular singing. Fitzgerald, sounding modern, sophisticated, and very smart, sang the melody straight, then offered a relaxed, jazz-inflected second chorus with delightful melodic improvisations, the band picking up her momentum. Surprisingly, this style earned her a reproach from

Metronome's George T. Simon, who wrote, "Ella Fitzgerald sings a swell straight chorus of 'The One I Love,' but then gets too tricky for her own good."[55] A few months later Fitzgerald covered Dinah Shore's torch song "Jim." Even though her version sank, she was practicing the docile ballad timbres of womanly devotion for a genre that would become increasingly popular in the next year.

★★★

THE MOST IMPORTANT EVENT for Fitzgerald's career in 1941 was winning a movie contract for a Hollywood feature film. *Ride 'Em Cowboy* was a vehicle for the comedy team of Abbott and Costello, a duo of a straight man and his sidekick, a goofy lovable cutup; they had already transferred their vaudeville comedy into several top-earning films in 1941. Released in 1942, *Ride 'Em Cowboy* was one of the top-grossing films of the year. The film put "A-Tisket A-Tasket" on the musical map once again, giving a mass audience a chance to learn what she looked like. In the words of *Variety*'s veteran editor Abel Green, "the grimmer the headlines about the war in Europe, the more Americans flocked to comedy, especially the low comedy, of which Abbott & Costello were undisputed top dogs."[56]

The plot of *Ride 'Em Cowboy* hinges on the familiar setup of city slickers venturing into the Wild West, Hollywood-style. (A writer of ersatz western novels earns his spurs and thereby wins the love of a skeptical cowgirl.) Ella joins the crew in the role of Ruby, the cook. As they arrive in Arizona by train, and then head out to the dude ranch, she gets up from her seat at the back of the bus—where else would she sit?—and strolls down the aisle looking for her yellow basket. She moves right along with the bus. Wearing an outfit good enough for Easter, she references Savoy dances by pointing her fingers in the air for "truckin'" and jabs her neck chicken-style on "peckin'." The well-known white vocal quartet the Merry Macs as cowboy crew ask, "Was it red? Was it green?" A boyish Lou Costello then appears improbably in the back window of the bus, asking, "Was it cerise?" Costello's inclusion helped ensure that the scene would stay in the film and elude Southern censors. In *Metronome*, Barry Ulanov found her "unabashed" and "cute as usual."[57]

Ride 'Em Cowboy had a mixed identity as a musically liberal yet socially conservative film. In Ella's second big number, "Rockin' and Reelin'," a big dance scene, she "rocks" as a Black swing singer while white dancers "reel" (as in the square dance, the Virginia Reel), encouraged to convert to swing—not white western swing already making its way into country music, but the real thing. Ruby jive-raps: "And we'll show you how they drop the square, / You know, back in Harlem on Sugar Hill." Savoy Ballroom dancers miraculously appear to demonstrate the "congeroo" for forty seconds in a separate insert, since they could not be shown dancing with white folks.[58]

Too bad that a better song written for Fitzgerald, "Cow Cow Boogie," was edited out in postproduction, which reinforced the contradictions of the music and the message. The lyrics spoke of "a swing half-breed" with a "knocked-out Western accent with a Harlem touch." She watched a version by Ella Mae Morse, recorded with Freddie Slack's orchestra in May 1942, which became a surprise hit, launching Morse's career and jump-starting a newcomer label, Capitol Records. Ella would get her chance to record the song two years later.

Industry racism tarnished Fitzgerald's breakthrough when Universal Studios distributed publicity materials that minstrelized her in a fabricated dialogue with the director, Arthur Lubin. In the dialogue, Fitzgerald—described as a "badly frightened newcomer" upset by a rodeo scene—says, "Mr. Lubin, I'se glad I done okay, this job sho am going to change my mode of livin'." A vigilant columnist for the *Baltimore Afro-American* objected:

> That, in the language of Hollywood's publicists, is belittling to a star revered as "America's queen of swing vocalizing," and embarrassing to all who know that Ella Fitzgerald couldn't be such a composer, rave-exponent of song, and such a public figure without a better mode of expression. . . . This writer has conversed with

Ella Fitzgerald enough to know that those words were expounded by the white man, and that Universal, nor any other studio wants the highest type of expression from colored players. It might change the players' and public's mode of thinking.[59]

Four months later the *Baltimore Afro-American* followed up, reporting, "Miss Fitzgerald was shocked when approached by the AFRO concerning the story." The paper also printed an apology from Universal Pictures: "This clearly was a case of overzealous writing, plus bad editing. We are extremely sorry that the story got into print and certainly will see to it that nothing of this kind ever happens again."[60]

★★★

THE SECOND IMPORTANT EVENT IN 1941 for Fitzgerald was a stay in Hollywood that renewed her friendship with Duke Ellington. In July he arrived at the Trianon Ballroom in South Gate, a suburb of Los Angeles, and Ella and the orchestra followed him there. A Gale press release bragged of ten thousand paid admissions from July 15 to 21.[61] Ellington was in town for the premiere of his new musical revue, *Jump for Joy*, which opened on July 10 at the Mayan Theater downtown. "We had front row seats," said Teddy McRae, who took Ella to see Ellington's progressive, satirical commentary on American popular culture, which would never play in New York in Ellington's lifetime.[62] She likely also met Alice (sometimes Alyce) Key, a dancer in the revue and a future journalist and community activist who would later bring her attuned social conscience to newspaper columns about Fitzgerald.

The big hit song from *Jump for Joy* was "I Got It Bad (And That Ain't Good)," attracting interest from several emerging singers, including Doris Day and Peggy Lee. Ellington's definitive version with Ivie Anderson was graced with a passionate alto saxophone solo by Johnny Hodges, the virtual second singer on the recording. It was the first song by Ellington that Fitzgerald covered: her interpretation was recorded at Decca's L.A. studio on July 31, 1941, and it registered her growth as a jazz singer—she sang a rich, ardent lyricism that left her early balladry far behind.[63]

★★★

AFTER EXTENSIVE SUMMER TRAVELS, Fitzgerald and the band returned to the Northeast for the usual fall round of Black theaters. At a vaude-pic date at Brooklyn's Strand Theater in September, *Variety* reported that the band did less "blasting music" and the audience "couldn't get enough of her warbling." But for the first time another act overshadowed her. The Ink Spots shared top billing, described as "obviously the big draw on the bill," while "Miss Fitzgerald's band is much the same as last season."[64] Fitzgerald's week at the Apollo, and even a return to the Famous Door, generated no further reviews in the customary press outlets.

Gale had endowed the Ink Spots with a huge promotional campaign, tapping a vein of enthusiasm among both Black and white audiences for genteel vocal harmony and novel delivery. In a September 1941 article about Gale for the *Saturday Evening Post*—titled, without apparent irony, "Harlem's Great White Father"—he touted his discovery of the vocal quartet as a career touchstone.[65]

Perhaps because of Gale's focus on other acts, the orchestra's relationship with management deteriorated over the fall of 1941. Newcomers to the group included two bebop pioneers, trumpeter Dizzy Gillespie and drummer Kenny Clarke. Each lasted about a fortnight. Gillespie later recalled, "Teddy McRae was the leader who took charge of everything; Ella just sang."[66] Dizzy also noted the Gale Agency's tight control over salaries. Clarke told a more dramatic story to Helen Oakley. Borrowing an advance for a new set of drums, he learned that the Gale Agency planned to withhold his pay until he repaid the debt. He had no money to live on and went on strike just before a gig:

> Ella took my side. She said that she wouldn't make the gig unless I played, and she told Gale to pay up. The argument went on for thirty minutes and the manager got furious—but I wouldn't

budge. Finally, Gale gave in, I got my check, and we went on and played. I really appreciated the way Ella stuck up for me. She saw Gale wasn't being fair.[67]

Gale could also insist on retrograde racial presentations, as when Fitzgerald was booked at the Bermuda Terrace in Boston's Brunswick Hotel from September 26 to October 18. The accompanying floor show was billed as a "20th Century Minstrel Show."[68]

Fitzgerald's future with the band depended entirely on Moe Gale's decisions. On the last night of the Brunswick Hotel date, he summarily fired Teddy McRae, Ella's friend and most important colleague. Frustrated by the poor salaries—a perpetual complaint about the Gale operations—and watching the band draw well, McRae felt he deserved better. He had taken his objections to the agency. "On the road you'd be working a long time," McRae said. "And they're making all that money, and they don't want to divide, you know. Look, give the guys a raise. This band should get more money!" Treating this as insubordination, Gale and Charles Buchanan went looking for his replacement. How quickly they fired him is not clear. Was Fitzgerald consulted, and was she as surprised as McRae himself that night? As McRae later recalled, "Gale comes in after the second show, and he has with him my friend Eddie Barefield. . . . So Barefield took over the band. . . . That night, 12:05, I came back to New York. That was the end of it with Ella."[69] McRae quickly joined Cab Calloway's band, and Fitzgerald returned to the Savoy for a four-week booking from October 24 to November 20.

In *Down Beat*'s account, Barefield was the band's "new pilot" while "Ella continues to handle the vocal assignments."[70] A solid and respected sideman on saxophone and clarinet, Barefield had worked in many dance bands since the early 1930s, including Fitzgerald's orchestra at various times in 1939 and 1940. In a later account, Barefield recalled, "She sang whatever I called for her to sing. I made arrangements for her and Dick Vance, and a few others made arrangements."[71] Others in the band, including Beverly Peer, said she chose her own songs. Fitzgerald's role in shaping her own repertory would remain a contested question for decades. Barefield's recollection evokes the classic description of the "girl singer with band" from the mid-1930s. Ella "sitting down"? It would be hard to fathom, considering the many years she spent trucking and Lindying at the Savoy and the Apollo.

Fitzgerald did her best to relate to the other band members as an equal, and some liked her more than others. Beverly Peer recalled, "Ella was always one of the boys," a view echoed by Bardu Ali:

> It never changed with her. She was just "Sis" with us, and we just took it as a matter of fact. Everybody else was . . . raving about her and things, and we just took it in stride, you know? Like it was supposed to be that. You know, nobody paid any attention to it at all. And she never changed, she was the same person, so we all got along. There was no case of anybody getting a big head or nothing like, she never did that. And the guys treated her the same way.[72]

Perhaps because they had known her longer, Peer and Ali had easier encounters than Ram Ramirez, who had joined the band by January 1940. "Oh man. One thing I know, she's not as nice as people say or think that she is," Ramirez would say. "When she came up she was tough. . . . *Yes she was!*"[73] She had to be to survive.

In early December 1941, Fitzgerald and the band were touring through industrial towns of Pennsylvania on the Warner Bros. theater circuit. They played Erie on December 5 and 6, then traveled 120 miles to Ambridge on December 7 for a show the next night. By the time they arrived in Greensburg for a date on December 9, the United States was officially at war. The band continued to meet the schedule, reaching Johnstown on the tenth.[74] Then came Detroit and a week-long vaude-pic date at the Colonial Theatre.[75]

In November Ella had invited a tall, handsome fellow Harlemite, twenty-eight-year-old Benny Kornegay, to join her on the band bus. He had been her suitor since the spring, and they married in St. Louis on December 26.[76] The band kept to its itinerary. She and Benny spent Christmas Eve in Columbus, Ohio, Christmas Day in Cincinnati, New

Year's Eve in Durham, North Carolina, and New Year's Day in Greenville, South Carolina.[77]

The day after her marriage, *Billboard* issued a heartfelt proclamation:

> We have a war to win. From now until the war is won, the music
> business shall be governed by considerations more important than
> the waxing of a hit record, the plugging of a song, the signing
> of a lucrative contract or the inconveniences of a one-nighter
> jump. . . . We make the songs that America sings. We must con-
> tinue to create these songs. We must take them into the camps,
> into the homes and into the hearts of the people. . . . A country
> can't win a war by singing but a song often means the differ-
> ence between low and high morale. This has been proved many
> times. . . . We've got to carry on.[78]

Now, as Ella Fitzgerald and Her Famous Orchestra returned to the
Savoy in early 1942, she would confront the implications of having two
home fronts, as an artist and as a wife.

Chapter 9

THE HOME FRONT

(1941–1945)

When questioned about her marriage by a reporter, "Miss Fitzgerald stated that she wanted her life to her own." She later called herself "stupid," claiming she had been provoked by a bet or a dare, either by the groom or by the guys in the band. But then lots of people were "stupid," if by that we mean shaken by the onset of World War II, which left no aspect of life untouched. Ben Kornegay told the press he hoped their life together would be "normal" and would not disrupt her professional career.[1] Ella, in an interview, showed that she had her priorities straight: "He understands when people like to do something, it's better not to try and stop them." She offered a glimpse of his appeal to her—"When I clown, he don't mind, and I'm always clowning"—then put on an apron: "But I have to learn to cook. We just started our apartment and I want to get into the kitchen. We've been eating in restaurants and he's getting tired of it."[2]

Soon she got tired of him. By April rumors of marital trouble surfaced in the Black press. Moe Gale hired private detectives to investigate Kornegay, who resisted a divorce.[3] Filing suit in October, Fitzgerald won an annulment in the New York State Supreme Court in January 1943.[4] The caption to an AP photo of her smiling exit from the courthouse quoted Honorable Justice Aaron J. Levy: "You just keep singing 'A-Tisket A-Tasket' and leave the men alone." This pat, seriocomic ending sounds like a publicist's confection, but Fitzgerald repeated the story in the 1980s. In April 1943 Dan Burley, a columnist for the *New York Amsterdam News*, alleged she paid $2,500 to get free from "Cigaret," Kornegay's nickname.[5] As it happened, they did have some future contact, and Kornegay made a life for himself in Harlem; in the 1960s Kornegay's charitable activities in Harlem's social clubs made the press.

★★★

FITZGERALD'S ORCHESTRA was a far more serious war casualty; over the first half of 1942, it suffered a slow demise and eventually collapsed. A January review of a date in Norfolk, Virginia, addressed her marginalization: "She's way past her peak in national popularity and you don't hear so much about her band these days. Despite her vigorous efforts to keep the Chick Webb ensemble alive, it is not a big timer on the metropolitan circuit anymore. But that doesn't always mean that it hasn't the stuff."[6]

In April Moe Gale terminated Fitzgerald's leadership of the orchestra, even ahead of its last dates. He hoped that Eddie Barefield could lead the band independently, and that Ella could reunite with them for part of each year and remain profitable on her own, especially in light of impending travel restrictions.[7] The military draft—up from 900,000 in 1941 to 3 million in 1942—was vastly expanding, and civilian travel was severely curtailed. Car companies ceased production of private vehicles in the spring of 1942, and gas, rubber, and oil were rationed.

The Office of Defense Transportation banned all domestic bus service on June 1, 1942. Gale had already anticipated the devastating consequences for Black bands, who depended on touring more than their white counterparts did.[8] In October 1942, in an op-ed for *Variety,* Gale asked, "Are colored bands doomed?"—but he had already answered the question by dooming hers.[9] He was still signing other bands, however, including the Cootie Williams Orchestra in September and Eddie Durham's draft-proof All-Star Girl Orchestra in October. All-girl bands, many of which had existed in the 1930s, were now suddenly in demand. The Williams and Durham bands would both figure into Ella's near future.

Mixed reviews accompanied the band's waning days. At the Los Angeles Orpheum in June, Fitzgerald's gross reportedly outperformed the Andrews Sisters and Jimmie Lunceford.[10] In the summer Ella Fitzgerald and Her Famous Orchestra took a farewell tour touching all regions of the country, and on July 30, 1942, they gave their last performance at the Earle Theatre in Philadelphia, with Bill "Bojangles" Robinson added to the bill. *Billboard* reported, "House hit a dandy $24,000 in face of the sweltering heat."[11] Reaching into her memory book, Fitzgerald sang "Mr. Paganini" along with the expected "A-Tisket A-Tasket."[12] The band was praised as "solid swingeroo . . . each tooter acting as if he's having a helluva time working."[13]

Not so for Eddie Barefield, the music director of the orchestra. "I just got disgusted," he said of Gale's management, which had a well-deserved reputation for underpaying musicians.[14] Some of the musicians blamed greed for the band's demise, while others were ambivalent. The breakup "was the best thing that ever happened to it," said Beverly Peer in one interview. In another, he said he wished Ella had persisted because the band deserved it.[15]

Fitzgerald hadn't recorded with her fifteen-member orchestra since 1941. The band included some well-respected musicians, but her Decca sides that year were mostly untethered from vital swing and burdened by mediocre material. Even the better songs by Ellington and Jerome Kern had tired arrangements. Only three of her 1941 recordings cracked the *Billboard* pop charts (including her own composition, "The Muffin Man"), none staying there for more than a week.[16]

Starting with a recording session on March 11, 1942, Moe Gale paired her with the Four Keys, a vocal harmony quartet he had recently signed in the wake of his success with the Ink Spots. Instead of a big band, she was now backed by four singers who accompanied themselves on instruments. The Four Keys included three Furness brothers—Bill on piano, Slim on guitar, and Peck on bass—plus Ernie Hatfield on drums. Gale recognized the trendiness of an urban Black pop style for mixed vocal and instrumental combos. In their earlier iteration as the Three Keys, the group had adapted Ella's choruses for their own arrangements.[17]

Unintended by management, the small group setting allowed Fitzgerald to shift toward her jazz roots, showing she knew who she was better than the people who were telling her who she should be. In late September 1942, when she and the Four Keys made their performance debut at the Aquarium Restaurant in Times Square, *Billboard*'s critic thought the new unit gave "the dusky chanteuse more elbow room."[18] *Variety*'s critic raved about how the combo gave "freer rein" to her "unusual ability for improvisation."[19] Fitzgerald and the group continued to tour, largely in the Black theater circuit. Their first billing at the Apollo on November 20, 1942, included a newcomer, Sarah Vaughan, who later said that Fitzgerald "stopped me from signing myself away to all of the agents around."[20] Fitzgerald and the Four Keys were enough of a success that in January 1943 Gale secured them a fifteen-minute sustaining radio spot on WJZ. By May the new pairing commanded a booking fee of $1,750, a first-tier salary.[21] For their February and June engagements at the Apollo, Eddie Durham's "All-Girl Band" had second billing.

"More elbow room" would seem an understated description for a Fitzgerald performance in March 1943, when a critic reported that she was "riffing 'Flying Home'" and "had the crowd begging for more."[22] She was vocalizing a famous solo by the tenor saxophonist Illinois Jacquet from the "high-jivin" bestseller released by Lionel Hampton and His Orchestra in 1942.[23] Jacquet's solo had already become a classic by the time Fitzgerald claimed it as a vocal novelty. In the Black community, the solo took on a life of its own. In his memoir Count Basie wrote, "Everybody remembers his solo on that record, and a lot of people can still hum it note for note."[24]

Jacquet's two-chorus tour de force on "Flying Home" lasted over a minute, mix-matching lyricism and heat. It opened with a phrase from "Ah! So Pure," an aria from the opera *Martha* by German composer Friedrich von Flotow, popular among America's many late-nineteenth-century opera lovers. "Ah! So Pure" had already had a makeover into a popular song, recorded by Connie Boswell and Bea Wain, which was probably how Jacquet heard it. In the first half of Jacquet's second chorus, he did little more than repeat one note with a brash, bold timbre that earned him the label of "honker" and much later "proto-rock-and-roller."

How Fitzgerald changed Jacquet's solo in 1943 is not known since she did not record "Flying Home" until 1945. But in a wordless scat chorus, she hummed her way into the instrumentalist's domain in a bold and prophetic act. It would take four more years for its influence to reach a wider world.

In these years, Decca was not very interested in scat singing from the only Black female singer on their roster. Instead they slotted Fitzgerald into the role of home-front sweetheart, a Black counterpart to the increasingly popular Dinah Shore, Peggy Lee with Benny Goodman, and Helen Forrest with Harry James. Female vocalists with all-female bands gained commercial opportunities because of the war, meeting a public need for comfort, loyalty, and reassurance by dispensing sentimental ballads.[25] "Many of the songs we sang in these years," Forrest wrote, "were sentimental songs aimed at wives and lovers separated by the war from their men in the service. A lot of the songs had to do with women waiting for their men to come home."[26] So did Fitzgerald's Decca assignments, which made only an occasional foray into urban Black pop. During the war, Fitzgerald sang Forrest's 1942 hits "I Don't Want to Walk Without You" and "I Had the Craziest Dream" in live performance as well. The two women had met in the late 1930s.

The seven ephemeral songs she had recorded with the Four Keys between March and July 1942 had already had the home-front style down pat. Billy Rowe wrote of her "famous crooning voice" and "that soothing manner that is Ella's alone."[27] In *Down Beat*, Mike Levin singled out the best of the lot: "Fitz fans will never recognize her version of 'All I Need Is You' recorded with the Keys on April 10 as the singing of Chick's vocalist. In the past few months, her whole style has changed from driving rhythm phrases to almost lush ballad style."[28]

Still, the absence of a solid hit record depressed Fitzgerald's overall standing in the music business. Her July 31, 1942, recording date with the Four Keys had been squeezed in just before a recording ban by the American Federation of Musicians (AFM), the powerful professional union, took effect the following day. She would not record again for over fifteen

months. Even in the jazz-oriented press, she declined in poll ratings. In
Metronome's reader poll at the end of 1942, Helen Forrest dominated the
"female singers" category with 718 votes, while Ella crashed at twelve
votes, to put her in eleventh place. Along with Billie Holiday (123 votes)
and Lena Horne (13 votes), Fitzgerald lagged far behind the white female
singers in the pop mainstream.[29] The next generation of African American female artists, among them Sarah Vaughan, Dinah Washington, and
Betty Carter, would help claim more room for Black voices after the war.

★★★

FITZGERALD'S CAREER OUTSIDE THE STUDIO reflected the challenges that
faced America's self-conception as the beacon of Western democracy.
Walter White, president of the NAACP, captured the essence of America's dilemma in his 1942 speech "War and National Policy":

> How can a Negro believe wholeheartedly that the cause he is
> asked to die for is worth dying for when daily he is confronted by
> insult, discrimination, and segregation? . . . We demand the right
> to live and work for our country in the defense industries and the
> right to die for our country without segregation or discrimination
> in the armed forces and on the same basis on all other citizens.[30]

This outlook led Black newspapers to vigorously promote and cover the
Double Victory campaign: victory against racism at home and against
fascism abroad.

Fitzgerald lived and worked in that Double V world. As a "morale
builder," many musicians contributed to the war effort through the
United Service Organizations (USO) by entertaining troops at home
and abroad. In 1941 segregation in the American military had often
constrained Fitzgerald's visits to troop sites. On June 3, she and the
orchestra had played for the all-Black Ninth and Tenth Cavalry at Camp
Funston in Kansas.[31] On June 21, they performed at a new Black officers'
club at Fort Huachuca in Arizona, which accommodated 4,500 African

American soldiers.[32] African American GIs suffered from major discrimination at the base. During the performance, soldiers "forc[ed] their way through windows, climbing over the balcony and rafters and using obscene language." The orchestra, thrown into chaos, "had to pick up their instruments and retire to the dressing room due to the lack of discipline."[33] The experience was harrowing. Race tensions would abate at Fort Huachuca in the next two years, when musicians like Irving Ashby and Babe Wallace were stationed there, and Lena Horne and Pearl Bailey both appeared there at USO camp shows.[34] But Fitzgerald did not return; nor did she mention this event in public.

Road travel in the South remained a war zone for Black Americans. In May 1944, nine days after a camp show at Barksdale Air Force Base in Louisiana, Ella performed at the Coliseum in New Orleans. There she met up with John Hammond, who was confronting racism at Camp Plauche, a troop-staging area outside the city. As he later wrote, "The troupe had just arrived from Atlanta, tired and unhappy with their accommodations in New Orleans. I had lunch with Ella in a miserable Black hotel while she told me her troubles." Hammond then booked her for a show he had engineered for an integrated audience in Camp Plauche's makeshift open-air theater.[35]

Perhaps her best experience from the war years was a memorable trip to the Tuskegee Army Airfield in Alabama (TAAF). This famous training site for African American pilots, established in 1941, was an important symbol of dignity for Blacks in the military. On June 17, 1944, Fitzgerald headlined the opening of the TAAF Theatre. Standing in a long white gown, next to officers, singing, and even dancing the Shorty George—an old dance step from her Savoy Ballroom era—Fitzgerald was treated as a heroine.[36]

In Harlem, Fitzgerald often participated in Double V activism through benefits. On June 25, 1942, at the USO Benefit Dance-Gala at the Golden Gate Ballroom, she joined Lena Horne and Hazel Scott, who were far better known for their public protests against discrimination in the military.[37] Fitzgerald nevertheless took a stand on various occasions. On March 30, 1941, the National Urban League presented a nationwide radio program about discrimination in the defense industry, using airtime donated by the

CBS radio network. Fitzgerald and Her Famous Orchestra appeared along with a host of Black stars including Marian Anderson and Bill Robinson and the bands of Duke Ellington, Louis Armstrong, and John Kirby.[38] Fitzgerald also "swung left," publicly supporting the campaign of Benjamin J. Davis, Jr., the Communist Party candidate for the New York City Council seat vacated by Adam Clayton Powell, Jr. At Davis's "Million-Dollar" fundraiser on October 24, 1943, Fitzgerald performed for about five thousand people along with Paul Robeson, Art Tatum, Billie Holiday, Hazel Scott, Coleman Hawkins, and Mary Lou Williams.[39] From November 1943 through December 1944, she was listed as a "contributing editor" or "contributor" on the masthead of the *Music Dial*, a Black-run radical left magazine, but her writing output was limited to two fluffy columns as "Jitterbug Interviewer" of Georgie Auld and Al Cooper.[40]

Fitzgerald contributed to the efforts of the Armed Forces Radio Service through radio broadcasts, including several *Jubilee* programs aimed at Black troops. In 1944 a *New York Amsterdam News* photo spread on "How Our Top Performers Join In to Give Boys Overseas a Break" featured her twice.[41] In 1945 and 1947 she also recorded government "V-Discs," which top recording artists made for soldiers abroad and that were prohibited from commercial sale.

The rise in race conflicts early in World War II also had an impact on Fitzgerald's career. The historian Neil A. Wynn writes, "In 1943 more than 240 racial incidents—ranging from 'hate strikes' and industrial conflicts to full-scale riots—occurred in forty-seven towns and cities," including the infamous Detroit riots and a Harlem riot on August 1 and 2.[42] Jack Schiffman, the son of the Apollo's owner, would write:

> One of its major results was that the many whites who had been traveling uptown to see the shows at the Apollo and the various nightclubs no longer went. The riot of 1943 engendered fear that has remained unshakeable. With the downtown movement of Black artists well underway, the riot succeeded in making ghetto Harlem more isolated than ever.[43]

That "downtown movement" spurred the establishment of Cafe Zanzibar, which opened July 8, 1943, on Broadway between 50th and 51st streets, recycling the glitzy floor shows and variety acts of the defunct Cotton Club. Unlike other major midtown nightclubs—the Latin Quarter, the Stork Club, and the Copacabana—the Zanzibar admitted Black clientele. Shortly before it opened, Porter Roberts in the *Chicago Defender* wrote, "Ella Fitzgerald has not done so hot since the great Chick Webb died. You know, kinda up here and down there (I mean in popularity)."[44] This new venue gave her a much-needed New York platform outside Harlem. On its opening night, the all-Black revue featured Fitzgerald along with Don Redman's band, several dancers and comics, vocalist Avis Andrews, a "sable-skinned eight-girl line" known as the Zanzibeauties, and Maurice Rocco, a boogie-woogie pianist famous for standing up at the keyboard. Allotted four songs, Fitzgerald chose "Put Your Arms Around Me Honey" (recently revived by Dick Haymes), "Summertime," "Murder, He Says" (a Hollywood novelty popularized by Betty Hutton), and the inevitable "A-Tisket A-Tasket" encore.[45]

The Zanzibar proved a stable New York venue for Fitzgerald during the war years, booking her as a regular for one- to three-month periods from 1943 through 1946. Other regulars included Duke Ellington, Louis Armstrong, and Cab Calloway. Handling its diverse crowd and cultivating an eclectic repertoire, she sang for white theatergoers coming in for nightcaps and for servicemen from across the country who were spending a night on the town with their young wives or girlfriends and having their photo taken before being deployed overseas. She also sang for middle-class African Americans who were beginning to socialize outside Harlem—even if, as Langston Hughes wrote, they were shunted to the worst tables in the house.[46] Fitzgerald was honing her extraordinary gift in reading an audience and forging a bond with them as they realized she understood what they needed to hear. She would turn this aspect of her genius into a cornerstone of her career.

★★★

FITZGERALD RESUMED HER DORMANT RECORDING CAREER on November 3, 1943, after Decca, staving off bankruptcy, became the first major label to sign a new agreement with the AFM. The session yielded "Cow Cow Boogie," the tune that was dropped from the Abbott and Costello film *Ride 'Em Cowboy* but that the white singer Ella Mae Morse rode to fame. Recognizing the song's jukebox appeal in the race market, Dave Kapp paired Fitzgerald with the Ink Spots, the era's most popular African American vocal group and a jewel in Decca's crown.[47] This record pairing was a long time coming, considering she had known the Ink Spots since 1937 and shared a date with them at the Park Central Hotel in 1939, just before their single "If I Didn't Care" launched their stardom. "Cow Cow Boogie" was a crossover hit, reaching number one on *Billboard*'s Harlem Hit Parade chart in February 1944 and number ten on its pop chart in March.

The price of crossover success was multiple reprimands in the music press for her descent into mediocrity. *Billboard*'s usually complimentary M. H. Orodenker panned the single, while *Down Beat*'s critic treated her as buried treasure submerged in pop dross: "It's good to hear Ella's voice again, even if the material isn't right up her alley. Is she trying to imitate that other Ella, Miss Morse, on *Cow Cow*? Heaven forbid! She used to do considerably better than just all right singing her own style! . . . Come on, Ella, you can do better than this!"[48]

She would do better indeed when paired with a new producer. In the spring of 1943, Milt Gabler assumed responsibility for Fitzgerald's career and would soon change her profile at the label. One of the most intuitive producers and respected hit makers in the music business, Gabler had known Fitzgerald since her Chick Webb years. His idiosyncratic devotion to traditional New Orleans jazz led Decca to hire him in 1941 to produce an archival reissue series. He had earned respect in the Black and the jazz worlds as the producer of Billie Holiday's anthem "Strange Fruit" on his own Commodore label in 1939. By 1944 Gabler had worked with Decca's major Black artists, including Holiday, the Mills Brothers, the Ink Spots, Lionel Hampton, Louis Jordan, and Louis Armstrong. His records with Fitzgerald would add luster to his contributions in 1940s Black popular music.

On August 30, 1944, Gabler reunited Fitzgerald with the Ink Spots for two tracks, demonstrating his superb instincts for commercial hits with "Into Each Life Some Rain Must Fall" and "I'm Making Believe."[49] Both were issued on the same single, which rose to the top of the Harlem Hit Parade and pop charts. "Into Each Life" went on to sell over a million copies. The clever lyrics by Doris Fisher supported a three-chorus arrangement, likely worked out by the musicians, which integrated Fitzgerald into the Ink Spots' unique novelty vocal style.[50] The high tenor lead singer, Bill Kenny, sings the first chorus straight; when Ella enters for the second chorus, the spare accompaniment shifts to a more swinging feel. For the third chorus, Orville "Hoppy" Jones signifies on Kenny's formality by repeating his lyrics in a "talking bass" voice with deadpan irony. That same "top and bottom" contrast had propelled their hit "If I Didn't Care" to the top reaches of the *Billboard* charts in 1939. On "Into Each Life"—its title and message adapted from a Henry Wadsworth Longfellow poem written in 1844—Ella's middle chorus adds a modernizing lilt and momentum. After Kenny's genteel singing, she sounds like an independent American girl upstaging a Victorian chaperone.

★★★

OUTSIDE DECCA, the Ink Spots remained a crucial part of Fitzgerald's professional success, because they were both managed by Moe Gale. When in January 1944 Gale brought on another client, Cootie Williams and His Orchestra, a regular at the Savoy Ballroom, he won the lottery. Sometimes dubbed "the Big Three Unit," co-opting the popular political nickname for the new wartime alliance of Roosevelt, Churchill, and Stalin, Fitzgerald, the Spots, and Williams proved a winning ticket. For the year 1944, *Billboard* reported that the package grossed over $500,000, thanks to rising disposable income among African Americans in the wartime economy. Elsewhere in the race-stratified marketplace, only Cab Calloway ($750,000) and Duke Ellington ($600,000) grossed higher, with Count Basie ($400,000) and Lionel Hampton ($350,000) next in line.[51] In 1945 the Big Three broke records at the Paramount Theatre.

For live dates, the Cootie Williams Orchestra backed Ella, the song choices often showing that they had become musically invigorating partners. With his innovative explorations of trumpet timbres, Williams had been a vital constituent of the "Ellington sound" from 1929 to 1940, after which he shocked jazz fans by leaving Duke to join Benny Goodman for a year. The musicologist Guthrie Ramsey credits Williams for an "eclectic repertory that resists the usual categories"—which made him an ideal colleague for Ella.[52] Williams had been friends with Chick Webb and played in Webb's band during his first stint at the Savoy.[53] Onstage Ella and Cootie inspired each other, and offstage, according to trumpeter Henry "Red" Allen, they sometimes "were having a scene together and Cootie used to get so drunk that Ella regularly had to carry him home."[54] Onstage they shared their love for Duke Ellington's songs.

At one of their first joint concerts, at the Orpheum in Los Angeles on April 25, 1944, she sang Duke Ellington's "Do Nothing Till You Hear from Me," which carried Williams's own history. The song originated as one of Ellington's well-regarded miniatures, "Concerto for Cootie," recorded in 1940, and it featured Williams when he was still in the band. The lyrics were added in 1943, and "Do Nothing" was identified with Ellington's band vocalist, Al Hibbler. A precious live air check of the song by Fitzgerald and Williams survives from the *AFRS Jubilee* radio program on May 5, 1944.[55] The format featured requests culled from letters sent by soldiers overseas. Fitzgerald lingered over just the right words—"so I've been seen with someone new"—to emphasize the bittersweet lyrics of a romantic tug-of-war.

The tour in 1944 was a generally happy time among compatible artists. Some of the musicians later recalled encountering typical Jim Crow indignities, such as denials of access to restrooms at gas stations, or white fans seeking Fitzgerald's autograph while white restaurants closed their doors. On the bus in their own world, making music, smoking pot, playing cards, they kept on. The musicians remembered Fitzgerald's amiability and passing travel time with her in card games of tonk and pinochle. The pianist and organist Bill Doggett, who had worked with Fitzgerald at the Zanzibar and now backed the Ink Spots, said, "Ella had Georgiana, her maid, with her. But we all soon got to know one another. She was real regular. . . . Everybody had all the respect in the world for Ella. . . . It was more like a family tour."[56]

Fitzgerald had grievances as an artist. She was used to being the only woman on a tour but not necessarily to being subjected to the whims of her partners. In a rare interview with Fitzgerald around 1944, which was published two years later in the *Los Angeles Sentinel*, the columnist Alyce Key criticized the decline in her recorded material:

> We had thought Ella had as little taste in her selection of songs as she has in her dress until we happened to run across her in Tucson, Arizona, a couple of years ago. We had been heard to remark it was a good thing Ella was such a great singer because she certainly would sing any and everything that came along. . . . Ella is, like no other singer we can think of, perfectly capable of handling a blues, a torch tune (and of course she is head and shoulders above any swing vocalist). . . . However, when we talked to Ella in Tucson, she told us she had very little choice in the songs she delineated. At the time she was on tour with Cootie Williams' band and the Ink Spots, and Ella told us that she was left whatever tunes the band or the Ink Spots didn't choose. Now How 'bout That?[57]

In this atmosphere Fitzgerald's professional relationship with Bill Kenny was difficult. They quarreled during their important four-week date at the Paramount in New York in March 1945. She had to accept her position on billings, with the Ink Spots in the top spot and Cootie Williams in the second slot many times. But Kenny's conduct onstage led to war. In the words of Carl Jones, a member of the singing group Delta Rhythm Boys, "She couldn't stand Bill Kenny showing off behind her on stage, flashing his gold rings while she was singing. She said, 'I'm not going to stand for that.' Then they had an argument. He said, 'I'm just as popular as you are.' So she refused to work with them anymore."[58] Jones spoke from his privileged position as her new collaborator at Decca when the sixth studio collaboration between Fitzgerald and the Ink Spots, in February 1945, turned into their last, despite their solid sales results and the pleasures of singing a Duke Ellington song. The Decca version of "I'm Beginning to See the Light" reached number five on the pop charts, outselling Ellington's own recording with Joya Sherrill. *Metronome* named it a top record of the year, and while white jazz critics unreasonably savaged Kenny's falsetto voice, they celebrated her. "Ella really tears this one apart; she's never done anything quite like it and her vocal is actually thrilling," wrote *Down Beat* in a review.[59]

Perhaps the success of this Ellington tune led Milt Gabler to pair her with the Delta Rhythm Boys, a more conventional, more jazz-oriented vocal quintet like the Mills Brothers. They had recorded with Count Basie and Jimmie Lunceford and had been with Decca since 1941. The change in orientation from the Ink Spots' novelty format to the jazz-influenced style of the Deltas gave Fitzgerald an opportunity to refresh her repertoire. She pushed Gabler to let her record a solid standard, "It's Only a Paper Moon," by Harold Arlen and E. Y. Harburg, at a moment when the Nat King Cole Trio was lifting this show tune out of obscurity and into the jazz-standard playbook. On March 27 she recorded it in an arrangement by the lead tenor, Carl Jones. Fitzgerald's version with the Deltas made *Billboard*'s pop and Harlem Hit Parade charts. A reviewer wrote, "Ella still has the best pipes in the business outside La Holiday, who is really so different in style that the two can't properly be compared."[60] Gabler conceded: "She loved the song and Nat's rendition and she wanted to do it," Gabler said. "She was right."[61]

Fitzgerald continued to tour with the Ink Spots and Cootie Williams right through 1945. They shared the last days of the World War II era together, celebrating V-E Day, May 8, 1945, at the Stanley Theatre in Pittsburgh and V-J Day on September 2 at the Royal Theatre in Baltimore. Their concerts were seemingly untouched by the momentous changes in climate around them. "Very few if any changes have taken place in the general run of the shows put on by this Big Three Unit since it was organized some months ago. There is great improvement in Cootie's leadership and in Ella's vocal renditions, but the Spots remain the drag of the show," ran a *Metronome* review of a one-week engagement at the Downtown Theater in Detroit for the week of August 10. But Fitzgerald was on the move in her own way. While Williams revamped "Do Nothing" and used the singer Eddie Vinson for jump blues, Fitzgerald was supplementing Decca fare by reviving "Flying Home." "It was a sender," wrote the reviewer.[62]

Exactly when Milt Gabler heard Ella Fitzgerald sing "Flying Home" in live performance is not known, but it allayed his concerns about a jazz date. With sufficient leverage from the success of her Ink Spots hits, Fitzgerald and Gabler recorded two takes—and nothing else—in a Decca studio on October 4, 1945. According to Gabler, a large ensemble of Decca's "great studio men" conducted by Vic Schoen adapted her arrangement on the spot. At a time when Decca was more conservative than ever, this brave act was the best he could do, leaving the recording in limbo, its marketability uncertain, and delaying its release for two years.

The Big Three ended the year with a three-month booking for Claude Hopkins's big new Cotton Club–like revue at Cafe Zanzibar starting on December 5. The Gale Agency touted a "new Ella" with a "complete new routine of songs" and a "new $2,800 wardrobe."[63] On opening night Billboard's reviewer lauded her "scorching opener of 'The Honey Dripper' in which she displays some of the best jump singing heard in these parts in a long, long time." She sang across her diverse repertoire, improvising on "Flying Home," "St. Louis Blues," and her seven-year-old "A-Tisket A-Tasket."[64] The Zanzibar was a perfect spot to mark a new era. "Many of the men who crowded into the square were on fighting fronts a year ago last night," wrote the New York Times. At the Zanzibar, some tables were reserved by scientists who had worked on the atomic bomb project at Oak Ridge, Tennessee.[65] The Great White Way of Broadway had returned to glory. The brownouts and curfews had ended. On New Year's Eve, Times Square theater and club owners promised to keep signs lit until sunup. The club's neon lights wrapped around its corner location, glowing its invitation to an eager crowd.

★★★

WHO WAS THE "NEW ELLA" that her manager promised? On the face of it, she seemed a lot like the old Ella—the underrated star who deserved better treatment and was staying in place despite being proclaimed the best in the business. The Gale Agency continued booking her mainly in Black theaters. In the jazz press, critics found good and bad in this or that recording, while claiming how "far ahead of all other singers on the air" she was, with her "wonderful scatting, as she and Cootie Williams played one of those question-and-answer games."[66] The Black press watched over her as a member of the community. They noted the inadequate promotion for her billings, her lack of radio time, and her complicity in accepting second-class status in general. Even doting Billy Rowe added his voice to this chorus. On January 16, 1946, he delivered a New Year's resolution for one of his favorite "daughters of Harlem."[67] "She should be the star attraction at the Zanzibar," he said, "not just a feature." Curiously, he blamed both Gale and Fitzgerald herself: "From what can be gathered, the super singer won't listen to reason, those smart sensible reasons that will take her out of the category of the band vocalist to individual starship. . . . Her talent is far too great to be given such a flippant brush-off, either by her or those concerned."[68] What provoked this outburst remains unknown, but it pointed to Ella's difficulties in changing her image as well as to the cultural importance of her success.

Only Ella Fitzgerald could chart a new course for herself, and by then she was on the move. Referring to the ballads of the war years, she later told a reporter, "I got tired of singing about long-lost loves."[69] She was pushing Decca harder, sparking talk of a "revival of this great singer," as George Simon wrote in May 1946.[70] The same month she was at the Apollo, singing the Gershwin song "Lady Be Good" her way.[71] In hindsight, the new Ella who was emerging would change both her career and her personal life—and, in her own determined way, transform vocal jazz.

Chapter 10

"GOING DIZZY"

(1945-1947)

On January 12 Decca ran a big ad, "Coming Your Way in 1946," featuring thirty-one musicians, including eight white female vocalists; Fitzgerald was the only Black female.[1] Decca's "race artist" gave the label a constituency of jazz fans and Black juke-box patrons, yielding a predictable return on their investment. She understood her role in the company, and the diversity of the recordings she and Gabler made shows that sometimes she used it to her advantage. Other times she found ways to register her complaints directly with him and sometimes with journalists. No longer identified as a "swing-song singer" or a "band singer," she ranged across the spectrum of Black popular music and jazz in unpredictable ways, often prompted by Gabler, sometimes taking the initiative herself.

For his part, Gabler balanced his duties to Decca while satisfying her ambitions as best he could. In the late fall of 1945 and early 1946, he put to use his considerable gift as a musical match-maker. First, he paired her with Louis Jordan, whom she had known since her Chick Webb days; he was by then a superstar in the Black pop market and one of Decca's biggest money-makers. With his "jump blues" style (not yet labeled "rhythm and blues"), Jordan had had several chart-busters in the war years. Recorded in October 1945 and released in May 1946, their novelty calypso "Stone Cold Dead in the Market (He Had It Coming)," reached number seven on the *Billboard* pop chart in July 1946, selling 250,000 copies and finishing the year as "top race record on the nation's juke boxes."[2] According to Milt Gabler, Fitzgerald, who had learned the Trinidadian murder ballad from her hairdresser, took a risk.[3] Fitzgerald later claimed, "Everybody who was interested in my welfare warned me that America wasn't ready for Calypso, but I liked the song. I asked Jack Kapp if I could record it."[4] Perhaps it was *her* version of calypso others might not be ready for—Decca had already helped pioneer a calypso craze in the late 1930s, and in 1945 Kapp's pet group the Andrews Sisters had catapulted the Trinidadian melody "Rum and Coca-Cola" to the top of the charts.[5] Both hits were helped by network bans on airplay—"Rum and Coca-Cola" for promoting alcohol, and "Stone Cold" for trivializing homicide, it was said, through the murder of an abusive husband by his battered wife. When using the song on live dates, Fitzgerald had fun impersonating Jordan.[6] Their musical chemistry also fit the B side of the recording, the ephemeral "Petootie Pie," which Benny Goodman praised as "the best jazz record of the last ten years. And it's relaxed, too."[7] *Band Leaders and Record Review* wrote that she turned Jordan into a "mere side dish."[8]

Gabler's next matchup, pairing Fitzgerald with Louis Armstrong on January 18, 1946, also yielded chart success, a tribute to Gabler's wisdom as he launched a historic partnership in vocal jazz. "We don't know whose idea it was to team these two great artists but believe us the combination is a natural," Alyce Key wrote in the *Los Angeles Sentinel*.[10] The duo covered two current pop hits: "The Frim-Fram Sauce," a novelty that Nat King Cole put on the jazz map, and "You Won't Be Satisfied (Until You Break My Heart)," a chart success for Doris Day.[10] Ella and Louis deliver audible smiles. They sing with such empathy and warmth that one critic wrote, "With good material what this pair couldn't do!"[11]

After that Gabler let Fitzgerald record the little-known Duke Ellington tune "I'm Just a Lucky So-and-So" with the pianist Billy Kyle and his trio.[12] Gabler let her be with a simple background that allowed her interpretive skills shine. In his review in May, George Simon wrote, "It looks like Decca is breaking down a little bit too. First they let Ella sing with Louis Armstrong, and now they're putting her with the right sort of backing. Now, if they'd only release her 'Flying Home'!"[13]

★★★

FITZGERALD STOPPED WAITING FOR DECCA. On its October 5, 1946, cover, *Billboard* announced that Ella Fitzgerald was "Going Dizzy": "This wistful-voiced singer is the latest convert to bebop. With the hope of becoming known as the leading femme bebop chanter, she is planning a tour, staring November 1, from coast to coast with Dizzy Gillespie."[14] That opportunity arrived after Moe and Tim Gale decided to sell a one-third minority share in the Gale Agency to Billy Shaw, Gillespie's agent. Gale was shocked by Fitzgerald's announcement. According to his son Richard, "When Ella started singing bop, my father was horrified. He wanted Ella to do this light pop stuff. He was thinking only commercially."[15] Fitzgerald's endorsement of Gillespie, which took courage and independence, changed her career and changed bop. Other swing musicians were criticizing bebop. Benny Goodman complained in *Metronome*, "I've been listening to some of the Re-bop musicians. You know, some of them can't even hold a tone. They're just faking. Bop reminds me of guys who refuse to write a major chord even if it's going to sound good."[16] They were "rejects," the African American swing band drummer Panama Francis said. "You couldn't dance to it."[17] Louis Armstrong told *Time* magazine, "Mistakes, that's all bop is . . . a whole lot of notes, weird notes . . . that don't mean nothing."[18]

Ella Fitzgerald ignored them and aligned herself with a serious modernist movement that demanded a profound rethinking of jazz's traditional relationship to popular music. Swing musicians typically preserved the classic twelve-bar blues and thirty-two-bar song forms. They retained its symmetrical phrase structure. (They "traded" fours and eights, not fives and sevens.) They controlled the level of dissonant harmonies. Listeners delighted in their individuality in improvisation because they experienced a shared literature and common language. Bebop made these norms an option, not a premise. Its leaders, Dizzy

Gillespie on his trumpet and the alto-saxophonist Charlie Parker, explored radical harmony and forms enough to spark a revolution and a counterrevolution. In 1945, when Gillespie recorded a tribute album to Jerome Kern, the Kern estate threatened litigation after Kern's widow found it disrespectful to her husband's original melodies.[19]

In the publicity surrounding Fitzgerald's tour with Gillespie, she reasserted her faith in bebop. In August 1946 the *Cleveland Call and Post* noted, "It is in keeping with her modest character that she, in an interview to correspondents of this paper, neglected to say anything about her own work and spent all of her time in praising Dizzy Gillespie. . . . She claims that Dizzy's spontaneous style and manner are in keeping with the way she likes to sing."[20] In the *Pittsburgh Courier*, Billy Rowe raised an eyebrow at Ella's claim that Dizzy was "the first musician since Louie Armstrong to come up with something new. Lionel Hampton, Count Basie and Jimmie Lunceford may not agree with her on that score."[21]

Fitzgerald had been interested in Gillespie's music since their friendship began in 1937, when they were both twenty years old. John Birks Gillespie had arrived in New York by way of Cheraw, South Carolina, and Philadelphia. He expected a steady job with Lucky Millinder, but Lucky kept him on "standby," as Gillespie put it, then stopped paying him altogether. Engagement at the Savoy helped soothe the moment: "Chick Webb took a liking to me and . . . used to let me sit in, in Taft Jordan's place, and take solos. I think I was the only one he used to let sit in like that."[22] In May 1937 he joined Teddy Hill's band, which worked alongside Webb at the Savoy. "We used to get off the stage at the Savoy Ballroom and start dancing," Ella recalled. "We'd jump off and start Lindy hopping."[23]

In 1939 Gillespie got a plum job with Cab Calloway, who traveled with his own train and paid well. But in August 1941 Dizzy was fired amid rumors he stabbed his boss in the leg during an altercation. By September 26 he had joined Ella Fitzgerald's orchestra, meeting up the drummer Kenny Clarke, a friend and a kindred bop innovator. Fitzgerald obliged Gillespie by having the band run through his new arrangement of the tune "Down Under."[24] Both men had left Fitzgerald's orchestra by mid-October 1941.

Fitzgerald's "Going Dizzy" depended on other experiences in the early to mid-1940s. "We all used to go and visit him," she said in 1987.[25] (Gillespie's apartment was a virtual classroom where he explained bop harmony and chord changes.) She followed him around to learn more:

> When they used to have the after-hours jam sessions at Minton's, and another place, I used to sneak in with them. And I feel that I learned what little bop I do have by following Dizzy around these different places. I feel that that was my education. He is a wonderful teacher, and I am very grateful to him. I probably never would have tried to bop, but I wanted to do what he was doing. We used to go in there and jam all night, and sometimes we'd go down to 52nd Street to the Three Deuces, and we'd sit up there and listen to Lady Day.[26]

In February 1946, when Fitzgerald was working at Cafe Zanzibar with Cootie Williams, Gillespie was booked nearby at the Spotlite Club on 52nd Street, where he did such good business that his sextet was augmented to a big band. That triumph led to the proposal for a joint fall tour, to run through the Deep South in December. Gillespie's previous Southern tour had barely survived, meeting with indifference from the "unreconstructed blues lovers down South who couldn't hear nothing else but the blues."[27] With Ella on the bill, he had a chance.

Gillespie's respect for Fitzgerald sometimes flummoxed the younger members of his band, who relegated her to the dated role of swing-song singer or pop stylist. Gillespie's young pianist, John Lewis, later said, "My appreciation for Ella wasn't as great as it should have been, although after Dizzy kept pointing it out to me every night, I got the message! At the time, in '46, along with the rest of the band, I was more interested in Sarah [Vaughan]."[28] So were many others, as Vaughan's recordings of "East of the Sun," "Mean to Me," and "Interlude"—all with Gillespie in the ensembles—differentiated her from Fitzgerald's generation, who had to plug songs through a straight vocal chorus to satisfy a sheet music publisher. Vaughan was seven years younger, and her approach to melodic paraphrase assumed the freedom Fitzgerald fought to earn. In July 1946 *Down Beat*'s Michael Levin credited Vaughan as the "first singer to distract the musicians from Ella Fitzgerald, Mildred Bailey and Billie Holiday in some time."[29] When Fitzgerald declared she was "going Dizzy," Sarah had already "gone."

From July through September, before the official joint tour, Fitzgerald headlined a few dates in the Midwest with Gillespie's "new re-bop band" in the package. They also cut their fees to appear together at a membership and equal rights drive for the New England NAACP.[30] The official tour got underway on October 18 with week-long engagements at two important Black theaters, the Howard in Washington, D.C., and the Royal in Baltimore. The bills included the drummer Cozy Cole and dancers from the musical *Carmen Jones*. Fitzgerald and Gillespie then ventured to the South and Southwest for a spell of one-nighters, playing mostly in segregated dance halls and an occasional theater in small cities with vibrant Black commercial districts, such as Nashville, Memphis, New Orleans, and Little Rock. Sometimes managers segregated the audience by running a rope down the middle of a room.

"Ella Fitzgerald Knocks Wacoans Stone Cold Dead," read a review from Waco, Texas. "Dizzy Gillespie has a talented troupe," but "the folks came out, really, to hear Ella Fitzgerald," who sang "I'm Just a Lucky So-and-So," "A-Tisket A-Tasket," "Stone Cold Dead in the Market," and "Lady Be Good."[31] For the beboppers, it was an uphill climb. James Moody remembered, "It was funny to see the reaction of the people to the band. Down there it was a little different because the people weren't quite aware of bebop, and they didn't know how to dance to the music at that time. So they would stand and look up at the band as if we were nuts."[32]

As was typical, the musicians returned with memories of random racism or the threat of violence. Moody recalled two tense encounters:

One time, down South, this guy was looking up and he said, "Where's Ella Fitzgerald?" He was mad because he didn't see Ella Fitzgerald yet. And we were playing. I think that night we kinda had to band together, to get out and leave there. It was down in one of those little towns down South somewhere. They didn't know what was happening.[33]

One time we got into a town late and the sheriff and his wife were there waiting for us. The wife said, "You know, Ella, I just love the way you sing," and the sheriff said, "Yeah, my wife loves the way you sing. Would you sing something for us?" I mean, Ella's on the bus! Ella was saying, "I'm tired. My voice is tired. I can't do it." They wound up leaving us alone, but they were pretty persistent.[34]

★★★

GEORGE GERSHWIN'S SONG "OH, LADY BE GOOD" was already a jazz standard when Fitzgerald began her scat interpretations in the spring of 1946, a few months before the joint tour with Gillespie. For a May performance at the Apollo with Willie Bryant's band, *Variety* noted, "Chirper who is at her best in a small club, warms large theatre immediately and can't beg off," singing "Lady Be Good" as an encore, "strictly as a vocal jam."[35]

What it sounded like on these dates is not clear, but a *Metronome* review of another Apollo date in September was headlined "Vocal Jam Best That Am":

The piece de resistance was, of course, Ella's now-famous vocal jam session on "Lady Be Good" and good for at least 6 sensational choruses. She has some set riffs now that would make many top musicians' eyes bug out and also offers a quick imitation of Slam

Stewart that is good for laughs. The whole thing packs more wal-
lop than any music business specialty to he heard around today.[36]

All this attention happened well before Fitzgerald recorded "Lady Be
Good" on March 19, 1947. Three days after the recording, Fitzgerald
sang it on WNEW's *Saturday Night Swing Club*, with the encouragement,
she said, of Gillespie and the show's host, Martin Block. Once again the
conservative climate at Decca delayed its release. In April, according
to the *Los Angeles Sentinel*, fan requests at record stores forced the issue,
along with audience approval at the Paramount and the Apollo.[37] Decca
announced the release in late June.[38] Gabler used the moment to liber-
ate "Flying Home," her shelved scat improvisation from 1945, as the
B-side.[39] A transformative moment for vocal jazz had arrived.

"Lady Be Good" was a singular moment of triumph, one that gave
Fitzgerald another chance to express filial gratitude. "I guess in a way
this record is a memorial to Chick," she told the liberal magazine *PM*,
because he had initiated her into his after-hour jam sessions.[40] In her
many performances of the song over the years, she would consistently
pay tribute to Gillespie. In 1956 she recounted, "By working with Dizzy
Gillespie, I got this arrangement on 'Lady Be Good' just by listening to
the way they played, and I tried to sing like that and it became a hit, and
so naturally I feel he was a great influence on me."[41] Indeed, the many
musical references woven into her improvisation include Gillespie's
compositions "Cool Breeze," "One Bass Hit," and "Oop Bop Sh'Bam."

After an initial negative review calling the record a "vocal exercise
that would delight only the re-bop menageries," *Billboard* reversed itself.
"Fitzgerald displays her versatility on this disk, going through seven
[actually six] scat choruses of the Gershwin evergreen which are just
as amusing as they are amazing. Disk already is breaking loose in race
locations. . . . This is jazz at its finest level."[42] In *Variety* George Frazier
proclaimed Fitzgerald "beyond the talents of any other female vocalist. . . . It's a stunning demonstration of imagination, beat, phrasing,
and humor."[43]

Down Beat gave its highest five-note rating, "the first time this column has ever fallen on its face so profoundly in the presence of a superior performance. . . . Miss Fitzgerald comes on with two quasi-scat sides which will be listened to just as avidly ten years from now as they are today."[44]

Fitzgerald's creative improvisation had its roots in "signifying," a distinctive African American cultural practice. In the words of Samuel Floyd, indebted to the scholarship of Henry Louis Gates, Jr., "signifying" is a process, practiced through "the transformation of preexisting musical material by trifling with it, teasing it, or censuring it . . . demonstrating respect for or poking fun . . . through parody, pastiche, implication, indirection, humor, tone play or word play."[45] Fitzgerald signified explicitly through her quotations. Sometimes she was obvious, intending to woo the audience with her satire; other times she was subtle, delivering messages for musicians. She took risks all the time. Jazz musicians and critics can be wary of excessive or overly explicit musical quotation—Leonard Feather, for example, reviewing Ella's live performance of "Lady Be Good" in mid-1946, found "too many familiar and borrowed licks."[46]

Nonetheless, in jazz improvisation musicians talk to one another in the present and the past by borrowing, quoting, and paraphrasing to honor and compete. For Fitzgerald, it was a joyous process. In the words of jazz scholar Katharine Cartwright, "her borrowings are remarkable for the rich diversity of her sources, the musicality with which she invoked them, the ingenuity with which she made the material her own, and her palpable enjoyment of the process."[47] In "Lady Be Good," we find a powerful example of Fitzgerald's aesthetic purpose in channeling her phonographic memory, reaching out to musicians at one level and multiple audiences on another. It is a timeless strategy, a perfect example of what Leopold Mozart advised his son Wolfgang to do—write both for *Kenner und Liebhaber*, the connoisseurs and the public at large.[48] A particularly famous event in "Lady Be Good" is her impersonation of bassist Slam Stewart, her colleague going back to the Slim and Slam days in the late 1930s and sustained during the war years, when they worked together on various Home Front charity events. She impersonated his use of the full string bow on his solos rather than plucking the bass with his fingers, and simultaneously humming his lines up an octave. The distinctive result sounded like the scat of a bumblebee, which she captured in the recording.

Fitzgerald brought her new style to jazz clubs and Black theaters in 1947. A June engagement at the Downbeat Club on 52nd Street received excellent notices, prompting predictions that her celebrity would revive business on the Street. She returned to the Downbeat later that summer.[49] An aircheck from a radio broadcast on August 5, 1947, at the Howard Theatre and released for the first time in 2000 exposes the delight that African American audiences took in "Lady Be Good." Backed by Ray Tunia at the keyboard, Ella's Slam Stewart impression produced a joyous uproar with cheers and whistles from an audience of connoisseurs.[50] When George Kirby, a noted African American impersonator, did his own takeoff on Ella's "Lady Be Good" at the Paramount the following year, he came on right after Fitzgerald herself.

***

Fitzgerald first performed at Carnegie Hall on March 15, 1947, for a gala benefit sponsored by the *Pittsburgh Courier*, singing "Lady Be Good."[51] On September 29 her involvement with bebop received a historic acknowledgment at this august venue when she joined Dizzy Gillespie's orchestra for a "Program of the New Jazz." (See Fig. 6.) Jazz musicians had appeared at Carnegie several times that year, but bebop was still controversial, and the trade press still used the term *jazz concert* self-consciously, as a sign of cultural recognition for the art form. Now considered a canonic event, the Carnegie Hall concert included outstanding works by Gillespie, George Russell, and Charlie Parker, his "guest star" in a quintet that broke off from the big band. Fitzgerald, who joined the orchestra for six tunes, "showed to advantage in a white tailored dinner gown," as *Down Beat*'s Michael Levin wrote in one of the few reviews acknowledging her contribution.[52]

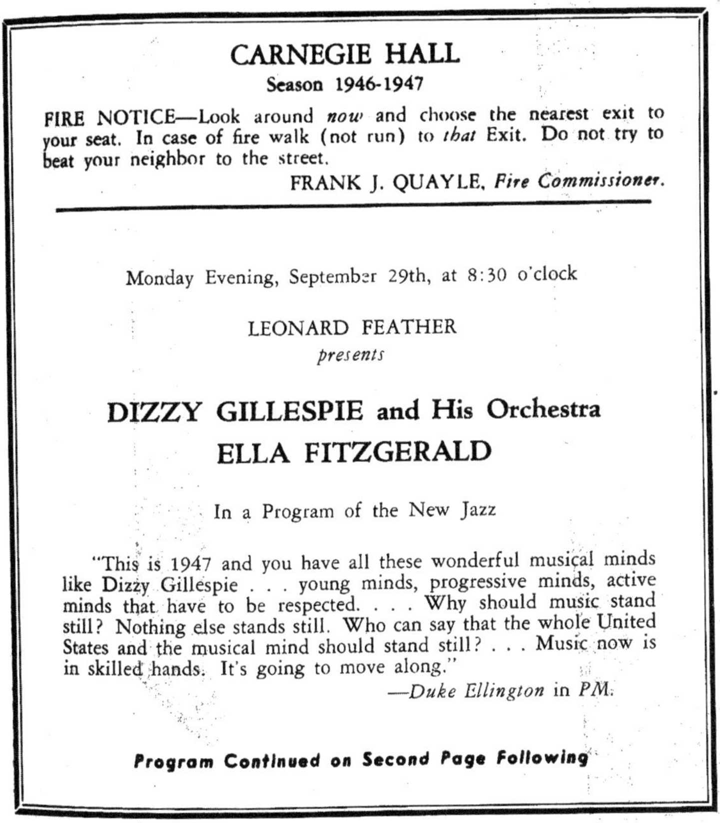

CARNEGIE HALL
Season 1946-1947

FIRE NOTICE—Look around *now* and choose the nearest exit to your seat. In case of fire walk (not run) to *that* Exit. Do not try to beat your neighbor to the street.

FRANK J. QUAYLE, *Fire Commissioner.*

Monday Evening, September 29th, at 8:30 o'clock

LEONARD FEATHER
presents

DIZZY GILLESPIE and His Orchestra
ELLA FITZGERALD

In a Program of the New Jazz

"This is 1947 and you have all these wonderful musical minds like Dizzy Gillespie . . . young minds, progressive minds, active minds that have to be respected. . . . Why should music stand still? Nothing else stands still. Who can say that the whole United States and the musical mind should stand still? . . . Music now is in skilled hands. It's going to move along."

—*Duke Ellington* in *PM.*

Program Continued on Second Page Following

Fig. 6. Title page of the program book for Dizzy Gillespie and Ella Fitzgerald's historic concert at Carnegie Hall, September 29, 1947. *Courtesy of Carnegie Hall Rose Archives.*

Fitzgerald picked her repertoire carefully, balancing the familiar with the new. Backed by the full band, she opened with "Almost Like Being in Love" from *Brigadoon*, a musical by Alan Jay Lerner and Frederick Loewe then in its sixth month on Broadway. In contrast to the hit versions issued by Frank Sinatra, Mildred Bailey, and Mary Martin, Fitzgerald purged sentimentality in an arrangement punctuated with brassy dissonance and bite. Her interpretation had subtle jazz phrasing, inflected melodic alterations, and inimitable swing—the approach she would later bring to perfection in her classic *Song Book* LPs.

She followed with a superb "Stairway to the Stars," eliciting initial audience applause in tribute to her past hit. The third tune was "Lover Man," associated with Billie Holiday's poignant eroticism and graced by a deep wistfulness. Then came the bop segment, with extensive scat improvisation on three tunes. Fitzgerald reprised both "Flying Home"—spiked with even more dissonance than in the recording—and "Lady Be Good," shouting "Slam Stewart!" to cue the audience into her joke. Ella and Dizzy closed by "trading fours" on the bop staple "How High the Moon," and Levin acknowledged her "giving Dizzy considerable competition on some chase choruses."[53]

During the concert, Gillespie overplayed the showmanship he had learned from Cab Calloway, and his stage-stealing manners during Fitzgerald's performance provoked both private and public criticism. In the *Chicago Defender*, Lillian Scott wrote, "Someone should tell Gillespie that the first principle of the stage is not to willfully distract attention from another artist."[54] Levin described him taking a bouquet meant for Ella and "doing mincing dance steps and in general stealing as much of the play from her singing as possible."[55] Even Louis Armstrong, no stranger to vaudeville mores, reproached Gillespie backstage: "You're cutting the fool up there, boy. Showing your ass."[56] We do not know how Fitzgerald reacted to charges that he was trying to upstage her. When discussing her bop "education," she expressed her gratitude and never breached jazz protocol by wavering from public loyalty. "I thank you, I thank you, I thank you," she sang to her audience in Carnegie Hall and to Gillespie as well.

Fortune had to smile again on "Lady Be Good" to reach a bigger audience. In November 1947 Dave Garroway—a nationally known DJ who would later become the founding host of NBC-TV's *Today* show—started playing "Lady Be Good" on the radio. "Dave Garroway, God bless him, played that record so often on his program in Chicago that I got to work every theater in the city," recalled Ella in 1983. "Bopping was a different thing and everybody wanted to hear it."[57]

Garroway also invited her onto his radio show, introducing her in his hip literary style, without the standard code words to describe a Black voice:

You don't have to be told about the strange and fantastic quality in her voice like a piece of fine and imported lace. It can be cold and then warm, hard and then soft, and it's a voice that always has a sharp edge to it, when it's soft it's not mushy. Ella's living in 1947 and knows more about a new idea in music maybe than most people. You may have heard it called bop, sometimes referred to as bop dead. But it's livin' and this is the world in which you and I live and Ella has done a thing with her voice in it that transcends anything that's ever been done close to it. . . . More verbal control with her voice than the Juilliard School hopes it has and some of the good people there.[58]

Garroway would treat Sarah Vaughan's guest appearances on his program in the late 1940s similarly, pretentiously or not. In the words of Vaughan biographer Elaine Hayes, he encouraged a "boundary-free style of listening, one that sought to eliminate racial, emotional and ultimately intellectual barriers, and he encouraged his audience to do the same."[59]

Fitzgerald did not rest easily on the other side of the river she had crossed. In an interview published in October 1947 in *PM*, she repeated Chick Webb's advice about "always getting there with the firstest with the mostest and the newest":

I think I'll keep singing jazz tunes for a while and then I'll look for something new. A lot of singers think all they have to do is exercise their tonsils to get ahead. They refuse to look for new ideas and new outlets, so they fall by the wayside. But there'll always be new ideas in jazz—just as long as there are enthusiastic kids trying to crash this business. I'm going to try to find out the new ideas before the others do.[60]

Chapter 11

ELLA'S MOON

(1947–1949)

When Ella Fitzgerald joined Dizzy Gillespie on his Southern tour, she did not invite a boyfriend along for the ride, as she had with Ben Kornegay in 1941. She was leaving no one behind, even if in 1944 and 1945 the press speculated about a few random guys. But on the Southern tour was Gillespie's twenty-year-old bassist, Ray Brown. "I never listened to singers much until I met [Ella]," he said. "I didn't dig 'em. Then after listening to her every night, constantly, I said to myself, something's happening!"[1]

Born October 13, 1926, in Pittsburgh, Ray Brown came from a middle-class family, his father employed as a Pullman porter.[2] Brown described his father as an avid Fats Waller fan and his mother as an admirer of Lucky Millinder. Pittsburgh had a particularly vibrant and consequential Black community, and its outstanding public school music programs produced such distinguished alumni as Earl Hines, Billy Strayhorn, and Erroll Garner. In June 1944, at almost eighteen, Brown had had to turn down a job with Cootie Williams, then on tour with Ella Fitzgerald and the Ink Spots, during their run at Pittsburgh's Stanley Theatre. As he explained,

> I went home and told my folks that I had this marvelous job, my big chance, and my mother said, "You can't go to work 'til you

finish school, your brother's going to college. Don't you want to go to college?" I said, "No." She said, "Well then you have to finish high school." My father said, "Yep, you got to." And so I had a double coronary and three fits and then I got over it.[3]

After graduating from Schenley High School and doing a stint arranging popular hits for the New Orleans–based territory band Snookum Russell, Brown headed for New York without a solid job offer.[4]

Upon his arrival on October 20, 1945, his life transformed with breathtaking speed. He headed for midtown Manhattan, where Duke Ellington was at the Zanzibar, Charlie Parker at the Downbeat Club, Don Byas at the Three Deuces, and Coleman Hawkins at the Spotlite with Thelonious Monk on piano.[5] Brown chose the Spotlite when he saw that his friend, pianist Hank Jones, was on the bill backing singer Billy Daniels. Dizzy Gillespie stopped by, and through Jones, Brown secured an unexpected audition. The next day in Gillespie's apartment, he impressed Charlie Parker, Bud Powell, and Max Roach—a daunting jury of giants—and got hired on the spot. When Brown called home, "my mother asked, 'Which of those bands did you go with? Andy Kirk? Lucky Millinder?' 'None of them, I took another job with Dizzy Gillespie.' She said, 'Who's that?'"[6]

Los Angeles patrons would ask "What's that?" when Gillespie's quintet with Parker, Brown, and the white musicians Al Haig on piano and Stan Levey on drums played Billy Berg's jazz club from December 10, 1945, into February—a landmark episode in bebop's struggle for acceptance. For Brown, bebop was instrumental music, pure and simple; vocal bop diluted its status, pushing it into commercialism. That attitude had deep roots in jazz history—it affected Ella's career with Chick Webb. At Billy Berg's, Brown and Gillespie shared the gig with two novelty jazz singers. Clubgoers loved Slim Gaillard, performing his hit "Cement Mixer, Put-Ti, Put-Ti," and Harry "the Hipster" Gibson, promoting his cult favorite "Who Put the Benzedrine in Mrs. Murphy's Ovaltine?" As Brown remembered the audience,

They didn't know what we were playing; they didn't understand it, and a guy asked us to sing. . . . A guy named Billy Berg, he said, "You're gonna have to sing or something." And I'll never forget, Bird wrote a couple of charts where the whole band was singing, you know. I don't know how Dizzy felt inside, because I don't think he really cared for that. I'm sure he didn't, but I'm sure he didn't transmit it to the guys in the band.[7]

Gillespie wrote, "Tempted as I felt to go upside Billy Berg's head for demanding that we sing as well as play, I stayed cool, and except for 'Salt Peanuts,' we didn't sing neither. Sea to sea, America in 1945 was as backward a country musically as it was racially."[8]

At the Spotlite from May 30 to June 13, 1946, Gillespie's reconstituted big band gave Brown opportunities to shine. "There was no other soloist featured as Ray was," according to the big band historian Jeff Sultanof.[9] Brown's signature tune, "One Bass Hit," was promoted as a repertory staple and featured in the 1947 film *Jivin' in Be-Bop*, aimed at an African American audience. In *Esquire*'s "All-American Jazz Band" poll at the end of 1946, Brown won the "new star" award along with Sarah Vaughan, Miles Davis, and Brown's Gillespie colleague Milt Jackson.[10]

Brown made his own transition to bebop through systematic study. After a month with Gillespie, he recalled,

I cornered him after the gig and said, "Diz, how'm I doin'?" He said, "Oh fine. Except you're playing the wrong notes." That did it. I started delving into everything we did, the notes, the chords, everything. And I'd sing the lines as I was playing them.[11]

Touring all over the country by bus with Gillespie and Fitzgerald, Brown realized that she sang the right notes. Ella and Ray fell in love and stayed in love when the tour ended in January 1947, returning to their separate professional lives, occasionally crossing paths. On March 15 they both appeared at a Carnegie Hall concert produced by the *Pittsburgh Courier*, honoring Lionel Hampton and other winners of its fourth annual All-Star poll.

That summer Ella and Ray became a public pair. After performing at the Howard Theatre in D.C. (August 1–7) and the Chanticleer Club in Baltimore (August 14–27), Ella returned to New York and stopped in at the Downbeat Club to see Ray at work with Dizzy Gillespie and His Orchestra. Of course, Dizzy asked her up. A now-famous photograph by William Gottlieb, published in the September 24 issue of *Down Beat*, captures Ella in the middle of a triangle. At the microphone, lost in song, her face is haloed by a feathery white hat. Dizzy gazes up at her with a comically besotted expression. Ray, playing bass in the background, looks concerned.[12] As well he might have been.

Shortly afterward Dizzy Gillespie fired Brown, which Brown attributed to his relationship with Ella. Little is known of her finances at this time, but judging from the box office notices and the revenue from big pop hits with the Ink Spots, she was doing well enough to indulge a new boyfriend. As Ray recalled, "It was, I think, bad for the band for me to show up in a $400 suit and a big Cadillac to come to the job, and the guys are making $67 a week."[13] By September 29, 1947, when Fitzgerald joined Gillespie's orchestra for their historic concert at Carnegie Hall, Brown had been replaced by Al McKibbon. However, two days earlier Brown was onstage at Carnegie as part of Norman Granz's Jazz at the Philharmonic (JATP) concert troupe, with stars including tenor saxophonists Coleman Hawkins and Flip Phillips, trombonist Bill Harris, pianist Hank Jones, and vocalist Helen Humes.

Ella and Ray got officially engaged amid this upheaval. In October 1947 the *Los Angeles Sentinel* reported she was "sporting a rock big enough to choke a cow from Ray Brown."[14] Professionally they went their separate ways. Fitzgerald toured the usual rounds of theaters, sharing bills with Dizzy Gillespie at Newark's Adams Theatre in October and Detroit's Paradise Theatre in November. Brown traveled with JATP from September to November, performing in some fifty cities.[15]

Finally, the couple reunited on November 13 at a JATP concert in Akron, Ohio. As soon as the JATP tour ended in November, Ella had a new rhythm section backing her on club dates, with Ray joined by Hank Jones on piano and Charlie Smith on drums—a knockout group. For the first time in her career, Ella rather than Moe Gale chose her accompanists and took more room for her own repertoire. From November 21 to 25, they worked at the Regal Theatre in Chicago with the Illinois Jacquet Sextette, her touring partner. Next came Youngstown, Ohio, from December 1 to 10.[16] "The night life was when the blacks and whites got together," recalled the manager of Youngstown's Cotton Club. "She appeared at a white club called the Merry-Go-Round on the west side of town, but afterwards she came to our after-hour place around 2:30 and stayed until 6 or 7 o'clock in the morning."[17]

Ray and Ella got married at city hall in Youngstown on December 10, 1947. Walter Winchell called her a "secret bride" correctly.[18] "The new Mrs. Brown (she will keep the name 'Ella Fitzgerald' for trade purposes) said to reporters: 'We are just plain people, and we only want to be happy like other plain people. You should see some of the knitting I have done to pretty up the home we will make together.' "[19]

On December 20 Mr. and Mrs. Brown had their first session together at Decca, with several horns added to the rhythm section of Brown, pianist John Lewis, and drummer Joe Harris. "No Sense," a pop song they had written together (her words, his tune), lived up to its title. The better "My Baby Likes to Be-Bop (And I Like to Be-Bop Too)" was perfect for a couple who had bonded just that way. What made the session historic was her first studio encounter with "How High the Moon," a staple of her repertoire for the next three decades. Milt Gabler recalled, "That was another one we heard her doing in a room . . . another great one, the bebop thing creeping in there."[20] Walter Winchell too reported on her singing the tune earlier that summer: "Ella Fitzgerald at the Downbeat. She toys with 'How High the Moon,' for a short, straight chorus, then riffs and jams, using her voice like one of the instruments for 5 minutes or more."[21] Gabler had the arrangement made from her performance routine, informally taped in his office.[22] This time Decca released it without much delay in April 1948, with "Vocal Be-Bop with Orchestra" on the label.[23]

Fitzgerald approached "How High the Moon" at an extraordinary level of ambition. Written in 1940 by Nancy Hamilton and Morgan

Lewis for an obscure Broadway revue, *Two for the Show*, set in wartime London during the Blitz, the song was an ethereal ballad sung by a couple grabbing a moment of escape. In the early 1940s jazz and pop musicians picked up on it, and in the mid-1940s instrumentalists borrowed its chord sequence—which could not be copyrighted under U.S. law—substituting entirely new melodies, later known as "contrafacts." Fitzgerald used all these approaches, incorporating "Ornithology," Charlie Parker's famous contrafact. Negotiating extreme changes of register, leaping up an octave like an acrobat, destabilizing the original song's four-bar phrase patterns through syncopation, Fitzgerald wove in quotations from various sources including "Poinciana," "Deep Purple," and "Rockin' in Rhythm."

While *Down Beat* gave it a four-star review, other jazz critics were skeptical of Fitzgerald's novelty approach, which seemed to compromise bebop's elevated artistic status.[24] Grading it B-minus, *Metronome*'s review read, "The biggest vocal talent of our time is both disappointing and brilliant on 'Moon.' Ella goes wrong in singing some cheap, coined lyrics."[25] Her lyrics convey that she was taking requests: "I'm singing it because you asked for it, and I'm singing it just for you." Jazz critics could not always appreciate how much she grew as an artist precisely from her awareness of the needs of an audience.

Fitzgerald's third conspicuous vocal experiment of 1947 occurred on December 23 with "Robbin's Nest," another excursion into recomposition. Composed by keyboardist Sir Charles Thompson and named after DJ Fred Robbins, the tune had become a jazz hit that spring as an instrumental.[26] Ella penned and sang the first recorded lyrics, backed by pianist Hank Jones, guitarist Hy White, bassist John Simmons, and drummer J. C. Heard. The lyrics transition to her scatted take on Illinois Jacquet's outstanding recorded solo, and she shifts between lyrical and bop modes without disturbing the flow, adapting the opening of Frédéric Chopin's "Heroic" Polonaise Op. 53, then making the rounds as a classical crossover melody.

In the late 1940s, few jazz critics would concede the bebop label to vocalists without qualifications and a renegotiation of categories.

In his 1949 book *Inside Be-Bop*, Leonard Feather, an editor at *Metronome*, acknowledged that "the same bop idiom that seemed unacceptable to some listeners when dished up in uncompromising orchestral style became popular when it was translated into the modified novelty form of bop vocals." He named precedents to Fitzgerald's scat performances, including recordings by Dave Lambert, Buddy Stewart, and Babs Gonzales. And in the wake of her "celebrated treatments" of "Lady Be Good," "Flying Home," and "How High the Moon," he documented the diffusion of bop idioms among popular vocalists including Mel Tormé, Nat King Cole, Jackie Cain, and Roy Kral. Yet no vocalists besides bandleader Billy Eckstine were listed in his appendix of biographical sketches, an unwitting erasure of the contributions of Anita O'Day and Sarah Vaughan.[27]

The singer Betty Carter acknowledged the impact of "Lady Be Good" and "How High the Moon" on her own beginnings. "That's what gave us females permission to dig in and do some improvising ourselves," said Carter. "It was no longer a man's world."[28] That even to this day Fitzgerald's stature remains unsettled in the jazz community speaks to the ongoing challenges that she—and jazz singing in general—poses to jazz historiography. Her deferential advocacy of Gillespie, and her practice of quoting, have blurred our understanding of the unique synthesis she forged over several years of assimilation and innovation. "It's her *own* bebop," the scholar Gunther Schuller told this author. "I think she just speaks as a bebop singer. She found a way to use licks and syncopation and adapted it to the voice. She was not going to imitate Dizzy. 'How High the Moon' I've heard many times. That one is so on target, and so relentless in its invention."[29]

★★★

THE MARRIAGE OF TWO MUSICIANS faced impediments in its very first year. In 1948 Ray Brown did not find work with JATP and Norman Granz. Further, he refused Dizzy Gillespie's offer to join his European tour in January 1948. "At that time, I was in a bit of a curl between her wanting me to travel with her as well," he said later. "She wanted me to travel with the trio; she had Hank Jones playing piano."[30] This left Moe Gale in control of Brown's schedule as well as hers.

In January Fitzgerald and Illinois Jacquet went on a three-week tour of one-nighters throughout the East Coast and Midwest. Their January 17 performance at Carnegie Hall, presented by DJ Fred Robbins and billed as a "One-Nite Stand Midnight Variety Concert," provoked the *New York Times* reviewer to pay cartoonish homage to the raucous audience: "The band sets the pace, but it is the listeners who break it up. They sway and clap in or out of rhythm, cheer and whistle, stand on the seats and even dance in the hallways and boxes, usherettes to the contrary notwithstanding."[31] The double-barreled tour reaped fabulous box office, serving as prime evidence that "jazz hasn't died," as *Down Beat* editorialized.[32]

In February Fitzgerald and the Ray Brown Trio began a two-year run, giving their musical partnership a chance to flourish. For the first time in her career, club bookings competed significantly with theater bookings. Box office results were mixed. In Los Angeles, her much-anticipated date at Billy Berg's was problematic. One review touted her survival amid a general slump, while another claimed her engagement was cut short, and she "speeded east as fast as she could scoot."[33] From April 21 to May 16, a movie and stage show appearance with Duke Ellington at the Paramount in Times Square got solid business. Coming on after a screening of the film noir thriller *The Big Clock*, Fitzgerald sang the recently released "Robbin's Nest" along with "Can't Help Lovin' Dat Man" and "Lady Be Good." Critics took sides, some pointing to adoring jazz fans, while another lamented that the music was "aimed at either hipsters or corn admirers. There is little in between to amuse the adult theater patron, who wants something understandable and still literate."[34]

In the summer and fall of 1948, gigs at reliable venues like the Apollo were interspersed with club dates, of which the biggest was at the Three Deuces on 52nd Street from June 10 to July 7. Ella "jammed" the place, according to *Down Beat*, and on opening night Moe Gale threw an event that made the cover of *Billboard*, celebrating her "tenth anniversary as a top attraction." The cover photo shows Ella flanked by her two handlers, manager Moe Gale and Decca "executive" Milt Gabler, jointly holding the cake.[35]

The music-making of Fitzgerald and the trio had matured through collective wisdom. Hank Jones recalled that the trio did their own "head arrangements," meaning they were not written down:

> We would all do it together. Ray Brown was an excellent arranger as far as his musical thinking was concerned. Some things I would do, some things he would do. And Ella had a very musical mind herself, a lot of ideas, a lot of input into anything that happened on the stage. Of course, much of the improvisation came right on the stage when she was playing—singing. I say "playing" because Ella thought like an instrument.[36]

At the Three Deuces, the young British pianist George Shearing played "intermission piano" and occasionally sat in for Jones. He would write in his memoir:

> Ray would lay down one of his solid bass lines, really ding-donging downstairs, and Ella would start singing "oop-oop-shooby-doop"—then I'd fall in behind her, gently harmonizing her vocal line with another three parts in the right hand of the piano, with Charlie Smith just swooshing away on brushes in the background. . . . I thought I'd died and gone to heaven. One piece we played was called *The Other Flying Home*, a real kind of walking thing, and we would swing everybody into bad health until three o'clock in the morning.[37]

In August Fitzgerald found an appreciative audience at the Apollo Theatre, sharing a bill with Boyd Raeburn's white orchestra. The Ray Brown Trio got a special mention in *Variety* for contributing "a couple of sizzlers as prelude" to Fitzgerald, who sang "How High the Moon" and some earlier Decca hits including "Mr. Paganini" and "Don't

Worry 'Bout Me."[38] Other times business was slow, as was a booking from August 31 to September 11 at Chicago's Rag Doll, a second-tier venue off the beaten track.[39] A Chicago fan, Max Braun, remembered the dingy scene fifty years later:

> The Rag Doll was a little place with stools around the bar. There were maybe fifteen people there. If fifty, it would have been full. There were two men talking loudly at the bar—I shut them down. The big gigs got down into the Blue Note down in the Loop. This was the time when Sarah Vaughan was very, very big. My take was that Ella was not doing that great.

Braun was also disappointed in the way she presented herself: "She looked like a streetwalker. She was dressed inappropriately for a very, very famous jazz singer at the time. She was wearing a wrap-around black skirt slit up to her hip, and a big red flower and a black blouse."[40] Nonetheless the *Chicago Defender*, expanding on a Gale Agency press release, ran the headline "Chicago Raves as Ella Fitzgerald Triumphs in Bon Voyage Date Here."[41]

★★★

THE "BON VOYAGE" that the headline referred to was for a tour of Britain. On September 14, 1948, Ella, Ray, and Hank Jones set sail for a month's bookings, centered around a plum opportunity at the Palladium, the London variety theater. Gale threw a farewell party at the Three Deuces, then a "big send-off for Ella Fitzgerald" at the Cunard Line's Hudson River pier with "thousands attending," according to the agency's news release. ("More like hundreds," said the local press.)[42] The promised first-class tickets on the *Queen Mary* turned out to be "tourist passage." Nonetheless, the British public, which had found solace in Glenn Miller's music and the USO camp shows during the nadir of the war, eagerly embraced Fitzgerald. The country was now experiencing, in the words of music journalist Val Wilmer, a "postwar feeling of optimism" embodied by jazz and American popular culture as a whole.[43]

Fitzgerald was among the first American singers to perform modern vocal jazz in Britain after the war. The U.K. Musicians' Union had embargoed American performers through protectionist measures designed to force reciprocal booking agreements. In the 1930s, live appearances of Louis Armstrong, Benny Goodman, Benny Carter, and Coleman Hawkins were rare events. Fitzgerald's visit was eased by a Ministry of Labour provision granting exceptions for "persons giving stage performances at music halls."[44]

Even before Britain entered the war in 1939, Fitzgerald had been somewhat known among its jazz buffs and record collectors. "All the American singers were our heroes," said British singer Beryl Davis. "I tried very hard to emulate Ella the most, trying to learn that special, clear Ella sound."[45] Fitzgerald's recording of "F.D.R. Jones," distributed through Decca's subsidiary label Brunswick, was a significant seller in the U.K. by 1940. After the war, British fans bought her Louis Armstrong duet "You Won't Be Satisfied" as well as "You Turned the Tables on Me," "Tea Leaves," and especially, "My Happiness."[46]

The Palladium's manager, Val Parnell, had been headlining one American entertainer after another, including Danny Kaye, Dinah Shore, the Andrews Sisters, and Betty Hutton. Fitzgerald was supposed to top the billing as well, but on the eve of her two-week run she learned she was among the many supporting acts for the legendary British singer Gracie Fields, who was performing live again after a multiyear hiatus. Fitzgerald told the American press she was "disappointed, misled" by earlier publicity. "There was never any question of Ella Fitzgerald topping the bill at the Palladium," retorted Parnell. "That is quite understood with her agent. . . . We had Gracie in mind all the time."[47] A critic for *Melody Maker* detected a "great nervous tension" in Fitzgerald's opening night performance.[48]

At the Palladium, Fitzgerald earned mixed and sometimes condescending reviews. Referring to her vocal jams, the uncomprehending *Times* reviewer wrote of "Miss Ella Fitzgerald the American coloured singer, whose naturally sweet voice she is content to use as a medium for those strange surrealist little pieces that connoisseurs of popular music like best."[49] The drummer from the Skyrockets, the Palladium house band, blamed her dicey reception on her "uncompromising modern style," but conceded that "she was left with the mere shreds of her own presentation."[50] Decca pushed her to program the novelty song "The Woody Woodpecker," a recent hit for Danny Kaye with the Andrews Sisters. "Ho-ho-ho ho ho! Ho-ho-ho ho ho!" bopped the bird from Walter Lantz's famous cartoon.

Fortunately, her final Palladium appearance on October 17 was on a different bill, part of a "Swing Session" series led by an outstanding swing bandleader, Ted Heath. Ella told the band, "You don't know what this means after singing 'Woody Woodpecker' for two weeks." Heath's bassist, Charles Short, reported, "Those 4,000-odd people who were at the London Palladium on that Sunday were the luckiest people in England. That day they heard the greatest jazz played in this country since Coleman Hawkins was here before the war." Ella said,

> They wanted a jam session, so they got it. I like to sing good ballads—you know the tunes you can sing with the right feeling— but if the people are yelling for swing, what can you do but give it to 'em. We gave a swing show, and they sure ate it up.

They heard "It's Magic," "How High the Moon," "Lady Be Good," "Oop-Pop-a-Da," "That's My Desire," and "Flying Home," earning a tumultuous standing ovation. Ray Brown shared the limelight, especially because of his close ties to Dizzy Gillespie, who had yet to appear in England despite an unsuccessful attempt to circumvent the U.K. Musicians' Union. Now here was Ray Brown as an unexpected emissary, and Ted Heath made the most of it, putting "One Bass Hit" on the program.[51] A paper reported that while Brown played, "Ella danced and jived in front of the orchestra."[52] It was a perfect honeymoon moment. "Mr. and Mrs. Brown," as they were listed on the manifest of the *Queen Elizabeth* ocean liner, bade Britain farewell on October 30.

★★★

THE OCTOBER 1948 *Metronome* published a test of their musical compatibility. Leonard Feather had inaugurated his "Blindfold Test" feature in 1946, and for this installment "Ella and Her Fella" reacted to ten unidentified recordings. Feather wrote, "There wasn't much disagreement between Mr. and Mrs. Brown," and they both favored the more modern records. Still, their reaction to the 1944 recording "Bean at the Met," by the Coleman Hawkins Quintet, illustrated the potential for conflict arising from affixing musical labels. They sound very married, and Feather's transcription caught the interruptions:

Ray: I'll give the record about two and a half [stars]; Hawk sounded good.

Ella: I give it three, because I liked the tempo, l like the—

Ray: It was a nice tempo but it didn't swing, though.

Ella: Well, I thought it was swinging. After all, it isn't supposed to be a bop record.

Ray: Well, what is bop?

Ella: I mean, it isn't real up-to-date.

Ray: But the date has nothing to do with swinging.

Ella: No, you don't understand me.

Ray: It isn't close to what's going on nowadays, though they did use a modern theme—you might call it a bop form of playing "How High the Moon," but as soon as you hear Teddy Wilson and Hawk, it—

Ella interrupting: Anyway, I liked it. Three stars.[53]

★★★

IN SEPTEMBER 1949 Ella and Ray bought a small single-family home at 104-47 Ditmars Boulevard in East Elmhurst, Queens, a rare suburban area welcoming upwardly mobile African Americans. The neighborhood included several celebrities, including baseball star Willie Mays and Fitzgerald's touring partner Illinois Jacquet, while Louis and Lucille Armstrong lived close by in Corona. It looked like she "had it all"—that fragile balance between love and work—when *Our World*, a photo magazine aimed at the Black middle class, described Ella and Ray as "an inseparable musical couple." The December 1949 feature included a photo from a recording session, captioned "Husband Ray Brown holds her hand during a break."[54]

Sometime that year Ella and Ray became parents, adopting the infant son of Ella's younger half-sister, Frances, who was twenty-three years old. The child was born James Williams Correy, but they renamed him Ray Brown, Jr.[55] Fitzgerald's publicist Virginia Wicks remembered, "The first time I saw him, he was in a little stroller, he was about maybe nine months old. [Ella] said, 'My sister gave him to me because she had other children and I had none.'"[56] Ella "had a condition which made it impossible for her to have children," according to Ella's cousin, Dorothy Johnson. "[Frances] had quite a bit of children," in Johnson's words, by the time she was twenty-three years old.[57] The reasons for this informal adoption are not known, but as Dorothy Johnson said, "in a family where those who had gave to those who didn't," informal adoption was culturally accepted.[58]

According to some authorities, the practice of informal adoption was prevalent then and remains accepted today among Black families.[59] Ray Brown, Jr., has said, "I was two or three when I was [legally] adopted. They went about things by the book." Yet the delay caused a rift when he was twelve or thirteen. "I remember being in a hotel when I was told I was adopted. It was very traumatic and probably very dramatic. But she held me, told me she loved me," and he knew it was true.[60] He did not know that Frances Correy was his mother until much later in life.[61]

Ella was fulfilling a deep wish and need in her life. She had treated children as a priority when she was with Chick Webb, telling one reporter "earnestly" in 1937 of her wishes to have a radio "kiddie broadcast" for "keeping children out of mischief."[62] In 1947 she proudly publicized her participation in the Foster Parents Plan, started during the war. "I adopted a little boy in Naples," she told reporters, showing them a photograph, and a clip of his picture even ran in the *New York Amsterdam News*.[63] Now she had a child of her own. While she was on tour, she relied on Aunt Ginny Williams and other extended family to help raise him.

★★★

ON APRIL 14, 1949, Ella Fitzgerald stepped into the role of opening night magnet when she helped launch Bop City, a large room seating around eight hundred at Broadway and West 49th Street. She was second-billed to headliner Artie Shaw, the clarinet virtuoso and bandleader. Shaw was remaking himself as a classical musician and conductor, and convinced Ralph Watkins, one of the owners of the club, and a longtime promoter and entrepreneur on the New York midtown jazz scene, to book in a forty-piece symphony orchestra—a class crossover that roped in the press, including *Time* and *Life*. There was Chinese food on the menu, a "milk bar" for underage customers, and a "big, interracial crew" of waiters, the *New York Age* reported.[64]

Among the celebrities inside were the cream of Black music's high society, including Billie Holiday, Billy Eckstine, Harry Belafonte, and Louis Jordan, along with prominent Black journalists (Dan Burley, Izzy Rowe) and white music business executives (Norman Granz, John Hammond, Milt Gabler). For Fitzgerald, it was a singular triumph, a homecoming among friends and her professional community. Photographs by *Life* reporter Martha Holmes, not published at the time, show a radiant performer gregariously circulating among her crowd. In one she greets Congressman Adam Clayton Powell, Jr., and his glamorous wife, the jazz keyboard stylist Hazel Scott. In another, she chats with Ralph Watkins and Symphony Sid.[65]

As it turned out, the opening was her night as much as Shaw's. *Life*'s brief account—headlined "Artie Shaw's Bop Flop"—was accompanied by two audience reaction shots, in which the same group of young men first scowl at Shaw (captioned "Shaw's arty efforts are greeted with bored looks and snickers") and then beam at Fitzgerald ("Ella Fitzgerald's singing gets a rousing round of 'bopplause'").[66] "It was Miss Fitzgerald who saved the show," wrote *Billboard*'s reporter.[67] *Variety* wrote that Fitzgerald, backed by her trio, "delivered the anticipated bop. Whether this brand of music is revolutionary or plain neurotic, Miss Fitzgerald performs with a superb artistry that registers beyond the cultist confines."[68] A *Down Beat* reporter caught how she saluted Billie Holiday in the audience by interpolating her nickname into a rendition of "Lady Be Good" ("Oh, Lady Day be good").[69]

The Bop City engagement led to an unexpected affirmation of her stature outside the jazz world. Attending the opening were the producers of the documentary newsreel series *The March of Time*, who tapped her to appear in the eighteen-minute episode *It's in the Groove*, devoted to the history of the phonograph in American music. Released in June 1949, the film began with Thomas Edison, moved on to the Original Dixieland Jazz Band and Paul Whiteman, and then featured white male stars on the current scene.[70] Since Guy Lombardo represented Decca, it was serendipity that she appeared at all. The best aspect is the voice-over during the brief clip from "How High the Moon," where Ella is backed by the Ray Brown Trio: "And as long as this country has such artists as Ella Fitzgerald making records, the recording industry will turn out millions of records annually which will find their way into American homes."[71]

Since the 1941 film *Ride 'Em Cowboy*, the American public had had only one previous opportunity to see Fitzgerald on screen: a July 18, 1948, appearance on Ed Sullivan's newly launched TV show, *Talk of the Town*, where she sang two numbers. TV was still in its infancy and concentrated in New York, but *The March of Time* had an estimated 28 million viewers across the country. For this mainstream audience, "How High the Moon" symbolized the authenticity of Black music and the parallel miracle of creative improvisation in vocal jazz. By flipping an allegedly radical style into a well-known popular song—in a documentary with no other Black performers or women—she demonstrated the power of her transcendent artistry. When she sang "Somewhere there's heaven, / It's where you are," she looked back at her husband. How high was the moon for Ella in 1949? At its peak, luminous and full.

Chapter 12

"THE SINGER AND THE LABEL ARE IN IT TOGETHER"

(1948-1953)

"Recording companies are a business and the singer and the label are in it together," Milt Gabler once said.[1] In the wake of her successful bop vocals, Decca gave Ella Fitzgerald more lavish promotion. In February 1949 it ran a splashy one-page ad in *Billboard* promoting her back catalog in three categories: "The Queen of Be-Bop," "Memorable Ballads," and her four-disk "Souvenir Album."[2]

"What is the Ella Fitzgerald style *today*?" asked *Ebony* magazine in a May 1949 feature story. She told the magazine that her admiration remained solid for "bop musicians like Parker and Gillespie," who "have more to say than any other musicians playing today," but she did not want to limit herself:

> Despite all of the things I've done, despite the different kinds of songs I sing, I still consider myself basically a ballad singer. I suppose it'll always be that way. I love ballads. Despite what they'll say, that will never change.[3]

To her mind, ballads were standard Tin Pan Alley fare from mainstream pop. But in a postwar era of rapid change in the music business,

Gabler had other ideas for her. A trendspotter, watching the charts like a speculator in the musical stock market, he shrewdly diversified her fare to exploit her skills as a cover artist with songs she would never have chosen on her own. In April 1948, four months after her studio recording of "How High the Moon," he assigned her "My Happiness," which had been an unpretentious career-launcher for the midwestern singing duo Jon and Sondra Steele. She recorded it a cappella to circumvent the AFM's 1948 recording ban; the Song Spinners supplied banal background harmony. Tim Gale, her booking agent and the brother of her manager, Moe Gale, recalled:

> She cut it under protest. . . . She was temperamental about what she sang. However, she would sing *anything* if her advisors were insistent. . . . I brought the dub backstage to her at the Paramount, and she said "It's a shame. A corny performance of a corny song."[4]

"My Happiness" turned into Fitzgerald's biggest solo pop hit in ten years.[5] *Billboard*'s reviewer found that she "was really a knockout as she leaves the bop department to do the hit ballad straight."[6] She returned to the timbres of her "peach-fuzz voice" of the early 1940s to sing this folklike ditty or "heart-song," to use a term from the early 1900s that fits this moment. When Ella performed the song as a duet with Bing Crosby on his radio show in 1949, they displayed a collaborative charisma that Decca neglected to tap. Crosby listed Ella's version of "My Happiness" as one of his top-ten favorite disks in *Jazz 1951: The Metronome Yearbook* singers' poll.[7]

Gabler remembered telling Fitzgerald that her jazz-oriented records, such as "How High the Moon" and "Lady Be Good," might sell 180,000 to 200,000 copies, but "My Happiness" would "[pay] the rent! . . . It would sell 500,000 to 600,000 records. That pays for all the good things we want to do, and you'll be in the black."[8] On her English tour in September 1948, audiences demanded the song, so she had to send for the sheet music and relearn the lyrics. After that she told Gabler she would not doubt his acumen again, but over the next five years, her skepticism increased.

Next on Gabler's agenda was another ditty outside the mainstream. On August 20, 1948, backed by unknown Decca studio musicians and a vocal harmony group, she recorded "It's Too Soon to Know" by the songwriter Deborah Chessler; it ranked in the top ten on the race charts for three weeks.[9] She was crushed, however, by another version, released on August 21 by the Orioles, an unknown close-harmony vocal group from Baltimore led by Sonny Til, a charismatic, sweet lead tenor. Fitzgerald was also beaten out by Dinah Washington, a rising young pop-blues singer who nearly matched the Orioles' success as their versions unexpectedly crossed over into the pop charts.

"It's Too Soon to Know" was what musicologist Albin Zak called "a warning shot, isolated at the time but prefiguring radical changes to come," with strong implications for Fitzgerald in particular.[10] It would be labeled "doo-wop," a style of Black pop reaching working-class Black Americans and a new, younger audience in northern cities who had migrated up from the South during and after World War II.[11] This audience would increasingly gravitate to singers who sounded more like them, with vernacular grains in their voices, as opposed to cultivated timbres like Fitzgerald's. In 1951 a columnist for the *Los Angeles Sentinel*, a Black weekly, would write, "This may come as a shock to the collective ego of such popular artists as Billy Eckstine, Herb Jeffries and Ella Fitzgerald—they don't rate on South L.A.'s hit parade. No, sirree bob. No."[12] When jazz fans heard Ella sing "It's Too Soon to Know" at the Royal Roost on November 27, 1948, she imbued it with the soul that the Decca arrangement lacked.[13]

Then it was back to home territory. In January 1949 Fitzgerald climbed onto Mother Goose's lap once again for "Old Mother Hubbard," a novelty bop nursery rhyme by the British swing singer Ray Ellington. In her Decca version, accompanied by Sy Oliver's orchestra, she sang a full chorus of scat improvisation, reaching her target sweet spot for "boppers as well as pop buyers," as *Billboard* put it.[14] On the cover of the sheet music, subtitled "Ella Fitzgerald's New Be-bop Song," a jolly Mother Hubbard points her finger to the sky in the old "trucking" gesture from the Savoy Ballroom. (See Fig. 7.) Over the next

Fig. 7. Cover of Ella Fitzgerald's bebop song "Old Mother Hubbard" sheet music. It depicts Old Mother Hubbard trucking on down to the cupboard, her fingers pointing to the skies in the gesture of the original swing dance step from "A-Tisket A-Tasket." This modernized nursery rhyme, recorded in 1949, proved popular among Ella's fans. *Courtesy of G. Schirmer.*

two years, Ella brought the tune to every conceivable venue, including jazz clubs like the Royal Roost and Birdland, stage shows at the Apollo and Paramount, and even Carnegie Hall.

In assigning her material, Gabler had to pay attention first and foremost to his mission as a Decca producer. He was particularly aware of the momentum in "hillbilly" music, which in 1949 *Billboard* rebranded less pejoratively as "country" and "country and western." Over a third of the pop singles sold in 1950 were rooted within this genre, to the surprise of the major labels.[15] Gabler said Ella was wary of these songs, yet he believed adamantly in her ability to recommercialize ethnic white styles for the Black charts. Hits he assigned to her included Floyd Tillman's "I've Gotta Have My Baby Back" and Red Foley's "M-I-S-S-I-S-S-I-P-P-I," to no avail. He had better luck with "I'll Never Be Free," which reunited Fitzgerald with Louis Jordan in a vocal duet.[16] The song had been a huge success for Tennessee Ernie Ford and Kay Starr, a jazz-rooted pop vocalist whose natural vocal twang suited country music. Ford and Starr's version would become one of Capitol's best-selling records of the decade. Decca's version had some traction in the R&B market, though Ella was again outcharted by Dinah Washington in another cover.

If Fitzgerald couldn't control all her studio recordings, live performance sometimes handed her an opportunity to signify on current trends. According to Tim Gale,

> She once played a club in Omaha when Frankie Laine's "Mule Train" was a tremendous hit. One of the biggest spenders in Omaha came in constantly and demanded that she sing it. She kept ducking it until finally the club boss begged her to please the money guy. Ella said to herself, "I'll sing it in such a way that he'll never ask for it again," and proceeded to do a burlesque so tremendous that on leaving town she kept it in the act and scored riotously with it everywhere—even at Bop City.[17]

Fitzgerald's "Mule Train" parody used one of her favorite vehicles for social commentary: an incongruous quotation, in this case from "The Donkey Serenade," a Rudolf Friml tune that originated as an aria in the 1937 film version of his Broadway operetta *Firefly*. "The Donkey Serenade" became a standard for operatic voices but was sometimes covered by pop singers like the Andrews Sisters. Tennessee Ernie Ford resurrected "The Donkey Serenade" as the B-side of his cover of Frankie

Laine's other big hit, "The Cry of the Wild Goose," which could explain how Ella made the connection. At Café Society in Manhattan, she reportedly cantered through the "Mule Train" lyrics—"all we do is clippity clop, never stop this clippity clop"—and mashed up Laine's two hits with the line "My heart goes where the mule train goes, / and the mule train goes where the wild goose goes."[18] In Toronto on March 10, 1950, Ella sang "Mule Train" in "baby voice to stop the show."[19] Perhaps she channeled Otto Harbach's worry that "I am just a fool / Serenading a mule."

The bulk of Fitzgerald's arrangements for Decca in the early 1950s depended on the traditions of big band swing. Ella and her key arranger, Sy Oliver—one of the few African American arrangers working for a major label—emerged from the same big band Harlem scene in the swing era. In the 1930s Oliver built his reputation working with Jimmie Lunceford and then revitalizing charts for Tommy Dorsey. Joining Decca in the late 1940s, Oliver was determined not to be relegated to the race record niche, and he had just been promoted to musical director when he began working with Fitzgerald.[20] Oliver was widely respected and in 1949 published *Sy Oliver's Self-Instructor Arranging Course*, which was excerpted in *Down Beat*.[21]

The fifteen sides that Fitzgerald and Oliver cut in 1949 and 1950 include some of her best work, including "Don'cha Go 'Way Mad," derived from the big band jazz instrumental "Black Velvet," written by Illinois Jacquet and Jimmy Mundy. Fitzgerald likely brought the song to Gabler, as she and Jacquet were often packaged together by the Gale Agency. Recorded on February 2, 1950, "Don'cha Go 'Way Mad" featured Fitzgerald and Oliver sparring in a vocal duet with novelty patter. The disk was listed among *Metronome*'s "Records of the Year," and the song remained in her repertoire.[22]

Jack Schiffman recalled asking Oliver, "Does she accept the arrangements as you write them?" He responded, "Hell, no. Ella knows exactly what she wants, and nobody tells her otherwise. If she's not happy with an arrangement I've done, she's perfectly capable of making one up herself!"[23] Toward the end of his career, Oliver remembered a typical session: "I hadn't seen Ella, she didn't know what the songs were half the time, but I knew her keys and I knew how she sang, and that was all I needed to know."[24]

Fitzgerald also worked with the white celebrity arranger Gordon Jenkins, yielding eight sides over two sessions in 1949. In *Billboard*'s annual "music-record poll" for that year, Jenkins ranked third among "The Year's Top Pop Artists," behind only Vaughn Monroe and Perry Como.[25] Gabler admired Jenkins for his innovative use of Eurocentric background voices and string-heavy arrangements, and he often added his backup singing groups to fussy things up even more. Even so, the Jenkins sides show off Fitzgerald's voice in its deeper range as she sought out richer, more lustrous timbres for her voice and her now ubiquitous vibrato.

For an album of songs from *South Pacific*, the hit musical by Rodgers and Hammerstein, Decca included the Fitzgerald-Jenkins recordings of "Happy Talk" and "I'm Gonna Wash That Man Right Outa My Hair."[26] *Variety* responded, "It's the first time the ballad, jazz, bop, and what-have-you singer ever used strings."[27] While Columbia scored a bestseller with the cast album, Decca's compilation sank. "We did it with four top artists," said Gabler, referring to Ella along with Bing Crosby, Danny Kaye, and Evelyn Knight. "You couldn't sell it."[28]

"Black Coffee," another Fitzgerald-Jenkins recording from 1949, lost out to Sarah Vaughan's equally lush orchestral version, which rated number one under the "rhythm and blues" heading in *Billboard*'s annual disk jockey poll.[29] *Down Beat* assigned four stars to the record, praising Jenkins for "accompaniment on both sides far better than Decca normally extends to its singers." For "I'm Gonna Wash That Man Right Outa My Hair," the reviewer added that Ella "makes 'Hair' sound like a song, a real feat. Truly some wench, our Fitzgerald."[30]

Decca had a reputation as a top label for rhythm and blues, and Gabler found some musical and commercial success pairing her in "double feature format" with other African American stars on the label's roster. With Louis Jordan, she propelled the April 1949 recording "Baby It's Cold Outside" into the top ten on both the rhythm and blues and the mainstream charts, even though it was competing with three other versions.[31] Jordan and Fitzgerald had worked all night on an arrangement, which Decca rejected, wanting to keep it simple.[32] Because of the song's success and the novelty of the collaboration, *Billboard* ran a photo of the couple on its May 28, 1949, cover. The song was banned briefly from NBC radio for its "suggestiveness," but the record found favor in *Seventeen*, whose circulation by 1949 reached 2.5 million American girls: "Just about our favorite for this month is this sensational recording of a wonderful song by Ella Fitzgerald and Louis Jordan." The review was addressed to "Teena," the magazine's composite prototype of its readership. Those daughters of flappers and jitterbug dancers were now buying more pop records than any other demographic.[33]

"My big thrill," Gabler later stated, "was to take a great artist and match them with a song and have it become a standard. You feel a certain type of material for an artist; you tell him or her what songs you think would be good for them and how you want to put a framework around them."[34] A fulfillment of this goal was the vintage tune "Dream a Little Dream of Me," a glowing duet reuniting Fitzgerald with Louis Armstrong on August 25, 1950, backed by Sy Oliver's orchestra.[35] Ella had made a specialty of her Armstrong impersonations and even issued a Decca novelty, "Basin Street Blues," released under the name "Ella 'Satchmo' Fitzgerald."[36] Returning to Decca in 1949 after a two-year hiatus, Armstrong was "back on pop tunes," as *Variety* wrote.[37] *Billboard* called "Dream a Little Dream of Me" a "future collector's item," and though it failed to capture chart play, it would find its public in France on Armstrong's next European tour.[38]

★★★

IF GABLER THOUGHT HE COULD "FEEL" POTENTIAL HITS for Fitzgerald, the singer had other ideas. In the February 1950 issue of *Down Beat*, columnist George Hoefer wrote that Fitzgerald "agrees that Decca has made some poor choices of tunes for her to wax. Some of her biggest successes were numbers she worked up herself."[39] In the April *Metronome*, in an interview by George Simon, a trusted critic, Fitzgerald went farther. Simon wrote, "Ella loves the old tunes, loves them more than the new things she too often is pressured into doing, despite her better judgment."[40] The "modesty" Simon touted as the virtues of this "wonderful woman," embodied in Herman Leonard's cover photo, sometimes obscured her tenacity in challenging Decca.

The wish list she shared with Simon included Cole Porter's "Easy to Love"; Harold Arlen's "Ill Wind"; "The Boy Next Door," Judy Garland's ingenue number in the 1944 Hollywood musical *Meet Me in St. Louis*; and the most esoteric choice, a new, unrecorded title by Benny Carter, "My Kind of Trouble Is You." With Porter and Arlen among these choices, her list fits with an early-1950s trend of record companies reviving oldies, retrofitted with new arrangements for new vocalists. A September 1950 *Variety* headline read, "Standards Become 'New' Hits."[41]

Milt Gabler was listening and provided her with a grand new opportunity with "old tunes" on her first ten-inch LP project, *Ella Sings Gershwin*, recorded September 1950 in duet with pianist Ellis Larkins.[42] The idea of a songbook album devoted to one songwriter of show tunes was not new, especially at Decca. When Jack Kapp died suddenly at the age of forty-seven in 1949, his obituary by Abel Green stated, "Jack Kapp had been putting emphasis on name composers, such as Berlin, Porter, Gershwin, Rodgers & Hammerstein and kindred anthologies."[43] While these 78 rpm albums often packaged songs originally released as singles, they nevertheless promoted the idea of Broadway and Hollywood show tunes as classic repertoire. In a now-forgotten 1939 package of three 78s, Decca released a Rodgers and Hart *Album of Song Hits* by its hugely popular singer Hildegarde, a glamorous "supper-club" personality. In 1949 Decca released a compilation album of Gershwin songs by Bing Crosby.

Fitzgerald already had shown her independent artistic interest in Gershwin's songs outside the studio. By this time, several Gershwin tunes showed up on live dates, including "Summertime," the ballad

"Embraceable You," and two rhythm songs, "Somebody Loves Me" and "I Got Rhythm."[44] She was ready for whatever Gabler proposed. His set list borrowed heavily from cabaret singer Lee Wiley, a pioneer in vocal jazz history for her 1939 set of eight Gershwin songs, rendered with modern flair and ingenuity.

Ellis Larkins, who enjoyed a reputation for accompanying singers in cabarets, was delighted when this project came to him out of the blue. "With her, there was no rehearsal, you just did it," he said.[45] Rather than an "accompanist," Larkins is better understood as a "collaborative pianist," the term now used in American classical conservatories. Raised by parents who loved classical music, Larkins, as a ten-year-old prodigy in 1934, played a movement from a Mozart concerto with the Baltimore City Colored Orchestra.[46] Barred by the color line from Peabody Conservatory, he received off-site private lessons from faculty members. Larkins recounted that when he came to New York in 1940, "I had every intention of being a classical pianist, but I started working as a jazz pianist simply out of the need for money."[47] He enrolled at Juilliard, and in 1943 his graduate recital for his master's degree was titled "Between Bach and Boogie Woogie."[48]

Such background helps explain why he later described his jazz approach as a form of counterpoint. "After a while, you sense where a singer is going and where she isn't," he told Whitney Balliett. "You lead her and you keep out of her way. The two voices—the pianist's and the singer's—should move side by side and contrapuntally, and it becomes a little game between them." (Balliett noted that after saying this, Larkins shook his cupped hands, as if shooting dice.)[49] For the Gershwin LP, Larkins occupied his left hand with rhythmic tricks in his syncopated stride piano style, while his right hand imbued his fills and filigree patterns with dissonant harmonies.

"My One and Only," from the 1924 Broadway musical *Funny Face*, exemplified the flow between them, as her bluesy gentleness contrasted with his brittle, angular chords. Fitzgerald allotted him a sixteen-bar half-chorus solo in the middle, and together they supplied a brilliant, original coda in a revisionist interpretation of a then-obscure show tune.

Fitzgerald believed in the artistic integrity of *Ella Sings Gershwin* and pushed it when she could. Just as "Lady Be Good" expanded the dimensions of vocal bop, *Ella Sings Gershwin* transcended conventions around the songbook concept, propelling show tunes into the realm of art songs. *Billboard* wrote:

> On the face of it, this is not what is called a "commercial" album, violating as it does the usual tabooes. That is, there's only a piano for accompaniment, songs include full verses as well as choruses, and tempos vary according to the mood of the singer. But—this album will sell, and sell long and strong simply because it's an irresistible work of art.[50]

Equally lavish praise came from Germany's foremost jazz specialist, Joachim-Ernst Berendt, who wrote that Fitzgerald sang with "a certainty and purity that is incomparable as far as the music goes—from La Scala in Milan to the Metropolitan Opera, from the elegant Hollywood nightclubs to Harlem's jazz cellars."[51] Berendt was echoed by British swing-era authority Stanley Dance, who reviewed the 1954 UK reissue on Brunswick: "This seems to us to be wellnigh perfect and to possess something of the timelessness of great art. . . . Ella's voice and artistry are so personal, so inimitable, as to be quite unique in our time."[52] Of course "great art" status can cripple sales, yet the album remains a treasured connoisseur's item, one of the best in a decade that would see the rise of the classic jazz LP. Ella felt protective about the album, watching its sales. Over a year after its release, on August 16, 1952, in a live broadcast from Birdland, she said, "I'd like to put in a little plug" for the album, which despite the praise did not receive the sales she wanted and needed.[53]

★★★

AFTER *ELLA SINGS GERSHWIN*, Gabler returned to Decca's policy of promoting Fitzgerald primarily as a conventional singles artist, recording twenty-three titles in 1951. Only one, the scat vehicle "Smooth Sailing," made an impression on the charts.[54] Using Arnett Cobb's tenor saxophone solo from his 1950 recording as a springboard, she treated the twelve-bar blues as a song without words, adding a few Gillespie-speed bop flourishes starting in the third chorus. She was backed by Bill Doggett's Hammond organ, a fresh, funky sound for her, along with vocal accompaniment by the Ray Charles Singers (a polished and reliable white vocal quartet, no relation to the singer). "Smooth Sailing" would remain in her repertoire through the 1960s. Gabler followed through in January 1952 with two more scat vehicles: a retooling of the Benny Goodman hit "Airmail Special" and a lesser attempt, her own composition, "Rough Ridin'."

In October 1951 Fitzgerald renewed her contract with Decca Records for five years. Considering the market power of this major label, even the rumor of her defection to Mercury hinted at her discontent, as well as the impact of her work with Norman Granz through Jazz at the Philharmonic.[55] The ongoing competition between Gabler and Granz would intensify over the next several years, turning into a major battlefield over Fitzgerald's future. That irritating Granz kept buzzing failure at Gabler, who later stated:

> He was trying to get her away from us, because he was using her at the JATP concerts, and we wouldn't release her from her contract. He wanted to buy her contract, and I said, "I won't even tell the boss about your offer because I love her just as much as you do, Norman, forget it!"[56]

In December 1951 *Down Beat* reported that Mercury's jazz catalog "already boasts Norman Granz' entire line of JATP stars, excepting Ella Fitzgerald."[57] Moe Gale had her sign the restrictive Decca contract, even though his ties with the label had waned. Gale, at a transitional moment in his career, was expanding his operations with new clients, including white singers. Fitzgerald's role in this muddy negotiation remains unclear, since no comments from her have survived.

In 1952, with five more years on the line, Gabler tried to please Fitzgerald in various ways, striking a balance between her taste and his business sense. Besides aiming for hit singles, he built her catalog by pairing standards like "I Hadn't Anyone But You" and "That Old Feeling" with new ballads. These singles typically disappeared, despite *Billboard*'s consistent praise for both singer and producer, and predictions of solid sales from her loyal fan base. Sometimes Gabler chose swing singer standards such as Helen Ward's 1936 hit with Benny Goodman, "Goody Goody," which became one of Ella's personal favorites.

On other occasions Gabler accepted ballads that she brought to his attention, including "Angel Eyes" by Matt Dennis. Dennis recalled:

> I was playing in a little nightclub in Reno, Nevada, in 1951, around Christmas, and Ella came there, too, to perform at a hotel there, and Hank Jones was her accompanist at the time, a wonderful pianist. I played "Angel Eyes," which was still unpublished at the time, for her, and that was the first time she heard it. This was on a Monday, I think, and she was opening two days later on a Wednesday, and she said, "I'd like to open with that song, use it as my opening number." I said, "Of course!" So Hank Jones learned the song overnight. I went to her opening night, and she introduced me on the floor and said "I'm going to record this." That was very nice![58]

Fitzgerald recorded "Angel Eyes" with Sy Oliver's orchestra in June 1952, and Decca released it in the spring of 1953.[59] It failed in the marketplace. Despite favorable predictions for Fitzgerald's single in the trade press, a plug from Dorothy Kilgallen, and even an onscreen performance by Dennis himself in the feature film *Jennifer*, "Angel Eyes" did not make a big sales impression.[60] A review in the September *Metronome* read, "The best singer of them all gives it a truly musicianly, heartfelt once-over, soft, sincere, the kind of singing that others use for a sample when they're really trying."[61] But "Angel Eyes" would stay in her repertoire for decades.

Reviewers loved her Caribbean-styled version of "My Bonnie Lies Over the Ocean," which foreshadowed the mid-1950s calypso craze.

The record also echoed the urban folk revival, which Decca was spear-heading by signing Pete Seeger and the Weavers. But increasingly in 1952, the notices of praise and approval for Fitzgerald's work in the jazz press and *Billboard* gave way to complaints about Decca's handling of her. Chicago DJ Fred Reynolds wrote, "Altho[ugh] she enhances everything she sings, what a waste of talent it is to have her plugging away on some of the trash she's been given to do just because it sounds commercial."[62] *Down Beat*'s review of "Oops!" and "Necessary Evil," two duets with Louis Armstrong, described the tunes as "deplorable" duds from the bottom of "the novelty barrel."[63]

Fitzgerald was also reproached for her covers of hits by Doris Day and Jo Stafford. Why was Decca still pursuing the old strategy of making covers for the race market? When Decca put out the LP *Top Tunes by Top Artists*, with contributions from Louis Armstrong, Bing Crosby, and the Mills Brothers as well as Fitzgerald, *Billboard* critiqued the strategy: "It would seem that in turning out such packages a label would attempt to stay more current than several of these tunes are, particularly when the songs were established by competitive artists."[64] A *New York Times* review in 1952 stated:

> This reviewer's reverence for Ella Fitzgerald prevents him from saying any unkind words about her latest record, "Ding Dong Boogie" and "Preview" (Decca). The greatest jazz singer of our day can never make a truly bad record, but this one is, shall we say, uninspired. "Ding Dong" seems to be slanted straight toward the juke-boxes and may it prosper well there. It's still several hundred cuts above anything they've got.[65]

By the laws of fairness, Fitzgerald's recording of "Mr. Paganini" from that same session ought to have offered some redemption. The beloved novelty, which Fitzgerald treated as a souvenir of Chick Webb and her youth, was expanded to two sides of one disk, changing tempos and showing off her scat virtuosity with a quotation from "A-Tisket A-Tasket."[66] It was "a tour-de-force," said Sy Oliver's wife, Lillian, a vocalist with the Ray Charles Singers, yet the record slipped away without much attention, then and even now, as an outstanding version of one of her favorite novelties.

★★★

THE YEAR 1953 was a turning point in Fitzgerald's Decca output, which shrank to only eleven titles in four sessions. She may have been sidelined for a few months getting treatment for vocal problems, perhaps nodules on her vocal cords. Ever loyal, Milt Gabler tried to please her. On the February 13 session with Sy Oliver's orchestra, Gabler hired two of Chick Webb's former sidemen, the outstanding lead trumpeter Taft Jordan and bassist George Duvivier, to remake "Blue Lou," one of Edgar Sampson's notable arrangements for the Webb orchestra. Vocalizing an instrumental swing classic, she expanded her tribute to Webb with a vibrant scat section, most likely adding her own lyrics. Rating it 74 out of 100, in the "good" range, *Billboard* found her "straining somewhat" in the scat section while praising the "tremendous impact" of Sy Oliver's arrangement and predicting a strong response from her fan base in rhythm and blues.[67] On the same session, Gabler recorded "I Wonder What Kind of a Guy You'd Be," a conventional thirty-two-bar pop song with lyrics by Fitzgerald, which slid by the wayside.

"One for her, one for them" (alternation between Fitzgerald's choices and his own commercial responsibilities) kept Gabler on track in the next session on June 11, when he assigned her "Crying in the Chapel." This country tune was touted by *Jet* magazine as "the fastest selling song since the 1951 'Tennessee Waltz' craze," referring to Patti Page's defining hit of the era.[68] "Crying in the Chapel" was a new hit for the Orioles, and once again Fitzgerald's style sounded old-fashioned by comparison. For the recording, Gabler assembled a studio facsimile of a gospel backup group, with trumpeter Taft Jordan, organist Bill Doggett, drummer Jimmy Crawford, and the Ray Charles Singers.

Validating Gabler's commercial acumen, "Crying in the Chapel" became Fitzgerald's biggest chart success since her match with Louis Jordan in 1949.[69] She could still extract kudos from the jazz press, including *Metronome*, where Bill Coss described her singing as "humble" and "sincere."[70] The reviewer for *New Musical Express* followed suit:

> Two real tear-jerkers sung very commercially by one of the finest jazz singers. The subdued backing is by the great Sy Oliver—what a set-up for a couple of commercial pops! Ella does a remarkable job of restraining herself and proves that however ordinary the melody and lyrics of a tune might be, a true artist still tries to sing them sincerely.[71]

Gabler later reflected on Fitzgerald's country covers as a continuation of Decca's race-conscious strategies in place since the 1930s:

> She didn't like those songs, and neither did I. But that was a pretty big seller, a surprising one for Ella; it sold records, which was good for Ella and good for the company. She did very well when she did that kind of material, and we were reaching for the black market with those songs, like a crossover.[72]

As with "My Happiness," she could get "a good piece of the business," as Gabler put it.[73] Yet "Crying in the Chapel" was an end to a beginning, as her last entry on the rhythm and blues chart for the rest of the decade. Younger Black audiences and white teenagers preferred the Orioles' version, propelling it onto *Your Hit Parade*.

In retrospect, the five years from 1948 to 1953 mark a low point of Fitzgerald's history at Decca. "We tried them all," Gabler later said[74]—country and western spinoffs, rhythm and blues, vocal group backings, big band arrangements, children's tunes, novelties—in quest of the cover that could secure some leverage in the record market, steal airplay, and keep Decca's ledgers balanced, delivered through her voice that mellowed the categories. Her post–"How High the Moon" discography in these years chronicles adaptation and innovation, artistic success and commercial failure. While few titles reached the *Billboard*

charts, the songs she helped turn into standards included some outstanding records and several songs that she would return to later in her career.
The biggest surprise, perhaps, is that the one album she released stands
out among the best jazz LPs of the era, a tribute to her own ideals for
herself as well.

For a cover story in the October 1953 issue of *Metronome*, Fitzgerald
talked candidly with Bill Coss about her profession and her art, register-
ing her deep discontent. She acknowledged receiving "all this acclaim,
much more than any other jazz singer has had," yet "such great and consistent talent is too often thwarted by Decca." As for *Ella Sings Gershwin*,
Coss observed, "she says that it was the only chance that she has ever
had to record with arrangements that really matched her ideas."[75] This
at a time when the hit single was touted as the key to gold, luxe pop was
at a peak, and jazz albums remained a fringe item.[76]

Despite her frustrations, however, she and Decca were "in it together"
with three more years to go.

Chapter 13

EARLY YEARS WITH JAZZ AT THE PHILHARMONIC

(1949-1952)

I f Ella Fitzgerald had had to count on hit singles for her income in the early 1950s, she might have left the business. Instead, she relied on her touring career, working two circuits booked separately. Moe's brother Tim Gale, who ran his own agency, organized her usual mix of clubs and mostly Black theaters for fifteen to twenty weeks a year. Norman Granz, running Jazz at the Philharmonic, put her on the burgeoning arena-auditorium circuit for another twenty weeks or so.[1]

Fitzgerald attained significant national reach with her Gale bookings, including many dates in the notoriously volatile climate of jazz clubs. In her itineraries, historic clubs like Birdland in New York City and the Blue Note in Chicago recurred, along with lesser-known venues like Storyville in Boston, the Celebrity Club in Providence, the Nightcap in Newark, the Powelton Café in Philadelphia, the Merry-Land in Washington, D.C., the Ebony Lounge in Cleveland, and the Tiffany Club and the Club Oasis in Los Angeles. In the winter of 1949, her booking at the Monte Carlo in Miami attracted press attention because its owners, with Tim Gale's support, flouted Jim Crow by bringing Black entertainment to a new section of the city. *Variety* reported that Fitzgerald played to "almost empty houses," and the Monte Carlo was soon shuttered.[2]

"For over fifteen years," wrote jazz pianist Billy Taylor, "from its beginning late in 1949 until it eventually closed in 1965, Birdland was the most important answer to a dying 52nd Street."[3] Broadcasts from this iconic basement jazz club have so far yielded the main cache of recordings of Fitzgerald's American club work from the early 1950s. In four dates from 1950 to 1952 we hear her sparkling mix of oldies and current pop hits spiked by occasional scat numbers inspired by jazz instrumentals yielding virtuoso results. For the bebop classic "Lemon Drop," written by pianist George Wallington and popularized through a 1949 arrangement for Woody Herman's band, Fitzgerald sang the theme's long, convoluted phrases, then launched into her solo.[4] Her 1949 rendition at the Royal Roost included a humorous quote from "Yes Sir, That's My Baby," which reappeared at Birdland in August 1952. Fitzgerald would expand on "Lemon Drop" on a few memorable occasions in the 1970s and '80s.

The drummer Roy Haynes, part of her trio in the summer of 1952, recalled, "Ella Fitzgerald was a great musician and was very verbal about what she wanted from me." In the course of the 1950s, he backed Sarah Vaughan for five years and worked a few dates with Billie Holiday. Comparing this triumvirate, he said, "I think Ella Fitzgerald was the hardest to play with because she sang fast tempos and could scat sing, sometimes taking a hundred choruses."[5]

Another account of her performance practice came from an unsigned review in the *Chicago Defender*. In May 1950 Fitzgerald was performing in Los Angeles at the Club Oasis,[6] and the reviewer wrote a description of her singing, focusing on the importance she attached to reading an audience:

> The house was packed—with celebrities and ordinary Joes and Janes. The applause had been heavy and sincerely appreciative: She had to do four or five encores. When it was all over, she wasn't flush with the feeling of another conquest. Rather she was "worried."

"I didn't know what to sing," Miss Fitzgerald said. "I was so nervous. I wonder if they liked me—you know, they like different songs in different cities. . . ."

"Oh, Ella," a female writer and fan said, "you're always so modest. You know you're good, why don't you just go on and act like it?"

Ella allowed as how that wasn't natural with her. And, that's another "in" to the "why" she stands so high. She's natural in her singing; when it appears that she's having fun, which is all the time, she's having fun. It's never just another appearance before a bunch of yokels.[7]

Behind the presence of naturalness stood fifteen years of adaptation and innovation. Her stage shows at prominent New York venues recycled hits from mainstream pop as needed. In March 1950, earning $3,800 for a week at the Paramount Theatre in midtown on a bill with Mel Tormé, she pleased the family crowd on school vacations with the novelty hit "If I Knew You Were Comin' I'd've Baked a Cake."[8] At the Apollo and at Detroit's Fox Theatre, she entertained mostly Black audiences with a parody of "Into Each Life Some Rain Must Fall," her Decca collaboration with the Ink Spots.[9] With the most diverse repertoire in the business, if an audience did not respond, whose fault other than hers could it be? Her aesthetic values stayed in place, as did her chronic anxiety.

★★★

IN FEBRUARY 1949 Fitzgerald began a new phase in her career by officially joining the all-star ensemble Jazz at the Philharmonic. Ray Brown, who joined JATP in 1947, said that Norman Granz "used to be after me all the time to get her to come with Jazz at the Philharmonic, and after a couple of years she finally did it."[10] It seemed like merely a lateral career move, but it was the beginning of a transformative relationship for both of them, and over time it would become a historic partnership, changing not only her career and her life but the course of American vocal jazz.

Born in 1918 to a poor Russian Jewish immigrant family, Norman Granz learned Yiddish as his first language. He grew up in three southern California communities, each with its own demographic. He lived first near Central Avenue, the main thoroughfare for the Black community, then in mostly white areas, mainly Long Beach. During high school, he lived in Boyle Heights, a Los Angeles community with a large Jewish population as well as Asian and Latino Americans—not unlike New York's Lower East Side. As an intense, intellectually curious teenager, he absorbed the neighborhood's leftist political values.[11] His close friend, Archie Green, the distinguished folklorist and labor historian, told Granz's biographer Tad Hershorn that they shared "New Deal culture," ranging from the all-Black productions of the Federal Theater Project to the liberal small magazines like the *Nation* and the *Atlantic Monthly* that they read at the public library.[12]

Living in Los Angeles, Granz was exposed to American popular songs more through Hollywood film singers than through Broadway stage stars. As he recounted to Hershorn, Granz adored the film musicals produced in their golden age, singling out *Top Hat*, which he saw twenty times in high school.[13] This 1935 film featured Fred Astaire tap dancing to Irving Berlin's songs with the aplomb of a jazz percussionist, and singing "I'm steppin' out my dear / To breathe an atmosphere / That simply reeks with class" in the title song.[14] "Class" fueled Granz's ambitious drive to become rich as fast as possible. Studying economics and philosophy at UCLA from 1939 to 1942, he worked his way through school in a punishing routine of jobs. Clerking at a stock brokerage firm, he was fired for being a "jew-boy" at a high point of anti-Semitism in the United States.[15]

At UCLA Granz became a jazz fan, then a "participant-observer" in the jazz life of African American musicians in Los Angeles. From 1930 to 1940, L.A.'s Black community doubled; its newcomers expanding what was already a thriving musical life amid severe segregation.[16] In the words of cultural historian Douglas Flamming, "At any given

moment, the community was only half-free and locked in struggle—
fighting to maintain and extend basic human rights."[17] This struggle
had its counterparts in the world of jazz. As a white man, Granz chose
the role of middleman, or mediator of a racial divide, brokering the
talent of Black musicians into Hollywood's parallel white world of
live entertainment. In his twenties, his passion for jazz earned him the
friendship of several African American musicians, among them pianist-
singer Nat King Cole, drummer Lee Young, and Lee's older brother,
tenor saxophonist Lester Young, all of whom appeared in the first jazz
concert Granz produced—a Sunday-afternoon jam session at the Trouville Club in June 1942.[18]

At this turning point in Granz's career, Fitzgerald entered it through
coincidence. Just when Granz needed out-of-town musicians to supplement the Trouville gig, she and her orchestra were playing the Trianon
Ballroom in South Gate, Los Angeles, and he hired her lead trumpeter,
Taft Jordan, and her clarinetist, Eddie Barefield. "I never used Ella," Granz
said later. "In those days I never dug Ella."[19] "Norman used to use all your
musicians out of the band," the jazz critic Leonard Feather remarked to
Ella in 1987. "That's right," she replied. "He'd never ask me in. That's
funny."[20] Maybe she was too vaudeville for him. At the Trianon, she and
Barefield even did "a bit of terping [dancing] that gets plenty of laughs,"
according to a *Billboard* reviewer.[21] At the Trouville, nobody danced, as
Granz insisted on arranging the tables for listening only.

The Trouville date established Granz's strategy of using jazz as a gateway for civil rights activism, a sociological strategy to combat segregation. Inspired by the activism of Black leaders like A. Philip Randolph
during the war, Granz pursued policies of radical resistance to racism.
While the club's owner, Billy Berg, had set a precedent by hiring Black
musicians, he still barred Black patrons—a situation Granz called "an
aberration."[22] Granz insisted on mixed-race seating, a policy he would
pursue for the rest of his career. At stake was equality of access to public accommodations, a right that would not be universally established
legally until the Civil Rights Act of 1964. Ahead were battlefronts across
the United States that he could not have imagined.

The Trouville event was a huge success. When Granz was drafted two months later, the *Los Angeles Sentinel*, a Black newspaper, sent him off with a fanfare as "the extremely likeable ofay" who could sponsor a jam session better than anyone else,

> and has made a place in our hearts because he has a thorough understanding of racial problems and not just in theory. His has been an almost one-man campaign in the Hollywood spots to practice democracy and stop preaching it. So the next time you walk into the Trouville, and you are immediately seated and served at the best available table in the house, drink an audible toast to Norman Grant [*sic*] of the United States Army, a friend we can ill-afford to lose.[23]

After receiving a medical discharge from the army in May 1943, Granz returned to running jam sessions at several clubs and a small hall in a Black neighborhood in L.A.'s Westside. His next business step would have a far-reaching impact. On July 2, 1944, he produced a jazz concert in downtown Los Angeles at the three-thousand-seat Philharmonic Auditorium, which had been home to the city's symphony orchestra since 1920. The concert featured all-star personnel on an eclectic swing-to-bop bill. When a printer's error on the program poster shortened "Jazz at the Philharmonic Auditorium" to "Jazz at the Philharmonic," Granz found his brand. The concert was a fundraiser for a civil rights cause célèbre: an effort to overturn the verdicts of the Sleepy Lagoon murder case, in which seventeen Mexican American youths were convicted in a travesty of justice.[24]

It took Granz a couple of years to put JATP on a solid footing, but by 1947 it was a top-grossing concert package with a stellar roster including Coleman Hawkins, Buck Clayton, Willie Smith, Trummy Young, Buddy Rich, and occasionally Illinois Jacquet and Flip Phillips.[25] The demise of many big bands around the end of World War II had left no shortage of top swing musicians looking for work. In 1947, inspired by the activism of Actors' Equity Association in the theater world, Granz exhorted bandleaders across the music industry to adopt a uniform anti-discrimination clause in their contracts with venue operators. The initiative failed because the music business needed the South to survive. But Granz received moral support for his efforts, especially in the Black press.[26] In May he was profiled in the NAACP publication *The Crisis*, which quoted his idealistic liberal rhetoric:

> Jazz is America's own. It is the music which grew out of a young and vigorous melting-pot nation. It is a product of all America, deriving much of its inspiration and creation from the Negro people. . . . Jazz is truly the music of democratic America. It is an ideal medium for bringing about a better understanding among all peoples.[27]

Fitzgerald encountered Granz mainly because of Ray Brown. Perhaps she had met Granz earlier, but in November 1947, she attended a JATP concert in Akron, Ohio, to visit her fiancé—and unintentionally stopped the show. When Granz introduced her in the audience, the audience clapped her right onto the stage. "People started clapping so it was unavoidable," Granz remembered. "I would normally not have done it, in deference to the singer I had, a great blues singer. And I don't know whether Ella was comfortable doing it either, because it was interfering with another artist, and they were friends on top of that."[28] He was talking about Helen Humes, Basie's former singer and the first vocalist to join JATP as a regular touring member, whom he hired the year before. Humes became "'the real phenomenon' of 1945–1946," Granz wrote in JATP's program book, and "an unrecognized singer of real merit."[29] The genial ex–Basie singer sang blues in a light, cultivated voice filled with amiable irony. In 1947 Mercury had just released her "Jet Propelled Papa," which she was singing on tour.

It was an awkward moment that Fitzgerald compressed into a long misleading sentence decades later: "People kept applauding and told me to sing, because Helen Humes was singing with the group then. The next thing I know I was with Norman."[30] Not quite. In 1948 Granz enlisted Sarah Vaughan for a substantial spring tour emphasizing bebop with a group that included Charlie Parker, Miles Davis, and Max Roach.

★★★

"AND NOW IT GIVES ME GREAT PLEASURE to introduce the greatest thing in jazz today, Miss Ella Fitzgerald," Granz said at her JATP debut on February 11, 1949, in Carnegie Hall.[31] He would repeat this phrase for the next eight years, and she would flourish in a context that facilitated her genius. The JATP mix of swing-to-bop artists echoed her own fluid approach to jazz. With Dizzy Gillespie's crew she had faced skepticism, but the JATP rosters included friends and admiring colleagues such as Coleman Hawkins, Buddy Rich, and her onetime lodger Lester Young.

Through JATP, Fitzgerald could carve out a special role for a jazz-woman in midcentury America. In the jam session finales, as the only woman onstage, she attracted special comment for her role challenging the caste system subordinating singers to instrumentalists. She also brought tremendous drawing power, no matter who else came and went in JATP's roster. At the same time, Granz extended her reach to mass audiences, which challenged her image as "Apollo's girl," as mentioned in *Time* in 1950, which described her "gently rasping voice" as standing "halfway between jungle wail and a jukebox jangle."[32]

Instead of the Apollo and other venues in movie houses with stage shows, JATP played jazz in arenas, auditoriums, and concert halls. It attracted diverse audiences whom Granz described as mostly Black, Italian, and Jewish, and often overwhelmingly loud.[33] The so-called Silent Generation of the Eisenhower era made a lot of noise before rock 'n' roll arrived. A few months after her Carnegie Hall debut, JATP played Boston's venerable Symphony Hall. "It would be a complete understatement to say it was a wildly enthusiastic audience," a reviewer wrote. "It was a constant race to see who would make the loudest noise, the audience or the musicians."[34] That image would cling to JATP concerts like lint, as critics attacked JATP musicians for using showboat techniques and creating an atmosphere too close to a mob scene.

At her JATP debut in Carnegie Hall in February 1949, Fitzgerald, backed by drummer Shelly Manne and her regulars Hank Jones and Ray Brown, sang two sets totaling nine numbers on a long bill that included Charlie Parker and Machito's Afro-Cubans orchestra.[35] She wanted this new audience to get to know her history, so she chose "I Got a Guy," introduced with Chick Webb in 1937; two Dizzy Gillespie–era hits, "Robbin's Nest" and "Ool-Ya-Koo"; and her new bop tune "Old Mother Hubbard." The sold-out eleven p.m. concert received scant press attention, and the *Down Beat* review by Mike Levin slighted it, obsessing about the disruptive audience.[36] The ballad "I've Got My Love to Keep Me Warm" was the only one of Ella's numbers that evening to survive into her later performances. She graced the melody with such a playful paraphrase that an arrangement in her 1958 *Irving Berlin Song Book* could not compete.

On the coast-to-coast tour of twenty-one cities from February 11 to March 31, reviews suggest Ella was finding her groove in bopping, or "vobopping," as one reviewer labeled it. Another reported that she "joined saxophonist Flip Phillips in an uproarious rendition of 'Perdido,'" with "her amusingly clever travesty on the 'bopping' idiom."[37] In Detroit, she worked up a duet called "Ella's Boogie" with trombonist Tommy Turk.[38] In St. Louis, she "came through with her sensational vobopping on 'Flying Home,' 'How High the Moon,' 'Robbin's Nest' and 'Perdido.'"[39]

The fall tour of JATP of fifty cities in twenty-nine states further strengthened her role as JATP's star. A recording from September 18, 1949 (not released for decades), is the only commercially available documentation of her work with JATP before 1953: it shows the pleasure and freedom she enjoyed in this new environment.[40] Backed by Hank Jones on piano, Ray Brown on bass, and Buddy Rich on drums, she sang an exceptional repertoire, including a very slow, sensual version of the Duke Ellington ballad "I'm Just a Lucky So-and-So"; George Gershwin's "Somebody Loves Me," which she treated as an exquisite miniature; an Armstrong impersonation on "Basin Street Blues"; and her usual bop vocals. In the finale of "Perdido," after solos by Charlie Parker and Tommy Turk, she stepped up for two choruses, offering what jazz theorist Tom Cleary has called a "dazzling example of melodic grace under the pressure of a rowdy audience."[41]

Fitzgerald added lyrics that generously plugged the forthcoming soloist, Flip Phillips, who was identified with the tune ("So blow, blow, Phillips, blow"). The mere mention of his name triggered his fans, but she kept on. Crowd noise was the focus once again in a *Down Beat* review by John S. Wilson, the future *New York Times* critic: "Despite the fact she seemed to have no face (due to the overhanging mike) and the constant uproar of her clients . . . Ella, of course, could be sunk in a well and she'd still sound good." Perhaps because she was a woman onstage, he compared the disrupters to "the old strip house habitues or, in the apt phrase of E. Y. Harburg, sons of habitues, and they're still attending the same orgiastic rites."[42]

In 1950 Fitzgerald toured with a smaller JATP ensemble in which Oscar Peterson also gained prominence. But she was the JATP star who provoked the most audience frenzy, raising the bar for jazz vocalists. A reviewer in Dayton, Ohio, wrote:

> You've got to hand it to Ella Fitzgerald . . . The boys with the horns were supposed to get most of the attention at Memorial Hall Thursday. . . . They were good; wonderful, in fact; but it was the hefty Ella who completely stole the show. And when you "cut" fellows like Coleman Hawkins, Oscar Peterson, Buddy Rich, Flip Phillips, Bill Harris, Lester Young and the bunch, you've done something. . . . The enthusiastic throng wouldn't let her leave the stage. She was it.[43]

Fitzgerald stayed "it," no matter who else came and went. The fall tour for 1951, with its arduous itinerary of forty-eight concerts in thirty-nine cities over ten weeks, found Fitzgerald with new colleagues noted for their stage-stealing showmanship: drummer Gene Krupa, tenor saxophonist Illinois Jacquet, and trumpeter Roy Eldridge. Even so, Fitzgerald frequently eclipsed them in newspaper reviews with such comments as "It was a good show, but Ella stole it," or "She was by far the standout," or "Singer Brings Gems of Songs," as if she were a solo artist.[44] In San Antonio, Fitzgerald and her friend Illinois Jacquet turned "Flying Home" into a competitive dialogue.[45] She learned to manage crowds. *Variety* praised her for taming them, noting that she "delivered her numbers in top form against great odds. The kids were yelling for the bop and scat numbers, but Miss Fitzgerald succeeded in quieting them somewhat with her ballads."[46]

What JATP offered was collegiality among musicians who spoke a common language and thrived through improvisational conversation. In 1950 Granz collaborated with the filmmaker and photographer Gjon Mili on a film about JATP. The film was unfinished, but surviving soundless footage shows Fitzgerald sitting among a quintet of players. Her face glows with concentrated pleasure as she scats her way into the session with a tune called "Blues for Greasy," probably intended as the jam session finale. She remains shadowed on the edge of the screen and enters somewhat shyly, taking four scat choruses. Even without sound, the clip captures a visual analogue of her vocal plasticity. No matter that Flip Phillips, whose "Perdido" she colonized, felt territorial, interrupting her twice, the second time successfully.[47]

Once she was onstage, her shyness left, as Oscar Peterson recounted in his loving memoir:

> Lester Young used to sidle up to me in the wings with his taste [alcohol] in one hand, the other holding his bottom lip with an aghast stare on his face, listen for a couple of choruses, take my arm, grunt, and say, "Sis is kicking ass out there tonight, ain't she, Lady P? Lester better go get his horn and get ready for the finale and things." . . .
>
> Fitz continued on her merry way unperturbed by anything or anyone. She sauntered through her show each evening with that same imperturbable musical confidence. On the finale each night, she courageously took on the front line horns, regardless of who they were. . . . Ella traded fours, eights, sixteens, or whatever they

wanted with them and never got hurt. As a matter of fact, on various nights when some of the horns got a smidgen careless, Fitz would run up over them and keep right on going.

"I told you about getting too sporty out there with Lady Fitz," Pres [Young] reminded Flip Phillips one night when he decided to stay at the mike and "fairground" as Pres put it.

"Geez," muttered Flip in disbelief, "I didn't think she'd get that rough!"

"Rough?" repeated Pres in sarcasm. "You stay out there long enough and Lady Fitz will really lay waste to your ass! Lester knows better. Lester lets Lady Fitz sing her little four-bar song, then Lester plays his four-bar song, and then Goodnight Irene. Lester's through!"[48]

★★★

To an outsider looking at the bond between Ella Fitzgerald and Ray Brown, she seemed to have struck an enviable balance between love and work. An April 1950 cover photo in Metronome by Herman Leonard showed a contented artist basking in the devotion of Ray, who was described inside as "her personal representative and husband"; a sidebar read, "big love: husband ray brown."[49] In 1951 the pair bought a larger home at 179-07 Murdock Avenue in St. Albans, Queens, a step or two up from East Elmhurst. But they were struggling to make a life together, and marital difficulties were rumored in the Black press. In June 1951 the New York Amsterdam News published a story about their "much-discussed long threatened breakup." It's unclear how much credence to give to maudlin details about Ella crying between sets and "a few of her thousands of friends coming back stage to pat her on the shoulder."[50]

Ray was "unavailable for comment," perhaps because he was touring with the virtuoso Canadian pianist Oscar Peterson and slowly disentangling himself from his wife's career. Peterson had joined JATP in the fall of 1949—a hiring that Ella had helped promote—and quickly became a major attraction. Ray Brown and Oscar Peterson formed a marvelous duo—their personal as well as musical affinity surfaced almost immediately—and their 1950 recordings made a splash in the jazz world, particularly an innovative version of "Tenderly." Peterson asked Brown to tour as a duo, but "Ray hesitated, because of his marriage," then "agreed to try it for awhile."[51] How long could a musician of Brown's gifts content himself with a background role in a singer's rhythm section? With the later addition of guitarist Barney Kessel to form the Oscar Peterson Trio, Brown would solidify his artistic partnership in one of the great chamber ensembles in twentieth-century jazz.

Ray admired Ella, as Virginia Wicks pointed out—how could he not have?—but "Ella was very aware that he was younger and very attractive and a wonderful musician."[52] The jazz organist Sarah McLawler, a casual friend of Ella's, witnessed a fray that ended with an imperative from wife to husband: "You're not going anywhere!"[53] But that was exactly the point: he was considering exit strategies with Peterson, and there was no denying that the marriage was in a slow demise. On August 11, 1951, on a bill with Duke Ellington at the Fox Theatre in Detroit, Fitzgerald almost fell apart.

> I was torching for my ex-husband and Duke told me . . . it's just like a toothache, it hurts. But when you take the tooth out, you miss the tooth but it won't hurt. You'll miss it but . . . It was so funny because I was getting ready to go on stage, and when he said it, I was getting ready to cry. And he said, "No, not now."[54]

Ellington was known as an incorrigible ladies' man, but she took his message of emotional discipline as wisdom. She got through the evening, winning "unanimous plaudits" according to *Variety*'s review.[55]

In the fall of 1951, more rumors made the papers. "Nobody knows what cooks with Ella Fitzgerald and her husband, Ray Brown," wrote Dorothy Kilgallen in her syndicated column in October. "One minute they are solid, next minute they are nowhere."[56] That same month Ella's old friend Izzy Rowe wrote in the *Pittsburgh Courier*, "The Ella Fitzgerald romance is off again, as she and hubby Ray Brown have decided that it's just not to be. It's particularly tough since he's with 'Jazz at the Philharmonic' too and they're thrown together even though they aren't speaking."[57] Three months later Rowe provided an update: "Ella Fitzgerald is beaming as she displays the ten-carat sparkler which hubby Ray Brown put in her Christmas glove announcing to the world that the six month's separation is over and he's back home to stay."[58]

The timing was propitious. Two months later Jazz at the Philharmonic embarked on its first European tour. A previously planned tour scheduled for March 1951 had been canceled, partly because, as *Variety* reported, Granz and Fitzgerald were in a "money wrangle" with her manager, Moe Gale.[59] With these issues sorted out, Granz could hardly wait to cross the pond and demonstrate the power of JATP's music in seven European countries. "Jazz at the Philharmonic is finally coming to Europe," announced *Melody Maker*.[60] On March 26, 1952, as JATP departed for Stockholm, a photograph captured its maiden voyage at the airport. Standing in front of the SAS plane were Ella and Georgiana Henry, her personal assistant, waving along with the JATP troupe that was about to conquer the Old World.

Chapter 14

EUROPE WITH JAZZ AT THE PHILHARMONIC

(1952–1953)

Ella Fitzgerald welcomed JATP's 1952 European tour as a new adventure. Back in 1948 she and Ray Brown, about a year into their marriage, had performed abroad in England on a virtual honeymoon trip. But back then she had been singing her Decca hits. This tour, she said later, was "one of my most exciting . . . this was more jazz."[1]

In March 1952, when Granz announced that his long-anticipated European tour was "finally going to happen," jazz was already "conquering" a continent eager to leave the war years behind, and jazz magazines were running stories about Europe-bound American musicians "getting into the act."[2] Through JATP, his record labels, and now his European touring, Granz was poised to become "a major catalyst" for what would soon be termed mainstream: small-group jazz occupying the space between swing and bebop.[3] JATP's annual tour would become a perennial fixture on the European jazz concert scene, continuing for the next sixteen years.

The historic European debut tour would last less than a month, but Granz piled on the dates. JATP gave fourteen concerts in seven days in Sweden and Denmark, closed a major jazz festival in Paris, and country-hopped with four dates in Holland, one in Brussels, two in Switzerland,

and two in West Germany.[4] Sweden was a great place to begin. Because the country had remained neutral during the war, it had maintained shipping contact with the United States, enabling Swedish musicians to keep up with American musical developments. Innovative jazz had caught on to such an extent that Dizzy Gillespie's 1948 Swedish tour had ten city stops.[5] By the time JATP arrived, Sweden arguably had Europe's most thriving jazz culture.[6]

"Daddy-O, it was the most," reported Ella Fitzgerald,[7] who had already contributed to vocal jazz in Sweden through her swing singer recordings. They made a deep impression on the country's foremost popular singer, Alice Babs, who would later collaborate with Duke Ellington. In her 1940 hit movie *Swing It, Magistern!* (Swing It, Teacher), Babs—who was seven years younger than Fitzgerald—evoked the girlish charm of "A-Tisket A-Tasket" on the title song and scatted a bit as well. As her daughter Titti Sjöblom recalled, "Mother was light years ahead of the others, and early to catch up with the American jazz."[8] At JATP's Stockholm concert, Babs came to greet her idol, who presented elegant arrangements of standards with Ray Brown and pianist Hank Jones.

Instead of praising Fitzgerald's bebop, as one might have expected, Swedish reviewers highlighted the ballad "Body and Soul." "Getting those simple lyrics to sound like love poetry demanded an artist of the highest class. . . . Ella sang the melody with true empathy," wrote a Swedish reviewer.[9]

After Copenhagen, JATP arrived in Paris on April 6. French esteem for Fitzgerald had deep roots. Django Reinhardt, the virtuoso "Gypsy" guitarist widely considered Europe's greatest jazz improviser, had recorded her early Decca repertoire in 1939. (He would even record the indestructible "A-Tisket A-Tasket" in 1950.) His vocalist, the child star Beryl Davis, later said, "I learned everything from Ella's records, and being so young, I was fearless."[10] After the war, Eddie Barclay, later a major French music producer, reported in 1948 from his music shop in Paris that Ella was one of only four "American singers who mean something, along with Bing Crosby, Frank Sinatra, and Billie Holiday."[11]

Most important, the French adored Louis Armstrong, and their Decca duet "Dream a Little Dream of Me," circulating in France by 1950, had become a particular favorite. In a 1951 poll by the French magazine *Jazz Hot*, Fitzgerald and Armstrong landed in first place for vocals.[12]

JATP, on its 1952 tour, was in Paris for Le Salon du Jazz, a ten-day festival commonly known as the Paris Jazz Fair. It would be Fitzgerald's first appearance in the French capital, at a time when the jazz audience was expanding from connoisseurs, intellectuals, and "bearded, duffle-coated left-bank youth," as *Life* described them, to the mass public. International jazz fairs reflected this trend, starting at Nice in 1948. The 1952 fair in Paris expanded the festivities to include jazz movies, lectures, and exhibits, booking Sidney Bechet for fans of traditional New Orleans jazz, Dizzy Gillespie for the avant-garde, and JATP for the mainstream middle. *Life* sent over a crew for a photo essay on "le jazz hot," comparing the enthusiasm of French youth for jazz to Sinatra worship in the early 1940s and singling out Gillespie and Fitzgerald as the hits of the fair.[13]

Fitzgerald also charmed prominent Parisian intellectuals, among them Boris Vian, an influential novelist, critic, and musician.[14] A frequent contributor to jazz journals and a habitué of Paris's avant-garde circles, Vian wrote: "The three great moments of my life had to be the concerts of Ellington in 1938, Dizzy in '48, and Ella in '52."[15] A private tape circulating among collectors preserves the JATP performance at the Salle Pleyel before two thousand people. Tidal waves of applause follow every song in Fitzgerald's set, and murmurs of recognition greet "How High the Moon" and "Lady Be Good." An imitation of Louis Armstrong in "Frim Fram Sauce" brought knowing laughter along with cheers. New material included the Gershwin standard "Somebody Loves Me." For "Body and Soul," she improvised a haunting cadenza just before the end. "She had the audience in the palm of her hand," wrote Mike Nevard of *Melody Maker*. "Here the rhythm section, backing her, stopped, and she lingered on the words, 'I'd gladly surrender myself to you, body and soul,' repeating them; dwelling on them. The audience was still as death."[16]

★★★

IN POSTWAR EUROPE, each country had its own cultural relationship with jazz. JATP rounded off its tour with two dates in Frankfurt, at a time when West Germans were struggling with their collective responsibility for Nazism in a process termed *Vergangenheitsbewältigung*, meaning "coming to terms with the past." For German jazz enthusiasts, jazz concerts had the potential to exorcise hateful Nazi propaganda epitomized in the infamous 1938 *Entartete Musik* (Degenerate Music) exhibition in Düsseldorf, with its oft-reprinted poster of a minstrelized blackface saxophone player wearing a yellow Jewish badge. The larger German public received jazz with far more ambivalence, resistance, and confusion. Werner Burkhardt, a future concert producer, said, "I am still grateful that the great Black jazz musicians—Ella and Louis, Oscar Peterson and not least Lionel Hampton—came to Germany so early. This was still complicated, by no means self-evident terrain for jazz musicians, who were mostly Blacks or Jews."[17]

In the early 1950s, Frankfurt was perhaps the most jazz-conscious German city. The Frankfurt Hot Club sponsored the first JATP concert. Its founder had gone to prison after being caught listening to jazz on the radio.[18] For a German populace still reeling from the war to encounter American jazz in halls historically dedicated to Beethoven required an emotional pivot. "The jazz audience was jubilant with pleasure," wrote the critic in the *Frankfurter Abendpost*, juxtaposing the sacred and the profane. "The international language of music gained a wild, dynamic force. As the experience of a Beethoven symphony leads the listener to the gates of eternity, jazz pushes man in front of the disconsolate doors of a cheap hotel of feelings." Perhaps in spite of himself, swayed by the virtuosity of JATP, he added, "The U.S. stars provoke the most remote points of jazz with masterly, often ice-cold perfection. The headshaking of the skeptics no longer carries weight. For the most attractive disease of our days [probably depression], jazz that night offered a consolation, if not a cure."[19]

JATP continued on to give an in-house concert for American troops stationed at the nearby Rhein-Main Air Base, and a benefit concert for patients at the 97th General Army Hospital. By the time JATP flew home, Granz was triumphant—the tour had secured his status as the country's most prominent and successful jazz impresario. He thanked the Scandinavians for their hospitality, praised the Belgians as "the hippest" audience, and chided the French as the noisiest. He appreciated that European fans had "contented themselves with waiting for 'How High the Moon' and 'Lady Be Good'" and showed taste in appreciating Fitzgerald's ballad singing. But he singled out for disapproval the "shrill requests" that often marred Fitzgerald's ballads "in the U.S. from that impatient few that (a) try to show how hip they are; or (b) have had poor upbringing."[20] His ire at rude interruptions of his star singer would worsen over the years.

★★★

IN THE FEW MONTHS between the JATP's European tour and U.S. tour in September 1952, Fitzgerald was occupied with bookings from Moe Gale—which included sixty-one cities. She knew her crowd and, as *Variety* reported, "didn't make last year's mistake of delivering too many ballads." While she incorporated Jo Stafford's summer hit "You Belong to Me," she concentrated on "sock" numbers including "Airmail Special," "Why Don't You Do Right?" and "St. Louis Blues." The tour package included drum battles between Buddy Rich and Gene Krupa, which likewise raised the musical temperature.[21]

JATP's national tour launched at Carnegie Hall with two packed shows in one evening, grossing $21,000. When Granz introduced "the great Billie Holiday" as a surprise guest, Oscar Peterson recalled, "the audience went berserk and gave her a standing ovation." Fitzgerald supported Holiday's guest appearance, but Peterson was surprised at Granz's "inexplicable" lack of courtesy in adding Holiday to the bill.[22] Peterson accompanied Holiday's first set, which he later described as "magnificent . . . a thing of beauty."[23] But her second set never got past the opening bars. Backstage, Holiday had taken enough heroin to precipitate a total collapse, which Ella witnessed firsthand.[24] Years later Tony Bennett named Fitzgerald's disciplined avoidance of the drug plague as a reason for her professional success.

On the road again, Fitzgerald got her usual plaudits in out-of-town reviews, although an Omaha paper took a sly dig that she "swung her weight around in a group of classic vocals."[25] Home for a few weeks around Christmas, she had a throat operation to remove nodules on her vocal cords, a common condition typically caused by overuse and stress. It kept her out of work until the end of January, when she made her debut at the jazz club Storyville. A reviewer from the *Harvard Crimson* assured the world that "her voice had lost nothing."[26]

★★★

EARLY IN 1953, JATP returned to Europe for its second tour, giving fifty concerts in thirty cities, this time including stops in Rome and London. The London concerts on March 8 were a personal triumph for Granz, who according to *Down Beat* became "the first American to present a jazz group in England in 18 years."[27] JATP performed at a benefit for recent flood victims on Britain's east coast; by covering all the expenses, he bypassed the Ministry of Labour's embargo on American musicians. The expert British jazz press lavished attention on their heroes, and photographers captured a rare assemblage of jazz women. In one photo, Ella stands with her hands characteristically folded in a proper position. Standing next to her is Adelaide Hall. Perhaps they reminisced about sharing the stage in the 1933 benefit for the Yonkers Federation of Negro Clubs. Also photographed were the renowned pianist and arranger Mary Lou Williams and the "Chi Chi Girl" Rose Murphy, whose comic delivery of ballads was spoofed by Ella in "I Can't Give You Anything But Love."[28]

Fitzgerald received the usual splendid reviews for her updated set, which was weighted toward rhythm and blues material ("St. Louis Blues," "Why Don't You Do Right?") along with vintage standards ("Imagination," "The Man I Love") and some vocal jams. In an interview with the British magazine *New Musical Express*, she conveyed her characteristic mix of worry, ambition, and total preoccupation with music. "Did you know I wrote songs? Latest one's called 'I Wonder What Kind of a Guy You'd Be.' Recorded it four weeks ago with Sy Oliver's Orchestra." Then she reflected on the concert. "My throat's so sore, and I'm afraid they didn't like it. But I really feel in a creative mood and if there'd been time, I'd have liked you to have heard 'Blue Lou.' "[29] She was working hard on this tune, a tribute and update to the classic Chick Webb instrumental. JATP guitarist Barney Kessel remembered,

> When we were touring Switzerland, instead of gossiping with the rest of the troupe on the bus, she and I would get together and she'd take some tune like "Blue Lou" and sing it every way in the world. She would try to exhaust every possibility, as if she were trying to develop improvisation to a new point by ad-libbing lyrically too, the way calypso singers do.[30]

Of all her colleagues on the tour, Oscar Peterson became her most devoted friend and admirer, notwithstanding his deep friendship with Ray Brown. "Were someone to ask me to choose my favorite Ella period, I would have to name the early 1950s as one of the strongest contenders," he later wrote. "Those nights of awed listening are as fresh in my memory as yesterday."[31] Since Hank Jones had failed to appear at the airport, Peterson was also thrust into the role of her accompanist.

In Sweden, she felt slighted when Oscar walked by her table without saying hello. She confronted him, furious, and Oscar said, "If you want to have this out, let's take it outside." In fact, he was suffering from his own case of nerves, worrying that she was displeased with his playing. Ella reassured him and told him, "Why, I even went out and picked out something real nice that I wanted to give you in order to say thanks."[32] Then ensued a mutually tearful reconciliation.

The March 13, 1953, performance for Swiss radio in Lausanne was a remarkable demonstration of Fitzgerald and Peterson's musical bond, aided by Ray Brown, drummer J. C. Heard, and guitarist Barney Kessel. The richness of Peterson's classically trained keyboard technique—all that big sound without any percussive backlash—and the rich harmonies enhancing every opening—freshened the frames of the standards. In breathtaking tempos, they dispatched Harold Arlen's "It's Only a Paper Moon" in two minutes, and then pared a minute from the Decca recording of "Lady Be Good." Finally a spectacular, four-minute treatment of "St. Louis Blues" upstaged everything else.

Expanding on her long history with W. C. Handy's classic, Ella sensuously heated up the opening twelve-bar choruses, while Oscar pounded out burlesque riffs on the piano. For a Latin-tinged "tango" chorus, she put castanets in her voice. At the start of the fourth chorus they doubled the tempo, and Ella delivered the classic blues lyrics with an R&B feel. Surprising perhaps everybody, she let out a screamer on a long note, which unlocked the door to a bopping scat. The whole was a thrilling exploration of modernist jazz singing.

JATP's reception in Germany was the highlight of the 1953 European tour, both for its musical triumph and for the context in which it occurred. Once again, among Germans, jazz evoked shame and hope. As Werner Burkhardt explained:

> Jazz was the first message of a completely new democracy. And the participation of the Germans—especially the young people—in this music was connected with a feeling of liberation. At last, you could hear again things that were forbidden before. What provoked so much enthusiasm about the musicians who still came

from swing at the time was the directness, passion and bluntness of their expression: that someone played in a one-to-one correspondence of who they were.[33]

What people found in the performances depended on what they sought. Reviewing JATP's Hamburg concert on February 27, a writer for the respected newspaper *Die Welt*, who had survived the Allied bombings and had been a fan for decades, remarked that "A-Tisket A-Tasket, I lost my yellow basket" was "one of the few records that I have mourned the loss of through a malicious bomb one night." Yet he insulted her: "They call her the 'Queen of Jazz'—but . . . the Queen was more like a good fat Negro mammy from *Uncle Tom's Cabin*." His putdown was the exception to the generally respectful praise elsewhere. A review of the same concert in the *Frankfurter Allgemeine Zeitung* said she handled both ballads like "Body and Soul" and bebop with a "smooth and warm voice."[34] A British critic on the scene described the audience as "lovers of music and plenty of it sitting spellbound. I admired too, the effortless way she sang. No frantic contortions of the body here. In fact, on a slow number, she just stands there and sings, hands clasped behind her back."[34] Her deportment appealed to a bourgeois German audience used to hearing recitals of lieder by Schubert and Schumann performed by classical singers whose formal body language, with hands folded at the waist, signified respect.

Fitzgerald's face stared out at German readers from the April 22, 1953, cover of *Der Spiegel* (The Mirror), a widely circulated weekly news magazine. Punning on the name shared by the Harlem theater of her discovery and the Greek god of music and arts, *Der Spiegel* labeled her "Apollos Mädchen" (Apollo's girl). In the cover photograph—captioned with her own words, "Die Leute mögen mich" (People like me)—she looks a bit loopy, holding a beer stein.

The long feature article inside, titled "Kennst du den Blues" ("Do You Know the Blues," alluding to a song by Schubert, "Kennst du das Land"), did not draw on an interview but rather synthesized material from two white expatriate writers, musician Mezz Mezzrow and the Marxist historian Sidney Finkelstein.[36] It described jazz as a musical form struggling as an underdog in American society and its artists as waylaid by drugs. Fitzgerald, as the "Queen of Jazz," occupied a peculiar niche in this survey, naming only one other female artist, Billie Holiday. Adding some misinformation about Fitzgerald's religion (calling her a pious Presbyterian) and making the usual comment about her weight (220 pounds), it quoted her mainly from the blurb from the JATP program booklet: "What Ella Fitzgerald says about her singing could hang over the bed of all modern jazz musicians who believe that snobbish Dadaism with sounds is enough: 'I always try to tell a story and sing only what I have experienced. Despite all of my bebop, I'm actually a ballad singer, and I always will be. And I try to bring the story that I sing to life because I believe that music is a narrative art.'"[37]

Back home, Fitzgerald aroused even more devotion in a cover story for *Metronome*'s October issue by the critic Bill Coss. This interview could serve as a template for the anomalies she projected both as an artist and as a woman that would be repeated throughout her lifetime: the gulf between her acclaim and her low opinion of herself, sometimes described as humility, here by Coss as "self-abnegation"; and her tolerance, expressed as appreciation for all kinds of music ("hillbilly" songs even), "as long as it's played well." Coss coined a phrase he would return to in later reviews: "So much timidity amidst so much grandeur." "No-one could get as much out of a lyric as Ella," he wrote. He quoted Fitzgerald's assessment of the state of jazz in Europe, which suggests a critical intelligence and acumen often obscured by the enigmatic persona she cultivated. "There are certainly modernists everywhere, not just in the Northern countries," she said, using a term that suggested her connoisseurship.[38]

★★★

PROFESSIONALLY, FITZGERALD WAS LIVING A DOUBLE LIFE, with Moe Gale on one side and Norman Granz on the other. Gale arranged a

national package tour for her from April 4 to May 11, 1953, with Frankie
Laine, Louis Jordan and His Tympany Five, and Woody Herman and
His Third Herd, along with a tap dancer and comic. Onstage at Car-
negie Hall, she hammed up "Stone Cold Dead in the Marketplace" and
"Side by Side" with Louis Jordan. She later reminisced:

> We had such good times when we all worked together on the tour
> with Frankie Laine, which was a beautiful tour. Everybody always
> traveled in the bus 'cause they wanted to be close together. When we
> traveled on the tour, Woody insisted on riding right in the bus with
> everybody and I thought that was so beautiful. We had a comedian,
> and he used to tell jokes on the bus, sing, and everything.[39]

The timing of the tour helped assuage her pain at the collapse of her
marriage to Ray Brown. All those emotional performances of "Body and
Soul" may well corroborate her inner upheavals during the 1952 tour,
which Oscar Peterson speculated "was perhaps the beginning of the end
of her marriage to Ray."[40] Ella and Ray were officially divorced in August
1953, but in an unusual challenge, they still had to work together in JATP.
Publicly they practiced mutual coexistence. *Jet* magazine wrote that Fitzgerald "still dines nightly with her bassist husband, Ray Brown."[41] In the
fall of 1953, the pair were on a marathon national tour with a new iteration of JATP, adding Ben Webster, Benny Carter, and Gene Krupa to the
lineup. They played jazz clubs in the Midwest and auditoriums in university towns for around thirty-eight dates in six weeks.

"Ray and Ella were professionals," Granz said.[42] But not always—
who could be? JATP required her to continue to make music with a
man she had loved and lost. On the band bus after their divorce, Peterson recalled, Fitzgerald witnessed Brown signing autographs for attractive young women:

> She still had feelings for him after the divorce. . . . She walked
> past him and got on the bus. For some reason, she hit me. I mean,
> I saw stars for a couple of seconds. She said, "I know what you're

up to, Oscar." I realized she wasn't, in essence, talking to me. She was talking to Ray.[43]

Privately Fitzgerald suffered grief. Sometime in 1953 in her New York office, Virginia Wicks overheard Ella sobbing and repeating to herself, "I won't let it stop me."[44] An unpublished blues number, "Throw It Out Your Mind," for which we have undated sheet music, bears lyrics attributed to her: "Throw it out your mind, forget it . . . Throw it out your mind and just be friends."[45] (See Fig. 8.) It reads like a self-help strategy. Then a more troubling incident occurred. She apparently made a halfhearted suicide attempt by climbing out of a hotel window when she got drunk with her cousin Georgie, who was in the room and pulled her back inside.[46] Years later Fitzgerald recounted the incident to a friend and then laughed and said, "That's funny."[47]

"Jealousy was one of my faults," Fitzgerald admitted in 1961, in a marriage where she had made mistakes. In a 1983 interview with Leonard Feather, she delivered an epitaph:

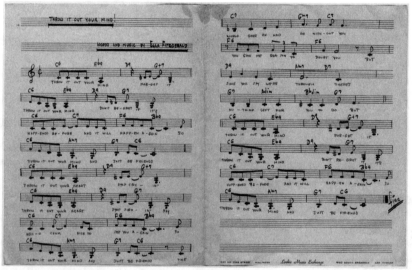

Fig. 8. Ella Fitzgerald's manuscript lead sheet for "Throw It Out Your Mind" from early to mid-1950s. She likely wrote this unpublished song upon her marital separation from Ray Brown. *Ella Fitzgerald Papers, NMAH.AC.0584, ser. 1, box 3, fol. 5. Archives Center, National Museum of American History, Smithsonian Institution. Courtesy of Ella Fitzgerald Charitable Foundation.*

I don't think [Ray Brown and I] really knew each other. I think
to have a successful marriage you have to have more than just—
you have to learn to love somebody. I mean really love them. . . . I
mean you have to understand them, you know. Well, you have a
good understanding of everything. At that time we didn't.[48]

★★★

ON OCTOBER 30, 1953, the JATP national tour ended in Honolulu.
That was by design, for Granz had arranged a dramatic postlude: a
three-week tour of postwar Japan, which was still occupied by American troops, with Emperor Hirohito still in place as a figurehead.
Japan's embrace of jazz had long rivaled Europe's in depth and complexity. Thousands of people gathered at the airport to give JATP an
unforgettable welcome that astounded them.[49] The surprise reception
included a motorcade parade. The tour reached fourteen Japanese cities. Only one incident marred the jubilation. At the Nichigeki Theater in Tokyo, while Fitzgerald was singing "Body and Soul," drunken
American marines harassed her from the balcony and shouted obscen-
ities including "Fuck you, Ella." After the concert, Granz tracked
them down, accompanied by Oscar Peterson and Benny Carter. As
Peterson described it:

> Like a shot in the dark, Norman uncoiled a left hook and knocked
> the marine back into the curtains behind him. . . . There was
> applause in the foyer from the Japanese audience. . . . The
> three . . . returned backstage to tell Ella, who was in tears, that
> the unasked-for favor had been paid back.[50]

Their final engagement in Tokyo on November 18 was broadcast
over the radio and, unbeknownst to Granz, was bootlegged and sold
without a license in Japan. In 1972 it was released as *JATP in Tokyo: Live
at the Nichigeki Theater 1953*.[51] The reissue was the earliest commercially
available performance of her "Body and Soul." Backed by Ray Tunia
on piano, Herb Ellis on guitar, Ray Brown on bass, and J. C. Heard on

drums, she sang the same arrangement as in Europe, one that validated the earlier reviews.

After the new year, she was off again on JATP's February–March European tour, with an itinerary that this time included Helsinki, Vienna, Zurich, West Berlin, and Kaiserslautern, an American military community in West Germany. While critics found fault with other performers, they praised her as usual. In Berlin on February 19, 1954, the *Berliner Zeitung* read:

> The young boys in the Sports Palace roared with enthusiasm when Ella spouted out their favorite number, "A-Tisket A-Tasket," bowed shyly and coquettishly showed a piece of pink petticoat. Then she put infinite melancholy and childlike tenderness in "Body and Soul." It moved even the most stubborn brooders to tears. . . . This music is a valid expression of our time. A time that is pushing for absolute top performance—a bit at the expense of individualism, of course. That is why Ella Fitzgerald is perceived as a refreshing oasis in the Jazz at the Philharmonic ensemble, precisely because of their almost oppressive technical accuracy and excellence. Ella's voice does not come from the throat, it comes from the heart. It does without cheap pop sentimentalism—and still stirs up.[52]

Norman Granz had long appreciated this force of nature who was mainstreaming American popular song in postwar Europe and attracting such attention, and the tours only increased his admiration for her. Likewise, the growing audiences in Europe made Fitzgerald appreciate his managerial acumen. In September 1953 Granz boasted to a *New York Times* reporter:

> She can run anyone out of room—unequivocally. She can do a ballad as well as the most commercial non-jazz singer there is today and she can scat with Louis Armstrong and she can make the same harmonic changes as any bopper can make and you can tune up

to her—she's got perfect pitch—and she improvises. Which means that what she does is fresh. It's not just a set, pat thing.[53]

In the middle of the Japanese tour in November 1953, Granz had taken a risk. Sitting next to Fitzgerald on the flight from Tokyo to Osaka, he proposed to become her manager. As he later recalled, "I had been thinking for years about taking over Ella's personal management. . . . Ella was afraid. She thought I was too much of a blow-top."[54] Nevertheless, she accepted his offer and agreed to a year's trial, in which Granz would forgo his fees. Considering how much time both would spend in the air, a plane was a fine place to make that deal.

Chapter 15

UPWARDLY MOBILE

(1954-1955)

The singer and her new manager were now a team. It remained for Ella to say farewell to the career profile that Moe Gale had long shaped for her: the focus on Black theaters, the occasional white-time venue (a venue catering mainly to a white demographic), and jazz clubs. Her final Gale bookings in the spring of 1954 again boxed her into old-fashioned vaude-pic dates, confirming her need for change.

On Easter weekend, Gale booked her at Loew's State in Times Square, packaging her with Julius La Rosa, a popular Italian American singer being promoted to teenagers as a romantic crooner. La Rosa sang his number-one pop hit, "Eh, Cumpari" ("Hey, Buddy"), while Fitzgerald sang "St. Louis Blues" and "Young at Heart," covering Frank Sinatra's best-selling single. She even calmed La Rosa's nerves before the audience of "jazz cultists, strays and waifs." The booking merely broke even.[1] Still, a $50,000 gross at Loew's State was no small feat when you could stay warm at home and watch *Beat the Clock*, Jackie Gleason, or Sid Caesar on Saturday night television.

Moe Gale "deserved to lose her," said Gale's son Richard. "He was happy to have her in a steady state."[2] Fitzgerald tolerated Gale's "bossiness," but publicist Virginia Wicks bristled at the way he talked about his Black clients "as if they were another class of people."[3] Milt Gabler criticized Gale's road management, which often failed to provide adequate sound systems and backstage accommodations. George Wein, who ran the Boston jazz club Storyville, remembered:

> In 1952, she didn't even have a serious manager. . . . Ella came over to the club to pick up her money. She was dressed so plainly that I almost didn't recognize her. When I handed her the envelope of cash, she thanked me humbly and tucked it into her coat. I could hardly believe that this consummate artist didn't have someone to handle her money and look after her interests.[4]

After Fitzgerald left Gale, she had a rude awakening: she was in arrears for a startling amount of back taxes. A 1961 memo from Granz to Fitzgerald stated, "Your financial position on January 1, 1956, shortly after I became your manager, was that . . . your liabilities were $46,255.90 more than your assets."[5] According to pianist Lou Levy, an accompanist for Fitzgerald, Granz settled the IRS bill.[6]

It fell to Norman Granz to redefine her career. His goal was to move her out of jazz clubs and into some of the country's top-paying nightclubs and hotel venues. As a famous jazz singer celebrated for scat improvisation, she occupied a particular cultural niche. To the mainstream audience, nothing would dislodge that primary identity, no matter how many ballads she sang. Granz's most important business decision for her was to embrace the broader label of "popular singer." In his words, she was finished with "52nd Street money."[7] He wanted to "make her a singer with more than just a cult following amongst jazz fans."[8] He told Leonard Feather, "It was a matter of pride with me, that she still hadn't been recognized—economically, at least—as the greatest singer of our time."[9]

The *Pittsburgh Courier* columnist Izzy Rowe agreed, addressing her friend directly in January 1955:

> You're head, shoulders, voice and talent above any other gal in the whole world of such entertainment. With a ten-foot pole they couldn't touch you or catch up to you in seven-league boots, but

something is wrong. You're not booked into the plush places; only now and then you get a guest shot on some TV show or radio program. Your records have found their way into millions of homes, white as well as colored, but you just can't seem to break through.[10]

"Breaking through" meant confronting the stigma around jazz, not only as Black music but as a lower-class form of expression. In 1952 the jazz writer and record producer Orrin Keepnews wrote, "Jazz is still very much of a social step-child in America, inhabiting a peculiar half-world."[11] The mid-1950s would bring greater social respectability to jazz in the form of concert presentations, media coverage, accredited college courses, and foreign tours sponsored by the U.S. State Department, yet jazz musicians and their fans were still broadly stigmatized as cultists, drug users, and social misfits. As the classical music critic George Marek wrote in *Good Housekeeping* in 1956, jazz fans were just starting to break through the stereotype of "misguided youth" who chose "to dress like a freak, to speak in juggling phrases that started with the word 'Man!,' to call something 'cool' when you meant 'good,' 'square' if you meant 'bad,' and generally to behave like a runaway idiot."[12]

Granz had weathered this kind of criticism in producing his JATP concerts, and he understood it was time for Fitzgerald to inhabit the "class nitery," the "upper-crust" nightclub, the "posh" or "plush" room in a five-star hotel. Class-consciousness in the 1950s, fueled by rising affluence, meant conspicuous fun for grown-ups. Among these elite venues whose floor shows received regular reviews in *Variety* were the Waldorf Astoria and the Copacabana in Manhattan, the Fontainebleau in Miami, the Mocambo and Ciro's in Hollywood, the Fairmont Hotel in San Francisco, and the Flamingo, Sands, and New Frontier in Las Vegas. Some had already hired prominent African American entertainers from the worlds of popular music and film, an elite group that included the elegant singer Nat King Cole and exceptionally beautiful women such as Lena Horne, Eartha Kitt, and Dorothy Dandridge. Dandridge confided to a friend, "Ella Fitzgerald is one of the most talented people in the world, and it embarrasses me that she cannot work the rooms that I work. The reason for it is so horrible. She's not sexy."[13] Despite the old fear Fitzgerald had expressed as "When a girl looks like me . . . ," Granz was certain that together they could transcend this career obstacle.

On May 25, 1954, Ella's new beginning was launched at Basin Street, a fairly new jazz club in midtown Manhattan. The event was coordinated by Virginia Wicks, who was considered one of the best publicists in the business. A former model, she had just been featured in a *Look* magazine photo spread as an outstanding "career girl/press agent."[14] "Ginny," as Ella knew her, was a trusted associate who conceived the Basin Street event as a tribute to Fitzgerald's nineteenth anniversary in the music business. "I hope I've gotten across that this is a sincere and justified tribute, and not a brassy promotion," Wicks told the press.[15] Decca chimed in, floating the figure of 22 million records sold in related press releases. Dorothy Kilgallen joked, "Invitations to the soiree look like bids to Buckingham Palace."[16] Attendees included movie star Audrey Hepburn and her fiancé Mel Ferrer, rising entertainers Eartha Kitt and Harry Belafonte (both clients of Wicks), and music businessmen Gale, Granz, John Hammond, and Decca president Milton Rackmil. The emcee, Steve Allen—host of TV's *Tonight* show, then still local to New York—offered comic relief and presented plaques and bouquets. Ella beamed as she heard telegrams from fellow musicians including Lena Horne, Billy Eckstine, Benny Goodman, Rosemary Clooney, Guy Lombardo, Lionel Hampton, Louis Armstrong, and Charlie Parker, whose telegram read, "If you'll forgive the pun, Ella Fitzgerald is strictly for 'The Bird.' "[17]

Speaking briefly to the gathering, Ella said, "I guess what everyone wants more than anything else is to be loved. And to know that you people love me and my singing is too much for me. Forgive me if I don't have all the words. Maybe I can sing it and you'll understand."[18] She sang, among other things, "A-Tisket A-Tasket," "Lady Be Good," "Who's Afraid (Not I, Not I, Not I)," the Gershwins' "A Foggy Day," and Rodgers and Hart's "My Funny Valentine."

At a time when classical music critics sometimes reviewed jazz events, and dedicated jazz journalists were almost nonexistent in mainstream newspapers, the *New York Times* dispatched its chief classical critic, Howard Taubman, to review the evening.[19] An admitted "stranger to these haunts," Taubman found much to disapprove of in the supporting groups led by Sam Butera and Louis Bellson, whose dueling trumpeters Charlie Shavers and Roy Eldridge, he wrote, "seemed to shy away from lyricism as if it were a commodity that would contaminate the place." When Fitzgerald came on,

> It became clear again that sheer insistence and noise were not necessarily the hallmarks of quality or success. For Miss Fitzgerald was simple and unaffected. Of course, she has know-how as an entertainer, but her personality is warm and she is not afraid of emotion. She stood there on the stage with a great natural dignity as important folks made a great do about her.[20]

Taubman may have undervalued Shavers and Eldridge, but he knew the value of dignity. He had long championed Marian Anderson, the great African American classical singer, whose integrity and unshakable poise were weapons in the struggle against racism in the classical music world.

A new variant of dignity brought Fitzgerald within Taubman's purview a few months later, when he covered the First Annual American Jazz Festival, soon to be known as the Newport Jazz Festival.[21] This historic event, produced by George Wein and held on July 18–19, 1954, in Newport, Rhode Island, was the first major multiday jazz festival in the United States. Encouraged by Newport residents Louis and Elaine Lorillard, and backed by their family fortune in tobacco, Wein modeled the event after the Berkshire Music Festival at Tanglewood, the summer home of the Boston Symphony Orchestra. He later described his rationale: "Let's put [jazz] on the level of classical music. Let's put it on a level of the arts that it deserves."[22]

Since the Gilded Age of the 1890s, Newport had been known as a summer retreat full of opulent mansions for the socialite rich. During the festival, some hotels refused rooms to Black clientele, who also endured surly attitudes at local restaurants. Within the Newport elite, support for the festival was mixed. While Newport's mayor told *Jet* magazine that it was "just about the greatest thing that ever happened to Newport," George Wein told *Esquire*, "There was a definite element against us. They resented jazz musicians coming into Newport."[23] In 1960 the writer Cleveland Amory, a sardonic loyalist to upper-class mores, would wryly describe the festival as guilty of "manslaughter in the second degree."[24]

On a wet, chilly Saturday evening around midnight, a crowd of seven thousand heard Fitzgerald introduced as a "vocal genius."[25] Wein would pay tribute to her many times in the course of her career. She was accompanied by pianist John Lewis, bassist Jimmy Woode, and drummer Shadow Wilson; her set included the ballad "Angel Eyes" and two jazz standards, "Lover, Come Back to Me" and "How High the Moon."[26] Reviews as usual emphasized the audience's reception of her, one recounting that "she came on to sing and steal the show" and another that she "aroused the audience to a frenzy."[27]

Following Newport, Ella went on tour with JATP in September and October 1954. In 1983 rare recordings of her live performances were released on LP.[28] She was in top form, brimming with jazz originality, luxuriating in her rich vibrato on love songs. Updating her repertoire, she included two show tunes from the Broadway musical *Pajama Game*—a tender rendition of "Hey There" and an inventive version of "Hernando's Hideaway," sparked especially by Buddy Rich on drums and delighting the audience. *Variety*'s reviewer misguidedly labeled "Hernando's Hideaway" as "a hoked-up version," perhaps because of the tempo changes in the middle along with her ebullient scat.[29] Reviewing the opening JATP concert in Hartford on September 17, George T. Simon in *Metronome* grabbed the moment to write about JATP's "polished performances," and "wonderful Ella," running a photo of her getting a bear hug from Dizzy Gillespie, who had joined the Granz operation.[30]

The mammoth tour closed at the Shrine Auditorium on November 8, with Ella bowing out early to open at the Tiffany Jazz Club in Los Angeles on November 5.[31] A *Billboard* reviewer wrote, "It's love at first song between Ella Fitzgerald and the jazz crowd at the murky Tiffany Club" with its "tight quarters," where she sang her JATP repertoire plus her impersonations and novelties.[32] But for better or worse, it was a jazz club, and she said so to her local press agent, Jules Fox, as he reported many years later in his memoir: "Jules, I know I make lots of good money at the jazz clubs I play, but I sure wish I could play at one these fancy places," along Sunset Strip in Hollywood.[33]

Who would have expected a *dea ex machina* from Hollywood to ful-fill her wish? In mid-November, accompanied by the photographers who followed her everywhere, Marilyn Monroe turned up at the Tif-fany Club. Photos of the two women in conversation soon appeared on AP and UPI wires, running in newspapers across the country.[34] As the captions made clear, Monroe was in the midst of a separation from her husband, the baseball player Joe DiMaggio, and was now out and about after a minor surgery. For Monroe's fans, Ella was a prop, although a useful reminder of Monroe's successful debut as a singer in the film musical *Gentlemen Prefer Blondes*. That film, in fact, had introduced Monroe to Fitzgerald's art; as one of her coaches suggested, she listened to no other vocalist in preparation. That made her a fan.[35]

For Fitzgerald's fans, the encounter sparked a friendship and an inter-vention that led from the Tiffany Club in November to the glitzy Sunset Strip celebrity nightclub, the Mocambo, in March 1955. Monroe prom-ised the Mocambo owner, Charlie Morrison, her presence front-row center during Fitzgerald's booking. It seems likely that Monroe reneged, but that mattered little once the contract had been signed.[36] In May 1955 *Down Beat* described Monroe as Ella Fitzgerald's "ardent" fan.[37]

In a 1972 article, Fitzgerald recalled not quite accurately:

> I owe Marilyn Monroe a real debt. . . . She personally called the owner of the Mocambo and told him she wanted me booked imme-diately. . . . She told him, and it was true, due to Marilyn's super-star status—that the press would go wild. The owner said yes, and Marilyn was there, front table, every night. The press went over-board. . . . After that, I never had to play a small jazz club again.

Fitzgerald added that Monroe "was an unusual woman—a little ahead of her times. And she didn't know it."[38] Ella could have been talking about herself.

In reviews of her Mocambo appearances, the issue of jazz as an obstacle to success surfaced consistently. "In her first mainstem date on the Sunset Strip, chirp Ella Fitzgerald surprises the odds makers to score a resounding success," wrote *Billboard*. "Ella offers a class act, not the up-tempo, driving scat she might give out with at the Blue Note or Birdland."[39] Yet the "class act" barely differed from her Jazz at the Philharmonic setlists, although she had cultivated more ballads in her repertoire, and at the Mocambo she included her modernist version of "Lover, Come Back to Me," reprised from the Newport festival. Photos of Ella's Mocambo engagement in *Jet* magazine showed her with white Hollywood celebrities Frank Sinatra and Judy Garland.[40]

Another breakthrough engagement came shortly afterward at San Francisco's Fairmont Hotel. The Fairmont's Venetian Room—a West Coast counterpart to the Empire Room at Manhattan's Waldorf Astoria—evoked a palazzo on the Pacific, and through the late 1960s it remained a last bastion for demanding formal dress on the opening night of a new act.[41] Fitzgerald was its first jazz booking, but for a vocalist associated with JATP, management demanded concessions. In late 1953, after rowdy fans at the San Francisco Civic Auditorium caused minor property damage, city authorities had banned JATP from further concerts there.[42] Calculating that a residency at the Fairmont would have value for Ella's future, Granz volunteered to cover any losses incurred by the hotel and persuaded her to accept a lower fee than usual. Her three-week booking began on April 5, 1955.

Variety laid out the stakes: "This is Miss Fitzgerald's first booking of this type, and the success of it will not only determine her draw in similar places but also the possibility of other jazz stars playing the Venetian Room."[43] She could "turn out to be a legend in her own time, like Louis Armstrong," *Variety* wrote, with a "non-show-business audience as far removed from the jazz concert hipsters as you can get."[44] Granz had been right, and Ella delivered. She sang Rodgers and Hart's "This Can't Be

Love" (a recent addition to her repertoire), the pop megahit "Teach Me Tonight," and two slow ballads, "Angel Eyes" and "Someone to Watch Over Me." Dorothy Kilgallen reported, "San Francisco was at Ella's feet so much so that a department store decorated its windows with a juke box and a loudspeaker playing her records."[45] The Fairmont would become a second home for Fitzgerald in the latter years of her career.

Her next conquest in the posh western circuit was the Flamingo Hotel and Casino in Las Vegas, where she opened on November 4, 1955. *Variety's* reviewer wrote she had found her groove, not "jazz-cool" but "modern cool," and was ready for exposure to broad audiences.[46] Then off she went for return visits to the "plush" Mocambo and the "swank" Fairmont. Who can doubt the power of class-consciousness on the human brain when considering the swerve in Fitzgerald's fortunes? The rooms changed, the press changed, the money changed—but she mostly did not. "One of the nicest things that Norman Granz has done is to start Ella Fitzgerald on a career in the plusher nightclubs," *Metronome* reported. "Still singing more or less the same routine, Ella's making a big hit in the big time circuit."[47]

★★★

FITZGERALD'S UPWARD MOBILITY TOOK PLACE during a volatile period in American race relations. On May 17, 1954, a week before Howard Taubman acknowledged her dignity at Basin Street, the Supreme Court ruling in *Brown v. Board of Education* prohibited race segregation in American public schools. Three days after the Basin Street event, Fitzgerald and Harry Belafonte headlined a fundraising benefit for the Brooklyn NAACP's Operation Freedom fund to fight segregation in schools, housing, voting, and jobs.[48] The bus boycott in Montgomery, Alabama, was still a year and a half away.

It would take another ten years for the Civil Rights Act of 1964 to legislate American apartheid out of public accommodations, including hotel rooms and entertainment venues. The experiences of Fitzgerald and the JATP musicians on the front lines illuminate the dynamics of a heightened political consciousness throughout the country, including backlash from white segregationists. The more famous she became, the more she drew press attention when racial discrimination was involved, and the more tenaciously Granz stayed the course "to use jazz for justice."

An incident in Hawaii in July 1954 proved his point. En route to Australia for a week's tour, she, pianist John Lewis, and Georgie Henry were bumped from their first-class seats into tourist class on an oversold Pan American flight. Was this international airline behaving like an Alabama bus company, seating passengers according to the tacit rule "white forward, colored rear"? Pan Am offered to reinstate Fitzgerald's first-class booking, but because her companions were not treated similarly, she refused. Three days after the incident, an Australian newspaper reported her arrival on Qantas Airways with "1,000 fans there to greet her."[49] Granz sued Pan Am for $270,000 in damages, triggering press stories throughout the United States and in Europe, Japan, and Brazil.

The next incident, which was even more disturbing, went unreported at the time. The 1954 national JATP tour had left the South pretty much alone, but Granz agreed to a benefit concert for the March of Dimes on September 27 at the County Hall in Charleston, South Carolina. A road veteran of the South before joining JATP, Fitzgerald was ready for what lay ahead. Despite its image of moderation and civility, Charleston had its white supremacist groups and was as polarized as any other city in the Deep South.[50] A few months earlier a local African American theater company had mounted a production of Gershwin's opera *Porgy and Bess*, touted as its Southern premiere, at the Dock Street Theatre. The company demanded mixed-race seating for the audience, but when the request was denied, the company shelved the production. An editorial in the *Charleston News and Courier* read, "In demanding that the audience be racially mingled, in disregard of South Carolina laws and customs, these Negroes in our opinion have not helped to promote good race relations. If upsetting these customs is the only terms on which they will participate, it is better that the project be abandoned."[51]

The JATP troupe arrived in Charleston in their chartered private plane, along with a ticket-seller from New York to ensure mixed seating. Ella recalled, "When the show started, the people were all staring at each other and so afraid that they couldn't even applaud."[52] After the show, Dizzy Gillespie recalled, the JATP musicians and crew sneaked out of the hall, while Ella's maid Georgie hastily stuffed receipts down the front of her dress.[53] The road manager, Pete Cavello, had noticed a crowd of local toughs gathering outside the stage door and kept the spotlight on Fitzgerald while the rest of the musicians packed up their instruments to make their getaway. Cavello recounted what happened next:

> We told the drivers, "Get us to the airport as fast as you can." These four limos went out like hell, man. It took them about five or ten minutes before they found out we were gone. . . . You never saw us load up a plane so fast in your life. As we get on the runway, we saw dozens of cars coming up this little road to the airport after us. We were up in the air looking down at the headlights, and I said, "Oh boy, that was one we got out of."[54]

A few things were left behind in the scramble, including one of Ella's shoes. "We got away with it," Fitzgerald recalled, "even though they ran us out of town after the show. . . . Let's face it, there were lots of things back then that you either had to overlook or you got angry and cried about."[55]

For JATP's six-week tour the following year, Granz booked several Houston venues: the City Auditorium, the Music Hall, and the Sam Houston Coliseum. At these venues sometimes Blacks were excluded, and sometimes they had to sit in the balcony or, more rarely, downstairs in designated sections.[56] Granz arranged for the sale of tickets on a first-come, first-served basis. He hired eight off-duty policemen for the evening.[57]

Two shows were booked for October 7, 1955, at the Houston Music Hall. The first one sold out—native son Illinois Jacquet helped the draw. The desegregated crowd filled the theater. Near the end of the first show, five plainclothes detectives from the vice squad of Houston's police department barged into Fitzgerald's backstage dressing room, brandishing guns. They were looking for a way to stop the show and make an arrest, by finding either drugs or gambling there. It was harassment plain and simple. When a police officer started for the bathroom, Granz stopped him, fearing he might plant drugs. The officer held his gun to Granz's stomach and said, "I ought to shoot you."[58]

Everyone backstage was arrested on gambling charges and brought to the police station. Granz quickly arranged for bail at ten dollars each, reminding the police that unless the musicians returned to the theater for the second show, they would have to deal with the uproar of angry customers.

International news coverage of the arrest threatened Fitzgerald's respectability by association, with headlines like "Vice-Squad Arrest U.S. Stars in Texas" in *Melody Maker* and "'Tisket-Tasket' Girl Has Dressing Room Dice Game Broken Up by Texas Vice Squad" in the *New York Amsterdam News*.[59] A widely disseminated press photo showed her sitting in the police station, hands folded and ankles crossed, being comforted by her cousin Georgie, her road companion. Stories drawn from the AP and UPI wire services described her fur coat and elegant dress and repeated that "Miss Fitzgerald dabbed tears from her eyes."[60] In Houston, the incident became an embarrassment. The local white press soon printed a rebuke from the police chief to his own vice squad, and by early November the charges were dropped.

Ella recalled the Houston incident a few times over the course of her life, with flashes of irony replacing anxiety. "Yeah, and I was the innocent one!" she says in Gillespie's memoir. "Yeah, sitting up eating pie [laughter]. They took us down and then when we got down there they had the nerve to ask for an autograph. That was quite an experience."[61] In 1973 she joked to an audience at the Houston Astrodome that it was her first trip to the city since "1955, when we had a little struggle. I wasn't shooting dice, of course, I was bobbing for apples."[62] In 1978, performing in Galveston, Texas, she said the police "took everybody including me. God bless the dead. Duke Ellington's manager had two gold dice made up in a bracelet to remind me of Houston."[63]

Fitzgerald did not typically repeat such stories or dwell on these experiences in public. Stoical and private, not perseverating on the past but conserving her psychological energy for her art and her craft, she eschewed political controversies. Nevertheless, in the heightened atmosphere of the mid-1950s, she began to speak out against Jim Crow policies in her own profession, particularly in television, a vital front in the growing struggle for equal opportunity.

Television mostly neglected Fitzgerald in its early years. The year after her 1948 appearance on Ed Sullivan's *Talk of the Town*, she guested on *Eddie Condon's Floor Show*, a jazz program networked on NBC. In 1950 she appeared on the DuMont network's *Cavalcade of Stars*, hosted by Jackie Gleason in a live vaudeville format, and in 1951 she appeared along with Cab Calloway on the low-budget ABC series *Kreisler Bandstand*. In 1952 she sang for two charity telethons, NBC's band series *Saturday Night Dance Party* and the NBC variety show *All-Star Revue*. In 1954, however, she had not appeared on American television in two years. When a British critic told her, "Baby, you're the greatest," she boomeranged the compliment: "If I'm so great, why don't I get a regular TV show like so many other stars do?" She quickly apologized, the critic noted, but the point had been made.[64] White vocalists, among them Mel Tormé, Jo Stafford, Dinah Shore, Perry Como, and Frankie Laine, along with lesser lights, had been granted the fifteen-minute format then current on American network television, backed by corporate sponsorship.

Fitzgerald publicly protested Jim Crow television in a remarkable interview published in the February 23, 1955, issue of *Down Beat* by Nat Hentoff, a jazz critic known for his liberal race politics. Sammy Davis, Jr.'s bid to host a TV show had been derailed when he insisted on an interracial cast of dancers and backup singers, and the network failed to find an underwriting sponsor.[65] It would take another decade for Davis to host a network variety series. Fitzgerald began by expressing her own personal ambitions:

> Like every singer my ambition for a long time has been to have a
> TV show of my own, but I don't like to think too far ahead. What

I mean is I don't know anybody who has one. Do you understand what I'm trying to say? Sammy Davis, Jr., for example. He didn't get his show, and no one certainly could get tired of looking at *him* for 15 minutes. Do you remember how great he was on the *Colgate Comedy Hour*? And there's Lena Horne, Jiminy Crickets! If *Lena* doesn't have a show of her own! We have so many wonderful artists who deserve a TV show. But I don't know . . . the way things are . . . someday maybe. . . . Even if it were just a New York program, so I could stay home a little. It's not that I don't like the road, but traveling all the time, year in and year out, isn't as easy on a woman as it is on a man.

She added, "I'd like a program that was like inviting the audience into my home," sketching out a plausible if somewhat didactic pilot for a fifteen-minute spot. Take a hit song and approach it two ways, drawing the audience into the experience of creative evaluation. Sing commercials, but make up new words each time. Invite talented kids to audition, as she had done at the Apollo as a teenager. A TV show could also revive her songwriting ambitions. "If I had a TV show of my own, I'd be real eager to write some music for it," she said. "Oh, I have gobs and gobs of ideas, but—well, you dream things like that, and that's what these are, you know—my day dreams."[66]

Over the next few years, she watched others fail, most notoriously Nat King Cole, whose NBC show began in 1956 but lasted little more than a year for lack of advertising. *Down Beat* journalist John Tynan asked her about Cole's show when it was picked up for national syndication, rekindling feelings of pride and indignation over the crippling race bias on television. "I'm so proud for him," she said. "Nobody deserves it more than he does. All I can say is that I hope I'm the first woman—" a sentence she left hanging.[67]

Chapter 16

"WE GOT ELLA!"

(1954-1956)

n May 1954 *Variety*'s critic told the worrisome truth that "Ella Fitzgerald has been unaccountably absent from the hit lists for the past couple of years, although generally recognized as one of the best song purveyors in the business."[1] If the trade didn't understand it, neither did she, nor Milt Gabler at Decca. Her six new singles (down from eleven in 1953) had the usual elaborate—some would say overblown—jazz-pop arrangements from Gordon Jenkins and Sy Oliver, including the small mixed-group background chorus fills that Gabler routinely used. While the singles got decent reviews in the music trade and jazz press, none of them arrived on any jukebox or LP chart.

One bright spot was Fitzgerald's special rapport with "Lullaby of Birdland," recorded on June 4, 1954.[2] By then George Shearing's instrumental was already a jazz standard. (RCA even put out an LP of twelve different versions.) She was the first to add lyrics to the tune, turning "Lullaby of Birdland" into a vocal-jazz classic so effectively that versions by Chris Connor and Sarah Vaughan would appear in the next eighteen months.[3] Sy Oliver gave her a midcentury modern arrangement that is a virtual sonic parallel to the two-toned sedans Chevy made that year—all orange and aqua with its opening flamboyant saxophone solo and decorous choral fills in the background. Even so, *Billboard* disapproved, describing it to be "not much . . . of interest to the mass market."[4]

In another landmark that year, Fitzgerald recorded her second LP, *Ella: Songs in a Mellow Mood*, as part of the festivities around Decca's celebration of its twentieth anniversary.[5] Here she was allowed to choose the tunes, Gabler said later.[6] She crafted a connoisseur's list of titles, mostly from the late 1930s, that do not fall into any one category except quality and the occasional surprise. Paired again with only Ellis Larkins at the keyboard, she sang outstanding versions of two warhorses, "Stardust" and "I'm Glad There Is You." Along with Rodgers and Hammerstein's "People Will Say We're in Love" from *Oklahoma!*, she resurrected "Baby, What Else Can I Do?," which she had introduced as conductor of the post–Chick Webb orchestra. Milt Gabler treated her as a classic, grouping his thirty-seven-year-old artist in tandem with fifty-one-year-old Bing Crosby and fifty-two-year-old Guy Lombardo, both of whom were about to retire from the label. Gabler described *Ella: Songs in a Mellow Mood* as "designed to withstand the test of time."[7]

Superlative notices in both the jazz and the trade press matched those for the earlier Gershwin album. In *Down Beat* Nat Hentoff effused that the LP was "one of the most rewarding experiences in the history of jazz recording."[8] An exceptional analysis of several tracks by British jazz writer Stanley Dance compared Fitzgerald's work on "Makin' Whoopee" to Duke Ellington's alto saxophonist, known for his sweet lyricism: "Ella blows it out soft and languorous, just as though she were a kind of Johnny Hodges." Dance added, "And may Granz one day put those two together," a wish that would come true three years later.[9]

Billboard told its record dealer readers that they could count on sales of Ella's LP from a magic duo of supporters: "aficionados of jazz—and there are plenty" and "pop buyers" who love standards.[10] But the album's conservative introspection could not compete with new trends in arrangements of standards. Solo piano lacked the coloristic appeal of orchestral mood music, which that year sent Jackie Gleason's *Music, Martinis and Memories* to the top five on *Billboard*'s LP charts. More important, the LP had neither a distinctive identity nor the thematic coherence that was sparking the "concept album" innovations of Frank Sinatra's *Songs for Young Lovers*, aided by Nelson Riddle's modern arrangements.

Small wonder then that by the end of 1954, Fitzgerald had reached such an impasse in her career that Gabler took an extraordinary step. He thought of Granz as the "other man" in a triangle, competing for the same woman, saying, "He kept her from being available to me."[11] But in December he felt sufficiently desperate and frustrated to write directly to Granz for advice:

> I believe it is very important that we have a meeting regarding the recordings of Ella Fitzgerald. You have been her representative for a long while and have never requested such a meeting with me concerning her repertoire. As her manager this should be one of your "first" interests as records are all important to a popular singer's career. Personally, you know how I feel about her, there is nothing I wouldn't do to help her sales at Decca. The time to do something for Ella is now![12]

He offered Granz a chance to work with him in the studio and sent a copy of the letter to Fitzgerald's home.

No response from Granz has survived. But two months later, interviewed by Nat Hentoff for *Down Beat* February 1955, Fitzgerald dealt Gabler an unpleasant surprise: she expressed recriminations both against him personally and against the label. She had her own way of looking at her career, independent of both Gabler and Granz, that their rivalry obscured but that had changed little since her Chick Webb years: she was anxious about being left behind.[13] Never mind her own complicity in choosing vintage for her LP; that repertoire suited the album format. But her contemporary preferences came through in her many live dates in New York, where she sang current hits like Frank Sinatra's "Young at Heart,"[14] Jo Stafford's top hit "Make Love to Me,"[15] Sammy Davis's "Hey There," and Judy Garland's "The Man That Got Away," doing "especially fine work" on those tunes, said *Metronome*.[16] Why would Gabler not let her sing those kinds of songs for her singles?

Especially, she asked Hentoff, why not "Teach Me Tonight," the big hit by Sammy Cahn and Gene de Paul? The song was perfect for her, another faux-schoolgirl seduction lyric with references to black-boards and learning the ABCs—in this case, of lovemaking. Gabler had assigned it to a younger, virtually unknown white newcomer, Janet Brace, whose recording, released in January 1954, sank. (Cahn joked later that it sold three copies—one to him, one to De Paul, and one to her.)[17] Then the DeCastro Sisters made the tune number one for months, followed by successful covers by Jo Stafford and Dinah Washington. As Fitzgerald said to Hentoff:

> It's been so long since I've gotten a show tune to do, except for the album. Or a chance to do a tune like "The Man That Got Away." Frank Sinatra came into Basin Street often while he was at the Copa, and he asked for that song every time. And he also asked, "How come, Ella, you don't have a number like *that* to record?"
>
> I don't know why myself. . . . I never do get a chance at the songs that have a chance. They give me something by somebody that no one else has, and then they wonder why the record doesn't sell. I'm so heart-broken over it. Maybe it's me, but there are so many pretty songs I *could* sing on record. I need a record out. I know that, but I don't know what they're doing at the record company. There must be something that I can make that people who buy records would like to hear. . . . I sure would like to record with someone who would give me something to record.[18]

"The Man That Got Away" was a Hollywood show tune by Harold Arlen, a favorite composer of hers, and a show-stopping torch that Judy Garland sang in the 1954 film remake of *A Star Is Born*.

Fitzgerald aired these views in the same Hentoff interview in which she had brought out her objections to racism in American television. She thus implicitly framed her Decca problems in terms of "white for-ward, colored rear," with white singers getting the strongest pop mate-rial with hit potential and Black singers left with ephemeral songs aimed at the jukebox.

As for the "album" Ella referred to, *Songs in a Mellow Mood*, she had further grievances against Decca:

> The album was something I was pleased with. It got such wonderful write-ups, and I remember when I was on the coast it seemed like everybody was playing it. But the disc jockeys claimed that the company didn't give them the record. In fact, we had to go out and buy the record and give it to those disc jockeys that didn't have it.

"Maybe it's because that record company is mainly interested in pictures now," she added, referring to Decca's recent acquisition of Universal Pictures.[19] The truth was, she had lost faith in Gabler's judgment and in Decca's commitment to her.

Granz and Gabler continued their epistolary sparring behind the scenes as well. At one point, Granz suggested that Gabler might consider starting a separate label and allowing Ella to record for both. Sarah Vaughan had such a double arrangement at Mercury; her jazz recordings were released on a subsidiary label, EmArcy. Gabler remained silent on that suggestion.

Then in the spring of 1955, Gabler took a dramatic step. Ironically, while Fitzgerald was thinking in terms of singles, he assigned her a new LP project, *Sweet and Hot*, a thematic album of standards from the 1930s and '40s, recorded in Los Angeles in April. The album juxtaposed the two sides of Fitzgerald's musical personality. The "sweet" A side had four arrangements by the commercially savvy André Previn, who was then the reigning staff musician at MGM Studios' fabled Arthur Freed Unit. The "hot" jazz-oriented B side, which could have been labeled "cool," featured four arrangements by Benny Carter, her old friend from Harlem days, now a respected and busy composer, arranger, and conductor, also based in Los Angeles.[20]

Sweet and Hot remains a little-known and underrated LP masterpiece, but both sides contained gems. Among the "sweet" highlights was the superb "It Might as Well Be Spring" by Rodgers and Hammerstein.

Previn's arrangements relied on Hollywood's luxe approach to orchestral femininity, with lush strings, pastelled flutes and oboes, and a triangle here and there. Previn skirted an "easy listening" style—it was written off as "Muzakian" in *Down Beat* but praised in *Metronome*.[21] The up-tempo "Lover, Come Back to Me" sported a tight, top-flight band arrangement controlling the horn traffic behind her. She imposed her own sophistication on the guileless banalities of Oscar Hammerstein, Jr.'s lyrics. For the original lines "The sky is blue / And high above," Ella substituted New York Yiddish: "You laid some spiel / I thought it was real." She and the band collaborated like Olympic skating pairs, switching off in counterpoint, then rebalancing again, in a version that clocks in at just under two minutes.

Gabler claimed "Lover, Come Back to Me" was "one of the greatest recordings she has ever made, and I feel it's a big one and should make the charts."[22] Before the LP was released, he issued it as a single, paired with "Old Devil Moon."[23] He must have been keenly disappointed by its review in *Variety*—perhaps the worst one she had ever received there—when a critic scolded, "Ella Fitzgerald, who rarely has made an inferior side, here comes up with a decidedly questionable cut of 'Lover Come Back to Me.' The double time tempo hardly fits the mood of this standard and the added hip talk together with the tricky vocalistics are on the irritating side."[24] Barry Ulanov, *Metronome*'s respected jazz critic, thought the sweet-hot mix made for "strange programming."[25] A critic in *New Musical Express* found "recurrent fault" in her breathing.[26] But the unnamed reviewer in *High Fidelity* got the point: "A practical lesson on how a great jazz singer can command a fantastic variety of voices and inflections and use them all with astonishing skill. There's very nearly a different Ella for each of these dozen tunes."[27]

Despite that tribute, *Sweet and Hot* faltered in the marketplace, largely because her marketing profile could not place the album into a consumer-friendly, up-to-date category. Further, the sweet-hot binary was old-fashioned, harkening back to the swing era and largely in disuse by 1955.

Thereafter Granz, the impresario of jazz, prodded Gabler, the Decca moderate, into considering more current pops for her singles. In July he wrote:

> I certainly wish something could be done to give Ella some material of the pop nature, instead of the standards alone. Certainly, for instance, the treatment that Sarah [Vaughan] has been getting at Mercury ought to presage some kind of comparable treatment from Decca. For example, I'm sure Ella could have wrapped up "Whatever Lola Wants" much better than Sarah. That's only one example, and I'm sure you know even more.[28]

★★★

IN 1955 FITZGERALD'S PROFESSIONAL FORTUNES got their most significant lift from her singing role in *Pete Kelly's Blues*, a feature film that paid homage to the roaring twenties. Produced and directed by TV celebrity Jack Webb, who starred as an L.A. police detective in the hugely popular crime show *Dragnet*, the film was set in 1927 amid the mob-run speakeasies of Kansas City, in a noir sound-world of blues and torch songs relieved by Dixieland jazz. The film did solid box office upon its late-July release, tying *East of Eden* and *The Seven-Year Itch* in thirteenth place for the year.[29]

Singer Peggy Lee carried the main musical responsibilities while playing the serious dramatic role of an abused gang moll. Nonetheless Fitzgerald's presence was a coup, and she had enough time and good material to make a strong impression through her understated performance. Cast as bland Maggie Johnson, owner of a joint called Fat Annie's, she sings the title song on screen, accompanied by her own pianist, Don Abney. And in the great novelty "Hard Hearted Hannah (The Vamp of Savannah)," she paid tribute to the singing comediennes of the 1920s.[30] "Hard-Hearted Hannah" would stay in her repertoire over the years. Jack Webb later said Fitzgerald was "the only one that stopped the previews by getting applause."[31] The *New York Times* reviewer wrote, "The wonderful Ella Fitzgerald, allotted a few spoken lines, fills the screen and sound track with her strong mobile features and voice."[32]

Reviewers generally overlooked Fitzgerald's obvious shortcomings as an actress, which she freely acknowledged. In 1958 she was asked why she found acting so hard. "Bashful," she said simply. "I'm just plain afraid to try. Oh, singing. That's different because it comes naturally, and I have the feeling that people will like it. But acting makes me nervous."[33] In 1974 she laughed off her own self-consciousness: "I was bothered by all the movie stars watching. Mr. Webb gave me my cue, and all I could answer was 'Huh?' I kept thinking, 'Here I am doing a scene with Joe Friday.' "[34]

Fitzgerald benefited from promotional tie-ins. The month of the film's release, Decca released the LP *Songs from Pete Kelly's Blues.* Fitzgerald had only three tracks out of twelve, and Peggy Lee's name and image dominated the cover, but the album garnered critical praise and charted in the top ten that fall. The film also gave Fitzgerald rare television exposure: on July 24, 1955, NBC's live Sunday-night program *The Colgate Variety Hour* plugged the film in a behind-the-scenes narrative about its making. It staged the title song as a production number, pairing Fitzgerald with trumpeter Ray Anthony, whose 1953 version of the *Dragnet* theme had renewed his career. Fitzgerald gave an earnest, effective performance.

★★★

REGARDLESS OF FITZGERALD'S SUCCESSES OR FAILURES, public complaints or private reproaches, nothing shifted Gabler's position regarding her contract, which obligated her to stay at the label for another year. But that fall Granz found an escape hatch, using leverage from his own exclusive contracts with drummer Gene Krupa and pianist Teddy Wilson, both from the original 1930s Benny Goodman trio. In the fall of 1955, Decca prepared the soundtrack LP for the film *The Benny Goodman Story*, a heavily promoted biopic from Universal Studios, but Decca forgot to secure licenses from Granz for Krupa and Wilson, who appeared in the movie and played on the soundtrack. When Decca compared the value of Fitzgerald's remaining contract to that of a soundtrack LP for a major film, there was no contest. The months-long negotiations were consummated in early January 1956.[35]

That month, during a booking at San Francisco's Fairmont Hotel, in a local radio interview, Fitzgerald announced the break with Decca without divulging names or details.[36] In 1992 Gabler recollected, "I was sorry to see her go. Norman finally got her away from me!"[37] In retrospect, Gabler had no real solution for his daunting problem: Fitzgerald was terrific in the studio, but her genius flourished in live dates, where she could express her originality over the course of an evening. No studio date could capture her stage energy. Consider her playlist, around this time, for a "Jazz à la Carte" series produced and hosted by Norman's brother, Irving Granz, at the Shrine Auditorium in Los Angeles. Backed by just her trio, her selections included "Cry Me a River," a song Decca passed over; "Lullaby of Birdland"; and for the closer, a dazzling "Air Mail Special," with a quotation thrown in from "Sixteen Tons," a crossover country-pop smash by Tennessee Ernie Ford. *Down Beat*'s John Tynan wrote that she "brought the audience to its feet in thunderous ovation," and reaffirmed her own "unquestionable right to the throne."[38]

The break did not leave Gabler empty-handed. In the aftermath, he mined his back catalog for songs that could potentially be released in LPs.[39] For *Lullabies of Birdland*, released on January 6, 1955, he assembled her acclaimed vocal jams from the 1940s along with newer material, her pioneering contributions on his label.[40] He continued to repackage Fitzgerald's singles with Decca into new LP albums, sometimes organized by arranger, other times marketed as her greatest hits. In 1993, in an elegant box set for her seventy-fifth birthday, Gabler ended his reminiscences with this tribute: "Happy 75 Ella. Look what we did, so long ago. So many ways to go, and we tried them all."[41]

★★★

"WE GOT ELLA!" shouted Granz in triumph in a flashy advertisement in the January 14, 1956, issue of *Billboard*.[42] The "we" was his new label, Verve, launched the previous December. Designed to shelter pop as well as jazz projects, Verve would soon absorb Granz's other labels Clef and Norgran. Throughout the mid-1950s, his combined jazz output would far exceed that of all other record companies.

In both the jazz press and even in Walter Winchell's column, the news of Fitzgerald's exit from Decca was accompanied by the announcement of her plan to make an album of Cole Porter songs. The critical importance of this project influenced Granz's decision to hire an arranger with major credentials in musical theater, although marginal credentials in jazz. Buddy Bregman became Verve's director and chief arranger. A nephew of the Broadway songwriter and producer Jule Styne, Bregman had been raised in musical theater. Extremely talented, he deserved to benefit from his family connections. By age twenty-five, he had amassed orchestration credits ranging from the TV adaptation of Cole Porter's musical *Anything Goes* to "I Need Your Lovin' (Bazoom)," a 1954 teen hit by Jerry Leiber and Mike Stoller for a young college-boy quartet, the Cheers.[43] Anita O'Day, who relocated from Norgran to Verve at the end of 1955, described Bregman as "a dark-haired, personable . . . playboy, Hollywood's arranger-of-the-moment who was riding a big hit with Gogi Grant's 'Suddenly There's a Valley.' "[44] Bregman recalled, "My first meeting with Ella was a bit strained—it was Ella, Norman and myself. She didn't say anything, but I could read her as he did all the talking, like: 'Who is this kid in jeans and a tee shirt—he certainly isn't a musician?!' "[45]

Fitzgerald recorded her first studio session with Bregman on January 25, 1956. Granz forgot about his pitch to Gabler and assigned her four tracks of unknown songs for singles. Many of the big band crew Bregman used would return for the Cole Porter project the following month. In the meantime, Fitzgerald started preparing for the new album. On February 2 at Zardi's, a popular jazz club in Hollywood, she conducted an experiment on a live audience.[46] As she explained in a

1958 interview, "When my current sponsor, Norman Granz, suggested I do something straighter like the Cole Porter songs, I didn't hesitate. I knew I could watch the faces at first."[47] The Zardi's setlist suggests that she and Granz had already discussed the possibility of a series of songbooks even before she began the Cole Porter project, for among its twenty-one titles are songs by Jerome Kern. Rodgers and Hart, George and Ira Gershwin, and Duke Ellington. Cole Porter turned up as a request. Other fare included a brilliant scat version of "Bernie's Tune," perhaps as a nod to Bregman; a Hollywood film song, "The Tender Trap," a hit for Frank Sinatra; and a reprise of "And the Angels Sing," a signature swing era tune for Benny Goodman, back on the public's radar because of *The Benny Goodman Story*. Perhaps she was doffing her hat to her old friend who had unwittingly provided the key to her exit from Decca.

As she sang, she observed her listeners' smiles and body language, their attentiveness and applause, to feel the vibe in the room and answer her perennial questions *Am I making them happy? Do they like me? Am I reaching everyone?* John Tynan answered: "Ella Fitzgerald sang up a happier storm than this reviewer had heard heretofore. Ella hit the capacity opening night crowd like the Basie brass section."[48] Now it remained for her to get down to work and learn the Cole Porter repertoire with Bregman as her guide. As Bregman would tell this author decades later, "I was never an Ella Fitzgerald fan, ever. As a kid, mother and dad used to take us to see jazz stuff all the time, go to the opera house. . . . I was more into Broadway shows, because of uncle Julie and all that. I'm still more Broadway than jazz."[49] Granz thought that background was perfect for the task ahead.

Chapter 17

THE COLE PORTER EXPERIMENT

(1956-1957)

On February 7, 1956, Fitzgerald stepped into the Capitol Records studio on Melrose Avenue in Hollywood to cut *Ella Fitzgerald Sings the Cole Porter Song Book*.[1] She had many mixed emotions. "At first the idea worried me. I felt it was a big investment for him [Granz] to make—if people didn't buy them, he'd lose a lot," she told one interviewer.[2] "To another she said the project gave her "a chance to do some recordings of songs that I've wanted to do and was afraid of, you know, like show tunes."[3] What was she afraid of? Perhaps it was the historical context of this repertoire. The name Great White Way, referring to the illuminated signage in New York's theater district, possessed an unintended racial irony. In the 1940s and '50s, apart from a few race-specific Black-cast shows—usually written by white songwriters—the color line generally kept Black actors, singers, and dancers out of both the Broadway stage and Hollywood screen musicals.[4] Thirty years later she offered further insight to this turning point in her career:

> In the fifties I started singing with a different kind of style . . . picking out songwriters and singing their songs. Cole Porter was the first. It was like beginning all over again. People who never heard me suddenly heard songs which surprised them because they didn't

think I could sing them. People always figure you could only do one thing. It was like another education.[5]

Fitzgerald educated others in turn. Even while she was still signed with Decca, Granz sketched out the Cole Porter project and went over Gabler's head, pleading with the label's vice-president to consider it:

> When I discussed it with Leonard Schneider and others at the company—not including Milt Gabler—and proposed a budget, they laughed at me. They said it wasn't material she could do. Or maybe they just didn't like the idea. Their lack of insight was amazing.[6]

In *Metronome*, the critic Dirk Schaeffer admitted that before he heard the *Song Book*, he found the Porter-Fitzgerald combination

> particularly ill-chosen. . . . Cole's songs have almost always been distinguished by a definite measure of intelligence—or the nearest a pop song can come to it. . . . Now, whatever praiseworthy [things] one may say about Miss Fitzgerald, intelligence is certainly the one quality to which her voice could never lay claim.[7]

Porter himself, according to his biographer William McBrien, "rather snobbishly doubted that Ella could make any sense of the allusions to the *monde* in his lyrics."[8] Chic insiders got the mischievous references in his *vers de société*, smiled at his *doubles entendres* and coded references to homosexuality, and identified with his musical portrayals of their *liaisons dangereuses*. In 1954 his lyrics had been published as a book of light verse, winning critical acclaim.[9]

In the liner notes to *Ella Fitzgerald Sings the Cole Porter Song Book*, Don Freeman reported that in the studio she was "slightly apprehensive. After every recording session, she'd ask, hopefully: 'Did I say all the words right?' She did, of course. You can hear them for yourself."[10] Even if "Heloise" became "Eloise" in "Just One of Those Things," she mastered "camembert," "Louvre," and "Tin-Pantithesis." How apt that the musical *My Fair Lady* was just opening on Broadway in March 1956. "The rain in Spain stays mainly on the plain," sings its heroine, Eliza Doolittle, purged of her lower-class Cockney accent. "I think she's got it!" cheers her coach, Professor Henry Higgins.

The more pressing issue concerned vocality. Porter wrote songs in many types for both male and female voices, including novelty songs, rhythm tunes, exotic ballads, torch songs, list songs, and closers for production numbers. They had originated on the stage, sung by "legitimate" or "legit" voices, as the jargon went, that is, delivered without amplification by singers who did not need a microphone to be heard over the pit orchestra. Porter's songs were most linked to two revered stage stars, Mary Martin, whose self-described "high-piping" voice cut through the pit orchestra, and Ethel Merman, Porter's favorite, whose belting style easily reached second balconies.[11]

By the time Fitzgerald was contemplating the *Cole Porter Song Book*, jazz and pop singers had shaped an alternative tradition for recordings. In the interwar years, pop singers, sometimes called "microphone singers" (among them Bing Crosby, Dinah Shore, and Frank Sinatra), had turned individual Porter titles into hit parade singles on 78 rpm and 45 rpm records. They treated standards as vehicles to project their own vocal personalities, extracting ballads out of context, rarely singing verses, and switching genders. Cabaret singers tended to view lyrics as scripts for interpretation, cultivating worldly personas to reach urban sophisticates, as Mabel Mercer did in her album of Cole Porter songs, released in 1955. Among jazz singers, including Ella, the jazz ideal opposed the very notion of a fixed score or stable melody. She herself had famously demonstrated this principle by expanding George and Ira Gershwin's "Oh, Lady Be Good" into a scat vehicle. It was reasonable for Bregman to assume she would explore Porter tunes with the same license.

Closing her ears to precedent, Fitzgerald found a third way that she called "a different style" and that we might characterize as curatorial: self-imposed simplicity. According to Bregman, "She was not interested in how other people did this or that song." During their rehearsals at Zardi's, she told him she wanted fidelity to the original melody, harmony, and lyrics. Bregman would sing through a song, then she would take that rendition as the template for her work. She had no need to infuse it with drama or her own personality. Instead, she said, "I'll just sing it, I'll just sing it exactly as you did." Bregman was so startled, he followed up. "I said, 'Don't you want to add?' Ella said, 'Nope, I want to do it exactly how it is.' "[12] By setting aside jazz techniques such as scatting and melodic paraphrasing, and by muting her own personality, she would clear space for a collective presentation of the songwriter's oeuvre.

We should not take her self-imposed simplicity too literally, as transcripts comparing the published originals to her versions show many alterations.[13] Nevertheless, she took a classical approach to material that had typically been treated as a chart rather than a score. At the same time, her roots in jazz and swing reframed the show tunes as midcentury modern songs rather than as antiquarian revivals.

Fitzgerald's profound contribution in rhythm—a legacy of the Harlem-Savoy swing—was to turn Cole Porter songs into swing songs. Fitzgerald modernized and enhanced Porter's melodies through "time," to use jazz shorthand, and rhythmic propulsion. In the three surviving takes of "Let's Do It," we can hear how one attempt just sounds better, with micro-timing so subtle that only a computer could notate it. In rehearsal she exclaimed, "That's swingin'!"[14]

As the arranger for this prominent project, Bregman faced daunting challenges. Arrangers such as Nelson Riddle, Benny Carter, Paul Weston, Billy May, and André Previn were turning Hollywood into a hub of modern jazz and pop orchestration. Bregman was a novice. "I felt sorry for Buddy—his having been elevated to the 'big-time' so early in life," said Milt Bernhart, a first-call Hollywood session trombonist hired for the *Song Book* studio crew. "Buddy practically went from college to Ella Fitzgerald in one jump. He had much to learn and he was forced to learn in the spotlight. Everybody was watching him."[15]

Bernhart judged that Bregman "did very well," producing serviceable arrangements, earning a major career boost, and securing his place in Fitzgerald's story. Working at high speed, he produced twenty-four charts for a sizable ensemble of first-rate studio freelancers, including JATP alumni Barney Kessel on guitar and Harry "Sweets" Edison on trumpet. He gave the other eight numbers small-group treatments, adding variety to the whole. Even Ella's discerning biographer Rainer Nolden, who felt Bregman's "arrangements rarely go beyond average, mediocre craftsmanship," singled out his "brilliant" work in the mid-tempo "What Is This Thing Called Love," dressed in the contemporary aesthetic of "cool jazz."[16]

Granz, for his part, made a major contribution by recognizing the importance of the songs' opening verses. They frame familiar melodies in a kind of recitative-aria parallel to opera, and including them imparted dignity to the project. Sometimes Fitzgerald resisted, and one time Granz recalled a "terrific row":

> It might take me a week later [longer] to convince Ella upon listening to the acetates that we ought to go back and do it again because I really wasn't pleased with it. I couldn't *make* her do it. If she said "No, that's the way I hear it," that's the end of it. I remember one time, "You're the Top," she just couldn't get the verse for whatever the reasons were, she couldn't get it. So we said, "Oh, do it without the verse," but I knew we were destroying something because the verse was an important verse. And Ella on her own two days later . . . called up and said, "I know you want me to do the verse so let's try it again."[17]

Granz was right. That verse was "not only a perfect introduction to the song but also a perfect introduction to the art of Cole Porter and in particular his rhyming genius," as music educator Rob Kapilow has written. Once she consented, Fitzgerald went on to master the verse's "virtuosic, erudite, quadruple rhyme."[18]

Despite the forethought he devoted to this project, Granz stubbornly insisted on a difficult, rushed production schedule of three marathon sessions on February 7, 8, and 9. His speed and decisiveness, and his confidence in his own judgment, were both a virtue and a fault. Later that year Fitzgerald publicly acknowledged her discomfort at having had to "rush" through the sessions.[19] Bregman also complained, as did the pianist Paul Smith, soon to be hired as Fitzgerald's accompanist. Smith recalled that the sessions were "just kind of *ground* out. . . . We'd run down the verse, just to make sure she knew it, and bang, we'd record it!"[20] Granz proudly told an English critic that there were "only three retakes in the whole lot."[21]

Amid all their haste, however, the collaborators inadvertently omitted Porter's most famous song, "Night and Day." Now that would have been an embarrassment. In a radio interview with Willis Conover, broadcast around the world over the Voice of America, Ella told him:

> We were flying, I think we were going to Germany, and . . . we started a conversation about—something about day and night, and all of a sudden Norman says, "Day and night? Oh, you mean 'Night and Day.' We didn't even record . . . Cole Porter's number one song." He says, "That's just like doing a [Hoagy] Carmichael album and [we] don't put 'Stardust' in there!" And he says, "Oh, we just gotta do it." He says, "I don't know how to face the man." In fact, he was supposed to meet Cole Porter in Italy. He says, "I think I'll have to go everywhere else but Italy, because we don't have the number."[22]

On March 25, after returning from Europe, they recorded "Night and Day" along with retakes for "You're the Top," "I Concentrate on You," and "Let's Do It."

Porter had telephoned Granz even before Ella's recording sessions, when he was writing "Now You Has Jazz," a centerpiece duet for Louis Armstrong and Bing Crosby in the 1956 film *High Society*. He had sought reassurance on his use of jazz vernacular, and after Granz helped him, he gratefully sent Granz a lead sheet inscribed "By Norman Granz and Cole Porter," which Granz had framed and hung in his Hollywood office.[23]

In February, before the album was released, the two men met in person in New York at Porter's fabulous penthouse apartment in the Waldorf Astoria. Granz was looking for a quotable endorsement and got the comment, "My, what marvelous diction that girl has," which was then widely circulated.[24] A few months later Granz recalled:

> I personally played these records for Cole Porter (who, I imagine, is a pretty good authority on Cole Porter), and he told me (believe me, quite professionally and not because he is a friend of mine), that this album was one of the finest he had ever heard, and he made the specific comment about one of the tunes that Ella breathed a new life into it for him—he never knew the tune was so good.[25]

But according to the author James Gavin, Porter wrote "withering letters of criticism" about interpretations of his songs by Fitzgerald, Frank Sinatra, and Lena Horne.[26]

After the recording sessions in Los Angeles, Ella did a memorable guest spot on *Stage Show*, a half-hour TV variety program on Saturday night hosted by the Dorsey Brothers. On February 11, 1956, she shared the evening with twenty-one-year-old Elvis Presley in his third appearance on national television.[27] He sang "Blue Suede Shoes" and "Heartbreak Hotel," which would make their way into her novelty repertoire the following summer.

Then she flew to New York for a few days before embarking on her next European tour with JATP. She caught up with her family, especially her son, Ray Jr., then six years old. Still living in the house on Ditmars Boulevard in Queens, she trusted her aunt Virginia, the head of the extended family of cousins, to raise him. Junior considered her his grandmother. Uncle Leon, Virginia's other son, lived close by, as did Georgiana Henry and her son Richard. Ella could go on tour and miss him without worry.

★★★

JATP OPENED ITS EUROPEAN TOUR on February 18 in Oslo, then performed in twelve German cities in twelve days. Usually ready to plug her new recordings on tour, Fitzgerald curiously left the Porter album behind, apart from singing the obvious "I Love Paris" in that city. Instead, she returned to her mix of ballads, impersonations of Louis Armstrong, and scat gems, this time including a raucous version of the rhythm and blues hit "I Want You to Be My Baby." In short, her material still reflected her Decca repertoire. A special moment of the tour came in Stockholm, when the city sponsored a free concert program for young teenagers called School Holidays Jazz.

Back in the States by the end of March, Fitzgerald returned to an uncharacteristic lull in her otherwise nonstop career. On April 9 she filled a guest spot on Steve Allen's *Tonight* show. Not much else transpired for her professionally until a two-night gig in early May at El Morocco in Montreal. In between, on April 18 in Washington, D.C., she granted one of her most casual and personal interviews to Willis Conover for the Voice of America broadcast. They ranged over a variety of professional topics, including Norman Granz:

Conover: That Norman Granz has certainly done a wonderful job of finding new outlets for appearances, hasn't he?

Fitzgerald: Yes, I will say this, that I think Mr. Granz works very hard, and that's one of the reasons everything seems to be so successful when we play over there, because it's all prepared for us, and all we have to do is go to work.

C: Specifically, what has Norman Granz done for you? You were already an established name and an established singing favorite before he became professionally aware of you, but since then, what can you credit Norman Granz with having done for you, Ella?

F: Well, I can credit him for getting some jobs and things that I always—places I wanted to play and was afraid to play, and he's given me a little more confidence in myself, and I've had a chance to do some recordings of songs that I've wanted to do and was afraid of, you know like show tunes, for instance. We have a Cole Porter album coming out with about thirty-four songs, and I do some ballads, I do novelties, and I do some of the sweet songs, and I even get a little sexy on a couple of songs [*both laugh*].

C: With Cole Porter lyrics it'd be hard to avoid I guess.

F: Yeah, I don't think some of them will ever reach the air, but they can get 'em in the stores for, uh, your own personal use [*both laugh*].[28]

In the interview, Fitzgerald names some singers who, as Conover put it, "deserved to be listened to," among them Martha Raye, Lena Horne, Margaret Whiting, Anita O'Day, and June Christy. She squinted at Elvis Presley, citing "Blue Suede Shoes" as an example of the power of a hit single, her particular obsession. Then she pretended to forget the title of his latest hit, "Heartbreak Hotel," mentioning "something about a hotel."

In the final segment, she named some favorite disks for Conover to spin, including Gerry Mulligan's 1952 quartet recording of "Frenesi," a progenitor of the "West Coast cool" sound; Dizzy Gillespie's "Ooh-shoo-be-doo-be" with singer Joe Carroll; Billie Holiday's "Good Morning Heartache"; Count Basie and Joe Williams's cover of "Roll 'Em Pete," which Ella sang earlier that year at Zardi's; Sarah Vaughan's "I'll Never Smile Again," from her recent landmark LP *In the Land of Hi-Fi*; Duke Ellington's "Jam with Sam," a blues jam and performance staple; and the Oscar Peterson Trio's "Swingin' Till the Girls Come Home." She also mentioned Frank Sinatra and Nelson Riddle's "Glad to Be Unhappy," recalling how one evening when Sinatra sat in the audience, she messed up the song from nerves.

★★★

UPON THE RELEASE OF THE COLE PORTER EXPERIMENT on May 15, 1956, the verdict came quickly: an unexpected rush of sales. In the June 2 issue of *Billboard*, Verve ran an ad touting that over fifty thousand double-LP packages, retailing at a high price point of $9.95, had been sold and that the pressing plant was in overtime production. "The year it came out, it was for us insane," Granz later recalled. Within a month, sales reached the 100,000 mark, and even in early 1959 the album still appeared in *Down Beat*'s top-twenty jazz LP chart.[29] *The Cole Porter Song Book* went on to become one of the best-selling jazz records of all time and was probably the most commercially successful release of Granz's career.

Three sets of liner notes lent cultural authority to the album package, which was presented in a gatefold format and looked like a coffee table book. The production had Granz's fingerprints all over it, with an excerpt from Fred Lounsberry's introduction to *103 Lyrics of Cole Porter* and an overview by jazz journalist Don Freeman, who praised Fitzgerald's "basic purity of sound, and of style; she sings honestly and truly." The cover photograph framed the singer against the 1950s palette of peach, gray, and aqua, dignifying her status as a modern, professional working musician. A Black woman without a white-woman hairdo, she poses assertively with hand on hip, holding a lead sheet in rehearsal. It was a perfectly calibrated package for upper-middle- and middle-middle-class affluent consumers listening to high-fidelity LPs on their fashionable home consoles.

Solid reviews flowed in. *Billboard* called it a "monumental issue," with the "real cream of Porter done here as they never have been done before. Jazz shops, 'class' shops, and plain record shops—stock up!"[30] *Down Beat*'s anonymous reviewer wrote, "Never has so much superior Porter received so musically illuminating a series of treatments in one recital as happily happens here."[31]

But there were enough dissenting views to warrant some reflection. Even her supporter *Metronome*'s Bill Coss read Fitzgerald's equipoise as blandness, suggesting that Porter's lyrics were "out of Ella's realm of experience." Frank Sinatra or Billie Holiday could "tell their own story" through Porter vehicles, but in "Love for Sale" Fitzgerald shortchanged his sexual sophistication "using the usually pretty embellishments which are her stock-in-trade, not knowing that you can add drama not ornament to those twisting lines."[32] Coss might have added

Fitzgerald's version of "Miss Otis Regrets," which did not equal Ethel Waters's 1934 recording.

In critics' debates, comparisons between artists can raise questions that harden into dogma—not because the questions lack merit or the answers lack truth, but rather because concentration on what is missing slights new ways of hearing and thinking. In his rebuttal letter to the editor, Granz explained that the album was "virtually a decathlon of singing. I don't believe any singer could have faced up to all the changes of mood, tempo, instrumentation and lyrical content as Ella did."[33] Granz had a point about the album's cumulative effort and impact, while Coss was still thinking in terms of singles.

Probably none of these men anticipated the extent to which Fitzgerald would serve as Porter's messenger. The Porter expert Robert Kimball credits this album with "introducing more people to Porter's songs than through any other recording at the time of its release."[34] The inherent tenderness of her voice emphasized the implicit humanity of his songs, mediating the remote sophistication in Porter's lyrics. As the composer-critic Alec Wilder wrote, "Porter's most quoted lines are all the East Side New York sophisticated kind. But no matter how distant or unrealistic, no matter how weary or cynical they may have been, Porter's lyrics were astonishingly softened and warmed by his music."[35] In retrospect, the album was more than the sum of its parts. Fitzgerald synthesized African American and Euro American singing practices to produce a hybrid model for a "jazz pop" performance of show tunes and a classic recording on its own terms.

★★★

BEFORE COSS REVIEWED THE *COLE PORTER SONG BOOK*, he met with Granz and Fitzgerald in the recording studio on June 25, 1956, to witness her first post–Cole Porter session. Coss was representing *Metronome* for the production of an LP, *Metronome All-Stars 1956*, underwritten by Granz. Since 1939 the magazine had sporadically sponsored studio recordings of its poll winners. The 1956 LP turned out to be a brilliant swan song for the series. Ella and Count Basie's band, as the number-one female vocalist and big band in the latest *Metronome* poll, were teaming up for the first time. Coss wrote that she arrived "protesting that she really wasn't a blues singer and that she felt rather awed about singing with the band anyway," then got to work.[36]

This little-known session remains one of Fitzgerald's most satisfying examples of musical friendship. She and Basie remade Basie's instrumental hit single "April in Paris," which had been released in January 1956. Part of its appeal came from trumpeter Thad Jones quoting "Pop Goes the Weasel" to launch his solo, and Basie speaking the lines "One more time" and "Let's try it one more once" after two false endings. Basie said, "As soon as that record hit the jukeboxes, everywhere we went, audiences started imitating that jive line I used for the tag."[37] In the remake with Fitzgerald, she quotes "Pop Goes the Weasel" along with Jones and usurps Basie's "jive line" for the second false ending. The band adds a "Jingle Bells" tag to the arrangement, in a tune about springtime. Fitzgerald would revisit the song several times in her career, keeping the amusing quotes and Basie signifiers intact.

Fitzgerald recorded three other tunes in the session with her friend Joe Williams, who had joined Basie in 1954 and was carving out an important career. Gifted with a powerful baritone and enormous vocal magnetism, Williams had placed a number of tunes on the rhythm and blues charts. His 1955 recording "Every Day I Have the Blues" was a massive hit for Basie and decisive in the band's reemergence. Williams had first heard Ella on radio broadcasts from the Savoy Ballroom in 1937, then saw her lead Webb's band after his death at Chicago's Regal Theater. They became friends in the mid-1940s. "It was always a thrill and a challenge to work with her," said Williams. "We used to challenge each other vocally: we used to spend an afternoon, just the two of us. We'd sit and drink and challenge each other—this was around 1946."[38]

The Fitzgerald-Williams session with Basie's band was jazz joy in action. They flirted in "Party Blues" before exchanging scat choruses:

Fitzgerald: Joe, you have no idea how long I've had to wait. . . . This is
the greatest thrill, being on this swingin' date.
Williams: Ella Fitzgerald, it sure is good to see you. . . . 'Cause baby girl
I love everything you do.

Later that year Granz issued "Party Blues" and "April in Paris" as a 45
rpm single.[39] Both tracks also appeared on *Metronome All-Stars 1956*, but
little attention was paid to this commercially negligible album. Basie
and Fitzgerald would return to the studio for Verve in a few years.
Fitzgerald continued to acknowledge her musical friendship with Williams by adopting and augmenting his hit rendition of "Roll 'Em Pete."
She added stanzas, like this one from a live JATP date in Seattle in
October 1956:

Joe Williams jazzed the blues with Count Basie's band
He's the singin'est, swingin'est singer in the land.[40]

In mid-June 1956 Fitzgerald resumed her usual bookings. At Basin
Street, her New York celebrity fans sat at ringside VIP tables marked
SINGER'S CIRCLE, and Dorothy Kilgallen spied singer Dick Haymes and
songwriter Johnny Mercer in the crowd.[41] In early July she made her
third appearance at the Newport Jazz Festival, where Duke Ellington
electrified the crowd with a twenty-seven-chorus blues solo by tenor
saxophonist Paul Gonsalves on "Crescendo and Diminuendo in Blue."
Rain drenched a brave audience at the Thursday-night opening, but
Fitzgerald performed Friday with about seven thousand in attendance.
According to Whitney Balliett, the other performers on the bill—
including the Brubeck quartet and a pickup group led by Buck Clayton
and Coleman Hawkins—were "like old beer, flat. The stunning exception was Ella Fitzgerald, who appeared, huge and shining in a pale purple gown and white fur wrap, and sang knee-loose and swaying, with
a strength and emotion not easy to forget."[42] She was working in her
Porter favorites, singing "Just One of Those Things" with the verse, "As
Dorothy Parker once said / To her boyfriend, 'Fare thee well.' " A little

rock 'n' roll helped raise the audience applause meter, as she wove in references to "Elvis, Elvis Presley" and his hit tunes "Blue Suede Shoes" and "All Shook Up." Jack Tracy described the audience reaction as "the only mass hypnotism of the evening."[43]

Less noticed was the impact of her sterling backup trio, with pianist Tommy Flanagan, bassist Benny Moten, and drummer Gus Johnson. Johnson was beginning a seven-year run with Fitzgerald, and Flanagan would come and go until becoming her regular accompanist in the mid-1960s. Both were learning what Johnson called "her little ways"—her perfectionism along with her social anxieties and her self-consciousness about her appearance. Johnson later gave this account of the trio's dynamic:

> I used to tell her all the time, "Go ahead and sing. Nobody's talking bad about you. They love you!" She wanted people to love her, and she's beautiful, to me, but she was always trying to improve herself in everything she did. When Tommy Flanagan came with the group, we were playing some club in Cleveland, and the first night he was doing the best he could when she turned around and like to scared him to death. I saw it happen and just told her, "Turn around!" I believe that pretty well shocked her, so afterwards I walked right behind her, waiting to hear "You're fired!" But she had evidently gotten over it. "This is his first night," I told her. "He doesn't know the numbers, and he's nervous."[44]

★★★

FITZGERALD'S SUCCESS BOOSTED GRANZ'S CAREER as a record producer to another level, and her career became increasingly important to him. A Los Angeles native, Granz never liked New York and suggested she relocate from Queens to L.A. as her bookings shifted toward the West Coast. Granz lived in Benedict Canyon in West Los Angeles, off Ventura Boulevard, and ran his businesses from a small office on 451 North

Canon Drive in Beverly Hills, producing recording sessions at Capitol Studios in Hollywood. Fitzgerald, as a Black American, had few choices of where to live in a city that practiced redlining and real estate segregation. Yet upper-middle-class African Americans prominent in "Black Hollywood" could buy single-family homes in certain pockets of the Los Angeles sprawl. On May 29, 1956, Fitzgerald closed on a house at 3971 Hepburn Avenue in Leimert Park, a racially mixed neighborhood in South Los Angeles. Built in 1950, the Spanish colonial home had over 2,500 square feet with three bedrooms and two and a half baths.[45] A photograph of Fitzgerald standing in front of her pleasant-looking home in September 1957 shows a stucco exterior on a tree-lined street. Ray Charles and his family bought a house on the same block in March 1958. His son Ray Charles Robinson, Jr., wrote that the neighborhood "was a mecca for upwardly mobile families of all races," especially for African American entertainers.[46]

She was leaving behind her home on Ditmars Boulevard in the "Black Gold Coast" of Queens, a community she knew. That neighborhood was home to many celebrities from the worlds of entertainment and sports, and it was close to New York City, the jazz epicenter of the world. There she had friends who would miss her when she was gone and notice when she occasionally landed home. There she had played pinochle at the home of singer-dancer Rosetta Williams, caught glimpses of Count Basie, offered a home to Lester Young as he moved from one place to another, and in 1953 invited "the entire Woody Herman Band" to dinner.[47] It was also near her relatives and their children, including the families of her cousin Georgiana Henry and her aunt Virginia Williams.

Still, moving seemed like the right thing to do, and she spent much of her career on the road anyhow. Ella's son Ray, then eight years old, made the three-day journey with her, by train from New York to Los Angeles. When asked about the move decades later, he thought the question was a tad foolish. "You go where the money is," he said.[48] Granz was her manager, agent, producer, label owner, and trusted adviser whose guidance had already proved essential. Los Angeles had its own cultural vitality and offered an easier way of life. She was on the move literally and figuratively. From gross earnings of about $168,000, her net after business expenses and income taxes was about $54,000.

On August 15, 1956, Granz produced an outdoor gala concert at the Hollywood Bowl in Los Angeles. In addition to Fitzgerald and the JATP troupe, he booked in Art Tatum and Louis Armstrong, enriching the evening. Tickets sold out. Twenty thousand people sat on wooden benches on the gently sloping hill that formed a natural amphitheater, the summer venue for the Los Angeles Philharmonic. The Bowl management had expanded its pop fare for stars like Frank Sinatra and Dinah Shore but generally ignored jazz, and this was its first recorded jazz concert.[49] Seeing his musicians at this prestigious site, Granz entered a state of grace about his beloved music:

> Suddenly I felt that after all the talk, and true talk it was, about "jazz and the smoke-filled rooms" and jazz's roots in the work fields and brothels, it was wonderful that evening to see that jazz finally found a proper place for itself, a sort of new dimension, where it could move great masses of people emotionally, and, in a way, beautifully and peacefully.[50]

Fitzgerald and Armstrong received equal billing as headliners. After the opening jam session and a memorable set of solo piano by Tatum, Fitzgerald closed out the first half of the concert with seven numbers, backed by pianist Paul Smith, guitarist Barney Kessel, bassist Joe Mondragon, and drummer Alvin Stoller. Two Cole Porter tunes, "Just One of Those Things" and "Love for Sale," were regulars in her setlist by this time, joining the warhorses "I Can't Give You Anything But Love," "Too Close for Comfort," and the scat feature "Air Mail Special." "She mowed down her audience, which was a large and varied one," the *Los Angeles Times* reviewer wrote.[51]

At the end of the concert, after Armstrong finished his set, Fitzgerald joined him onstage. The two reprised the Decca tune they had waxed ten years earlier, "You Won't Be Satisfied (Until You Break My Heart)," with Fitzgerald ad-libbing some lyrics to Armstrong's mellow trumpet noodling. Then they launched into an old Chick Webb favorite, "Undecided," at a freeway tempo. "To see such greats as Louis (Satchmo) Armstrong with his trumpet and froggy voice, Ella Fitzgerald, the one and only, as Der Bingle [Bing Crosby] and thousands of others call her, get together, they make your hair stand on end, and this night was no exception," wrote the *Chicago Defender*'s Hazel Washington.[52]

Granz would issue the concert on the double album *Jazz at the Hollywood Bowl*, which was Fitzgerald's first live recording issued on a commercial label. The album received solid reviews but did not have much market impact. Still, the end of the concert, when Fitzgerald joined Armstrong, revealed hidden potential. The next day the two friends went into a recording studio to make an album of duets for Granz.

Armstrong's very presence represented a coup for Verve. In 1955 his manager, Joe Glaser, had eliminated exclusive record contracts from his business model, severing ties with Decca in 1955 and Columbia in 1956. Promising Armstrong a spot on the Bowl concert in exchange for some precious studio time, Granz swept in like an eagle to make a recording that would enhance Fitzgerald's public profile almost as much as the Cole Porter album.

Chapter 18

SING ME A STANDARD

(1956-1957)

"Perhaps Armstrong's ideal partner was Ella Fitzgerald, who herself was one of his greatest fans," wrote the jazz historian Dan Morgenstern, who knew them both.[1] This new recording was about to demonstrate Norman Granz's awareness of Fitzgerald's genius for empathic collaboration. A title with "Ella and _____" was proving to be a formula for greatness. He had witnessed this repeatedly with "Ella and Oscar" on JATP tours in the early 1950s. He united "Ella and Basie" for the first time for *Metronome All-Stars 1956*. Now it was "Ella and Louis," a strategic move pairing her with a figure of greater renown.[2]

To record the album's eleven cuts, Granz allotted one afternoon—August 16, 1956. Oscar Peterson, Herb Ellis, Ray Brown, and Buddy Rich made up the stellar rhythm quartet. The setlist included both standards and show tunes, a repertoire slighted in Armstrong's playbook at Decca. "Louis simply had the tune played for him," Granz later recalled, "there was no procrastination whatsoever. That was all improvised, all 'head' [arrangements]."[3] Their list included Hoagy Carmichael's "The Nearness of You," Vernon Duke's "April in Paris," and Gershwin's "A Foggy Day (In London Town)." Ella "deferred to Armstrong to make the final choices on the songs and keys," even if they were not her keys.[4] On Irving Berlin's "Cheek to Cheek," she and Louis turn into the vocal counterpart of Ginger Rogers and Fred Astaire, evoking their courtship choreography in the film musical *Top Hat*. "Now Mama, dance with me," Louis ad-libs; when he transfers the baton to her, he says, "Sing it Ella, swing it," and she responds with a slightly different intensity, showing off her fabled swing, pushing the time forward. It was enchanting.

The honey-mustard blend of their voices was enhanced by the "great deal of admiration each had for the other," as Ella's son, Ray Brown, Jr., stated. "It's almost like listening to an inside joke because it seems like they're giggling at everything, there's just this joy that the two of them shared."[5] "Louis Armstrong was a lesson of love," Fitzgerald said in 1986. "This was a man everybody loved, no matter what he did. He just had that 'way' and that 'want.'"[6] Not really. Was she indifferent to the controversies his stage persona provoked among both Black and white cultural critics?[7] Oscar Peterson reflected,

> Ella was a very proud person, you know . . . and, certainly, racially, she was proud, you know. She could be insulted very easily and, as we say, would "feel a draft" very easily. Now she's in the studio with Pops, who, at that time many people associated him with being a form of Uncle Tomism. . . . Most of it she found funny, you know. It didn't bother her.[8]

Knowing her temperament, Peterson had insight.

> And she wasn't tolerating him. It wasn't a matter of her tolerating him. She just got a kick out of the way he approached, for instance, the lyrics to some of these tunes and the way he'd attach a mm-hmm on the end of something, which I'm sure she wouldn't even think of doing. He'd be singing and she'd look over and she'd just hold her head in her hands and just cover her mouth, you know. But she knew that was Pops and she loved him.[9]

At the time she gave him a photo of herself inscribed, "To Satchomouth, the greatest person I know."[10]

Fitzgerald said later, "Louis was the type of person—like same way that he talked to you, that's the same way he played. That's why it was such a ball to work with him. You never felt like you were actually doing a recording date. We just had a ball. We went in and whatever came out that was it."[11]

> [He] would go through all the motions just like he would on stage, and it was just such a thrill to watch and listen to him, so I would come in all wrong in the songs and we'd have to make it over, you know. [Imitating Louis] "That's all right, Ella." That's what we did. That's the way we did all our albums. . . . When we made records, I never made the record right. I'd be so busy watching him, you know, he had those rolled down socks.

The socks appear on the well-known album cover. Ella wears gingham. The pair are seated on folding chairs and appear without any typography save the Verve logo.[12]

Praise-filled reviews accompanied the album's release in October 1956.[13] It remained a top seller well into 1957 and has since become a classic LP.

***

FITZGERALD'S CREATIVE SURGE continued through late August and September 1956, when she recorded *Ella Fitzgerald Sings the Rodgers and Hart Song Book*, celebrating the dazzling legacy of this songwriting team for Broadway musicals from 1925 to 1942.[14] Drawing on the 1951 piano-vocal collection *The Rodgers and Hart Song Book: The Words and Music of Forty-Seven of Their Songs from Twenty-Two Shows and Two Movies*, Granz and Fitzgerald included thirty-five songs encompassing both the familiar ("With a Song in My Heart," "Lover," "Manhattan," "My Funny Valentine," "Where or When," and "Blue Moon") and the esoteric and seldom-heard ("A Ship Without a Sail," "To Keep My Love Alive").[15]

With the success of the Cole Porter album, "she could have a big band, she could have strings, she could have any damned thing she wanted," Granz later said.[16] Whether she asked for it or not, Buddy Bregman, in vastly improved arrangements, gave her an orchestra worthy of Rimsky-Korsakov's tone poem *Scheherazade*, with eleven violins, harp, glockenspiel, flutes, French horn, and tubular bells. The arrangements, which Ella found "so pretty," reflected the Hollywood taste for what musicologist John Howland aptly calls "luxe pop," the midcentury synthesis merging "standard big band instrumentation with lush, urbane, string-based backgrounds."[17] A few tracks used just a rhythm section led by pianist Paul Smith. *Billboard* found that "Wait Till You See Her," a duet of one chorus lasting about a minute with guitarist Barney Kessel, was "alone . . . worth the price of the album."[18] That Granz followed that track with a brassy "Lover" shows his producer's acumen. In an era of rigidly defined sex roles and stigmatized homosexuality, Ella changed the lyrics to "Wait Till You See Him," while "Have You Met Miss Jones?" became "Have You Met Sir Jones?" Granz said he argued for "Miss Jones," but "Ella was very firm . . . and I didn't think it warranted a stand on principle."[19] In the near future, Anita O'Day would use "Sir Jones" and Sarah Vaughan would sing of "Old Jones."[20]

In contrast to such conservatism, Fitzgerald embraced two songs by Rodgers and Hart that challenged stereotypes of ingenue innocence. "The Lady Is a Tramp" pilloried class conformity in high society and glorified the liberated milieu of "hobohemia." Ella cherished the song and would take it on JATP tours; her most famous interpretations would follow in the 1960s.

Ella's other favorite was "Bewitched, Bothered, and Bewildered," in which her voice illustrated the lyrics as seduction on its own terms. We are "bewitched" by her lustrous beguiling voice, which "moved with the ease, purity, and grace of a well-developed operatic singer," in the words of vocal expert John H. Haley. "Unlike most popular singers, she was capable of transfixing her listeners, placing us in a virtual trance, based upon the sheer uncanny beauty of flowing tone she could serve up in a ballad." How she did this was a "mystery."[21] She so dominated this song that Lorenz Hart's then-controversial lyrics, which dare to celebrate lust, receded into the background. An older, self-aware woman embarks on an adulterous affair with a younger playmate she knows is a "cad" or a "heel." The lyrics were routinely censored, as in Doris Day's hit version in 1950. But Granz allotted over seven minutes for Fitzgerald to sing all the refrains, an act duly noted at the time. Later in 1956 Fitzgerald said, "I got real sexy on that one," joking about her sexual charisma.[22] In a later live performance at Mister Kelly's in Chicago, after singing "Those ants that invaded my pants," she apologized, "It was on the record!"[23]

Released in January 1957, *Ella Fitzgerald Sings the Rodgers and Hart Song Book* surpassed even the commercial success of the Cole Porter album. Fitzgerald earned the respect of the composer himself. Richard Rodgers had objected to many swing treatments of his songs and in 1953 took to the *San Francisco Chronicle* to complain about "the enormous amount of distortion visited upon our tunes by performing artists, both vocal and instrumental." But in 1958 he gave her a significant endorsement: "Whatever it is Ella does to my songs they sound better."[24]

The critical reception was diverse, as some still registered doubts about her emotional intelligence. The widely read Irving Kolodin still took her to task for "A-Tisket A-Tasket," giving her a "most improved" award: "For a lady who made her first fame in terms of a nursery rhyme . . . Fitzgerald has come a long way to deal on even terms with the verbal niceties of 'It Never Entered My Mind.' "[25] *Metronome*'s Bill Coss detected a "certain amount of faking (that is, pretending of knowledge), when the lyrics deal with subjects obviously out of the normal ones that befall human beings. . . . (we're with Anita [O'Day], who says, 'who dreamed up the idea of Ella singing *and then my heart stood still*')."[26]

★★★

THOSE WHO KNEW FITZGERALD only from records might have been shocked to hear her concert on September 1, 1956, at the Sunset Auditorium in Carmel, California.[27] Ignoring most of her songbook material, she covered current popular singles by Julie London ("Cry Me a River") and Frank Sinatra ("Love and Marriage"). For "Autumn Leaves," she told the audience, "It's so pretty, I would like to do this song even though I don't know the lyrics." She impersonated Louis Armstrong singing "Sixteen Tons," ad-libbing "That doesn't go into a concert, but we decided to do something to cheer you up." Inventing a medley on the phrase "Saturday night," she referenced Duke Ellington's "Don't Get Around Much Anymore" ("Missed the Saturday dance . . .") and Frank Sinatra's "Same Old Saturday Night" and "Saturday Night Is the Loneliest Night of the Week," confiding to the audience, "I dance too."

★★★

IN JANUARY 1957 the gossip columnist Dorothy Kilgallen, a longtime Ella booster, wrote that her

> schedule has become so crowded she can't even count on Sundays for relaxation any more. Sunday the 27th, for example, will begin with her daily Swedish lesson (Ella departs next month on a concert tour of Scandinavia and Europe), followed by four shows at the Paramount, a sandwiching-in of rehearsals and performance on the Ed Sullivan TV Show, and as a finale a midnight salute to the President and Mrs. Eisenhower during the ANTA's [American National Theatre and Academy] "White House Serenade" from the Waldorf.[28]

None of this happened because she had a sudden onset of acute appendicitis, which, befitting her increased celebrity, got coverage everywhere from the *New York Times* to the *Pittsburgh Courier* to the French *Jazz Magazine*. She convalesced for a month with her aunt Virginia Williams in Queens. "When I woke up in the hospital," she said, Virginia's "was the first face I saw. She'd take care of the kids all day and come back to sit with me in the hospital all night. She just loves you back to well."[29]

By March Fitzgerald resumed limited bookings, and on March 24 she appeared on *The Ed Sullivan Show*. In April she had bookings in Jamaica and Panama with Oscar Peterson. The rescheduled European tour, the most extensive to date, lasted from April 23 through early June, reaching thirty-four cities. Granz issued no recordings from the tour, but in the early twenty-first century archival footage of full concerts from European state-owned television stations became commercially available and filled the vacuum. In Amsterdam, Stockholm, and Brussels, she glowed in front of adoring audiences, backed by the superior musicianship of pianist Don Abney, bassist Ray Brown, guitarist Herb Ellis, and drummer Jo Jones. But she limited her stage patter to frequent thank-yous.

Fitzgerald's relationship with Norman Granz remained solid, despite some memorable arguments. "When we were in Italy," Fitzgerald remembered, "they liked 'Lullaby of Birdland.' [But Granz] didn't like 'Lullaby of Birdland,' and he didn't want me to sing 'Lullaby of Birdland.' I was determined I was going to sing it. And I went on the stage, and he went on the stage and sat and wouldn't let the fellows play or nothing."[30] Likely referring to the same tour, Granz recalled that "we had a terrible flare-up. It was in Milan; she didn't sing 'April in Paris,' her big hit record there; instead, she let the audience shout her into 'Lady Be Good.' When she came off I yelled and she yelled and we didn't speak for three days."[31]

Back home, Fitzgerald still toppled barriers in jazz's continuing struggle for cultural inclusion. On June 13 she debuted at the Copacabana, designated "New York's most important night club" by *Down Beat*.[32] The Copa was Frank Sinatra's favored New York venue, and Black vocalists Billy Eckstine, Nat King Cole, Harry Belafonte, Eartha Kitt, and Pearl Bailey had preceded her there. But the Copa's manager, Jules Podell, called her engagement an "experiment" for a jazz singer in "unfamiliar surroundings."[33] She was back at the Copa the following year, and on her opening night she welcomed Sinatra, Johnny Mathis, and Vic Damone, who "to the delight of the audience . . . joined Ella in a song fest."[34]

Fitzgerald's most important date in the summer of 1957 was the Newport Jazz Festival, which broke its attendance record. Granz had an exclusive contract to record the festival and produced a special live album, *Ella Fitzgerald and Billie Holiday at Newport*, pairing Fitzgerald's July 4 appearance with Holiday's on July 6. But the potential landmark record turned into a disappointment, as neither singer was at her best. Still, Fitzgerald generated sparks for the crowd of about ten thousand in her scat closer, "Air Mail Special," making humorous references to Davy Crockett, Harry Belafonte's "Banana Boat Song," and Dean Martin's "That's Amore."[35]

A few days after Newport, Fitzgerald joined Louis Armstrong and Lionel Hampton at the Warner Theatre, a four-thousand-seat movie palace in the gambling resort of Atlantic City. On July 9, as she stood in front of a half-filled auditorium, an audience member rushed onstage and attacked her. According to press reports, the attacker was William Edward Fitzgerald, a psychotic drug addict who mistook her for his errant wife. Nevertheless, Fitzgerald handled her second show, and the incident became another experience to be scatted away. Fitzgerald and Armstrong did just that on July 26, while recording their sequel duet LP, *Ella and Louis Again*. In their rendition of "Stompin' at the Savoy," a five-minute tour de force romp about the good old days, he said, "One more, Ella, one more," goading her into an extra chorus. "What'll we do, what'll we do?" she asked. "One more, don't grab your coat now." Then he ad-libbed, "When we was in Atlantic City—no, we won't talk about that!"[36]

Norman Granz rewarded Ella Fitzgerald's brilliant year by scheduling a solo date on July 20 at the Hollywood Bowl. While jazz concerts had become commonplace since Granz had first broken the barrier, only a handful of jazz artists, such as Erroll Garner and Dave Brubeck, had been the solo attraction on a concert bill in a large American venue. For the first half of the Hollywood Bowl concert, Fitzgerald was backed by a 102-piece orchestra playing Frank DeVol's luxe pop arrangements of swing era standards. For the second half, she was accompanied only by a jazz rhythm section. No live recording was issued, but four days later Fitzgerald and DeVol recorded several songs, and their further sessions in 1957, 1958, and 1959 were combined for three albums, *Like Someone in Love, Get Happy!,* and *Hello, Love.*[37] Also from the July 24 session, but issued as a single, was DeVol's fresh update of "A-Tisket A-Tasket" as a mambo, which she liked and brought to her club dates. In these albums, Fitzgerald cultivated what might be termed her "rom-com voice," luxuriating in the beauty of its pampered prime, with melodic refinements and tender nuances that exuded the warmth of the mink coats she loved. In his *Down Beat* review of *Like Someone in Love,* Dom Cerulli wrote, "Fifteen lovely ballads are mounted in a setting more beautiful than platinum," evoking John Kenneth Galbraith's wry comment in his 1958 bestseller, *The Affluent Society,* "Wealth is not without its advantages."[38]

★★★

DESPITE THE WARM PUBLIC ACCLAIM SHE RECEIVED, Fitzgerald the woman freely acknowledged the gaps in her private life. Since the collapse of her marriage to Ray Brown in 1953, she had not found a steady someone, though rumors occasionally surfaced in gossip columns.[39] In the late 1950s, at her request, Buddy Bregman arranged a date for her with Pete Rugolo, the white arranger associated with Stan Kenton and his former band singer June Christy. Rugolo was thrilled to meet her, cooking a gourmet Italian dinner. "She had a crush on him," Bregman recalled.

> She talked very soft, said "It's nice to meet you." He goes back in the kitchen, she turns to me, "Honey, I've got a headache. Maybe I should go." I said, "No, you can't do that, it's rude." I said to myself, "This is a disaster." She said, "You need to take me home. I want to go home, Buddy, let's go home." She was very smart in that world of her singing, but the social aspect of it is not good.[40]

In June 1957 she told a New York tabloid, "I guess I pick them wrong. But I want to get married again. I'm still looking. Everybody wants companionship."[41]

Later that summer she had a candidate in mind. On her way to a gala benefit in Monte Carlo on August 4, she detoured to Oslo to meet Thor Einar Larsen, a handsome twenty-nine-year-old concert promoter whom she met during a JATP tour. When she arrived in Oslo, they became a public couple. Fitzgerald flirted with the press, saying she wished to marry him, and photos of the happy-looking couple appeared in newspapers. It seemed harmless enough until a front-page story appeared on July 29 in the Norwegian tabloid *Verden Gangs*. The headline read, "Ella Fitzgerald's name is Mrs. Larsen. Secretly married to a Norwegian for two years."

Larsen called it "nonsense," and a photo published on July 30 in another Norwegian paper, *Morgenposten*, was captioned "Ella har ingen norsk ektemann" ("Ella has no Norwegian husband"). Ella flew on to Monte Carlo, expecting Larsen to follow, but the publicity had engendered scrutiny of his past, exposing an unsettled court case. Within a week Larsen was arrested at the airport in Gothenburg, Sweden, on charges of stealing money from a previous fiancée.[42]

Fitzgerald learned about Larsen's secret past from a reporter's phone call. From Monte Carlo, she wrote an intimate letter to Virginia Wicks, her publicist.

August 6, 1957
Hello Virginia,
Received your wire today. Thanks for the consolation. Yes, I have faith. I know he couldn't do anything wrong to me because I believe he loves me. . . . We could have gotten married in Paris in June, but I talked it over with Norman & Georgie. I hope you understand this. I'm so nervous and upset. We all agreed we should wait a little longer & not rush into anything. That was our own little secret. As Mr. and Mrs. we meant no harm to anyone. I guess we really hurt our own selves.

After chronicling the sequence of events, she continued:

Hope this hasn't bored you but wanted you to know I've never done anything to be ashamed of and I'm not ashamed now. Of course, they're making a big thing out of him being in Prison all because he gets with me. Don't know how he feels about me now because he might blame me for him being in prison. Maybe he feels if all this publicity hadn't happened, he'd be alright. He told me he loved me very much—next day when I called him. . . . I've tried to contact him but they won't let me speak to him. No matter what. None of us is an angel. I had dinner with his sister. We had so much fun. They even told me . . . they felt that I really loved him. If he doesn't love me . . . anything I understand. No regrets![43]

Larsen was soon sentenced to five months of "hard labor."[44] At the end of the month, Fitzgerald issued a statement to restore dignity to both Thor and herself, printed in the *Pittsburgh Courier*: "It's true I was very fond of him. I thought he was a wonderful person. . . . Yes, we did discuss marriage, but we wanted to be sure and only time could give us the answer. The invitation to visit came from Thor and his sister. I was thrilled and happy when I arrived." She blamed publicity for precipitating his arrest. "For that I am sorry and hold no bitterness toward him. He gave me and all the members of the JATP troupe every reason to like and respect him when we were in Europe."[45]

Virginia Wicks recalled,

There were words between Norman and Ella. I think that Norman realized before Ella did that Larsen was taking advantage of her. He felt the guy was after her money only. Granz was the kind of guy who would try to prove it to her, and he did. From then on it wasn't the same. I felt grief. She was angry with him, saying, "You don't run my life. You don't run my personal life. You don't know what goes on."[46]

"We feel for Ella," wrote veteran African American reporter Dolores Calvin. "After searching for the 'right man' for so long and just when she thought she'd found him . . . up comes a cruel blow and he's off to jail . . . which means she could hardly remain an esteemed public figure if she accepted him now."[47] Many years later Ella told the CBC, "It wasn't a scandal, it was just at the time that people did not accept the fact of the racial situation."[48] In 1986 she reflected on television, "Well, I think all women have pitfalls. We all have skeletons in the closet. I used to be a little too romantic. Sometimes you learn from it, and sometimes it comes out in our songs."[49]

★★★

WHAT BETTER ANTIDOTE TO A LOVE AFFAIR GONE AWRY than a heavy dose of work, in this case a series of one-nighters on a JATP tour of twenty-one American cities from September 14 to October 25. The tour marked the end of JATP's presence in American life: box office grosses were declining, and a younger generation of jazz fans were turning away from the swing-to-bop synthesis championed by Granz in favor of new styles like hard bop and cool jazz. Among the blitz of live recordings Granz issued as his grand finale was *At the Opera House*, an LP assembled from dates in Chicago and Los Angeles.[50] It was her first and only album issued by Granz with JATP, and it could aptly have been titled "Ella Fitzgerald Sings the JATP Song Book." Backed by the Oscar Peterson Trio with Jo Jones added on drums, the selections included a luminous three-and-a-half-minute version of "Bewitched, Bothered, and Bewildered"; classic Tin Pan Alley tunes and swing song novelties; and scatting and jamming on "Stompin' at the Savoy" and "Lady Be Good." Granz wrote in the liner notes, "Incidentally, I submit that Ella's performance of 'Stompin' At The Savoy' is irrefutably the most incredible, brilliant jazz vocal performance ever put to wax."[51] Released in July 1958, *At the Opera House* earned a five-star review from Dom Cerulli in *Down Beat*. "There must be many to whom Ella is until now largely a great ballad singer," he wrote. "This LP should help explain why she keeps knocking over poll after poll as a jazz singer."[52]

JATP's departure from the national scene did not threaten Fitzgerald's career. On the contrary, Granz claimed she could command higher fees as a single: "She was better off not touring with Jazz at the Philharmonic and going on her own, even though I was her manager."[53] Her future was secure in any case. As he told Leonard Feather:

Now that she's on my own label she'll make more records during the first year than she made in the whole nineteen years she was with Decca; what's more, she'll have complete freedom to record anything she likes. Eventually I want Ella to make enough bread so she can afford to take a couple of months off every year; if she can make two hundred grand a year, and without dieting, why should she knock her brains out? That's what I'm looking out for—that, and her dignity, which hasn't been respected enough.[54]

All in all, 1957 was another breakthrough year. In an article by May Okon in the New York *Daily News*—a rare instance of Fitzgerald being interviewed by a white female reporter from the media mainstream— Ella assessed her life as an artist and a woman. She confessed to shyness and persistent stage fright. On the subject of her weight, she had her script worked out: "I know I'm no glamour girl, and it's not easy for me to get up in front of a crowd of people. It used to bother me a lot, but now I've got it figured that God gave me this talent to use—so I just stand up there and sing."

May Okon asked about Ella's "other" career, being a mother. Once again, Fitzgerald spoke like an enthusiastic mother up to a point. Work took precedence, and she did not apologize for her priorities.

I sure would like to spend two or three months there every year with my son, Ray Brown, Jr. Ray's seven now, and I don't worry about him because he's taken care of by my aunt, who raised me. I decorated the new house myself, and I'd sure like to be fiddlin' around in the kitchen making Ray things he likes to eat. I've been thinking that it would be nice if I had a television show out there and could spend more time with Ray. I don't think I'd ever give up the tours, though. Oh, being on the road gets rough some- times, but I'd sure miss singing to the people.[55]

As she stood at the threshold of a new stage in her art and career, she was satisfied: no worries and no regrets.

Chapter 19

FLOUTING CATEGORIES

(1957–1958)

n 1958, after the end of the American touring of Jazz at the Philharmonic, Ella Fitzgerald began a challenging stage in her career, going
out almost exclusively as a "single." The "compellingly versatile artist," as *Time* magazine called her that year, was the poll-winning,
box-office-record-setting leader in a field no one could quite figure
out.[1] Was she a popular singer, a jazz singer, or both? For her September
concert at Carnegie Hall, John S. Wilson's review in the *New York Times*
reveals how stubbornly this binary was lodged in critical discourse and
how strongly she challenged its legitimacy:

> It was more of a "pop" program than a jazz program. . . . Miss
> Fitzgerald is thoroughly at home in the worlds of both "pop"
> music and jazz and she moved readily between the two. There is
> such a strongly rhythmic feeling in her delivery that even when
> she is staying close to the composer's lines on a ballad, she seems
> to be injecting implications of swing. . . . This was both "pop"
> singing of a high order and jazz singing of an equally high order.[2]

His juggling act shows how much was invested in such binaries just
at a moment when they seemed to be dissolving. In the mid-to-late
1950s, a special moment of "peaceful coexistence"—to borrow a com-

mon phrase from Cold War politics—was at hand. Fitzgerald's art had long traversed pop and jazz in her unique fashion, and as she entered her vocal prime, her artistic fluidity coincided with this jazz-pop rapprochement. She was now more commercially viable and artistically respected in this blossoming "jazz pop" or "pop jazz" context, however inchoately or inconsistently these genre terms were understood at the time.

A jazz-pop apotheosis could be registered in the explosion of LP releases by established and upcoming vocalists, and the increasing prevalence of standards, particularly show tunes, in their core repertoire. Debates about the definition of jazz singing persisted, especially among jazz critics, and indeed would continue into the 1960s, but marketplace realities also mooted them. In the July 1958 issue of *Metronome*, devoted to "Singers and Vocalists . . . In and Out of Jazz," the editors wrote, "There will be argument here about jazz singing and what it is. . . . The fact of the matter is that it grows harder each month to definitely point to jazz singers as separate from the rest, because more singers of taste continually appear."[3]

"'Jazz Singer' Tag Covers a Wide Artist Roster on Wax," read an astute *Billboard* headline the following month. The survey article pointed out what everybody knew: that vocal jazz was now largely dominated by women, both as artists and as consumers. "From the standpoint of sales, Ella Fitzgerald, Chris Connor, June Christy, Sarah Vaughan and Anita O'Day have all done exceedingly well," went the article, though some singers were making studio concessions: "In the marketplace most of them are avoiding scat and improvisation, although in concert this works." She too seemed to fit that profile since the *Song Books* promoted her ballad standards, outshining *At the Opera House*, her only live album on Verve. The article noted that the *Song Books* "scored heavily," most recently with *Ella Fitzgerald Sings the Duke Ellington Song Book*.[4] *Billboard* seemed to find the choice of Ellington unremarkable, perhaps overlooking its radical nature.[5]

★★★

IT "CAME AS A GREAT SURPRISE TO EVERYBODY," the British music writer Benny Green wrote, "when the news went public that Fitzgerald and Granz were planning a Duke Ellington Songbook."[6] It had been assumed that next up would be one of the other "Big Six" songwriters of show tunes for musicals, perhaps Jerome Kern, Irving Berlin, George Gershwin, or Harold Arlen. Instead, the choice of Ellington asserted the canonic stature of a jazz composer, arranger, and bandleader who was known mainly through his own recordings. Ellington's stage output was minimal: it included the two-month run of the revue *Jump for Joy* (1941) in Los Angeles and the four-month run of *Beggar's Holiday* (1946) on Broadway. More to the point, his songs existed mainly in their own private musical universe. While Ellington was considered a "popular song writer" in the music trade, his songs were recorded mainly by his own band vocalists or "sung" by his virtuoso band members as "vocal instrumentals." He had an impressive presence on *Billboard* charts, which listed seventy titles between 1929 and 1954, including his own covers of hits by other songwriters; yet a *Billboard* survey of popular songwriters in 1950 showed that the public at large knew a few of his titles, and few vocalists outside his orchestra recorded his songs in the 1940s.[7]

Ella Fitzgerald was an exception. In the 1940s and early '50s, she had proved her enthusiasm for Ellington's songs both in Decca 78 rpm singles and on live dates. Especially noteworthy was her fondness for the little-known "I'm Just a Lucky So-and-So," which she recorded in 1946; she even brought the tune to an important JATP Carnegie Hall concert in September 1949.[8] "How High the Moon," hecklers shouted from the audience; "all right," she said, then quieted them with a sensuous reading of this gem. By 1951 she had seven known Duke Ellington songs in her book. It seems logical that in November 1956, as John Tynan wrote, she would have "suggested to Norman Granz, her personal manager, that she do an album of Ellington tunes."[9] Already on September 4, 1956, she had recorded fourteen of his songs in one afternoon. Her backing sextet had two outstanding obbligato players, the violinist Stuff Smith and the tenor saxophonist Ben Webster, a former Ellingtonian and Fitzgerald's JATP touring partner. As with previous *Song Books*, she mixed well-known titles ("Sophisticated Lady," "Prelude to a Kiss," "Solitude") with esoteric material like the modernist ballad "Azure." She scatted the rhythm tune "Cotton Tail," exploiting Webster's 1940 solo. "Solitude," treated in an intimate duet backed by guitar, emerged as a highlight on the Jazz at the Philharmonic national tour in the fall of 1956.[10]

Whether alone or in collaboration with Fitzgerald, who at the least gave her consent, Granz expanded the idea of one LP into a massive new *Song Book* project, which he pitched to Ellington that fall. Conceiving *The Duke Ellington Song Book* on a grand scale as a four-LP package, Granz enlisted the composer and his band in a brave move. "It would have been stupid not to use him. I wanted the band very badly for Ella," he later stated.[11]

But the choice was "stupid" in another way—a triumph of hope and ambition over common sense. The climate around Ellington's song oeuvre was complicated by creative drama. He flourished through collective collaboration and spontaneous composition. Ellington, according to a feature writer for the *Saturday Evening Post* in 1943, "doesn't write down his intricate 'standards.' He may jot down a scrap of a melodic theme, but he does not like to be bothered with manuscripts, and is the despair of his publisher, a plump Broadway character named Jack Robbins."[12] Long an admirer of Ellington's band, Granz understood this well, yet he did not plan accordingly. In the fall of 1956, the Granz office dispatched requests for new arrangements, specifying Ella's keys, assuming the responsibility would fall mainly on Billy Strayhorn, Ellington's creative partner, whom Ellington trusted with the core of his vocal compositions. Considering that Ellington's book bulged with arrangements tailored for individual members of the Ellington operation, it seemed reasonable to expect solid results.[13]

Several months later, from June 24 to 27, 1957, Ellington's orchestra joined Fitzgerald for their first session at the Fine Recording Studios in New York. Expected to supply new arrangements for fifty slots on three LPs, Strayhorn showed up with only thirteen titles prepared, Ellington with just four, leaving a vacuum of thirty-three titles. Chaos ensued. Ellington talked about "tonal personalities." How would he handle Fitzgerald's personality as an outsider, a newcomer to the group? Strayhorn talked about the "Ellington Effect," wherein "each member of his band is to him a distinctive tone color and a set of emotions, which he mixes with others equally distinctive, to produce a third thing."[14] It took four days to complete seventeen titles.

In 1963 Norman Granz described the process:

> Duke would ask Ella what key she was in and she would tell him the key and he would have to transpose and there would be a lot of furious writing to change the key. Then Ella would try and fit in and the band would get swept along by its own memories of just how it ought to play, and so Ella, as you can hear on some of the songs was fighting for her very life with Cat Anderson hitting those top notes or even fighting Johnny [Hodges] on something else. Really at one point she became so nervous and became almost hysterical, that she began to cry. Duke went over to her and said, "Now, now, baby" in his most gentle tones, "Don't worry, it'll all turn out fine."[15]

In 1965 the usually discreet Fitzgerald confirmed the gist of his remarks: "It was a panic scene, with Duke almost making up the arrangements as we went along. Duke is a genius. I admire him as much as anyone in the world; but doing it that way, even though it was a lot of fun at times, got to be kind of nerve-racking."[16]

Additional accounts emerged later. In the liner notes of the 1999 CD reissue, sidemen from the session paid tribute to her adaptation. "Ella gave the impression that she was on hand to do whatever Duke or Billy wanted her to do," recalled trombonist John Sanders. "She was so gracious that you would think she was just the band vocalist . . . sitting quietly, waiting her turn whenever they wanted her." Trumpeter Willie Cook reflected, "Ella was so well liked by the guys. She sang her songs in a way that made people realize what the song was actually standing for. She could get with whoever musicians that she was working with and fit in just like a glove with whatever they were playing."[17]

In the end, musical empathy and trust—the essence of the jazz experience—along with musical genius transformed a virtual experiment into a landmark treatment of Ellington's oeuvre. Highlights of the June sessions included a fresh arrangement of Juan Tizol's classic "Caravan," with the first chorus marked "Samba Not Swing!" on the parts, and the second in swing double-time; a renewed "Take the 'A' Train" with brilliant scat and her bop compatriot Dizzy Gillespie sitting in; and an exceptional version of Strayhorn's modernist chart for "Day Dream," suffused with warmth. Ellington wrote a finale, "The E and D Blues (E for Ella, D for Duke)," though Strayhorn had contributed enough for "B is for Billy" to get his share. She traded phrases with several horn soloists; in the words of Fitzgerald specialist Thomas Cleary, it was "Ella's gift for leaving space within her own improvising and using that space to listen to and immediately echo other players that ultimately holds it all together."[18] Together D and B composed a sixteen-minute orchestral suite, *Portrait of Ella Fitzgerald*, and in his florid verbal introductions to each movement, Ellington called her "beyond category," a term he used to protect his own artistic freedom and to honor a favorite few. Completion of the project required another small-group session on October 17, including a retake on Strayhorn's masterpiece "Lush Life," this time with Oscar Peterson on piano instead of the composer.

Norman Granz spared no expense in marketing *The Duke Ellington Song Book,* with a twelve-page essay by Leonard Feather amid many photographs. As a practical measure, he sold the expensive package in two separate double-LP volumes. Despite the hefty price tag, the box set reached number eight on *Billboard*'s "Best Selling Jazz Albums" for May 1958 through April 1959.[19] As part of the publicity campaign, Granz set up a joint concert at Carnegie Hall on April 6, 1958. Dietrich Fischer-Dieskau, the famous German *Lied* singer and a frequent touring artist in the United States, changed his travel plans to get there. "Ella and the Duke together! One just doesn't know when there might be a chance to hear that again," he said.[20] But the evening had its problems, echoing the studio sessions. *Billboard*'s Bob Rolontz noted, "Ella sounded good with the [Ben] Webster combo but missed with the ork, and the concert ended on a note of chaos."[21]

As for the album, in general, the mainstream press used words like *monumental* and *encyclopedic* for it, alongside accolades for her singing. At the *Saturday Review*, Irving Kolodin called her "the greatest jazz vocalist known to history,"[22] while John Tynan of *Down Beat* called the set "an absolute must for any library."[23] A young Martin Williams, already a formidable critic, thrust her into the pantheon of greatness, noting that "her rhythm is impeccable, her musicianship superb, and at her best she can state and vary a melodic line as effectively as almost anyone in jazz—even the Armstrong of the Thirties."[24]

But the jazz press had its dissenters. *Metronome*'s Bill Coss reiterated his *idée fixe* about her lack of emotional intelligence: "I question the use of several of the songs, because their lyrics were outside Ella's understanding."[25] *The New Yorker*'s Whitney Balliett offered a conservative assessment: opposing the contemporary jazz-pop synthesis, he idealized Armstrong and the late-1930s-early-'40s recordings of Billie Holiday as pinnacles of jazz singing and insisted that just as Anita O'Day and Billy Eckstine had voices that were too cultivated for jazz, Fitzgerald suffered from the same handicap. Her voice took on "a soft edge that often blots out whatever jazz expression it once had."[26] She was a "peerless popular singer," no more, no less.

It would take time for the importance of the *Song Book* to emerge. In the words of Bob Blumenthal, the jazz critic who wrote liner notes for the reissue of the *Ellington Song Book* in 1988, "Ella Fitzgerald was the most important person outside of the Ellington orbit in establishing his songs. To me that was the most important thing she did for Ellington [through which] she underscored the importance of jazz in American popular song."[27]

★★★

THE *SONG BOOK* PROJECTS continued to evolve with each new entry. Irving Berlin, the most famous American songwriter of the first half of the century and by then an institution, contacted the Granz office to promote himself as Fitzgerald's next subject. Granz was already researching him, as were others in the recording business in anticipation of the celebration of Berlin's fiftieth year in music.

On March 13 and 19, 1958, Fitzgerald recorded thirty-two Berlin songs in Los Angeles with Paul Weston's studio orchestra, sometimes augmented with strings. A consummate studio musician and innovative arranger, Weston had worked with Tommy Dorsey in the 1930s and heard Ella with Chick Webb at the Savoy Ballroom. Since 1952 he had helped guide the career of his wife, the singer Jo Stafford. Fitzgerald's pianist, Paul Smith, who played on Weston's other studio dates, described his style as "cool and polite, sophisticated commercial jazz" and got Weston to import Ella's experienced rhythm section into the studio band.[28] By excluding Irving Berlin's anthems "God Bless America" and "White Christmas," they made room for such rarities as "I Used to Be Color Blind," "(Let's Go) Slumming on Park Avenue," and "How's Chances?"[29]

In an interview from 1958, Fitzgerald alluded to her approach. "Simplicity wins out most of the time," she quipped, "just like in women's clothes," and ballads give "people a chance to hear the voice more."[30] The album was not yet released when a London reporter popped the standard jazz-pop question: "Ella, do you find yourself compromising between your jazz sense and the melody?" She answered by equivocating: "Not necessarily. I've made an album of Irving Berlin and in some of those tunes we swing a little. But I prefer ballads because you tell a story more. The fast ones, however, do help to break it up. But you must always make the melody clear." Sometimes that led to blandness, as in "Supper Time," seemingly oblivious to its original meaning as a song protesting lynching in the early 1930s.[31] This exchange did not acknowledge other shifts in Fitzgerald's approach.

Fitzgerald had, in fact, scatted Berlin's "Blue Skies" right out of the album. Instead, the recording was released on *Playboy* magazine's compilation LP *The Playboy Jazz All-Stars*.[32] It was a loss for the Berlin *Song Book*. After an unusual opening vocal cadenza and lyric chorus, Fitzgerald scatted for two and a half choruses—quoting fragments from "Star Dust," Wagner's wedding march from *Lohengrin*, and Gershwin's *Rhapsody in Blue*—before returning to the lyrics for the final half-chorus. It would become one of her celebrated treatments. In the words of the musicologist Jeffrey Magee, she "redefined what it meant for a singer to perform "Blue Skies.""[33]

Fitzgerald modeled her treatment of "Alexander's Ragtime Band" on other precedents. Weston said, "It was Ella's idea to do the corny Jolson imitation and ham it up."[34] Decca had released the LP *The Immortal Al Jolson* earlier that year. More likely, Ella was channeling Ethel Merman, who sang "Alexander" on the memorable Ford Anniversary two-hour TV special on June 15, 1953, its soundtrack released on an LP that year. If so, she got Merman's accent and raucous exuberance down pat.

In 1959 the freshly minted National Academy of Recording Arts and Sciences (NARAS) issued the first Grammy Awards, *Ella Fitzgerald Sings the Irving Berlin Song Book* won "Best Female Vocal Performance" while her *Ellington Song Book* won "Best Individual Jazz Performance."

★★★

IN APRIL 1958 FITZGERALD MET THE CHALLENGE of her first major European tour officially as a solo artist, without JATP. Most of the time she worked with her trio, pianist Lou Levy, bassist Max Bennett, and drummer Gus Johnson. On several dates, Granz added the Oscar Peterson Trio or other JATP colleagues to the bill. In Paris, the photographer Jean-Pierre Leloir captured Fitzgerald dressed as a fashion plate. Granz issued no live albums from the tour, but thirty years later her performance in Rome on April 25, which had been recorded, was released as *Ella in Rome: The Birthday Concert*, achieving great acclaim and sales.[35] The concert captured her core repertory of show tunes and Tin Pan Alley standards. Her tour de force on "St. Louis Blues" deserves special comment. The "extraordinary variety of [fourteen] source references in Fitzgerald's 1958 scat solo represents a mini-typology of quotational practice in jazz," Katharine Cartwright, a jazz theorist, has written. It revealed the profound autobiographical nature and intellectual strengths of Fitzgerald's creative improvisation.[36]

In May, with the Oscar Peterson Trio, Stan Getz, Coleman Hawkins, Sonny Stitt, and Roy Eldridge, Fitzgerald toured England for two weeks of one-nighters. The musicians' arrival was marred by customs delays and a protracted search of their luggage, which drew significant publicity, beginning with an event that soured her triumphant return to a country where she had a large fan base. The Associated Press dispatch read, "Miss Fitzgerald came out fuming and said she had been 'socially insulted,' that she had been searched as though she were a criminal."[37] In *Melody Maker*, Maurice Burman recounted a press conference at the Dorchester Hotel where she faced down nineteen photographers flashing at her. Granz told Burman that Fitzgerald was "scared of" flashbulbs, but it is hard to know what he meant—was he referring to her sensitive eyes, a harbinger of future troubles, or to the disruption of invasive cameras? Meanwhile she fielded questions and maintained order: "I can only do one thing at a time. I can't look in all directions at once." Addressing Burman she said, "And you let me finish one question before you ask the next." So much for the "shy" singer, as she was so often described by American reporters and herself as well. When asked stale questions about which other singers she admired, she refused to answer, and when Burman prodded her about her breathing—disrupting phrases and one time even a single word, she broke out, "What! I've never noticed it— no one's ever told me that before." In his words, he broke through the "plump, gentle, and cuddly" persona in performance, presenting an alternative image offstage: "she is slimmer, younger looking and very alert. She has great dignity and a fierce pride."[38]

In June Fitzgerald was back in the States for a return gig at the Copacabana in New York. A *Variety* reviewer, praising her as "one of the great singers of this era," applauded her "vein of musical originality that makes every song an event."[39] In July she joined forces with Louis Armstrong and the Oscar Peterson Trio at the outdoor Carter Barron Amphitheater near Washington, D.C., a venue she would return to many times. Then it was back to Europe for some exceptional dates in the convivial atmosphere of summer festivals. At the Festival Mondial du Jazz in Belgium's Knokke Casino, she featured different songbook composers in three consecutive concerts honoring Rodgers and Hart, Ellington, and George Gershwin, whose *Song Book* project was still in planning stages. The following night she joined Sarah Vaughan for a friendly scat contest on "Lady Be Good" and "How High the Moon," a historic match of two elegantly gowned women who rarely appeared together. A photograph from that evening remained a treasured souvenir for her, framed and mounted in her living room at home.[40] Fitzgerald and other JATP stars also headlined the first jazz festival sponsored by the city of Cannes, with Granz in his element as impresario.[41] In a charming mix of serious music appreciation and tourist publicity, Cannes officials filmed Fitzgerald singing Ellington's "Just Squeeze Me" and George and Ira Gershwin's "How Long Has This Been Going On?" on a boat ride along the French Riviera.

★★★

FITZGERALD'S FIRST NATIONAL TOUR as a solo artist without Jazz at the Philharmonic marked a milestone in her career. As a prelude, on August 16, 1958, she and Paul Weston gave a *Song Book* concert at the Hollywood Bowl, split between the works of Cole Porter and those of Irving Berlin. A rave in the *Los Angeles Times* confirmed that Hollywood had become her home crowd: "The one woman in the popular field who could do it, of course—and probably the only woman singer of any kind of equal drawing power, except possibly Maria Meneghini Callas—was Ella Fitzgerald."[42] Then she was off, partnered with the Oscar Peterson Trio, on a whirlwind tour of twenty-two U.S. and Canadian cities in twenty-three days.[43] The billing varied from "An Evening with Ella Fitzgerald" to "Ella Fitzgerald and Her Song Book Show." Granz tinkered with her stage persona, asking her to sit on a barstool like a cabaret singer for ballads, which she learned to tolerate. Another change brought a reproach from *Variety*'s reviewer: "Granz's production furbelows with the lights to set a mood, like opening Miss Fitzgerald on a dark stage, is corny and unnecessary. Her voice is enough of a mood-setter."[44]

A review of Fitzgerald's act at the Fairmont Hotel in San Francisco, which ran for three weeks starting October 28, could have been written by Granz himself. Backed by her quartet, or sometimes by the house orchestra led by Ernie Heckscher, the singer "without peer" sang "mostly oldies," including esoteric tunes like Frank Loesser's "The Lady's in Love with You" and Irving Berlin's "Russian Lullaby" and "You're Laughing at Me." The familiar "Angel Eyes" and "How High the Moon" kept fans happy. With the wisdom and expertise of more than twenty years onstage, she was "relaxed and friendly at the mike."[45]

At home Fitzgerald presented a familiar face to interviewers, whose reports stressed her modesty and shyness. An AP report by William Glover was typical, in which she said she didn't collect her own records because "I thought I might be thought conceited," adding, "Some of my own big albums seem just too long, but the public certainly doesn't seem to feel that way." She reiterated her belief that "this rocking thing is passing, like all trends."[46] That conservative persona was reinforced by her four American television appearances in 1958.

In April, on the "spectacular" *Swing into Spring*, a nostalgic salute to the swing era starring Benny Goodman, Fitzgerald was paired with Jo Stafford.[47] Their requisite duet on "St. Louis Blues" epitomized the commercial vocal jazz that television producers deemed traditional for the medium and that the jazz community generally dismissed. Not by coincidence, a W. C. Handy biopic of the same title, starring Nat King Cole, was released the next day, with Ella making a cameo appearance as herself. The film had disappointing critical results. But sometimes her star shone through the small screen, especially when the host inspired her. Fitzgerald's guest appearance on *The Frank Sinatra Show*, telecast from Los Angeles on May 9, drew accolades. Sinatra and Fitzgerald sang a memorable version of "Moonlight in Vermont," drawing on Billy May's arrangement on Sinatra's 1958 album *Come Fly with Me*. They blended as a unit, both looking fulfilled and even joyful, after the perfectly sculpted performance that turned a standard into an art song. They admired each other and it came through their music making. In an interview, Fitzgerald told syndicated TV columnist Steven H. Scheuer:

> When I was traveling with the Chick Webb band, the boys used to tease me about the crush I had on Frank. When we were both in New York, I used to go down to the Paramount Theater in the afternoon and sit in the front row to gape at Frank. I just couldn't get enough of that man's voice. Tommy Dorsey would walk out on the stage, spot me in the first row, and groan, "Not you again."[48]

In a preview of the special, Scheuer caught the vibe. "Frank's never been more at ease on his show than tonight, with guest Ella Fitzgerald," he wrote.[49] A new pair, "Ella and Frank," made the scene.

Fitzgerald's last TV appearance for 1958 sums up the cultural ambitions hovering over the *Song Book* projects. On December 3 the *Kraft Music Hall* TV show, hosted by veteran comedian Milton Berle, elevated both the songwriters and the singer to the stature of "Art" literally and figuratively. As a preview described it, "The *Milton Berle Show* gets a bit arty tonight, when Ella Fitzgerald comes in to sing. Not that Ella is arty, but the background against which she'll sing is. They've borrowed six original oils, valued at $100,000. Each ties in with part of a song Ella will sing, and some tricky electronics will be used to make the most of this intriguing idea."[50] The preview also hyped the technological breakthrough of color TV. The stage set reproduced the album cover of *The Irving Berlin Song Book*: Fitzgerald was seated at a French bistro table with a bottle of white wine, while the camera closed in on genuine French twentieth-century paintings by Utrillo, Dufy, Vlaminck, and Derain.[51]

★★★

In November 1958 the syndicated jazz columnist Ralph Gleason elicited an unusually candid and important interview from Fitzgerald, filled with her usual self-deprecating humor along with a forceful defense of her art.[52]

"You know what I'm trying to do? I'm trying to be myself," she repeated. She considered her success with the *Song Book* LPs a victory over prejudice: "It's a good feeling for me to do something new. Like the Broadway tunes and the songbooks I've done. Some people thought maybe I shouldn't do them, or couldn't do them, so it was a challenge. I did them and they were successful." She reflected on her struggles with the stereotype of the sexual nightclub chanteuse. Her model for glamour, Lena Horne, had revived her career in 1957 with highly stylized and sensual presentations at New York's Waldorf Astoria Hotel;[53] Ella had experimented along these lines, only to recognize their irrelevance. One anecdote she relayed to Ralph Gleason confirmed the value of her resistance to having her womanhood defined by others, and to the sales strategy of defining her audience through what feminist historians would later call "the male gaze."

> I'm not a glamour girl and I'm not a dancer. I'm just me. I could do all the acting with a song, all the stuff with the hands and those gimmicks if someone showed me and I learned it. But it's not me. You want to hear a funny story? I did it once in Chicago. I was singing "Witchcraft" . . . and I acted it all out with the gestures and my gown down off one shoulder. And when I finished, some guy in the audience said, real loud, "That's fine. Now let's hear Ella Fitzgerald do it!" I was so embarrassed![54]

Her versatility had similar integrity at its core. She recognized it as innate to her nature. It was not a pose, and if it helped give her more fans, so be it. As she said to Ralph Gleason, "I'm not going Hollywood. I'm not changing. I'm trying to sell records and give the people something they can hum; some familiar melody. . . . I'm just trying to be myself out there and get over some of that self-consciousness I have. I try to give the audience a little bit of everything. I sing current popular tunes and even some rock 'n' roll. And I do a little Dixieland. The people seem to like it, and I know it's been good for me. I'm feeling so good these days, so ambitious."[55]

Chapter 20

MIDCENTURY MODERN
TRIUMPHS

(1959)

The year that followed Ella Fitzgerald's declaration of independence from category turned into a high point of her career. In 1959 she released three important LP projects and enjoyed a surge of television appearances. Four of her LPs made *Billboard*'s list of thirty-five best-selling jazz albums from May 1958 through April 1959.[1] Her manager, Norman Granz, who once said that she could have whatever she wanted, was choosing material to challenge her voice in its prime to acknowledge her need for variety across the jazz-pop continuum.

Jazz fans worried that Ella was "going commercial" after her success "at top hotels and supper clubs," as Ralph J. Gleason wrote in November 1958, but they were reassured by *Ella Swings Lightly*, a connoisseur's album recorded that month and released in March 1959.[2] The album paired her, for the first time, with Verve's hot new arranger Marty Paich, a staple on the West Coast jazz scene. It would prove an enduring and influential pair-up, with ninety Paich arrangements now in her collection at the Library of Congress. She was backed by Paich's Dek-Tette, an eleven-piece ensemble that debuted in 1956 on a well-regarded LP with Mel Tormé. The Dek-Tette's eight horns included French horn and tuba, hardly standard fare for a pop album. Equally nonstandard were the "sixteen oldies," as *Billboard* summed up the selections;[3] they included esoterica like "720 in the Books," which refers to the big band "book" of the 1930s bandleader Jan Savitt. "Little Jazz" was a scat tribute to Roy Eldridge. "Teardrops from My Eyes" had an R&B-style backbeat. "You Hit the Spot" was first sung by Fitzgerald in 1936 for a Chick Webb transcription. "This is Ella at her very best," wrote *Metronome*'s Jack Maher.[4] The album won a Grammy for "Best Jazz Performance, Soloist," before jazz vocalists had their own category.

Porgy and Bess, Fitzgerald's last studio collaboration with Louis Armstrong, was recorded in August 1957 but was withheld from release until mid-1959 so it would coincide with the release of MGM's blockbuster Hollywood film version.[5] The actor Sidney Poitier, like many in the Black community, believed the opera's libretto reinforced negative stereotypes about African Americans, but he accepted the role of Porgy after an initial rejection.[6] In this controversial climate, Fitzgerald and Armstrong's double LP was one of many adaptations of Gershwin's masterpiece by Black artists who put their own stamp on it.[7] A version by Harry Belafonte and Lena Horne, along with an instrumental rendition by Miles Davis and Gil Evans, joined the Fitzgerald-Armstrong release on *Variety*'s list of fifty best-selling albums of 1959.[8]

"Norman had the nerve to tell me the truth about myself," Ella would say in 1962. "He told me I wasn't limited to singing jazz or blues or pops. He said I could sing anything I tried."[9] *Porgy and Bess* demanded that Fitzgerald expand her understanding of her gift to encompass opera, and she later condensed two glorious pieces—the aria "I Loves You, Porgy," and Bess's part in the duet "Bess, You Is My Woman Now"—into a medley for live dates. The challenging arias required her to negotiate what is known in vocal pedagogy as the "passage" between registers, and disguise the transitions between lower, middle, and head tones. She never learned the opera singer's technique of depressing the larynx to glide from bottom to top. Instead she relied on falsetto and a lighter tone, adapting her vocal equipment as needed. She said, "I wonder if I can make it," perhaps more to herself than the audience on August 10, 1958, when she performed the medley at the Chicago jazz club Mister Kelly's:

We'd like to get real serious for a moment, and try to do a medley of *Porgy* for you, ladies and gentlemen. Just in case you should like it we have an album coming out soon. I have to plug the albums. We have an album coming out with Louis Armstrong, and we do *Porgy and Bess*. We sing a little of everything in it. And it's not a real jazz album, but you know, very pretty. I wonder if I can make it. Hmm? Everybody's so quiet, it frightens me. You'll hear the bad notes [laughter]. . . . This is *different*. You don't get this all the time.[10]

"You don't get this all the time" is one of Ella Fitzgerald's classic understatements. The double-LP project, which compressed a four-hour opera into fifty-four minutes, respected its fusion of European opera and a range of Black folk music—gospel, street cries, blues, novelty—all filtered through jazz improvisation. Russell Garcia, who conducted his own symphonic arrangements, knew the opera's internal workings, having already conducted the first jazz LP version for the Bethlehem label in 1956. Garcia's role was limited, however, as Ella and Louis sometimes used head arrangements instead of fixed charts, and they also altered the voice parts, turning the soprano solo "Summertime" into a duet with trumpet solo. Ira Gershwin, who liked the album enough to hand out copies to his friends, told a reporter that hearing Fitzgerald singing male parts—in Porgy's "The Buzzard Song," for example—"was quite a surprise, I must confess, but I found it effective in this case."[11] Sometimes Fitzgerald and Armstrong ditched the libretto, getting rid of its most egregious dialect. In the comic novelty song "It Ain't Necessarily So," for example, she discarded "De'tings dat yo' li'ble / to read in de Bible," in favor of "The things that you're liable / To read in the Bible." "Ella was so proper that she had wanted to sing 'It *isn't* necessarily so,'" Granz recalled.[12] For her, it was about more than being proper, as incorrect grammar fed stereotypes of primitive Black folk. She and Louis dissolved the lyrics into scat anyway.

Reviewing the Fitzgerald-Armstrong *Porgy and Bess* in the *Saturday Review*, Irving Kolodin wrote, "A new compound is created that is wonderful."[13] The Black columnist Dolores Calvin thought Fitzgerald's dignity acted as a counterweight to the "Jezebel" stereotype of hypersexuality attributed to Black women.[14] In the film, where Hollywood star Dorothy Dandridge played Bess, Calvin wrote that the "the press boys" were "getting more disgraceful every day. . . . They're trying to portray it as an all-sex drama with Bess more as a streetwalker than a girl in love with Porgy." Not so, however, with the "beautiful LP albums featuring Louis Armstrong etc., which they waited so long to put on the market at the time of the premiere."[15]

At Mister Kelly's in Chicago, Fitzgerald expressed her impatience with the libretto, making fun of "Summertime," the opera's most famous song, by invoking her own work ethic as an ironic counterweight to the lyrics. As her trio continued playing the chord sequence, she broke into a spoken interlude:

> They say summertime, the living's easy. What makes it easy? You have to go out and work. So you go out and you do a day's work. It's so warm, it's so hot, you perspire. Yes, you perspire and you perspire. What do you get? Perspiration. But you don't mind it because it's summertime and the living's *easy*. So you say, "I think I'll go down, let's, let's go down and dig the real *cool* sounds at Mister Kelly's. You come into Mister Kelly's and you taste a while. Yes daddy, you drink awhile. And you drink. What do you get? The check. You don't mind it, 'cause it's summertime and the living's easy. What do you care, your daddy's rich, you got a good-lookin' mother. Imagine, everybody with a good-looking mother and a rich daddy. Summertime. That's what the song says—livin' *easy*. [laughter] Oh yeah![16]

"Oh Ella, she perspired, she didn't sweat," said a musician colleague. "And she stuck it to you all the same."[17] She would go on to sing a poignant traditional rendition of "Summertime" through the 1980s.

★★★

Ella Fitzgerald with the Chick Webb Orchestra, Paramount Theatre in New York, August 1938. The late Adelaide Cromwell (1919–2019), a pioneering African American scholar and professor of sociology at Boston University, recalled: "I remember Ella . . . in a white shirt and a black skirt, like a schoolgirl. Of course, she wasn't anything to look at. It was the singing. But Ella's voice was so overwhelming you couldn't sing the songs she sang" (interview by the author, May 3, 2010). *Ella Fitzgerald Collection, Archives Center, National Museum of American History, Smithsonian Institution.*

Chick Webb, formal studio portrait, c. 1936. *Pictorial Press Ltd., Alamy Stock Photo.*

Taken at the Paramount Theatre during a photo shoot for a feature by Earl Wilson in the *New York Post*, August 18, 1938. The story was prompted by the success of "A-Tisket A-Tasket." Neither the photo nor the story flattered young Ella, who looks like she needs the protective touch of Chick Webb. *Photograph by Gilles Petard / Redferns, Getty Images.*

Left to right: Mildred Bailey, Ella Fitzgerald, Count Basie, and Helen Humes at the Savoy Ballroom, c. 1940. Both Bailey and Humes were important figures in defining the role of female vocalists with big bands, and Count Basie would tour with Fitzgerald in the 1970s. *Photograph by Otto F. Hess. Courtesy of The New York Public Library.*

Ella Fitzgerald, who announced she was "Going Dizzy" in 1946, steps up as a guest to sing at Dizzy Gillespie's date at the Downbeat Club in New York. This iconic photo was shot by William Gottlieb in August 1947. *Courtesy of William P. Gottlieb / Ira and Leonore S. Gershwin Fund Collection, Music Division, Library of Congress.*

Ella Fitzgerald and Ray Brown. The very married couple lean into each other, glowing with love. Taken in either 1949 or 1950, this photo is most likely connected to a JATP concert at the Syria Mosque in Pittsburgh. *Teenie Harris Archive, Carnegie Museum of Art, Getty Images.*

Norman Granz (in the foreground) with John Hammond to his right and Flip Phillips sitting opposite. They are listening to Ella Fitzgerald at the opening of the Bop City nightclub in New York on April 14, 1949. "We called him 'eyebrows,'" Ella once said. Taken by the *Life* photographer Martha Holmes, the photo did not run in the magazine. *The* Life *Picture Collection, Shutterstock.*

Ella Fitzgerald in Paris. Too tired to get up from her table after a JATP concert at the Salle Pleyel on May 2, 1957, she managed to "sing for her supper" from her seat in this cover photo for the French *Jazz Magazine*, June 1957. *Ella Fitzgerald Collection, Archives Center, National Museum of American History, Smithsonian Institution.*

Norman Granz and Ella Fitzgerald working on a *Song Book* project, late 1950s. *Ella Fitzgerald Papers, Archives Center, National Museum of American History, Smithsonian Institution.*

Ella Fitzgerald and Louis Armstrong working on their album *Ella and Louis*, c. 1956. *Courtesy of Bridgeman Images.*

Ella Fitzgerald in her dressing room at the Masonic Auditorium in San Francisco, sharing the evening with Duke Ellington in 1966. *Photo by and courtesy of James W. Blackman.*

Ella Fitzgerald with Keter Betts (bass), Bobby Durham (drums), and Tommy Flanagan (piano), one of the most important trios of her career and all good friends, 1967. *J. Paul Getty Trust and Ella Fitzgerald Papers, Archives Center, National Museum of American History, Smithsonian Institution.*

Ella Fitzgerald and Duke Ellington working on "Azure" (a 1937 song composed by Ellington with lyrics by Irving Mills) for the recording of the album *Ella at Duke's Place* in 1965. Ella first recorded the song in the 1957 album *Ella Fitzgerald Sings the Duke Ellington Song Book*. *Photo by Michael Ochs, Getty Images.*

Ella Fitzgerald surrounded by her nephew, Michael Williams; nieces Janice Gilmore and Karen Gilmore (children of her deceased sister); and son, Ray Jr., c. 1966. *Ella Fitzgerald Collection, Archives Center, National Museum of American History, Smithsonian Institution.*

Ella Fitzgerald performs at Lucerna Hall in Prague at the height of her "Soul" period, 1969. *Photograph by Miroslav Zajíc / Corbis, Getty Images.*

Ella Fitzgerald with Arthur Fiedler, the conductor of the Boston Pops Orchestra, in May 1973. She credited him for fostering her appearances **with pops orchestras** through this debut performance. *Photograph by Michael Peirce. Courtesy of Boston Symphony Orchestra.*

Ella Fitzgerald and Count Basie in a concert with the San Antonio Symphony in December 1979. *Photograph by and courtesy of Tad Hershorn.*

Joe Pass and Ella Fitzgerald in Jones Hall, Houston, October 28, 1983. This photo, taken by Tad Hershorn, was used as the cover for the 1987 Pablo album *Easy Living*. *Courtesy of Tad Hershorn.*

Ella Fitzgerald with Jim Blackman. The first photo (*left*) was taken in 1962 when a young fan met his idol. The second (*right*) was taken c. 1985 at the Paul Masson Winery, Saratoga, California. *Courtesy of James W. Blackman.*

Ella Fitzgerald in concert at the Paul Masson Winery, Saratoga, California, July 20, 1985. According to Jim Blackman, she especially liked this photo. *Courtesy of James W. Blackman.*

Left to right: Mary Jane Outwater (vice president of Salle Productions), Ella Fitzgerald, Mary Cavello, and Pete Cavello (Ella's road manager) at Ella's front door on North Whittier Drive, April 1989. The group was headed to the Society of Singers gala in Los Angeles, where Ella received the first Ella Award. *Photograph by and courtesy of James W. Blackman.*

Ella Fitzgerald celebrates her sixty-ninth birthday on April 25, 1986, in Eugene, Oregon.
Photograph by and courtesy of James W. Blackman.

Ella Fitzgerald at a rehearsal for the tribute to Sammy Davis, Jr., escorted by Eddie Murphy and Michael Jackson, November 1989. *Photograph by and courtesy of James W. Blackman.*

Ella Fitzgerald was the toast of the entertainment and jazz worlds at the "Hearts for Ella" tribute held on February 12, 1990, in Avery Fisher Hall at Lincoln Center. After the star-studded program, she surprised everyone by singing two songs. At the conclusion of the evening, Ella gathered with some friends, including (*left to right*): Quincy Jones, Bobby McFerrin, Lena Horne, and trombonist Al Grey. *Photograph by and courtesy of Tad Hershorn.*

Ella Fitzgerald with Paul McCartney at the 1990 Grammy Awards in Los Angeles. She performed and recorded many hit songs by John Lennon and Paul McCartney in the mid-1960s. Her version of "Can't Buy Me Love" reached the UK charts in 1964. *Pictorial Press Ltd., Alamy Stock Photo.*

Ella Fitzgerald rehearses with Frank Sinatra in December 1990, when Sinatra received the Ella Award from the Society of Singers. That night, they sang "The Lady Is a Tramp." *Photograph by and courtesy of James W. Blackman.*

IN EUROPE FROM APRIL 11 THROUGH MAY 17, Fitzgerald followed familiar itineraries, playing major concert halls. Far less predictable were her American circuits, where she was presented like a jazz "everywoman," singing everywhere with everybody and promising everything. An ad for a Chicago concert claimed that her setlist would range from "jazz to popular tunes, and from ballads to classics of Americana."[18] At the Riviera Theater in Detroit, she worked with Nat King Cole, and at the Latin Casino in Philadelphia, she was billed alongside the slapstick Three Stooges.[19] In Eugene, Oregon, she performed at a homecoming dance for the state university.[20] At the Starlight Room of the Waldorf Astoria, she sang "I've Grown Accustomed to His Face," gender-switching the hit from the Broadway musical My Fair Lady. At the Lorton Penitentiary in Virginia, she waived her fee and sang "chorus after chorus of the blues" for the inmates.[21] Writing about her appearance at the Playboy Jazz Festival in Chicago, Gene Lees of Down Beat noted that she topped all the other performers, including Coleman Hawkins, Chris Connor, and Louis Armstrong, and earned the only standing ovation.[22] At the Hollywood Bowl, she collaborated with Nelson Riddle in a concert of Gershwin songs for around twenty thousand people. At the Philharmonic Auditorium in Los Angeles, she gave a "one-woman concert" in a benefit sponsored by the elite African American sorority Delta Sigma Theta. A review in the Los Angeles Times praised her genuineness and sincerity, making her into a quintessentially American heroine: "Though she may take liberties with her songs, Ella's on-stage deportment is refreshingly free of 'personality' gimmicks or mannerisms. She is herself, remains natural and unaffected at all times."[23]

★★★

THE DEARTH OF LIVE RECORDINGS from this period makes the extant tapes from her television appearances all the more valuable. A fixture in the jazz-pop world, she was mainstreamed on television as an adult contemporary fare for bourgeois taste— "middle brow," as it was known then and even now, routinely scorned by serious jazz fans.[24] The year

1959 was "somewhat fruitful for sepia greats," said the *Chicago Defender*, especially for Fitzgerald, who "appeared on practically every major program on the three chains."[25] In the Black world, she was an icon of visibility in a complicated racialized environment. The African American feminist bell hooks would later recall, "When we sat in our living rooms in the fifties and early sixties watching those few Black folks who appeared on television screens we talked about their performance, but we always talked about the way the white folks were treating them."[26]

In a remarkable but little-known performance on February 10, 1959, she was paired with Duke Ellington on NBC's *Bell Telephone Hour*; the "American Festival" program also featured opera singer Risë Stevens and two principals from the New York State Ballet, Jacques d'Amboise and Melissa Hayden. With the experience of the *Duke Ellington Song Book* as a foundation, Fitzgerald soared through an eleven-minute medley, as Ellington at the piano joined her regulars Jim Hall on guitar, Wilfred Middlebrooks on bass, and Gus Johnson on drums. For *New York Times* critic John P. Shanley, "Ella and The Duke" were the "principal delight" of the program. A UPI wire review agreed, singling out "Do Nothing Till You Hear from Me" ("a stunner—packed with feeling and flow") and "I'm Beginning to See the Light" ("luminous").[27]

Fitzgerald's TV dates for 1959 were otherwise unexceptional yet satisfying. Most of her appearances on variety shows were carefully mediated: she typically sang material chosen to harmonize with the hosts, who in 1959 included Dinah Shore, Eddie Fisher, Pat Boone, and Frank Sinatra. For the *Dinah Shore Chevy Show*, the two women, who had become friends, tried to salvage a syrupy blues medley. Yet even that earned approval in the Black press just because Ella held up the visibility of the race. In the *Chicago Defender*, TV critic Hazel A. Washington took note: "Their rendition of 'Blues in the Night' flooded the office of Ella's hostess with congratulatory mail from across the nation. I'd like to take some credit for Dinah's use of Negroes on her show, since I pointed it up to her and her sponsors."[28] Fitzgerald fared well on the second episode of *Swing into Spring*, a heavily promoted, hour-long TV special showcasing Benny Goodman on April 10. *Billboard* summed up the program as "a lightly swinging, tasteful hour of musical nostalgia, circa the '30s and early '40s."[29] Sharing the vocal spotlight with Peggy Lee, Fitzgerald was allotted six songs including a chorus of the Gershwins' "'S Wonderful" and a rare outing of the Rodgers and Hammerstein show tune "The Gentleman Is a Dope."

Three telecasts at the end of the year highlighted Fitzgerald as an interpreter of the songs of George Gershwin, coinciding with the release of her major five-LP project, *Ella Fitzgerald Sings the George and Ira Gershwin Song Book*.[30] A program titled "The Music of George Gershwin," hosted by Ira Gershwin and telecast on the *Bell Telephone Hour* on November 20, let her sing "Summertime." It was tarnished by racism when the sponsors insisted that Fitzgerald's white guitarist, Herb Ellis, be replaced by an African American lest they be perceived as endorsing social integration. When Granz refused, the TV cameras obscured Ellis's image in the background, provoking Granz to pay for a full-page ad in *Variety* condemning the cowardice of the sponsors and producers.[31] In that climate, when Pat Boone invited Fitzgerald to his show on October 29, he was "bombarded by calls and letters" from his relatives "for having a Negro as a guest," he later said. It raised his civil rights consciousness.[32] Small gestures loomed large. On his TV special "An Afternoon with Friends," Frank Sinatra's admiration enabled him to give an overview of her repertoire on December 13. Her rendition of the ballad "There's a Lull in My Life" showed off her lush chest-tone low notes as they carved out lyrics and ornamented the melody. She gave two minutes of scat to Gershwin's rhythm song "Just You, Just Me." In their duet "Can't We Be Friends," Sinatra kept his arm around her as she did loving impressions of one African American diva after another—Pearl Bailey, Lena Horne, Dinah Washington, and Dakota Station. The final segment of the show featured a medley of two more Gershwin songs in Nelson Riddle's sweet arrangements, all prefaced by an exceptional plug for her new *Song Book*. The five-LP album went for the incredible price of $100. "I ran right out and grabbed me a few," Sinatra said.[33]

★★★

THE MORE FITZGERALD ESTABLISHED HER AUTHORITY in interpreting Broadway show tunes, the greater her impact on the canon that would later be reframed as the Great American Songbook. Her leadership occurred at a high point of interest in standards. As Milt Gabler observed in November 1959, "The companies are recording more great standards than ever were recorded in the history of the business. . . . There is such a demand for long-play music that some of the standard songs have been recorded on every label six or seven times in the last couple of years—some more than that."[34]

From the initial skepticism around the Cole Porter project to Ira Gershwin's investment in her role, *Ella Fitzgerald Sings the George and Ira Gershwin Song Book* stands as a major benchmark of her achievement. In 1956 she had mentioned her envy of the "happy closeness" between Riddle and Frank Sinatra. Now she got her turn as Riddle supplied fifty-two new arrangements. He respected her musicianship, and he respected Gershwin's original score to a point; but as befitted a midcentury modern arranger, he added his own complex chords to Gershwin's harmonies and slowed down many tempos (most notably in "Lady Be Good" and "Love Is Sweeping the Country"). He considered it his responsibility as an arranger to study Fitzgerald's "personality," and through timbre he portrayed her as amiable and direct. His consistently "feminine" orchestrations for her, gilded with harp, celesta, flutes, and strings in high registers, contrasted markedly with his hypermasculine approach with Frank Sinatra on similar repertoire. And in contrast to Sinatra's active involvement in the studio, Fitzgerald said that with Riddle,

> He just got the keys on them [the songs,] and each day we did so many arrangements and completed the album. I never, ever did much talking to Nelson, because Nelson is the type of arranger that you really don't have to worry about what's going to happen to the song. You just go out and sing, 'cause you know the arrangement's going to be beautiful, and it's left up to you for what you do.[35]

Fitzgerald and Riddle's signature sound in the *Gershwin Song Book* was previewed when Verve released a single of "But Not for Me,"[36] which had also been adopted as the title song for a feature film starring Clark Gable. The movie's ads and posters included the line, "Gershwin Wrote the Title Song . . . Ella Fitzgerald Sings It!" Even by 1959 standards, *Billboard* found it "sentimental," yet it was irresistibly so for many, opening with a captivating gesture of sweeping strings and soon adding harp and celesta. Fitzgerald delivered a fashionably slow version of the melody, sculpting every phrase with loving warmth, relishing the low chest tones that marked her voice in its prime, and relaxing into Gershwin's short phrases, unconcerned about breath control. The single charted well in the United States and Britain, winning a Grammy for "Best Vocal Performance, Female" in November 1959.[37] Her "happy closeness" with Riddle would blossom into dates with symphony orchestras and albums featuring their partnership in the early 1960s, and she even became "Auntie Ella" to his children.

The distinguished stature of the Gershwin project owed much to the special relationship between Ira Gershwin and Norman Granz, who would later call their collaboration his "most fruitful" experience as a producer.[38] The two men had become friends during the *Porgy and Bess* project in 1957, when Gershwin initiated contact to complain about the many jazz instrumental projects of the Gershwins' songs, which by definition neglected their lyrics.[39] For Ella's *Gershwin Song Book*, Ira retrieved some forgotten songs. Among the four recorded premieres was "The Real American Folk Song (Is a Rag)," the brothers' first collaboration, heard on Broadway in 1918. Ira made fastidious changes to verses and refrains to eliminate specific references to shows, and he gender-switched lyrics written for male characters. Ira's assistant and biographer Lawrence Stewart described his investment in the project as "an unusual departure for him," as he normally preferred not to be involved or show favoritism.[40] When she flubbed a lyric, he said he liked it better her way. And in one of her most widely quoted endorsements, he famously said, "I never knew how good our songs were until I heard Ella Fitzgerald sing them."[41] By including Lawrence Stewart's musicological treatise on

Ira Gershwin's lyrics, Granz emphasized the dignity of popular music as worthy of scholarly focus.[42]

The music trade treated the project with respect, even a bit of awe for the "superlative packaging and first-rate production, a project occupying more discs than a complete set of Beethoven's nine symphonies and marketed with comparable grandeur."[43] With supreme confidence, Granz did not name either the musicians or the songwriters on the cover. Instead, emulating a marketing strategy then in fashion for classical LPs, he commissioned a painting by the French modernist Bernard Buffet. Verve marketed the entire recording at three price points—$25 in monaural for mainstream consumers, $30 in stereo for audiophiles, and a $100 limited edition for "status seekers"—to borrow the title of a contemporary bestseller by social critic Vance Packard—with a deluxe walnut wood box, pearlized leather LP sleeves, more Bernard Buffet prints, and authentic autographs from Fitzgerald, Riddle, and both Gershwins.[44] In 1996 Granz reflected, "If I were working for a major label they would have thrown me out. . . . But that was the luxury of owning my own company and doing what I thought would help my artist. So I didn't really care if five LPs sold or not. I knew ultimately it would retrieve its cost."[45]

The reviews offer an informal survey of the cultural importance of the standards in an era of newly won respect for American song. Many critics elevated the project to a plane of monumentality as Fitzgerald placed her imprint on the legacy of a great American composer—not just a songwriter—far more definitively than had her earlier album with Ellis Larkins. Some dissenting reviews doubted the merit of the undertaking and expressed skepticism about her stature. Were the brothers Gershwin really worth all this fuss? In the *San Francisco Examiner*, jazz critic C. H. Garrigues called *Ella Fitzgerald Sings the George and Ira Gershwin Song Book* "possibly the most impressive tribute ever paid to a singer by a recording company" and "even for those of us who think comparatively little of Gershwin this is a beautiful collection."[46] Did it not demonstrate, as John S. Wilson wrote in *High Fidelity*, that "Miss Fitzgerald's association with jazz has been more a matter of circumstance than inclination, for her primary talent is her treatment of warmly melodious ballads"?[47] Why celebrate a body of work that exalted the national mythology of "the American dream," Don Heckman asked in the highbrow *Jazz Review*, with its "sugar-plum world of happy endings"? Ira Gershwin was too uxorious, too bourgeois; and as for Ella, she still believed in Mother Goose: "For the little orphan girl who leaped to nation-wide attention with 'A-Tisket A-Tasket,'" wrote Heckman, "the myth must be a part of everyday life, a dream fantasy that she relives every time she steps on a stage to receive the unabashed enthusiasm of audiences throughout the world."[48] Perhaps he should have recalled what Fitzgerald had said about Billie Holiday, that "Billie wasn't like what people say. She was [seen] like that because of her songs, not the other way around."[49]

In December Ella was home in Los Angeles. She could read the news about her latest Grammy Award, circulated around December 1, attend a surprise party for Frank Sinatra on December 9 that she and the rest of the cast arranged, listen to herself on radio, and prepare to share Christmas with her ten-year-old son, Junior.[50] She had only one concert in the area, a one-woman show being promoted fiercely by Audrey Franklyn scheduled for December 26 at the Santa Monica Civic Auditorium. It was advertised as a two-and-a-half-hour marathon. By then, Norman Granz had taken up permanent residence in Switzerland. He assured Fitzgerald he would come back for major performances, but this year her Santa Monica concert was not one of them.

Chapter 21

"IT'S QUITE A PROBLEM TRYING TO PLEASE EVERYONE"

(1960-1964)

E lla Fitzgerald said little in public about Norman Granz's decision to leave the United States. She trusted him, and he remained a responsible manager. Moreover, he invested her money, and by 1961, organized her business dealings into a separate operation, Salle Productions (*Ella's* spelled backward). In his small office on North Canon Drive, two devoted executive assistants, Mary Jane Outwater and Margaret Nutt, ran the business side of her career. Ultimately Mary Jane helped the forty-three-year-old mother in absentia run her home. According to Oscar Peterson, Norman recognized how Ella needed supportive female companionship,[1] so "the office" took over Granz's watch.

The real shocker was Granz's decision, at the peak of his influence in the record business, to sell Verve. He once cited exhaustion as the reason for divesting a label less than five years old.[2] Granz was cagey, and in September 1960 he denied his intentions to sell the label.[3] Frank Sinatra was reportedly interested in buying the label, but Granz balked, especially at Sinatra's stipulation that Granz run the European side of the operations.[4] There was too little trust between them to untie the inevitable knots in business negotiations.[5] In December 1960 Metro-Goldwyn-Mayer Records bought Verve for around $2.8 million. Stories about their mutual animosity surfaced later. In advance of Fitzgerald's 1959 appearance on Sinatra's TV show, according to a musician on site, Granz had offered suggestions for repertoire, which led to Sinatra throwing him off the set.[6] On other occasions, Granz reportedly expressed disdain for Sinatra as a singer.[7] There would be no "Ella and Frank" studio LPs, as there had been with "Ella and Louis," then or ever.

"Granz to Keep Watch over Ella," said *Billboard*,[8] referring to the Verve sale. The contract provided that Fitzgerald would remain protected within MGM operations for six years, while Granz retained supervisory rights on her recording projects. The two of them operated in their own space. In 1961, when Creed Taylor assumed the artistic direction for Verve, he was not interested in working with Granz in any case, considering him a technically careless producer in the studio.[9] "Norman and Ella operated completely independent of any MGM pressure," he later said. "No one at the company would dare get between Norman and Ella."[10] Taylor soon brought remarkable new energy into Verve, especially through bossa nova with Stan Getz, a former collaborator with Ella, but that would happen adjacent to if not totally outside her studio sessions.

★★★

IN THE SHORT RUN, Granz's physical removal from the American scene gave Fitzgerald increasing autonomy on the road in shaping her repertoire and balancing her sets.[11] In February 1960 she flew to Minneapolis for a date at Freddie's Jazz Club. When a young reporter met her at the airport, she was warding off a cold and warded off the reporter as well:

Reporter: Commence interview. The family stuff, question one.
Miss Fitzgerald's answer: I'm very seldom home. I collect recipes, watch TV. Ray plays the piano. I love music. I have a few friends—the people who like to sit and play cards and listen to music and watch TV. These are a few close friends and my cousins. I have a cold. I went to bed at 3 a.m., caught the plane at 5 a.m. I haven't slept. I'm tired. I've got to see a doctor tomorrow. Please, I don't want any more interview.

Reporter: It was a 20-minute ride back to town. I shut up. Miss Fitzgerald shut her eyes. And the "greatest" made it through three shows
at Freddie's last night.[12]

Staying for two sets on February 2, Will Jones, the respected columnist for the *Minneapolis Star Tribune*, couldn't believe what he was hearing:

"Somebody requested a song I don't know," said Ella Fitzgerald to
her loving audience. The song asked for was "Mack the Knife,"
but that didn't stop her. Miss Fitzgerald sang the song anyway,
improvising her own lyrics. "It's not for a lady to sing this song /
And that's why Ella sang the lyrics all wrong." And on she went,
chorus after chorus, loosely, uninhibitedly creating phrases, and
swinging all the way. There were references to Bobby Darin.
There was a bit of Louis Armstrong's growl.[13]

The story of "Ella and Mack" stands as a sequel to "A-Tisket
A-Tasket"—another unlikely angel delivering that magic "hit." The
murder-ballad had a bizarre and extensive history. "Captain MacHeath"
was a villain in John Gay's subversive 1728 ballad opera *The Beggar's
Opera*, an English missile lobbed at the Italian opera popular among the
British elite at the time. In 1928 Bertolt Brecht, the librettist, and Kurt
Weill, the composer, adapted Gay's work and renamed it *Die Dreigro-
schenoper* or *The Threepenny Opera* and nicknamed the captain "Mackie
Messer," German for "Mack the Knife"—the star of one of the most
popular songs in Weimar Germany. And so "Mack the Knife" stayed
in the translation in the American composer Marc Blitzstein's off-
Broadway production of *The Threepenny Opera* in 1955. The following
year Louis Armstrong gentrified "Mack" for a hit single; three years
later a young, white rock 'n' roll newcomer, Bobby Darin, swaggered
his arrangement into a number-one single on *Billboard*'s pop chart, winning a Grammy for "Record of the Year."[14]

"I would like to present 'Mack the Knife,' especially at my first concert in Berlin because it is a German song," she told Fritz Rau, the Ger-

man concert promoter for JATP's tour in February and March. With Granz in South America, Rau wavered. "Normally I would say in such an important concert, especially the Berlin one, that you shouldn't start this experiment. But after we went over the lyrics, we were both sure, yes, it's okay."[15] She practiced reeling off the roll call of oddball names in Mack's harem of prostitutes and victims—Sukey Tawdry, Jenny Diver, Polly Peachum, Lucy Brown.

On February 13, Fitzgerald arrived at West Berlin's Deutschlandhalle arena, filled with around twelve thousand East and West Germans, about a year and a half before construction of the Berlin Wall. Her bassist Wilfred Middlebrooks, a relative newcomer, recalled:

> We had played Brussels earlier, flown to Berlin and been up for 22 hours. We were all so tired we couldn't hold our heads up, when Ella turns around and says, "Let's do 'Mack the Knife.'" My heart sank. . . . We were in front of too many people to try something crazy, and I knew Ella didn't know the tune . . . but before I could say any more she had turned around and was announcing it. I looked at Paul and he just grinned.[16]

At the end of the second chorus, she gave Paul Smith, the pianist, a hand signal to shift the key from G major up a half step. By the fourth chorus, she had forgotten the words. Middlebrooks remembered thinking, "Well, she's about as lost as she can get, Louis Armstrong will show up any minute, because when Ella got lost in a swing number, she usually fell back on her Louis imitation."[17]

Louis showed up, and so did Bobby Darin and so did the Ella whose forgetting earned "neverending thunderous applause," in the words of Fritz Rau.[18] The more "mess" she made, the greater the charm of the contrast between her honesty and her artistry, and the more she remade it a "woman's song." Afterward she worried that Norman "was going to scream because I was putting in a song when I didn't know the lyrics."[19] But Norman recognized a phenomenon when he heard one. After listening to Rau's tape in March, he released a 45 rpm single paired with another song from the evening, the German-themed song, "Lorelei," on the B side. "Mack" debuted on *Billboard*'s rhythm and blues chart on May 23, peaking at number six, and crossed over to the top forty, reaching number twenty-seven. In July the single topped the Berlin Hit Parade.[20] Even Blitzstein praised Ella's "darling goofy" rendition, "with all my careful lyrics handsomely messed up."[21]

Fitzgerald was on fire that night. "How High the Moon" synthesized around twenty-five allusions to other songs, from "A-Tisket A-Tasket" to "Poinciana," "Deep Purple," "Ornithology," and Irving Berlin's "Heat Wave."[22] As with "Stompin' at the Savoy" from 1957, Granz released "How High the Moon" as two sides of a 45 rpm single. Then he released the Berlin concert as *Ella in Berlin: Mack the Knife*, which stayed on *Billboard*'s pop album charts for fifty-one weeks and became one of her best-selling albums.[23] In 1961 she received a Grammy for "Best Vocal Performance, Single Track Female" and "Best Vocal Performance, Album Female." All this from taking a request and singing what she called "a gag."[24]

"Mack the Knife" as a single and an album "kept Ella's career spiraling upward," Paul Smith said.[25] After the European tour, she made a quick trip to São Paulo, Brazil, in April.[26] "Three days off in six weeks," Fitzgerald said, back in Los Angeles, during her television interview for *Person to Person* on June 3, 1960, a tribute to her fame. In a segment hosted by Charles Collingwood, she introduced Aunt Virginia and Junior. Stiffly she walked from room to room, squandering time pointing to her wall of autographs, a practice that she had begun in 1936 and had carried on for decades. There was "Miss Dinah Shore who I just love so much." She pointed to the photo of Sarah Vaughan dueling with her in Brussels—"I call her Sassy, I feel more closer to her that way." Then to Nat King Cole, Louis Armstrong, "Frankie Boy," and Norman Granz, "that's the 'eyebrows' they call him." When asked if she had a trophy room, she said, "I don't like to keep too many around, I don't like to feel I love me that much." Nevertheless she was proud of her four Grammys, which had come from "fellow workers." Who had helped her? Collingwood asked. The perfectionist answered, "Friends who could tell me when I was doing something wrong, when you know you are not that great." She advised younger singers to cultivate many styles beyond the hit that launched them.[27]

In the spring of 1960, Fitzgerald debuted in her first serious film role in *Let No Man Write My Epitaph*, adapted from a novel by the radical African American writer Willard Motley. The role of a dope-addicted junkie saloon singer was out of her range; she coped adequately but not sufficiently well to justify much camera time. "Hear Ella Sing 4 All-Time Favorites" ran the ads, but the film preserved only snippets. While the movie enjoyed respectable success, the LP Granz salvaged to dovetail with the film was a commercial flop.[28]

The year ended with more jet travel to Australia and New Zealand, accompanied by Mel Tormé and the Lou Levy Quintet. Fitzgerald had last visited Australia in 1956, leading to the lawsuit against Pan American Airlines. Although one critic felt entitled to label Fitzgerald "the mammy of U.S. vocalists," the Australians were ready to welcome her again.[29] Her concert took place on December 4, 1960, at the Embers Club in Melbourne. It was taped for the Australian TV series *BP Super Show*, sponsored by British Petroleum, and was broadcast in January 1961. The hour-long program showed her as a nervous woman in a no-frills hairstyle, ignoring the cameras and offering no patter. She displayed no stylized body language and had no particularly graceful way of moving onstage or off. Nevertheless she enchanted her listeners. Then it was on to New Zealand for three concerts—"pristine, unknown territory" for jazz, Norman Granz said.[30]

Back in Los Angeles for Christmas with eleven-year-old Ray Jr., she enjoyed her new, larger home on North Sierra Drive for a few weeks. She tucked in a songbook recital on January 6, 1961, at the Shrine Auditorium. And then she was off to a grand inaugural gala evening, produced by Frank Sinatra as a benefit to defray campaign debt for John F. Kennedy. She had campaigned for the presidential candidate with Sinatra that fall and looked forward to sharing the spotlight with a grand parade of American performers, including Nat King Cole, Harry Belafonte, Ethel Merman, and Mahalia Jackson. That evening she sang "But

Not for Me" in her pearliest ballad voice. By then Mother Nature had turned Republican, bringing a major snowstorm to Washington, D.C., and preventing a television broadcast on NBC.[31]

At the private party afterward, she was assigned a seat at Sinatra's table next to his buddy Sammy Cahn, her old Decca colleague, but never claimed it. As Cahn later wrote, she "was always terribly nervous at such affairs."[32] The next night, accompanied by her road manager, Pete Cavello, cousin Georgiana Henry, and new friend Phoebe Jacobs, then working at Basin Street East, Fitzgerald sang at three different inaugural balls. Jacobs recalled her trudging through the slush and snow with her long chiffon dress tied up and her satin shoes covered with white trash bags. "She didn't complain," Jacobs remembered. Fitzgerald later said, "I think meeting President Kennedy—that warm handshake of his— was one of the greatest thrills" and joked that her elaborately beaded white satin dress with train was her "wedding gown, which I wore for President Kennedy's Inaugural Gala."[33] Ella "was so American," said Jacobs. "She was so dignified and so proud. They were going crazy that she was coming over, and she was ecstatic that they wanted her."[34]

★★★

AMID A GENERAL BOOM FOR LP SALES, and with the success of "Mack" as security, Fitzgerald and Granz anticipated a welcoming climate for their new albums, with settings ranging from Hollywood big-band-plus-strings arrangements to small groups to the occasional live set. In fact, *Ella in Berlin* deceived both her and her manager because it was an end, not a beginning, to her presence on the *Billboard* popular charts. While her albums produced solid sales over time as catalogue satisfying her fan base, she rode a roller-coaster of hits and misses traversing the continuum of jazz-pop. The pop establishment liked some, the jazz world others, while she helped sustain the relevance of vocal jazz especially for female singers through the transitional early 1960s.

The hybrid jazz-pop genre had worked for Fitzgerald brilliantly in the late 1950s, but sustaining it turned into a bigger challenge than either she or

Granz anticipated. How could it have been otherwise? Jazz had changed, and so had pop, and so had the cultural and political milieu. Granz's conservative taste stayed fixed on mainstream jazz from the swing-to-bop era that JATP had helped establish as the norm. Fitzgerald as always was driven by Chick Webb's advice to stay current. In 1963 she said, "It's quite a problem trying to please everyone."[35] Was it artistically desirable, or even possible?

Canon building continued with *Ella Fitzgerald Sings the Harold Arlen Song Book*, a two-LP set of twenty-four songs released in 1961, at the time when Arlen himself was lamenting the sharp decline of interest in his craft.[36] Its sales reflected that trend even as critical acclaim justified the continuation of the *Song Book* project as "bound to take its place alongside other classic 'Song Book' efforts."[37] "I was scared all the way through 'Stormy Weather,'" Fitzgerald told the *New York Herald Tribune*. "I knew this was Ethel's (Waters) song and I kept remembering how great she sang it."[38] The composer loved Fitzgerald's interpretations, lavishing praise and expressing gratitude for the spotlight she shined on him. "I never thought that after the pommeling 'Stormy' has taken over the years that I'd be able to sit and hear it as for the first time," said Arlen, buttressing the authority of her work.[39]

Granz chose Billy May as the arranger, noted for his collaborations with Frank Sinatra. He had known Ella since 1939, when "she was a young lad of a girl," he said, singing with the Chick Webb band.[40] Norman and Ella, he recalled, argued sideways:

> When we did the Harold Arlen songbook, Ella was very upset that Norman insisted on doing "Over the Rainbow." She said Judy Garland had done it so definitively. When we got to the bridge, she started [goofing around] a little. So Norman called me into the booth and said, "Look, she's blowing it off, and I know why. But I don't want to get into a thing. So I'm going to tell her the pickup on the drums was bad and we have to do it again. But don't tell her I didn't like the performance." So I went into the studio and said we had to do another one. Then Ella comes over to me and says, "I know what he said. He said the drums were too loud and we gotta

do another one. But he didn't like the way I sang it." She read him perfectly. That kind of shit was going on the whole time.[41]

For "Over the Rainbow," Granz prevailed on her to sing the rarely included verse, which separated her sufficiently from Garland's performance to make it viable and distinctive.[42]

Her next studio LP, *Clap Hands, Here Comes Charlie!*, released in December 1961, returned her to the small-group jazz format.[43] Reinforcing Fitzgerald's conservative taste, its setlist was shaped by an autobiographical subtext: it was a subtle tribute album to her cohorts in the 1930s and '40s. The title tune had been Chick Webb's drumming showcase in 1937. "My Reverie" evoked Bea Wain, Larry Clinton's "girl singer." Fitzgerald revisited her own Decca hits "I Got a Guy" from 1937 and "The One I Love Belongs to Somebody Else" from 1941. She honored Billie Holiday with "Good Morning Heartache" and "You're My Thrill"; and Sarah Vaughan with "Signing Off," which Vaughan had memorably recorded with Dizzy Gillespie in 1944—few had sung it since. *Clap Hands* sold well enough and garnered excellent reviews among jazz critics. In *Down Beat*'s review, John Tynan took the opportunity to disparage the "ponderous orchestras" of the Hollywood arrangers.[44]

Granz then returned exactly to that milieu, with conventional anthologies of standards from the 1930s and '40s, aimed at mainstream audiences, in big band arrangements by Nelson Riddle. For Fitzgerald, it was another chance to record the many tunes Decca had deemed outside her purview. The November 1961 and April 1962 sessions in Los Angeles yielded two LPs, *Ella Swings Brightly with Nelson* and *Ella Swings Gently with Nelson*.[45] Neither cracked the *Billboard* list of top LPs, yet the Hollywood music establishment awarded *Ella Swings Brightly* a Grammy for "Best Solo Vocal Performance" of 1961.

★★★

FITZGERALD'S WORK ETHIC matched Granz's prodigious energy. For a tour starting in February 1961, he launched an empire-building itinerary, with dates in Turkey, Greece, Yugoslavia, Iran, and Israel, where she would sing Hebrew translations of her songs.[46] Britain, where Granz consistently paired her with Oscar Peterson, supported multicity tours, and this time the U.K.'s Granada TV network broadcast an entire recital.[47] In a review from this tour, the British jazz pianist Robin Douglas-Home focused on the sheer sound of her voice with an explicitness rarely seen in the American press: "The sound is pure, almost child-like. The voice, now velvet, now husky; swoops and plunges with uncannily perfect control, caressing a phrase here, jumping an octave there. The texture is as airy and light as a willow-warbler's spring song."[48]

With so much work in Europe, Fitzgerald adopted Copenhagen as a surrogate home. Like other jazz artists who formed small expat communities throughout Europe as oases from American racism, Fitzgerald found respite there. In Beverly Hills, when she wanted to purchase a single-family luxury home but came up against whites-only real estate covenants, Granz had purchased the property in his name.[49] Still, as *Jet* magazine reported, "a group of citizens held a protest meeting but found out too many citizens were happy to have the noted jazz singer as a neighbor."[50] Copenhagen offered her privacy especially for her romantic relationships. In November 1961 a feature story in *Ebony* magazine emphasized that she cried when she was alone, lest one think that a career satisfied an unmarried woman, and it quoted her: "You can have love of family, love of children and all that, but you've got to have your man."[51] But according to Paul Smith, in Copenhagen she was involved with a "little Danish guy [who] was much younger than she was, and he was about half her size. It was a kind of live-in boyfriend type of thing." Lou Levy described him as "a real young, blond, rosy-cheeked, blue-eyed Dane."[52] For three years she held a fashionable apartment in Klampenborg, a northern suburb of Copenhagen, with a view overlooking the sea. *Berlingske Tidende* reported, "It is her intention to settle down here between her many tours. . . . Here there is peace and quiet."[53]

Compared to her European tour, which booked her into arenas and large concert halls, in her U.S. itinerary in 1961 she performed for United Nations diplomats; college kids at the University of Maryland and at Lawrence College in Appleton, Wisconsin, where she ate at a local diner and posed with a waitress; and at the exclusive Forest Hills Tennis Club in Queens, where eleven thousand fans heard many "Fitzgerald surprises" including "a humorous take off on a ridiculous rock and roll record of 'Blue Moon.' "[54] The term *diverse* appeared in many reviews, as she floated above and through popular music genres, incorporating new repertoire through the jazz axiom "It ain't what you do, it's the way that you do it," as she sang in 1937 and kept close to her heart.

On April 13, 1961, Fitzgerald opened a three-week booking at Basin Street East, her first New York club date in three years. The venue, which jazz record producer George Avakian called "pretty much the top night club in the country for what the trade classifies as a 'class jazz act,' "[55] had been the scene of Peggy Lee's career renaissance, and Fitzgerald followed one of Lee's triumphant month-long stands.[56] *Variety* reported that she won over the crowd "without vocal gimmicry and without physical embellishments" in a program of "diversified material" including "Mack the Knife" and "Lorelei."[57]

Perhaps the audience rapport at Basin Street East encouraged Granz to return to live recordings, which the public adored.[58] He had already accumulated many tapes, including several from Berlin that could have formed a sequel but that remained in the vaults. Creed Taylor said, "If an Ella project did not make it to LP, it was completely Norman's call."[59] Apparently, Granz was waiting for a hometown location, Crescendo, a jazz club on Sunset Strip with a history of live recordings by Louis Armstrong, Mel Tormé, and George Shearing. In marched folks from the Hollywood celebrity A-list—Audrey Hepburn, Rock Hudson, Natalie Wood—their entrances filmed for a publicity reel and for a photo feature by Louella Parsons in *Modern Screen* magazine.[60] The *Los Angeles Times* review found that "she has never been better. . . . The opening-night audience soon realized it, too and wildly applauded each number. . . . She simply mows down an audience. . . . She belted, she crooned, and ended with a wild outburst of jazz singing that left auditors shouting for more."[61]

Granz documented Ella's stand at the Crescendo with systematic thoroughness, recording every night from May 11 to 21, 1961—a total of 138 tracks, from which twelve were chosen for the LP *Ella in Hollywood*.[62] He seemed more invested in the live experience of documenting her oeuvre than in getting the results to a satisfactory LP, even resorting to the dubious tactic of adding artificial applause from a larger hall no less, which compromised the intimacy of the space holding around two hundred people. Still, the results of a date in an American venue planned for a timely release made this LP valuable. The album consisted of a mix of ballads and vocal jams, including Billy Strayhorn's "Take the 'A' Train," which ran for nine and a half minutes with her longest scat solo on record.[63] Her bassist, Wilfred Middlebrooks, claimed that her "'A' Train" solo was unrehearsed and that she spontaneously appropriated licks by Ray Nance, Dizzy Gillespie, and Clark Terry.[64] Fitzgerald again spoofed the doo-wop hit version of "Blue Moon" by the Marcels, telling the crowd, "If you can't beat 'em, join 'em, so we did." Her old friend "Mr. Paganini" was also released as a single, charting briefly in *Billboard* and boosting album sales.[65]

Diversified was the bon mot of choice, for a repertoire that pleased some and alienated others.[66] If Granz had so desired, he could have issued another songbook titled "Ella Fitzgerald Sings the Ella Fitzgerald Songbook." But he let that opportunity slide. The full potential of documenting her range of styles, especially the epigrammatic takes on Tin Pan Alley classics as well as songbook fare gave a special aura to a subsequent curated CD box set (an acclaimed CD box set from 2009, *Twelve Nights in Hollywood*; its producing editors chose fifty-five unreleased tracks, remastered the originals, and restored the club ambience).[67] That said, the record released in 1961 languished in sales. Leonard Feather chose *Ella in Hollywood* to represent Fitzgerald in his article "The Essentials of a Jazz Record Library" for *HiFi/Stereo Review*. He led off, "The question 'Is Ella Fitzgerald a Jazz Singer?' can hardly be better answered than in these sides taped before a very live audience at the Crescendo in Hollywood. . . . Ella defines jazz singing in every phrase of every tune."[68]

★★★

"Is Ella Fitzgerald a jazz singer?" was a ubiquitous question among jazz critics in the early 1960s. How could this be when during these years (and beyond) she was held up as an icon in the national mainstream, winning every major poll in the female-jazz-singer category in both the jazz and trade presses and outpacing rivals by huge numbers? The answer is that there is not one answer: it would bring us too far afield from Ella's story to fully explain the complicated reasons for the marginal status of jazz singers, whose history is only now being explored by contemporary historians in many disciplines, analyzing the intersectionality of race and racism with gender and sexism and juggling it with music theory and pedagogy, no less.[69] Instead, we begin with what Fitzgerald herself thought about the question, because with her usual courage, she tackled it head on.

In 1961, in a little-known important interview for the *Los Angeles Times* on September 24, the story highlighted how "Ella Fitzgerald answers the critics who say she's just not a jazz singer anymore with some of her thoughts on music."

> I've heard where music critics say I'm not just a jazz singer anymore. But we all try to grow and improve. What is jazz, anyhow? I don't know. To me jazz is music. Anyway, as they said, I have changed. I sing what the public likes. Sometimes you sing what you like, sometimes you sing what you don't like. . . . I try to do a little bit of everything. You get a wonderful release. Even rock 'n' roll. Hillbilly music. Anything, if it's played well. When I get requests I get a kick out of doing something I don't know and making up lyrics for it. Personally I like the pretty songs. The fast numbers are just a happy feeling and nobody really listens unless you're bopping. Me, I'm a lover of sweet music—sweet and semi-swing. . . . I don't do everything perfect since I just kid around on the stage. It's part of me and it's what the people want of me.[70]

"What the public likes" did not mean pandering. She based her priorities on "accessibility," which has deep roots not just in jazz and popular music but in the myriad ways the performing professions evolved across the American musical landscape. In the words of the distinguished music historian Richard Crawford, "Accessibility seeks out the center of the marketplace. . . . And it invests ultimate authority in the present-day audience. Performers driven by accessibility seek most of all to find and please audiences and to increase their size."[71] With her phonographic memory she infused whatever she chose from wherever she wanted and made it work.

In the early 1960s, Fitzgerald's music making also triggered controversy around her instrumental voice. How much weight, for instance, should critics attach to the sheer beauty of her vocal instrument or to classical elements such as her range and purity of tone in a jazz tradition where—in the words of German jazz authority Joachim Berendt—"some of the most important jazz singers have voices which are almost ugly"? In *The New Jazz Book*, translated into English in 1962, Berendt wrote, "The dilemma of jazz singing can be expressed as a paradox: all of jazz derives from vocal music, but all of jazz singing is derived from instrumental music. . . . Nothing more flattering can be said of a singer than that he or she understands how to treat the voice as an instrument." He praised Fitzgerald as the best representative of "sounding like a horn" through her improvisational scatting.[72] By contrast, the American journalist Nat Hentoff dismissed Fitzgerald's scatting as facile virtuosity and as an inappropriate intrusion into the domain of instrumentalists.[73]

Another factor in the volatility of Fitzgerald's reputation centered around the emergence of a binary opposition between Billie Holiday and Ella Fitzgerald, as though they represented mutually exclusive vocalities, and further that one had to choose between them as symbols of excellence. Some critics addressed this question by advocating stylistic tolerance, while others proposed a Cold War, either-or mindset. This approach grew more urgent in the early 1960s, after the death of Billie Holiday in 1959 gave rise to assessments of that loss.[74] Who would have expected its longevity or even expansion in the jazz world into the 1990s? A prominent critic, Francis Davis, would write in 1994 about its impact: "It is virtually impossible to listen to one without also hearing the other; they seem to demand that we make a choice. And . . . a preference for one of these singers at the expense of the other reveals something about a person's outlook on life, not just his taste in music."[75] This makes the following few examples have more than topical relevance. In a 1961 review of *Clap Hands, Here Comes Charlie!*, George T. Simon wrote,

> On records, as well as in person, some jazz singers try to convince the listener with dramatic intensity that nobody can possibly know the trouble they've seen or seem to be feeling. Others take themselves and their sad songs more lightly. Instead of overselling, they undersell, and still they manage to get across their personal messages of love or loneliness with equally complete conviction.
>
> Master, or mistress, of the latter style is Ella Fitzgerald. Compare her quiet, resigned, relaxed treatments of "Good Morning Heartache" and "You're My Thrill" with the far more dramatic and intense Billie Holiday versions, with which most jazz fans are familiar, and you'll agree there's more than one honest jazz way to sell a song.[76]

Reviewing *Ella Swings Brightly with Nelson*, *Down Beat*'s Richard Hadlock—also a musician—mooted the issue of sexual charisma for what he described as a disembodied voice.

> That contemporary jazz writers still bicker in public about Miss Fitzgerald's standing as a jazz singer suggests a need for judging this remarkable woman with a slightly different method from that one [*sic*] might to, say, Billie Holiday. The latter was a story-teller who made most of her fans fall in love with her; Ella is a musician, to be enjoyed much as one would enjoy Johnny Hodges or Bobby Hackett. She thinks notes rather than words, and is, in a way, less a singer (in the storytelling sense) than is a

highly emotional instrumentalist such as Ben Webster. It is not unusual to enjoy her work thoroughly without giving a passing thought to her womanhood.[77]

Perhaps the most influential antagonist to Fitzgerald was Nat Hentoff, who attracted attention among his peers for his total devotion to Billie Holiday. Exploiting the notion that she sang like a "little girl," wih her fist still grasping her yellow basket, he treated her as if her ingenue voice defined her personality, not just her persona. In his liner notes for *The Best of Ella Fitzgerald* in 1959, he called her a "pretty bird," a "lamb," and "an innocent with the musical capacity of a sweet wizard." He embellished this idea: "It is not that Ella does not sing jazz; but she is happier, I feel, in the less naturalistic pop world, where she can sing popular songs and standards in a jazz-influenced style and never meet anything more forbidding than the *Wizard of Oz*."[78] Whatever intellectual authority she possessed was obscured by Hentoff's beguiling literary bravado. His piece received an even wider circulation when it was republished in 1960 in the anthology *The Jazz Word*.[79]

In such a climate, it was not surprising that a dispute emerged in the music trade press between pro– and anti–Ella Fitzgerald advocates. Hentoff had a forum for his extremism in 1962 when *HiFi/Stereo Review* seized the moment for an official debate over the question "Is Ella Fitzgerald a great jazz singer?" "NO," said Hentoff, the confident radical; "YES," said Leonard Feather, the moderate.[80] Her "little-girl" charm camouflaged emotional immaturity. By contrast, his paragon, Billie Holiday, "never approached Ella's instrument-like facility, but there was not the slightest doubt about the complex nature of a human personality when Billie sang. . . . Ella too often sounds like a child, and although popular music is based on the fantasies of actual or arrested adolescents, the essence of jazz has certainly never been for children." Hentoff's wife, Margot, later recalled that when they attended her concert around this time, Ella spotted them in the audience and gave them a "sarcastic smile."[81]

Leonard Feather spoke for Fitzgerald's credentials as a great jazz singer.

By then, a seasoned producer, historian, and syndicated jazz critic in the mainstream press, Feather cited his 1956 poll of one hundred leading jazz musicians and singers, in which "she received sixty-six votes as the greatest female jazz singer of all time, followed by Billie Holiday with twenty-three and Sarah Vaughan with twenty-one votes." Then he made room in the musical universe for two shining stars. While conceding precedence to Holiday—"To my mind, no greater jazz singer than Billie Holiday has ever lived"—he asserted that Ella Fitzgerald need not be demeaned through a false binary opposition.

> But Ella Fitzgerald is peerless in jazz on another level; she has virtues that are not to be sought, and certainly not to be found, in Billie or anyone else. Hers is a different vitality, a different not a lesser range of emotions—emotions that reach most listeners as completely as Billie's emotions reached hers. To suggest that comparative measures must be used in evaluating the contribution of either artist is to suggest that only one means may be used to reach an artistically perfect end.[82]

The jazz press reflected the struggles of women in a marginalized jazz-pop field to establish their own practices and traditions in a male-dominated critical environment. As one of the few women or African Americans writing for the jazz press, Barbara Gardner in "Thoughts on Female 'Jazz Singers,'" published in the *Down Beat Music '63* yearbook, asked why "recognized and respected critics and reviewers who will readily decline to define jazz split into atomized factions when discussing who should be considered a jazz singer or if, really, anyone should"? Her polite deflation of entitled male critics suggests latent currents of resistance that would surface at large when Betty Friedan's feminist manifesto, *The Feminine Mystique*, was published the following year. Critics were in effect trying to control jazz singing as a form of "women's work," conflating tensions around style with confusions around gender identity in a male-dominated field. "Sounding like a horn" had for decades conferred stature on those women who, as Gardner wrote, could "infuse their performances with the emotional and creative charge identified with instrumental jazz," which was understood to be "men's work."[83]

In this context, Fitzgerald was the most noted living representative of "women's work" in jazz. Gardner noted her hybridity both as a jazz singer and as a popular singer. Jazz-pop did not have sufficient integrity, in her mind, to resolve Fitzgerald's dual identity with jazz critics. She well knew that labeling a singer a "popular singer" was a demotion in status and a strategy to mark boundaries.[84]

Fitzgerald's ambiguous status may have thwarted her participation in the first all-jazz concert at the new Lincoln Center for the Performing Arts on November 11, 1962. Lincoln Center had been slow to include jazz in its programs, but around the end of 1961 it formed a three-man jazz advisory committee comprised of jazz pianist Billy Taylor, composer Gunther Schuller, and BMI public relations director Russell Sanjek to remedy the problem.[85] In October 1962 the columnist Leonard Lyons reported that for a lunch with Norman Granz and Duke Ellington at Philharmonic Hall, Fitzgerald was denied access because "Lincoln Center says that Ella Fitzgerald is not a jazz singer"; Ellington, after an "incredulous smile . . . threw back his head and laughed: 'Ella Fitzgerald is not a jazz singer? Ella?'" Once Ellington stopped laughing, "he wondered whether his own music would meet the test."[86]

Whether or not Lyons was accurate, the climate around Fitzgerald's status made the story credible. In *Down Beat* one member of the Lincoln Center committee explained that "evenings at the center should be creative evenings, not just a one-night stand, and that is the commission we have from the center. We feel that the hall should be a challenge to the artist."[87] Fitzgerald would not perform in Philharmonic Hall until a few years later.

The question of Fitzgerald's stature in jazz followed her to Europe in the spring of 1962. In Paris, where she garnered major critical attention, "Ella Fitzgerald is telling the press here that she is not a musician but a singer," *Variety* reported, "and that she does not consider herself a jazz figure either. She just sings her own way."[88] French critics exempted her from the hypersexualized discourse they typically meted out to other female artists.[89] In April, during her month-long British tour, Fitzgerald elaborated on her approach to a reporter:

> I hate being typecast. Maybe I'm more of a jazz singer than a pop one. I don't care to restrict myself. I like to sing what I feel. . . . Sometimes when I've sung a pop [song] someone asks me, "What's the matter, Ella, are you going square," and I've given them my answer. "No, I'm not going square. I'm going versatile." . . . I like to surprise and please my audiences. I'm sensitive and can feel whether people really enjoy a song. It's quite a problem trying to please everyone. Some come to hear jazz, others to hear numbers from the song books. I try to include as many jazz items into my repertoire as I can, but all the time, I'm trying to broaden my field. I have to move with the times. I don't want to stand still. I must keep experimenting, trying new ideas, and new songs.[90]

★★★

FITZGERALD'S FLEXIBILITY FIT THE TIMES. The economic climate for jazz musicians showed signs of decline in 1962, yet for the record industry as a whole, as Leonard Feather wrote, "commercially, it was a year without precedent, a new era that saw jazz artists intermixed with pop stars on the best-seller lists every week."[91] Granz kept his eye on new match-ups and themes, pivoting from one approach to another, filling the bins at record stores and the options on "Record of the Month" clubs. Fitzgerald was "always looking for unusual material to record," wrote George T. Simon. When Granz issued a Brazilian bossa nova–style single with her "Desafinado" on one side and "Stardust Bossa Nova" on the other, Simon claimed that "Stardust Bossa Nova" evoked a Latin version of "Stardust" that Chick Webb had played at the Savoy Ballroom with Fitzgerald pitching in on claves, gourds, and cowbells.[92] Taking a cue from the huge success of Ray Charles, Granz enlisted rhythm and blues organist Bill Doggett for Ella's LP *Rhythm Is My Business*, released in September 1962. Doggett's arrangements drew on his big band swing roots while including "Hallelujah, I Love Him So," which had been an R&B hit for Charles.[93]

Slow record sales in 1962 demanded intense touring to make up revenue shortfalls, so Granz kept her on the road. After the European tour, she performed at familiar venues such as the Flamingo in Las Vegas and the Basin Street East in New York, then in May did a national tour of small cities. During her June engagement at the Crescendo in Los Angeles, *Variety*'s reviewer wrote, "It's time for a re-appraisal of Ella Fitzgerald who has been waxing merrily along in this business for over 27 years." Somehow "ageless Ella" had turned into a "glamor gal—gowned in an incredibly designed black creation of expensive simplicity, offset by long, white gloves—she clutches a peach-colored chiffon kerchief to dab her beads of perspiration; and she is coiffed in the very latest fashion, complementing her face and figure."[94]

The pace of touring with JATP in Europe caught up with Granz, who contracted hepatitis and convalesced in Reykjavik, Iceland, for three months on his way back to the States. Fitzgerald sent him a note: "Gee, I wish I could have come by, but as you know, I was not allowed, so *please*, please take care and do as they say. I'll miss you very much, but will get things fixed and taken care of (the music). Well, you are a good man, Norman. I mean that from my heart, in spite of our quarrels. I guess we're too good and think about other people too much."[95]

Paul Smith characterized the JATP tour as "the most grueling forty-six weeks of my life. We worked every single day. Most days we did two concerts, many of those in different cities. How her heart, lungs, and voice held up is beyond me. We ended that tour in Seattle at the World's Fair. After the last concert, Stan Levey and I took off our tuxedos, threw them into the closet and swore we were never going on the road again."[96]

Not Ella Fitzgerald. After a week at home, she was ready for more.

Chapter 22

GENERATION GAPS

(1963-1965)

"So little girl, how does it feel to be back in New York?" asked Fred Robbins, Ella's old DJ friend, in a long interview in April 1963.[1] Her last few months had been particularly busy, with a prominent date at the Santa Monica Civic Auditorium, annual visits to Basin Street East and the Deauville in Miami Beach, and several weeks touring Europe.[2] On April 10 she had opened the renovated Royal Box in the Hotel Americana in midtown Manhattan to strong reviews. Occasionally supplemented by eight string players in the hotel's house band, her quartet now included pianist Tommy Flanagan, bassist Jim Hughart, and veteran drummer Gus Johnson, while trumpeter Roy Eldridge provided mostly obbligato work. "Is there any kind of particular feeling, Ella, when . . . you sing for the first time in a new room?" Robbins asked. "Are you used to it by now, this marvelous love and respect and adoration that you've accomplished all over the world?" Hardly one to sanction complacency, the sin that feeds mediocrity, boredom, and failure, she replied, "I don't think anybody ever reaches the complete top, because I don't think there's anyone that's really always right in good form." "Any singer," she told Robbins, "could catch a cold, get nervous when a fellow singer walks into the room, or read the crowd wrong." Further, as she reminded patrons at the Royal Box, "I'm on Verve Records, and I haven't had a hit since 'Mack the Knife.'"[3]

The interview then swerved into contemporary politics, at a time when the media was reporting frequently on the Southern Christian Leadership Conference (SCLC), led by Martin Luther King, Jr., and their heroic campaign to desegregate public space in Birmingham, Alabama. Robbins asked the globe-hopping artist if she still believed in jazz as democracy's messenger. Fitzgerald, who generally avoided politics in interviews, replied,

> It's a sad thing to say in a way. I'm not a politician or anything, and I don't attempt to be, but I wish that music could mean as much and could bring as much happiness and bring people together in certain parts of our own country as it does in the other countries. . . . It makes you feel so bad to think that we can't go down through certain parts of the South and give a concert like we do overseas and have everybody just come to hear the music, enjoy the music, and sit and enjoy each other because of the prejudice thing that's going on.

She then described her embarrassment when asked about U.S. race relations by overseas journalists.

> Why don't you play down in so and so? or You don't play in Alabama. Why can't you have a concert and music is music? Why can't they be sharing it down South? Why can't we? Why do we go to Japan, why do we go to Paris, and all the different places, and the people just come because they want to hear the music? And why can't we do the same thing in our own country?

Fitzgerald elaborated further on her ambitions to do radio and television, where she "could just get to children, and because children coming up is where the roots have got to be planted." She concluded, "This is unusual for me, but I'm so happy that you had me [talk] instead of singing for a change, I got a chance to get a few things off my chest."[4]

Fitzgerald's public and private activities on behalf of social justice dated back to 1936, when Chick Webb's orchestra played a benefit for the Scottsboro Boys at the Savoy Ballroom. In the 1940s she had joined benefit rallies for progressive political candidates and visited military bases. In the 1950s she had helped raise money for the NAACP, and with Granz as her manager, she had been thrust into the front lines of the battle to desegregate public spaces. On October 1, 1961, at the Shrine Auditorium in Los Angeles, Fitzgerald, backed by the Paul Smith Trio, gave her first solo concert benefit for the NAACP. "It's something I've always wanted to do," she told the *Los Angeles Times*. "I have a son and feel that people must learn to live with and love one another. Until people know these things . . ." She left that sentence unfinished.[5]

In May 1963 she donated $1,000 to the SCLC, which had just achieved a historic victory to integrate public accommodations in its Birmingham campaign.[6] On June 15 at the Crescendo in Los Angeles, she and the club owner, Gene Norman, held a benefit for the SCLC. "Even the musicians donated their pay for the night to this crucial cause," Ella said, "and everyone went out of their way at added expense to make sure that the Crescendo was packed that night so that I could show my deep support."[7] For a "Salute to Freedom" concert in Birmingham on August 5, Fitzgerald was listed along with Ray Charles, Johnny Mathis, and Nina Simone on the concert poster, but she did not appear. She also missed the March on Washington on August 23, even though she was named among the many performers headed there.[8] An anecdote later surfaced according to which she had declined to join, saying, "March, no sirree. My feet are killing me. I'll do what I do best—sing."[9]

A younger generation of activists wanted their famous stars to march with them, but Fitzgerald was a shy, retiring person who avoided public tumult in general. But now she was risking irrelevance as she insisted on the power of music to communicate her goals outside political activism. A *Chicago Defender* headline typical of the Black press in 1963 read, "Do Top Entertainers Dodge Peace Parades, Integration Protests?" The writer, Bob Hunter, wrote:

This is not to say that Negro stars are not fighting segregation in their own way. They are. The really big ones will not play dates at clubs which refuse service to the race. They also stand behind the NAACP, the Urban League and CORE (Congress of Racial Equality). However, when it comes to that personal touch—active participation—the people in question are nowhere to be found. . . . Direct participation by Negro stars is the answer to many of the racial problems in this country.[10]

While Fitzgerald was not as outspoken as many young people in her audience would have liked her to be, she nonetheless reached out to them in her venue choices, expanding beyond fancy hotels and expensive jazz clubs. In July 1963, with Duke Ellington also on the bill, she made her second appearance at Ravinia, the estate in Highland Park, Illinois, where the Chicago Symphony held its family-friendly summer season. On July 22 she hit the Convention Center at Asbury Park, New Jersey, in a summer lineup that included Ray Charles and a Hootenanny Festival with Odetta. She had first visited Asbury Park in 1938, singing swing songs to her peers. Now she had to captivate a partially filled hall with her scatting. "Few of her younger fans are familiar with this form of jazz vocalizing," the local New Jersey reviewer wrote.

When Miss Fitzgerald swung into "Take the 'A' Train" and "Stompin' at the Savoy," the room came alive. She lifted lines from other songs, and quoted television commercials, without losing a note. She twists! And shimmies! Both dance steps were done in fun as parts of songs, and evoked cheers from the audience, many of whom had never seen her in person before. Their knowledge of Ella Fitzgerald was limited to hearing her recordings and watching her occasional television appearances.[11]

★★★

HOW MUCH WOULD THEY REALLY HAVE KNOWN about her from those network TV appearances? By this time, Fitzgerald was averaging around four or five guest spots a year, a notable exception to the widespread exclusion of African Americans from television. Along with Louis Armstrong and Duke Ellington, she remained in the top tier of jazz attractions on TV variety programs, ranging from the hip late-night talk shows hosted by Johnny Carson and Steve Allen to prime-time shows hosted by the personable Dinah Shore, the raffish Las Vegas swinger Dean Martin, and the middle-of-the-road yet versatile Andy Williams. As Fitzgerald said in 1965:

> On each of these shows I did something of a different type; yet each time I probably reached certain people who said, "Now that's the way I dig her; that's the real Ella." On another show I might do a little bopping and someone else will make the same kind of remark. Yet I don't want to feel that everything must be in any one of those grooves or that any one is the real Ella.[12]

Usually backed by excellent TV studio orchestras, Fitzgerald typically split her time between swing songs and standards from the 1930s and '40s like "Body and Soul," "Them There Eyes," and "I Got It Bad (And That Ain't Good)." She told Leonard Feather that *The Dean Martin Show* "was a ball. Les Brown has the band on it, and they had picked out a couple of things for me, but I always have to say to myself, 'What's it got that's gonna make me feel like I *want* to sing?' And so Les said, 'Just sing whatever you feel like singing,' so we wound up doing things like 'Mean to Me,' and 'Time After Time.'"[13] On different episodes of *The Andy Williams Show*, she stretched out on "Sweet Georgia Brown" and duetted with Williams on "Let's All Sing Like the Birdies Sing," a bland novelty with Disneyland origins. She covered "Midnight Sun" in full diva operatic trappings, singing the line "Your lips were like a red and ruby chalice" amid six sparkling pedestaled candelabras.

In Dinah Shore's ambitious TV specials, Fitzgerald was notably relaxed and enjoyed the harmonizing medleys with her old friend. *Variety*'s review called their celebrated 1960 duet "the high spot—perhaps the musical high spot of the season."[14] In other Shore segments, she seemed more ill at ease. On one she and Dinah vied with Joan Sutherland, the emerging coloratura soprano opera star, on "Lover, Come Back to Me." Sutherland stole the spot. In another program, Shore, Fitzgerald, and Gordon and Sheila MacRae bravely managed a medley of country and western tunes.

Fitzgerald's appearances on *The Ed Sullivan Show* rank high among her best television work. She could sing what she wanted, and Granz negotiated twenty-minute time slots for her, much more than guests were typically allotted.[15] Columnist Dave Hepburn of the *New York Amsterdam News* wrote in 1963 that Sullivan was still making a "valiant effort to use the best Negro talent he can find and it is one of his saying that he has received no hate messages from the South because of it. This is hard to believe."[16] In one outstanding moment on February 2, 1964, the show paired her with Sammy Davis, Jr., in their only known TV duet. Davis set it up in a chat with Sullivan: "You know, Ella Fitzgerald, I know her, she's like family, but I have never sung with her." After they performed the Gershwin brothers' "'S Wonderful" with scatting and genuine interactive spontaneity, Sullivan told the audience, "There are a lot of youngsters here, and when these youngsters grow up, the people at home can say that they saw the two of you together, heard the two of you together." Then, facing Fitzgerald and Davis, he sang the phrase, "You're wonderful, you're marvelous," and Ella teased back, "Oh, listen to him sing," in her lyrical speaking voice. As benign as this episode appears today, at the time it tested the limits of tolerance in mainstream entertainment for vocal jazz improvisation. Racist stereotypes about primitivism were always at hand. One Pittsburgh newspaper columnist wrote that the duet "raised goose-flesh. Spellbinding, that's what it was," but an editorialist in Mason City, Iowa, found it "revolting" as Fitzgerald and Davis would "wriggle, scream, and put out with strange noises. Are the days of melody and harmony never to return?"[17]

★★★

FITZGERALD'S FINAL TWO *SONG BOOK* projects for Verve were *Ella Fitzgerald Sings the Jerome Kern Song Book*, recorded in 1963 and released in

1964, and *Ella Fitzgerald Sings the Johnny Mercer Song Book*, recorded in 1964 but not released until 1965.[18] Due to flagging interest from Granz and perhaps resistance from Verve, both projects were restricted to one LP, with no bravura gatefold productions, no studio photos, and no extensive liner notes. For both projects Granz hired arranger Nelson Riddle, filling out the usual big band with strings for the Kern but cutting out strings for the Mercer.

In September 1965, on the *Bell Telephone Hour*, Fitzgerald sang Nelson Riddle arrangements in a tribute to Jerome Kern. She told Leonard Feather it was "a song book type of appearance; that was one side of Ella. The song book material is beautiful, but with these show tunes you have to stick to a certain type of material and a certain approach, and sometimes you can't do too much with these numbers before you get away from the essence of the tune."[19]

Careful planning helped *The Jerome Kern Song Book* represent Kern's broad achievement while avoiding the default "greatest hits" format. The twelve titles chosen balanced the "European" Kern, influenced by Victor Herbert's operettas, with the "American" Kern, who learned to swing while writing for Fred Astaire movie musicals.[20] Three tunes came from the pivotal film *Swing Time*, with lyrics by the witty Dorothy Fields, including "The Way You Look Tonight." Also included were "All the Things You Are" and "Yesterdays," two jazz standards whose soaring melodies and complex harmonies endeared them to singers of all manner of voices. Two lesser-known titles, "Remind Me" and "You Couldn't Be Cuter," echo choices made by Margaret Whiting in her weightier, outstanding precedent, *The Jerome Kern Song Book*, initiated by Granz and released on Verve in 1960. In *Down Beat*, John S. Wilson wrote of Fitzgerald's "affinity" for Kern in "her warm, fresh and glowingly lovely treatments," while in *Saturday Review*, Martin Williams praised Riddle's "miraculously relevant taste in scoring for strings."[21]

The Johnny Mercer Song Book celebrated a lyricist instead of a composer. Mercer's collaborators included the great songwriters of the era, and Riddle's lean, classical style left room for Paul Smith to improvise fills at the piano. Among the album's highlights are poetically intimate arrangements of "Midnight Sun" and "Early Autumn." Commenting decades later on her rendition of "Early Autumn," the accomplished arranger Johnny Mandel observed:

> She's listening to the background, and she's blown away. She just loves it, and she's really gotten into it. She's got this beautiful curtain of sound that Nelson set up. It's the kind of sound he got on [the Frank Sinatra LP] *In the Wee Small Hours*—it's very atmospheric. It's one of those times when everything's going right.[22]

Riddle later added strings to the Mercer arrangements, so that they could be performed along with other *Song Book* material in "pops" concerts with symphony orchestras, a format Fitzgerald would increasingly exploit in the 1970s.

In May 1965, before the Mercer LP was even released, ASCAP bestowed an award on Fitzgerald "in recognition of her outstanding interpretations of Great Songs in the ASCAP Repertory and for her unique series of Recorded Song Books."[23] As music historian Larry Stempel has written of the *Song Book* canon, "Perhaps nothing did more to fix the name and the idea in the popular mind than a series of LP recordings that began with the release of *Ella Fitzgerald Sings the Cole Porter Song Book* in 1956." These eight albums "collectively have come to represent the heart of the American Songbook."[24]

Yet in the mid-1960s, Fitzgerald had so much to say outside the *Song Book* repertoire. Granz knew that pairing her with a big band and returning her to her swing roots could elicit her best studio work. Count Basie, who had recently recorded albums with Frank Sinatra and Sarah Vaughan, was the perfect choice, and Quincy Jones the ideal arranger. Recorded in July 1963, *Ella and Basie!* included nostalgic tunes from her pre-Granz years as well as "Shiny Stockings," a signature Basie instrumental from the 1950s, to which she added her own lyrics.[25] Quincy Jones vividly recalled,

Ella Fitzgerald was a shy, almost withdrawn person, so she liked arrangements that allowed her to cut loose and be free. When I arranged "I'm Beginning to See the Light" for Ella with Basie's band, I put a tag repeat on the end of the song that allowed Ella to do her thang. Before we started the song, I said to Basie, "Let's take Fitz to church when we hit the vamp at the end," which got a laugh out of Basie because he knew how timid Ella was. Sure enough, when we hit the vamp Ella was testifying. She was dead in the pocket and was wailing so hard that she didn't want to give it up. She wailed on and on; she didn't want to give up a drop. Each chorus was better than the last, until she and the band were getting musically drunk on each other. She was groovin' and shakin' booty so hard that I couldn't stop the band. I just kept conducting them through the coda until she had had her say.[26]

★★★

HAVING HER SAY MEANT STAYING IN THE PRESENT, as popular music changed and evolved in a dizzying parade of styles in the mid-1960s. Fitzgerald's early interest in the Beatles, beginning with their first American tour in January 1964, foreshadowed a deepening involvement with rock—a development few of her fans and jazz critics would have anticipated. Most jazz critics, along with most of the cultural establishment, generally condescended to the Beatles and their teenage-girl fans, but when Ella arrived in England on March 20 for a three-week tour with Oscar Peterson, she headed straight for Abbey Road. By then the Beatles accounted for 60 percent of all record sales in the United States. She endorsed them as solid musicians worthy of her attention. When a British journalist asked Fitzgerald about the Beatles hit "Can't Buy Me Love," she said, "I like it. And I'd like to record it. Seems to me to be such a good tune and it's almost a blues sequence."[27] On April 7 she was at the Abbey Road Studios with Norman Granz, arranger-conductor Johnny Spence, and the savvy Beatles producer George Martin to turn

"Can't Buy Me Love" into a shiny, big band swing tune.[28] In May the Beatles returned the compliment in a press story bannered "Beatles Say Ella's Song's a Knockout!" The following month they added, "We're flattered."[29] Back in February, John Lennon had told DJ Fred Robbins, "She's great. It took me years, I couldn't understand what people liked about her. And then I heard this record [unidentified] and I thought it was great. I asked somebody who it was. . . . I didn't believe him. I thought it was [an R&B singer. Before that] I hated her!" Just like, he said, he had hated Frank Sinatra. Robbins quickly moved on.[30]

Ella understood the power of the Beatles partly from listening to her son, Ray Brown, Jr. Now fifteen years old, he was playing drums on weekends in a rock combo called the Skins, a bit of gossip relayed by Walter Winchell.[31] "I loved the Beatles," Ray recalled. Fitzgerald composed and recorded her own song, "Ringo Beat," as a tribute not exactly to the skills of drummer Ringo Starr but to the rock beat he represented.[32] "She wanted to do it," Granz said, distancing himself. The backbeat-heavy arrangement by her former JATP mate Barney Kessel used a studio combo and a girl vocal group; she insisted that Verve release it as a single for the jukebox market. She made it a vehicle for tolerance. Her lyrics push one generation into another, as if Ringo Starr belonged in the same lineup as Gene Krupa, the "drummer boy": "So don't knock the rhythm of the kids today / Remember they're playing the Ringo Way." If that is what Ray Brown, Jr., needed right then, then a mothering singer delivered. On November 29 she gave the song prime-time exposure on *The Ed Sullivan Show*, along with "Day In, Day Out" from *The Johnny Mercer Song Book* and the novelty war-horse "Old MacDonald." *Billboard* gave the single perfunctory respect in a section aimed at "Middle Road" DJs, but it sank into oblivion.[33]

Fitzgerald made a more musically ambitious foray into the Beatles' world when she introduced "A Hard Day's Night" into her repertoire.[34] The global hit had a blues-like sequence that made it another "natural for her," according to Beatles expert Walter Everett, who added that the Beatles "liked it, considering it one of the best reinterpretations of their material."[35] A filmed concert from Copenhagen in 1965 shows her bending the song to her will. "Thank you, Beatles fans," she told the audience. "We thought we would put it in because it's one of the top tunes. And it *is*, I wish *I* had part of it." That same year she said of the present pop scene, "I won't put it all down. I don't care what people say about the Beatles, they've proven they do know some kind of music, and I'd love to make an album of their songs."[36] This hope was never realized, but she went on to record "Something," "Got to Get You into My Life," and "Hey Jude." By then a number of jazz stars, including Carmen McRae, Duke Ellington, and Count Basie, had capitulated to the market upheaval and recorded their own versions of Beatles songs.

Back in January 1964, as the Beatles were "invading" the United States, Louis Armstrong's cover of the Broadway show tune "Hello, Dolly!" was quietly released. In April Fitzgerald followed Armstrong's lead, recording her own version. In May Armstrong's single reached the top spot on *Billboard*'s pop chart, and in June the original cast album for *Hello, Dolly!* reached number one on the album chart, temporarily usurping the Beatles' reign. Fitzgerald's version became the title track for her LP *Hello, Dolly!*, released in August.[37] The liner notes by Leonard Feather stated the truth in a dubious compliment: "There are singers who wouldn't touch a tune associated with the current hit lists. Not Ella." The LP also registered the impact of a newcomer, Barbra Streisand, who posed a double challenge as both a Broadway star and a popular singer. Streisand's signature ballad "People," from the musical *Funny Girl* by Jule Styne and Bob Merrill, would stay in Fitzgerald's playbook for decades. Later that year Streisand edged Fitzgerald into second place for female vocalist in *Playboy* magazine's reader poll after a nine-year run. Fitzgerald also used the *Hello, Dolly!* LP to revisit "How High the Moon" at a slow tempo and to record her lyrical interpretation of "Memories of You," a Black Broadway show tune by Eubie Blake and Andy Razaf. The LP reached only number 146 on *Billboard*'s LP chart and did not earn more than perfunctory notices.

Ella at Juan-les-Pins, recorded live at the fifth annual Festival Mondial du Jazz Antibes on the French Riviera in July 1964, focused on classic repertory along with the newer material she performed.[38] In addition to her trio, Roy Eldridge, with his muted trumpet obbligatos, added a sensuous sheen to the evening glow, especially on the request number "St. Louis Blues," taken at a slow, erotic tempo. A patter of easy, humorous ad-libs sustained the flow of her sets, and she improvised the lyrics about the crickets chirping away in the background while the band punched in "I Got Rhythm" changes. "Ella Swings Out with Crickets," read the UPI dispatch. Could anyone want better press than that?[39] A high point of Fitzgerald's live recordings from the 1960s, the LP betrayed Granz's desultory approach to recording, as he confessed in his liner notes that he had had "no intention to record the concert" and that for the album he had to rely on a tape from French television. The package earned strong reviews,[40] yet on its February 1965 release, the LP failed to make the charts.

In 1965 Granz was cutting down on his management duties even more, handing over U.S. bookings to his brother Irving. Norman did accompany her on dates in January and February, marked by her now-annual return to the Americana's Royal Box. She reached mainly African American audiences at the Syria Mosque in Pittsburgh, and Nelson Riddle's orchestra backed her at the Hyatt Burlingame Theatre in California. Still, her domestic appearances were starting to seem like preludes to the main action abroad, an impression reinforced by newspaper reports. In April, when she touched down in Warsaw, cheers of "Long Live Ella! Long Live Jazz" filled her plane-side reception; she sold out two nights at the Palace of Culture.[41] *Down Beat* took the occasion to note that in Poland, "jazz was included in public schools' music appreciation classes, something seldom done in this country."[42] In Munich, a photo showed her beaming among a crowd of high school boys and holding their bouquet of flowers. "Paris was wonderful," she said. "Dublin this year was just unbelievable. I just stood there onstage and cried; the audience was just too much. We played Hamburg, and they wouldn't let me off; of course, they are very, very music-conscious there."[43] Granz taped the March 26 Hamburg concert and released it as *Ella in Hamburg*.[44] In attendance was local resident Werner Burkhardt, who wrote in the liner notes for the German release: "What has formed between Ella and the people of Hamburg is almost a familial confidence, because of which unnecessary glamour can be done away with."[45] Sporting a blond wig— half Jackie Kennedy and half Marilyn Monroe, and rendered on the album cover in a pop-art style evoking Andy Warhol's prints of both— Fitzgerald was playing with her own image in freer ways.

"A Hard Day's Night" was a regular feature of the tour, and she sang the line "I've been working like a dog" with a knowing smile, glancing back at her fellow musicians. The villain was overwork, as she performed as many as eighteen consecutive days with two shows a night in one city after another.[46] This daunting schedule finally caught up with her in April, when she collapsed onstage in Munich, and Granz had to cancel a reported $20,000 in European bookings.[47] Fitzgerald explained, "We were running from one town to another, and I began to feel I just couldn't take it. One night I thought I was about ready to faint onstage. Gus Johnson had to lead me off, and I was almost literally trying to climb the backstage walls."[48] Shortly after the incident, in an interview, she made a rare public rebuke of Granz, delivered via the euphemism "some people," exposing a fault line in their relationship:

> I don't like this anymore. A concert artist would never agree to do as we do. . . . You're afraid if you say "No," people will say you don't appreciate what they've done for you. Some people get very angry when you're ill. But, working every day on a voice, you can't expect it to be perfect. It's a God-given talent—you shouldn't abuse it. I don't think I want to anymore.[49]

Rarely did she advocate for herself so forcefully and publicly on an issue that hounded so many jazz careers. Why did she follow such a hectic schedule? Was it because her high fees required two shows a night for a presenter to make money? Or did it come from her own need for an audience? True enough, like Duke Ellington and Louis Armstrong, she had a prodigious appetite for work. When someone accused Granz of "doing nothing but killing Ella Fitzgerald," the drummer Jo Jones, who toured with Ella in 1963 and 1964, replied, "She *will not*, as of today, sit down. She just got to be out here. Let's go! She's Ringling Brothers, she's carrying a load, you know."[50] This time she sat down on the advice of her doctor, and Granz issued a new policy statement limiting her travel and nightclub appearances in the States. But the problem remained a constant source of friction between Granz, her traveling musicians, and her divided selves.

With rest, Fitzgerald recovered in time to resume a quieter summer schedule, which included appearances at the Carter Barron outdoor theater near Washington, D.C., and at Ravinia again with Nelson Riddle. The highlight of the season was an outdoor concert on July 10 at the Greek-columned Lewisohn Stadium of the City College of New York, with Riddle conducting the Metropolitan Opera Orchestra. Demolished in 1973, the eight-thousand-seat amphitheater had long promoted classical music to the masses. "Ella Fitzgerald Does Met Proud," ran the *New York Times* review:

> She didn't sing "Aida," but there were plenty of triumphal choruses from America's Golden Age of Jazz. George Gershwin and Cole Porter were heard most often . . . in a stunning display of her own virtuosity, spontaneity, and supreme mastery of the jazz idiom. . . . Such a combination of musicality, technique, and humanity is rare on any stage. The Met had a good night.[51]

★★★

WEAKER SALES OF FITZGERALD'S ALBUMS were taking a toll on her confidence, as revealed in a candid and expansive *Down Beat* interview with Leonard Feather in November 1965—one of the most important of her career. She said of her European tour, "I needed that boost overseas, because I felt like nothing was happening here. And it was great, until the overwork caught up with me."[52] "Nothing" meant unfilled halls and indifferent audiences.

With the trend like it is now, the teenage sounds and everything, it's almost like you're afraid. There's nothing worse in life for a performer than to go out there and do nothing with an audience. I'm very self-conscious about people not liking me. I had gotten in a rut for three or four months at home, and I just began to feel like, well, I don't have it, you know, when you don't have a big hit record going for you. It took Gus [Johnson] and a lot of people to convince me that those things aren't everything.[53]

Yet she mentioned various album projects with enthusiasm. For his part, Granz, increasingly alienated from the scene in the United States, publicly predicted the demise of mainstream jazz. He had made a strategic decision for her to return to familiar collaborations, suggesting new projects with Duke Ellington.

The Ellington sessions, which were due to begin a week later, seemed hopeful at just the right time. Feather left the interview convinced that Fitzgerald had recovered her spirit. "She smiled broadly when I left," he said. "See that wasn't so bad, was it?"

Chapter 23

A JAZZ OASIS IN A CHANGING SCENE

(1966-1967)

I n 1966 MGM-Verve did not renew Fitzgerald's contract—an event that would have been inconceivable at the beginning of the decade. "For the first time in 30 years Ella Fitzgerald is a freelance chirp," *Variety* announced in July. She had successfully navigated the shoals of the first "British invasion" and Beatlemania, but the advent of serious adult-rock pushed the old standards onto dry land.[1] Jazz reached audiences mainly through new instrumental hybrids. Thus, her work no longer fit Verve's business model, especially at her accustomed fees of as much as $25,000 per album. The label enjoyed a banner year in 1966, with instrumentalists like Stan Getz, Jimmy Smith, and Wes Montgomery successfully adapting to jazz-pop settings, but by mid-1966 her *Jerome Kern Song Book*, released in 1964, was already deleted from its back catalogue.[2] So much for the hallowed *Song Book* series.

Fitzgerald approached her last studio album for Verve, *Whisper Not*, recorded July 1966, with some ambivalence about the viability of her jazz-pop aesthetic.[3] Sounding a rare note of cynicism, she told Leonard Feather (who had written the lyrics for the title track, a 1950s jazz standard by Benny Golson), "This album gets a little back to the jazz thing. It probably won't sell very well, there're too many tunes in it that I like."[4] But it had its own special qualities, finding her welcoming the fresh pianism of Jimmy Rowles in the studio for the first time, yielding an album highlight on "Spring Can Really Hang You Up the Most." Venturing from established *Song Book* composers, the eclectic mix of twelve tunes included "Wives and Lovers," a clever tune in waltz time, and the first of several songs she would adopt by Burt Bacharach and Hal David. By making that choice, she was advocating for their inclusion into the domain of standards, appreciating this innovative songwriting team "bringing an American Songbook sensibility and sophistication to Teen Pan Alley," in the words of jazz journalist Marc Myers.[5] The now-dated advice prodded married women not to forget their duties, asserting that "wives should always be lovers too," reflecting both the slick masculinity promoted for men in *Playboy* and the sexualized feminism for women in *Cosmopolitan* magazine, recently revamped by its new editor, Helen Gurley Brown. Fitzgerald took the chart on the road for a plum European tour with Duke Ellington, arranged by Granz at just the right moment.

★★★

IN RETROSPECT, Fitzgerald's renewed collaboration with Duke Ellington from 1965 to 1967 solidified her still underacknowledged historical position as the most important twentieth-century champion of his vocal legacy. "She just did his stuff like nobody else," remarked her son, Ray Brown, Jr.[6] The authority of pairing the composer with a singer he admired so profoundly yielded a deeply satisfying artistic body of work that in its refinement surpassed *The Duke Ellington Song Book* itself. Over the next few years, she would record memorable, sometimes dazzling versions of his songs. Granz deserves credit for once again facilitating the collaboration, especially because he believed "Ella was an artist of the same stature as Duke, so he was delighted to work with someone that was his equal."[7] "When you talk about Ella and Duke, you've got to thank Norman because he put them together," said the jazz historian Dan Morgenstern.[8] The synergy between Ella and Duke was plain to see in their first joint appearance on *The Ed Sullivan Show* on March 7,

1965. Facing Ellington with a hand resting on the piano, Fitzgerald sang "Do Nothing Till You Hear from Me" in such an intimate fashion that they seemed alone together rather than being watched by 25 million Americans.

A few months later, from October 17 to 20, in the midst of one of Ellington's creative surges, they recorded the LP *Ella at Duke's Place* in a Hollywood studio, previewed in *Down Beat* as "the meeting of giants."[9] Ellington's trombonist Buster Cooper later recalled:

> Ella idolized Duke and [Billy] Strayhorn as human beings and for their creativity. She would just listen to everything they'd say. We ran down the charts once and she caught them. She has the greatest ear in the world. . . . Duke did most of the piano playing. It was a collaboration; he would always be checking, "Oh, now—how do you feel? Is it comfortable for you?" He would always go in the direction of his artists, and he respected her ability so much.[10]

With most of Ellington's jazz standards already recorded for *The Duke Ellington Song Book*, the new project focused on more esoteric songs in novel presentations. On the original LP labels for *Ella at Duke's Place*, the first side was headlined—by Ellington, no doubt—"The pretty, the lovely, the tender, the hold-me-close side," while the second side was "The finger-snapping, head-shaking, toe-tapping, go-for-yourself side." Opening with three modernist ballads by Billy Strayhorn—"Something to Live For," "A Flower Is a Lovesome Thing," and "Passion Flower"— the first side could also have been aptly described as "the wistful, the erotic, the mysterious." With Strayhorn suffering from esophageal cancer, Ellington drafted Jimmy Jones for arrangements. An experienced pianist who had previously worked with Sarah Vaughan and Joe Williams, Jones soon joined Fitzgerald's trio through 1967. "Norman Granz stole me away from Ellington," Jones said. "We all wound up being booked together."[11]

Switching personalities on side B, Fitzgerald went overboard in a dazzling display of scat virtuosity on "Cotton Tail," in dialogue with tenor saxophonist Paul Gonsalves. The album was released in February 1966 to an enthusiastic reception, including a four-and-a-half-star review in *Down Beat*. "A musical masterpiece," wrote Hazel Garland, devoting her entire column to it.[12] Despite being nominated for a Grammy in 1966 for "Best Vocal Performance, Female," *Ella at Duke's Place* remains one of her lesser-known albums.

On October 31, without much fanfare, Duke and Ella made their first joint public appearance since 1959 at Stanford University, filling about 40 percent of the ten-thousand-seat Frost Amphitheater in Palo Alto. As jazz made further headway into American higher education, overcoming years of indifference and prejudice, the concert was part of a series, Stanford Jazz Year, that left a big cultural footprint and in later years would be cited as a benchmark.[13] In contrast to typical university bookings of performers for dances and homecoming games, a politically and musically progressive group of college students initiated this series to bring jazz to a conservative community. Student organizer Rick Bale later recalled that some administrators "worried that jazz would attract the 'wrong element' to campus," while "others felt the subject wasn't serious enough for an elite campus." But Duke and Ella "were so happy to be together," said Bale.[14] Hired as a series consultant, the jazz critic Ralph J. Gleason wrote a rapturous review for the *San Francisco Chronicle*: "I have never heard her sing as well as she did Sunday afternoon. . . . 'Don't go!' she cried out to a couple who had to leave during her solo set. 'I'm gonna sing with Duke! You'll miss it!' "[15]

In early November another bout of illness, unspecified but likely related to fatigue, sidelined Fitzgerald for two weeks at Cedars Sinai Hospital in Los Angeles. Then it was back to business as usual.[16] She appeared at UC Berkeley's homecoming football game along with pianist Ramsey Lewis, who was riding high with his hit "The 'In' Crowd." Senior Jim Blackman was an eyewitness from the stands: "How wonderful it was in the midst of the early Beatles phenomenon and the burgeoning popularity of rock 'n' roll that the University of California chose Ella for their big game concert. The Harmon gymnasium was packed, and Ella looked great wearing a blond wig, à la Dinah Washington. She held the crowd in thrall for the duration of her set."[17] Fitzgerald rejoined Ellington on November 21 at the Academy of Music in Philadelphia, then brought her trio to the Hotel Fairmont's Venetian Room at the end of December for her annual three-week gig with Ernie Heckscher's orchestra.

★★★

OVER THE COURSE OF HER EUROPEAN TOURS with Duke Ellington, Ella Fitzgerald experienced the kind of success that deepened her own sense of purpose about her cultural "work," so to speak. She was forging a persona with ethical charisma. Her 1963 comment asking "why can't they be sharing," which pertained to the American race divide, expanded to the generational divide in 1964 with her early championship of the Beatles as "good composers." By the end of 1966, the obsessive European touring that Granz prescribed gave her experiences that justified her belief in music as a "universal language." "It brings people closer together," as she was quoted in 1967.[18] That was one theme that emerged from the reception she and Ellington enjoyed on their European tours.

The first tour Granz arranged for Fitzgerald and Ellington lasted from January 28 to February 28, 1966, opening in Frankfurt, West Germany. The tour exceeded Granz's expectations, and at its end he took out a full-page ad in *Variety* stating, "This has been the most successful jazz tour I have presented in Europe since 1950."[19] Their Paris concerts on January 28 at the Salle Pleyel were so successful that Granz added two more on February 11. *Melody Maker*'s review was titled "Infallible Ella Walks Off with Duke's Concert," while *Le Monde* critic Lucien Malson, an Ellington devotee, described Ella as singing "in a state of grace."[20] Still, her pairing with Ellington elicited the old grievance about the inferiority of singers versus instrumentalists. Before their U.K. performances, critic Vic Bellerby argued that even a vocalist of Fitzgerald's stature would dilute Ellington's authority.[21] In response, a critic for *The Stage* wrote, "Once again, Duke Ellington and Ella Fitzgerald have confounded those critics who put performers into pigeonholes.

Jazz and pop together in one concert? But at the Royal Festival Hall their two styles merged into a supremely integrated show."[22] Fitzgerald's tour repertoire included Strayhorn ballads, the Billie Holiday warhorse "Lover Man," Ellington's "I'm Just a Lucky So-and-So" and "C-Jam Blues" (repackaged as "Duke's Place"), and a selection or two from the *Song Books*, often Cole Porter's "Let's Do It." Newer material included the bossa nova she loved—"Só Danço Samba," a hit from the landmark 1964 bossa nova LP *Getz/Gilberto* by Stan Getz and João Gilberto.

At home, Fitzgerald now frequently offered mission statements, burnishing her reputation as a globe-trotting ambassador for American cultural democracy. For her March 14 to April 2 engagement at the Royal Box in the Hotel Americana, gossip columns noted the UN diplomats coming to her show, and she was honored at a UN reception hosted by some of the countries she visited on the tour. According to newspaper reports, "Miss Fitzgerald said her purpose was 'to promote world brotherhood through song and do something that might help this tired, old world.'"[23]

Ella and Duke renewed their collaboration in a high-profile concert at the Newport Jazz Festival on July 3, closing out the Sunday night lineup. Treated as the "grand lady" and "the big star," as one reviewer wrote, she was also watching newcomers claim the spotlight, particularly Nina Simone.[24] In his *Down Beat* review, Dan Morgenstern noted Fitzgerald's "kaleidoscopic 'How High the Moon,'" which had everything, from opera to the Beatles, thrown in," and the encore of "Imagine My Frustration," with a Hodges solo and Ella dancing a "modified frug," a variant on the twist. Morgenstern concluded that Ellington and Fitzgerald "made Sunday night at Newport everything a jazz festival concert should be: a joyous and inspiring occasion."[25]

In late July Granz virtually co-opted the seventh annual Antibes Jazz Festival in Juan-les-Pins for four nights of "Duke and Ella" projects. Mike Hennessey wrote in *Down Beat*, "Four concerts by the best band in the world, three by the best singer in the world—perhaps it is a little churlish to ask more of a festival."[26] Veteran jazz promoter Jacques Muyal noted that for the European tour earlier that year, "The music and concerts were so great that Norman and Frank Ténot [a French jazz critic] convinced Jacques Souplet, the festival director, to yield the time so that they could make a movie on the subject."[27] That fall *Variety* reported Granz's intentions to release three LPs and a film that was then being edited in Cologne; "If the ninety-minute feature plans don't jell, he will also have a one-hour version for a tv spec."[28] In 1967 Granz settled for a double-LP release and a documentary on National Educational Television (NET), shortening the title simply to the name for the French Riviera, *Ella and Duke at the Côte d'Azur*. A mammoth eight-CD package with seventy-eight unissued tracks was released in 1997.[29]

Granz, who so idealized collective reinvention as the essence of jazz, opened the double LP with Fitzgerald's rousing performance of "Mack the Knife." As he explained in his liner notes, "Instead of an umpteenth rendition of it, it becomes a classic, definitive version by the band's and Ella's amalgam of swing. There was no arrangement, head or written: the band simply fell in and started to riff behind her."[30] But the treasure of the set was the spectacular "Só Danço Samba," retitled "Jazz Samba," which Ella had expanded into a six-minute tour de force. It ended with her clever scat improvisation imitating Latin percussion instruments. Backed by claves and maracas, she spoke in tongues to her audience, whispering her secrets, backed by rim shots on drums—a virtual jazz counterpart to experimental vocal techniques that would develop among the classical avant-garde in the later 1960s and '70s.

Fitzgerald's contribution to the Côte d'Azur projects was affected by the unexpected death of her forty-one-year-old sister, Frances Correy Gilmore, from cancer.[31] When the two had last seen each other is hard to say, although Ella had been a witness at her sister's wedding in 1954.[32] According to Dorothy Johnson, Frances was a quiet woman who had not moved from New York to Los Angeles with the rest of the family. A reporter on the scene reported that when Fitzgerald received the news, she "was ready to go on with the concert scheduled for the third night, but impresario Norman Granz arranged for her to fly home at once and the organizers agreed to extend the Festival by one day so that Miss Fitzgerald could make her two appearances. After attending the funeral, she returned on the fifth day and made an appearance which was as magnificent as it was unexpected."[33]

Months later she told a Danish reporter, "After my sister died, it was hard to perform with Duke Ellington's orchestra when I returned to the tour in Europe. But I said to myself, 'You must go out and sing for her. That is the way you can express your feelings.'"[34] Fitzgerald called her Côte d'Azur performances "the best therapy in the world."[35]

Yet on the scene, her fragile emotional state led to a temporary rift between Ellington and Granz. Fitzgerald left the stage after the first half. In the second half, Granz pleaded from the wings to bring her back, but Ellington ignored him, knowing, as an observer, Renée Diamond, said, that she "wasn't in any condition to perform."[36] Ella's bassist Jim Hughart later described Granz as "arrogant and abrasive" and said, "She was afraid to confront Norman. I can't imagine that Norman was unaware of that fact." Hughart also recalled overhearing Duke talking to Ella about Norman: "It [will] be all right, sweetie, completely ignore him."[37]

Fitzgerald and Ellington had one more joint booking in 1966 at the Greek Theatre, an outdoor arena in Hollywood, from September 14 to 23. In a *Los Angeles Times* interview beforehand, gossip columnist Joyce Haber affirmed the Svengali myth, referring to Fitzgerald's "child-parent relationship with manager Granz." She also quoted Ella on the upcoming concerts:

> I never played there. I've been there only once, two years ago, to see Jerry Lewis. You always hear of people like [Harry] Belafonte singing there, so this will be quite a thrill to me. . . . I'll sing "A Hard Day's Night." That's not my kind of song but it did all right for me and there will be kids in the audience. . . . We also have a new arrangement of "These Boots Are Made for Walkin'." We're going to do it a little different than What's-her-Name does it.

"What's-her-Name" was Frank Sinatra's daughter Nancy Sinatra. Haber segued to the man himself, chastising Frank for calling Ella "technically terrible" in *Life*: "When it's Ella Fitzgerald you can be certain it will be different. And furthermore, I think What's-her Name's father, What's-his-Name, owes Ella not only an apology but a retraction."[38] Portions of the Greek Theatre engagement were televised locally, and Granz recorded the last evening on September 23, 1966, which went unreleased until 1994.[39]

Granz organized one more "Ella and Duke" tour in Europe, launching in Milan on January 15, 1967, and making a solid British finish in March. In London, Princess Margaret, a jazz fan, came backstage, and the publicity photo showed Fitzgerald beaming with pleasure. "The princess is someone who puts you right at ease," Fitzgerald said. "Her favorite was 'You've Changed,' which has beautiful lyrics." "You've Changed" was her latest tribute to Billie Holiday, replacing "Lover Man" in her setlists. To a newspaper reporter, Fitzgerald described the tour as "beautiful" and singled out her reception in Germany: "In Dusseldorf, the audience refused to go home. Finally, I went backstage, changed my clothes, and when I came out, they were still there. Of course, I sang another song for them."[40] Jimmy Jones remembered,

> With Ella, doing the one-nighters the way we did it, I would say, "Boy"—talking to myself now—"Say Jones, I hope you can make it tonight." And it would be one of the best performances, and I don't even know where the energy came from. And the chemistry worked. We had one experience in Hamburg, Germany, where we're just getting standing ovations, one after another. We went back and changed our clothes to go to the airport, and they wouldn't let us leave. They just came around and stood around the stage, you know? We were so tired, but the people loved it, and you had to give it to them, you know.[41]

In the hoopla and celebrity aura surrounding the tour, a souvenir menu titled *La Soirée Extraordinaire 1967 d'Ella Fitzgerald*, from an elegant hotel in Gstaad, Switzerland, listed among its fare "Le Caviar 'Sophisticated Lady,' " "L'Essence de Canard Sauvage 'Old MacDonald' Piroski," and the dessert "Les Fraises Fraîches Fauchon 'Air Mail Special.' "

In the middle of the tour, on January 25, Fitzgerald gave a sold-out midnight concert at the Friedrichstadt-Palast in East Berlin, before a public that was ruled by the fiercest dictatorship in the Soviet bloc. During the Cold War, any appearance by a Western artist in East Germany carried political significance: almost two years earlier, Louis Armstrong had played a highly celebrated date at the same venue. Before three thousand people, Fitzgerald mixed standards by Ellington, Porter, Gershwin, and Mercer with a few "new sounds," as she called them, including "These Boots Are Made for Walkin'," adding a characteristic comment about wishing she could match its sales. The comment likely mystified the audience, who in Fitzgerald's own recounting "knew most of the records like with Louis Armstrong and of course 'Mack the Knife,' so I mean the Ella they loved [was from] the *old* records, not from the real pop tunes."[42]

East German critics were enthusiastic, writing of her mastery of "all possible means of modern jazz vocalism" and comparing her "vigorous, unsentimental style" to the blues singers of the 1920s: "Whatever Ella Fitzgerald sings, whether she improvises freely or sings a melody accentuated by text, every interpretation carries the unmistakable characteristics of her personality."[43] Through a UPI wire story, the American public read that the Allgemeiner Deutscher Nachrichtendienst, the official East German news agency, called her performance "phenomenal" and observed that the "ovations did not stop."[44] Did the applause carry a political message? Rock music had already been censored, and after Fitzgerald's performance, jazz too lost favor with the East German government under Walter Ulbricht, which decreed that all popular music on radio and television must be sung in German.[45] Ruth Hohmann, a rare East German jazz vocalist who was dubbed "the Ella Fitzgerald of the East," weathered the crackdown and would still be performing long after the fall of the Berlin Wall.[46]

★★★

THE YEAR 1967 FOUND FITZGERALD back in the United States amid cultural turmoil and divides between Black and white popular music; jazz was struggling to survive as an alternative to both. As a Black artist, Ella searched for new ways to satisfy the musical taste of an ever-fragmenting generation. Meanwhile in a burst of sentimental enthusiasm for his native land, Granz mounted a tour that began with Duke Ellington and ended with James Brown.

After his success with Fitzgerald and Ellington in Europe, Granz decided they would anchor a revival of Jazz at the Philharmonic in the United States after a ten-year absence. "I know it may sound corny," the patriotic expatriate said, "but this is my main reason for this one last American tour—and I think this will be the last. I simply want to give the kids a chance to hear some real jazz."[47] Not to his taste the avant-garde led by John Coltrane and the postbop experiments of Miles Davis, whose tours he promoted in Europe. The itinerary from March 25 to April 29 stretched from Boston to Denver, and a second round of West Coast dates began on June 24. Granz went all out with an extravagant three-part format, starting with an hour of the Oscar Peterson Trio plus Coleman Hawkins, Benny Carter, Clark Terry, and Zoot Sims, followed by an hour of Ellington's orchestra, then a complete set of Fitzgerald with her trio.

The tour's critical reception made earlier controversies over Fitzgerald's status as a jazz singer seem moot, as jazz itself had become more commercially marginal. With jazz now thinking only of its survival, the critics no longer had the luxury of expelling someone like Ella. Nor did they maintain genre distinctions so rigidly, even as she confounded them. Still, she could be attacked for singing too much or too little jazz, or for too much or too little pop, proving that the mark of a successful compromise is dissatisfaction from both sides. In his review of the kickoff concerts of the tour at Carnegie Hall, The New Yorker's Whitney Balliett praised her as "an excellent and funny scat-parodist" who, when trading breaks with drummer Sam Woodyard, "had sticks and snares and cymbals in her voice," despite the seemingly necessary avowal of her secondary status to

Billie Holiday.[48] In the *New York Times,* John S. Wilson wished for "less scatting and ad-libbing."[49]

What a time for Granz to try to turn back the clock! The old Tin Pan Alley standards and show tunes were being overwhelmed by a tidal wave of talent and innovation, from the Beatles and their innovative studio art to James Brown and Aretha Franklin in soul, Bob Dylan and Simon and Garfunkel in folk-rock, and Burt Bacharach, Hal David, and their muse Dionne Warwick in adult contemporary genres. By the end of the tour, Fitzgerald registered Black nationalism and Black Power. In her audience patter, she adopted catchphrases from Black nationalism and soul to reach out to Black youth. She shouted "Let's tell it like it is," while the lyrics "If it ain't got that swing" turned into "If it ain't got that soul." Addressing a crowd in Oakland, she said,

> We'd like to and it's all in fun, ladies and gentlemen, we'd like to give you our interpretations of the new sounds, and we hope you enjoy them as much as we enjoy trying to sing them. The new rock and soul. You'd better believe, you'd better wha wha wha—it makes no difference [under her breath] to James Brown. You'd better keep the faith baby, keep the faith, baby, and everything will be all right. It don't mean a thing if you ain't got that soul, daddy. I couldn't beat 'em, that's why I join 'em. . . . We're so glad you enjoyed that. We'd like you to know we enjoy soul, too.[50]

Oakland, with its large Black population, was home to the Black Panther Party and a mecca of radical Black nationalism;[51] the city designated June 30, 1967, "Duke Ellington Day" in honor of this concert.

Then Granz was finished with nostalgic interventions. After a grand date at the Hollywood Bowl on July 1, JATP exited the American scene. The tour had ended up with a small profit, but Granz said he would not repeat the experiment. In 1975 his thwarted pride and frustration with sparse audiences surfaced in the title he gave to a four-LP album drawn from the final concerts of the tour: *The Greatest Jazz Concert in the World.*[52] In the fall of 1967, Fitzgerald and Ellington went their separate ways. That year the Ella of the *Song Books* was acknowledged when on October 15, she received ASCAP's Pied Piper Award, recognizing her support for "the good music of today and the great songs of our musical past." The ceremony that evening included performances by artists spanning the century from Eubie Blake and Noble Sissle to Burt Bacharach.[53] With Rodgers at the piano, "Ella thrilled everyone by singing some of his songs," reported Hazel Garland.[54]

Fitzgerald soon extended her efforts to reach new audiences. The foray into James Brown foreshadowed Fitzgerald's immersion in soul, the new style of Black popular music sweeping the country in the late 1960s. "Ella is singing material unworthy of her," wrote John L. Wasserman of the *San Francisco Chronicle* in a review of her three-week booking at the Fairmont Hotel around Labor Day. To her already diverse repertoire, she added "I Can't Stop Loving You," a hit for Ray Charles, "wailing" as she "threatened to turn the sedate Venetian Room into a revival meeting."[55] A newspaper columnist reported, "Despite SRO crowds every night in the Venetian Room, and unanimous rave reviews, the first lady of song, Ella Fitzgerald, remains sensitive to the tiniest criticism. 'There's always somebody you're not getting through to,' says the worrisome Ella."[56] Whose fault could that be but hers?

Interpreting current material risked her reputation as the archetypical jazz singer, as she was usually still cast on network television. Having won a Grammy Award for Lifetime Achievement in March 1967, she appeared on May 24 in *The Best on Record*, an hour-long prime-time Grammy special on NBC, singing "Satin Doll" and "Don't Be That Way," backed by Les Brown's band. *Variety* reported that the "nearly immortal" Fitzgerald was "the only artist spotlighted on more than one number" in "one of the best-produced, fastest-paced specials to come to the home screens in months."[57] On the promotional LP *1966 Grammy Award Winners*, issued by the National Academy of Recording Arts and Sciences to radio and TV stations, Ella's performances appeared alongside those of Louis Armstrong, the Beatles, Ray Charles, Eydie Gormé, and the jazz guitarist Wes Montgomery.

Television remained the ultimate conduit to mass acceptance. On

November 13 twenty-five million people watched her sing with Frank Sinatra on his TV special *A Man and His Music + Ella + Jobim*.[58] A previous Sinatra special from 1965, marking his fiftieth birthday, had been treated as a public milestone in American culture, and in 1966 his massive hit "Strangers in the Night" had reaffirmed his star power. *A Man and His Music + Ella + Jobim* allowed his gifts as the swinging singer with jazz taste to shine, and it reunited both Frank and Ella with Nelson Riddle, the program's musical director and arranger. Their medleys stole the show. The first one allowed them to play with contemporary songs, ending with harmonizing on the 1964 Little Anthony and the Imperials hit "Goin' Out of My Head" in a glitzy and climactic arrangement. The second medley was the tour de force, honoring jazz and the big band era. On "Stompin' at the Savoy," she was permitted a chorus of scat autonomy while Sinatra sat near her feet on the edge of the stage in homage. Exchanging lines on "The Lady Is a Tramp," an "infectious contagion of rhythmic rapport encompassed the stars and their audience alike in an electrifying experience in the field of popular music," as the *New York Times* TV critic Jack Gould wrote. "Viewers could sense how one professional thrives on the challenge of another professional."[59]

Quietly, around this time, Frank and Ella were working on a joint album, but no LP materialized. Neither artist left any account, but according to Nelson Riddle's biographer Peter Levinson, Sinatra, Fitzgerald, and Riddle rehearsed for three days after taping the television show. Then the project was "abruptly canceled" after an argument between Sinatra and Granz.[60] Granz—apparently mistaking the date—told Elliot Meadow two decades later, "I never was able to record Ella with Sinatra either. In the late '50s they were both at their peaks, but a meeting was contractually impossible. Later on in the early '60s they started an album together but never finished it."[61] Fitzgerald appreciated Sinatra but sometimes seemed bemused by the hero worship surrounding him. In 1969 Billy Taylor complimented *A Man and His Music + Ella + Jobim*, which was still being telecast in reruns, and she replied, "Oh I had a ball with that, too. . . . Yeah, I had a ball with the master [laughter]."[62]

While the show was being taped, her envy and ambition surfaced in the *Los Angeles Sentinel*, a Black newsweekly. "I'd like to have my own television show someday," she said. "'Just Plain Ella' would be the format." So much for Sinatra, as the rest of the interview paid tribute to Duke Ellington:

> The Duke and I have a musical rapport that just won't quit. Duke keeps on growing; his music today is still 20 years ahead. . . . I don't want to be considered—like the song says—"As Cold as Yesterday's Mashed Potatoes." I want to stay with it. On television, on records, on tour—I want to sing.[63]

★★★

FITZGERALD'S DEFINITIVE SWERVE into current popular styles was displayed on November 22 when she debuted in "Great Performers at Philharmonic Hall," a mostly classical recital series at Lincoln Center in New York. The series, which was inaugurated in 1965 with the Duke Ellington Chamber Ensemble as its first jazz offering, was an important moment in her career; a younger Norman Granz might have grabbed the opportunity for a live LP. In the *New York Times*, a feature by John S. Wilson previewing the concert was titled "Ella Changes Her Tunes for a Swinging Generation," and she had a platform for her views:

> Music today has a different beat. . . . Unless you sing today's songs, all there is is the standards, the old show tunes. What new show tunes are there? "Hello, Dolly"? It has that old beat, it's an old type song. Can you think of anything else that's come out of Broadway? Or out of the movies? . . . No matter where we play, we have some of the younger generation coming to the club. It's a drag if you don't have anything to offer them.[64]

With Bobbie Gentry's "Ode to Billie Joe," which she sang on the Sinatra show, she went overboard: "It's one of the first songs since

'Mack the Knife' that I really like to do." She kept up with teenage hits through her eighteen-year-old son and sixteen-year-old niece, laughing while admitting, "They made a Monkees fan out of me." She continued, "At home, there's a 'Do Not Disturb' sign on each of their doors. They've each got their own bag going on their phonographs. My niece loves the Supremes, Martha and the Vandellas, Marvin Gaye—the whole Motown bit. Ray likes jazz trios."[65]

A Monkees fan? The boy-band quartet, formed by a casting agency to emulate the Beatles, had found success in 1966 with their network TV show and their first single, "Last Train to Clarksville," despite journalists lambasting their manufactured beginnings. Ray Brown, Jr., recalled telling his father that his mother approved of the Monkees. "She must have said that for your benefit," he replied.

> My father felt that rock and roll—"These people are terrible and awful." Ella could say, "You know what? They're working." On the Monkees, she liked them. We watched the TV show. You know what? They served a purpose, they made money, they had a TV show, they made records, they made music. They were not the evil empire.[66]

In his review of the Lincoln Center performance, John S. Wilson, lamenting "an air of superficiality" on several songs, checked off her new repertoire ("Sunny" and "Goin' Out of My Head") and acknowledged her jazz expertise while singling out "gentle ballads" as her true calling. He was particularly won over by her rendition of "On a Clear Day (You Can See Forever)," written by Burton Lane and Alan Jay Lerner for a 1965 Broadway musical of that title: "The full warmth of her voice and the skill with which she wove beckoning lines of true, pure sound gave 'On a Clear Day You Can See Forever' an amazing sense of melting beauty."[67]

As 1967 ended, Fitzgerald was home for Christmas and New Year's. Earlier that year the Hawaiian columnist Cobey Black revealed the family side of Fitzgerald, seldom glimpsed in the jazz press. When she knocked on her door, she was met by a "shyly smiling, expansive woman in a blue housecoat and comfortable slippers." No recaps about the Apollo debut were necessary—"Let's just chat."[68] The mood was relaxed and cozy.

The interview offered some touching details about Fitzgerald's blended family. After the death of her sister, Frances, the birth mother of Ray Brown, Jr., she had assumed guardianship of Frances's three daughters, ranging in age from four to sixteen. At the time she told her friend Phoebe Jacobs that she felt the need to work as hard as ever. "I have to get back to work," she said. "Who is going to support all these kids?"[69] They were all living with her in Beverly Hills, and a year later it seemed to be working. Ray Brown, Jr., who had learned of his adoption some years earlier, did not know that Frances Correy was his biological mother; nor would he until several years later. To him, the new arrivals were cousins, and the new family settled in.[70]

Ella let these personal details slide, instead focusing on her son's determination to "really study music." His father, Ray Brown, had left the Oscar Peterson Trio and settled in Los Angeles. She doted on the youngest, Karen, a five-year-old who was taking ballet lessons and refused to take off her ballet slippers. She said she cooked a French veal stew to share with her girlfriends. She wanted a "comfortable home" where the children weren't banished from the furniture and visiting men would not have to "take off their shoes so they won't ruin the white rug."

But not even that family could compete with the other— "the audience":

No matter how tired you may feel or how blue, once you go on stage, an entirely different feeling takes over: the audience belongs to you and you to them and you both forget everything else. Singing for me is like talking to someone, someone close to you.[71]

Starting December 28 Fitzgerald was at the Cocoanut Grove for a three-week engagement. She invited children in for a special performance. Her busy publicists reached the feature writers in the African American press: "It was a jam-packed Cocoanut Grove matinee for teenagers and the smaller ones Saturday when Ella Fitzgerald played a special matinee for them alone," wrote Gertrude Gipson in the *Los Angeles Sentinel*, who brought a young relative to the event: "Our Shonte is still oooh! . . . 'n' . . . ah'n."[72] Ella was so proud of this feat. Let others court nostalgia; she lived the gift of the present. Out went a press release, which quoted her almost two years later: "Music changes with each generation and I'm changing right along with it. I have tried to communicate with them as a performer, and I believe I've succeeded. When I held a concert for teenagers at a nightclub in Los Angeles, a friend warned me that not more than 15 kids would show up. Well, they filled the place—1200 of them."[73] She never stopped counting.

Chapter 24

REINVENTING HERSELF

(1968-1969)

I n the late 1960s, Ella was determined to stay current. Despite threats of extinction for the endangered species known as "jazz singer," or perhaps because of them, she integrated soul and rock into her live performances. In her opening remarks to audiences, to frame this eclectic repertoire, she referred to the "now sounds" and the "new sounds." In Western Europe, as in the United States, 1968 was a year of student protests, anti–Vietnam War demonstrations, and youth culture. In Fitzgerald's European tour, starting January 27 and covering twenty countries in twenty-five days, the "New Ella" was generating a drama all her own. A February 11 concert in the Deutschlandhalle, filmed for German national television, exploded with the creative energy that Berlin audiences seemed to evoke in her, matching the level of the fabled "Mack the Knife" date in the same venue eight years before.[1] Backed by the Tee Carson Trio and delivering some expected fare, including a great rendition of "Summertime," the New Ella moved squarely into soul territory for the finale, a risk-taking ten-minute expansion of Ray Charles's global hit from 1962, "I Can't Stop Loving You."[2] The trio established the urgent, backbeat-heavy rhythm, then dropped out as Ella delivered a seductive, gospel-infused melisma. Then she stopped and looked back at her trio. Had they missed a cue? The audience was unsure how to respond. "Soulsville!" she cried with playful irony. She and the band continued joking with each other, confident the audience would indulge her.

Five minutes in, the band dropped out again, and Fitzgerald sang in a preaching church style with the drummer punctuating the end of each line:

All I want is respect, in the morning.
In the evening,
Give it to me all night long, give me respect.

Fitzgerald was no doubt signifying on Aretha Franklin, the reigning Queen of Soulsville, whose single "Respect" had been a number-one hit the previous summer and would become an intersectional anthem for both the Civil Rights and Women's Liberation Movements in the 1970s. As the historians Darlene Clark Hine and Kathleen Thompson have written, Franklin "was perfect for the new age of black women who were clearly part of popular culture . . . able to assert their determination to claim their place in the world,"[3] just as Fitzgerald would assert her right to be "just me."

Ella let her spirit take over, tapping into a confessional flow as the drummer kicked back in behind her. Then six and a half minutes into the performance, in a shocking moment of identity crisis—as if she were waking up from a spell—she confessed in a normal speaking voice, "Oh, this ain't my bag." Unaccompanied, she began singing the opening lines of the Vernon Duke and Ira Gershwin standard, "I Can't Get Started." Twenty seconds later she was back in church, addressing Berliners like a Black congregation. Pointing to the front row, she sang to one woman after another, "Do you love your man?" a paraphrase of "Do you love Jesus?" No woman responded *ja* or *nein*, and Ella broke character again, laughing and saying, "And there is silence." If they wouldn't answer, she would, with the band vamping again:

I wanna talk about my man, yeah.
I wanna preach about my man, yeah.

Oh, oh [hollering, moaning]
Cuz I'm the woman, cuz I'm the woman with the, with the skinny legs
Yeah, yeah, cuz I'm the woman with the little skinny legs, yeah yeah
Oh yeah, oh yeah, oh yeah, oh no, alright
I can't stop lovin' you.

Among the thousands in attendance, perhaps not a single person understood this reference to her youth in Harlem, when, as she told an interviewer, "my legs were so skinny, I used to wear boots so nobody could see the bottom of my legs."[4] She trusted her audience to love and accept her, which in turn allowed her to take risks that made the second half of her Berlin performance so magical. Even her trio stood and applauded her. Whether Fitzgerald repeated "I Can't Stop Loving You" in this way is not known. After the tour, her subsequent renditions lost their edge, turning the song into a good-natured, novelty crossover with an edge of parody, lacking the power and psychodrama of her Berlin vocal jam.

Setlists for the rest of the European tour remained built on both old and new: Cole Porter, Ellington, and Gershwin, along with a bossa nova, current pop hits, a medley, and an excursion into R&B territory. In Budapest, her concert at the two-thousand-seat Erkel Theatre was booked by a private agency, bypassing the Communist bureaucracy. Ticket demand was over fifty thousand, even though the concert was carried live on the radio. A journalist based in Eastern Europe wrote that it was "one of the most exciting musical events in postwar Hungary."[5] Fitzgerald told *Jet* magazine, "Our arrival was televised on a national hookup throughout Hungary. I've never seen such press coverage."[6]

★★★

"ARETHA'S GOT HER BAG GOING WITH SO MUCH SOUL," said Fitzgerald in a fascinating exchange with her friend Billy Taylor, the jazz pianist and educator, on WLIB, a New York radio station aimed at Black audiences. "Oh boy, she's got so much soul she could lend me a little. I never had that kind of soul."[7] In response, Taylor, who had played with Fitzgerald in the early 1950s, contested narrow applications of *soul* as a marker of Black cultural authenticity:

> I can't let that statement stand unchallenged. To me soul is so many things. Aretha certainly has what is the current way of putting it in terms of soul—she's directly related to the gospel feeling in music, but to me, to hear you sing the blues, to do some of the things more in the Negro tradition, I hear the same quality but in your way, and to me, it's the same as—well, Charlie Parker and Art Tatum had soul, but I don't think you would listen to them in the same way as you would listen to Ramsey Lewis. I heard you do "Misty" . . . and there's no mistaking this is Ella Fitzgerald's kind of soul going into a very beautiful composition by a jazz pianist [Erroll Garner]. It makes what you do very special for me.

Ella answered, "Right, thank you for helping me [laughter]. Well you got me out of that!" Later noted for his advocacy of jazz as "America's classical music" in the 1970s, Taylor stressed the continuity of African American expressive culture, regardless of marketplace genres.[8] The conversation soon returned to the controversial issue of tolerance for popular music. "I think we should stop fighting," she said. "Why are we trying to put down some of the music going on now? Is it because we don't do it, because we don't like it? We must learn to like some of it. . . . I don't think jazz is gone." Taylor replied that she led by example.

The Billy Taylor interview occurred during her booking at the Rainbow Grill in Rockefeller Center. The press coverage piled on with praise, raving about her youthful vitality in the year of her presumed fiftieth birthday.[9] On May 30 her performance was broadcast on WNEW's *Make Believe Ballroom*, hosted by radio personality William B. Williams, a champion of standards. The show began with a dazzling "The Lady Is a Tramp" and ended with "Ray's Idea" from her Dizzy Gillespie years. "We made a little swing arrangement out of it," she joked with Williams. "There's no lyrics—it's psychedelic lyrics."[10] She also sang her new composition "He Had a Dream" in memory of Rev. Martin Luther King, Jr., who had been tragically assassinated on April 4. "It's very simple, nothing jazzy, nothing fancy like that," she told Billy Taylor. "I don't know if it's that beautiful. . . . It's simple enough so there's not a lot a mush. . . . He's not the type of man who believed in too many fiery things, so I made it soft."[11]

Despite her iconic status, Fitzgerald still treated each performance as a trial of her ability to satisfy her audience. Every performance meant a fresh challenge. When listeners met her with indifference or refused to respond, she was undone. Audience chatter and cigarette smoke at ringside tables remained sore points when patrons came to socialize as well as listen. The Rainbow Grill, on the sixty-fifth floor of 30 Rockefeller Plaza, initially billed her engagement as "Ella Fitzgerald Sings for Dancing," but it changed its policy at her insistence. Backed by the Tee Carson Trio, she told management that she expected people to listen, and she got her wish.[12] It took courage to make that demand. As she told Billy Taylor, "I was afraid because the first night I thought people would want to hear a dance band . . . but it's great. . . . We start out with a routine where I just do requests. . . . I get to do a lot of ballads. . . . They just want to sit and listen."[13] One night in November 1968, at another prominent New York venue, the Royal Box, that trick of turning a nightclub into a listening room failed. "I've never seen an artist more bitterly disappointed in her audience," wrote a columnist in attendance:

> The room quiets and she begins to chat about her sidemen. A voice tells her "we've heard it. Sing." Ella turns and quietly and not unkindly says, "But you're not being fair to the people who haven't heard it." . . . The lovely "Devil Moon" is marred by talk in isolated sections of the room. "I'll cut out the ballads for you people," Ella warns.
>
> She tries an impeccable "Have You Met Miss Jones?" and abruptly cuts it off. "Maybe I'd better stop this tune. Everybody's laughing. Maybe something's wrong." . . . "We love you, Ella,"

a woman shouts behind me. . . . Tears well up. "It's kind of hard. You want to mix the songs. And everybody's laughing. I just don't know." . . . Despite her doubt and unhappiness there are no flaws in the tour de force that follows.[14]

The spring of 1968 brought the fulfillment of a long-held ambition: her own hour-long television special, titled *Something Special: The Ella Fitzgerald Show*. The carefully crafted program, with Fitzgerald backed by the Jimmy Jones Trio, the Duke Ellington Trio, and Ellington's full orchestra, focused on standards with a heavy dose of Ellingtonia. She delivered an elegant "Summertime," a vivid "Just One of Those Things," and a less adventurous "I Can't Stop Loving You." As she had envisioned in previous interviews, she welcomed viewers to her home, sitting in her garden, straining for the professional intimacy of Dinah Shore.

In the Black press, the ever-loyal entertainment columnist Hazel Garland wrote, "Don't bother to call me Friday, November 29 between the hours of 9 and 10 p.m. I'll be glued to my set watching 'The Ella Fitzgerald Show' which is to be aired on local ABC-TV affiliate here."[15] The reviews predictably praised her voice while gently criticizing the hostessing concept, which did not help further distribution by the independent production outfit, Screen Gems. As the show was purchased by local affiliates rather than programmed on the national network, its airings varied by location, with rebroadcasts as late as 1975. Just as impactful were Fitzgerald's appearances on network variety programs, including, from 1968 to 1970, those of Ed Sullivan, Pat Boone, Joey Bishop, Carol Burnett, Glen Campbell, Andy Williams, Flip Wilson, and Tom Jones, along with the nostalgia series *The Hollywood Palace*.

By this point in her career, Fitzgerald was more widely acknowledged as a "citizen-artist"—no firebrand but nonetheless civic-minded and politically engaged. In September 1968 in San Francisco, photographers snapped her portrait in front of Grace Cathedral, where she joined a fundraising rally to aid the secessionist state of Biafra in the Nigerian Civil War.[16] A few days later she appeared at the Hunters Point Co-op to lend her support to a struggling Black-run, working-class enterprise. "I came down because I was invited," she told a reporter. "I hope this visit, in a little way, can be encouraging because I wish these things could be done all over. And they can be. You just have to get the pride and do it. It can be done."[17]

In New York in November 1968, the elite Black sorority Alpha Kappa Alpha recognized her iconic status by finally making her an honorary member. The AKA sisters sponsored a "dinner party" in her honor for fifteen hundred people at the Coliseum. Coretta Scott King was among the vice-chairs, and committee members included Frank Sinatra, Dionne Warwick, Count Basie, Richard Rodgers, Aaron Copland, and Massachusetts senator Edward Brooke. At the ceremony, she was also presented with New York City's first Cultural Award for "exceptional achievement in the performing or creative arts."[18]

She was known around the world, making hefty sums as a performing artist; her daily activities were deemed newsworthy and New York celebrated her life as a civic event. Who needed a record label? She did.

★★★

AFTER HER VERVE CONTRACT TERMINATED, Fitzgerald took a while to get back into a recording studio. Granz convinced Capitol to sign her for a one-LP-at-a time deal, as executives waited to assess her market traction. Her first three Capitol LPs were recorded in February, July, and December 1967—the year rock surpassed "adult" in LP sales—and her final Capitol LP in May and June 1968. During this Capitol period, the gap in repertoire between her studio recordings and live performances was wider than at any time since her Decca years. In a series of missteps, her executive producer, Dave Dexter, downplayed her adherence to "the Negro tradition," in Billy Taylor's words. Dexter's history with Fitzgerald extended way back to 1938, when he had reviewed her for *Billboard* as "the dusky chanteuse with the Webbmen" at a vaudepic date in Kansas City.[19] Employed at Capitol since 1943, Dexter had extensive jazz credentials but is better remembered among rock historians for mishandling the release of Beatles singles amid the skeptical climate greeting them in 1962 and 1963.

Fitzgerald's first Capitol release was *Brighten the Corner*, an album of hymns for the mainstream market overseen by Ralph Carmichael, and using his choir and orchestra. A leading figure in contemporary Christian music, Carmichael had carved out a similar territory for Nat King Cole.[20] Fitzgerald described the album as the fulfillment of a long-standing wish to make a religious record, though her comments also suggest a desired respite from the extroversion of soul and gospel: "I sing them [hymns] quietly, the way that I feel they are supposed to be sung," she told a newspaper critic. "I am not trying to do it as others have done it."[21] Walter Trohan, in the *Chicago Tribune*, illustrated a conservative interpretation of her album of hymns. In the wake of terrible race riots in the summer of 1967 and the rise of Black Power, he praised *Brighten the Corner* for encouraging "racial cooperation," contrasting Fitzgerald's "spiritual devotion and poetic feeling" to "the look of sullen hate which so many Negroes cast at any and all whites, even those who would help them."[22] *Brighten the Corner* cracked *Billboard*'s Top 200 LP chart for two weeks.

In 1970 Fitzgerald reflected on it:

> Yes, it was wonderful. It's so very different from what I otherwise sing, and it's given me a possibility of telling people that show people have another life as well. People always believe we do nothing apart from drinking, or just sit having a nice time together. But a lot of us have a family, and when they're done with a hard day's work, we rush home. That proves that we are people, who just have a somewhat different job than most.[23]

On its heels came *Ella Fitzgerald's Christmas*, an LP of Christmas carols.[24] Her third Capitol release was *Misty Blue*, an album of country and western songs in orchestral arrangements with strings and backup singers.[25] Dexter's agenda, according to *Billboard*, was "to re-establish the veteran vocalist as a fresh, new commodity with the new generation of record buyers who have no prior knowledge of Miss Fitzgerald's past."[26] He also had in mind the crossover success of Ray Charles's landmark 1962 album *Modern Sounds in Country and Western Music*, as he hired Sid Feller, who produced the Charles LP, to arrange *Misty Blue*. With his uninspired choices, Dexter seemed almost determined to play to Fitzgerald's weaknesses. "I doubt that her album will have the response of Charles's," wrote the reviewer for *Soul* magazine. "Ella's venture into country is smooth and straight in the Ella tradition. It's not so much that she adapted herself to country music as it is that she took some country tunes and adapted them to her style—a beautiful and consistent style."[27] The album sank, though one song, "I Taught Him Everything He Knows," nudged the charts.

In his 1976 memoir, Dexter described Fitzgerald as "diffident and uninterested" or as listening "suspiciously" or "morosely" to his suggestions.[28] In late 1967 he visited her home on North Sierra Drive, toting an enlarged color print of her from a costly photo shoot. "A housemaid opened the door," he recalled. "I asked if I might see Ella for a moment. She turned and yelled to someone that 'a man named Dexter wants to see you for a minute—can you come to the door?' 'Not today,' Ella—or someone—hollered from inside." He left, unsure what had happened or too chagrined to admit he did. He was not alone in her strategic brush-offs.[29] Unknown to him, she could answer the telephone, hear a voice, and disguise her own. "Is that you, Ella?" a friend once asked, catching her in the act.[30]

Dexter's repentance was her final Capitol album, *30 by Ella*, which returned to jazz but also failed, dulled by its formulaic concept: a series of medleys arranged by the eminent Benny Carter.[31] Dexter then secured a prime television spot on *The Lawrence Welk Show*, aimed at a musically conservative, older white audience perfect for his agenda. Norman Granz torpedoed the deal, saying, "Welk's the lowest pay in the industry, I wouldn't book Fitzgerald's ex-husband for that money." At the end of her two-year Capitol contract, with little of the $100,000 advance recouped, Dexter did not raise the issue of extending her deal.[32]

Disappointed with the Capitol albums, Granz countered by producing his own live album.[33] In February 1969 he taped Fitzgerald live at the Fairmont Hotel in San Francisco with Tommy Flanagan's trio and Ernie Heckscher's orchestra; it was released as *Sunshine of Your Love* on the German MPS label.[34] The title track, a big hit for the British rock group Cream, had already been covered by R&B singers. It was a perceptive choice, recognizing that rock aesthetics had something to offer jazz. Vibraphonist Gary Burton, an early experimenter in fusing jazz and rock, recalled, "I had grown up in an age when rock musicians were considered musical idiots by those who were well-trained. Yet with Cream, here were guys who were superb musicians. All of the guys from Cream knew how to play jazz and the blues."[35]

Other tracks included the Beatles' "Hey Jude," the requisite bossa nova, retro titles from the swing era, and a moving performance of Bacharach and David's "A House Is Not a Home," as yet relatively undiscovered. Fitzgerald's "soul" vocal style was increasingly apparent, perhaps compensating for postmenopausal changes in her voice, which was losing its youthful sheen. Soul idioms could offer new sources of drama, with more swooping into notes, expanded dynamics on single pitches, and greater abandon and intensity.

Fitzgerald's next LP, *Ella*, recorded in May 1969, was her first for Reprise Records.[36] Granz had signed her to the label in 1968 but still absented himself as a producer. Another makeover was coming, according to the label: "Isn't it about time somebody did something about ELLA? Somebody has. Reprise."[37] Richard Perry, a young producer at the threshold of a significant career, assembled a congenial list of tunes including Motown choices ("Get Ready," "Ooo Baby Baby"), a recently minted Bacharach ("I'll Never Fall In Love Again"), a Beatles tune ("Got to Get You into My Life"), and folk-rock ballads from newcomer singer-songwriters Harry Nilsson ("Open Your Window") and Randy Newman ("Yellow Man"). Among her recording crew in London was pianist Nicky Hopkins, a session player for the Rolling Stones, some of whom apparently dropped by. Multitracking both the vocals and instrumentalists on his rock arrangements, Perry lavished his ambitions on this project at a moment when techno-savvy producers were taking on the authority of "auteurs" in studio postproduction, challenging ideals of spontaneity in live performance and slighting jazz improvisation.

A review by Robert Christgau, an influential new-guard rock critic, reflected this broad change in aesthetics. Calling her earlier rock covers "embarrassments," Christgau praised Perry for suppressing "the habitual inclinations of a genius" and for persuading her "to sing straight and forget the doobie-doobie-doobie. . . . It's the long-awaited union of a great singer and a great music, a treasure, and it would never have happened if it weren't for Richard Perry."[38] Such cavalier dismissals of the historic practices of vocal jazz were increasingly widespread. "When Ella sings in that pure cool voice, she is just great," wrote a Florida journalist in 1971. "But when she reverts to that obsolete scat singing from another era, Lord help us."[39]

Perry took great pride in the *Ella* LP and was disappointed by the lack of promotion. His collaboration with Fitzgerald was scheduled for a second album in late 1969, but it was never completed, allegedly because Granz objected to the change in musical direction.[40] Fitzgerald also had qualms, according to her son, Ray Jr.: "I remember the recording sessions with Rick Perry. I was amused. I don't believe my mom was as thrilled as I was. He had her do multi-tracking of vocals. This was a different approach to recording. It did not appear to be her cup of tea."[41] Nonetheless Fitzgerald kept a few songs from the album in circulation, most notably "Get Ready," which had been a major R&B hit for the Temptations in 1966. With new charts for her trio, she brought the song to TV spots in 1969, updating her image through recent Motown memories.

★★★

FITZGERALD'S 1969 EUROPEAN TOUR, covering twenty-two cities from May to July, brought some of the "New Ella" including renditions of "Sunshine of Your Love" and the Blood, Sweat & Tears hit "Spinning Wheel." Her first-ever Prague concert, broadcast on state television, took place ten months after the Soviet Union invaded Czechoslovakia and suppressed the liberal reforms enacted by Alexander Dubček under the slogan "socialism with a human face." "Among those who applauded hardest were young Czechoslovak Army officers in uniform," wrote the *New York Times* correspondent, of the concert. "Some Russian also was heard among the 3,000 people crowding the Lucerna Auditorium . . . but no Soviet uniforms were seen in the audience."[42]

The climax of the tour was her first appearance at the Montreux Festival in June. A film of her performance, later released on DVD,[43] documented her charming a jazz crowd into submission. The radically diverse set included Jerome Kern's "I Won't Dance," delivered with the energy of Ginger Rogers's tap-dance routine in the 1935 film *Roberta*. For "Sunshine of Your Love," she compensated for the lack of electric guitar with sheer energy, including a mock-confession: "I'm screamin', I'm shoutin', I'm hollerin' here in Montreux, I'm ashamed of myself." No one was fooled. The vocal jam finale borrowed from several points in her career timeline, even throwing in "A-Tisket A-Tasket."

After Montreux, Fitzgerald and the Tommy Flanagan Trio settled down for the month of July in Copenhagen at the Glassalen (Glass Hall) in Tivoli Gardens, which seated around one thousand. Booked into a variety format, she went from Montreux's discriminating fans to a broad family public. "I like reaching people who can't afford those high price festival tickets," she told a reporter.[44] Danish critic Bent Henius, amazed with her "fantastic success," wrote that she "has actually gotten better over the years—more mature and emancipated."[45] Her month-long stay was a homecoming of sorts, since she was had lived in Copenhagen in 1961. Anders Stefansen, a concert promoter who worked with Granz, recalled that she had many friends in Copenhagen, and she enjoyed the music scene so much that she and Granz considered buying a local jazz club.[46] She socialized with drummer Ed Thigpen's family and the community of expatriate American jazz musicians who had fled American racism. She also brought over her son, Ray Jr., her two nieces Karen Gilmore and Eloise Young, and Eloise's infant daughter, Valerie.

Earlier that year Fitzgerald discussed her parenting style in a particularly frank interview for the ABC-TV show *For Blacks Only*. "He had to grow up by himself," she said of Ray Jr., who had graduated from Beverly Hills High School the previous year.

> But he has done a pretty good job by himself. . . . Believe me, sometimes I want to hit him on his head. They think they know everything, too. We sorta have a system in our house. Whenever I think he's gone too far, I ground him. Take his wheels away. . . . I put my foot down, otherwise you don't get respect. . . . I feel I'm out here working, hitting these boards, and when I go home, I want that respect.[47]

"Nobody toured like my mother," Ray Jr. observed as a middle-aged adult. His mother's layovers at home rarely lasted longer than ten or twelve days, with a few weeks around Christmas. In the summers, he split his time between his father and his stepmother, Ray and Cecilia Brown, and Fitzgerald. Coping with neglect yet proud, loving, and defensive of his mother, over time he would travel his own path to acceptance and find his own musical identity:

> Nobody ever seemed to focus on the time that we spent together. That time was so intense. And I think she tried even harder when she was home to connect with me. . . . She would talk about little things, about growing up in a neighborhood with all different types of people, the importance of people getting along. About walking down the street with her mother and having a less than appreciative attitude, and her mother dealt with that. I know that there are obviously people she didn't get along with. As far as she dealt with me, you know, I can't say that there was any unfairness.[48]

Fitzgerald frequently commented on her son's aspirations, and she wanted him to be focused and purposeful. Some strain was suggested in the *For Blacks Only* interview:

> He plays the drums and is studying to be a music teacher. He went from the drums, to the guitar, back to the drums; now he

feels he sees a future being a music teacher. Never know what he's going to be. I don't think I should try to push him. Let him be what he wants to be. I do know he wants to go on the road.

In the next few years Ray Jr. would do just that. He made music with a band, followed a girlfriend to Seattle, and like many of his generation, worried about getting drafted in the Vietnam War.

At the close of the 1960s, Fitzgerald's plan to stay current had mostly succeeded. She juggled the Old and New Ella as needed, and her audience recognized that she had carved out a new direction for herself without forsaking her past. At Ravinia in August 1969, the African American critic for the *Chicago Defender* praised her *Song Book* concert with Nelson Riddle conducting the Chicago Symphony Orchestra for "10,000 persons of all ages, religions and races."[49] On November 22, at Philharmonic Hall in Lincoln Center, she appeared once again in the "Great Performers" series, with an overflow audience seated onstage. "The concert was an absolute gas to many in the audience, who like Miss Fitzgerald's change of pace singing, and a disappointment to those nostalgic enough to yearn for the Ella of old," wrote the classically trained critic Perdita Duncan for the *New York Amsterdam News*. "Even that Fitzgerald gem from the past, 'A-Tisket A-Tasket,' was sung in the modern manner, with only a hint of that glowing delivery which once tugged at the heart."[50] Her strategy was working, but at a price. How long could she sustain this approach?

Chapter 25

KEEPING ON

(1970-1972)

n the early 1970s, when she was in her early fifties, Ella Fitzgerald had recurrent problems with her vision that threatened not only her career but her emotional and physical well-being. That she soldiered on through crises that could have justified early retirement was inevitable given how she lived her life onstage. It was "30 years of facing those powerful lights," she said after weathering a physical and emotional breakdown in the winter of 1970. At the time it did not seem worrisome and appeared to be easily remedied, as she explained: "It got to where I had to keep closing my eyes all the time. I was very nervous. Finally, I canceled all my bookings and went into the hospital. I was off two-and-a-half months."[1] Her hiatus drew little if any press coverage at the time. Whatever medical treatment she received is not known. Nevertheless, it marked the onset of a chronic condition that was slowly unmasked as a symptom of diabetes, which would compromise her career for the next three years in dramatic public incidents. Since few knew about the issue, her return to performing was not treated as a "comeback" or a "recovery." That would come later.

A second challenge she faced concerned the viability of her belief that it was her duty, indeed her mission as an artist, to engage the popular music of her time. She had been saying for decades "I will not be left behind," but the question was how to achieve this goal in the midst of so much stylistic change while sustaining her own identity as "Ella," recognizable by her first name alone. She was willing to take risks. Big press accompanied her two-week date at the Waldorf Astoria's Empire Room in April 1970, where she continued undaunted along her "now sound, new sound" path with a jazz-rock repertoire. That night the AP reviewer, Mary Campbell, accepted the new along with the old as genuine: she was still Ella, and that was "the biggest compliment of all. It's like speaking of a beloved relative, somebody not seen often enough but who, when seen, never lets you down. And of course everybody knows whom you are talking about." Campbell heard "those incredible jazz riffs that seem to rush out from nowhere and subside just as quickly in songs like 'Spinning Wheel.' Who else could do that?"[2] Celebrities came in to see and be seen. In one touching incident, she introduced Louis Armstrong, who had just played the Waldorf after months of illness; "Louis joined her in the front of the band, put an arm around her neck, dislodging one of her earrings and endangering her wig, took the mike away from her and said, 'Relax while I do "Mack the Knife," and think up something we can do together.'"[3] *Variety* reported that "had not some subtle pressures been exercised, he would have taken over the entire session."[4] She rallied and beamed at him in photos of what would be their final duet, for Armstrong died the next year.

The gulf between the public response and that within the jazz world widened in 1970. *Down Beat* had recently expanded its coverage to include rock, gospel, and R&B, but editor Dan Morgenstern, reviewing her appearance at the Newport Jazz Festival in July, lamented the change in her:

> Ella works hard, a little too hard, perhaps, and I, for one, don't much care for her current emphasis on contemporary material. Granted that every performer, and especially the ladies, desires to be up-to-date, and that such tactics may help to find new audiences. Yet, it can be done without abandoning established practices, and tonight I missed Ella's beautiful ballads.[5]

In the same magazine four months later, that moderate tone yielded to outright rejection of her "inferior material" at the Now Grove (formerly the Cocoanut Grove) club in Los Angeles. "She was not the Ella that we in the jazz community can relate to," the reviewer Harvey Siders wrote. "Why she stoops to singing the awkward constructions of Bacharach and the Beatles is unfathomable." Yet even he acknowledged her connoisseurship in reinventing Bacharach's "Raindrops Keep Fallin' on My Head."[6] From her perspective, Fitzgerald was demonstrating the viability of jazz as musical practice to reach across genre boundaries, rather than remaining confined to traditional repertoire choices.

The brilliant date at the Now Grove would hold a place of honor in Fitzgerald's life as one of her last public appearances with Duke Ellington and His Orchestra. Their bond remained a touchstone of her career. When Ellington died in 1974, Fitzgerald left a jazz cruise ship to attend his funeral on May 27 at the Cathedral of St. John the Divine in New York City. A short TV clip from ABC's national news showed her singing a few mournful phrases of "(In My) Solitude," accompanied by Billy Taylor on piano, Lisle Atkinson on bass, and Jo Jones on drums.[7] Afterward she sang the hymn "Just a Closer Walk with Thee."[8]

On *The Andy Williams Show* on October 17, 1970, she and her host duetted decorously on Otis Redding and Steve Cropper's "(Sittin' On) the Dock of the Bay."[9] On Flip Wilson's comedy show in November, she returned to "Lady Be Good" and duetted with Wilson on a blend of "The Glory of Love" and "Makin' Whoopee."[10] In December, on *This Is Tom Jones*, hosted by the white British singer then at the peak of his popularity, the two sat in twin rocking chairs singing the 1963 soul standard "Sunny."[11]

A more important substantive renewal began with her collaboration with Count Basie, engineered by Norman Granz. After their nine-day tour of Argentina and Chile in September 1969, they barnstormed Europe.[12] Returning to the big band milieu of her youth, and musicians whom she had known since her Chick Webb years, gave her new motivation, while for Basie it was a lifeline at a time of professional ebb: "Norman is my man. Period."[13]

On April 21 Fitzgerald wrote to her New York friend Phoebe Jacobs from Frankfurt, "We've been doing very well over here. Basie and the band and myself. Everybody gets along so well."[14] Their synergy sparked coverage through mass media, capturing her artistic bravado in this transitional period.[15] (It would take decades for Americans to hear her work from these years.) The West Germans went overboard in documenting her presence, using a birthday concert on April 25 in Frankfurt as the centerpiece of an ambitious documentary, *Ella Fitzgerald in Deutschland 1970*, which was broadcast on German state television.[16] It captured not only her performances but backstage footage and interviews with Granz and her trio. She romped through "Crazy Rhythm," singing that she had "gone crazy for the new kind of sound" and alluding to "Aretha Franklin and Tom Jones, too." In duet with pianist Tommy Flanagan, she sang a sensuous interpretation of Cole Porter's "I Concentrate on You." Flanagan, who had rejoined Fitzgerald as pianist and artistic director in 1968 and would stay with her until 1978, had learned that she needed room to roam. As he said later, "I think she demanded that," and he brilliantly mastered the "head arrangements" with few written charts as guides.

A recording of her concert in Hungary on May 20, 1970, released in 1999 as *Ella Fitzgerald in Budapest*, exemplified these challenging programs.[17] Never mind her mission to please everyone—she was having a great time indulging herself with the security of her "fellas," who had learned to ride the wave of her imagination. She changed Rodgers and Hammerstein's "Hello Young Lovers" into a bossa nova: "Hey lovers," she ad-libbed. An extraneous word or two could arrive from nowhere, as when "The Girl from Ipanema" veered briefly into her "Gotta Do the Moon Walk" followed by "Fly Me to the Moon."

Fitzgerald's international success was exhilarating to Granz, who relished the tours that brought her to Europe, his home. During her 1970 tour, Granz—who had by then established a reputation as an international art collector—made a special, indeed rather extraordinary request of Pablo Picasso, a valued friend since 1968: to draw a souvenir portrait sketch of his star, even though Picasso had not met her. Picasso claimed he did not know what she looked like, but nevertheless he sketched a line drawing on the back page of a random art catalog, which Granz treasured. In an oft-repeated anecdote, perhaps from this same time, Granz said he offered Fitzgerald the chance to meet Picasso in Juan-les-Pins. She replied, "I'm busy. I'm darning my stockings, and I have some other things I'm sewing, so I can't go." When Granz relayed this to Picasso, he responded, "That's great. Now I really want to meet her!"[18] Was it diffidence or indifference to his celebrity that produced this flimsy comical excuse? Picasso and Fitzgerald did meet later on, and in the 1980s she sported a huge pendant she said was given to her by "Mrs. Picasso."[19]

★★★

THERE WERE OFFSTAGE CHALLENGES AS WELL. Social and political change made untenable her habitual reticence and discretion. She had already lambasted the well-known American journalist Mike Wallace, telling another reporter in 1968 that Wallace had asked her "sarcastic and stupid questions" such as "Why does everyone say they love you?"[20] The standard American interview about her political and cultural views left so much unasked, especially in an era of the Black nationalist revolution. In June 1970 a young Danish reporter, Chris Wammen, asked her to speak about the current scene, which made her angry and defensive. He pushed her, and she pushed back, and he was reduced to calling himself a "stupid reporter" at the end of the interview. On the political front, he asked if her views had shifted from the nonviolence of Martin Luther King, Jr., to the Black Power ideology of Eldridge Cleaver, the Black Panther Party leader then in exile:

> I don't believe in violence. On the other hand, I can't say if Cleaver is wrong. I would rather stay out of it. I am not a politician, so I don't want to talk about Cleaver or anybody else. I only want to talk about Ella. And I do not like that people categorize me and make me say things about other people. I can only speak for myself.[21]

Another subject was the sexual revolution, which had given Denmark, along with Sweden, a reputation for "free love" norms.

Wammen: Are you not impressed by the big free spirit in Scandinavia?

Fitzgerald: If people get sex the way they need it, then it's all to the good. I don't live here, so I don't know what it's like.

Wammen: There must have been some development—in the USA as well—from 1938, when you were discovered in Harlem, to today.

Fitzgerald: A man is a man, and a woman is a woman. I do not think anything has happened in that area.

Wammen: But the social conventions have become less restrictive.

Fitzgerald: I do not know anything about that. I can, after all, only speak for myself. But I would rather not talk about sex. It is not part of my politics. I am not a sex singer. The crucial thing for me is the rhythm. . . . There are just certain things that I don't want to talk about. One has to have some privacy, and I don't want to try and sell something that I cannot even quite explain myself. I have achieved a certain respect, and I want to maintain that respect.[22]

As it happened, just around this time, Fitzgerald had a love affair with a New York man, Ray Wallace. "She was a sensuous woman," Phoebe Jacobs said of her friend.[23] On April 21, 1970, Ella wrote, "[I] missed my family and my guy. Guess I became close to them by being home longer."[24] She kept letters and a photograph of Wallace, a handsome African American man who appeared to be in his thirties or forties, posed in front of baseball trophies—an athlete, appealing to a baseball fan like Ella. She was possessive, as she had said in her interview with *Ebony* in 1961 and repeated some years later. She added a bittersweet note to an interviewer in 1976:

I think my big problem about falling in love was that I was always traveling. I'd be in one place, and they'd be in another. I think it's beautiful if two people understand each other. Understanding is as important as loving. Sometimes you love too soon and you don't understand, and as you go along, you wonder why you love at all.[25]

Despite her refusal to discuss sex and politics in the interview with Wammen, Ella answered a survey questionnaire by mail when she was asked to contribute to a book on the opinions of prominent women. Published in 1972 as *Open Secrets: Ninety-Four Women in Touch with Our Time*, the book focused on the emergent women's movement. Editor Barbaralee Diamonstein asked her prominent interviewees about "male supremacy," "male chauvinism," and "oppression." Fitzgerald took the task seriously, even overriding some editorial changes from her presumptuous publicist.[26] The overall impression is of a woman whose commitment to family ties and duties was formed in the 1940s and '50s but who accepted sex outside marriage. How much her answers related to her career versus her life is hard to say, even though some of her answers refute the stereotype of her acquiescence to Norman Granz. Still, a new generation wanted more candor than she provided in her old-school palliatives of covert power.

Men treat you as an equal? *Yes and no.*

"Women's Liberation?" *What else but that women want to be free from something or other? From what? If you ask me, there's some good in it, and some bad.*

Speak freely when you disagree with a man? *More freely. Most men will let a woman talk, and that's just what I do.*

Living in a man's world? *No, because as most of us know—there's always some smart woman behind every successful man. Also women today don't sit back. They do what they want to do—if it's taking care of a man, they do a good job. And men love it.*

If women had more political power? *Who really knows? Most women are telling the men what to do, anyhow.*

If you had real power? *I'd teach people everywhere to learn to live side by side, together, share, do together, all things including worship.*[27]

★★★

FITZGERALD HAD MORE SOFT POWER than she knew as a cultural mis-
sionary for tolerance and equality. In 1967 *Harper's Bazaar,* an elite fashion magazine with a circulation of around 425,000, included Fitzgerald
in their publication of *100 American Women of Accomplishment.* Her entry
reflected the transition from national treasure to international human-
itarian. "Music is the Universal language. . . . It brings people closer
together. And that is Ella, only Ella's very personal province."[28] The
Pittsburgh Courier quoted her: "I'm so glad the different schools of music
'dig' me because music has no boundaries, actually."[29] In February 1971,
after she concluded a set at the fashionable Elmwood Casino in Windsor, Ontario, with Jackie DeShannon's 1969 flower-power hit, "Put a
Little Love in Your Heart," she talked to a reporter more expansively
than usual about her cultural mission. "The love-your-neighbor theme
is one that Ella embraces and talks about privately as well as on stage,"
the reporter noted. And perhaps delivering a message to Norman
Granz, Fitzgerald said she wanted to record children's songs in several
languages: "I don't see why I shouldn't. I've been called Auntie Ella all
over the world and am a godmother in just about every country."[30]

A new album, *Things Ain't What They Used to Be (And You Better Believe
It),* recorded in 1970 and released in 1971, addressed race relations.[31] A staple of Duke Ellington's repertoire, the title song had a special agenda.
Dating from 1942, it had been handled primarily as an instrumental and
identified with alto saxophonist Johnny Hodges. Fitzgerald's rendition
revived Ted Person's original lyrics, quoted by Granz in the album notes:
"Got so weary of bein' nothin'," and now "Can see a glow / Announcin',
things ain't what they used to be." Granz added, "It's uncanny how prophetic they were in terms of how things have turned out, and inevitably
how they must continue. . . . For black and white alike, and especially
blacks, things not only ain't what they used to be, they never will be."[32]
Fulfilling her obligations to the Reprise label, Granz oversaw the project, hiring arranger-conductor Gerald Wilson, a master at integrating
big band swing with rock and soul. Wilson included electric piano and

Fender bass in his studio orchestra, providing a bloated arrangement on "Sunny" and a more polished treatment of the Afro-Cuban jazz standard "Manteca." In his syndicated review Leonard Feather wrote, "Ella is back home with her jazz family."[33]

Ella took one of the album's songs, "Mas Que Nada," to her free concert on July 12, 1971, in New York's Central Park, where she and Oscar Peterson attracted an estimated 200,000 people and Dizzy Gillespie was a surprise guest.[34] Here was one occasion when a mass audience of Americans heard the Ella Fitzgerald that Europeans knew from her touring. In an unusually favorable review in the *New York Times*, John S. Wilson described the "two extremes of her unique manner of vocalizing—a 'Body and Soul' that was a masterpiece of subtly built variations that took her from the very top to the rich, strong bottom of her range, and a slam-bang, eruptive version of 'Mas Que Nada' full of clicks, shouts and mutters that came on like a happy Saturday night brawl."[35] Later that month she sang an unusual date with her trio at an outdoor arena in Baalbek, Lebanon, not far from Beirut. "How well I remember that breezy July 1971 night when Ella mesmerized us," wrote journalist Magda Abu-Fadil in 2014. "It was magical, under the stars in the open-air temple of Bacchus. We couldn't get enough of the performance and gave 'the lady' a well-deserved 20-minute standing ovation."[36] After a stop in Rome, she reached the French Riviera for an evening concert at the Théâtre de Verdure de Nice, another outdoor site. Granz taped the concert, releasing it on the LP *Ella à Nice* in 1972.[37]

After the concert, Fitzgerald crashed for the second time with serious eye problems. Unable to see, she was rushed to Paris. The issue was retinal damage, a symptom of advancing diabetes that threatened blindness. Granz arranged for a private jet and accompanied her back to Boston. Her career would be sidelined for several months. If only she would take better care, Granz's friend Jacques Muyal, a French jazz concert producer, heard him complain. "She never believed in doctors," said Muyal. "This was tremendously frustrating for Norman, who was very concerned about her health."[38] Her stay at the Massachusetts Eye and Ear Clinic in Boston set a pattern of frequent eye check-ups that would follow for the rest of her life. According to newspaper reports, she was "briefly blinded" and underwent an operation to repair a "vitreous hemorrhage in her right eye."[39]

Loyal Arlie Small, her personal assistant and traveling companion since 1962, was also dealing with diabetes. She had been on leave but came up from Queens to comfort her. After spending four days with Ella, Arlie wrote to her friend Jim Blackman, "There she was, there alone with only Norman Granz and his girlfriend there in Boston and no one else to visit. . . . It was good for both of us and my prayers were answered when [on] the second day of my visits they had removed the patches from her eyes and she saw me."[40] "They were like sisters," recalled Small's niece Robin Robinson, who grew up thinking "Auntie Ella" was indeed related to her.[41] Grateful for the newly developed laser treatments she received, Fitzgerald did a benefit concert for the Retina Foundation in late October, one of many.

This time, after a four-month recuperation, Fitzgerald's return to the stage received some special attention. "Hello, glad to be back again, Ella," captioned her photo-ad in *Fabulous Las Vegas* (a weekly magazine delivered gratis on the Strip), when she began a month's booking at the Flamingo Hotel in November 1971. Relying on her vintage repertoire, she told the audience, "the charts have been changing so fast, I don't know which of the new songs to do, so we'll try some of the old ones." That was a rare admission.[42] She went back, in particular, to "Begin the Beguine" because "everybody seemed to like hearing Cole Porter again and I got good write-ups."[43]

By the early 1970s, Ella was a fixture in a slowly changing scene in Las Vegas. She was singing not only to middle-class white people but to a new audience demographic being courted by hotels—middle-class African Americans in the "New Black Entertainment Capital of the World."[44] What a "drastic change," *Billboard* had noted earlier that year, for Las Vegas hotels to "openly solicit black patrons."[45] The litany of praise that Fitzgerald accumulated in the press could seem habitual, but John S. Wilson remained skeptical in his review of her Carnegie Hall concert on May 13. Yes, she was in "fine fettle" with the Tommy Flanagan Trio, "but rewarding as her ballad singing is, her way with material at faster tempos still has a casual, disinterested air as though her mind were a million miles away. It is this manner that often gives her the appearance of not even knowing what the song is about."[46] Her vision problems may have contributed to this impression.

★★★

PERHAPS THE PLEASURE OF WATCHING "ELLA AND BASIE" dazzle crowds in one major European city after another prompted Norman Granz to come out of retirement. He started a new record label, naming it Pablo in honor of Picasso, which precipitated a change in Fitzgerald's artistic trajectory, as he had so often done before. He dramatically jumped into the fray by booking a concert for June 2, 1972, at the Santa Monica Civic Auditorium. The date was billed only for Fitzgerald and Basie, but Granz privately arranged for a sound truck and assembled a future roster for his label. "I know you came to see Ella and the Count but you're going to get more than you bargained for," he told the audience.[47] Then came the Jazz at the Philharmonic All Stars, an ensemble with musicians from JATP's glory years including Oscar Peterson, Ray Brown, Stan Getz, and Roy Eldridge, along with future Pablo leaders Harry "Sweets" Edison and Eddie "Lockjaw" Davis.

Fitzgerald, the "star" of the evening in Granz's presentation, provided a magical finish, bringing a message of Black activism to older white listeners in a format they could absorb. Her playlist underscored the impact of Black pop culture with her funky scat treatment of "Street Beater," the theme from the Redd Foxx TV sitcom *Sanford and Son*, which had debuted in January. In her Cole Porter good-luck charm, "Begin the Beguine," she interspersed names of the great swing era bandleaders, ending with Chick Webb. Introducing "Indian Summer," the ballad Tommy Dorsey made famous in 1939, she said, "I wonder how many remember this one." (Not many, judging from the tepid applause.) In "Shiny Stockings," a signature tune for the Basie band, Fitzgerald sang her own lyrics and "chatted" with the Count in their easygoing style, trading phrases backed by his crisp, tight band. She could still shake up a jazz crowd without the rock ballads.

Billboard reported that Fitzgerald's covers of contemporary material "shocked—literally shocked the stilled audience," performing Carole King's ballad "You've Got a Friend," which she described as a future standard, and Marvin Gaye's "What's Going On," a powerful anthem addressing the Vietnam War and the despair and violence within urban Black communities.[48] Her rendition captured the impressionistic, ambient dialogue and jazzlike phrasing of Gaye's classic record. Two years later she told a reporter, "I also dig Marvin Gaye. When I sang his 'What's Goin' On?' some people said 'Why are you doing that? It's a protest song!' I told them, 'I don't find it that way. To me, it's good music.'"[49] She would bring that message to a vast television public on the talk show of Johnny Carson in 1974.

The concert's grand finale was an eleven-minute "C Jam Blues." After Fitzgerald's scat solo, each of the JATP All Stars had their say, then "traded fours" with Ella in imitative, gregarious dialogues that displayed her skill and confidence and charmed the audience into applause and laughter. According to Fitzgerald scholar and music theorist Thomas Cleary, her scat work on "C Jam Blues" demonstrates how she had become "increasingly daring, agile and innovative as a soloist in her later years."[50] Decades later this performance still stood out in the memory of Ray Brown, who found it "very representative of what she was doing."[51]

A third health crisis occurred shortly after this triumphant display of her powers. The buzz and energy around the Santa Monica concert carried into a European tour, but after a performance in Verona, Italy, she suffered another hemorrhage in her left eye. The Massachusetts Eye and Ear Clinic saved her vision, but the best the doctors could say was that her eyesight was "functional."[52] She canceled all dates through October, and at least one columnist, Bill Lane of the *Los Angeles Sentinel*, questioned her decision to continue working at all. "She is already a landmark of wonderment and endearment all over the world where she has fans by the million. . . . [Entertainers] regard those crowds as their only true friends. But those adoring crowds also do not like to see their favorites stumble and fall incessantly, acting as if they have failed to hear that five-o'clock whistle blow."[53]

Fitzgerald rallied and retained some functional vision, but this time the experience had diminished her. In December 1972 Hazel Garland wrote of "a much smaller, older-looking Ella Fitzgerald," adding loyally that "there is only one Ella and she is still the 'First Lady of Song' as far as I am concerned."[54] Fitzgerald now had to wear unusually thick eyeglasses, both offstage and on. In public she remained her stoical self, spinning her recovery as a mix of fun and games at home with a little redecorating and self-improvement thrown in. "I've got more cookbooks than the library," she told a reporter. "I'm a very good diet cook."[55] To learn Brazilian Portuguese, she hired Oscar Szmuch, a native speaker and teacher, to give her six months of home lessons twice a week. As Szmuch recalled, "Ella was a good student. The funny thing is she was so humble." She told him, "I intimidated her!"[56]

Real life as she knew it returned in the fall. Fitzgerald described her relief: "When the doctor said I could go back to singing, my mouth went around my ears."[57] On November 29 a TV audience witnessed her renewal on *All Star Swing Festival*, a Timex-sponsored tribute to Louis Armstrong hosted by Doc Severinsen, the popular bandleader on *The Tonight Show Starring Johnny Carson*.[58] Originally taped in front of a live audience at New York's Philharmonic Hall on October 23, this grand reunion included Duke Ellington, Dizzy Gillespie, the Dave Brubeck Quartet, and Benny Goodman. Ella got good notices, delivering a sporty "Lady Be Good" with Count Basie at the piano, a playful "Goody Goody," a "Hello, Dolly!" for Armstrong, and a nuanced "Body and Soul," the hit of the evening. Jazz singer Betty Carter remembered,

> Ella Fitzgerald can swing like nobody else. I mean she can really romp and romp. This is what Ella is good at. Like the other night, I heard her on television. She has perfect pitch. She came out of a phrase on "Body and Soul," and when she ended up, she was right.[59]

For the finale, the band played "One O'Clock Jump" as all the musicians assembled onstage. As the credits rolled, Fitzgerald started dancing in place, and Dizzy Gillespie darted from the wings and spun her into a lindy.

Ella ended the year with two special bookings near home. At the Circle Star Theatre in San Carlos, California, she had a joyous and well-received week-long reunion with Count Basie and His Orchestra. Then she shared a six-day run with the Oscar Peterson Trio at the Los Angeles Music Center, where she was advertised as "America's Affectionate Empress of Song."[60] She recapitulated many numbers from the Santa Monica concert, and for her encore she romped through "C Jam Blues" with Peterson. Leonard Feather, by then entrenched as her advocate, called the evening a "hearteningly reassuring occasion . . . as if the audience's emotions were iron filings and Ella Fitzgerald a magnet of limitless power." The concert wasn't labeled a comeback, but it proclaimed her recovery from her fourth crisis in four years. She wore her thick glasses, "the better to see an audience that had been growing dim during the fight for her vision."[61] She had a plan; she had unlimited courage to tackle contemporary music from jazz to TV commercials. What more did she really need? That another swerve in a new direction would happen in the next year or so did not seem likely to her or anyone else at the time.

Chapter 26

"YOU CAN ALWAYS LEARN"

(1973-1978)

I n April 1973, just shy of her fifty-sixth birthday, Ella Fitzgerald was
interviewed by a young reporter to promote a gig at the Flamboyan
Hotel and Casino in San Juan, Puerto Rico. The reporter wrote
of "the great lady . . . looking as cool as her music" and "the earth
mother of music" who resembled "everybody's favorite aunt" offstage.
Warming to the interview, Fitzgerald focused on jazz music education
to counter the declinist narrative on the state of jazz in the early 1970s.
"Now kids are more music conscious," she said. "There's a lot of talent
coming out of colleges and universities. . . . They have the right systems and everything. . . . They know a lot about music which makes it
easier to sing with them. I can even sing jazz to them. Kids today have
rediscovered jazz."[1] Jazz education had grown dramatically in American
high schools and colleges throughout the 1960s, and in 1971 it reached
a milestone with the formation of the International Association of Jazz
Educators. "By the end of the 1970s, they had succeeded with hundreds
and hundreds of high schools and colleges," recalled Gary Burton, the
jazz vibraphonist. "Suddenly I found myself playing in South Dakota in
a high school cafeteria."[2]

Education and the renewed enthusiasm for jazz among young people
became staples of Fitzgerald's public conversation, driven by her own
perpetual self-improvement program. "I always feel like I'm learning,

if I can do one song different," she told the San Juan reporter. "Because music is such a funny thing. You can always learn." The reporter echoed, "When Ella sings, when she moves on stage, it's like learning how to live."[3]

Around this time Fitzgerald was prominently featured in a TV advertising campaign. The Memorex Corporation, pushing its cassette tapes, came up with the gimmick of a high singing voice shattering a wineglass, followed by a cassette recording duplicating the feat, with the tagline, "Is it live, or is it Memorex?" The first ads in 1971 used opera singers, but Fitzgerald was brought in to appeal to a wider audience, and her image proliferated in magazines and merchandising displays. She recalled,

> They asked me to do the ending of "How High the Moon." I just kept singing, "High, high, the moon," doing the ending. And when the glass broke, they said "That's the one!" Then I got the job. . . . A lot of people say, "Did you really break the glass?" We had to prove that. They had lawyers there.[4]

On another occasion she said, "I broke thirteen glasses. When I broke the first one, they didn't expect it, and they didn't even have the tape running."[5] A delighted Memorex executive remembered, "Ella took it to another level," giving the audience "the picture, voice, character and warmth in one package."[6] The TV ads showed her scatting before delivering the glass-shattering high notes, carrying the message of jazz improvisation as a magical force despite its vulnerability in the music business. She soon became informally known throughout the country as "the Memorex Lady." In Memorex sequels, she was joined by Count Basie, Nelson Riddle, and in 1979, a new pop star, Melissa Manchester. Even though Manchester crowded out her face, *Jet* ran a squib, "Ella Can't Live Down Memorex Tag."[7]

Fitzgerald found another, more substantive avenue to the general public in her appearances with American symphony orchestras, typically in the "pops" concert format outside the usual subscription series. The breakthrough came in 1973, when the celebrity maestro Arthur Fiedler invited her to sing for his Boston Pops Orchestra. Granz had never recorded Fitzgerald with a full-scale symphony orchestra, and she later testified that Fiedler had "started a whole new thing for me."[8] While the Boston Pops had introduced "light classical," Fiedler had earned a reputation for his interest in show tunes and jazz.[9] He told her he was an admirer of her *Cole Porter Song Book*, especially "Too Darn Hot."[10]

Fitzgerald's first concert with Fiedler was recorded at Boston's Symphony Hall and televised on the PBS series *Evening at Pops* on May 23, 1973, giving her major public exposure. George Shearing, Dave Brubeck, and Dizzy Gillespie had preceded her on the series, which was then in its fourth year. After the orchestra played Charles Ives's *Variations on "America"* and some Broadway standards, Fitzgerald, dressed in feathers befitting a swan, was brought on for a varied repertoire including her rousing "That Old Black Magic," her scat on "Lemon Drop," a Duke Ellington medley, "Good Morning Heartache" in honor of Billie Holiday, Gershwin's "'S Wonderful," and a current pop hit, "People."[11] She told the audience, "I'm a little nervous, because it's such a thrill working with him."[12]

She had some reason to be. Johanna Fiedler, the conductor's daughter, would write that her father "would find himself lost; Ella Fitzgerald, Sarah Vaughan, and Dizzy Gillespie with their freewheeling improvisational styles were especially challenging."[13] The assistant conductor, Harry Ellis Dickson, wrote, "A perfectionist herself, Ella ran head-on into Arthur, and Symphony Hall shook. Her music was arranged for full orchestra, but not the way Arthur preferred it for the Boston Pops. It was too loose." Another danger was her poor eyesight. "She could barely see the podium. . . . She sang from memory, never once referring to the music, which she could not have seen clearly, anyway." Dickson added that Fiedler "had no concept of what was happening" when Fitzgerald was scatting, but "even we long-hairs realized it was an artistic manifestation of jazz at its finest."[14] The *Evening at Pops* concert inaugurated an ongoing collaboration between Fitzgerald and Fiedler, which included dates outside Boston and her return to Symphony Hall in 1976 for a televised benefit concert for the Eye Research Institute. True to form, she sent him little notes of congratulation when the occasion called for it. Whatever his jazz shortcomings, Fiedler played a leadership role in bringing cultural awareness to the role of the pops format itself.

The "pops" concert was a classic American hybrid incorporating European "light classical" music and new works by Hollywood composers like Henry Mancini and Nelson Riddle. A new generation of white American symphonic musicians increasingly assimilated jazz in this format—they could "swing" better than jazz partisans typically granted. Other jazz–pop singers were exploring this crossover terrain, notably Sarah Vaughan, who began collaborating with Michael Tilson Thomas in 1974. After a concert with the New Jersey Symphony, Fitzgerald told a skeptical BBC interviewer that the orchestra was "made up largely of . . . young people" and that "the brass section was just out of sight. And we were so surprised because they were really swingin'. Some of them actually play in little jazz groups when they're not playing the symphony."[15]

Fitzgerald sang pops concerts with six other symphony orchestras in 1973, a pattern that continued throughout the decade. The late 1960s and '70s witnessed major growth in public and private funding for American orchestras, including, by 1973, over $80 million from the Ford Foundation alone.[16] In St. Louis on October 21, Leonard Slatkin conducted a pops "Sunday Festival of Music" featuring Fitzgerald and Gershwin's songs.[17] The previous month she sang Ellington tunes on an all-jazz program with the Cincinnati Pops, conducted by the "Prince of Pops" conductor, Erich Kunzel. Before the concert, a local critic heard an orchestra musician remark that "she looks like everybody's grandmother." "Maybe," retorted the critic. "But Ella Fitzgerald doesn't sing like anybody's grandmother. There's springtime in her voice."[18]

Fitzgerald was also proud that her pops concerts were breaking class barriers:

> I think it's a beautiful thing, because this way I feel that it gives
> the younger people a chance to really, not just hear jazz, but we

get a chance to present jazz as part of American music, as well as the classical music that they hear. And I think it's beautiful because then they begin to appreciate it a little more than they would if they feel that it's just something that they shouldn't know.[19]

Through pops concerts, Fitzgerald served as an ambassador for musical and social integration in a space rife with contradictions. In 1973 she gave a little-known concert in Byram, New Jersey, with the Newark-based New Jersey Symphony Orchestra, conducted by Henry Lewis, one of the few African American conductors then on the scene.[20] Yet overall, American symphony orchestras were barely integrated, which was particularly galling in light of government and foundation support for them. A 1974 poll of fifty-four orchestras, including all the major ones, found only sixty-seven minority musicians out of a total of almost 4,700.[21] As Dizzy Gillespie wrote of classical orchestras, "They're in the red all the time, but when we play with one, it gets in the black."[22]

★★★

FITZGERALD'S RECORDING OPPORTUNITIES expanded as Norman Granz's 1972 experiment in Santa Monica found solid footing in 1973 after a rocky start. His strategy of marketing the album *Live at Santa Monica* as a mail-order item failed miserably; "I couldn't give them away," he later said. But then a German executive from PolyGram in Hamburg heard the LP and decided to rescue the operation; had he not done so, Granz's Pablo Records would have remained a whim rather than a reality. As Granz's biographer writes, Granz was "coaxed back into the studio. Granz flew to Hamburg a free man and returned a player in the record business once more."[23] Pablo Records, founded in 1973, developed into a major label delivering mainstream jazz within the American market, and Fitzgerald benefited in the most unexpected way: Granz signed the guitarist Joe Pass to the Pablo roster. Pass was twelve years younger and unknown beforehand, but in him she found a muse and a partner who gave her a new outlet for her creativity. Over the next decade, reviewers and fellow musicians would comment on the special quality of their duets. Sometimes, in some negative critiques of Fitzgerald's singing, Pass would even be treated as an antidote to her jamming and scatting. He helped Fitzgerald discover what might be termed a modern cabaret style, which they perfected together. In austere duo settings, she honed her skills as a diseuse, cultivating expressive intimacy.

Joe Pass had a reputation for working with singers. In 1971 he backed Carmen McRae at Donte's Jazz Club in North Hollywood, resulting in the widely praised live recording *The Great American Songbook*—a title that helped codify an emerging historical category. In her liner notes, McRae wrote, "Joe Pass, without a doubt, is the greatest living jazz guitarist."[24] In 1973, with Granz as producer at Pablo, Pass recorded his classic solo album, *Virtuoso*. As Tad Hershorn wrote, "No artist coming into Pablo Records rose further and faster than Joe Pass as Granz began managing his career and mixing him in among the giants of jazz on records and in live performance, as he had done with [Oscar] Peterson to such consummate effect."[25] At first, Fitzgerald said, "We never took it seriously as far as us working together," but an important duet recording soon followed.[26] Recorded on August 28, 1973, and released in 1974, *Take Love Easy* encompassed nine standards. Pass's strumming halo of chords, placed high above her voice, illuminated her elegant twists and turns of famous melodies, compensating for any vocal aging.[27]

The recording session took Granz's spontaneous approach to an extreme. Pass could not quite believe the situation he encountered. Without a rehearsal, they both read from lead sheets—sometimes in pencil, and in one case in different keys—and Granz refused to allow second takes. Granz picked the tunes, and Joe and Ella worked out the keys.[28] Fitzgerald remembered, "We went in the studio late at night without knowing what we were going to do. But we were lucky, we got it right the first time, and sometimes it can take you months or years."[29] A few months later she smiled the experience into a gentle memory: "On the album we do songs that are what we call sexy. It's a little softer album with Joe Pass, our guitarist, and it's just the two of us. . . . You can see from the title, it's more of a love album."[30] Critics were relieved to hear Fitzgerald retreat from her soul-rock explorations, and the album won the Deutscher Schallplattenpreis, West Germany's version of the Grammy. In a four-and-a-half-star *Down Beat* review, Jon Balleras wrote, "This is a record to be savored late at night, at subdued volume, for its dominant mood is relaxed and muted, suggesting a kind of intimate conversation between Fitzgerald and Pass that we are fortunate to overhear. Ella sheds all her coy, little girlish mannerisms for this encounter."[31]

★★★

FITZGERALD'S FIRST FULLY ACTIVE POSTRECOVERY YEAR was 1974, filled with events, interviews, studio recordings, and a busy performance schedule in the United States, including an extensive European spring tour with concerts televised in several countries and glamorous appearances in Las Vegas with Frank Sinatra and Count Basie. She was back with renewed energy.

The year began with an all-star studio date with horn players Clark Terry, Zoot Sims, Eddie "Lockjaw" Davis, and Harry "Sweets" Edison added to a rhythm section of Pass, Flanagan, Ray Brown, and Louie Bellson. The LP title, *Fine and Mellow*, paid tribute to Billie Holiday's composition in the wake of the successful biopic *Lady Sings the Blues*, starring Diana Ross. The subtitle, *Ella Fitzgerald Jams*, acknowledged the added horns and rollicking spirit of tunes like Ellington's "Rockin' in Rhythm," along with the subversive send-up of the Gershwins' torcher "The Man I Love." Held back for five years, the album won a Grammy when released in 1979.[32]

On January 18 Fitzgerald gave a concert at New York's Avery Fisher Hall in conjunction with receiving a major honor: the Lincoln Center Medallion, previously bestowed on Dmitri Shostakovich, Fred Astaire, and Andrés Segovia. The presenter mentioned the Apollo Theatre as contributing to her beginnings, and she told the audience, "Without the Apollo and the fans throughout the years, this couldn't have happened."[33] The evening included a rare performance of "Checkered Hat,"

Norris Turney's whimsical tribute to Johnny Hodges, which according to John S. Wilson's *New York Times* review "brought out her most
expressive singing."[34]

The European tour from January 22 to April 11 was a feat of endur-
ance, taking in nine countries and forty-five cities, fourteen of them
in Germany. In March a reporter in Helsinki asked about her renewal:

EF: Well, I've just been sitting home listening to music, and enjoying
    some of the songs of today. Actually, I haven't been that far away
    from music, because I've been studying—trying to do some things,
    get arrangements together for coming back overseas.
Reporter: They say that your style has become much easier after that.
EF: You think so? Oh, well I think I'm a little more relaxed because
    I'm just happy, you know, that I can see everybody, and everybody
    seems to be so full of love and warmth, and I feel like a different
    person when I'm working.[35]

Recordings from the tour reveal a let-loose spirit on some novelties, jams, and unconventional arrangements of standards. In the medley
"Different Kinds of Music" on *Live in Cologne 1974* she parodied classical
music, Dixieland, country and western, the Basie and Ellington orchestras, and the *Soul Train* TV show, climaxed by an exuberant "It Don't
Mean a Thing (If It Ain't Got That Swing)."[36] "Ella Fitzgerald: The First
Lady of Jazz," a program taped for German Television ZDF, with no
audience present and Norman Granz in the control booth, shows off a
slow ballad treatment of "How High the Moon," with Fitzgerald lean-
ing on the piano in a duet with Tommy Flanagan.[37]

Bassist Keter Betts remembered that after thirteen weeks of touring,
"We were basically a family. . . . We're talking about four musicians on
stage—Joe Pass, Tommy Flanagan, Bobby Durham, myself, and then
Ella. . . . And then there was the lady who was traveling with Ella. It
was six people against the world. Every place we'd go, hither and yon-
der, our purpose was to go in there and conquer."[38] The tour wrapped
up with a two-week engagement at Ronnie Scott's jazz club in London,

and their closing evening on April 11 was broadcast on the BBC-TV series *Omnibus* and released on the Pablo album *Ella in London*.[39] This performance is a prime example of Fitzgerald's artistic development in her fifties, showing off the complete artist-entertainer as close to her audience as possible. In *Melody Maker*, Max Jones wrote, "Just about everyone who talks or writes about Ella Fitzgerald on this visit to London comments on the amount of laughter and friendly chit-chat in her present act, and on her stage disposition: less aloof and nervous than it appeared to be in the past. That is after they're done praising her singing, now more emotional than it used to be."[40]

Her voice had improved with her health, sounding less strained on the high notes and richer overall. After easing into the set with the old jazz novelty "Sweet Georgia Brown," Fitzgerald showed off a range of interpretations, from the British favorite, Cole Porter's "Everytime We Say Goodbye," to her bebop scat showcase "Lemon Drop." Her arrangements included more comic bits incorporating the musicians, as in her extended version of "The Man I Love." "Tell me all about him, Keter, tell me about my man," she said, and Betts answered with improvised bass lines impersonating a gossipy friend. Joe Pass also shone, especially when she took a difficult request to sing "The Very Thought of You," by the British composer Ray Noble, as a duet, even though she hadn't performed the song in years. While the flow of "thank you, thank you, ladies and gentlemen, thank you" still filled the space between songs, so did more stage patter and bolder interactions with her audience. In her wailing "Happy Blues" finale, she roared, "There's a little bit of soul in Ella, there's a little bit of soul in me," claiming the blues her way. She exuded even more independence in a *Washington Post* interview with the African American journalist Hollie I. West after she along with Count Basie and Oscar Peterson had charmed a middle-class Black audience at Shady Grove the following year. She was sticking with her script, saying little not already printed elsewhere many times: not wanting to be left behind, learning from the younger generation, embracing change as wise aging. West wrote it all down as the words of the so-called "New Ella," although it was actually the familiar "Adaptive Ella." Yet she did say something different on this occasion, displaying a refreshing healthy dose of ego: "I don't expect everybody to love my style of singing. For every one of those who don't like me, there are those who like me."[41] Undoubtedly, this inner integrity contributed to the aura of renewal despite her aging voice.

By mid-decade, few commented about Fitzgerald's aging voice, even if some critics noted the loss of that "little girl" quality. Instead, most reviews emphasized her bursts of renewal and newfound maturity in the wake of her eye problems. After a London concert with the Count Basie Orchestra in 1975, she could read in the *Guardian* that "it is probably true to say that her voice is clearer and stronger now than it has been for some time."[42] Norman Granz helped Fitzgerald forge a legacy of her late blooming voice in her fifties through several Pablo recordings released in the mid- to late 1970s. They followed a predictable course in tandem with Granz's attitude toward LP projects at this time. The establishment of the Pablo label and his discovery of Joe Pass had helped renew him as well, but only so far. He let the music projects come to him in a way. Live recordings were easier than studio recordings. Turn on the tape equipment over the course of, say, a famous jazz festival, maybe in partnership with an official national radio station or television channel, cut and paste a bit, and voilà: an album. Why not? He had the resources at hand: Fitzgerald's genius at reading an audience and extraordinary empathy she established with Count Basie's band, the stimulating creativity of her duets with Joe Pass, and a stable of former JATP musicians ready to fill in the gaps to make the occasional studio session happen.

Even so, it has to be said, recordings tell only part of the story that with some luck just may enhance and truly document Fitzerald's artistry in new ways as the tapes of loyal collectors become accessible to a new generation of jazz historians. Many collectors taped her TV shows in Europe and her live performances in other halls. Indeed, a few devoted, extraordinary collectors now possess private archives of live materials beyond the scope this biography can handle. We have yet to fully comprehend how she improvised her way out of vocal decline.

Private collectors' tapes have preserved the magic Fitzgerald possessed at her most famous outing in 1975 at the Uris Theatre (now the Gershwin Theatre)—when she and Count Basie and His Orchestra were invited to join a glamorous, highly publicized billing with Frank Sinatra in his post-retirement comeback. "Miss Fitzgerald walked on and pounced on 'Too Close for Comfort,' tearing it apart with vocal excitement," the AP reviewer wrote. Chick Webb's spirit flowed between her and Basie's percussionist Butch Miles, wowing an audience of her contemporaries. She and Sinatra reprised their classic duet on "The Lady Is a Tramp." Gross profits cleared a million, and the producers ran an ad quoting lavish reviews in *Variety*.[43]

Other high points of 1975 included a set of standards at the Montreux Festival in July, yielding the live Pablo LP *Montreux '75* with Tommy Flanagan in peak form.[44] In October she toured Germany in a Granz package titled Pablo Jazz Festival, and remarkable footage later emerged of a duet concert with Joe Pass in Hannover.

Fitzgerald recorded *Ella and Oscar* with Oscar Peterson and her ex-husband Ray Brown in May 1975.[45] Her marriage to Brown had long ago drifted far into the distance, yet their ability to make music together endured. She then resumed her ascetic alliance with Pass for her next studio LP, *Fitzgerald & Pass . . . Again*, recorded in January and February 1976.[46] With Pass exclusively on acoustic guitar, this LP stands at the high point of their musical empathy, as Pass also believed.[47] He accepted her suggestion to record "Tennessee Waltz," a massive hit for Patti Page in 1950, and they changed the 3/4 rhythm to 12/8, bending the melody in a subtle update. Echoing Fitzgerald's JATP colleagues from the 1950s, Pass remembered her obsession with repertoire: "Sitting in the car, backstage, in a restaurant, she's humming! She always has a tune on her mind. It's like a preoccupation with her. She's always got a melody going on in her head. It's always a piece that you've forgotten all about, haven't played in a long time or heard in a long time."[48] In February 1977, the year she turned sixty, *Fitzgerald & Pass . . . Again* earned Fitzgerald her first Grammy for a new recording in sixteen years. The category, "Best Jazz Vocal Performance," was newly instituted, confirming that the professional drought plaguing jazz vocalists might just be waning.[49]

★★★

IN THE DECADE OF THE AMERICAN BICENTENNIAL, Fitzgerald, often described as a "legend," continued to symbolize racial harmony as well as musical excellence. Coming of age in the era of Franklin D. Roosevelt, admiring Mary McLeod Bethune, and then embracing the leadership of Martin Luther King, Jr., she remained a liberal universalist who believed in music as a colorblind global blessing. Although she stayed away from controversy, sometimes it found her, as when she accepted an invitation from President Gerald Ford to entertain at a White House event honoring the Bicentennial on July 20, 1976.

The event, reported in the press but not televised or otherwise drawing much attention, was essentially a dinner with entertainment held for the Washington diplomatic corps. In a concert shared with country singer-songwriters Tammy Wynette and Roger Miller, she sang her Gershwin, Porter, and Ellington. The *Washington Post* reported that Miller "would have stolen the White House show completely except that he was followed by Ella Fitzgerald, who stayed nervous all the way through but sang all the better for it. . . . Ella admitted that she was 'all nervous because I feel like I'm doing an audition in front of our President.' "[50] Ford was not considered a champion of civil rights, and Fitzgerald told an interviewer that her political friends "called me a traitor, but I thought it was one of the greatest honors—singing before all the ambassadors. Who would have turned that down?"[51] Three months later, in October, she gave a festive weekend concert for the Congressional Black Caucus, singing Ellington and ending with the treat of "Ease on Down the Road" from the Black Broadway musical *The Wiz*.[52]

Fitzgerald's sense of responsibility to the Black world was shaped by the traditional ideals of service that she grew up with in Yonkers. In a long interview in November, Fitzgerald spoke of civic duty in language that reflected the Yonkers social clubs of her youth, echoing a late-nineteenth-century motto of her mother's generation, "Lifting as we climb," from the leaders of the National Association of Colored Women's Clubs.

We've been doing quite a few benefits lately. In fact, this has been quite a year of benefits, but I don't mind. I'm always happy to try to be around to do something for somebody who needs help. I deeply believe that none of us can get along without the help of others. After all, it took someone [Chick Webb] to help me. Doing a benefit gives me a good feeling. I figure that if the little people will get it together to do something constructive and they think enough of you to ask to help, and you're supposed to be the "big" person, then you shouldn't complain at all. . . . You should simply do it.[53]

Fitzgerald consistently channeled her philanthropy largely outside the white world, without aligning herself with any political movement or controversy. The act of composing "He Had a Dream" in memoriam to Martin Luther King, Jr., in 1968 was her first and only effort at translating her social conscience into song. Thereafter she lent her name and talents to fundraising efforts, often high-profile charity events within the upper echelons of African American society in New York and Los Angeles. Occasionally, all that she needed to do was show up in person, as at a star-studded Hollywood tribute to Fitzgerald in October 1976 to benefit the National Association for Sickle Cell Disease, though she accepted Mel Tormé's invitation to join him onstage for a scat routine.[54] In New York in 1977, she headlined a benefit to raise money for medical fellowships for minority students. An account in the *New York Amsterdam News* idealized the virtues of womanhood that endeared her to her generation in the Black community at large:

She is not well-known, except by those closest to her, for her humaneness and profound humility. Of course, she realizes that the world considers her "great" and a "star"; but she never gloats in that fact. Instead, she expends her energies doing whatever she can to help others accomplish their goals and aspirations.[55]

Spending more time at home, Fitzgerald became more active in liberal Hollywood causes, especially in the wake of the 1965 Watts riots.

She belonged to a women's organization called Neighbors of Watts, organized in 1969 and run by both Black and white women from the Hollywood entertainment community. This organization was dear to Fitzgerald's heart because it opened child care centers in the poorest Black and Spanish-speaking neighborhoods of Compton and South Central Los Angeles, helping working mothers. In March 1976 she persuaded Norman Granz, with his new touring outfit, the Pablo Jazz Festival, to donate the box office proceeds from a concert at L.A.'s Shubert Theatre.[56] In 1979 she helped start the Ella Fitzgerald Child Care Center in Compton, donating money and time over the ensuing years.

Occasionally Fitzgerald accepted invitations to sing or otherwise help with events supporting the recognition of jazz in American colleges and universities. In October 1974 she sang at a benefit inaugurating the Ella Fitzgerald Performing Arts Center at the University of Maryland's Eastern Shore campus, located in a predominantly African American area, and she continued her support afterward. In 1975 she took part in the annual Black Musicians Conference at the University of Massachusetts Amherst, along with Max Roach and Archie Shepp.[57] In October 1977 she was in Kansas City to support the founding of the Charlie Parker Memorial Foundation Hall of Fame. The weekend of concerts and testimonials honored Count Basie, who also received an honorary doctorate from the University of Missouri.[58]

Though her repertoire had shifted back toward jazz and the Great American Songbook, Fitzgerald stuck with her pattern of staying current with new material. She had her nieces as "informants" about current pop stars and named singers outside of the jazz mainstream in the same sentence as the in-crowd. She said Barry Manilow was "big in our house, along with Phoebe Snow, Dionne Warwick, and Melissa Manchester." In 1974 she grouped "Carmen" and "Sarah" with Helen Reddy, who had won a Grammy as the best pop vocalist the previous year for her feminist anthem "I Am Woman."[59] There is no record to date of Fitzgerald adopting that song into her book, but she was listening.

On a Grammy Awards show in February 1976, her scat improvisation with Mel Tormé won the biggest ovation of the evening. From 1975 to 1977 she appeared yearly on *The Mike Douglas Show*, and on April 28, 1976, she guested on *The Tonight Show Starring Johnny Carson*. In the November 1977 episode "Dinah and the First Ladies" from Dinah Shore's last variety show, *Dinah!*, she appeared along with Lucille Ball, Beverly Sills, and Elizabeth Taylor and turned in a solid jazz performance on "I'm Beginning to See the Light."[60] But thereafter, starting around 1977, she appeared less frequently on American television programs, signaling a decline in her public appeal.

In 1978 Tommy Flanagan, at the age of forty-eight, quit his post as her artistic director. He had played a crucial role within the most stable rhythm section of her career, along with Keter Betts and Bobby Durham. In 1973 Fitzgerald had called him a "genius," and she later attested that he "really started getting me singing what I heard inside and what I wanted to get out."[61] In 1975 she marveled that the trio "never know what I'm going to sing, how I'm going to sing and when I'm going to sing. But they're right there—all the time."[62] In the mid-to-late 1970s Flanagan's musical weight increased further in their collaborations.

When asked why he left Ella, he cited health, money, travel, and commercialism. "Her repertoire can't change that much because she is identified with certain things," he said shortly after striking out on his own. "What she likes to do is really be current—do commercial things. That's okay, but I don't care for that myself."[63] Flanagan soon advanced his career trajectory with widely praised duo and trio albums, knowing he had satisfied one of the greatest singers of the twentieth century. He kept the birthday presents she had given him, including a gold Rolex Oyster watch and a gold ID bracelet, and in 1993 he recorded a tribute album, *Lady Be Good . . . For Ella*.[64]

Fitzgerald carried on, but she was reading increasingly frank comments about her age, and writers' high praise for her relaxed confidence in 1974 and 1975 became less evident in later reviews. Reporters might be granted only fifteen minutes backstage and never get past her standard stump speech. In a 1978 interview at the Spoleto Festival USA in Charleston, South Carolina, Fitzgerald displayed the classic insecurities of her earlier years. "I don't know why people like me," she told the reporter, Elizabeth George. "How can I know? I suppose it's the music really." George wrote:

She pondered each question carefully before replying in a deceptively casual manner. And always with a smile. . . . She fiddled with an engraved, gold pendant from Duke Ellington. . . . Though she tried to avoid giving opinions, some gentle badgering uncovered her two favorite songs—"Nobody Does it Better" and "People." Those are her current favorites. She sang both for the Spoleto audiences. Neither sounded like their original hit recordings. They were better. They were sung only the way Ella can sing them. . . . A question about her retirement plans brought on almost a hurt expression from the First Lady of Jazz. "What would I do if I wasn't a singer. It's something I enjoy doing. I won't quit."[65]

At other times, the press gave her powerful reinforcement. After her Carnegie Hall concert for the Newport Jazz Festival on June 24, 1978, John S. Wilson wrote in the *New York Times*:

Her special triumph . . . was "Angel Eyes," sung with a depth of feeling that one has not expected from Miss Fitzgerald in the past, projected with the purest of her rich, warm tones and developed with great sensitivity for the mood. It brought the audience roaring to its feet in one of the biggest demonstrations of the evening, and Miss Fitzgerald, tearing through her glasses, remarked happily, "I'd better keep that one."[66]

What better proof could there have been that she still had much to offer? She was no longer young, but others her age or older were still out there, including her friend Count Basie, who was using a motorized wheelchair to negotiate the stage. One time, probably in 1978, Basie called and asked to visit her new estate on North Whittier Drive in Beverly Hills. Phoebe Jacobs arrived for a visit to find the Basie band bus parked in front. Ella explained its presence. "Bill called," Ella told her, saying that he and his band were "on our way to Japan, we want to stop off. Can you make us some sandwiches?"[67]

Chapter 27

"PUSH ME, PUSH ME"

(1979-1985)

E lla Fitzgerald enjoyed a remarkably fruitful sixtieth decade. With age came not only recognition from the public at large but also freedom within. In 1981, when asked that irritating question, she answered: "Retire? I don't think about it. If you just stop everything, and sit, you're losing part of your life."[1] In 1983, when she was sixty-five, she said, "I've always been very fortunate to have musicians who push me, and who inspired me to the point where you have to grow. That's how I feel about the business. I feel like if you don't have some kind of inspiration, you're nothing. It's like push me, push me."[2]

"A woman of valor who can find? . . . Strength and dignity are her clothing; and she laughs at the time to come."[3] Even some of her fiercest critics experienced her curiosity anew, recognizing a musical woman of valor. When John S. Wilson reviewed her September 6, 1979, concert at Radio City Music Hall, he reminded the reader that "one sometimes wondered if she knew what the words meant." Yet she "revealed an unexpected, free, fresh interpretive ability," and concluded, "Miss Fitzgerald's career may be entering an autumnal blossoming in which she reaches audiences and performance levels that were beyond her before."[4]

Earlier that year Fitzgerald had reached an American television audience through the special *Previn and the Pittsburgh*, which aired on April 3, 1979, on PBS and meshed conversation with live performance.[5] She felt at ease with its host, André Previn, whom she knew from LP and television projects from the late 1950s; he was now the artistic director of the Pittsburgh Symphony Orchestra. Conversing with him, she trotted out familiar anecdotes about "Snakehips Tucker" and the Apollo auditions, and she even repeated her usual "I'm not a musician." The urbane Previn affected the appropriate double-take at that remark. Backed by the Paul Smith Trio, she sang nine songs, almost all of them *Song Book* standards. On Ellington's "I'm Just a Lucky So-and-So," she did a few dance steps and inspired the audience to clap along with the beat: she had reached them. Previn went to the piano, backing her skillfully, and in an extemporaneous lyric, she thanked him, then sang an introspective version of "Like Someone in Love." She and Previn would share other collaborative projects, including benefit performances and even an LP in the 1980s.[6] As happened with TV specials, encore rebroadcasts reached many more viewers in later years.[7]

Fitzgerald's collaborations with Count Basie remained a wellspring of delight. Granz channeled their musical friendship into projects and touring that continued into the early 1980s. On December 9, 1979, they illuminated the TV special *An Evening with Ella Fitzgerald*, part of the *Soundstage* series produced by Chicago's PBS affiliate. In addition to Basie, the personnel included her trio led by Paul Smith and the Pablo All-Stars Joe Pass, Roy Eldridge, and Zoot Sims. Granz, overriding the regular production team, barred the usual live audience.[8] The wisdom of this decision was seen in the most dazzling segment, featuring Fitzgerald and Basie immersed in musical intimacy and oblivious to their surroundings. In "Honeysuckle Rose" she interacted with Basie's beguiling piano musings and scatted with effortless mastery. Then she improvised on Basie's theme, "One O'Clock Jump," for perhaps the first and last time.

Earlier in 1979 Fitzgerald recorded two Pablo LPs with Basie's orchestra, *A Classy Pair* in studio with Benny Carter's arrangements, and *A Perfect Match* live at Montreux—her last great statements fronting a big swing band.[9] The highlight of the Montreux performance was "Basella," a ten-minute romp adapting Ellington's "C Jam Blues."

Trading four-bar phrases with tenor saxophonist Eric Dixon and trombonist Booty Wood, she incarnated their respective instruments, to the crowd's delight. In the final choruses, as Stanley Dance noted, "her musicianship is even more glorious as she goes up over the final ensembles like a high storming trumpet."[10]

The pantheon of two eventually reached network television on May 18, 1981, when Ella and Basie performed a medley of hits from the big band era for a one-hour *Grammy Hall of Fame* special on CBS television. The program was watched by 14.9 percent of America's households—some 30 million people.[11]

The year 1979 ended with a grand flourish when Fitzgerald was named one of five recipients of the Kennedy Center Honors, a lifetime achievement award for performing artists. In the awards' second year, she was following in the footsteps of Marian Anderson. In a ceremony televised on December 2, Fitzgerald was joined by the actor Henry Fonda, the modern dance choreographer Martha Graham, the playwright Tennessee Williams, and the classical composer Aaron Copland.[12] With First Lady Rosalynn Carter substituting for President Jimmy Carter, who was then wrestling with the Iran hostage crisis, Fitzgerald sat in the President's Box and watched her friend Peggy Lee introduce her part of the program: "Ella Fitzgerald has become the standard by which the rest of us are measured."[13] After a tribute video, Count Basie and His Orchestra, Joe Williams, and Peggy Lee captured the joy of vocal jazz, ending with Jon Hendricks, another pioneering singer, joining them for a paraphrase on Basie's theme song "One O'Clock Jump."

Fitzgerald was thrilled and moved to tears.[14] "You know, you sometimes say these awards don't mean anything, but that's not true. It's always nice to know somebody likes what you do, and it's nice when they tell you," she told an interviewer the following year. "It's a once-in-a-lifetime thing, and it does mean something. I was crying, and I asked Tennessee Williams—he was sitting beside me—for his handkerchief, and I told him I thought I would just keep it as a souvenir of that night. He said, 'Oh no, you don't. You can't have that handkerchief. I'm keeping that one for myself because it's got Ella Fitzgerald's tears in it.'"[15]

★★★

AROUND 1981 FITZGERALD MADE FURTHER CONCESSIONS to age in her touring schedule. In Europe, the grueling six-week blitzes of one-night stands were replaced by shorter hops and three to four performances per week. She told a reporter she was home more often but maintained deep ties to Europe, where fans nourished her sense of well-being:

> How else could you have the opportunity to meet people all over the world and to find people who love you? I've been able to see the world, and everywhere I go it's like another home because I have friends there. It's amazing how loyal the fans are. I have one in Manchester, England, who writes me all the time, even sent me a piece of her son's wedding cake. Another in Scotland who writes all her letters in poetry. A man in London who sends me jams and teas. Another in Norway who always sends me cards for Valentine and Christmas.[16]

On her European itineraries in the early 1980s, concert halls in England and Germany remained solid bases of operation, and for five nights in April 1981 she and Peterson filled the mammoth London Palladium.[17] In July came an unusually vibrant performance at the Edinburgh Playhouse Theatre with Brian Fahey Radio Orchestra. The concert was released on LP, a rare chance to hear Fitzgerald with a classical pops orchestra in Europe.[18] The following year, at London's Royal Festival Hall, she sang with her trio and the full Basie band. "The voice is as flexible and young as ever," wrote Mike Hennessey. "She delighted a warmly responsive audience by singing the neglected verse of 'Blue Moon' and made a minor masterpiece of 'In a Mellotone,' backed only by Keter Betts' briskly walking bass."[19]

Most professional entertainers calculate and adapt to their audiences, and Ella had insisted on doing so as a virtue for decades, yet the breadth of her range in the 1980s seems ever more stunning. When she appeared in London at Grosvenor House with Oscar Peterson in July 1980, the reviewer described her classical restraint.[20] In the United States, where intense competition for a small jazz fan base persisted, her itineraries maintained their usual stunning range of venues in all regions of the country—from a pops concert in Cincinnati to a White House state dinner on October 13, 1981, for King Juan Carlos of Spain at the request of President Ronald Reagan.[21]

Starting in 1981, Fitzgerald performed several times at the Kool Jazz Festival, George Wein's renamed Newport Jazz Festival, now a traveling affair. Outside New York City, the depth of her experience allowed her to handle audiences of all sorts, a skill few could emulate.[22] On June 13, 1982, kicking off the Kool Jazz Festival in Pittsburgh, she faced around ninety thousand people jammed into Point State Park for the free concert. According to local critic Bob Karlovits, the audience included "badly behaved kids who wouldn't have known Ella Fitzgerald from Olivia Newton-John." He then described her step-by-step conquest of the "restless" crowd. It was genius at work, showing off her years of listening to people listening to her.

> Ella took an audience that could easily have gotten ugly and made it mellow. . . . The warmup act by the Jimmy Rowles Trio didn't soothe anyone. The shouts grew louder and coarser. . . . She put her first clamps on the audience by opening the concert with "We are Family" [a song that had become an anthem for the Pittsburgh Pirates]. That was just to get everyone's attention, though, and she immediately went into "There Will Never Be Another You." . . . The growl that opened the second chorus brought a round of applause and when she closed the number with one of those upper-register pokes that make your eyeglasses vibrate, the crowd responded heartily. . . . "In a Mellow Tone" gave her a vehicle for her famous scat-singing. . . . Playing the instruments in pantomime and swaying gracefully in her long, deep blue gown, she had the audience clapping and moving with her. . . . "Misty" had some people singing and dancing. . . . Her humor and custom-fitting of lyrics also drew heavy response. . . . By the end

of the concert, most of the crowd was on its feet. From gray-haired senior citizens to shirtless teens, the throng seemed to forget the hassles of the early evening and drew Ella out for three encores.[23]

Fitzgerald benefited from her new pianist, Jimmy Rowles, who had worked with Billie Holiday and Peggy Lee. Initially hired to replace Paul Smith for a month-long European tour in 1980, Rowles quickly adapted and stayed for about two years, suggesting songs for her repertoire. In 1982 he told Leonard Feather, "Ella changes her mind about tempo—one night she'll want it this way, tomorrow night that way—but it's a joy to work with her."[24] The singer Carol Sloane, who was in a serious relationship with Rowles and traveled with him, observed that "Ella loved Jimmy," calling him "my gray boy, white with lots of black inside of him."[25]

★★★

To FUNCTION IN SUCH VOLATILE TOURING CONDITIONS, Fitzgerald relied especially on Pete Cavello, her skilled and devoted road manager. Keter Betts also played an important role as a confidant to whom she turned for support. Rounding out Fitzgerald's informal network of intimates were her women friends, who traveled with her mainly as companions, especially the stalwart Arlie Small. On February 29, 1980, at the Fairmont Hotel in New Orleans, Fitzgerald asked the crowd to sing "Happy Birthday" to "my dear friend, Arlie Small."[26] In Arlie's last letter to Jim Blackman on March 17, 1980, she wrote, "I love the road, but I don't know just how long I can continue." Sadly, she died the following month from a heart attack at the age of fifty-eight. Keter Betts, who referred to Small, Cavello, and the trio as "the family," said, "That was hard on all of us. It was just the six of us—Ella, Arlene, Pete, and the trio."[27] The New York Amsterdam News, reporting that Ella flew in for the funeral, described Small as "her Girl Friday."[28]

June Norton, a professional singer who had worked with Duke Ellington sporadically, stepped into the breach. Norton recalled that she virtually hired herself. When Ella's nieces didn't step into the breach, she soon found herself on the road with her: "As the companion, and as a secretary and intermediary, anything I could do to make it easier for her to do what she had to do. When I see her get a little sad, to cheer her up, because Arlie had been with her a long time. She didn't need to be alone or with a stranger, she needed to have a friend."[29]

After six months, Norton was replaced by Judy Bayron Cammarota, who stayed for the next six years, through 1986. Like Norton, Cammarota initiated her hiring by a phone call. She had met Ella around 1940, when she played trombone with the famous integrated women's swing band the International Sweethearts of Rhythm.[30] They shared a booking at the Howard Theatre, and their friendship grew from the coincidence of having the same birthday. "That was when I was fifteen, and I've known her ever since," recalled Cammarota. They could rattle each other, and Carol Sloane said she occasionally helped defuse tension between them. Cammarota recalled Ella's long-standing fear of exclusion from the group, and after a visit from her sister, she heard Ella say, "What was you and your sister talking about? Were you talking about me?"[31] In San Francisco, according to Jim Blackman, Ella dedicated a performance of "Nobody Does It Better" to Cammarota, out of suspicion that she was having a love affair with one of her sidemen.[32] "Ella had an edge," André Previn once said, and sometimes the women taking care of her on the road felt it.[33] Then would follow apologies, little notes, presents, and forgiveness.

Jim Blackman, then in his thirties, was a fan who crossed the boundaries to become a friend and then even virtual family member. For years he had traveled to see her perform, and then, starting in May 1981 at the Fairmont Hotel in New Orleans, she began acknowledging his presence. "Ella bragged about having this fan all over the world who adored her," he said. Blackman witnessed a large sample of her audiences, remembering, "There were always young people there." Blackman developed a special relationship with Fitzgerald in the 1980s. After he moved to San Francisco in 1982, he caught her increasingly long annual visits to the Venetian Room, where he watched her transform that grand ballroom seating around 450 people into a cozy parlor. Night after night he noticed "subtle changes throughout each performance of the same song," along with the humorous banter, taking of requests, and calling up visitors like Tony Bennett for impromptu duets that felt like family reunions. Blackman recalled that when musicians from the San Francisco Symphony came, "She threw in a bunch of classical melodies, including operatic and symphonic melodies in her solos." He believed she did it without much forethought.[34] On April 12, 1983, the atmosphere was celebratory, as the California State Senate had passed a formal resolution honoring Fitzgerald for her illustrious career.[35]

When he visited her at home for the first time, she was living at 908 North Whittier Drive in Beverly Hills. She had purchased this grand estate around 1978, prompted in part by a series of burglaries at her previous home on North Sierra Drive.[36] Her new Spanish colonial home had six thousand square feet of living space in two wings. Palm trees shaded the circular drive in front, and in the back, the pool house had been refurbished as a cozy rehearsal space. Here she lived a life of relative ease, as Mary Jane Outwater in the Salle Productions office handled most of the daily operations and maintained the house. "Mary Jane loved Ella and would do anything for her," said Blackman. Oscar Peterson recalled, "Mary Jane became, rather than just her private secretary, a companion, in a lot of ways."[37] The "office" was Fitzgerald's professional family, so to speak, and sometimes she chafed under their efforts to protect her privacy. An old friend, Marian Bruce, found herself shunted away from visits, by whose orders it was unclear. Blackman reported Ella's advice: "Don't tell them you're coming up."[38]

Outside the Salle Productions office, Fitzgerald had a large extended family with a complicated network of relationships. The core triangle of Fitzgerald, her aunt Virginia Williams, and her cousin Georgiana remained intact in Ella's later years. Ella bought Virginia a home in Baldwin Hills, an upper-middle-class Black neighborhood in South Los Angeles. Dorothy Johnson, Virginia's unexpected last child, born in 1943, remembered "Auntie Ella":

My mother, my sister, and Ella . . . they were three the hard way. They stuck together. Ella spoke her mind. She was gonna tell you however she felt about it. She could be outspoken. She and my mother would do a lot of talkin' and laughin' at her house or she came down to my mother's house and sometimes she sent Chester [her chauffeur] to come and get her and bring her up. Every record Ella sang, my mother had a copy.[39]

Belonging to a different generation, Dorothy Johnson found herself a bit of a loner in a family whose early history she had not experienced. Georgie would tell her, "She's moody; don't go down to Auntie's today." Of her mother she said, "You couldn't ask her nothin'. . . . Leon [Dorothy's older brother] wouldn't say nothing about his mother. It's raised up in you. My family was secretive." By then her nieces Janice and Karen, who lived with Ella through the 1970s, had moved on, although Eloise's young daughter Valerie, a grandniece, remained with her.

No family is immune from tragedy; in Ella's life, the worst heartbreak arrived in late February 1982, when a grandnephew, Karen Gilmore's two-year-old son from a brief marriage, died. Karen was living with a new boyfriend, and allegations of child abuse were published in the press without the event ever being linked publicly to Fitzgerald.[40] Pete Cavello's family helped Fitzgerald cope with her grief. Not long afterward Fitzgerald was on the road with the Jimmy Rowles Trio, focusing on repertoire for her album *The Best Is Yet to Come*, which included her first recording of Billie Holiday's classic "God Bless the Child"—an apt outlet.[41] On March 5, where she appeared as part of the fifteenth annual Lionel Hampton Festival at the University of Idaho, she managed the date in a state of grief using the concert as consolation. She told Lyn Skinner, "Doc, I can't tell you why but for some reason I was supposed to be here." The jazz artists really believe in the spirit that's touching you. And she just said, "I felt the spirit knock and I was supposed to be here." So there she was. At a late reception, "Everybody wanted to have a chance to shake her hand," which she did from 1:30 to 4:00 in the morning. Then she asked, "'Would you like to have an Ella Fitzgerald quote that you can use when you're teaching young people?' Tell it to me. 'Here it is. Don't Ever Wish for the End of the Phrase. Think about that.'"[42] Skinner learned afterward that she had revealed her sorrow to the students driving her to the airport.

★★★

QUESTIONS DIRECTED AT ELLA ABOUT RETIREMENT seemed foolish and premature even as she turned a public sixty-five. Where was she supposed to answer them? Certainly not "in flight" in the lounge of an airborne Continental Airlines jet as a promotion for its first-class service, embarking from Chicago. Passengers received the new album *The Best Is Yet to Come*, and Continental commissioned a print poster from the well-known artist LeRoy Neiman, captioned "Ella in Flight." *Jet* magazine updated the number of albums sold from the repeated 20 million to 40 million. It reprinted standard Ella-isms, sloughing off the legend label, admitting that travel made men and friends impatient, and naming her favorite soap operas (*Ryan's Hope* and *The Edge of Night*). When the plane landed in Denver, she scatted "Lady Is a Tramp," hearing shouts from the crowd, "Work!" and "Don't stop, Mama."[43] Privately she told Leonard Feather, "I want to feel like each day I learn something else. Because otherwise then you just get stale with what you're doing. . . . and it's like you're not learning. But a new song, it's a little inspiration."[44]

In the 1980s, the climate for vocal jazz had grown increasingly favorable. Veterans like Betty Carter and Sarah Vaughan bolstered their careers, and a new generation of artists like Al Jarreau and the Manhattan Transfer revitalized the commercial potential of jazz-pop singing. At the Grammy Awards broadcast on February 23, 1983, Ella presented Miles Davis with his award for "Best Jazz Instrumental Performance, Soloist." Entering to a standing ovation, she was joined at the podium by the Manhattan Transfer, a vocal quartet that explicitly built on her legacy. Together they sang a one-and-a-half-minute version of "How High the Moon," backed by guitar, piano, bass, and drums. Janis Siegel's arrangement gave Ella a full chorus to scat against the group's harmonies, garnering another standing ovation. Siegel, who first met

Fitzgerald in 1976, recalled her amazement during rehearsal when Ella asked them if what she did was all right.[45]

Interviewers encountered Fitzgerald taking stock of her career. For a *Washington Post* feature she said, "Of course, as you get older, you start worrying about your vibrato and all that. But by taking some of my songs down a tone or two, I can do a full show without straining. And in the past few years, I've developed some low notes that I've never had before."[46] But even these valiant adaptations could not camouflage vocal erosion. Stephen Holden, an influential *New York Times* critic, took note in a review of her November 25, 1983, Pablo Jazz Festival concert with Oscar Peterson and Count Basie's orchestra at Avery Fisher Hall:

> There are few sights more unsettling than watching a great performer begin to falter in old age. When that artist is a musical Rock of Gibraltar like Ella Fitzgerald, one is reminded that all things, including even our most cherished symbols of permanence, must indeed pass. Miss Fitzgerald . . . is by no means finished as a singer. But many of her celebrated vocal trademarks . . . have crumbled. And her serene, achingly lovely soprano has acquired a wide, wobbly vibrato.[47]

Granz, meanwhile, was urging her to retire, in his characteristically blunt manner. Virginia Wicks reported that he vented his frustrations to her in 1981 or 1982, saying, "I have told Ella, 'You don't need the money! You don't need the money!'"[48] Wicks said she was "hurt for both of them":

> Norman was annoyed with her for several reasons. . . . I think Norman wanted her to stop singing and recording and playing dates some years prior, after she had her throat operation. He felt that she had enough money to live marvelously the rest of her life and why did she keep going. And of course Ella was hurt by his talking to her about that, and she felt she was singing just as well and wanted to keep singing one way or another.[49]

Still, from 1980 to 1983, Granz met his obligations as her record producer, through four LP projects that revisited formats from their past
successes while exploring new repertoire or new approaches to arrangements. The double LP *Ella Abraça Jobim*, recorded in September 1980
and March 1981, assembled nineteen songs, many of them unique to this
collection.[50] Her cabaret style was buoyed by beguiling arrangements
in a contemporary Brazilian feel, and the fifteen-piece studio orchestra
included virtuoso musicians from Brazil, Mexico, and Peru, as well as
jazz soloists Joe Pass, Clark Terry, Zoot Sims, and Toots Thielemans.
The album speaks to her ongoing sense of purpose and need to challenge herself, as she told an interviewer in 1984: "I like to feel like I can
try something else. Like we tried the Brazilian album. I think it's a good
idea when you learn. I think when you just stand still you find yourself
getting stale, and there's nothing to look forward to."[51]

Next came her standards album *The Best Is Yet to Come*, recorded in
February 1982 and reuniting her with Nelson Riddle.[52] Rather than
lament the loss of her original *Song Book* voice, she adapted, often lean-
ing on those "low notes" she was discovering. Granz had tired of the
conventional big-band-plus-strings format, and Riddle assembled an
eccentric ensemble including four flutes, eight cellos, and four French
horns. He remained a skillful word painter, opening up "Deep Purple"
with cello timbres to complement her new low range. *The Best Is Yet to
Come* earned Fitzgerald her twelfth Grammy (in the category of "Best
Jazz Vocal Performance, Female") at the 1984 ceremonies. "Too slick
and polite for my taste," carped *Down Beat*'s Jack Sohmer, blaming Riddle's "static arrangements."[53]

Riddle's account of the recording process belied the image of Fitzgerald as a passive conduit for Granz's taste:

> As far as the songs are concerned, Norman brings a list of songs
> which represent his choice of material for her to record, and Ella
> brings a list of tunes which she would like to sing, and they sit
> down, whether at his office or her home, and thrash the thing out.
> Norman has as many complaints about her choices as she has about

his, and whenever I'm present at one of these "song siftings," I am constantly amused, because through all the fuss and feather shines the respect and affection they have for each other. It seems obvious to everyone but the two principals.[54]

In 1983 she told her old friend Leonard Feather that "Granz has an irascible side" that she had "learned to live with." She further explained, "The idea was, get him to do the talking for me and I'd do the singing. I needed that. Sometimes we'd argue and wouldn't speak for weeks on end, and he'd give me messages through a third party, but now I accept him as he is, or I may just speak my mind. We're all like a big family now."[55]

In March 1983 Ella and Norman met in the studio for a far easier task: to record her and Joe Pass for their third duet album, *Speak Love*, still one of her least-known projects.[56] She added four songs to her recorded repertory, including Kurt Weill's classic "Speak Low," Count Basie's "Blue and Sentimental," and "At Last," a signature R&B hit for Etta James. "The Thrill Is Gone" showed off the virtuosity Fitzgerald and Pass inspired in each other, with an arrangement sequencing the 1931 torch-song standard with the minor-blues song of the same title that was immortalized by B. B. King in 1969.

The next project for Pablo was *Nice Work If You Can Get It*, an album of George Gershwin songs with André Previn on piano and Niels-Henning Ørsted Pedersen on bass, recorded May 23, 1983.[57] It courted inevitable comparisons with prior outings, when Granz had brought rough tapes to Ira Gershwin. On the scene, Michael Feinstein recalled that Ira had feigned approval: "Ira knew that if he didn't appear to love it, Norman might not release the record." For Feinstein, as for others, "the glow of Ella's voice had diminished, and for whatever reason the recording somehow just didn't gel."[58] In England, jazz critic Derrick Stewart-Baxter delivered a sensitive, eulogistic tribute:

I don't know when I have been so close to tears as when I first heard it. Here is an old, old lady, with little or nothing more to give, except a big heart and supreme artistry. Alas, time has caught up and she, poor dear, has little left to give us. Every bar she sings sounds like an effort—it is heart rending—but I would not be without this disc for "all the tea in China" (as the saying goes).[59]

Beyond the studio, a richer life in live performance remained for Fitzgerald. Granz recognized that her audience had "built up an appreciation for Ella, which in many cases has nothing to do with her records."[60]

Also beyond the studio was her multifaceted role as artist-citizen. In 1983 Jim Blackman asked her how she, a liberal Democrat, could sing for President Reagan. "Ella put me in my place," said Blackman. "She said, 'Well, it doesn't matter who the president is. It's always an honor to sing at the White House.'"[61]

Fitzgerald continued to participate in multiple benefits. As Phoebe Jacobs explained, "She believed, 'If they need me, I am there.' Somebody would call. Or they needed something in the veterans hospital, she would go."[62] Her charitable activities in Los Angeles remained focused on Neighbors of Watts, which ran a benefit in her honor in 1986. On March 21, 1984, at a gala dinner dance, Fitzgerald accepted the Whitney M. Young, Jr., Award from the Los Angeles chapter of the Urban League "for her outstanding contributions toward the improvement of racial equality." She was the first woman to receive the award in its eleven-year history, and her predecessors included Sammy Davis, Jr., Berry Gordy, and Sidney Poitier. A new generation of Black Hollywood stars gathered and danced to the music of Count Basie's orchestra, in what was apparently Basie's final performance before his death the following month.[63] The Urban League event generated a lavish photo spread in the *Los Angeles Sentinel*.[64] Ella responded, "Getting awards from my peers inspires me, makes me work harder."[65]

Fitzgerald's professional life increasingly centered on easily accessible venues, including the Marin Civic Center in the Bay Area, the Universal Amphitheatre in Hollywood, and the Paul Masson Winery in Saratoga. On April 12, 1985, during a benefit concert for the Faulkner Hospital in Boston, she tripped and fell. Joking with the audience, she continued to sing from her fallen position and finished the tune. After being escorted offstage to recover, she returned to finish the concert, earning an AP photo.[66] The fall was publicly attributed to a sprained ankle. That summer she kept her festival dates in Europe, with stops in Paris, Stockholm, Rome, London, and the Hague for the North Sea Jazz Festival.

In August her health issues became far more serious. A few days after a concert at Wolf Trap, the spacious outdoor venue near Washington, D.C., she was admitted to the hospital for "shortness of breath" and "some fluid in the lungs."[67] The concert was later televised on PBS, and she showed no signs of impending trouble. In a review of the TV broadcast, Jon Pareles of the *New York Times* found she "takes daredevil chances with every song":

> Demurely snapping her fingers, she darts in and around the beat, leaps from register to register and transforms the sound of her voice from Louis Armstrong's trumpet (in "Lucky So and So") to a melodic drum (in a scat-singing workout on "A Night in Tunisia"). She's light and playful in "Too Close for Comfort," torchy in 'They Can't Take That Away from Me," and she whoops it up in "Lullaby of Birdland." . . . The occasional imperfections show that she's still inventing on the spot.[68]

Fitzgerald treated the incident as a blip, despite the grim diagnosis of heart failure. She lost weight and began to look elderly and frail rather than merely older.

Her first public performance after the hospital stay came the following month in front of fourteen thousand people at the Hollywood Bowl, where she had not appeared in a dozen years. Backed by her trio and Nelson Riddle's thirty-five-piece orchestra, she "exuded an impression of radiant good health to match her perennial good spirits," as Leonard Feather wrote, though he added that her wobbly vibrato was "intrusive enough to be disconcerting to some lifelong admirers."[69] As time went on, critical diplomacy was increasingly abandoned, though some reviewers found new layers of her artistry to appreciate. Reviewing a June 1986 concert at Avery Fisher Hall, John S. Wilson singled out her rendition of "God Bless the Child": "The sensitivity and shading of her interpretation of this moving song was something quite apart from the usual facets of her singing and equally apart from Miss Holiday's version. To undertake the song was a particular challenge for Miss Fitzgerald and she emerged with a lovely, low-keyed triumph."[70]

In 1986 Fitzgerald was the subject of a pioneering half-hour television documentary, *Ella on Ella: A Personal Portrait*, for a set of programs profiling superstars by *Essence*, an African American women's magazine founded in 1970. Under the editorship of Susan Taylor, *Essence* had expanded its reach to the Black middle class and began a syndicated TV series in 1984.[71] Fitzgerald told her stories for a new generation, and Quincy Jones, validating vocal jazz as part of the core of jazz tradition, said: "Ella is an extension of what the beginnings of jazz are all about. It came from vocals. It came from instruments trying to emulate black vocal music. And Ella took it back to where it started."[72] With such glory, why contemplate retirement? In July 1986 she told the *Washington Post* she had slowed down enough to "know what's in my house," adding, "I'd feel embarrassed if I got out there and felt my voice was going. I'd let it go. That's what's so beautiful nowadays—you have the chance to keep going. I don't crochet, I don't knit. I love to sing. I love people. That's just me."[73]

On July 16 she performed at the Artpark, an outdoor family venue in Lewiston, New York, near Niagara Falls. "She'd been a little breathy at the concert," recalled her drummer Gregg Field. "The next morning at the Hilton, I'm standing at the desk checking out and the elevator doors open, and Ella is collapsing in Pete Cavello's arms, and she's saying, 'I can't catch my breath!' "[74] On August 19 Fitzgerald entered Cedars Sinai Medical Center in Los Angeles, and on September 3 she had quintuple-bypass cardiovascular surgery. Along with the incident in Niagara, AP and UPI issued widely distributed dispatches about her health usually based on press releases from Cedars Sinai Hospital or from the Salle office.[75]

The following year Ella told Leonard Feather, "It's funny—when I came to, I thought I'd been on a boat ride. I was saying to people, 'Boy, that sure was a terrible boat ride!' And they just fell out laughing at me. I now know all the soap operas."[76] Her inner circle assumed her career was over, and Salle Productions canceled all future engagements and terminated the contracts of her sidemen.[77] How she would fare after the necessary several months of recovery was open to question—unless you asked her.

Chapter 28

"DON'T EVER WISH FOR THE PHRASE TO END"

(1986-1996)

or a few months after the surgery, Ella could do little but rest, watch soap operas on an old TV in her bedroom, and listen to other singers. "At home I've got all kinds of records," she told an interviewer. "I like the young guy who lost all that weight—Luther Vandross. And the young girl with that new album—Whitney Houston. There are so many good ones now."[1] In April 1987 she described the recovery process to Leonard Feather:

> Most of the time I'm supposed to have my legs up. So just sitting like that could drive you crazy, and then I had the feeling like I couldn't do nothing else. I was getting bored and feeling like, "Oh gosh, when I am gonna be able to sing again?" And I just felt so bad. And the doctor said, "Why don't you have some rehearsals?" So then that's what we started doing. The first time that Paul [Smith] said we could have a rehearsal, I was so glad.[2]

If she needed a sign of hope for her voice, a random rehearsal provided it. Singing "Take the 'A' Train" in her den, her high note triggered a smoke alarm in the kitchen. They thought the alarm came from across the street, but a few minutes later Paul Smith answered the door and was greeted by the Beverly Hills Fire Department. "It was hilarious," said Ella in the Associated Press account. "I said, 'Is it Memorex or is it an alarm?'"[3]

On March 21, 1987, Fitzgerald's comeback began tentatively with a performance close to home, at El Camino College in Torrance, California. She sang a set of sixteen standards but left dissatisfied. "After the concert Ella came up to me," Jim Blackman recalled. "She said, 'I bet you wish you hadn't come down to see this tonight.' It was possibly the worst time I ever saw Ella. The audience was awful. There was tepid applause but not enough that would rile her up and get her to react."[4]

Her 1987 summer of recovery began in earnest on June 24 with a triumphant concert at Avery Fisher Hall in New York as part of George Wein's JVC Jazz Festival. In his *Boston Globe* review, Ernie Santosuosso called her "smashing comeback" the "lead story" of the festival.

> Fitzgerald seemed adrenalized by the cheering sell-out crowd and the transformation was dramatically heartening. As the crowd sent up repeated ovations, she paused and announced: "You are the therapy I've needed." . . . Her first four vocals seemed to be warm-ups, and then she went all-out on "It's All Right with Me," in which she seemed to be making a personal statement as well. Then, it was apparent she had turned the corner on the next tune, a hat-hoisting rendition of "In a Mellow Tone." . . . Fitzgerald . . . was now in total command on a couple of sambas, "Água de Beber" and "One Note Samba," and scatted wildly on "Manteca." With Pass accompanying, she sang a half-dozen standards and . . . brought her return to Manhattan to an explosive, heartwarming climax with the vocalese-scat interpretation of "Flyin' Home" and was accorded a tidal wave of cheers as she encored with "Mack the Knife."[5]

Santosuosso reported a huge set of twenty-two songs. On July 5, to close out the Montreal International Jazz Festival, Fitzgerald sang to a capacity crowd of three thousand. Longevity and diversity reframed

Fitzgerald's concerts into homages to vocal jazz. "The show was a whirlwind course in jazz history," wrote the reviewer, naming Gershwin, Rodgers, Duke Ellington, and Dizzy Gillespie.[6]

★★★

FOR THE REST OF THE 1980S and into the '90s, the constant touring she had sustained right through her sixties yielded to around seven to fifteen dates a year. She was "beset by health problems in recent years," captioned a photo in a September 1987 montage.[7] But she remained a box office wonder. Besides her favored hotel venues in San Francisco and Toronto and scattered university dates, she played the Hollywood Bowl from 1988 to 1992 and routinely sold out large halls. In New York City her draw at Radio City Music Hall made *Billboard*'s "Boxscore of Top Concert Grosses" every year from 1989 to 1992. Few women or Black artists made these lists, and she was the only jazz singer represented, yet she was slotted alongside the likes of rock and pop stars Eric Clapton, Bryan Adams, the Pet Shop Boys, and Bon Jovi—a remarkable achievement.[8]

The 1980s are often characterized as a "neoclassical" era in jazz, when musicians explored and negotiated the music's history as a wellspring for the present. Fitzgerald—a virtual encyclopedia of jazz practice and repertoire—was burnishing her legacy and remained popular and influential at a time when a new generation of fans and musicians were eager to understand the vocal jazz tradition she had pioneered. At the same time, the impact of her performances depended far more on her vocal courage. Audiences of these late years valued her spontaneity and the exhilaration of her signature scatting. At her Carnegie Hall concert on June 24, 1988, the AP reporter noted that the crowd "seemed to be mostly in their 20s and 30s. . . . There were spontaneous standing ovations and cheering at particularly telling bits of scat singing, growling imitations of Louis Armstrong and triumphant high notes."[9]

"She's 70—going on 17," began Steve Zipay's long review of her Radio City Music Hall concert on February 11, 1989. "Boys and girls," she told the audience, "this is home. I'll try to mix in a little of everything tonight. . . . The only thing I don't have is rap—but I'll try anything once!" Reported Zipay, "And later she did."[10]

Such virtuosity rarely reached the mainstream American public, which typically regarded her as an aging, generic emblem for jazz when it noticed her at all. Occasionally, however, the vast power of television reminded everyone that she was still a vital artist. On January 16, 1988, she left a strong impression on the NAACP's Image Awards show, where she received the first-ever President's Award for lifetime achievement. After singers Nancy Wilson and Al Jarreau reprised "A-Tisket A-Tasket," a tiny old lady was led to the stage to a standing ovation. The longer she spoke, the younger she seemed:

> This is such a great honor. Such a thrill, with all the talent that we've had here tonight. Aren't you proud of them? I am [applause]. . . . Thank you and I'm so proud to be in a class with all of these younger ones coming up. They ain't gonna leave me behind, I'm learning how to rap! They told me to sing something, the only thing I know that I could do. I haven't rehearsed with the band.[11]

Then she courted the crowd with Stevie Wonder's classic "You Are the Sunshine of My Life," humming like a soul singer, shaping words through dynamics, scatting a bit, and patting her hand on the podium while the camera panned the celebrity audience to prime emotional reactions.

Attending that night was her friend Dionne Warwick, who won the NAACP award for "Entertainer of the Year," and Warwick's niece Whitney Houston. Ella had already met Houston at a Grammy Awards ceremony in the mid-1980s, as recalled by Pete Cavello's daughter Kathy, who was backstage afterward:

Whitney came over to me and she referred to Ella as our aunt. She goes, "I want to be just like your aunt one day." I didn't know who this person was. And then Ella came over and said, "She's going to be a big star one day. And us ladies [Ella and Dionne], we're going to mentor her and make sure to get her straight because this girl is so talented."[12]

On October 6, 1989, Fitzgerald performed in Paris for Le Gala du Siècle, the centennial show of the historic Moulin Rouge cabaret in Montmartre. The program included French idols Charles Aznavour and Charles Trenet, along with white American stars Donald O'Connor, Lauren Bacall, and Mickey Rooney. Fitzgerald and Ray Charles, representing Black American music, polished off the blues "Route 66" in a duet that got up to speed by the end. "Come on, Ella," "Let's go, Ella," "I love you, Ella," he said on the televised special.[13]

Fitzgerald appeared far more tentative in another network TV cameo on November 13, 1989, when she closed a two-hour tribute to Sammy Davis, Jr., benefiting the United Negro College Fund. Escorted to the stage by Michael Jackson and comedian Eddie Murphy, she looked elegant but sang a dull "Too Close for Comfort."[14] Feeling tired, she greeted Sinatra, who had opened the program, in her dressing room, but avoided contact with the many artists waiting in the green room. After securing Michael Jackson's autograph for her nieces, she left before the group photo, while Jim Blackman took out plates of food from the catered dinner to eat at home.[15] At the 32nd Grammy Awards show on February 21, 1990, Fitzgerald was joined by Natalie Cole at the podium to present the "Album of the Year" award to singer Bonnie Raitt. Ella had known Natalie since her childhood, and Natalie's father, Nat King Cole, had been honored with a posthumous "Lifetime Achievement" award. At the podium they sang only a cursory, half-minute version of "Straighten Up and Fly Right," Nat Cole's 1943 hit, which Fitzgerald had covered since at least 1961.[16]

★★★

FITZGERALD'S BATTLE WITH DIABETES had been largely hidden from the public. It is not clear when she first heard the diagnosis of "having sugar," as it was often referred to in the African American world, but Arlie Small mentioned "borderline" diabetes in the early 1970s, and Ella herself mentioned it to Leonard Feather in March 1987. Her side effects associated with Type 2 diabetes can be traced back at least to the early 1970s, when she suffered from eye problems. In the 1980s the disease led to heart and circulation trouble, and in the 1990s, to kidney damage requiring dialysis.

In August 1987 one of her toes was amputated.[17] The operation seemed minor compared to bypass surgery, yet it increased the potential for falls, and her concert stages were marked with white tape. In July 1988 she fell on the wooden apron of the stage at the Hollywood Bowl. Several thousand people gasped at once, among them James Standifer, a music professor at the University of Michigan. When Fitzgerald appeared in Ann Arbor the following year, Standifer interviewed her and mentioned the incident, revealing her emotional bond with her audience:

Standifer: There was one lady in front of me and she said, "Oh, my Lord, God," and they had to get a doctor for her because they were fanning her, you know, like in the old black churches. . . . But that night! And to see you sing after that, I mean, how did you . . . ?

EF: It was funny. My heart doctor, my foot doctor, my [regular] doctor—they were all sitting in the front row. They told me I had to learn how to sit on a stool and not stand during a two-and-a-half-hour concert.

Standifer: This would drive me nervous. This is not Ella—sitting and singing. You've given love for a long time to this country, and I'll even be a little bit selfish—to black people, too. I think my daughter thinks that. She said, "Dad, I want to be like Miss Fitzgerald." So, every kind of concert you have, I bring her. . . . So, you've given a great deal of love. More than perhaps you've ever received.

EF: Oh, no. I don't think so. . . . I don't think I could work if I felt that I wasn't satisfying the audience.[18]

Every concert was a challenge. How many steps to the stage? Could she find a comfortable position on that uncomfortable saloon stool? She also struggled with memory loss. During the rehearsal for a pops concert with the San Francisco Symphony on August 3, 1989, pianist Mike Wofford had to play the melody of "Blue Moon" in a vain attempt to prod her memory. "Let's leave it," she said in frustration. At the concert itself, she rallied.[19] The following year she rejoined the San Francisco Symphony, and conductor Andrew Massey recalled,

> By that time, Ella had suffered a lot of damage from diabetes, and could not walk all that well. So to get on stage, she had to take my arm as I helped her up over a couple of steps out onto the stage. The hall was of course filled to its 3,000 capacity with people who had paid quite a bit and were thrilled to see her. For me, just to be there, hearing the instantaneous roar of the crowd, as we stepped into view, Ella on my arm—the roar was not for me, of course— brought tears to my eyes. . . . On a couple of occasions she didn't seem at all sure which song came next, even as the intro began. So I had to lean over to her to tell her. But the singing was as solid as ever. . . . Backstage, she sat in her dressing room and members of the San Francisco Symphony came to her to pay homage sincerely, and she was so humble. "I can't believe players in this great orchestra are being so kind to me." We had no problem believing![20]

★★★

FITZGERALD'S RECORDING PROJECTS had subsided along with her itineraries, but in 1988 her younger self magically reappeared with a discovery from the Verve vaults. Unearthed by the historian-DJ Phil Schaap, *Ella in Rome: The Birthday Concert*, which had been recorded on April

25, 1958, surged to number one on jazz best-seller lists.[21] "Some little guy found a tape of me, and now I'm number one," Fitzgerald told the youthful crowd at Carnegie Hall in June. Before the concert, Schaap played the recording for her. "She was 100 percent positive the record was a catalyst to the reactivation of her career at this time," he said. "She agreed with me it was her best ever '[I Loves You] Porgy.' She loved it!"[22]

After a three-year absence from the studio, and feeling fully recovered from her surgery, Fitzgerald decided to challenge herself and Norman Granz with what turned out to be their last LP project, *All That Jazz*, recorded in Los Angeles in March 1989.[23] Jazz critic John McDonough asked to attend the sessions, but Granz declined. "Sorry," he wrote McDonough. "It's her first session in a long time, and she's not that sure of herself or how well it will go. She'd rather not."[24] Granz had been urging her to retire, but nevertheless he found a way to frame a declining voice and highlight her musical integrity with top musicians and fresh material, including standards she hadn't recorded in decades and other songs with autobiographical resonance. "The Jersey Bounce" was by Tiny Bradshaw, the bandleader who had backed her at the Harlem Opera House in 1935. "My Last Affair," a ballad she first recorded for Decca in 1936, had competed for play with renditions by her swing sisters Billie Holiday and Mildred Bailey. "Little Jazz" was a wordless scat tribute to Roy Eldridge, who had died a month earlier. "Just When We're Falling in Love" was a reworking of the bebop tune "Robbin's Nest," with lyrics substituted by Jon Hendricks in 1952. Fitzgerald had sung "Robbin's Nest" in 1949 at the Royal Roost with her husband, Ray Brown, who rejoined her for the *All That Jazz* sessions forty years later. A newcomer on the roster, pianist Mike Wofford, remembered:

> Ray Brown was kind of telling everybody what to do. She just kind of let Ray do his thing. He was an assertive guy. He was brilliant at putting together head arrangements. That last album is not prime top Ella, with her loss of range and power, but I think it is pound for pound up there with some of her best recordings. . . . She didn't have to be Ella. She could just have a good

time being with the guys, like [Harry] Sweets [Edison], Benny Carter, Al Grey. It was just like a jam session that turned into a record. That's basically what it was.[25]

Reviewers accepted the tradeoff of wisdom and loss, more or less. In the consequential UPI syndicated review, Ken Franckling wrote, "The pipes aren't quite what they were when the marvelous Ella Fitzgerald was in her prime, but the reigning queen of jazz singers still knows how to ride a swinging beat."[26] In the *Boston Globe*, Michael Ullman found her voice listless, sometimes off-pitch, and "unnerving" despite the brilliant accompaniment.[27] In January 1992 Fitzgerald returned to the studio and recorded several tracks that were never released, as she was unhappy about the quality of her voice.

Despite the mixed reviews, *All That Jazz* won the 1990 Grammy for "Best Jazz Vocal Performance, Female."[28] That same year the academy bestowed multiple awards, including "Album of the Year," on the Quincy Jones CD *Back on the Block*, a multimovement oratorio organized around his own stylistic journey, with an ecumenical message about the continuities of African American music. Along with solo and scat passages from the likes of Miles Davis, Dizzy Gillespie, and Sarah Vaughan, Jones mixed Ella's scatting into the rap movement "Jazz Corner of the World" as well as into his inventive arrangement of "Birdland," a jazz-fusion standard by keyboardist Joe Zawinul. One of the biggest joys of the album, Jones said, was going back to his roots. "I recorded with Ella thirty years ago. It was like going home to a big family."[29]

Fitzgerald flew to New York City for one of the greatest musical tributes she enjoyed in her lifetime: a three-hour concert titled "Hearts for Ella" on February 12, 1990, at Avery Fisher Hall, benefiting the American Heart Association. "I wanted her to know we hadn't forgotten her," said producer Edith Kiggen, who collaborated with Ella's friend, the eighty-two-year-old Benny Carter, who assembled a "dream band" and served as music director. Among Carter's innovative ideas was to have Billy Byers arrange Fitzgerald's classic 1947 improvisation on "Lady Be Good" for the band, demonstrating its musical excellence and logic.

"When she goes into her improvisations on that record, everything she does following the opening chorus of that song is a composition," Carter told *Newsday*.[30] Kiggen explained that she "didn't want any lady singers" at the concert, unintentionally evoking the long road Fitzgerald had had to travel for acceptance as a jazzwoman. Kiggen added, "The whole deal is not about singing but about music." In a brilliant stroke, she asked Itzhak Perlman, a celebrity classical violinist with crossover jazz chops, to co-host the evening with Lena Horne, who declined to sing.[31] Among the performers were Cab Calloway, Melissa Manchester, the Manhattan Transfer, and Bobby McFerrin.

At the end of the show, Fitzgerald claimed the spotlight. "If she needs me to carry her on stage, I will," Dizzy Gillespie was heard to say earlier.[32] She sang "Honeysuckle Rose," then traded fours with Joe Williams and Clark Terry on "Lady Be Good." A critic from the *Chicago Tribune* wrote, "Fitzgerald turned inward, pulling out vocal runs that were as inventive and joyful as they were six decades ago."[33] Reviews strained the thesaurus of superlatives, with Leonard Feather writing of "an ovation that verged on levitation."[34] Traveling to the airport for the flight back to Los Angeles with her nieces Janice and Karen, she expressed familiar gratitude for the musical validation from "musicians," meaning instrumentalists. She had taken a previous award from the Society of Singers in stride, but as Jim Blackman recalled, "she couldn't get it out of her head that musicians had flown in from all over the country to sit in a band in a tribute to her. 'Where would I be without them, without the *musicians*, because that's who I came up with.'"[35]

Three weeks later Fitzgerald began her last round of tours in Europe. Her London stay in March 1990 included three nights of sold-out concerts at the Royal Albert Hall, with a promotional tie-in for the branding launch of Jazz FM, which called itself "Britain's First Jazz Radio Station." A marketing survey for the new station had determined that 60 percent of the British public didn't like jazz, but Ella, Billie Holiday, George Benson, and Nat King Cole had much better polling numbers. "I hope the regular jazz people will be patient," a radio executive told a reporter, implying that Fitzgerald's music was a commercial concession.[36]

Condescension surfaced again during a TV talk show hosted by Michael Aspel. After singing Cole Porter's "It's All Right with Me," she took the interview chair, and the conversation turned to soap operas. Fitzgerald said she would someday like to perform the theme from *Neighbours*, the Australian hit soap. Aspel raised his eyebrows at this lowbrow idea and mocked the melody. Fitzgerald held her ground, turning away from Aspel to address the studio audience. "I think it's a pretty song," she said. "But the lyrics, I'm listening to the lyrics. I mean, to think you have a neighbor and you love each other and you share things. That was the main reason I liked the song, 'cause I felt that that's something that we should all try to be, neighbors, where we share and love each other." Then she retook the stage for Burt Bacharach and Hal David's "A House Is Not a Home."[37]

For the *Evening Standard*, a London tabloid, Fitzgerald was interviewed by Caroline Phillips, a celebrity journalist with a reputation for candid, sometimes insulting, sometimes astute portraits. Phillips described Fitzgerald as a wise soul, "gentle and serene" and "irrepressible," yet possessed of "self-irony" and protective of her privacy in a manner that had stymied American interviewers for decades: "There's a palpable feeling that this lady's real delicate; that she could be easily offended—and just shut her mouth; a mouth that's full of politesse."[38] For the *Observer*'s Clancy Sigal, Ella hopped around on one foot to demonstrate her balance exercises. "She is a conservative woman," wrote Sigal, and in a rare moment of reproach, she criticized the younger generation as spoiled and neglected.[39]

For the Royal Albert Hall concerts, she was backed by Count Basie's posthumous band, directed by Frank Foster. The *Financial Times* review began:

> The old lady was carefully supported on to her stool. She stared myopically around the vast auditorium. The audience collectively suspended criticism in favour of respect for the past—and then got the shock of their life. Ella Fitzgerald, rising 72, launched into a

version of "Too Close for Comfort" with as much verve and attack as a Spitfire.[40]

Two months later Fitzgerald returned to Europe with Joe Pass and the Mike Wofford Trio for several prestigious dates, some of them broadcast live on radio and television. In Munich the concert was televised, and in her vocal jam on "A Night in Tunisia" she sounded vibrant and delighted with herself. "Every concert a little reunion," wrote Hans Ruland, who produced a two-hour retrospective on Fitzgerald for his radio program, *Jazz Welle*. He wrote of her thick glasses and "little small steps" and was "visibly shocked by her condition." How extraordinary that she called him to say thank you and ask what she could do for him. They met at her hotel the next day:

> She was just happy to be able to speak to someone who knows and loves her world. It quickly becomes clear how lonely a person can be who is worshipped by millions. And how dependent the stars are on their audience. She wanted to get on the stage every day, but the doctors had given her a rest period of at least five days between each performance. For her this means sitting in the hotel for five days, waiting. The accompanying musicians cannot afford this luxury, take on other obligations in between, and only join her on the evening of the next performance.[41]

Fitzgerald received even more attention in France, where she had come to symbolize both individual artistry and the Black experience in music. In 1987 the very popular French pop singer France Gall released her single of Michel Berger's "Ella, elle l'a" ("Ella has it"). It reached the top of the charts in Austria, Germany, and France, its lyrics comparing Ella to "joy" itself, suggesting that she articulates the history of African American people "swinging / between love and despair."

Before her concert at the Palais des Congrès de Paris on May 28, 1990, French culture minister Jack Lang awarded Fitzgerald the nation's high honor as Commandeur des Arts et des Lettres. She also collected another French Gold Record for *Pour l'amour d'Ella*, a double-CD compilation on Verve.[42] That summer exhaustion prevented her from traveling to the Netherlands for the North Sea Jazz Festival, which had planned a "Gala for Ella" in her honor.[43]

Fitzgerald's health declined over the next two years. On July 15, 1992, she appeared at the Hollywood Bowl for the last time in a concert conducted by her friend Benny Carter. "Her superb rendering of 'Good Morning Heartache' would surely have drawn a smile of approval from Billie Holiday," wrote Don Heckman in the *Los Angeles Times*.[44] On August 2 at the Circle Star Theatre in San Carlos, California, her foot was bandaged, and she sang the second set from a wheelchair. Scrambling to keep the lyrics straight in "Sweet Georgia Brown," she repeated the phrase "two left feet" and laughed at her condition as well as her mistake.[45]

On November 28, 1992, Ella Fitzgerald gave her last known public performance at the gala opening of the Kravis Center for the Performing Arts in West Palm Beach, Florida. Actor Burt Reynolds emceed, and Ella joined an elite roster of artists including the comedian Lily Tomlin, the Alvin Ailey American Dance Theater, and classical musicians Roberta Peters, Isaac Stern, and Leontyne Price. Sitting in a wheelchair with her bandaged foot in plain view, Fitzgerald somehow managed to upstage them all, at least according to one review praising her "indomitable spirit" and "miraculously supple voice."[46] Mike Wofford, Keter Betts, and Bobby Durham backed her on a set that included "Do Nothing Till You Hear from Me," "What Will I Tell My Heart," "Angel Eyes," "Good Morning Heartache," "As Time Goes By," "A House Is Not a Home," and a medley from *My Fair Lady*.[47]

In December she was unable to attend the White House ceremony to receive her Presidential Medal of Freedom, the country's highest civilian award. She was the fourth jazz artist to receive the award, following Duke Ellington in 1969, Eubie Blake in 1981, and Count Basie in 1985. Her citation captured the essence of her mainstream reputation, praising not only her "trademark scat" but her iconic status worldwide: "As a cultural ambassador, her impressive vocal range stretches across oceans and political boundaries."[48]

The year 1993 brought an end to Fitzgerald's career. In July, after beginning dialysis for kidney damage, she suffered the amputation of one leg below the knee. In September the other leg was also removed below the knee. For reasons never explained, the operations were withheld from the press and remained a secret until the following year. The *Los Angeles Sentinel* claimed to break the story in March 1994, and its coverage emphasized her diabetes and its disproportionate risk to Black Americans. A "Salute to Ella Fitzgerald" concert and dinner for the American Diabetes Association in February had raised money for its African American outreach program, but Fitzgerald did not attend.[49] Her birth year was still thought to be 1918, and she also had to miss the many tributes planned for her seventy-fifth birthday.

★★★

COLLECTIVE MEMORIES ABOUT HER AND HER WORK were turning into history for a new generation. Reissues devoted to Fitzgerald's early years with Chick Webb began to surface in 1992, prompting the reinvestigation of music that was difficult to find or had been minimized as a prelude to her Verve years. Gunther Schuller's magisterial 1989 study *The Swing Era* barely mentioned Fitzgerald's name and dismissed "A-Tisket A-Tasket" as a "dreadful bit of silliness."[50] Pressed on his lack of coverage, Schuller demurred, saying there wasn't room to cover two singers, and he had chosen Billie Holiday.[51] Reissues broadened the public discussion, and 1993 saw major releases championing her musical legacy at a time of strong consumer demand for older jazz. Milt Gabler, who had won a Grammy for reissuing Billie Holiday's work on Decca, supervised *75th Birthday Celebration*, a two-CD set on the GRP label compiling thirty-nine tunes from 1938 to 1955, including her two million-platter sellers, her famous vocal jams, and varied backgrounds from famous arrangers.[52] Verve issued *First Lady of Song*, a three-CD compilation covering the late 1950s and '60s.[53] In 1994 Verve followed up with the

U.S. release of a lavish multi-CD box set, *The Complete Ella Fitzgerald Song Books*, with extensive commentary from Benny Green and John McDonough.[54] A single-CD spinoff, *The Best of the Song Books*, stayed on the *Billboard* charts for two years.[55]

The complete edition helped further codify the notion of the Great American Songbook, the modern canonization of the Broadway and Hollywood songwriters of the first half of the twentieth century. Many important developments had prepared the way for Fitzgerald's LPs to be understood as vanguard achievements and monuments to American art. The discipline of American music studies expanded greatly in the 1970s, providing a foundation for scholarly acceptance and revisionist evaluations of popular music. Alec Wilder's *American Popular Song: The Great Innovators, 1900–1950*, a formalist study of songs through their scores rather than their interpretations, was published in 1972 and found a receptive audience among the sophisticated listening public as well as scholars.[56] In 1980 Benny Green's *High Fidelity* article "The Ella Fitzgerald/Norman Granz Songbooks: Locus Classicus of American Song" championed Fitzgerald and Granz as key links in the chain from the songbooks as commerce to the songbooks as art.[57] Calling the *Song Book* recordings "classical" implied their function as models, which other singers had long understood.

★★★

FROM 1987 TO 1991, as she rallied back from bypass surgery, her social life included the quasi-professional activities of the Hollywood community. Being home more, even if not by choice, meant she was more available for undemanding friendships that sustained her sense of well-being. She had neighbors. She had intimates in her family. She had close friends and helpers who understood her moods and tolerated her occasional possessiveness and tireless need for reassurance.

"I'm going to a little jazz concert next door on Saturday," Ella told Jim Blackman in December 1990. Her neighbor Dr. Levisman had invited her to his young son's recital in his backyard. Blackman attended along with Ella and her grandniece Valerie, Blackman recalled:

> We went next door to the doctor's house. She was supposed to be resting her voice. I knew what was going to happen and it happened just as I suspected it would. The doctor came up to Ella and asked her if she would like to sing, and she told him that she didn't want to because she was getting ready to perform the next day and was just relaxing. The quartet was playing "Watermelon Man," and Ella turned to me and said, "Well, maybe I can sing a little if I had a microphone." When one arrived, she scatted her way through the song.[58]

The next day Fitzgerald attended a glitzy event in Beverly Hills for the Society of Singers (SOS), a philanthropic nonprofit set up by the Hollywood establishment to offer financial assistance to professional vocalists. Frank Sinatra was presented with a Lifetime Achievement Award, which the SOS had named the "Ella" award in honor of Fitzgerald, the first recipient in 1989. A day removed from "Watermelon Man" in Dr. Levisman's backyard, she sang "The Lady Is a Tramp" with Sinatra in a memorable duet that was captured on video.[59]

Another neighbor who was allowed into her private world was the young singer Joyce Garro, who moved two houses away around 1989 and soon became a loving, loyal neighbor. Garro's friend Bea Wain, a former band singer just five days younger than Fitzgerald, had known Ella since the late 1930s, and they could talk shop and swap road memories with relish. Phoebe Jacobs remained a close, trusted friend. She and Wain described expeditions in Fitzgerald's Rolls-Royce, where Ella sat in the front seat next to her driver, Chester Matlock, and they would joke about onlookers wondering what the maid was doing there. "Look pretty, Phoebe, because they think you're somebody and they figure I'm the maid."[60]

In her later years, Ella often sang "A House Is Not a Home," adding the lyric "without a man" and underscoring the absence of a permanent guy in her life. Clifford "Bobby" Booker, a pediatrician from Washington, D.C., helped ease the loneliness of her last years. "My father and Ella had a romantic relationship from time to time for many, many years," said Claudia Booker. "Norman would have my dad travel with her. Her feet got to be in terrible shape, and with her toes and fingers getting numb, she was losing her balance. Dad just started to travel with her overseas. They wouldn't let her go without him."

Bobby Booker's affair with Ella began in the early 1950s, during the first of his six marriages. She was playing the Howard Theatre, and he was tending bar at the Stage Door nearby. "He had every jazz record you could get your hands on," said Claudia. "Whenever Ella was in town, he would disappear for days. One time my mother hosed him when he got out of the car." In 1988 Ella asked Claudia, "Do you remember meeting me? He snuck me down to the house and made you promise not to tell your mother."[61]

Booker was a more active presence in the 1970s, accompanying Fitzgerald to the White House Bicentennial concert in 1976 and to the Kennedy Center Honors in 1979. His surviving letters and postcards from the 1980s suggest the limits of the relationship. On January 9, 1984, apologizing for missing a concert, he wrote:

> I heard you loud and clear when you said "mi casa es su casa" and I was reassured that I was cared for. I just hated the way we ended that phone call. I realize that you are very sensitive because as you know I'm sensitive too. I hate to see time pass that could be more joyfully used, but that's what's happening now. I know you care and I hope you know I care. Your friendship has always been a part of my life. Call or write soon. I need that. Bobby B.

He sent pictures of his grandchildren. She once tried out the signature "Mrs. Ella Fitzgerald Booker" on a piece of stationery, and as Jim Blackman recalled, she sang "A House Is Not a Home" in several concerts during the late 1980s and early '90s with Bobby in the audience. Clifford Booker died in October 1995 from prostate cancer.[62]

Fitzgerald's extended family remained an important part of her life. She lost Virginia Williams in 1989 and Georgiana Henry in 1994, but the nieces and their children stayed in the area, and she supported them financially. She also took in Eloise Young's daughter Valerie, handling the disorder that goes with children. "I probably would have had a smaller place," Fitzgerald told Leonard Feather in 1987, "but I got a whole lot of nieces and nephews . . . and that's a whole lot of company." Her joy of having a grandchild helped mend the frayed ties with her son, Ray Jr., who was living in Sitka, Alaska, and leading a small band. Fitzgerald met her daughter-in-law, Margaret, for the first time at the wedding, but she told Feather she was catching up on family life. "Young Ray and his wife have a nice little house there and I think he's happy," she said. "I haven't been there."[63] Ray's daughter Alice, almost two, had visited Grandma Ella a couple of times. Phoebe Jacobs recalled an elaborate birthday party for Alice, and Ella traveled with a photograph of herself and her granddaughter. In 1990 she expressed pride in her son's musicianship. "I felt so bad he got into the rock 'n' roll thing. Dropped out of college in his last term, he wanted to be a teacher. Now he's a singer himself. Doesn't sound so bad, I have to admit."[64] "She loved that boy," Phoebe Jacobs said.[65]

Fitzgerald did not hide her regrets over the price she had paid for her life on the road. In 1990, after Ella received the Commandeur des Arts et des Lettres in Paris, the established jazz singer Dee Dee Bridgewater approached her during a reception at the American embassy:

> Everybody was having their champagne and there was Ella Fitzgerald sitting alone on the sofa and nobody's paying attention to her. So I went over to her. The point that she made to me was how she really wished she had spent more time with her son, how she had missed him growing up. And she hoped that I would not do that—that I would take time for my children and my personal life.[66]

After the terrible amputations in 1993, Fitzgerald was homebound except for visits to Cedars Sinai for dialysis and rides with Chester. Friends made pilgrimages for the last visit. Norman Granz, both loyal and alienated at the end of their historic partnership, came occasionally. According to Granz's biographer Tad Hershorn, "He had long had frictions with Fitzgerald over his belief that her family took advantage of her."[67] Fitzgerald's cousin Dorothy Johnson said that Ella talked about Granz "like a boss who came into town." Virginia Wicks said, "She was a bit, I think, resentful of his authority and his being aware of more personal things in her life. And how she spent her money. . . . I was very hurt for those two."[68] By this time, his responsibilities over her finances had been transferred to her private estate lawyer, Richard Rosman, who helped set up the Ella Fitzgerald Charitable Foundation in 1993. At some point in 1995, Ray Brown, Jr., and his family came to live at North Whittier Drive. That year her beloved Keter Betts visited for the last time. "Her son brought her down," he said. "We sat there. She was in and out, in and out, you know." Also that year Bea Wain remembered taking a ride with Ella on her birthday and hearing her name all the musicians on the CDs played in the car.[69]

Lillian Randolph, a nurse attendant, recalled Fitzgerald discussing her love for Dizzy Gillespie, scatting and humming to herself, and listening to her own recordings, which she had rarely done in earlier years. Ella would think she was on her way to an audience and would ask when the car was coming. " 'Get me a dress for my performance,' she told me around four o'clock almost every day." Randolph would diligently find her a dress, a wig, and matching shoes, gently reminding her that the doctor did not want her to work. At other times Randolph wheeled her around her home to revisit her past. "She wanted to see her things, she wanted to see her golden records. She wanted to see pictures—Louis Armstrong on her piano, the Ink Spots, an autographed picture of the Andrews Sisters, a photo of Connie Boswell, Dean Martin, an autographed picture of Duke Ellington." When Chester took Ella out for rides, often to Santa Monica, he'd play her CDs in the car and sometimes remind her, "That's you."[70]

Ray Brown, Jr., did "a remarkable thing," Bea Wain recalled. "When Ella was dying, I sat on her bed and sang to her. We all had our little moments with her. She was in bad shape. He hired a trio of top musicians to play downstairs while she was upstairs in bed. I thought it was the most wonderful touch. There were three guys and they played downstairs. It was wonderful."[71]

Ella Fitzgerald died on June 15, 1996, at home. On June 20, Ray Jr. held a private service in the backyard of North Whittier Drive with about eighty-five people in attendance, followed by a cortège to Inglewood Park Cemetery. The funeral ceremony at the headstone was simple and brief in accordance with the practice of Jehovah's Witnesses, Ray Brown, Jr.'s religion at that time. Jim Blackman and Phoebe Jacobs attended along with several extended family members. Among the musicians were Gladys Knight, Quincy Jones, Stevie Wonder, Dionne Warwick, and Nancy Wilson. Ray Brown and Arlie Small's niece Robin Robinson served as pallbearers. Norman Granz was conspicuous in his absence, and his name was not mentioned on the funeral program. Granz had called Oscar Peterson to relay the news of her death and could only muster the words, "She's gone."[72]

The high point of the service was the performance by Keter Betts. Virginia Wicks recalled:

> It was so moving and he spoke briefly. Keter Betts played a bass solo on "Poor Butterfly." And then all of a sudden when he stopped playing, a bird began to sing, and it sung and it was absolutely beautiful. And not only I could feel it, but I felt it from other people who were there who loved Ella.[73]

So many people "loved Ella" in different ways. "Who's your favorite jazz singer—after Ella of course." "The greatest thing in jazz today." "She has ears like Dixie Cups." "Ella's kicking ass out there." "She's like one of us." "She has no clue of her own importance." "She's the greatest thing in jazz." "Oh, Ella," a Pullman porter said, putting his hand over his heart, as he realized she was a passenger on *his* train.

In 1987 she had told Leonard Feather:

I was sitting in a store the other day and a lady saw me and said, "Oooh—my dreams have come true! It's my singing lady!" And I looked my worst—I had my sneakers on, and an old skirt. But she stopped and said, "We love you," and then another girl came, and soon everybody was asking me for autographs. I said to myself, "Well, you can't beat this kind of love." I've got about three bags of mail here that I haven't even answered yet—people who wrote me in the hospital. You start thinking, was it all worth it? And I say, yes.[74]

"I really always wanted to be a dancer." "Chick Webb didn't want me." "I don't want to just sing bop." "I love to sing ballads." "I *like* Old MacDonald." "Push me." "I need to see their faces." "It looks like a 'Lady Be Good' audience." "Sing pretty for the people." "The album's available at all record stores." "I'll try." "I won't be left behind." "I know why people like me. They like the songs I sing." "Some old, some new, some we know, some we don't."

Thank you, thank you. Thank you, ladies and gentlemen, thank you. Thank you.

ACKNOWLEDGMENTS

Ma fin est mon commencement	My end is my beginning
Et mon commencement ma fin	And my beginning my end.
Et teneure vraiement.	And throughout it holds true at heart.

—Guillaume de Machaut, Rondeau, c. 1390

I have been grappling with this project for many years, lifted up by Ella Fitzgerald's voice all the while. My debts exceed what I can properly set out here. But "beyond category," to borrow Duke Ellington's ever-useful phrase, are James W. Blackman and Tad Hershorn, whose friendship and support surpassed what any writer could possibly have expected. Jim Blackman supplemented his personal recollections with musical tapes from his private archive. Tad Hershorn, archivist and distinguished biographer of Norman Granz, shared his expertise and wisdom in many ways, as well as his partisanship: we enjoyed debating the question of influence between Norman and Ella, echoing their sparring. Their constant encouragement enabled me to keep on.

Their commitment flowed partly from their love of Ella Fitzgerald, an experience I also had working with Christine McKay, archivist of the Schomburg Center for Research in Black Culture. She dazzled me with her brilliant research skills in genealogy. I thought we had concluded our work when she told me that she was persisting in her search for information about Tempie Fitzgerald, Ella's mother, and Frances Correy, Ella's sister. On her own initiative, she tracked down their burial sites in Oakland Cemetery (Yonkers, New York) in 2020.

Other highlights over the years involved Fitzgerald's family and friends. Ray Brown, Jr., greatly encouraged me, writing in our first email exchange that his mother "would be pleased" by my promise to take a deep scholarly dive into her life. As it turned out, I did that with only parts of her life, especially the early years, perhaps influenced by his trust in me to safeguard the gift of his mother's scrapbooks from the late 1930s and '40s as well as his own memories. Dorothy Johnson, Virginia Williams's last child and Ella's first cousin, shared family memories and photographs. The late Phoebe Jacobs, executive vice president of the Louis Armstrong Educational Foundation, talked about her close relationship with Ella many times, once in the unexpected venue of an Upper East Side nail salon staffed by Russian American women who turned out to be avid Fitzgerald fans; as they eavesdropped, they interrupted with titles of their favorite songs. I met the late Virginia Wicks, a pioneering jazz publicist, while she was confined to her bed in her home in Los Angeles. Still finding intense pleasure in life, Virginia communicated empathy about aspects of managing Ella and her relationship with Norman Granz. I also benefited from Carol Sloane's wisdom as we shared many lunches at a local Italian restaurant in Stoneham, Massachusetts, where pictures of pop and jazz singers hung along the walls and their voices played in the background: "Listen to the way that word is shaped," she instructed me. "That's Carmen." Or how a phrase moved with lift: "That's Ella."

I have other vivid memories of encounters—those worthy of the label "interviews" are labeled as such in the notes—among them one with the unique Buddy Bregman, as we ate deli sandwiches in his Los Angeles apartment crammed with memorabilia. Many other communications, best described as ongoing conversations, provided background and context for the biography. In the jazz world, I benefited from the vast knowledge of Dan Morgenstern both before and after he ended his tenure as director of the Institute of Jazz Studies (IJS) at Rutgers

University. I relished the special IJS comradery, which included Vincent Pelote, Elizabeth Surles, and Wayne Winborne. They organized an important tribute to Ella Fitzgerald in 2017. During one panel session, I sat next to Richard Wyands, a pianist who had played with Ella; he demonstrated his artistry on the keyboard.

I reserve a place of honor for the time I spent with some extraordinary musicians who worked with Ella. It was total serendipity that brought me to Paul Smith when he was performing solo piano sets at a hotel in Rancho Palos Verdes not far from Los Angeles. In 2012 I knew too little to ask him the right questions, but we marveled together over the 2009 Verve release of *Twelve Nights in Hollywood*; among the twenty-five or so posthumous live CDs released in the last twenty-five years, this one stands out. I talked with bass player Jim Hughart, who played dates with Duke Ellington and Fitzgerald at the Côte d'Azur in 1966 and saw the darker side of Norman Granz, and with the drummer Gregg Field, who impressed Ella as a prodigy in the 1970s; Ray Brown, Jr., and I were at the Hollywood Bowl tribute "To Ella with Love" by the Count Basie Orchestra in 2017, in which Field joined the band and joyfully made music. Mike Wofford sensitively described Fitzgerald's final concerts and a late recording session when Ray Brown took charge. Other recollections about "Ella's fellas," as they were sometimes called in the press, came from proxy family members Kelly Peterson, Jennifer Betts, and Denise Thigpen.

The roll call of musical meetups took place on several other relevant occasions. André Previn described the backstage scene at the TV date *Swing into Spring* with his four Oscar statuettes glowing in the dusk in his New York apartment, thanks to Ellen Highstein, director of the Tanglewood Music Center. During her tenure as director, she arranged a concert of selections from Fitzgerald's *Song Books* using the great classical musicians in residence, brilliantly organized by Lee Musiker.

Other performers and people on the scene illuminated different periods. The fine big band singer Bea Wain shared tales of friendship in Ella's later years; they shared repertoire in the 1930s. The lindy expert dancer Norma Miller, Richard Gale, the son of Ella's manager Moe Gale, and

James Patterson, student of Webb's flutist Waymon Carver, talked about the 1930s. Mae Arnette, a Boston singer, and Sarah McLawler, a New York–based organist, reminisced about the 1950s, as did George Wein on his years at the Boston club Storyville. Rick Bale added background to concerts on the college scene in the Bay Area.

I have memories of telephone conversations with Nat Hentoff, who readily admitted his preference for other singers, of course Billie Holiday but also Ivie Anderson and Anita O'Day. It was too early on for me to probe the binary split between "Billie and Ella" in which Hentoff played an important role—a debate I know he would have enjoyed. I was far better prepared to challenge the composer, conductor, and musicologist Gunther Schuller, whose brilliant scholarship had inspired me as well as a generation of his peers and whose biography will eventually be written. His exclusion of Fitzgerald from his massive *The Swing Era* was, in his words, a consequence of there not being "room" enough for her, although his genuine and unbidden praise for her vocal bop delighted me. Others in the jazz world I especially thank include John McDonough, an expert jazz writer who interviewed Norman Granz at length and contributed authoritative overviews of Fitzgerald's career both during and after her lifetime. He generously shared with me transcripts of his interviews with Norman Granz and Oscar Peterson. I also want to thank Bob Blumenthal for an early conversation about biography, and Devra Hall Levy for details about the music business.

Ella Fitzgerald's many years in Los Angeles formed a separate stream of her life from 1957 to 1996. Fran Morris Rosman, a leading figure at Ella Fitzgerald Charitable Foundation, proved to be an indispensable fount of information and resources. She directed me to folks outside the music world, among them Oscar Szmuch, who gave Brazilian Portuguese lessons to Ella; and Lillian Randolph, a nurse attendant caretaker for Fitzgerald in her last months. I also thank Richard Rosman for his contributions and for arranging my meeting with Margaret Nutt, who took a vow of silence that day. I reached people associated with Fitzgerald's own company, Salle Productions, among them Mary Jane Outwater's children, Christopher Outwater and Edwin Outwater. I had the pleasure of knowing Joyce Garro, a devoted neighbor of Ella's in Beverly Hills and an active jazz-pop singer, who was a very special resource. Jim Blackman arranged a lunch with Pete Cavello's family and a talk with his wife, Mary, as well as an early interview with Robin Robinson, niece of Ella's good friend Arlie Small.

Among the music journalists, historians, practitioners, and scholars who contributed their expertise and support, I must acknowledge the inspiration of my deceased friend and colleague at Northeastern University, Leonard Brown. As a musician and ethnomusicologist, Leonard had a special holistic vision of music. I thank my other former Northeastern colleagues as well, including Anthony De Ritis, Junauro Landgrebe, Hilary Poriss, Ron Smith, Tisha Stadnicki, and Ronald Bruce Smith. In my field of American music studies, the historian Marva Griffin Carter proved to be an exceptional colleague and friend; among her many acts of generosity, she arranged a roundtable of friends and colleagues in Atlanta who had a special interest in Ella Fitzgerald. Lara Pellegrinelli, both as a graduate student and now as a music journalist, gave me a jump start on this project. Kay Shelemay and Tammy Kernodle offered special encouragement. I want to single out Stephanie Crease, who shared her work on Chick Webb even before it was published, as well as her historical expertise. I'm thankful for the many different kinds of help I received from Jane Bernstein, Enzo Capua, Geoffrey Block, Tom Everett, and Elaine Hayes; from Larry Hamberlin, who read early drafts of several chapters; and from Joseph Horowitz, Jeff Magee, Ingrid Monson, Max Noubel, Howard Pollack, Lewis Porter, Kristen Turner, Michael Ullman, Christie Jay Wells, and Elizabeth Wood.

Many collectors contributed their expertise and shared unpublished materials under their purview. At the top of the list is the exceptional Michel Macaire in Tours, France, who collects materials about Ella Fitzgerald with a special focus on her European career. He extended his generosity by supplying data from his thousand-page reference work in progress, which grounded many dates in this book. I relied on the help of John Hasse, Cynthia Hoover, Wendy Shay, and Kay Peterson at the Smithsonian National Museum of American History; Mark Horowitz at the Library of Congress; John Favareau, chief archivist at the Yonkers Public Library; Anna Kijas, a virtuoso Web researcher as well as head music librarian at Tufts University; Benjamin Knysak at the RIPM; David Coppen at the Eastman School of Music; Keith Pawlak at the Nelson Riddle Collection, University of Arizona; Garth Reese at the University of Idaho; Laura Schieb at Dartmouth College; and Charles Wash, director of the National Afro-American Museum and Cultural Center in Wilberforce, Ohio.

I supervised research with many assistants over the years. In the United States, I thank Sam Baltimore, Susan Bay, Zachary Cadman, Fred Carroll, Lauren Corcoren, Alex Cowan, Kathryn Heidemann, Ben Hoffman, Michael Li, Yenndie Lin, Lucille Mok, Joy Nesbitt, Diane Oliva, Richardson Smith, Tamar Sella, Abbey Siegel, and Francesca Toto. For reviews in Danish and German newspapers, I relied mainly on Martin Lauge Christensen and also Elizabeth Sorensen and Bruce Kirmmse. In Sweden, I received help from Alva Svenson, who acting on her own initiative located Titti Sjöblom, the daughter of the singer Alice Babs.

I owe a debt of gratitude to two editors at W. W. Norton. Maribeth Payne signed this book, and upon her retirement, she led me to Tom Mayer, whom I thank especially for his astute critiques of early drafts, and to his assistant Nneoma Amadiobi. My need to meet his insistence on succinct prose led me to Evan Spring, who offered not only valuable editorial help but also his expertise in jazz history. Will Myers helped me, as did Bruce Kluger, who extended a special assist at the very end. Minji Kim practiced wizardry in dealing with the final stages of this manuscript.

My collective of friends and extended family cheered me on by asking encouraging questions or exercising tact in inquiring about progress. Among them are Barbara Schectman, the late Herbie Weiss, Eleonore Weiss, Joyce Antler, and the opera singer Shiri Hershkovitz. Others I am grateful to include Robbie Apfel, Martha Bayles, Cheryl Brown, Jerry Cohen, Virginia Eskin, Ellen and Roger Golde, John Holland, Phyllis Karas, Debra and Mike Kaufman, Judy and Jonathan Knight, Rob Kirsch, Louis and Roberta Kurlantzick, Ian McMahon, Jana Porter, Judy Pollner, Nicholas Puner, Laura Rock, Peggy Seeger, Jack and Kay Shelemay, Bennett Simon, Joan and Rob Stein, Betty Torphy, and Elizabeth Woodhouse. I owe a special debt of gratitude to my biography reading group in Boston, the "Bios," who have been together as pillars of encouragement for one another for over thirty-five years: Joyce Antler, Frances Malino, Susan T. Quinn, Megan Marshall, Roberta Wollons, and the late Lois Rudnick.

My extended family always took an interest in this project, including my brother, the fine musician David Tick; my sister-in-law, Elizabeth Ronan; my sister, Beth Wagner; my nephews, Chris, Pat, and Mark Oleskey; and my nieces, Sarah Tick (who named her daughter Ella) and Noemie Tick.

My family, who thought my laptop grew out of my hip, accepted Ella Fitzgerald as a rival for my time and energy for more years than expected. They conveyed mostly loving tolerance, and I continue to thank, as my haven in the world, my daughters, Erica Grossman and Allison Oleskey; her husband, Jeff Pressman; and my grandchildren, Liv, Aria, and Ella, all of whom ask Alexa to play Ella. My beloved husband, the rock of my life, Stephen Oleskey, acted as counselor, editor, adviser, and life coach; I have been sustained by his devotion and integrity. We plan to grow even older together with Ella Fitzgerald, dancing "Cheek to Cheek."

APPENDIX

Ella Fitzgerald's Charted Hot Singles, 1936–1954

Adapted from Joel Whitburn, *Pop Memories 1890–1954: The History of American Popular Music Compiled from America's Popular Music Charts 1890–1954* (Menomonee Falls, Wis.: Record Research, 1986), 159–61; and J. Wilfred Johnson, *Ella Fitzgerald: An Annotated Discography; Including a Complete Discography of Chick Webb* (Jefferson, N.C.: McFarland & Co., 2001).

Record Title	Lyricist (L) & Composer (C)	Date Charted	Peak Position	Weeks Charted	Label & Number
1. Sing Me a Swing Song (And Let Me Dance)	Stanley Adams (L), Hoagy Carmichael (C)	7/24/1936	12	1	Decca 830
2. (If You Can't Sing It) You'll Have to Swing It [aka. Mr. Paganini]	Sam Coslow (L, C)	12/19/1936	20	1	Decca 1032
3. Goodnight My Love with Benny Goodman	Mack Gordon (L), Harry Revel (C)	1/16/1937	1	13	Victor 25461
4. Dedicated to You with the Mills Brothers	Sammy Cahn (L), Saul Chaplin, and Hy Zaret (C)	4/10/1937	19	1	Decca 1148
5. Big Boy Blue with the Mills Brothers	Peter Tinturin, Jack Lawrence, and Dan Howell (L, C)	4/24/1937	20	1	Decca 1148
6. If You Ever Should Leave	Sammy Cahn (L), Saul Chaplin (C)	7/10/1937	12	4	Decca 1302
7. All Over Nothing at All	Jack Lawrence (L), Arthur Altman (C)	8/14/1937	20	1	Decca 1339
8. Rock It for Me	Kay Werner and Sue Werner (L, C)	2/19/1938	19	1	Decca 1586
9. I Got a Guy	Marion Sunshine (L, C)	6/11/1938	18	2	Decca 1681
10. A-Tisket, A-Tasket	Ella Fitzgerald and Van Alexander (L, C)	6/18/1938	1(10)	19	Decca 1804
11. I Found My Yellow Basket	Ella Fitzgerald and Van Alexander (L, C)	11/12/1938	3	6	Decca 2148
12. Wacky Dust	Stanley Adams (L), Oscar Levant (C)	11/12/1938	13	4	Decca 2021
13. MacPherson Is Rehearsin' to Swing	Marion Sunshine (L, C)	11/12/1938	14	1	Decca 2080
14. F.D.R. Jones	Harold Rome (L, C)	11/26/1938+	8	6	Decca 2105
15. Undecided	Sid Robin (L), Charlie Shavers (C)	3/18/1939	8	4	Decca 2323
16. T'ain't What You Do (It's the Way That Cha Do It)	Sy Oliver and James ("Trummy") Young (L, C)	3/25/1939	19	1	Decca 2310

Title	Songwriters	Date			Decca
17. Chew, Chew, Chew (Your Bubble Gum)	Ella Fitzgerald, Buck Ram, and Chick Webb (L, C)	5/6/1939	14	1	Decca 2389
18. I Want the Waiter (With the Water)	Kay Werner and Sue Werner (L, C)	9/2/1939	9	3	Decca 2628
19. My Wubba Dolly	Kay Werner and Sue Werner (L, C)	10/28/1939	16	1	Decca 2816
20. The Starlit Hour	Mitchell Parish (L), Peter DeRose (C)	4/20/1940	17	3	Decca 2988
21. Sing Song Swing	Charles L. Cooke (L, C)	4/27/1940	23	2	Decca 3126
22. Imagination	Johnny Burke (L), Jimmy Van Heusen (C)	5/18/1940	15	3	Decca 3078
23. Sugar Blues	Lucy Fletcher (L), Clarence Williams (C)	6/1/1940	27	1	
24. Shake Down the Stars	Eddie De Lange (L), Jimmy Van Heusen (C)	7/6/1940	18	2	Decca 3199
25. Five O'Clock Whistle	Josef Myrow, Kim Gannon, and Gene Irwin (L, C)	11/30/1940+	9	5	Decca 3420
26. Louisville, K-Y	Sonny Skylar (L, C)	2/1/1941	23	1	Decca 3441
27. Hello, Ma! I Done It Again	Leo Robin, (L), Ralph Rainger (C)	3/15/1941	26	1	Decca 3612
28. The Muffin Man	Ella Fitzgerald (L, C)	8/2/1941	23	1	Decca 3666
29. Cow-Cow Boogie with the Ink Spots	Don Raye (L), Gene De Paul and Benny Carter (C)	3/11/1944	10	8	Decca 18587
30. When My Sugar Walks Down the Street	Gene Austin, Irving Mills, and Jimmy McHugh (L, C)	3/11/1944	27	1	
31. Once Too Often	Mack Gordon (L), James V. Monaco (C)	7/8/1944	24	2	Decca 18605
32. I'm Making Believe with the Ink Spots	Mack Gordon (L), James V. Monaco (C)	11/4/1944	1(2)	17	Decca 23356
33. Into Each Life Some Rain Must Fall with the Ink Spots	Allan Roberts and Doris Fisher (L, C)	11/11/1944	1(2)	17	

Title	Writers	Date	Pos	Wks	Label
34. And Her Tears Flowed Like Wine	Joe Greene (L), Stan Kenton and Charles Lawrence (C)	1/6/1945	10	5	Decca 18633
35. I'm Beginning to See the Light with the Ink Spots	Don George, Duke Ellington, Harry James, and Johnny Hodges (L, C)	4/28/1945	5	6	Decca 23399
36. It's Only a Paper Moon with the Delta Rhythm Boys	E. Y. "Yip" Harburg and Billy Rose (L), Harold Arlen (C)	8/25/1945	9	3	Decca 23425
37. You Won't Be Satisfied (Until You Break My Heart) with Louis Armstrong	Freddy James and Larry Stock (L, C)	4/6/1946	10	2	Decca 23496
38. Stone Cold Dead in the Market (He Had It Coming) with Louis Jordan	Wilmoth Houdini (L, C)	7/6/1946	7	6	Decca 23546
39. (I Love You) For Sentimental Reasons with the Delta Rhythm Boys	Ivory "Deek" Watson (L), William Best (C)	12/7/1946+	8	14	Decca 23670
40. Guilty	Gus Kahn (L), Harry Akst and Richard A. Whiting (C)	4/12/1947	11	4	Decca 23844
41. My Happiness with the Song Spinners	Betty Peterson (L), Borney Bergantine (C)	6/19/1948	6	21	Decca 24446
42. Tea Leaves with the Song Spinners	Morty Berk, Frank Capano, and Max C. Freedman (L, C)	6/19/1948	24	2	Decca 24446
43. Baby, It's Cold Outside	Frank Loesser (L, C)	6/11/1949	9	13	Decca 24644
44. Can Anyone Explain? (No, No, No) with Louis Armstrong	Bennie Benjamin and George Weiss (L, C)	11/18/1950	30	1	Decca 27209
45. Smooth Sailing	Ella Fitzgerald (Scat), Arnett Cobb (C)	9/8/1951	23	6	Decca 27693
46. Trying	Billy Vaughn (L, C)	9/27/1952	21	4	Decca 28375
47. Walkin' by the River	Robert Sour (L), Una Mae Carlisle (C)	11/29/1952	29	1	Decca 28433
48. Crying in the Chapel	Artie Glenn (L, C)	9/5/1953	15	4	Decca 28762
49. Melancholy Me	Howard Biggs and Joe Thomas (L, C)	3/6/1954	25	1	Decca 29008
50. I Need	Ralph Care and Sol Marcus (L, C)	5/29/1954	30	1	Decca 29108

NOTES

Introduction

1. Joe Smith, *Off the Record: An Oral History of Popular Music* (New York: Warner Books, 1988), 15–16.

2. David W. Hazen, "Singer Lacks Time for Play: Ella Fitzgerald Pinochle Love," *Oregonian*, July 17, 1940, 6.

3. Bruce Crowther and Mike Pinfold, *Singing Jazz: The Singers and Their Styles* (San Francisco: Miller Freeman, 1997), 140.

4. "Ella Fitzgerald. Her Vocal Versatility Continues to Amaze Musicians," *Ebony*, May 1949, 45–51.

5. Oscar Peterson and Richard Palmer, *A Jazz Odyssey: The Life of Oscar Peterson* (New York: Continuum, 2002), 158.

6. Ella Fitzgerald, *The Complete Ella Fitzgerald Song Books*, Verve 519832–2, 1993, multiple CDs.

7. Judith Tick, "Ella Fitzgerald in Soulsville," NPR, September 6, 2019.

8. Georgia Bryan Conrad, *Reminiscences of a Southern Woman* (Hampton, Va.: Hampton Institute Press, 1900).

9. Bud Kliment, *Ella Fitzgerald* (Danbury, Conn.: Grolier, 1988), 8.

10. Judith Tick, *American Women Composers Before 1870* (Ann Arbor: University of Michigan Press, 1987).

11. Lillian Johnson, "Ella Fitzgerald's Hardest Job Was to Get Folks to Listen!" *Baltimore Afro-American*, October 9, 1937, 10.

12. Oscar Peterson, *A Jazz Odyssey: My Life in Jazz* (New York: Continuum, 2002), 155, 157.

13. Katharine Cartwright, "'Guess These People Wonder What I'm Singing': Quotation and Reference in Ella Fitzgerald's 'St. Louis Blues,'" in David Evans, ed.,

Ramblin' on My Mind: New Perspectives on the Blues (Champaign: University of Illinois Press, 2008), 281–327.

14. John McDonough, "What Becomes a Legend Most," *Down Beat*, June 1993, 22.

15. George E. Pitts, "Ella Has Yearning to Be TV Actress," *Pittsburgh Courier*, June 2, 1962, 14.

16. David Ake, *Jazz Cultures* (Berkeley: University of California Press, 2002); Eric Porter, *What Is This Thing Called Jazz? African American Musicians as Artists, Critics, and Activists* (Berkeley: University of California Press, 2002); Eileen M. Hayes and Linda F. Williams, *Black Women and Music: More than the Blues* (Urbana: University of Illinois Press, 2007); and Nichole T. Rustin and Sherrie Tucker, eds., *Big Ears: Listening for Gender in Jazz Studies* (Durham, N.C.: Duke University Press), 2008.

17. Don Alpert, "The Ella Formula: I Sing It the Way I Feel It," *Los Angeles Times*, September 24, 1961, A5.

18. Howard Reich, "An Underrated Legend: Depths of Ella Fitzgerald's Artistry Remain Misunderstood," *Chicago Tribune*, June 19, 1996.

19. Eneid Routte, headline unknown, *San Juan Star*, April 15, 1973, 5 (from clippings file).

20. William Johnson, "Bella Ella," *Times-Tribune* (Scranton, Penn.), November 4, 1985, C1.

Chapter 1: Young Ella (1917–1932)

1. David Nicholson, "Jazz Gets Sell-Out Crowd," *Daily Press* (Newport News, Va.), June 29, 1992, A2.

2. David Nicholson, "Rain, Jazz Open First Day of Hampton Festival," *Daily Press* (Newport News, Va.), June 27, 1992, A1.

3. David Nicholson and Chuck Bauerlein, "Aretha Zips Through Her Set," *Daily Press* (Newport News, Va.), June 28, 1992, A4.

4. "Fifty Years of the Hampton Jazz Festival: And All That Jazz," *Daily Press* (Newport News, Va.), June 18, 2017, 23.

5. Nicholson, "Jazz Gets Sell-Out Crowd."

6. Nicholson and Bauerlein, "Aretha Zips Through Her Set."

7. Sam McDonald, "Worshippers at the Shrine of Ella," *Daily Press* (Newport News, Va.), May 10, 1998, 11.

8. Gene Lees, *Singers and the Song II* (New York: Oxford University Press, 1998), 152.

9. McDonald, "Worshippers at the Shrine of Ella," 11.

10. William Fitzgerald's draft registration card lists his date of birth as January 10, 1884. "Tempie" was a more common name than "Temperance" at the time. "Popularity Over Time: How Many Girls Have Been Named Tempie," https://www.babynameshub.com/girl-names/Tempie.html.

11. Ella's birth certificate was located by Diane L. Richard, Mosaic Research and Project Management, www.mosaicrpm.com. The civil rights leader Ella Baker was born in Littleton.

12. *Newport News, Hampton, Phoebus and Old Point, Va. Directory* (Newport News,

Va.: Hill Directory Co., 1917), 7, http://archive.org/details/newportnewshamp t1917unse/.

13. Laborer: Newport News City Directories from 1916 through 1919. On the grain ship, see the birth certificate. Transfer wagon and longshoreman are from the 1920 Census. I am grateful to Jay E. Moore, librarian archivist at the Mariners' Museum and Park, Newport News, Va.

14. "Hampton Incidents," *Southern Workman* 46, no. 6 (Hampton, Va.: Hampton Normal and Agricultural Institute, 1917), 361.

15. Jane E. Dabel, "Domestic Workers," in Darlene Clark Hine, ed., *Black Women in America*, 2nd ed. (New York: Oxford University Press, 2005), 362–63.

16. Parke S. Rouse, Jr., "Having Community Roots a Plus Now Missed by Many," *Daily Press* (Newport News, Va.), September 13, 1981, C3.

17. Parke S. Rouse, Jr., "Ella Fitzgerald Is Cited as Best," *Daily Press* (Newport News, Va.), February 3, 1980, C1.

18. Richard Crawford, *America's Musical Life: A History* (New York: W. W. Norton, 2001), 487–89; Lyn Udall and Karl Kennett, *Stay in Your Own Backyard* (New York: W. Witmark & Sons, 1899).

19. "Skilled Negro Labor," *Southern Workman* 46, no. 8 (Hampton, Va.: Hampton Normal and Agricultural Institute, 1917), 424.

20. Parke S. Rouse, Jr., "1918 Was Year That Changed History and Our Community," *Daily Press* (Newport News, Va.), October 11, 1981, C3.

21. Newport News City Directories, 1916, 104; 1918, 118; and 1919, 158.

22. Lynn Abbott and Doug Seroff, *Ragged but Right: Black Traveling Shows, "Coon Songs," and the Dark Pathway to Blues and Jazz* (Jackson: University Press of Mississippi, 2007), 143.

23. Fred Carroll, "Research Notes on Newport News," prepared for this author.

24. Lawrence Schenbeck, *Racial Uplift and American Music, 1878–1943* (Jackson: University Press of Mississippi, 2012), 114.

25. John V. Quarstein and Parke S. Rouse, Jr., *Newport News: A Centennial History* (City of Newport News, n.d.), 102–3.

26. "Many Servants Are Without Jobs Here," *Daily News*, April 14, 1921.

27. Quarstein and Rouse, Jr., *Newport News*, 118.

28. Ella Fitzgerald, interview by Steve Allen, c. 1971–74, Satchmo Collection, Louis Armstrong House Museum.

29. Antonio Correia Borges is listed in "List of Manifest of Alien Passengers for the United States, S.S. Sch. Carleton Bell, sailing from Brava, C.V., June 2, 1917," http://interactive.ancestrylibrary.com/Print/8758/MAT944_6-0548/3125324?land scape=false&sou, and his World War I draft registration card is under the name Antonio Coreia, September 12, 1918, date of birth September 5, 1898. Thanks to Christine McKay for this information.

30. Bruce D. Haynes, *Red Lines, Black Spaces: The Politics of Race and Space in a Black Middle-Class Suburb* (New Haven, Conn.: Yale University Press, 2001), 6.

31. Ibid., 33ff.

32. Gene Lees, "Ella by Starlight," *Gene Lees' Jazzletter* 11, no. 1 (January 1992): 1.

33. Paula Giddings, *When and Where I Enter: The Impact of Black Women on Race and Sex in America* (New York: William Morrow, 1996), 133.

34. Harold A. Esannason and Vinnie Bagwell, *A Study of African-American Life in Yonkers from the Turn of the Century: An Overview* (Elmsford, N.Y.: Harold A. Esannason Graphics, 1993) 20.

35. Information from Ella Fitzgerald's school registration card. The entries in the Yonkers City Directories of 1929 and 1930 read as follows: "Corey Antonio (Tempie) lab h72 School apt. apartment 15." His brother Raymond lived in apartment 7.

36. "Eight Taken as Disorderly: Four Negro Women Among Those Arrested," *Yonkers Statesman*, May 7, 1928, 5; and "Raid Nets 2 Women and Man as Disorderly," *Yonkers Statesman*, March 12, 1928, 1.

37. Leonard Feather, "Ella," *Los Angeles Times*, January 30, 1983, 1.

38. Joel Siegel, "Ella at 65: A Lot to Be Grateful For," *Jazz Times*, November 1983, 11.

39. "Words of the Week," *Jet*, October 21, 1985, 38.

40. Stuart Nicholson, *Ella Fitzgerald: The Complete Biography*, updated ed. (New York: Routledge, 2004), 23.

41. Haynes, *Red Lines*, 14.

42. Ella Fitzgerald, interview by Leonard Feather, April 23, 1987, Ella Fitzgerald Project, Leonard Feather Collection, University of Idaho. The author has a partial transcript of an interview dated January 15, 1983. Its provenance is confused and is listed as Cassette 53–55. I was not able to hear the originals in time for this book, but probably they would clarify dates.

43. Nicholson, *Ella Fitzgerald* (2004), 23.

44. Barbaralee Diamonstein, *Open Secrets: Ninety-Four Women in Touch with Our Time* (New York: Viking Press, 1972), 136.

45. Esannason and Bagwell, *Study of African-American Life in Yonkers*, 18.

46. The "politics of respectability" is an influential concept developed by Evelyn Brooks Higginbotham in *Righteous Discontent*. See Paisley Harris, "Gatekeeping and Remaking: The Politics of Respectability in African American Women's History and Black Feminism," *Journal of Women's History* 15, no. 1 (Spring 2003): 212–20.

47. "Yonkers, N.Y.," *New York Age*, June 14, 1930, 8; reprinted in Ruth Curtis, "Yonkers," *Chicago Defender*, June 14, 1930, 11.

48. "She Who Is Ella," *Time*, November 27, 1964, 86–91.

49. Records at Yonkers Public Schools.

50. Nicholson, *Ella Fitzgerald* (2004), 23.

51. Ibid.

52. Lees, "Ella by Starlight," 1.

53. David W. Hazen, "Singer Lacks Time for Play: Ella Fitzgerald Pinochle Love," *Oregonian*, July 17, 1940, 6.

54. Quoted in Jim Haskins, *Ella Fitzgerald: A Life Through Jazz* (London: Hodder & Stoughton, 1991), 150.

55. Ella Fitzgerald, interview by Leonard Feather, January 15, 1983, Ella Fitzgerald Project, Leonard Feather Collection, University of Idaho.

56. Ella Fitzgerald, interview by Steve Allen, c. 1971–74, Satchmo Collection, Louis Armstrong House Museum.

57. U.S. Census, 1930; William Barlow, *Voice Over: The Making of Black Radio* (Philadelphia: Temple University Press, 1999), 19.

58. The movie Ella saw was probably *The Big Broadcast* of 1932, a Hollywood musical featuring Bing Crosby and incorporating screen cameos by the Boswell Sisters doing their experimental "Crazy People" and the Mills Brothers singing their hit "Tiger Rag."

59. Fitzgerald interview by Feather, January 15, 1983, Ella Fitzgerald Project.

60. Lees, "Ella by Starlight," 3.

61. Laurie Stras, "White Face, Black Voice: Race, Gender, and Region in the Music of the Boswell Sisters," *Journal of the Society for American Music* 1, no. 2 (2007): 207ff.

62. George T. Simon and Friends, *The Best of the Music Makers* (New York: Doubleday, 1979), 82.

63. Nicholson, *Ella Fitzgerald* (2004), 27.

64. Thomas Brothers, *Louis Armstrong: Master of Modernism* (New York: W. W. Norton, 2014), 348–49.

65. Smith Ballew and His Orchestra, "Sing You Sinners," Okeh 41384, 1930, W. Franke Harling (music), Sam Coslow (words). It charted in March 15, 1930, at number 18, staying for two weeks. See Joel Whitburn, *Pop Memories 1890–1954* (Menomonee Falls, Wis.: Record Research, 1986), 44.

66. "Ella on Ella: A Personal Portrait," *Essence* (television program), NBC, April 26, 1986, Paley Center for Media, https://www.paleycenter.org/collection/item/?q=first&p=248&item=T:08316.

67. Mel Heimer, "My New York," *Daily Notes* (Canonsburg, Penn.), April 29, 1958, 4.

68. "Ella on Ella," *Essence*.

69. George T. Simon, "Ella Fitzgerald," *Metronome*, April 1950, 14.

70. "Ella Fitzgerald Is Radio and Film 'Must' to All But Powers," *Chicago Defender*, May 30, 1950, 21.

71. Nicholson, *Ella Fitzgerald* (2004), 31.

72. Constance Valis Hill, *Tap Dancing America: A Cultural History* (New York: Oxford University Press, 2010), 134.

73. Nicholson, *Ella Fitzgerald* (2004), 32.

74. Bob Lucas, "Ella Fitzgerald: The Debt She Can't Wait to Repay," *Black Stars*, January 1972, 42. For "I used to go," see Fitzgerald interview by Feather, 1983.

75. Charles Gulliver, in *Ella Fitzgerald: Something to Live For* (documentary), American Masters Digital Archive (WNET), November 24, 1998, https://www.pbs.org/wnet/americanmasters/archive/interview/charles-gulliver.

76. Ibid.

77. Brian Seibert, "Overlooked No More: Earl Tucker, a Dancer Known as 'Snakehips,'" *New York Times*, December 18, 2019, D6.

78. Ralph Matthews, "Still Singing the Blues," *Baltimore Afro-American*, November 3, 1934, 6.

79. "Whitman Sisters," *Performing Arts Encyclopedia*, Performing Arts Databases, Library of Congress, http://memory.loc.gov/diglib/ihas/loc.music.tdabio.156/default.html.

80. Hill, *Tap Dancing America*, 105.

81. Siegel, "Ella at 65."

Chapter 2: Amateur Nights (1933–1935)

1. Marilyn E. Wiegold, *Yonkers in the Twentieth Century* (Albany: State University of New York Press, 2014), 82; Robert Marchant, *Westchester: History of an Iconic Suburb* (Jefferson, N.C.: McFarland & Co., 2018), 241.

2. "Novice Driver Runs into Pole with 7 in the Car," *Herald Statesman* (Yonkers), October 11, 1932, 2.

3. Ella Fitzgerald, interview by Leonard Feather, January 15, 1983, Ella Fitzgerald Project, Leonard Feather Collection, University of Idaho.

4. "New York State Personal Notes," *New York Age*, March 25, 1933.

5. "Substantial Sum Netted by Revue," *New York Amsterdam News*, January 25, 1933, 10; "Poor Get Aid of Theatrical Folk," *New York Amsterdam News*, January 18, 1933, 10; "Yonkers Federation of Clubs Benefit," *New York Age*, January 28, 1933, 9.

6. "Negro Federation Sponsor Program," *Herald Statesman* (Yonkers), January 20, 1933, 5.

7. Iain Cameron Williams, *Underneath a Harlem Moon: The Harlem to Paris Years of Adelaide Hall* (London: Continuum, 2020).

8. "The Crooning Blackbird" (advertisement), *New York Amsterdam News*, January 18, 1933, 8.

9. Artie Crier, "Yonkers," *New York Age*, January 28, 1933, 8.

10. Tommy Seay, "Westchester Chatterbox," *New York Age*, September 5, 1936, 12.

11. "New York State Personal Notes," *New York Age*, March 25, 1933.

12. Russ Immarigeon, "The 'Ungovernable' Ella Fitzgerald," Prison Public Memory Project, October 29, 2014, https://www.prisonpublicmemory.org/blog/2014/the-ungovernable-ella-fitzgerald.

13. Some alumni from Riverdale recall Fitzgerald singing in the choir there, as recounted in Melba Butler, "There Is Home: A Case Study of the Colored Orphan Asylum in New York City," Ph.D. diss., City University of New York, 2012, 107.

14. Nina Bernstein, *The Lost Children of Wilder: The Epic Struggle to Change Foster Care* (New York: Pantheon, 2001), 9.

15. Richard Firestone, "In Memoriam: Fannie French Morse: 1866–1944," *Sociometry* 7, no. 1 (February 1944): 76–78.

16. Milton Bass, "Ella Fitzgerald," review of Music Barn concert, *Berkshire Eagle*, July 1, 1957, 13. The musicians were Don Abney (piano), Ray Brown (bass), Herb Ellis (guitar), and Jo Jones (drums).

17. "Small Town Vignette," *Chatham Courier*, June 27, 1957, https://www .fultonhistory.com/Fulton.html.

18. Nina Bernstein, "Ward of the State: The Gap in Ella Fitzgerald's Life," *New York Times*, June 23, 1996, sec. 4, 4. This article broke the story of the Hudson School and helped spur research into the institution.

19. Russ Immarigeon, conversation with the author, September 5, 2018. Immarigeon, who has conducted extensive archival research, stated that the quality of the recordkeeping fell off in the mid-1930s.

20. "Yonkers, N.Y.," *New York Age*, May 26, 1934, 8.

21. Hank O'Neal, *The Ghosts of Harlem: Sessions with Jazz Legends* (Nashville, Tenn.: Vanderbilt University Press, 2009), 295.

22. *Essence* interview, quoted in Jim Haskins, *Ella Fitzgerald: A Life Through Jazz* (London: Hodder & Stoughton, 1991), 26.

23. The discovery of Tempie's death certificate ("Tempie Fitzcorrey," Yonkers City Clerk's Office, New York) resulted from Christine McKay's first locating the gravesite and tombstone in Oakland Cemetery in Yonkers. Leonard Feather gave 1934 as the date in "The Three Graces of Jazz. Ella, Billie, Sarah," in Ken Williamson, ed., *This Is Jazz* (London: Newnes, 1960), 148. I think it likely that Ella believed that the accident two years earlier caused Tempie's death. Her statements about infections and such after the accident might have led to the conclusion of cause and effect. Later, jazz writers placed Tempie's death in 1932. However, the unsettling coincidence of the death date and the date of the accident has yet to be fully explained. In an interview, Ella mentioned her mother singing "Object of Affection," which came out in 1934. See Richard Harrington, "In the Key of Ella," *Washington Post*, May 6, 1988, B1.

24. Stuart Nicholson, *Ella Fitzgerald: The Complete Biography*, updated ed. (New York: Routledge, 2004), 32.

25. Ibid.

26. Phoebe Jacobs, interview by the author, December 7, 2009. Virginia Williams's daughter Dorothy Johnson supported this contention.

27. Phoebe Jacobs and Jim Blackman, interview by the author, March 27, 2011.

28. Ray Brown, Jr., interview by the author, November 18, 2018. According to the U.S. Census for 1920, Georgiana Williams's Social Security card application on July 3, 1941, lists her birthplace as Richmond, Va.; her birthdate as March 13, 1913; her mother as Virginia Davis; and her father as Charles Williams.

29. Viola Bagwell (Yonkers resident who knew Correy), conversation with the author, October 2009.

30. The U.S. Census for 1920 lists Virginia Williams with her daughter Georgie (age six) and Leon (age two).

31. George Ornstein, "The Cause of Death Among Negroes: Tuberculosis," *Journal of Negro Education* 6, no. 3 (July 1937): 303–13.

32. For Central Harlem population statistics, see "Harlem's Shifting Population," *Gotham Gazette*, September 2, 2008, http://www.gothamgazette.com/index.php/ city/4077-harlems-shifting-population.

33. Morris Sussman's slogan is cited in Ralph Cooper and Steve Daugherty, *Amateur Night at the Apollo: Ralph Cooper Presents Five Decades of Great Entertainment* (New York: HarperCollins, 1990), 62.

34. Shirley Greenes, Oral History interview, 2009, Columbia Center for Oral History.

35. "Apollo Joins Other Houses: Another Theatre on 125th Street to Play Negro Acts and Revues," *New York Amsterdam News*, January 17, 1934, 7.

36. George Norford, "Amateur Night," *New York Amsterdam News*, April 28, 1934, 6.

37. Greenes interview. See also "Colored Vaude Tilt Resumes in Harlem," *Billboard*, May 22, 1934, 41.

38. J. F., "Harlem Amateur Night," *Billboard*, November 24, 1934, 9; *Quad-City Times* (Davenport, Ia.), January 1, 1935, 5; *Times-Tribune* (Scranton, Penn.), May 13, 1936.

39. For Robinson, see Norford, "Amateur Night." Ellington is mentioned in *Herald Statesman*, December 12, 1934, 11.

40. Abel [Green], "Apollo, Harlem," *Variety*, November 13, 1934, 17.

41. Jeff Kisseloff, *You Must Remember This: An Oral History of Manhattan from the 1890s to World War II* (Baltimore: Johns Hopkins University Press, 1989), 317–18.

42. Gene Lees, "Ella by Starlight," *Gene Lees' Jazzletter* 11, no. 1 (January 1992): 3.

43. Leonard Feather, *From Satchmo to Miles* (New York: Stein & Day, 1972), 88.

44. Barbaralee Diamonstein, *Open Secrets: Ninety-four Women in Touch with Our Time* (New York: Viking Press, 1972), 135.

45. Named as Doris and Frances in "Ella on Ella: A Personal Portrait," *Essence* (television program), NBC, April 26, 1986, Paley Center for Media, https://www .paleycenter.org/collection/item/?q=first&p=248&item=T:08316.

46. Tommy Seay, "Westchester Chatterbox," *New York Age*, September 5, 1936. On the carfare, see Thomas Seay, "Westchester Chatterbox," *New York Age*, February 20, 1937.

47. Seay, "Westchester Chatterbox," February 20, 1937.

48. Hoagy Carmichael with Stephen Longstreet, *Sometimes I Wonder* (London: Alvin Redman, 1966), 239.

49. Gerold Frank, *Judy* (New York: Harper & Row, 1975), 58.

50. "Edwards Sisters Hot Dance Team," *Chicago Defender*, December 22, 1934, 8.

51. Cooper and Dougherty, *Amateur Night at the Apollo*, 86–87.

52. Greenes interview.

53. Norma Miller, interview in Jeff Kaufman, dir., *The Savoy King: Chick Webb and the Music That Changed America* (documentary), 2012.

54. Ella Fitzgerald, interview by Sidney Fields, "Songbird Is Missing a Note," *New York Mirror*, June 21, 1957.

55. Diamonstein, *Open Secrets*, 135.

56. Lillian Johnson, "Ella Fitzgerald's Hardest Job Was to Get Folks to Listen!," *Baltimore Afro-American*, October 9, 1937, 10.

57. "Apollo to Feature Bennie," *Pittsburgh Courier*, November 17, 1934, A9.

58. Norman David, *The Ella Fitzgerald Companion* (Westport, Conn.: Praeger, 2004), 10.

59. Chris Albertson, *Bessie*, rev. expanded ed. (New Haven, Conn.: Yale University Press, 2004), 227.

60. John McDonough, liner notes to *The Complete Chick Webb & Ella Fitzgerald Decca Sessions (1934–1941)*, Mosaic Records MD8-252, 2013, 4–5. This excellent essay includes McDonough's unique experience hearing the story about Henderson as a reminiscence between Fitzgerald and Benny Carter.

61. Ibid.

62. John Hammond, "Counterpoint," *Melody News*, November 1, 1934, 10.

63. "Believe It Beloved" (with George Whiting, Nat Schwartz, and J. C. Johnson), recorded in November 1934, stayed on the *Billboard* charts for eleven weeks, peaking at number five in April 1935.

64. Teddy Wilson interview (January 27, 1983), quoted in Barney Josephson and Terry Trilling-Josephson, *Café Society: The Wrong Place for the Right People* (Urbana: University of Illinois Press, 2009), 53.

65. Feather, *Satchmo to Miles*, 89.

66. Jeffrey Magee, *The Uncrowned King of Swing: Fletcher Henderson and Big Band Jazz* (New York: Oxford University Press, 2005), 95.

67. Nicholson, *Ella Fitzgerald* (2004), 38.

68. "Lost in a Fog," recorded by Bob Crosby (with Tommy Dorsey) and Connie Boswell (with Jimmy Grier) and Coleman Hawkins in 1934; Fitzgerald's version is on *Hello Love*.

69. Joe Smith, *Off the Record: An Oral History of Popular Music* (New York: Warner, 1988), 15.

70. "Willie Bryant, not Chick Webb, Gave Ella Fitzgerald Her First Start," *Chicago Defender*, November 11, 1939, 21. For the date of February 1, 1935, as Bryant's booking, see "Headliners Feature the Harlem Opera House Bill," incorporated into the digitized listing "Bill Robinson Signs for Role in RKO Feature," *New York Amsterdam News*, January 19, 1935, 10.

71. Stephanie Stein Crease, *Rhythm Man: Chick Webb and the Beat That Changed America* (New York: Oxford University Press, 2023). I am indebted to the author for giving me access to a prepublication copy.

72. "Tiny Bradshaw Will Top Opera House Bill," *New York Amsterdam News*, February 16, 1935, 10.

73. Ella Fitzgerald, interview by Leonard Feather, *Down Beat*, November 18, 1965.

74. Feather, *Satchmo to Miles*, 89.

75. Ted Fox, *Showtime at the Apollo* (New York: Holt, Rinehart & Winston, 1983), 89.

76. Ted Yates, "Harlem on My Mind," *Baltimore Afro-American*, March 2, 1935, 9.

77. Leonard Feather, "Ella's Good Heart Is Strong Again," *San Francisco Examiner*, May 7, 1989. The Boswell Sisters also recorded the tune with Pinky Tomlin, the songwriter.

78. Joel Siegel, "Ella at 65: A Lot to Be Grateful For," *Jazz Times*, November 1983, 11.

79. Jim Cleaver, "A Welcome Look at Dave Dexter's 'Playback,'" *Los Angeles Sentinel*, January 13, 1977, A7.

80. "The Object of My Affection," on Ella Fitzgerald, *Live at Chautauqua*, Dot Time Records DT8001, 2015, CD.

81. "Bradshaw, Pops and Louie and Alice Hits," *New York Amsterdam News*, February 22, 1935.

82. "Cab Calloway to Top Opera House Show," *New York Amsterdam News*, February 23, 1935, 10.

83. "Cab Packs 'Em In," *Chicago Defender*, March 2, 1935, 9.

84. Naresh Fernandes, "The Indian Who Discovered Ella," *Taj Mahal Foxtrot*, April 27, 2013, http://www.tajmahalfoxtrot.com/the-indian-who-discovered-ella/.

85. Bardu Ali quotes are from Johnny Otis, *Listen to the Lambs* (Minneapolis: University of Minnesota Press, 2009), 158.

Chapter 3: Into Chick Webb's Orbit (1935)

1. Ella Fitzgerald, interview by Leonard Feather, January 15, 1983, Ella Fitzgerald Project, Leonard Feather Collection, University of Idaho.

2. Stephanie Stein Crease, *Rhythm Man: Chick Webb and the Beat That Changed America* (New York: Oxford University Press, 2023). I am indebted to the author for giving me access to a prepublication copy.

3. Quoted in ibid.

4. Jeff Kaufman, dir., *The Savoy King: Chick Webb and the Music That Changed America* (documentary), 2012.

5. "Display Ad 46," *New York Amsterdam News,* February 2, 1927, 11.

6. William Barlow, *Voice Over: The Making of Black Radio* (Philadelphia: Temple University Press, 1998), 23.

7. Abel [Green], "Rose Danceland," *Variety*, December 21, 1927, 54; reprinted as "Webb's Orchestra Is Mainstay of Rose Danceland," *Baltimore Afro-American*, January 7, 1928, 7.

8. Christi Jay Wells, "'Lindy Hopper's Delight': The Chick Webb Orchestra and the Fluid Labor of Whitey's Lindy Hoppers," in *Between Beats: The Jazz Tradition and Black Vernacular Dance*, chap. 3 (New York: Oxford University Press, 2021).

9. "Moe Gale Dies; Impresario," *New York Times*, September 3, 1964, 29; Jonathan Karp, "Blacks, Jews, and the Business of Race Music," in Rebecca Kobrin, ed., *Chosen Capital: The Jewish Encounter with American Capitalism* (New Brunswick, N.J.: Rutgers University Press, 2012), 142.

10. "New Booking Co. Organized," *Plaindealer* [Topeka], November 13, 1931.

11. "Chick Webb on a Radio Chain Hook-Up Daily," *Chicago Defender*, August 25, 1934, 8; "Bands on the Air," *Metronome*, April 1934, 22.

12. Russell Sanjek, *Pennies from Heaven: The American Popular Music Business in the Twentieth Century*, updated by David Sanjek (1988; reprint New York: Da Capo Press, 1996), 127.

13. Benny Carter interview in Hank O'Neal, *The Ghosts of Harlem: Sessions with Jazz Legends* (Nashville, Tenn.: Vanderbilt University Press, 2009), 162.

14. "Hot Orchestrations," *Melody News*, December 1, 1934, 2.

15. Allison McCracken, *Real Men Don't Sing: Crooning in American Culture* (Chapel Hill, N.C.: Duke University Press, 2015).

16. "Harlem Chirpers Prove It's Sweet Singing Fans Prefer," *Chicago Defender*, May 18, 1935, 7. Hopkins had played the Savoy with Orlando Roberson on May 25, 1934.

17. Paul Eduard Miller, "Ivie Joined the Duke for Four Weeks, Stays with Band for Twelve Years," *Down Beat*, July 15, 1942, 31.

18. Dorothy Anderson, "The Yawning After," *Baltimore Afro-American*, February 23, 1935, 8.

19. For an introduction to the growing literature on this topic, see Elizabeth F. Loftus, *Eyewitness Testimony* (Cambridge, Mass.: Harvard University Press, 1979).

20. Stanley Dance, *The World of Swing* (New York: Scribner's, 1974), 87.

21. Stuart Nicholson, *Ella Fitzgerald: The Complete Biography*, updated ed. (New York: Routledge, 2004), 54.

22. Ibid.

23. Lillian Johnson, "Ella Fitzgerald's Hardest Job Was to Get Folks to Listen!," *Baltimore Afro-American*, October 9, 1937, 10.

24. "Formality Marks Yale Promenade," *New York Times*, March 9, 1935, 20; "Whiteman's Baton to Guide Over 1500 Down Gala Path of 'Different' Prom," *Yale Daily News*, March 8, 1935.

25. Mario Bauzá, interview by Smithsonian, September 9–10, 1992, Smithsonian Jazz Oral History Program, National Museum of American History.

26. Sidney Fields, "Songbird Is Missing a Note," *New York Mirror*, June 21, 1957.

27. Nicholson, *Ella Fitzgerald* (2004), 54.

28. Eva Jessye, "Chorus Girl Has Helped Glorify Modern Woman: Manager of Dixie Jubilee Singers Says Chorines Have Forced Recognition of Colored Woman," *Pittsburgh Courier*, August 25, 1928, A1.

29. Al Feldman changed his name legally to Van Alexander in 1939. See Kaufman, dir., *The Savoy King*.

30. Thomas Seay, "Yonkers-Town Goes to Harlem Town," Westchester Chatterbox, *New York Age*, September 5, 1936, 12.

31. Cheryl Lynn Greenberg, *Or Does It Explode? Black Harlem in the Great Depression* (New York: Oxford University Press, 1991), 3.

32. Tom Cassidy, "Harlem Race Riot. Police Fire on Mob," *Daily News* (New York), March 20, 1935, 3.

33. "Harlem Relief Is Poor; Misery Caused Race War: With Thousands Out of Job," *Chicago Defender*, March 30, 1935, 1.

34. "802 Planning Monster Benefit Which May Last for 12 Hours," *Billboard*, April 6, 1935, 4.

35. Charles Hiroshi Garrett, *Struggling to Define a Nation: American Music and the Twentieth Century* (Berkeley: University of California Press, 2008), 154.

36. "Chick Webb Battles Big White Band in Harlem," *Norfolk Journal and Guide*, May 4, 1935, 15; Christopher J. Wells, "'Spinnin' the Webb': Representational Spaces, Mythic Narratives, and the 1937 Webb/Goodman Battle of Music," *Journal of the Society for American Music* 14, no. 2 (2000): 176–96.

37. Fitzgerald's Social Security application on September 6, 1935, gives her address as Hotel Braddock, New York, and her birthday as April 25, 1918.

38. "Chick Webb and His Gang to Hold Spotlight Tonight at Sunset Casino," *Atlanta Daily World*, October 25, 1935, 3.

39. "Little Chick and His Chicks Score Again," *New York Amsterdam News*, November 16, 1935, 12.

40. A 1937 photograph shows Fitzgerald and Linton onstage at the Apollo. "The Theater Where Ella Fitzgerald Got Her Start," *New York Times*, June 25, 2020.

41. "Out of Billy Rowe's Harlem Note Book," *Pittsburgh Courier*, November 6, 1937, 21.

42. Johnson, "Ella Fitzgerald's Hardest Job."

43. Fitzgerald interview by Feather, January 15, 1983, Ella Fitzgerald Project.

44. Quoted in Nicholson, *Ella Fitzgerald* (2004), 63–64.

45. Ibid., 56.

46. Ibid., 37.

47. Ted Yates, "Harlem on My Mind," *Baltimore Afro-American*, March 9, 1935, 9; "Proceeds of Dance for Scottsboro Aid: Defense Committee Gives Dance to Aid Boys," *New York Amsterdam News*, February 22, 1936.

48. "Ruby Bates, Heroine of Scottsboro Case, Goes Unrecognized at Dance," *Norfolk Journal and Guide* (Norfolk, Va.), February 29, 1936, 3.

49. Charles Bowen, "On the Air," *Baltimore Afro-American,* March 7, 1936, 11.

50. Mary Lou Williams's autobiographical account ran in several installments in the British magazine *Melody Maker* from April to June 1954.

51. George T. Simon, "Pick-Ups," *Metronome*, January 1936, 27.

52. "Billy Rowe Reviews Theatricals for 1935," *Pittsburgh Courier*, January 4, 1936, A7.

53. Ronald Garfield Welburn, "American Jazz Criticism, 1914–1940," Ph.D. diss., New York University, 1983, 229. Welburn has an important interview with Billy Rowe, 227–42.

54. Leonard Feather, *From Satchmo to Miles* (New York: Stein & Day, 1972), 88.

55. Ernani Bernardi quoted in Leonard Feather, "Ella's Good Heart Is Strong Again," *San Francisco Examiner*, May 7, 1989.

Chapter 4: Swing-Song Singer (1935–1936)

1. Sidney Fields, " 'Songbird' Is Missing a Note," *New York Mirror*, June 21, 1957.

2. "Amusement Machines: 10 Best Records," *Billboard*, October 26, 1935, 77; "10 Best Records for the Week November 30," *Billboard*, December 7, 1935, 66.

3. Geoffrey Mark Fidelman, *First Lady of Song: Ella Fitzgerald for the Record* (New York: Citadel Press, 1994), 14.

4. Robert O'Meally, *The Jazz Singers* (Washington, D.C.: Smithsonian Collection of Recordings, 1998), 51–52.

5. Abel Green, "Swing It!" *Variety*, January 1, 1936, 188.

6. Ida Mae Ryan, "Along Radio Lane: 'Swing' Artists Enliven Rhythm Over WOR—Lewis-McAvoy Fight Put on Air," *New York Amsterdam News*, March 14, 1936, 8.

7. Albert Murray, *Stomping the Blues* (New York: McGraw-Hill, 1976), 106.

8. Roi Ottley, "Popularity Runs in Cycles, Says Savoy Exponent of Swing," *New York Amsterdam News*, February 13, 1937, 10. Webb makes a similar claim in Leon Hardwick, "Swing Is Newer Form of Old Art—Chick Webb: Noted Drummer, a Native Baltimorean Has Always Felt Swing," *Baltimore Afro-American*, October 16, 1937, 10. Ottley wrote the best-selling *"New World A-Coming": Inside Black America* (New York: Literary Classics, Inc., 1943).

9. *Harlem-Savoy* is a term from Marshall Stearns, "New Records," *Tempo*, December 1936, 13.

10. "Musikers Unabridged Dictionary of Jazz Terms," *Metronome*, February 1936, 21; Franklyn Frank, "'Swing' Terms New Vogue in Gay Nite Life," *Atlanta Daily World*, March 18, 1936, 2. See also Tom Dalzell, *Flappers 2 Rappers: American Youth Slang* (Mineola, N.Y.: Dover, 2012), 35. The term *crack canary* is from "Music-Nite Clubs: Swing Stuff," *Variety*, February 19, 1936, 61.

11. Gabler quoted in Stuart Nicholson, *Ella Fitzgerald: The Complete Biography*, updated ed. (New York: Routledge, 2004), 84.

12. "Musikers Unabridged Dictionary," 21.

13. Some early mentions include: "Betty Elliott, Radio 'Swing' Singer," *Atlanta Constitution*, September 11, 1935. Eileen O'Day is called a "clever little blond swing singer" in F. Langdon Morgan, "Oriental, Chicago," *Billboard*, April 18, 1936, 17. See also Cornelius Vanderbilt, Jr., "American Films' and Tin Pan Alley's Influence Noticed Around the Globe," *Variety*, September 23, 1936, 36. Billie Holiday is described as a "top ranking swing singer" in "TAPS," *Tempo*, April 1937, 9. An obituary for Holiday's father calls her a "star swing singer." Mildred Bailey is said to be a "star swing singer" in "The Great Red Father and the Rockin' Chair Lady," *Down Beat*, July 1938, 6.

14. Edward Duke Ellington, *Music Is My Mistress* (New York: Doubleday, 1973), 100.

15. "Joe Disk" [pseud.], "Wax Impressions," *Tempo*, February 1936, 7.

16. Donald Clarke, *Billie Holiday: Wishing on the Moon* (Cambridge, Mass.: Da Capo Press, 2002), 104, 106.

17. Teddy McRae (tenor sax) and John Trueheart (guitar).

18. "All My Life," Brunswick 8116, 1938. Sidney Mitchell (lyrics), and Sam H. Stept (music). Ella Fitzgerald is credited with "vocal chorus."

19. George T. Simon (pseud. Gordon Wright), "DISCussions," *Metronome*, May 1936, 40.

20. Joel Whitburn, *Pop Memories 1890–1954* (Menomonee Falls, Wis.: Record Research, 1986), 436, 459. According to *Billboard*, Wilson's version peaked at number thirteen and charted for two weeks.

21. Ross Firestone, *Swing, Swing, Swing: The Life and Times of Benny Goodman* (New York: W. W. Norton, 1993), 136.

22. Whitburn, *Pop Memories*, 159.

23. Van Alexander and Stephen Fratallone, *From Harlem to Hollywood: My Life in Music* (Albany, Ga.: BearManor Media, 2009), 28.

24. Whitburn, *Pop Memories*, 579, lists only the Webb version on the charts.

25. Edgar Greentree, "Discussion," *Down Beat*, August 1936, 8.

26. Van Alexander, interview by the author, June 1, 2010.

27. Marc Myers, "Interview: Van Alexander (pt. 1)," *JazzWax*, May 2, 2012, http://www.jazzwax.com/2012/05/interview-van-alexander-part-1.html.

28. Alexander and Fratallone, *Harlem to Hollywood*, 27–28.

29. Kitty Grime, *Jazz Voices* (London: Quartet Books, 1983), 48–49.

30. Will Friedwald, *A Biographical Guide to the Great Jazz and Pop Singers* (New York: Pantheon, 2010), 382.

31. John Hammond, " 'Raves' and 'Razzes' on Recent Record Releases," *Down Beat*, December 1936, 23.

32. Bruce Crowther and Mike Pinfold, *Singing Jazz: The Singers and Their Styles* (San Francisco: Miller Freeman, 1997), 124.

33. Friedwald, *Biographical Guide*, 644.

34. "Tritone," in *Harvard Dictionary of Music*, ed. Don Michael Randel, 4th ed. (Cambridge, Mass.: Harvard University Press, 2003), 1679. The interval is also commonly called the "augmented fourth."

35. She ended the second break with a wild leap from D down to G# before the horns reentered and solidified this dissonant chord, as noted in Catherine M. da Silva, "The Influence of Dizzy Gillespie's Bebop Style on Ella Fitzgerald's 'Flying Home,' 'Lady Be Good,' and 'How High the Moon' Solos," Ph.D. diss., Five Towns College, 2013, 128.

36. The *Ed Sullivan* appearance was on July 18, 1948.

37. Ella Fitzgerald, interview by Leonard Feather, January 15, 1983, Ella Fitzgerald Project, Leonard Feather Collection, University of Idaho.

38. Mario Bauzá, interview by Porter Roberts, quoted in Stephanie Stein Crease, *Rhythm Man: Chick Webb and the Beat That Changed America* (New York: Oxford University Press, 2023), n.p. I am indebted to the author for giving me access to a prepublication copy.

39. Teddy McRae, interview by Ron Welburn, January 1981, transcript, 231, 334, Jazz Oral History Project, Institute of Jazz Studies, Rutgers University.

40. Crease, *Rhythm Man*, n.p.

41. Ken Vail, ed., *Swing Era Scrapbook: The Teenage Diaries and Radio Logs of Bob Inman, 1936–1938* (Lanham, Md.: Scarecrow Press, 2006), 78–79.

42. "Music-Nite Clubs: Swing Stuff," *Variety*, February 19, 1936, 61.

43. William Barlow, *Voice Over: The Making of Black Radio* (Philadelphia: Temple University Press, 1999), 31, 33–35.

44. "Pick-Ups Roasts and Toasts," *Metronome*, June 1935, 21.

45. "Music: Swing Stuff," *Variety*, March 4, 1936, 58.

46. Charles Bowen, "On the Air," *Baltimore Afro-American*, March 14, 1936, 10.

47. "Krupa, Wilson Winners," *Metronome*, January 1937, 22.

48. Sondra K. Wilson, *Meet Me at the Theresa: The Story of Harlem's Most Famous Hotel* (New York: Atria, 2004), 189ff; Billy Rowe obituary in *Jet*, October 13, 1997, 18.

49. "Out of Billy Rowe's Harlem Note Book," *Pittsburgh Courier*, April 4, 1936, A9.

50. Several tour dates are listed in Ron Fritts and Ken Vail, *Ella Fitzgerald: The Chick Webb Years & Beyond* (Lanham, Md.: Scarecrow Press, 2003), 9–12.

51. Van Alexander and Stephen Fratallone, *From Harlem to Hollywood: My Life in Music* (Albany, Ga.: BearManor Media, 2009), 24.

52. McRae interview by Welburn, 332.

Chapter 5: The Second Feature (1936–1937)

1. Mack Gordon is listed in www.jazzstandards.com. Both Gordon and Revel are profiled in the Songwriters Hall of Fame, www.songhall.org. Among their best-known songs before 1936 are "Did You Ever See a Dream Walking?" and "You Hit the Spot."

2. Teddy McRae, interview by Ron Welburn, January 1981, transcript, 229, 333, Jazz Oral History Project, Institute of Jazz Studies, Rutgers University.

3. Ross Firestone, *Swing, Swing, Swing: The Life and Times of Benny Goodman* (New York: W. W. Norton, 1993), 128–29.

4. H. M. Oakley, "Goodman's Playing Defies Adequate Description," *Down Beat*, August 1935, 4.

5. Ward's account of her relationship with Goodman is in Firestone, *Swing, Swing, Swing*, 184–86.

6. "Rivals? Why Ethel Gave Ella Her Biggest Thrill!" *Baltimore Afro-American*, October 16, 1937, 10.

7. "Backstage with Homer Canfield," *Monrovia News-Post* (Calif.), November 12, 1936, 6.

8. J. Cullen Fentress, "Fentress' Gab Stuff," *California Eagle*, November 20, 1936; John McDonough, liner notes to *Chick Webb & Ella Fitzgerald Decca Sessions (1934–1941)*, Mosaic Records MD8-252, 2013, 8-CD set.

9. Stuart Nicholson, *Ella Fitzgerald: The Complete Biography*, updated ed. (New York: Routledge, 2004), 63.

10. Data taken from listings in *Billboard* and *Variety* beginning in December 1936.

11. John Hammond, "'Raves' and 'Razzes' on Recent Record Releases," *Down Beat*, December 1936, 23.

12. "Goodnight My Love" was broadcast from the Savoy on January 30, 1937, according to Ken Vail, *Swing Era Scrapbook: The Teenage Diaries and Radio Logs of Bob Inman 1936–1938* (Lanham, Md.: Scarecrow Press, 2005), 113.

13. George Hoefer, "Singer 'Evelyn Fields' on Trancs Really Ella Fitzgerald," *Down Beat*, February 24, 1950, 15; J. Cullen Fentress, "Fentress' Gab Stuff," *California Eagle*, November 20, 1936.

14. "'Rockin' Chair Lady' Appears at Surf with Red Norvo's Band," *Globe-Gazette* (Mason City, Ia.), April 21, 1937, 36.

15. Nicholson, *Ella Fitzgerald* (2004), 63.

16. Anthony Barnett, liner notes to *Let's Listen to Lucidin Presents Stuff Smith and His Lucidin Orchestra Featuring Ella Fitzgerald*, AB Fable ABCDI-024, 2010, CD; "Stuff Smith's Band, Radio Reviews," *Variety*, January 27, 1937, 31.

17. Broadcasts from January 22, 29, and February 5, 25, 1937, listed in Vail, *Swing Era Scrapbook*, 109, 112, 116, 125. Ken Jessamy, "No Air Commercials for Colored: Nix Products with Sepians," *New York Amsterdam News*, March 20, 1937, 10.

18. Marshall Davis, "Real Truth About Teddy Wilson and Benny Goodman," *Pittsburgh Courier*, November 28, 1936, 18.

19. John McDonough, eavesdropping on a private conversation in 1967, overheard Benny Carter ask Fitzgerald, "John Hammond had tried to hire you away from Webb. Isn't that about the way it happened?" Ella replied, "Yeah, that's it," with a "reclusive smile." McDonough, "The History of the Songbooks," liner notes to Ella Fitzgerald, *The Complete Ella Fitzgerald Song Books*. Verve 314–519832–2, 1993, 16-CD box set, 5.

20. "Benny Goodman Offers $5,000 for Ella's Contract, but Chick Webb Says 'No Sale,'" *Pittsburgh Courier*, December 5, 1936, 21.

21. "Ella Fitzgerald Returns to Chick Webb Again," *Pittsburgh Courier*, January 2, 1937, A7.

22. Ingrid Monson, *Freedom Sounds: Civil Rights Call Out to Jazz and Africa* (New York: Oxford University Press, 2007), 314.

23. "Out of Billy Rowe's Harlem Note Book," *Pittsburgh Courier*, December 5, 1936, 23.

24. Porter Roberts, "Praise and Criticism," *Pittsburgh Courier*, December 19, 1936, A7.

25. Edgar T. Rouzeau, "The Truth About Ella's $5,000 Offer: Chick Webb Denies Benny Goodman Offered to Buy Fitzgerald Contract; Wilson, Hampton Sign for Another Year," *Pittsburgh Courier*, January 16, 1937, A1.

26. Ibid.

27. Roi Ottley, "Popularity Runs in Cycles, Says Savoy Exponent of Swing," *New York Amsterdam News*, February 13, 1937, 10.

28. "Benny Didn't Try to Lure Ella Away," *Baltimore Afro-American*, October 16, 1937, 10. Additional relevant columns include "Around Harlem with Archie Seale," *New York Amsterdam News*, January 23, 1937, 9; and Moses, "Footlight Flickers."

29. Vivian Morris, "Harlem Beauty Shops," field report for the folklore division of the Federal Writers' Project, April 19, 1939, Library of Congress.

30. Frank Byrd, "Celebrities of Both Races Attend New York Broadcasting Studio Party," *Pittsburgh Courier*, February 13, 1937, 20.

31. Thomas Seay, "Westchester Chatterbox," *New York Age*, February 20 and March 6, 1937; "1,500 Hear Singing of Ella Fitzgerald," *Herald Statesman* (Yonkers), February 20, 1937.

32. Benn Hall, "125th Street Apollo N.Y.," *Billboard*, April 17, 1937, 18.

33. "Radio, Stage, Screen," *New York Age*, April 17, 1937, 9.

34. Al Moses, "Footlight Flickers, Swing Bands-Swing Music," *Norfolk Journal and Guide*, April 24, 1937, A16. See also "Entertainment World: New York," *New York Amsterdam News*, April 24, 1937, 16.

35. On Markham, see Frank Cullen et al., *Vaudeville Old and New: An Encyclopedia of Variety Performers in America* (New York: Routledge, 2007), 723–25.

36. For other autographs, see "To 'Ella.' Sincerely Edna Mae Harris, Noble Sissle's Orchestra, 1936–37"; "To Ella. Lucky Millinder"; "To Ella Fitzgerald. The greatest of all swing singers, Wishing you the greatest success from Norton and Margo." The author is grateful to Ray Brown, Jr., for providing access to the privately held scrapbook.

37. Markham imitations show up in Fitzgerald's version of "Mack the Knife."

38. *Whoopi Goldberg Presents Moms Mabley*, HBO documentary, 2013.

39. "Jacky Mabley Steals Chick Webb Revue at Chi's Regal Theatre," *Chicago Defender*, June 26, 1937, 11.

40. Helen Oakley, "Call Out Riot Squad to Handle Mob at Goodman-Webb Battle," *Down Beat*, June 1937, 1, 3.

41. Monk Rowe, interview by Helen Oakley Dance, February 12, 1998, Fillius Jazz Archive, Hamilton College.

42. "Chick-Benny—Oh, Man!" *New York Amsterdam News*, May 22, 1937, 20.

43. Billy Rowe, "Chick and Ella Hit at Loew's: Marching On to Greater Glory in Return Date on Broadway," *Pittsburgh Courier*, September 25, 1937, 21; "Out of Billy Rowe's Harlem Note Book: Give Me the Rhythm of the Typewriter," *Pittsburgh Courier*, September 11, 1937, 20.

44. Ashton Stevens, "Ziegfeld Would Have Starred Ella, Chick!: Ashton Stevens Lauds Artistry of Famous Pair," *Pittsburgh Courier*, December 4, 1937, 20.

45. "Rivals? Why Ethel Gave Ella."

46. Stevens, "Ziegfeld Would Have Starred Ella, Chick!" "Miss Otis Regrets" by Cole Porter had been recorded brilliantly by Ethel Waters three years earlier.

47. Stevens, "Ziegfeld Would Have Starred Ella, Chick!"

48. "Webb Sings for Records and Songs," *Billboard*, November 20, 1937, 15.

49. Martha Sherrill, "Ella Fitzgerald's High Note," *Washington Post*, April 11, 1989, D1.

50. "Leonard Bernstein," *Rolling Stone*, no. 592 (November 29, 1990), 79.

51. Wayne Enstice and Janis Stockhouse, *Jazzwomen: Conversations with Twenty-One Musicians* (Bloomington: Indiana University Press, 2004), 40.

52. "Top Jazz Singer Tells How She Got That Way," *PM*, October 24, 1947, 16.

53. *The Glory of Negro History*, Smithsonian Folkways FC7752, LP.

54. Marshall Stearns, "New Records," *Tempo*, January 1937, 8.

55. Catherine Tackley, *Benny Goodman's Famous 1938 Carnegie Hall Jazz Concert* (New York: Oxford University Press, 2012), 88.

56. The Yiddish word *schmear* was accepted in band and music arrangement primers.

57. David E. Sumner, *The Magazine Century: American Magazines Since 1900* (New York: Peter Lang, 2010), 88–89.

58. "The Story of a Song: 'Bei Mir Bist Du Schon' Now Heads Best-Sellers," *Life*, January 31, 1938, 39; "Amusement Machines: The Week's Best Records," *Billboard*, January 29, 1938, 77; Marshall J. Stearns, "Webb Wows Decca," *Tempo*, February 1938, 10.

59. "Fitzgerald's vocal girlhood, a departure from the black women blues and gospel singers prized by critics, thus became one significant means through which critics explained the Webb band's simultaneous turns toward commercialism, femininity, and whiteness." Christopher J. Wells, "'A Dreadful Bit of Silliness': Feminine Frivolity and Ella Fitzgerald's Early Critical Reception," *Women and Music: A Journal of Gender and Culture* 21 (2017): 55.

60. George T. Simon (pseud. Gordon Wright), "Discussions," *Metronome*, March 1937, 31.

61. John Hammond, "Did Bessie Smith Bleed to Death Waiting for Medical Aid?" *Down Beat*, November 1937, 15.

62. St. Clair Bourne, "'Blues'—'Swing': Death of Bessie Smith Marks Close of 'Blues Era,'" *New York Amsterdam News*, October 16, 1937, 18.

63. George T. Simon, "Roasts and Toasts in Which Some Get Slapped on the Back and Others in the Face," *Metronome*, January 1938, 20.

64. "Top Jazz Singer Tells How She Got That Way," *PM*, October 24, 1947, 16.

Chapter 6: "Truckin' On Down the Avenue" (1938)

1. "Chick Webb–Count Basie in Harlem 'Battle,'" *Chicago Defender*, January 15, 1938, 18.

2. "Out of Billy Rowe's Harlem Note Book: The Notebook's Hall of Fame . . . Count Basie," *Pittsburgh Courier*, May 1, 1937, 18.

3. "Stuff Smith Moves, Holiday Joins Count Basie," *Down Beat*, May 1937, 5.

4. Maurice Zolotow, "Music: Band Reviews—Count Basie and Band," *Billboard*, June 19, 1937, 12.

5. Norma Miller and Evette Jensen, *Swingin' at the Savoy: The Memoir of a Jazz Dancer* (Philadelphia: Temple University Press, 1996), 102.

6. "Chick, Basie Battle It Out in Swingtime," *New York Amsterdam News*, January 22, 1938, 16.

7. Susannah McCorkle, "The Mother of Us All," *American Heritage* (February–March 1994): 60–73.

8. "Webb 'Cuts' Basie in Swing Battle," *Down Beat*, February 1938, 2.

9. "Chick, Basie Battle It Out," 16.

10. Stephanie Stein Crease, *Rhythm Man: Chick Webb and the Beat That Changed America* (New York: Oxford University Press, 2023), n.p. Helen Oakley Dance, interview by Patricia Willard, MSS 62, Box 18, Stanley Dance and Helen Oakley Dance Papers, Yale Music Library; Helen Oakley Dance, interview by Oren Jacoby, in *Benny Goodman: Adventures in the Kingdom of Swing*, PBS American Masterworks, March 10, 1993.

11. "Colored Band Biz Becoming Big Biz," *Billboard*, April 2, 1938, 13.

12. Stanley Dance, *The World of Swing* (New York: Scribner's, 1974).

13. Harry "Sweets" Edison, interviewed in Stanley Dance, *The World of Count Basie* (New York: Scribner's, 1980), 105.

14. Sarah Jane Deutsch, "From Ballots to Breadlines 1920–1940," in Nancy F. Cott,

ed., *No Small Courage: A History of Women in the United States* (New York: Oxford University Press, 2000), 454.

15. For "historic dissonance," see Sherrie Tucker, *Swing Shift: "All Girl" Bands of the 1940s* (Durham, N.C.: Duke University Press, 2000), 2.

16. Linda Dahl, *Stormy Weather: The Music and Lives of a Century of Jazzwomen* (New York: Limelight Editions, 1988), 122ff; Lewis Erenberg, *Swingin' the Dream: Big Band Jazz and the Rebirth of American Culture* (Chicago: University of Chicago Press, 1998), 85–86; "More Midwest Bands Using Gal Singers," *Billboard*, July 23, 1938, 13.

17. Donald Bogle, *Brown Sugar: Eighty Years of America's Black Female Superstars* (New York: Crown, 1980), 61.

18. Ted Toll, "The Gal Yippers Have No Place in Our Jazz Bands," *Down Beat*, October 15, 1939, 18; "Why Women Musicians Are Inferior," *Down Beat*, February 1938, 4.

19. "Femme Warblers Complain Wages Don't Pay for Their Fingerwaves," *Variety*, July 13, 1938, 1.

20. This argument draws on Tammy Kernodle, "Black Women Working Together: Jazz, Gender, and the Politics of Validation," *Black Music Research Journal* 34, no. 1 (Spring 2014): 27–55.

21. Bruce Crowther and Mike Pinfold, *Singing Jazz: The Singers and Their Style* (San Francisco: Miller Freeman, 1997), 69.

22. Ibid.

23. Mario Bauzá, interview by Smithsonian, September 9–10, 1992, Smithsonian Jazz Oral History Program, National Museum of American History.

24. Lillian Johnson, "What Does Billie Holiday Wear?," *Baltimore Afro-American*, October 23, 1937, 8.

25. Norma Miller, interview by the author, January 10, 2010.

26. "Ivie Anderson Raves About Ella Fitzgerald in Exclusive Interview; Admits She's 33 Years Old," *Norfolk Journal and Guide*, November 27, 1937, 18.

27. Maxine Sullivan, interview by Sally Placksin, in Placksin, *American Women in Jazz, 1900 to the Present: Their Words, Lives, and Music* (New York: Seaview Books, 1982), 122.

28. Ron Fritts and Ken Vail, *Ella Fitzgerald: The Chick Webb Years & Beyond* (Lanham, Md.: Scarecrow Press, 2003), 25.

29. Richard Vacca, *The Boston Jazz Chronicles: Faces, Places, and Nightlife 1937–1962* (Belmont, Mass.: Troy Street, 2012), 40–41.

30. "Webb Slays 'Em in Boston," *Metronome*, March 1938, 12.

31. George Frazier, "Hackett's Nervousness Regrettable as Hell . . . And Artie Shaw's 'Goodmanish' Band Chief Objection," *Down Beat*, April 1938, 14; George Frazier, "Boston Wakes Up; Acclaims Chick Webb at Lavaggi's," *Tempo*, March 1938, 6.

32. John Chilton, *Let the Good Times Roll: The Story of Louis Jordan and His Music* (Ann Arbor: University of Michigan Press, 1992), 58–59.

33. Ibid., 55.

34. Stuart Nicholson, *Ella Fitzgerald: The Complete Biography*, updated ed. (New York: Routledge, 2004), 72.

35. Chilton, *Let the Good Times Roll*, 57.

36. "'Swing Here to Stay,' Bandleader Webb and Ella Fitzgerald, Vocalist, Agree," *Harvard Crimson*, February 23, 1938.

37. "Bedecked Amphitheatre Is Scene of 'Elbow Room' Prom Tonight," *Yale Daily News*, March 11, 1938.

38. "Chick Webb to Hospital for Operation: Only a Minor Matter, Says Swing Master," *Chicago Defender*, April 9, 1938, 18. For the "serious operation," see "Band Briefs, Boston," *Tempo*, June 1938, 19; "Chick Webb Recuperates in N.Y. Hospital," *Chicago Defender*, April 16, 1938, 19.

39. Arnold Shaw, *The Street That Never Slept: New York's Fabled 52nd Street* (1971; reprint New York: Da Capo Press, 1977), 246.

40. Ella Fitzgerald, "ASCAP Presents the Billy Taylor Interviews," Performing Arts Research Collections, Recorded Sound, LDC 42656, New York Public Library.

41. Van Alexander and Stephen Fratallone, *From Harlem to Hollywood: My Life in Music* (Albany, Ga.: BearManor Media, 2009), 35.

42. Gerald Nachman, *Raised on Radio* (New York: Pantheon, 1998), 170.

43. "Tommy Dorsey, Benny Goodman, Jack Hylton, Bert Ambrose, Harry Roy, Django Reinhardt, Louis Levy, Teddy Stauffer, James Kok, Carroll Gibbons, Ray Noble, die Mills Brothers, Sophie Tucker, Judy Garland—das waren die Stars, die uns auf Platten interessierten," in Jimmy Jungermann, *Ein Porträt* (Wetzlar: Pegasus Verlag, 1960), 6–7.

44. Arnold Shaw, *Let's Dance: Popular Music in the 1930s* (New York: Oxford University Press, 1998), 174.

45. Beverly Peer, interview by Loren Schoenberg, 1991, quoted in Nicholson, *Ella Fitzgerald* (2004), 72.

46. Garvin Bushell, *Jazz from the Beginning* (Ann Arbor: University of Michigan Press, 1988), 102.

47. Jack Schiffman, *Uptown: The Story of Harlem's Apollo Theatre* (New York: Cowles, 1971), 186.

48. James C. Burke, "Swing Exponents Make Jitterbugs of Maconites," in Ron Fritts and Ken Vail, *Ella Fitzgerald: The Chick Webb Years & Beyond 1935–1948* (Lanham, Md.: Scarecrow Press, 2003), 32.

49. "Southern Mosaic: The John and Ruby Lomax 1939 Southern States Recording Trip," Library of Congress, https://www.loc.gov/collections/john-and-ruby -lomax/about-this-collection/.

50. Paul Miller, "Scott One of the Most Vital Forces in Jazz," *Down Beat*, July 1938, 18.

51. Marshall Stearns, "New Records," *Tempo*, July 1938, 16.

52. Anita O'Day and George Eells, *High Times Hard Times* (New York: Hal Leonard, 1989), 27.

53. Leonard Feather [pseud. Rophone], "The Sillysyllabic School of Song," *Melody Maker*, July 30, 1938.

54. Teddy McRae, interview by Ron Welburn, January 1981, Jazz Oral History Project, Institute of Jazz Studies, Rutgers University.

55. Walter Winchell, "On Broadway," *Charleston Daily Mail* (S.C.), August 18, 1938.

56. Onah L. Spencer, "'Ol' Satchelmo' Makes Movie as Duke Recovers & Chick Breaks Records," *Down Beat*, September 1938, 2.

57. Isadora Smith, "Chick Webb to Halt Road Tour for Week at N.Y. Paramount," *Pittsburgh Courier*, August 13, 1938, 21.

58. Isadora Smith, "Chick and Ella Set Attendance Record at the Paramount," *Pittsburgh Courier*, August 20, 1938, 20.

59. "'Alex' Socko $75,000 2d Week, Other B'way Grosses Good; 'Sailor'-Webb Orch. Nifty $40,000, '4's a Crowd 75G," *Variety*, August 17, 1938, 9.

60. "The Screen: At N.Y. Paramount," *Brooklyn Daily Eagle*, August 11, 1938.

61. "$1,000 Increase to Chick" and "Page for Chick Webb," *Baltimore Afro-American*, September 10, 1938, 10.

62. Abel Green, "Paramount, N.Y.," *Variety*, August 17, 1938, 54.

63. "Out of Billy Rowe's Harlem Note Book," *Pittsburgh Courier*, August 13, 1938, 11.

64. Earl Wilson, "A Tisket, a Tasket, the Wrong Colored Basket," *New York Post*, August 15, 1938.

65. Earl Wilson, "That's Earl for Today," *Evening Standard* (Uniontown, Penn.), July 6, 1961, 16.

66. Leonard Feather (pseud. Rophone), "Hot Record Revived," *Melody Maker*, March 25, 1939.

67. Bardu Ali, interview by Steve Allen in *Satchmo: The Story of Louis Armstrong*, BBC 2 (radio documentary), December 1974, Satchmo Collection, Louis Armstrong House Museum.

68. I. P. Reynolds, "Atlanta Sees Chick and Ella," *Atlanta Daily World*, September 7, 1938.

69. Burke, "Swing Exponents," 32.

70. Onah L. Spencer, "Chick Webb's $25,000 Gate Breaks Benny Goodman's Record," *Down Beat*, December 1938, 2.

71. "Chick Webb Improving in Hospital," *Baltimore Afro-American*, November 12, 1938, 9. Beason is mentioned in "Band Briefs: Washington," *Tempo*, November 1938, 22.

72. Burm. "Variety House Reviews: Hipp, Balto," *Variety*, October, 26, 1938, 44.

73. Lillian Johnson, "Light and Shadow," *Baltimore Afro-American*, November 5, 1938, 12.

74. "Chick Webb to Go to Johns Hopkins," *Pittsburgh Courier*, October 22, 1938, 21.

75. "Chick Webb Leaves Baltimore Hospital," *Pittsburgh Courier*, November 12, 1938, 21. The tour dates are from Fritts and Vail, *Ella Fitzgerald*, 33–35.

76. "Apollo, N.Y.," *Variety*, January 18, 1939, 44.

77. Examples include Daniel Richman, "Night Club Reviews: Glass Hat, Hotel Belmont Plaza, New York," *Billboard*, March 18, 1939, 19; Bill Chase, "All Ears," *New York Amsterdam News*, December 3, 1938.

78. Van Alexander, *From Harlem to Hollywood*, 42.

79. "Top Jazz Singer Tells How She Got That Way," *PM*, October 24, 1947, 16.

Chapter 7: Chick and Ella (1939)

1. "Apollo, N.Y.," *Variety*, January 18, 1939, 44.

2. "On the Bandwagon," *Bandwagon*, January 1939, 2.

3. "Inside Stuff—Orchestras," *Variety*, February 22, 1939, 40. Details vary from $1,500 to $2,000 a week, the latter in Onah L. Spencer, "Louis Armstrong Set to Record Famous Old Bert Williams Tunes," *Down Beat*, January 1939, 4.

4. Billy Rowe, "Chick Webb Is Signed for Park Central Job," *Pittsburgh Courier*, November 5, 1938, 20.

5. "Night Club Reviews: Cocoanut Grove," *Variety*, February 1, 1939, 40.

6. Al Monroe, "On the Avenue," *Chicago Defender*, February 18, 1939, 11.

7. Floyd Snelson, "Harlem: Negro Capital of the World," *New York Age*, February 4, 1939.

8. M. H. Orodenker, "Cocoanut Grove, Park Central Hotel, New York," *Billboard*, February 4, 1939, 28.

9. Irving Kolodin, "The Dance Band Business: A Study in Black and White," *Harper's Magazine*, June 1941.

10. "Ella Opens 'Nitery'; Cab Goes to Central Park," *Pittsburgh Courier*, July 3, 1943, 20.

11. "Chick Webb," in Stanley Dance, *The World of Swing* (New York: Scribner's, 1974).

12. Daniel Richman, "Paramount," *Billboard*, March 18, 1939, 22; Hobe, "Variety House Reviews: Paramount, N.Y.," *Variety*, March 15, 1939, 45.

13. Herb, "Fox-Philly," *Variety*, April 19, 1939, 52. Joel Whitburn, *Pop Memories 1890–1954* (Menomonee Falls, Wis.: Record Research, 1986), 395. Peak position number three, charting on July 23, 1938. "Tutti Frutti," copyright Doris Fisher and Slim Gaillard, *Catalog of Copyright Entries: Part 3 Musical Compositions Including List of Copyright Renewals*, 1938, new series, vol. 33, no. 10 (Washington, D.C.: United States Government Printing Office, 1939), 1894.

14. "Chick Webb's Checkup at Johns Hopkins Hosp.," *Variety*, March 29, 1939, 30.

15. Count Basie, *Good Morning Blues: The Autobiography of Count Basie* (New York: Random House, 1985), 226.

16. N.K., "News . . . Boston," *Metronome*, June 1939, 26.

17. "Apollo, N.Y.," *Variety*, May 31, 1939, 37.

18. M. Oakley Stafford, "Informing You," *Hartford Courant*, May 5, 1951; originally published in *Hartford Daily Courant*, January 1, 1939, 4.

19. Heywood Henry quoted in Stuart Nicholson, *Ella Fitzgerald: The Complete Biography*, updated ed. (New York: Routledge, 2004), 76. It's not clear who instigated the rumors that the two were engaged. A gossip columnist spied a diamond ring on her hand. It was a present from Moe Gale, as she later admitted, though her fling with Henry lasted a few months.

20. Teddy McRae, interview by Ron Welburn, January 1981, Jazz Oral History Project, Institute of Jazz Studies, Rutgers University.

21. Ibid.

22. "Chick Webb's Show Goes On as He Dies in Baltimore," *Montgomery Advertiser*, June 18, 1939.

23. McRae interview by Welburn, 401–2.

24. Nell Dodson, "10,000 Bid Farewell to Chick Webb," *Baltimore Afro-American*, June 24, 1939, 1.

25. Lillian Johnson, "From Newsboy to King: The Story of Chick Webb," *Baltimore Afro-American*, August 26, 1939, 11.

26. AP, "Chick Webb, Band Leader, Dies at 30," *Hartford Daily Courant*, June 18, 1939.

27. "Chick Webb Is Dead: Negro Orchestra Leader Victim of Tuberculosis," *New York Times*, June 17, 1939, 19.

28. "Chick Webb, Just Hitting Peak, Dies at 30 Following Operation," *Variety*, June 21, 1939, 41.

29. "Bar Rest," *Metronome*, July 1939, 26.

30. Barry Ulanov, "Cootie Calls Chick Greatest Leader," *Metronome*, July 1941, 46–47.

31. Leonard Feather (pseud. Rophone), "Commercialism Was Too Strong for Chick Webb," *Melody Maker*, July 8, 1939.

32. David Green, *Shaping Political Consciousness: The Language of Politics in America from McKinley to Reagan* (Ithaca, N.Y.: Cornell University Press, 1987), ix.

33. John McDonough, historical overview and commentary, in *The Complete Chick Webb and Ella Fitzgerald Decca Sessions (1934–1941)*, Mosaic MD8-252, 2013, 8-CD box set.

34. E.g., Garvin Bushell, *Jazz from the Beginning* (Ann Arbor: University of Michigan Press, 1988), 102–3; Taft Jordan interview in Dance, *World of Swing*, 87; and Dick Vance in Burt Korall, *Drummin' Men: The Heartbeat of Jazz; The Swing Years* (New York: Schirmer, 1990), 32–33.

35. "Top Jazz Singer Tells How She Got That Way," *PM*, October 24, 1947, 16.

36. Michael Levin, "Swing," *Harvard Crimson*, April 28, 1939.

37. "Ella May Be New Boss of Chick Webb's Band," *Pittsburgh Courier*, June 24, 1939, 21; "Will Ella Fitzgerald Be Same Minus Chick?" *Chicago Defender*, July 15, 1939, 20; "What Next for Ella Fitzgerald?" *Norfolk Journal and Guide*, June 24, 1939, 16.

38. David W. Kellum, "Backstage with the Scribe," *Chicago Defender*, June 24, 1939, 20.

39. Al Monroe, "Ella Fitzgerald Rejects Offers to Marry," *Chicago Defender*, July 15, 1939, 20.

40. George T. Simon, "Record Reviews," *Metronome*, May 1946, 30.

41. Richard Gale, interview by the author, May 19, 2009.

42. Bernie Woods, "The Dance Band Parade," *Variety*, January 3, 1940, 125.

43. Jim Haskins, *Ella Fitzgerald: A Life Through Jazz* (London: Hodder & Stoughton, 1991), 58.

44. Beverly Peer, interview by Steve Allen in *Satchmo: The Story of Louis Armstrong*, BBC 2 (radio documentary), December 1974, Satchmo Collection, Louis Armstrong House Museum.

45. M. H. Orodenker, "Music: Review of Records," *Billboard*, March 30, 1940, 12.

46. Isadora Smith, "Chick's Band Willed to Ella," *Pittsburgh Courier*, July 1, 1939, 21.

47. Advertisement, *Billboard*, July 9, 1939.

48. "Ella Clicks at Loew's State," *New York Amsterdam News*, July 15, 1939.

49. Ibid.

50. Scho., "Loew's State," *Variety*, July 12, 1939, 45.

51. "Death Reminders Eliminated," *Variety*, July 26, 1939, 40.

52. Will Friedwald, liner notes to Ella Fitzgerald, *In the Groove*, Buddha Records 74465-99702-2, 2000, CD.

53. The playbill is reprinted in Ron Fritts and Ken Vail, *Ella Fitzgerald: The Chick Webb Years & Beyond 1935–1948* (Lanham, Md.: Scarecrow Press, 2003), 35. This version also alludes to Gene Krupa's recording on Brunswick with Leo Watson. I thank Vincent Pelote for this observation.

54. D. Antoinette Handy, *Black Women in American Bands and Orchestras* (Metuchen, N.J.: Scarecrow Press, 1981), 41– 44.

55. "Top Jazz Singer Tells."

Chapter 8: Orchestra Leader (1940–1942)

1. Bernie Woods, "The Dance Band Parade," *Variety*, January 3, 1940, cited in George T. Simon, *Glenn Miller and His Orchestra* (New York: Thomas Y. Crowell, 1974), 13.

2. Gunther Schuller, *The Swing Era: The Development of Jazz, 1930–1945* (New York: Oxford University Press, 1989), 661.

3. Gold, "Grand Terrace, Chi," *Variety*, October 4, 1939, 40.

4. Sam Honigberg, "Ella Fitzgerald," *Billboard*, October 21, 1939, 12.

5. "Hep Hep" belongs to Cab Calloway's hit "The Jumpin' Jive (Hep, Hep!)." The others are on *In the Groove*, Buddha Records 74465 99702 2, 2000, CD.

6. Sam Honigberg, "Grand Terrace, Chicago," *Billboard*, October 14, 1939, 17.

7. "Say Ella Fitzgerald Is Wed to Len Reed," *Chicago Defender*, October 14, 1939, 21.

8. Bill Reed, *The Leonard Reed Story: Brains as Well as Feet* (Albany, Ga.: BearManor Media, 2015).

9. "J-Bugs Storm Tenn. Race Trot, Giving La Ella Terrif $3,500," *Billboard*, December 16, 1939, 13.

10. "Swing Street Getting Ready for the Grave as Pop Talent Supplants Jive," *Billboard*, February 24, 1940, 9.

11. "Ella Bids Adieu to Roseland," *Pittsburgh Courier*, March 16, 1940, 21.

12. "Ella Fitzgerald Opens 'Famous Door' Before Visiting Celebrities," *Pittsburgh Courier*, April 20, 1940, 21.

13. "Baker Signs 10-Year Glaser Pact," *Down Beat*, April 15, 1940, 4.

14. "Bands Ask Top Money," *Billboard*, March 9, 1940, 3, 9–10.

15. "Sampson-Ella Riff: 'Too Many People,'" *Down Beat*, December 1, 1939, 1.

16. Teddy McRae, interview by Ron Welburn, January 1981, transcript, Jazz Oral History Project, Institute of Jazz Studies, Rutgers University.

17. "Money Discord Snags Carter-Fitzgerald," *Variety*, May 8, 1940, 51.

18. Morroe Berger, Edward Berger, and James Patrick, *Benny Carter: A Life in American Music*, 2nd ed. (Lanham, Md.: Scarecrow Press, 2002), 188.

19. "New York News by Ed Flynn," *Down Beat*, May 15, 1940, 20.

20. Norman E. Jones, "Recalls Courier's 50th Year, Bill Nunn Marks His 40th Year," *New Pittsburgh Courier*, December 14, 1985, 5.

21. William G. Nunn, "'Will Keep My Orchestra,' Ella Tells Courier," *Pittsburgh Courier*, May 11, 1940, 21.

22. Ibid.

23. "Babe Wallace Will 'Front' Fitzgerald Band on Tour," *Pittsburgh Courier*, June 1, 1940, 21.

24. "Bands Ask Top Money," *Billboard*, March 9, 1940, 3, 9–10.

25. Paul Eduard Miller, "Money Invested in Swing Music Will Keep It Alive," *Down Beat*, April 15, 1940, 6.

26. Lou Schurrer, "Ella Goes 18,000 Miles Touring 36 States," *Down Beat*, October 1, 1940, 18. Fritts and Vail, *Ella Fitzgerald, The Chick Webb Years & Beyond 1935–1948* (Lanham, Md.: Scarecrow Press, 2003), 51, mention only Dayton, Ohio, and Chicago; "Negro Blues Singer Here Thursday Night," *Hattiesburg American* (Miss.), June 12, 1940; "Music Reviews: On the Stand, Ella Fitzgerald (Reviewed at the Rainbow Ballroom, Denver)," *Billboard*, August 24, 1949, 12.

27. Harvey G. Cohen, *Duke Ellington's America* (Chicago: University of Chicago Press, 2011), 130.

28. "203 Lose Lives in Fire at Natchez," *Southern Advocate*, April 27, 1940.

29. Leon Lewis, "Ella Fitzgerald Exists from New Orleans Dance Tattered and Torn by Frenzied Mob," *Pittsburgh Courier*, June 29, 1940, 21.

30. Beverly Peer, interview by Steve Allen, in *Satchmo: The Story of Louis Armstrong*, BBC 2 (radio documentary), December 1974, Satchmo Collection, Louis Armstrong House Museum.

31. Beverly Peer, quoted in Jim Haskins, *Ella Fitzgerald: A Life Through Jazz* (London: Hodder & Stoughton, 1991), 67.

32. David W. Hazen, "Singer Lacks Time for Play: Ella Fitzgerald Pinochle Love," *Oregonian*, July 17, 1940, 6.

33. "Becomes Member of A.S.C.A.P.," *Pittsburgh Courier*, September 21, 1940, 20.

34. Isadora Smith, "Ella Fitzgerald Breaks 'Em Down at Apollo; Becomes Member of Musical Society," *Pittsburgh Courier*, September 21, 1940, 20. Smith names these songs: "A-Tisket A-Tasket," "Chew Chew Your Bubble Gum," "You Showed Me the Way," "Please Tell the Truth," "I Found My Yellow Basket," and "O Boy, I'm in the Groove."

35. McRae interview by Welburn, 280.

36. "Apollo, N.Y.," *Variety*, September 18, 1940, 38.

37. Sam Honigberg, "Vaudeville Reviews: Club Tropicana, New York," *Billboard*, October 26, 1940, 23; Isadora Rowe, "Ella Fitzgerald and Band Will Open New Broadway Nite Club," *Pittsburgh Courier*, October 12, 1940, 20.

38. Malcolm Johnson, "Café Life in New York," *New York Sun*, October 30, 1940.

39. "N.Y. Musicians' Local Forces Nitery Payoff," *Variety*, November 13, 1940, 52; "Poor Business: Negro Employment Down," *Billboard*, November 23, 1940, 1.

40. Billy Rowe, "Theatrical News," *Pittsburgh Courier*, November 9, 1940.

41. Major Robinson, "Club Starring Ella Fitzgerald Closes," *Chicago Defender*, November 9, 1940, 21.

42. Joe Cohen, "Academy of Music, New York," *Billboard*, December 7, 1940, 23.

43. "Ella Renewed at Hub Hotel," *Swing*, February 1941, 32.

44. Dan Burley, "Negro Bands Are Not Doomed Says Millinder," *New York Amsterdam News*, December 21, 1940, 20.

45. Ibid.; Gayle Wald, *Shout, Sister, Shout! The Untold Story of Rock-and-Roll Trailblazer Sister Rosetta Tharpe* (Boston: Beacon, 2008), 60.

46. Sam Honigberg, "Music Reviews: On the Stand, Ella Fitzgerald," *Billboard*, November 9, 1940, 12.

47. "Top Music Machine Records of 1940," *Billboard*, January 11, 1941, 9.

48. Geoffrey Mark Fidelman, *First Lady of Song: Ella Fitzgerald for the Record* (New York: Citadel Press, 1994), 34–35.

49. "T Ella GRAM" (advertisement), *Billboard*, October 26, 1940, 11.

50. Barrelhouse Dan, "Outstanding 'Commercial' Records," *Down Beat*, November 15, 1940, 15.

51. Leonard Feather (pseud. Geoffrey Marne), "The Wax Works," *Swing*, December 1940, 26.

52. M. H. Orodenker, "Review of Records," *Billboard*, March 30, 1940, 12.

53. Will Friedwald, *A Biographical Guide to the Great Jazz and Pop Singers* (New York: Pantheon, 2010), 172.

54. Schuller, *Swing Era*, 689.

55. George T. Simon (pseud. Gordon Wright), "DISCussions," *Metronome*, March 1941, 32.

56. Abel Green, *Show Biz: From Vaude to Video* (New York: Henry Holt, 1951), 495.

57. Barry Ulanov, "Ride 'Em Cowboy,' *Metronome*, April 1942, 19.

58. "Dancers Will Be Screened with La Ella," *Pittsburgh Courier*, July 19, 1941, 20.

59. E. B. Rea, "Uncompromisingly Yours: What Price Glory in Filmdom?" *Baltimore Afro-American*, April 4, 1942, 13.

60. Dan Thomas, "This Wouldn't Happen, If," *Baltimore Afro-American*, August 29, 1942, 10.

61. Fritts and Ken Vail, *Ella Fitzgerald: The Chick Webb Years*, 54. They give the dates as spanning one week, but this is contradicted by "Trianon 10,000 for Ella Fitzgerald on 2-Weeker at Calif. Spot," *Billboard*, August 9, 1941, 13. Dave Dexter, Jr., "Big Band Boom Has California on the Jump," *Down Beat*, August 15, 1941, 3; Lawrence F. LaMar, "Queen Ella: First Lady of Swing Follows Duke Ellington in Coast Spot," *Chicago Defender*, July 19, 1941, 20.

62. McRae interview by Welburn.

63. Ella Fitzgerald, "I Got It Bad and That Ain't Good," Decca 3968, 1941, 78 rpm.

64. "Strand, B'klyn," *Variety*, September 10, 1941, 38.

65. Maurice Zolotow, "Harlem's Great White Father," *Saturday Evening Post*, September 27, 1941, 37.

66. Dizzy Gillespie and Al Fraser, *To Be, or Not . . . to Bop* (New York: Doubleday, 1979), 133.

67. Mike Hennessey, *Klook: The Story of Kenny Clarke* (Pittsburgh: University of Pittsburgh Press, 1990), 36.

68. Fritts and Vail, *Ella Fitzgerald*, 56.

69. McRae interview by Ron Welburn, quoted in Stuart Nicholson, *Ella Fitzgerald: The Complete Biography*, updated ed. (New York: Routledge, 2004), 91.

70. "Barefield New Pilot of Ella Fitzgerald Ork," *Down Beat*, November 1, 1941, 3.

71. Nicholson, *Ella Fitzgerald* (2004), 91.

72. Beverly Peer, interview by Steve Allen, c. 1971–74, transcript, Satchmo Collection, Louis Armstrong House Museum.

73. Nicholson, *Ella Fitzgerald* (2004), 64.

74. "Orchestra Routes" and "Bands on Tour—Advance Dates," *Billboard*, December 6, 1941, 14.

75. "Two Detroit Spots Doing Strong Biz; 'Folies' Big 21G," *Billboard*, December 13, 1941, 25.

76. She later described the marriage as the result of a random bet and said that her band friends were upset. Joel E. Siegel, "Ella, the 'Lady Be Good,' " *Washington Post*, June 4, 1983, D1.

77. "Band Bookings," *Variety*, December 17, 1941, 52, and January 14, 1942, 38.

78. "A Job for All," *Billboard*, December 27, 1941, 28.

Chapter 9: The Home Front (1941–1945)

1. "Ella Fitzgerald, First Lady of Swing, Weds," *Pittsburgh Courier*, January 3, 1942, 21.

2. Leslie Gourse, *Louis' Children: American Jazz Singers*, updated ed. (New York: Cooper Square Press, 2001), 256. Gourse does not identify the source of the interview.

3. Stuart Nicholson, *Ella Fitzgerald: The Complete Biography*, updated ed. (New York: Routledge, 2004), 86.

4. "Ella Fitzgerald Wins Annulment of '41 Marriage," *Variety*, January 13, 1943, 39. The still inaccessible court file is *Fitzgerald v. Kornegay*, 31604–1942.

5. "Dan Burley's Back Door Stuff," *New York Amsterdam News*, April 10, 1943, 13.

6. Lem Graves, Jr., "She Rocks 'Em in Norfolk," *Norfolk Journal and Guide*, January 31, 1942, 15.

7. "Ella with Band Part of Time," *Down Beat*, May 1, 1942, 8; "Music: Gale Sets Campaign for Barefield Band," *Billboard*, April 4, 1942, 20.

8. "Two Mgrs. of Negro Bands May Merge . . . War Especially Hard on Traveling Colored Talent," *Variety*, June 17, 1942, 41.

9. Moe Gale, "Orchestras: Colored Bands Doomed?" *Variety*, October 7, 1942, 42.

10. "Ella Fitzgerald Big 15G in L.A.," *Billboard*, July 4, 1942, 17.

11. "Sepia Bill Dandy $24,000 in Philly; T. Dorsey off Big," *Billboard*, August 8, 1942, 14.

12. Mildred Martin, "Bill Robinson, at Earle, Spry as Ever," *Philadelphia Inquirer*, July 25, 1942, 16.

13. Shal., "Earle, Philly," *Variety*, July 29, 1942, 55.

14. Eddie Barefield, interview by Ira Gitler, Jazz Oral History Project, Institute of Jazz Studies, Rutgers University.

15. Beverly Peer, interview by Loren Schoenberg, 1991, as quoted in Nicholson, *Ella Fitzgerald* (2004), 92; Peer, interview by Steve Allen, in *Satchmo: The Story of Louis Armstrong*, BBC 2 (radio documentary), December 1974, Satchmo Collection, Louis Armstrong House Museum.

16. The singles were "Louisville, K-Y," "Hello, Ma! I Done It Again," and "The Muffin Man." Joel Whitburn, *Pop Memories 1890–1954* (Menomonee Falls, Wis.: Record Research, 1986), 160.

17. M. H. Orodenker, "The Reviewing Stand: The Three Keys," *Billboard*, March 2, 1940, 12; "Drops Baton: Teams with Keys," photo ad, *Norfolk Journal and Guide*, September 5, 1942, A1.

18. "Pertinent Facts About Artists Represented in This Year Book," *Billboard*, September 26, 1942, 96.

19. Elie., "New Acts—Ella Fitzgerald," *Variety*, September 23, 1942, 48.

20. Elaine M. Hayes, *Queen of Bebop: The Musical Lives of Sarah Vaughan* (New York: HarperCollins, 2017), 32.

21. "Salaries for Names Soar," *Billboard*, May 22, 1943, 16.

22. "Apollo, N.Y.," *Variety*, March 3, 1943, 41; Leonard Feather, "Stage Show Reviews," *Metronome*, April 1943, 20.

23. "Billy Rowe's Notebook: Headlines of Tomorrow," *Pittsburgh Courier*, June 6, 1942, 20.

24. Count Basie, *Good Morning Blues: The Autobiography of Count Basie* (New York: Random House, 1985), 257.

25. "Birdies Flee Band Cages," *Billboard*, January 30, 1943, 21.

26. Helen Forrest and Bill Libby, *I Had the Craziest Dream* (New York: Coward, McCann & Geoghegan, 1982), 136.

27. "Billy Rowe's Notebook: Personal Observations," *Pittsburgh Courier*, May 9, 1942, 20.

28. Mike Levin, "Record Reviews," *Down Beat*, June 1, 1942, 18.

29. "Helen Forrest Way, Way Ahead," *Metronome*, January 1943, 33.

30. Roi Ottley, *"New World A-Coming": Inside Black America* (Boston: Houghton Mifflin, 1943), 247.

31. "Soldiers to Hear Ella Fitzgerald Chirp Hot Songs," *Chicago Defender*, May 31, 1941, 20.

32. "Black Troops Engage in Own Mock Battle at Fort Huachuca: 90% of 4,500 Soldiers in Army Only Six Months," *Atlanta Daily World*, June 6, 1941, 1.

33. "368th Infantry Corporal Scores 'Barbarism' at Ft. Huachuca Dance," *Cleveland Call and Post*, July 5, 1941, 7B.

34. "Lena Horne Here for Theatre Dedication," *Apache Sentinel*, August 20, 1943. For more on Fort Huachuca's musical life, see Annegret Fauser, *Sounds of War: Music in the United States During World War II* (New York: Oxford University Press, 2013), 121.

35. John Hammond with Irving Townsend, *John Hammond on Record: An Autobiography* (New York: Penguin, 1981), 254; Dunstan Prial, *The Producer: John Hammond and the Soul of American Music* (New York: Farrar, Straus & Giroux, 2006), 181ff.

36. "Entertain at TAAF Opening," *Norfolk Journal and Guide*, June 17, 1944, 12.

37. Maureen Honey, ed., *Bitter Fruit: African American Women in World War II* (Columbia: University of Missouri Press, 1999), 319–20.

38. "To Broadcast Defense Jim Crow Protest: Urban League Program Will Feature Stars," *Chicago Defender*, March 29, 1941, 9.

39. "Showlife's Top Artists in Million Dollar Show for Ben Davis, Jr., at Golden Gate Ballroom," *New York Amsterdam News*, October 16, 1943, 7B.

40. For Auld, see "Jitterbug Interviewer," *Music Dial*, November 1943, 10, and for Cooper, December 1943–January 1944, 12.

41. "How Our Top Performers Join In to Give Boys Overseas a Break," *New York Amsterdam News*, October 28, 1944.

42. Neil A. Wynn, *The African American Experience During World War II* (New York: Rowman & Littlefield, 2010), 73.

43. Jack Schiffman, *Harlem Heyday* (Buffalo: Prometheus, 1984), 66.

44. Porter Roberts, "Praise and Criticism," *Chicago Defender*, July 3, 1943, 19.

45. Joe Cohen, "Zanzibar with $2,500 Budget Bows as Biggest Sepia Nitery Operation Since Cotton Club," *Billboard*, July 17, 1943, 16; Scho., "Zanzibar, N.Y.," *Variety*, July 14, 1943, 88.

46. Langston Hughes, "Theaters, Clubs, and Negroes," *Chicago Defender*, September 23, 1944, 12.

47. Nicholson, *Ella Fitzgerald* (2004), 97.

48. "Record Reviews," *Down Beat*, March 1, 1944, 8.

49. Ella Fitzgerald and Ink Spots, "I'm Making Believe / Into Each Life Some Rain Must Fall," Decca 23356, 1944, 78 rpm.

50. Nicholson, *Ella Fitzgerald* (2004), 99.

51. Paul Secon, "More $$ for Negro Musickers," *Billboard*, February 3, 1945, 13.

52. Guthrie P. Ramsey, Jr., *Race Music: Black Cultures from Bebop to Hip-Hop* (Berkeley: University of California Press, 2003), 67.

53. Barry Ulanov, "Cootie Calls Chick Greatest Leader," *Metronome*, July 1941, 20.

54. John Chilton, *Ride, Red, Ride: The Life of Henry "Red" Allen* (New York: Continuum, 1999), 193.

55. Ella Fitzgerald, *On the Air*, vol. 3, *1944–1947*, Masters of Jazz MJCD 169, 2000, CD.

56. Nicholson, *Ella Fitzgerald* (2004), 98.

57. Alyce Key, "Keynotes," *Los Angeles Sentinel*, April 4, 1946, 20.

58. Carl Jones, interview by Jason Gross, 2001, www.furious.com/perfect/delta rhythmboys.html.

59. "Ella Fitzgerald—Ink Spots," *Down Beat*, May 1, 1945, 8; "Records of the Year," *Metronome*, January 1946, 31.

60. Cliff Starr and Dave Fayre, "Waxing Wise," *Band Leaders*, November 1945, 31.

61. Milt Gabler, liner notes to Ella Fitzgerald, *75th Birthday Celebration: The Original Decca Recordings*, GRP GRD-2-619, 1993, 2-CD set, 22.

62. Hodges, "Cootie-Ella-Ink Spots," *Metronome*, September 1945, 28.

63. "A New Ella to Hit Zanzibar," *Baltimore Afro-American*, November 17, 1945, 10.

64. Paul Ross, "Zanzibar, New York," *Billboard*, December 15, 1945, 32. She sang "St. Louis Blues," "It's Only a Paper Moon," and "Is You Is or Is You Ain't My Baby?"

65. Meyer Berger, "Noisiest Throngs Since '41 Welcome New Year in City," *New York Times*, January 1, 1946, 1, 3.

66. George T. Simon, "Cootie Williams. This Fella's for Ella," *Metronome*, February 1946, 32.

67. Rowe used the byline of the "sons and daughters of Harlem" for some of his columns.

68. "Billy Rowe's Notebook: Conversation Piece," *Pittsburgh Courier*, January 19, 1946, 13.

69. "Top Jazz Singer Tells How She Got That Way," *PM*, October 24, 1947, 16.

70. George T. Simon, "Ella, Now Making Records That Are Stellar," *Metronome*, May 1946, 30.

71. Leonard Feather, "Ella Fitzgerald—Willie Bryant, Apollo," *Metronome*, July 1946, 39.

Chapter 10: "Going Dizzy" (1945–1947)

1. "Coming Your Way in 1946," advertisement in *Saturday Evening Post*, January 12, 1946, 86.

2. "First Annual Music-Record Poll," *Billboard*, January 4, 1947, 55.

3. John Chilton, *Let the Good Times Roll: The Story of Louis Jordan and His Music* (Ann Arbor: University of Michigan Press, 1992), 117.

4. "Top Jazz Singer Tells How She Got That Way," *PM*, October 24, 1947, 16.

5. H. Arlo Nimmo, *The Andrews Sisters: A Biography and Career Record* (Jefferson, N.C.: McFarland & Co., 2004), 211; " 'Stone Cold' Is Dead on the Nets," *Billboard*, August 10, 1946, 17.

6. Chilton, *Let the Good Times Roll*, 118, 128.

7. Goodman quoted ibid., 118.

8. "Records on Review," *Band Leaders and Record Review*, October 1946, 40.

9. Alyce Key, "Keynotes," *Los Angeles Sentinel*, April 4, 1946, 20.

10. Ella Fitzgerald and Louis Armstrong, "You Won't Be Satisfied / The Frim Fram Sauce," Decca 23496, 1946, 78 rpm.

11. Don C. Haynes, "Diggin' the Discs with Don," *Down Beat*, April 22, 1946, 16.

12. Ella Fitzgerald, "I'm Just A Lucky So-and-So," Decca 18814, 1946, 78 rpm.

13. George T. Simon, "Ella, Now Making Records That Are Stellar, Quite Different from Her Basket That Was Yella," *Metronome*, May 1946, 30.

14. "Ella Fitzgerald 'Going Dizzy,' " *Billboard*, October 5, 1946, 32.

15. Richard Gale, interview by the author, 2009.

16. George T. Simon, "B.G. Explains," *Metronome*, October 1946, 12.

17. Hank O'Neal, *The Ghosts of Harlem: Sessions with Jazz Legends* (Nashville, Tenn.: Vanderbilt University Press, 2009), 37.

18. "Satchmo Comes Back," *Time*, September 1, 1947, 32.

19. Ira Gitler, *Swing to Bop: An Oral History of the Transition in Jazz in the 1940s* (New York: Oxford University Press, 1987), 293.

20. "Ella Will Tour with Gillespie," *Cleveland Call and Post*, August 31, 1946.

21. "Billy Rowe's Notebook: What the Other Guys Have to Say," *Pittsburgh Courier*, August 31, 1946, 22.

22. Dizzy Gillespie and Al Fraser, *To Be, or Not . . . to Bop* (New York: Doubleday, 1979), 64.

23. Gene Lees, "Ella by Starlight," *Gene Lees' Jazzletter* 11, no. 1 (January 1992): 4.

24. Information on "Down Under" from Leonard Feather, *Inside Jazz* (New York: Da Capo Press, 1977), 24. Dates of arrival and departure are from Ron Fritts and Ken Vail, *Ella Fitzgerald: The Chick Webb Years & Beyond 1935–1948* (Lanham, Md.: Scarecrow Press, 2003), 56–57.

25. Ella Fitzgerald, interview by Leonard Feather, April 23, 1987, Ella Fitzgerald Project, Leonard Feather Collection, University of Idaho.

26. Gene Lees, *Singers and the Song II* (New York: Oxford University Press, 1998), 154.

27. Gillespie and Fraser, *To Be*, 223.

28. Stuart Nicholson, *Ella Fitzgerald: The Complete Biography*, updated ed. (New York: Routledge, 2004), 114.

29. Michael Levin, "Notes Between Notes," *Down Beat*, July 1, 1946, 5.

30. "Ella Fitzgerald, Dizzie Gillespie in New England NAACP Fight on Bias," *Cleveland Call and Post*, September 28, 1946.

31. "Ella Fitzgerald Knocks Wacoans Stone Cold Dead," *Waco Tribune-Herald*, December 1, 1946.

32. Gillespie and Fraser, *To Be*, 269.

33. Ibid.

34. Jim Haskins, *Ella Fitzgerald: A Life Through Jazz* (London: Hodder & Stoughton, 1991), 87.

35. "Apollo, N.Y.," *Variety*, June 5, 1946, 24.

36. Allen, "Fitzgerald-Williams Vocal Jam Best That Am," *Metronome*, November 1946, 42.

37. "Ella Records 'Lady Be Good,'" *Los Angeles Sentinel*, April 3, 1947.

38. Gillespie and Fraser, *To Be*, 273; "Advance Record Releases," *Billboard*, June 21, 1947, 118.

39. Ella Fitzgerald, "Oh, Lady Be Good! / Flying Home," Decca 23956, 1947, 78 rpm.

40. "Top Jazz Singer Tells How She Got That Way," *PM*, October 24, 1947, 16.

41. Ella Fitzgerald, interview by Willis Conover for the Voice of America, August 17, 1956, Voice of America Music Library Collection, RWB 3068 B3, Library of Congress.

42. The unfavorable review was in "Record Reviews," *Billboard*, July 12, 1947, 30; the favorable review was in "Record Possibilities," *Billboard*, July 19, 1947, 34.

43. George Frazier, "Jocks, Jukes and Disks," *Variety*, June 25, 1947, 40.

44. "Diggin' the Discs with Mix," *Down Beat*, July 2, 1947, 15.

45. Henry Louis Gates, Jr., *The Signifying Monkey: A Theory of African-American Literary Criticism* (New York: Oxford University Press, 1988); Samuel A. Floyd, *The Power of Black Music: Interpreting Its History from Africa to the United States* (New York: Oxford University Press, 1995), 8.

46. Leonard Feather, "Ella Fitzgerald—Willie Bryant," *Metronome*, July 1946, 39.

47. Katharine Cartwright, "'Guess These People Wonder What I'm Singing': Quotation and Reference in Ella Fitzgerald's 'St. Louis Blues,'" in David Evans, ed., *Ramblin' on My Mind: New Perspectives on the Blues* (Urbana: University of Illinois Press, 2008), 282.

48. Elaine Sisman, "Observations on the First Phase of Mozart's 'Haydn' Quartets," in Dorothea Link and Judith Nagley, eds., *Words About Mozart: Essays in Honour of Stanley Sadie* (London: Boydell and Brewer, 2005), 35–37; and Cartwright, "'Guess These People Wonder,'" 281ff.

49. "Street Starts to Jump," *Down Beat*, July 2, 1947, 2.

50. Ella Fitzgerald, *On the Air*, vol. 3: 1944–1947, Masters of Jazz MJCD 169, 2000, CD, track 13.

51. George F. Brown, "Courier's Carnegie Music Hall Concert Smash," *Pittsburgh Courier*, March 22, 1947, 1.

52. Michael Levin, "Dizzy, Bird, Ella Pack Carnegie," *Down Beat*, October 22, 1947, 1.

53. Ibid.

54. Lillian Scott, "Square Sees Gillespie Rebop at Carnegie Hall," *Chicago Defender*, October 25, 1947, 18.

55. Levin, "Dizzy, Bird, Ella," 3.

56. Geoffrey C. Ward and Ken Burns, *Jazz: A History of America's Music* (New York: Knopf, 2000), 348.

57. Joel E. Siegel, "Ella, the 'Lady Be Good,'" *Washington Post*, June 4, 1983, D1.

58. *The Dave Garroway Show* (radio program), NBC, November 23, 1947, Recorded Sound Reference Center, RWB 4871 B1-2, Library of Congress.

59. Elaine Hayes, *Queen of Bebop: The Musical Lives of Sarah Vaughan* (New York: HarperCollins, 2017), 94.

60. "Top Jazz Singer Tells How She Got That Way," *PM*, October 24, 1947, 16.

Chapter 11: Ella's Moon (1947–1949)

1. Leonard Feather, "Ella and Her Fella," *Metronome*, October 1948, 28.

2. U.S. Census 1940, Pennsylvania, Allegheny County, Pittsburgh, Ward Five.

3. Alwyn and Laurie Lewis, "Ray Brown Interview," *Cadence*, September 1993, 14.

4. Alyn Shipton, *Groovin' High: The Life of Dizzy Gillespie* (New York: Oxford University Press, 1999), 150.

5. Jimmy Butts, "Where They're Playing," *Jazz Record*, October 1945, 13.

6. Shipton, *Groovin' High*, 149–51.

7. Dizzy Gillespie and Al Fraser, *To Be, or Not . . . to Bop* (1979; reprint Minneapolis: University of Minnesota Press, 2009), 249–50.

8. Ibid., 50.

9. Jeff Sultanof to the author, August 29, 2015.

10. "Esquire's All-American Jazz Band, 1947," *Esquire*, February 1, 1947, 45.

11. Shipton, *Groovin' High*, 152.

12. "Ella Keeps It on the Beat," *Down Beat*, September 24, 1947, 5.

13. Shipton, *Groovin' High*, 193.

14. "Hitting the Nite Spots," *Los Angeles Sentinel*, October 30, 1947, 21.

15. Tad Hershorn, "Chronology and Itineraries for Norman Granz," James "Tad" Hershorn Collection on Norman Granz, Institute of Jazz Studies, Archival Collections, IJS.0081, Rutgers University.

16. Ron Fritts and Ken Vail, *Ella Fitzgerald: The Chick Webb Years & Beyond 1935–1948* (Lanham, Md.: Scarecrow Press, 2003), 85.

17. Isadore Blakeny, interview by Michael Beverly, April 29, 1999, transcript, African-American Migration to Youngstown Project, Oral History Program, Youngstown State University.

18. Walter Winchell, "Broadway," *Charlotte Observer*, December 16, 1947, 36.

19. W. L. Driskell and Artie Mae Smith, "Ella Fitzgerald Wanted to Keep Marriage at Youngstown a Secret," *Cleveland Call and Post*, December 20, 1947, 7B.

20. Stuart Nicholson, *Ella Fitzgerald: The Complete Biography*, updated ed. (New York: Routledge, 2004), 122.

21. Walter Winchell, "On Broadway," *Tampa Bay Times*, June 20, 1947.

22. Nicholson, *Ella Fitzgerald* (2004), 122.

23. Ella Fitzgerald, "How High the Moon," Decca 24387, 1948, 78 rpm.

24. "Record Reviews," *Down Beat*, May 5, 1947, 15

25. Peter Dean, Barbara Hodgkins, and Barry Ulanov, "Record Reviews," *Metronome*, June 1948, 35.

26. Illinois Jacquet shares a composer credit for "Robbin's Nest," but Thompson claims sole authorship in Stanley Dance, *The World of Count Basie* (New York: Scribner's, 1980), 333–34. The DJ's name was "Robbins," but Decca did not use that for its title.

27. Leonard Feather, *Inside Be-Bop* (New York: J. J. Robbins and Sons, 1949), 39–40.

28. Bruce Crowther and Mike Pinfold, *Singing Jazz: The Singers and Their Styles* (San Francisco: Miller Freeman, 1997), 140.

29. Gunther Schuller, interview by the author, December 7, 2011.

30. Gillespie and Fraser, *To Be, or Not*, 272.

31. Carter Harman, "Jazz at Midnight Pays Its Own Way," *New York Times*, February 1, 1948, 7.

32. "Tour Loot Proves Jazz Hasn't Died," *Down Beat*, March 10, 1948, 10.

33. George Fletcher, "Jazz in Hollywood," *Record Changer*, May 1948, 15; Dave Dexter, "For Sale: Virtually Any Hollywood Nitery," *Capital News*, April 1948, 2.

34. Bill Smith, "Paramount, New York," *Billboard*, May 1, 1948, 42.

35. "Mildred, Ella Boff in NYC," *Down Beat*, July 14, 1948, 4; Cover photo, *Billboard*, June 26, 1948.

36. Jim Haskins, *Ella Fitzgerald: A Life Through Jazz* (London: Hodder & Stoughton, 1991), 93.

37. George Shearing, *Lullaby of Birdland: The Autobiography of George Shearing* (New York: Continuum, 2004), 97.

38. Edba., "Apollo, N.Y.," *Variety*, August 18, 1948, 41.

39. For the press release, see Ron Fritts and Ken Vail, *Ella Fitzgerald: The Chick Webb Years & Beyond 1935–1948* (Lanham, Md.: Scarecrow Press, 2003), 91. See also Pat Harris, "I Don't Like to Sing Bop Most," *Down Beat*, September 22, 1948, 1.

40. Max Braun, interview by the author, April 17, 2015.

41. "Chicago Raves as Ella Fitzgerald Triumphs in Bon Voyage Date Here," *Chicago Defender*, September 4, 1948, 9.

42. James Hicks, "Big Town," *Baltimore Afro-American*, October 2, 1948, 4.

43. Val Wilmer, *Mama Said There'd Be Days Like This* (London: Women's Press, 1989), 40.

44. Martin Cloonan and Matt Brennan, "Alien Invasions: The British Musicians' Union and Foreign Musicians," *Popular Music* 32, no. 2 (May 2013): 294.

45. Richard Grudens, *Jukebox Saturday Night: More Memories of the Big Band Era and Beyond* (n.p.: Celebrity Profiles, 1999), 160.

46. "On the Beat," *Melody Maker*, November 6, 1948.

47. "Gracie, Ella, Harmonia Rascals Give the London Palladium Sock Finale," *Variety*, October 6, 1948, 50; "Palladium, London," *Billboard*, October 16, 1948, 47.

48. As cited in Haskins, *Ella Fitzgerald*, 100.

49. "London Palladium: Miss Gracie Fields," *Times* (London), October 5, 1948.

50. George Fierstone, "My Seven Years at the Palladium," *Melody Maker*, December 13, 1952, 3.

51. Ted Heath, *Listen to My Music*, vol. 3, *1947/48*, Hep HEPCD 61, 1999, CD; Charles Short, "At Last! A Successor to Jimmy Blanton," *Melody Maker*, October 30, 1948, 3.

52. Fritts and Vail, *Ella Fitzgerald*, 93.

53. Feather, "Ella and Her Fella," 18, 28–29.

54. "Ella Fitzgerald, "First Lady of Song," *Our World*, December 1949, 2.

55. Ray Brown, Jr., interview by the author, December 1, 2009.

56. Virginia Wicks, interview by the author, December 5, 2009.

57. Dorothy Johnson, interview by the author, August 23, 2012.

58. Dorothy Johnson, interview by the author, November 15, 2022. Nicholson, *Ella Fitzgerald* (2004), 63, writes that Fitzgerald "allegedly had an abortion" that made pregnancy impossible.

59. Leonor Boulin Johnson and Robert Staples, *Black Families at the Crossroads: Challenges and Prospects* (San Francisco: John Wiley & Sons, 2004), 252.

60. Ray Brown, Jr., to the author, November 11, 2022. Dorothy Johnson recalls that Ray was very angry at learning about this fact rather late in his life.

61. Dorothy Johnson interview by the author, November 15, 2022.

62. Lillian Johnson, "Ella Fitzgerald Hasn't Let Success Spoil Her," *Baltimore Afro-American*, October 9, 1937, 5.

63. "Ella Fitzgerald's Adopted Son," *New York Amsterdam News*, November 30, 1946, 11.

64. Bill Chase, "Bop City Opening Bopsolutely Mad," *New York Age*, April 23, 1949, 8.

65. Martha Holmes, "Ella Fitzgerald, at Bop City 1949," photo, https://jazzinphoto .wordpress.com/tag/martha-holmes/.

66. "Artie Shaw's Bop Flop: His 'Symphony' Music Lays Egg at New Nightclub," *Life*, May 30, 1949, 81.

67. Bill Smith, "Bop City, New York," *Billboard*, April 23, 1949, 48.

68. "Artie Shaw's Bop City Hop a Flop," *Variety*, April 20, 1949, 39.

69. "Much Confusion as Ella, Shaw Open Up Bop City," *Down Beat*, May 20, 1949, 16.

70. "'March of Time,' Films Doc of Record Business," *Billboard*, May 21, 1949, 20.

71. "Ella Fitzgerald Bops for Documentary Wax Film," *Baltimore Afro-American*, May 28, 1949, 6.

Chapter 12: "The Singer and the Label Are in It Together"
(1948–1953)

1.   Milt Gabler, liner notes to Ella Fitzgerald, *75th Birthday Celebration: The Original Decca Recordings*, GRP GRD-2-619, 1993, 2-CD set.

2.   "The Great Ella Fitzgerald: Everybody's Favorite Singer," *Billboard*, February 5, 1949, 17.

3.   "Ella Fitzgerald," *Ebony*, May 1949, 45–46.

4.   Leonard Feather, "Ella Meets the Duke," *Playboy*, November 1957, 42.

5.   Ella Fitzgerald, "My Happiness," Decca 24446, 1948, 78 rpm; Landon Ladd, "About Town," *Kansas City Times*, August 16, 1948, 2.

6.   "Record Reviews," *Billboard*, June 12, 1948, 117.

7.   Crosby-Fitzgerald duet on *Kraft Radio Show*, November 9, 1949; "Singers' Choice," *Jazz 1951: The Metronome Yearbook* (New York: Metronome Corporation, 1951), 24.

8.   Stuart Nicholson, *Ella Fitzgerald: The Complete Biography,* updated ed. (New York: Routledge, 2004), 139.

9.   Ella Fitzgerald, "It's Too Soon to Know," Decca 24497, 1948, 78 rpm.

10. Albin Zak, *I Don't Sound Like Nobody: Remaking Music in 1950s America* (Ann Arbor: University of Michigan Press, 2010), 91.

11. Guthrie Ramsey, *Race Music: Black Cultures from Bebop to Hip-Hop* (Berkeley: University of California Press, 2003), 24–25.

12. A. S. "Doc" Young, "Inside South L.A.," *Los Angeles Sentinel*, January 11, 1951.

13. Ella Fitzgerald, *Royal Roost Sessions with Ray Brown Trio & Quintet*, Cool & Blue Records C&B-CD112, 1993, CD.

14. Ella Fitzgerald, "Old Mother Hubbard," Decca 24581, 1949, 78 rpm; "Record Reviews," *Billboard*, April 2, 1949, 44.

15. Russell Sanjek, *Pennies from Heaven: The American Popular Music Business in the Twentieth Century* (New York: Da Capo, 1996), 240.

16. Ella Fitzgerald and Louis Jordon, "I'll Never Be Free," Decca 27200, 1950, 78 rpm.

17. Feather, "Ella Meets the Duke," 42.

18. Bill Coss, "Ella Fitzgerald, Café Society," *Metronome*, September 1951, 20.

19. "Casino, Toronto," *Variety*, March 15, 1950, 56.

20. "Oliver Joining Decca as a Musical Director," *Variety*, February 23, 1949, 36.

21. Sy Oliver and Dick Jacobs, "Arrangers' Corner," *Down Beat*, January 28, 1949, 18.

22. Ella Fitzgerald and Sy Oliver, "Don'cha Go 'Way Mad," Decca 75802, 1950, 78 rpm; "Records of the Year," *Jazz 1951: The Metronome Yearbook* (New York: Metronome Corporation, 1951), 22.

23. Jack Schiffman, *Uptown: The Story of Harlem's Apollo Theatre* (New York: Cowles, 1971), 77–78.

24. Joe Smith, *Off the Record: An Oral History of Popular Music* (New York: Warner, 1988), 20.

25. "Fourth Annual Music-Record Poll," *Billboard*, January 14, 1950, 15.

26. Ella Fitzgerald, "Happy Talk / I'm Gonna Wash That Man Right Outa My Hair," Decca 24639, 1949, 78 rpm.

27. "Ella Strings Along," *Variety*, April 27, 1949, 43.

28. Milton Gabler, "Reminiscences," November 1959, transcript, p. 60, Columbia Center for Oral History, Columbia University.

29. Ella Fitzgerald, "Black Coffee," Decca 24646, 1949, 78 rpm; "Favorite Records by Categories," *Billboard Disk Jockey Supplement*, October 22, 1949, 26.

30. "Record Reviews," *Down Beat*, July 1, 1949, 15.

31. Ella Fitzgerald and Louis Jordan, "Baby, It's Cold Outside," Decca 24644, 1949, 78 rpm.

32. "NBC Lifts Network Ban on Jordan-Fitzgerald Hit," *Baltimore Afro-American*, May 14, 1949, 6; George Hoefer, "The Hot Box," *Down Beat*, February 24, 1950, 15.

33. Kelly Schrum, "'Teena Means Business': Teenage Girls' Culture and *Seventeen Magazine*, 1944–1950," in Sherrie A. Inness, ed., *Delinquents and Debutantes: Twentieth-Century American Girls' Cultures* (New York: New York University Press, 1998), 141.

34. Milt Gabler, liner notes to Billie Holiday, *The Complete Decca Recordings*, GRP—GRD2-601, 1991, 2-CD set.

35. Ella Fitzgerald and Louis Armstrong, "Dream a Little Dream of Me," Decca 27209, 1950, 78 rpm.

36. Ella "Satchmo" Fitzgerald, "Basin Street Blues," Decca 24868, 1950, 78 rpm.

37. "Decca Puts 'Satchmo' Back on Pop Tunes," *Variety*, September 7, 1949, 41.

38. "Record Reviews," *Billboard*, September 30, 1950, 35.

39. Hoefer, "Hot Box," 15.

40. George T. Simon, "Ella Fitzgerald: The Greats' Great," *Metronome*, April 1950, 14.

41. "Standards Become 'New' Hits," *Variety*, September 13, 1950, 43.

42. Ella Fitzgerald, *Ella Sings Gershwin*, Decca DL 5300, 1951, LP. The long-playing, microgroove, "unbreakable," 33⅓ rpm vinyl record was introduced commercially in 1948, and in the early LP years, popular music was directed to the ten-inch

version, with room for about 13.5 minutes per side. *Ella Sings Gershwin* was also issued in 78 and 45 rpm formats as folios of four singles.

43. Abel Green, "Jack Kapp Brought a New Kind of Showmanship to Disk Biz," *Variety*, March 30, 1949, 37.

44. For "Embraceable You" and "I Got Rhythm," see Koll., "Vaudeville: Unit Review—Ink Spots Unit," *Variety*, January 19, 1944, 56. For "Summertime," see Scho., "Vaudeville: Night Club Reviews—Zanzibar, N.Y.," *Variety*, July 14, 1943, 88. For "Somebody Loves Me," see Edba., "House Review: Apollo, N.Y.," *Variety*, September 14, 1949, 54.

45. As quoted in Norman David, *The Ella Fitzgerald Companion* (Westport, Conn.: Praeger, 2004), 193.

46. *The Storm Is Passing Over: Celebrating the Musical Life of Maryland's African-American Community from Emancipation to Civil Rights* (traveling and online exhibition), 2008, Johns Hopkins University.

47. Whitney Balliett, *American Musicians II: Seventy-One Portraits in Jazz* (Jackson: University Press of Mississippi, 2005), 327.

48. Jeni Dahmus (Juilliard School archivist) to the author, September 9, 2013.

49. Balliett, *American Musicians II*, 328.

50. "Album and LP Reviews," *Billboard*, March 31, 1951, 40.

51. Joachim-Ernst Berendt, *Das Jazzbuch* (Hamburg: Fischer Bucherie, 1953), 62.

52. Stanley Dance, "Lightly and Politely," *Jazz Journal*, June 1954, 11.

53. "Bob Snyder Visits Stars in Jazz," *Bob Snyder Show* (radio program), NBC, August 17, 1952, Recorded Sound Reference Center, RWC 6653 A1-2, Library of Congress.

54. Ella Fitzgerald "Smooth Sailing," Decca 27693, 1951, 78 rpm; "The Year's Top Rhythm & Blues Records," *Billboard*, January 12, 1952, 22.

55. "Ella Fitzgerald, Decca Renew," *Billboard*, October 20, 1951, 18.

56. Ted Fox, *In the Groove: The People Behind the Music* (New York: St. Martin's Press, 1986), 95.

57. "Mercury Goes on Jazz Spree," *Down Beat*, December 28, 1951, 1.

58. Will Friedwald, *A Biographical Guide to the Great Jazz and Pop Singers* (New York: Pantheon, 2010), 158–59.

59. Ella Fitzgerald, "Angel Eyes," Decca 9-28707, 1953, 78 rpm.

60. Dorothy Kilgallen, "The Voice of Broadway," *St. Louis Post-Dispatch*, July 6, 1953, 30.

61. "Angel Eyes," *Metronome*, September 1953, 27.

62. Fred Reynolds, "Platter Chatter," *Chicago Daily Tribune*, August 25, 1952, A6.

63. Pat Harris, "What's on Wax," *Down Beat*, February 22, 1952, 14.

64. "Album and LP Reviews," *Billboard*, October 4, 1952, 45.

65. J.J.M., "Popular Field," *New York Times*, September 21, 1952, 10.

66. Ella Fitzgerald, "Mr. Paganini," Decca 28774, 1952, 78 rpm.

67. Ella Fitzgerald, "Blue Lou," Decca 28671, 1953, 78 rpm; "Popular Record Reviews," *Billboard*, May 2, 1953, 40.

68. "Orioles Score Hit With 'Crying in the Chapel,'" *Jet*, September 17, 1953, 55.

69. Ella Fitzgerald, "Crying in the Chapel," Decca 28762, 1953, 78 rpm.

70. "Record Reviews: Popular by Bill Coss," *Metronome*, October 1953, 27.

71. Reg Owen, "Bach and Bop—So What?" *New Musical Express*, October 23, 1953, 5.

72. Nicholson, *Ella Fitzgerald* (2004), 153.

73. Ibid., 179.

74. Gabler, liner notes to Fitzgerald, *75th Birthday Celebration*.

75. Bill Coss, "Ella!" *Metronome*, October 1953, 13, 29.

76. The term *luxe pop* is borrowed from John Howland, *Hearing Luxe Pop: Glorification, Glamour, and the Middlebrow in American Popular Music* (Berkeley: University of California Press, 2021).

Chapter 13: Early Years with Jazz at the Philharmonic (1949–1952)

1. Bob Rolontz, "Bumper Crop of Disk Names Slated to Hit Arena-Auditorium Trail," *Billboard*, May 24, 1952, 17.

2. "Sepia Talent Policy Fails to Pay Off in Miami Beach; Monte Carlo Folds," *Variety*, February 16, 1949, 53; "Agency Head Raps Racial Lines in Booking Talent," *Pittsburgh Courier*, March 26, 1949, A8. The Gale Agency won an antidiscrimination award from B'nai B'rith in 1949; see "Gale Wins Anti-Jim Crow Award," *Cleveland Call and Post*, May 7, 1949, 9B.

3. Billy Taylor and Teresa L. Reed, *The Jazz Life of Dr. Billy Taylor* (Bloomington: Indiana University Press, 2013), 127.

4. Ella Fitzgerald, *The Enchanting Ella Fitzgerald: Live at Birdland, 1950–1952*, Baldwin Street Music, BJH 309, 2000, CD.

5. David Schroeder, *From the Minds of Jazz Musicians: Conversations with the Creative and Inspired* (New York: Routledge, 2018), 98.

6. Located at 3810 S. Western Avenue, the Oasis hosted Dizzy Gillespie later that year, https://theconcertdatabase.com/venues/club-oasis?field_date_value=&order=title&sort=asc.

7. "Ella Fitzgerald Is Radio and Film 'Must' to All but Powers," *Chicago Defender*, May 20, 1950, 21.

8. June Bundy, "Paramount," *Billboard*, April 8, 1950, 51.

9. "Apollo, N.Y.," *Variety*, June 6, 1951, 22.

10. Ray Brown, Sr., *Ella Fitzgerald: Something to Live For* (documentary), American Masters Digital Archive (WNET), April 3, 1999, https://www.pbs.org/wnet/americanmasters/archive/interviews/494. Accessed April 11, 2021, but this interview is no longer available.

11. Tad Hershorn, *Norman Granz: The Man Who Used Jazz for Justice* (Berkeley: University of California Press, 2011), 16; George J. Sanchez, *Boyle Heights: How a Los Angeles Neighborhood Became the Future of American Democracy* (Berkeley: University of California Press, 2021), 5.

12. Hershorn, *Norman Granz*, 19.

13. Ibid., 171.

14. Todd R. Decker, *Music Makes Me: Fred Astaire and Jazz* (Berkeley: University of California Press, 2011), 3.

15. Carey McWilliams, *A Mask for Privilege: Anti-Semitism in America* (Piscataway, N.J.: Transaction, 1948), 143ff.

16. Catherine Parsons Smith, *Making Music in Los Angeles* (Berkeley: University of California Press, 2007), 175.

17. Douglas Flamming, *Bound for Freedom: Black Los Angeles in Jim Crow America* (Berkeley: University of California Press, 2006), 3.

18. Hershorn, *Norman Granz*, 43–44.

19. Norman Granz, interview by John McDonough, September 12, 1978, unpublished transcript supplied to the author.

20. Ella Fitzgerald, interview by Leonard Feather, April 23, 1987, Ella Fitzgerald Project, Leonard Feather Collection, University of Idaho.

21. "Trianon, South Gate, Calif.," *Billboard*, June 20, 1942, 12.

22. Norman Granz, interview by Elliot Meadow, February 27, 1987, transcribed by Tad Hershorn, January 2001, James "Tad" Hershorn Collection on Norman Granz, Institute of Jazz Studies, Archival Collections, IJS.0081, Rutgers University.

23. Hershorn, *Norman Granz*, 46–47. The undated clipping, attributed to the *Los Angeles Sentinel*, was supplied to Hershorn by Grete Granz.

24. Hershorn, *Norman Granz*, 25, 56–60.

25. Ibid., 102.

26. For comments from bandleaders, see "Richard, Open That Door and Let Ol' Man Jim Crow Go!," *Baltimore Afro-American*, February 22, 1947, 3.

27. "Granz and the Jazz Philharmonic," *Crisis*, May 1947, 144.

28. Norman Granz, interview by Tad Hershorn, May 21, 2001, Hershorn Collection on Norman Granz, Rutgers University.

29. Helen Humes did not appear on any JATP releases.

30. Fitzgerald interview by Feather, January 15, 1983, Ella Fitzgerald Project.

31. Hershorn, *Norman Granz*, 139.

32. "Apollo's Girl," *Time*, April 3, 1950, 71.

33. Hershorn, *Norman Granz*, 118–19.

34. J.H., "Granz Group and Audience Shiver Symphony Timbers," *Boston Daily Globe*, September 26, 1949, 7.

35. The program is reconstructed in Leif Bo Peterson and Theo Rehak, *The Music and Life of Theodore "Fats" Navarro* (Lanham, Md.: Scarecrow Press, 2009), 250–55. See also Hershorn, *Norman Granz*, 139.

36. Mike Levin, "With a Hoot and a Howl, JATP Kicks Off Another," *Down Beat*, April 8, 1949, 12.

37. Glenn Pullen, "Ella Fitzgerald Is Song Hit of Jazz by Granz," *Cleveland Plain Dealer*, March 7, 1949, 14.

38. "Jazz at Philharmonic Patrons Get 'Moving,'" *Detroit Tribune*, March 5, 1949, 15.

39. Charles Menees, "Record Attendance at Jazz Concert," *St. Louis Post-Dispatch*, March 14, 1949, 15.

40. *Jazz at the Philharmonic: The Ella Fitzgerald Set*, Verve 815147, 1983, LP.

41. For a transcript of and commentary on Fitzgerald's solo, see Thomas J. Cleary's

blogpost "Ellavolution: Ella Fitzgerald's Evolution as an Improviser," *Birdfeed*, November 23, 2021, https://blog.uvm.edu/tgcleary/2021/11/23/ellavolution-ella -fitzgeralds-evolution-as-an-improviser/.

42. John S. Wilson, " 'JATP' Kicks Off at Carnegie," *Down Beat*, October 21, 1949, 3.

43. Dale Stevens, "Ella Is Tops on Jazz Show," *Dayton Daily News*, September 29, 1950, S30.

44. "Famed Singer Steals Honors in EP Show," *El Paso Times*, November 3, 1951, 17; "Singer Brings Gems of Songs," *Oregonian*, November 10, 1951, 4; Don Freeman, "Norman Granz Jazz 'Sends' Sellout House," *San Diego Union*, November 23, 1951, A3.

45. "Jazz Revived by Granz Group," *San Antonio Express*, November 2, 1951, 2.

46. "Granz Concert Plenty Noisy—From the Aud; But Sock B.O. Anyway," *Variety*, September 19, 1951, 53.

47. Hershorn, *Norman Granz*, 153; *Norman Granz Presents Improvisation*, Eagle Eye Media EE39060-9, 2007, 2-DVD set.

48. Oscar Peterson, *A Jazz Odyssey: The Life of Oscar Peterson* (New York: Continuum, 2003), 156–58.

49. George T. Simon, "Great," *Metronome*, April 1950, 13–14.

50. "Ella Weeps over Break with Hubby," *New York Amsterdam News*, June 9, 1951, 1.

51. Peterson, *Jazz Odyssey*, 67.

52. Virginia Wicks, interview by the author, December 5, 2009.

53. Sarah McLawler, interview by the author, September 23, 2010.

54. Fitzgerald interview by Feather, January 15, 1983, Ella Fitzgerald Project.

55. Tew., "Fox, Detroit," *Variety*, August 15, 1951, 20.

56. Dorothy Kilgallen, "Voice of Broadway," *Shamokin News-Dispatch*, October 13, 1951.

57. "Izzy Rowe's Notebook: Sons and Daughters of Harlem," *Pittsburgh Courier*, October 5, 1951, 18. Isadora "Izzy" Rowe inherited the byline of the "Notebook" in 1951 when her husband, Billy Rowe, became New York City's first Black deputy police commissioner.

58. "Izzy Rowe's Notebook: '52's for Females," *Pittsburgh Courier*, January 12, 1952, 16.

59. "Granz Cancels Europe in Money Wrangle," *Variety*, March 7, 1951, 43.

60. "Jazz at the Phil. for Scandinavia, France—and Britain?," *Melody Maker*, March 22, 1952, 12.

Chapter 14: Europe with Jazz at the Philharmonic (1952–1953)

1. Ella Fitzgerald, interview by Steve Allen, 1971–74, pt. 1, transcript, Satchmo Collection, Louis Armstrong House Museum.

2. Marshall Stearns, "The Conquest of Jazz," in Stearns, *The Story of Jazz* (New York: Oxford University Press, 1956); Leonard Feather, "Top U.S. Stars Europe-Bound," *Down Beat*, July 13, 1951, 1. By the end of 1952, artists who had visited Europe included Louis Armstrong, Duke Ellington, Dizzy Gillespie, and Sarah Vaughan. Billie Holiday arrived in 1954.

3. For "a major catalyst," see Alyn Shipton, *A New History of Jazz*, rev. and updated ed. (New York: Continuum, 2007), 465. For a historiographic discussion of the term *mainstream*, see Ronald Radano, *New Musical Figurations: Anthony Braxton's Cultural Critique* (Chicago: University of Chicago Press, 1994), 14n29, 30.

4. "JATP Registers Solidly Abroad," *Down Beat*, May 21, 1952, 1.

5. Dizzy Gillespie and Al Fraser, *To Be, or Not . . . to Bop* (1979; reprint Minneapolis: University of Minnesota Press, 2009), 326–30.

6. Michael McEachrane, ed., *Afro-Nordic Landscapes: Equality and Race in Northern Europe* (New York: Routledge, 2014), 68.

7. Stearns, *Story of Jazz*, 292.

8. Titti Sjöblom, interview by and correspondence with Alva Svenning, April 8, 2016. I am grateful to Svenning for her initiative in finding Ms. Sjöblom and providing this material.

9. "Ljudlig Publicfest; Ella's 'Body and Soul' JATP-Kvällens Top" ("Loud Festivity in the Audience; Ella's 'Body and Soul,' JATP Highlight of the Evening"), *Göteborgs-Tidningen*, 1952, 195.

10. Beryl Davis sang "Undecided" and "Don't Worry 'Bout Me." Paul Balmer, *Stéphane Grappelli: A Life in Jazz* (New York: Bobcat, 2003), 120.

11. "Claim French Don't Yet Get with Bop," *Down Beat*, October 7, 1949, 3.

12. Robert Bonaccorsi, *Jazz en France, 1945–1962: Photos from Paris Match with Two CDs* (Paris: 2014), 12–13, includes "Dream a Little Dream of Me" as its representative example for 1950 with reference to the Decca recordings. "French Jazz Poll Again Has Some Odd Results," *Down Beat*, February 22, 1952, 3.

13. "Le Jazz, Still Hot in Paris," *Life*, April 28, 1952, 125.

14. Boris Vian numbered among his friends Jean-Paul Sartre, Simone de Beauvoir, and the young singer and actress Juliette Gréco.

15. Boris Vian, "Revue de Press," *Jazz Hot*, June 1952, 17; Rashida K. Braggs, *Jazz Diasporas: Race, Music, and Migration in Post–World War II Paris* (Berkeley: University of California Press, 2016), 222n2.

16. Mike Nevard, "JATP Brings Paris Fair to a Glorious End," *Melody Maker*, April 12, 1952, 4.

17. Werner Burkhardt, interview by Claus Lochbihler, *JazzZeitung*, March 2003, http://www.jazzzeitung.de/jazz/2003/03/dossier-burkhardt.shtml.

18. "Germans Stomping on the Rhine as Jazz Invades Reich Kultur," *Variety*, May 28, 1952, 45. The author is grateful to Meredith Soeder for research on the newsletters of Frankfurt Hot Club. Meredith Soeder, "Jazz in a Transatlantic World: Legitimizing American Jazz in Germany, 1920–1957," Ph.D. diss., Carnegie Mellon University, 2017.

19. [Title missing], *Frankfurter Abendpost*, April 21, 1952. Translations supplied by Meredith Soeder from personal notes as excerpts.

20. "Granz Tells Story of Tour; Lauds European Jazz Fans," *Down Beat*, June 4, 1952, 1, 17.

21. "Granz's 'Jazz' in 21G Tee-Off," *Variety*, September 17, 1952, 50.

22. Oscar Peterson, *A Jazz Odyssey* (New York: Continuum, 2002), 169.

23. Tad Hershorn, *Norman Granz: The Man Who Used Jazz for Justice* (Berkeley: University of California Press, 2011), 159.

24. Virginia Wicks, interview by the author, December 5, 2009.

25. "Jazz Artists Play Explosively but Eloquently at Tech Concert," *Evening World-Herald* (Omaha), October 25, 1952.

26. Robert J. Schoenberg, "Ella Revisted. At Storyville," *Harvard Crimson*, January 30, 1953. Two numbers, "Why Don't You Do Right" and "Mean to Me," from a broadcast at Storyville in Boston on February 7, 1953, were added as bonus tracks to a rerelease of *Ella Fitzgerald at Mr. Kelly's 1958* on Essential Jazz Classics EJC55721, 2017, 2-CD set.

27. "Granz Is First to Crack British Ban on U.S. Orks," *Down Beat*, April 8, 1953, 1.

28. "Jazz at the Phil Comes to Town," *New Musical Express*, March 13, 1953, 1.

29. "Quotes from the Stars," *New Musical Express*, March 13, 1953, 9.

30. Kitty Grime, *Jazz Voices* (London: Quartet, 1983), 49.

31. Peterson, *Jazz Odyssey*, 156.

32. Ibid., 161.

33. Burkhardt interview by Lochbihler.

34. Rainer Nolden, *Ella Fitzgerald: Ihr Leben, Ihre Musik, Ihre Schallplatten* (Waakirchen: Oreos Verlag, 1986), 66.

35. Bill Crozier, "This Is What a JATP Concert Is Like," *New Musical Express*, March 6, 1953, 10.

36. Milton "Mezz" Mezzrow and Bernard Wolfe, *Really the Blues* (New York: Random House, 1946); Sidney Finkelstein, *Jazz: A People's Music* (New York: Citadel, 1948).

37. "Kennst du den Blues," *Der Spiegel*, April 22, 1953.

38. Bill Coss, "Ella!" *Metronome*, October 1953, 13, 29.

39. William D. Clancy, *Woody Herman: Chronicles of the Herds* (New York: Schirmer, 1995), 187.

40. Peterson, *Jazz Odyssey*, 161.

41. "New York Beat," *Jet*, October 22, 1953, 64.

42. Norman Granz, interview by Tad Hershorn, May 23, 2001, Hershorn Collection on Norman Granz, Rutgers University.

43. Hershorn, *Norman Granz*, 205.

44. Virginia Wicks, quoted in Hershorn, *Norman Granz*, 205.

45. MS lead sheet for "Throw It Out Your Mind" in The Ella Fitzgerald Collection, 1935–1997, MC 104, ser. 1, box 2, fol. 4, Institute of Jazz Studies, Rutgers University; and in Ella Fitzgerald Papers, NMAH.AC.0584, ser. 1, box 3, fol. 5, Archives Center, National Museum of American History, Smithsonian Institution.

46. Jim Blackman to the author, June 27, 2016. Blackman learned about it from Judy Cammarota, Ella's traveling companion in the 1980s.

47. Jim Blackman, telephone conversation with the author, January 17, 2010.

48. Ella Fitzgerald, interview by Leonard Feather, April 23, 1987, 97, Ella Fitzgerald Project, Leonard Feather Collection, University of Idaho.

49. Hershorn, *Norman Granz*, 206.

50. Peterson, *Jazz Odyssey*, 122.

51. *JATP in Tokyo: Live at the Nichigeki Theater,* Verve 2615 015, 1972, 3-LP set.

52. Nolden, *Ella Fitzgerald: Ihr Leben,* 66.

53. Gilbert Milstein, "Hot Jazz Promoter: Norman Granz Didn't Dig Music at First, But Now He Is Big-Time Impresario," *New York Times,* September 20, 1953, 7.

54. Leonard Feather, *From Satchmo to Miles* (New York: Da Capo Press, 1984), 181.

Chapter 15: Upwardly Mobile (1954–1955)

1. "Vaude Has Gotta Be Top-Drawer Nowadays to Draw—Joe Vogel," *Variety,* April 28, 1954, 49.

2. Richard Gale, interview by the author, May 19, 2009.

3. Virginia Wicks, interview by the author, December 5, 2009.

4. George Wein and Nate Chinen, *Myself Among Others: A Life in Music* (Cambridge, Mass.: Da Capo Press, 2003), 94.

5. Norman Granz to Fitzgerald, August 1, 1961, Ella Fitzgerald Papers, Smithsonian Institution.

6. Stuart Nicholson, *Ella Fitzgerald: The Complete Biography,* updated ed. (New York: Routledge, 2004), 170.

7. Tad Hershorn, *Norman Granz: The Man Who Used Jazz for Justice* (Berkeley: University of California Press, 2011), 213.

8. Lee Jeske, "Ask Norman," *Jazziz,* November 1996, 59–60.

9. Leonard Feather, *From Satchmo to Miles* (New York: Stein & Day, 1972), 181.

10. "Izzy Rowe's Notebook," *Pittsburgh Courier,* January 29, 1955, 18.

11. Orrin Keepnews, "Jazz and America," *Record Changer,* August–September 1952, 34.

12. George Marek, "From the Dive to the Dean: Jazz Becomes Respectable," *Good Housekeeping,* June 1956, 120.

13. Donald Bogle, *Dorothy Dandridge: A Biography* (New York: Amistad, 1997), 256.

14. Joseph Morschauer, "Career Girl Press Agent," *Look,* January 26, 1954, 51–55.

15. "Inside Stuff: Music," *Variety,* May 12, 1954, 46.

16. Dorothy Kilgallen, "Joe Hits a Homer in TV Deal," *Washington Post and Times Herald,* May 14, 1954, 45.

17. Ken Vail, *Bird's Diary: The Life of Charlie Parker* (Chessington, Surrey, U.K.: Castle Communications, 1996), 159.

18. "Any Style Will Do," *Newsweek,* June 7, 1954, 82.

19. Taubman got the assignment even though John S. Wilson had joined the *Times* in 1952 as its first popular music critic. Wilson would later move into jazz criticism. Hubert Kupferberg, a classical music critic, reviewed jazz for the *New York Herald Tribune.*

20. Howard Taubman, "Singer's Party: Ella Fitzgerald the Star of Her Own Evening," *New York Times,* June 6, 1954, 7.

21. Howard Taubman, "Newport Festival: Jazz Goes Respectable in Resort Town," *New York Times,* July 25, 1954, 7.

22. "So the Story Goes: George Wein on the Birth of the Newport Jazz Festival,"

Jazz Blog, August 8, 2016, https://www.jazz.org/blog/so-the-story-goes-george
-wein-on-the-birth-of-the-newport-jazz-festival.

23. Burt Goldblatt, *Newport Jazz Festival: The Illustrated History* (New York: Dial Press, 1977), 13.

24. Cleveland Amory, *Who Killed Society?* (New York: Harper & Bros., 1960), 18–19.

25. Lillian Ross, "You Dig It, Sir," *New Yorker*, August 14, 1954, 31; reprinted in Robert Gottlieb, ed., *Reading Jazz: A Gathering of Autobiography, Reportage, and Criticism from 1919 to Now* (New York: Vintage Books, 1996), 686ff.

26. James T. Kaull, Jr., "Jazz a Howling Success in First Newport Festival," *Newport Daily News*, July 19, 1954.

27. Howard Taubman, "Newport Rocked by Jazz Festival," *New York Times*, July 19, 1954, 21; Whitney Balliett, "New Name Dropping at Jazzy Old Newport," *Saturday Review*, July 31, 1954, 24.

28. *Jazz at the Philharmonic: The Ella Fitzgerald Set*, Verve 8151471, 1983, LP; reissued B0024612-02, 2016, CD.

29. Herm., "'Jazz at Philharmonic' Kicks Off New Season with Peak 23G Gross," *Variety*, September 22, 1954, 49.

30. George T. Simon, "Music USA," *Metronome*, November 1954, 6.

31. Kap., "Tiffany. Los Angeles," *Variety*, November 10, 1954, 61.

32. Spielman, "'Capsule Comments,' Ella Fitzgerald Tiffany Club, Los Angeles," *Billboard*, November 17, 1954, 10.

33. Jules L. Fox and Jo Brooks Fox, *The Melody Lingers On: Scenes from the Golden Years of West Coast Jazz* (Santa Barbara, Calif.: Fithian Press, 1996), 86.

34. For the AP wire photo, see "Marilyn in Good Shape Again," *News-Review* (Roseburg, Ore.), November 26, 1954, 14; for the UP photo, "Looking Fit and Well-Groomed," *Waco News-Tribune*, November 20, 1954, 11, https://en.wikipedia.org/wiki/File:Ella_Fitzgerald_and_Marilyn_Monroe_at_Tiffany_Club_1954.jpg.

35. An anecdote of Hal Schaefer related in Will Friedwald, *A Biographical Guide to the Great Jazz and Pop Singers* (New York: Pantheon Books, 2010), 171.

36. See "Marilyn Monroe & Ella Fitzgerald," *Immortal Marilyn*, August 28, 2015, http://www.immortalmarilyn.com/marilyn-monroe-ella-fitzgerald. According to the article, Monroe "couldn't have been [there]. There are absolutely no accounts or records of her taking a flight to LA from March 15–21. She was living in New York at the time. . . . Ella states the press went overboard. Except there are absolutely no pictures from that week of Marilyn in Los Angeles." A review of Ella's Mocambo debut in "Ella Fitzgerald a Big Hit," *Jet*, April 7, 1955, 60–61, includes pictures of many celebrity guests.

37. "New Work for Ella Fitzgerald," *Down Beat*, May 4, 1955, 27. See also Lois Banner, *Marilyn: The Passion and the Paradox* (New York: Bloomsbury, 2012), 2; and "Marilyn Monroe & Ella Fitzgerald," *Immortal Marilyn*.

38. Gloria Steinem, "Growing Up with Marilyn," *Ms. Magazine*, August 1972, 104.

39. Friedman, "Ella Fitzgerald, Mocambo, Hollywood," *Billboard*, March 26, 1955, 16.

40. "Ella Fitzgerald a Big Hit," 60–61.

41. "Hotel's Outpost for Live Talent," *Billboard*, May 6, 1967, SF30.

42. Ralph J. Gleason, "San Francisco Officials Throw JATP Concerts Out of City Auditorium," *Down Beat*, December 2, 1953, 1.

43. "Ella Fitzgerald Sets Pace with Frisco Date," *Variety*, March 30, 1955, 57.

44. Rafe, "Fairmont, San Francisco," *Variety*, April 13, 1955, 69.

45. Dorothy Kilgallen, "Broadway Grapevine," *News-Herald* (Oil City, Penn.), April 19, 1955.

46. "Flamingo, Las Vegas," *Variety*, November 9, 1955, 48.

47. "Music USA," *Metronome*, July 1955, 6.

48. "Brooklyn NAACP Show to Star Ella, Harry," *New York Amsterdam News*, May 15, 1954, 24.

49. "U.S. Singer Arrives—First-Class," *Sydney Morning Herald*, July 26, 1954.

50. William D. Smyth, "Segregation in Charleston in the 1950s: A Decade of Transition," *South Carolina Historical Magazine*, April 1991, 99–123.

51. Ellen Noonan, *The Strange Career of* Porgy & Bess: *Race, Culture and America's Most Famous Opera* (Chapel Hill: University of North Carolina Press, 2012), 245.

52. Joel E. Siegel, "Ella at 65: A Lot to Be Grateful For," *JazzTimes*, November 1983, 10.

53. Dizzy Gillespie and Al Fraser, *To Be, or Not . . . to Bop* (1979; reprint Minneapolis: University of Minnesota Press, 2009).

54. Hershorn, *Norman Granz*, 236–37.

55. Siegel, "Ella at 65."

56. William H. Kellar, *"Make Haste Slowly": Moderates, Conservatives, and School Desegregation in Houston* (College Station: Texas A&M University Press, 1999), 43–45.

57. Aimee L'Heureux, "Illinois Jacquet: Integrating Houston Jazz Audiences . . . Lands Ella Fitzgerald and Dizzy Gillespie in Jail," *Houston History* 8, no. 1 (Fall 2010): 6–8.

58. Hershorn, *Norman Granz*, 244–45.

59. "Vice-Squad Arrest U.S. Stars in Texas," *Melody Maker*, October 22, 1955, 1; "'Tisket-Tasket' Girl Has Dressing Room Dice Game Broken Up by Texas Vice Squad," *New York Amsterdam News*, October 15, 1955.

60. "Jazz Philharmonic Artists Throw Snake-Eyes but Get Back in Game," AP, as printed in *Fort Worth Star-Telegram*, October 8, 1955, 1.

61. Gillespie and Fraser, *To Be*, 411.

62. Nicholson, *Ella Fitzgerald*, 254.

63. Bob Grace, "Ella Fitzgerald 'Spoiled by People's Love,'" *News* (Port Arthur, Tex.), November 26, 1978.

64. "Andy Salmieri's American Air-Mail," *New Musical Express*, October 1, 1954, 4.

65. Al White, "Sammy Davis Jr., Meets It in Bid for Interracial Television Show," *Chicago Defender*, April 24, 1954, 19.

66. Nat Hentoff, "Ella Tells of Trouble in Mind Concerning Discs, Television," *Down Beat*, February 23, 1955, 2.

67. John Tynan, "Ella: It Took a Hit Album to Make Miss F. a Class Nitery Attraction," *Down Beat*, November 28, 1956, 13.

Chapter 16: "We Got ELLA!" (1954–1956)

1. Herm Schoenfeld, "Jocks, Jukes and Disks," *Variety*, May 19, 1954, 46.

2. Ella Fitzgerald, "Lullaby of Birdland," Decca 9-29198, 1954, 45 rpm.

3. Will Friedwald, *The Great Jazz and Pop Vocal Albums* (New York: Pantheon Books, 2017), 140–41.

4. "Popular Records," *Billboard*, July 10, 1954, 30.

5. Ella Fitzgerald and Ellis Larkins, *Ella—Songs in a Mellow Mood*, Decca DL 8069, 1954, LP.

6. Milton Gabler, "Cold Cash Can Make 'Hot Seat' Not So Bad," *Billboard*, August 28, 1954, 16.

7. Ibid.

8. Nat Hentoff, "Jazz Reviews," *Down Beat*, October 6, 1954, 12.

9. Stanley Dance, "Lightly and Politely: Ella 'n' Ellis," *Jazz Journal*, April 1955, 6.

10. "Reviews and Ratings of New Popular Albums," *Billboard*, August 28, 1954, 64.

11. Milt Gabler, interview by Loren Schoenberg, 1992, cited in Stuart Nicholson, *Ella Fitzgerald: The Complete Biography,* updated ed. (New York: Routledge, 2004), 177.

12. Milt Gabler to Norman Granz, December 13, 1954, Milt Gabler Papers, Smithsonian Institution.

13. Nat Hentoff, "Ella Tells of Trouble in Mind Concerning Discs, Television," *Down Beat*, February 23, 1955, 2.

14. Jose, "House Review: LaRosa, Fitzgerald, Bobbysoxers Too in 1st Loew's State Show Since '47," *Variety*, April 21, 1954, 61.

15. "Talent Review: Ella Fitzgerald," *Billboard*, June 5, 1954, 1.

16. George T. Simon, "Music USA," *Metronome*, November 1954, 6.

17. Sammy Cahn, *I Should Care: The Sammy Cahn Story* (New York: Arbor House, 1974), 176.

18. Hentoff, "Ella Tells of Trouble."

19. Ibid.

20. Ella Fitzgerald, *Sweet and Hot*, Decca DL 8155, 1955, LP.

21. "Jazz Reviews," *Down Beat*, December 28, 1955, 16; Barry Ulanov, "Fine Singers Galore . . . and a Decca Package," *Metronome*, April 1956, 34.

22. Milt Gabler to Norman Granz, June 8, 1955, Milt Gabler Papers, Smithsonian Institution.

23. Ella Fitzgerald, "Old Devil Moon / Lover, Come Back to Me," Decca 9-29580, 1955, 45 rpm.

24. Herm Schoenfeld, "Jocks, Jukes and Disks," *Variety*, July 13, 1955, 42.

25. Ulanov, "Fine Singers Galore."

26. Mike Butcher, "In Modern Mood," *New Musical Express*, April 27, 1956, 9.

27. "Reviews," *High Fidelity*, February 1956, 105.

28. Norman Granz to Milt Gabler, July 5, 1955, Milt Gabler Papers, Smithsonian Institution.

29. James Gavin, *Is That All There Is? The Strange Life of Peggy Lee* (New York: Atria, 2014), 178.

30. For example, Fanny Brice and Florence Mills.

31. Michael J. Hayde, *My Name's Friday: The Unauthorized but True Story of Dragnet and the Films of Jack Webb* (Nashville, Tenn.: Cumberland House, 2001), 112.

32. H.H.T., "Webb Plays the Blues," *New York Times*, August 19, 1955, 10.

33. "Ella Fitzgerald Says She Is Bashful as an Actress," *Atlanta Daily World*, April 22, 1958, 2.

34. Gavin, *Is That All There Is?*, 173.

35. Tad Hershorn, *Norman Granz: The Man Who Used Jazz for Justice* (Berkeley: University of California Press, 2011), 215–16.

36. "Ella Fitzgerald Sez She's Quitting Decca," *Variety*, January 11, 1956, 53.

37. Nicholson, *Ella Fitzgerald*, 178.

38. John Tynan, "All-Star Coast Concert Turns Away 1,000," *Down Beat*, March 7, 1956, 33.

39. The lists are in Milt Gabler Papers, Smithsonian Institution.

40. Ella Fitzgerald, *Lullabies of Birdland*, Decca DL-8149, 1955, LP.

41. Liner notes to Ella Fitzgerald, *The 75th Birthday Celebration: The Original Decca Recordings*, GRP GRD-2-619, 1993, 2-CD set.

42. "Verve Records," *Billboard*, January 14, 1956, 41.

43. Hershorn, *Norman Granz*, 216–17.

44. Anita O'Day and George Eells, *High Times Hard Times* (New York: Putnam, 1981), 228.

45. Buddy Bregman, interview by Bruce Kimmel, December 2, 2009, http://www.haineshisway.com/interview-section/interview-buddy-bregman/.

46. Ella Fitzgerald, *Ella at Zardi's*, Verve 00602557980516, 2017, CD. The trio were Don Abney (piano), Vernon Alley (bass), and Frankie Capp (drums).

47. "Ella Fitzgerald Says She Is Bashful as an Actress," *Atlanta Daily World*, April 22, 1958, 2.

48. John Tynan, "Caught in the Act: Ella Fitzgerald," *Down Beat*, February 1956, 8.

49. Buddy Bregman, interview by the author, February 24, 2010.

Chapter 17: The Cole Porter Experiment (1956–1957)

1. Ella Fitzgerald, *Ella Fitzgerald Sings the Cole Porter Song Book*, Verve MGV-4001-2, 1956, 2-LP set.

2. Dick Kleiner, "Record Shop," *Appeal-Democrat* (Marysville, Calif.), August 26, 1957.

3. Ella Fitzgerald, interview by Willis Conover for the Voice of America, August 17, 1956, Voice of America Music Library Collection, RWB 3068 B3, Library of Congress.

4. Eileen Southern, *The Music of Black Americans: A History*, 3rd ed. (New York: W. W. Norton, 1997), 560.

5. Joe Smith, *Off the Record: An Oral History of Popular Music* (New York: Warner Books, 1988), 15–16.

6. Norman Granz, interview by John McDonough, March 6, 1989, James "Tad" Hershorn Collection on Norman Granz, Institute of Jazz Studies, Archival Collections, IJS.0081, Rutgers University.

7. Dirk Schaeffer, "Footnotes on Jazz," *Metronome*, November 1956, 49.

8. William McBrien, *Cole Porter: A Biography* (New York: Knopf, 1998), 370.

9. Fred Lounsberry, *103 Lyrics of Cole Porter* (New York: Random House, 1954).

10. Don Freeman, liner notes to *Ella Fitzgerald Sings the Cole Porter Song Book*.

11. Mary Martin, *My Heart Belongs* (New York: Morrow, 1976), 19.

12. Buddy Bregman, interview by the author, February 24, 2010.

13. See, for example, "From This Moment On," transcript, in Norman David, *The Ella Fitzgerald Companion* (Westport, Conn.: Praeger, 2004), 112–14.

14. A recording session added to a reissue of *The Complete Ella Fitzgerald Song Books*, Verve Records 314519832-2, 1993, 16-CD set, CD 2, track 19.

15. Will Friedwald, liner notes to *The Complete Anita O'Day Verve/Clef Sessions*, Mosaic MD9-188, 1999, 9-CD set.

16. Rainer Nolden, *Ella Fitzgerald: Ihr Leben, ihre Musik, ihre Schallplatten* (Waakirchen: Oreos Verlag, 1986), translated by Meredith Soeder.

17. *Out of the Norm: The Life and Times of Norman Granz* (18-part radio series), BBC 2 Radio, aired December 2003 to January 2004.

18. Rob Kapilow, "Which Comes First, the Music or the Lyrics? 'You're the Top,'" in Don M. Randel et al., eds., *A Cole Porter Companion* (Urbana: University of Illinois Press, 2016), 87.

19. John Tynan, "Ella: It Took a Hit Album to Make Miss F. a Class Nitery Attraction," *Down Beat*, November 28, 1956, 13.

20. Stuart Nicholson, *Ella Fitzgerald: The Complete Biography*, updated ed. (New York: Routledge, 2004), 185.

21. Mike Nevard, "Oh, Mr. Porter (Your Lyrics Are SO Poetic)," *Melody Maker*, April 21, 1956.

22. Fitzgerald interview by Conover.

23. Leonard Feather, "Jazz Millionaire," *Esquire*, January 1957, 112.

24. Ted Gioia, *The History of Jazz*, 2nd ed. (New York: Oxford University Press, 2011), 346.

25. Norman Granz, "Letter to the Editors," *Metronome*, November 1956, 12, 34.

26. James Gavin, *Intimate Nights: The Golden Age of New York Cabaret* (New York: Back Stage Books, 2006), 109.

27. Peter J. Levinson, *Tommy Dorsey. Livin' in a Great Big Way: A Biography* (Cambridge, Mass.: Da Capo Press, 2005), 290. It is not yet known what Ella sang that evening. See Paley Center Archives, https://www.paleycenter.org/collection/item/?q=&p=1&item=T:65025.

28. Fitzgerald interview by Conover.

29. "Jazz Best-Sellers," *Down Beat*, February 5, 1959, 22.

30. "Package Reviews," *Billboard*, June 2, 1956, 22.

31. "Popular Records," *Down Beat*, June 27, 1956, 18.

32. Bill Coss, "Record Reviews," *Metronome*, September 1956, 26.

33. Norman Granz, "Letter to the Editor," *Metronome*, November 1956, 12, 34.

34. Robert Kimball, liner notes for Ella Fitzgerald, *The Cole Porter Song Book*, Verve VE-2-2511, 1976 (reissue), 2-LP set; Album Liner Notes, http://albumlinernotes .com/Cole_Porter_Songbooks.html.

35. Alec Wilder, *American Popular Song* (New York: Oxford University Press, 1972), 224.

36. Bill Coss, liner notes to *Metronome All-Stars 1956*, Verve MG V-8030, 1956, LP.

37. Count Basie and Albert Murray, *Good Morning Blues: The Autobiography of Count Basie* (New York: Random House, 1985), 318.

38. "Joe Williams on Ella Fitzgerald," quoted in Will Friedwald, liner notes to *The Ultimate Ella Fitzgerald*, Verve 539 054-2, 1997, CD.

39. "April in Paris / Party Blues," Verve Records 89172x45, 1956, 45 rpm.

40. *Jazz At The Philharmonic Seattle 1956*, Acrobat Music ADDCD3074, 2012, 2-CD set.

41. Dorothy Kilgallen, "Gina's Hubby Handy Guy to Have 'Round," *Washington Post and Times Herald*, June 24, 1956, J15.

42. Whitney Balliett, "Jazz at Newport: 1956," *Saturday Review*, July 28, 1956, 25.

43. Jack Tracy, "Newport Festival: Friday," *Down Beat*, August 8, 1956, 17.

44. Gus Johnson in Stanley Dance, *The World of Count Basie* (New York: Scribner's, 1980), 295.

45. Information about the house comes from the author's on-site visit with William and Marilyn Ezell, c. 2015.

46. Ray Charles Robinson, Jr., *You Don't Know Me: Reflections of My Father, Ray Charles* (New York: Random House, 2010), 43.

47. "New York Beat," *Jet*, July 9, 1953, 65.

48. Ray Brown, Jr., interview by the author, December 2016.

49. "Hollywood Bowl History," n.d., https://www.hollywoodbowl.com/about/the -bowl/hollywood-bowl-history.

50. Norman Granz, liner notes to *Jazz at the Hollywood Bowl*, Verve MG V-8231-2, 1958, 2-LP set.

51. Albert Goldberg, "Huge Bowl Audience Enjoys Jazz Concert," *Los Angeles Times*, August 16, 1956.

52. Hazel A. Washington, "This Is . . . Hollywood," *Chicago Defender*, August 25, 1956, 15.

Chapter 18: Sing Me a Standard (1956–1957)

1. Dan Morgenstern, "Louis Armstrong and the Development and Diffusion of Jazz," in Marc H. Miller, ed., *Louis Armstrong. A Cultural Legacy* (New York: Queens Museum of Art, and Seattle: University of Washington Press, 1994), 141.

2. Ella Fitzgerald and Louis Armstrong, *Ella and Louis*, Verve MGV-4003, 1956, LP.

3. Ricky Riccardi, *What a Wonderful World: The Magic of Louis Armstrong's Later Years* (New York: Vintage, 2012), 143.

4. Tad Hershorn, *Norman Granz: The Man Who Used Jazz for Justice* (Berkeley: University of California Press, 2011), 222.

5. Ray Brown, Jr., interview by the author, December 1, 2009.

6. Joe Smith, *Off the Record: An Oral History of Popular Music* (New York: Warner Books, 1988), 15.

7. Krin Gabbard, *Jammin' at the Margins: Jazz and the American Cinema* (Chicago: University of Chicago Press, 1996), chap. 6.

8. Oscar Peterson, interview by John McDonough, 1997, courtesy of McDonough.

9. Ibid.

10. "Young Ella Fitzgerald in Performance," photo, n.d., Louis Armstrong House Museum, https://collections.louisarmstronghouse.org/asset-detail/1045316.

11. "Ella on Ella: A Personal Portrait," *Essence* (television program), NBC, April 26, 1986, Paley Center for Media, https://www.paleycenter.org/collection/item/?q=first&p=248&item=T:08316.

12. But the managing editor of the *Los Angeles Sentinel*, Stanley Robertson, called it "very poor taste. Don't tell me that Verve just HAD to run that photo with Louis and rolled down socks and Ella looking like she just finished scrubbing some floor." Stanley Robertson, "Sentinel Platter Parade," *Los Angeles Sentinel*, November 22, 1956, B5.

13. Nat Hentoff, "Jazz Records," *Down Beat*, November 14, 1956, 24; "Review Spotlight on Jazz Albums," *Billboard*, October 13, 1956, 26.

14. Ella Fitzgerald, *Ella Fitzgerald Sings the Rodgers and Hart Song Book*, Verve MGV-4002-2, 1957, 2-LP set.

15. *The Rodgers and Hart Song Book* led to a successful series of sheet music books. See Peter Schwed, *Turning the Pages: An Insider's Story of Simon & Schuster, 1924–1984* (New York: Macmillan, 1984), 21–22.

16. Norman Granz, interview by John McDonough, March 6, 1989, courtesy of McDonough.

17. John Tynan, "Ella," *Down Beat*, November 28, 1956, 13; John Howland, *Hearing Luxe Pop: Glorification, Glamour, and the Middlebrow in American Popular Music* (Berkeley: University of California Press, 2021), 84.

18. "Packaged Records Buying Guide," *Billboard*, February 2, 1957, 28.

19. Hershorn, *Norman Granz*, 223. Jim Blackman recalled hearing Fitzgerald sing "Have You Met Miss Jones?" at the Fairmont Hotel in the early 1980s, telling the audience she was not "that way." Jim Blackman, interview by the author, April 21, 2022.

20. Anita O'Day and Billy May, *Swing Rodgers and Hart*, Verve MGV-2141, 1960, LP; Sarah Vaughan, *The Divine One*, Roulette SR52060, 1961, LP.

21. John H. Haley, "Reflections on the Voice of Ella Fitzgerald," July 3, 2022, https://www.highdeftapetransfers.ca/blogs/news/relections-on-the-voice-of-ella-fitgerald.

22. Tynan, "Ella," 13.

23. Recorded on August 10, 1958, and released on Ella Fitzgerald, *Live at Mister Kelly's*, Verve B0008923-2, 2007, 2-CD set.

24. Rodger's complaint in *San Francisco Chronicle* was repeated in "Take It Easier on Our Tunes, Fellas, Richard Rodgers Asks of Arrangers," *Down Beat*, July 15, 1953, 3; "People at the Top of the Entertainment World," *Life*, December 22, 1958, 168.

25. Irving Kolodin, "Rodgers and Hart, Ella and Ellington," *Saturday Review*, March 16, 1957, 43.

26. Bill Coss and Jack Maher, "Record Reviews," *Jazz Today*, April 1957, 30, 32.

27. Monterey Jazz Festival Collection, ARS.0018, box 107, reel 3, Stanford University Archive of Recorded Sound, Online Archives of California, www.oac.cdlib.org.

28. Dorothy Kilgallen, "Voice of Broadway," *Anderson Daily Bulletin* (Ind.), January 21, 1957, 4.

29. Sidney Fields, "Songbird Is Missing a Note," *New York Mirror*, June 21, 1957.

30. Ella Fitzgerald, interview by Leonard Feather, April 23, 1987, Ella Fitzgerald Project, Leonard Feather Collection, University of Idaho.

31. Leonard Feather, "Ella Meets the Duke," *Playboy*, November 1957, 42.

32. "Music News: International Ella," *Down Beat*, May 16, 1957, 10.

33. "Copa Books Ella in 'Test' Date," *Variety*, April 17, 1957, 51.

34. "Jive-Jots of the Week," *Kansas City Plain Dealer*, July 11, 1958, 6.

35. Ella Fitzgerald and Billie Holiday, *At Newport*, Verve MGV-8234, 1958, LP.

36. Ella Fitzgerald and Louis Armstrong, *Ella and Louis Again*, Verve MGV-4006-2, 1947, LP.

37. Ella Fitzgerald and Frank DeVol and His Orchestra, *Like Someone in Love*, Verve MGV-4004, 1957, LP; Ella Fitzgerald, *Get Happy!*, Verve MGV-4036, 1959, LP; Ella Fitzgerald, *Hello Love*, Verve MGV-4034, 1959, LP.

38. Dom Cerulli, "Music in Review: Popular Records," *Down Beat*, February 20, 1958, 21.

39. Dorothy Kilgallen, "'Baby Doll' Bombshell Upsets All Plans," *Washington Post and Times Herald*, May 9, 1956, 26.

40. Buddy Bregman, interview by the author, May 24, 2009.

41. Fields, "Songbird Is Missing a Note."

42. "Love Swindle Jails Ella Fitzgerald's Mate," *Cleveland Plain Dealer*, August 16, 1957, 1.

43. Fitzgerald to Virginia Wicks, August 6, 1957, courtesy of Wicks's daughter Christina Bayles.

44. "Jail Ella's 'Mate' in Love Gyp," *Chicago Defender*, August 13, 1957, 1.

45. "Ella Thought Friend a Wonderful Person," *Pittsburgh Courier*, August 24, 1957, A17.

46. Virginia Wicks, interview by Tad Hershorn, April 2003, in James "Tad" Hershorn Collection on Norman Granz, Institute of Jazz Studies, Archival Collections, IJS.0081, Rutgers University.

47. Dolores Calvin, "Seein' Stars," *Arkansas State Press*, August 30, 1957, 8.

48. "Ella Fitzgerald on Her Career and Forbidden Love," CBC, 1980, https://www.youtube.com/watch?v=oWxWbig9oiA.

49. "Ella on Ella," *Essence*.

50. Ella Fitzgerald, *At the Opera House*, Verve MGV-8264, 1958, LP.

51. Norman Granz, liner notes to Fitzgerald, *At the Opera House.*

52. Dom Cerulli, "Record Reviews," *Down Beat*, September 18, 1958, 36.

53. Hershorn, *Norman Granz*, 263.

54. Leonard Feather, "The Jazz Millionaire," *Esquire*, January 1957, 114.

55. May Okon, "She Still Gets Stage Fright," *Daily News* (New York), September 8, 1957, Sunday news sec., 4.

Chapter 19: Flouting Categories (1957–1958)

1. "What Ella Does Best," *Time*, June 23, 1958, 67.

2. John S. Wilson, "Granz Presents a Jazz Concert," *New York Times*, September 13, 1958, 11.

3. Bill Coss, "Singers and Vocalists . . . In and Out of Jazz," *Metronome*, July 1958, 12.

4. Ella Fitzgerald, *Ella Fitzgerald Sings the Duke Ellington Song Book*, Verve MGV 4008-2 and MGV 4009-2, 1957, 4-LP set.

5. Ren Grevatt, "Disk Jockey Special: 'Jazz Singer' Tag Covers a Wide Artist Roster on Wax," *Billboard*, August 18, 1958, 20.

6. Benny Green, *Such Sweet Thunder: Benny Green on Jazz* (New York: Scribner, 2001), 387.

7. Lacking a definitive study of Ellington's presence as both a composer and interpreter of pop vocals, my qualified claim is based on the following: Jack Burton, "The Honor Roll of Popular Songwriters: Duke Ellington," *Billboard*, March 25, 1950, 42, and April 1, 1950, 46; seventy entries in Joel Whitburn, *Pop Memories 1890–1954* (Menomonee Falls, Wis.: Record Research, 1986); seventeen titles in Whitburn's *Top R&B / Hip-Hop Singles 1942–2004* (Menomonee Falls, Wis.: Record Research, 2006); and individual song profiles in *Second Hand Songs*, https://secondhandsongs.com.

8. *Jazz at the Philharmonic: The Ella Fitzgerald Set*, Verve 815147, 1983, LP. Mack David wrote the lyrics to "I'm Just a Lucky So-and-So."

9. John Tynan, "Ella: It Took a Hit Album to Make Miss F. a Class Nitery Attraction," *Down Beat*, November 28, 1956, 14; John Edward Hasee, *Beyond Category: The Life and Genius of Duke Ellington* (New York: Simon & Schuster, 1993), 325–26.

10. "Solitude" is singled out by John S. Wilson, "Music: Intellectual Jazz," *New York Times*, September 17, 1956, 23; and George Wein, column in *Boston Herald*, September 17, 1956.

11. "Verve Sights Set on Quality," *Billboard*, January 6, 1958, 19; Norman Granz, interview by John McDonough, July 27, 1997, courtesy of McDonough.

12. Maurice Zolotow, "The Duke of Hot," *Saturday Evening Post*, August 7, 1943, reprinted in Zolotow, *Never Whistle in a Dressing Room* (New York: E.P. Dutton, 1944), 295.

13. Walter van de Leur, *Something to Live For: The Music of Billy Strayhorn* (New York: Oxford University Press, 2002), 188. David Hajdu's fascinating biography *Lush Life: A Biography of Billy Strayhorn* (New York: Farrar, Straus & Giroux, 1996) explores the complex creative relationship between Strayhorn and Ellington.

14. In the *Down Beat* Jubilee tribute issue to the Duke: Leonard Feather, "The Full Ellington Story Up to His Silver Jubilee," *Down Beat*, November 5, 1952, 1.

15. Norman Granz, "In My Opinion," *Jazz Journal*, November 1963, 18.

16. Leonard Feather, "Ella Today (and Yesterday Too)," *Down Beat*, November 18, 1965, 23.

17. Patricia Willard, liner notes for expanded CD reissue of *Ella Fitzgerald Sings the Duke Ellington Song Book*, Verve 559-248-2, 1999, 3-CD set.

18. Thomas Cleary to the author, August 26, 2020.

19. "Best Selling Jazz Albums," *Billboard*, June 29, 1959, 22.

20. Henry Pleasants, *The Great American Popular Singers* (New York: Simon & Schuster, 1974), 169.

21. Frank Büchmann-Moller, *Someone to Watch Over Me: The Life and Music of Ben Webster* (Ann Arbor: University of Michigan Press, 2006), 169.

22. Irving Kolodin, "Duke Ellington and Queen Ella," *Saturday Review*, April 12, 1958, 50–51.

23. John Tynan, "Record Reviews," *Down Beat*, May 15, 1958, 26.

24. Martin Williams, "This Month's Jazz," *American Record Guide*, July 1958, 478.

25. Bill Coss, "Singers and Vocalists . . . In and Out of Jazz," *Metronome*, July 1958, 25.

26. Whitney Balliett, "Close But No Cigar," *New Yorker*, April 5, 1958, 133ff.

27. Bob Blumenthal, interview by the author, January 14, 2021; Blumenthal, liner notes for Ella Fitzgerald, *Ella Fitzgerald Sings the Duke Ellington Song Book*, Verve 837035-2, 1988, 3-CD set.

28. Stuart Nicholson, *Ella Fitzgerald: The Complete Biography*, updated ed. (New York: Routledge, 2004), 209.

29. Ella Fitzgerald, *Ella Fitzgerald Sings the Irving Berlin Song Book*, Verve MGVS-6005-2, 1958, 2-LP set.

30. William Glover, "Ella Fitzgerald Is Putting Emphasis on Ballads Now," *Richmond Times Dispatch* (Va.), August 24, 1958, 93.

31. "Supper Time," which Ethel Waters premiered in the 1933 revue *As Thousands Cheer*, dealt with lynching. Donald Bogle, *Heat Wave: The Life and Career of Ethel Waters* (New York: HarperCollins, 2011), 224–25.

32. *The Playboy Jazz All-Stars*, Playboy PB 1957, 1957, 2-LP set.

33. Jeffrey Magee, "Irving Berlin's 'Blue Skies': Ethnic Affiliations and Musical Transformations," *Musical Quarterly* 84, no. 4 (Winter 2000): 570.

34. John McDonough, liner notes to *The Complete Ella Fitzgerald Song Books*, Verve 314519832-2, n.d., 16-CD set, 103.

35. Ella Fitzgerald, *Ella in Rome: The Birthday Concert*, Verve 835-454-2, 1988, CD.

36. Katharine Cartwright, "'Guess These People Wonder What I'm Singing': Quotation and Reference in Ella Fitzgerald's 'St. Louis Blues,'" in David Evans, ed., *Ramblin' on My Mind: New Perspectives on the Blues* (Champaign: University of Illinois Press, 2008), 297–300.

37. "British Search U.S. Jazz Group," *Chicago Daily Tribune*, May 3, 1958, 1.

38. Maurice Burman, "ELLA," *Melody Maker*, May 10, 1958, 5.

39. Jose, "Night Club Reviews: Copacabana, N.Y.," *Variety*, June 11, 1958, 55.

40. Ella Fitzgerald, interview by Charles Collingwood, *Person to Person*, 1960, https://www.youtube.com/watch?v=jtPgNQ9AX14.

41. "Cannes Segues from Pix to Jazz Fest via International All-Star Airlift," *Variety*, July 30, 1958, 102.

42. Albert Goldberg, "Near-Capacity Bowl Hears Ella Fitzgerald," *Los Angeles Times*, August 18, 1958, 75.

43. "Granz Maps Fitzgerald, Ellington Treks," *Billboard*, September 15, 1958, 6.

44. Gros, "Ella Fitzgerald Pulls 'Em, Peterson Trio Chases 'Em in New Granz Jazz Show," *Variety*, September 17, 1958, 68, 72.

45. Stef, "Fairmont, San Francisco," *Variety*, November 5, 1958, 68.

46. William Glover, "Reviewing Records," *Herald-Sun* (Durham, N.C.), July 27, 1958, 5D.

47. Ella Fitzgerald, Benny Goodman, and others, *Swing into Spring*, Sandy Hook SH 2057, 1981, LP.

48. Steven H. Scheuer, "Ella Fitzgerald Sees Self on TV," *Manhattan Mercury* (Kan.), May 11, 1958, 1B.

49. Steven H. Scheuer, "TV Key," *Arizona Republic*, May 9, 1958, 8.

50. "Television's Best Bets for Tonight," *Wichita Beacon*, December 3, 1958, 34.

51. "TV Roundup: Dinah Shore May Curtail Video Activity," *Philadelphia Inquirer*, December 3, 1958, 39.

52. Ralph Gleason, "Styles of Glamour Singers Come and Go, but Ella Fitzgerald Remains Just Herself," *Boston Globe*, November 30, 1958, A9.

53. James Gavin, *Stormy Weather: The Life of Lena Horne* (New York: Simon & Schuster, 2009), 258, 265.

54. Gleason, "Styles of Glamour," A9.

55. Ibid.

Chapter 20: Midcentury Modern Triumphs (1959)

1. "Best Selling Jazz Albums," *Billboard*, June 29, 1959, 22. Number eight was *Ella Fitzgerald Sings the Duke Ellington Song Book*; number thirty was *Ella Fitzgerald Sings the Irving Berlin Song Book*; number thirty-one was *Ella and Louis*; and number thirty-four was *Ella & Louis Again*.

2. Ralph J. Gleason, "Ella's Audiences Are Glad She's Not Going 'Commercial,'" *Indianapolis Star*, November 30, 1958; Ella Fitzgerald, *Ella Swings Lightly*, Verve MG V-4021, 1959, LP.

3. "The Billboard Spotlight Winner of the Week," *Billboard*, March 9, 1959, 26.

4. Jack Maher, "Record Reviews," *Metronome*, May 1959, 33.

5. Ella Fitzgerald and Louis Armstrong, *Porgy and Bess*, Verve MG V-4011-2, 1959, 2-LP set.

6. "Poitier Will Play Porgy in Picture," *Los Angeles Times*, December 11, 1957, A13.

7. Ellen Noonan, *The Strange Career of* Porgy and Bess: *Race, Culture, and America's Most Famous Opera* (Chapel Hill: University of North Carolina Press, 2012), 280.

8. "Album Best Sellers of 1959," *Variety*, December 30, 1959, 40.

9. George E. Pitts, "Ella Has Yearning to Be TV Actress," *Pittsburgh Courier*, June 2, 1962, 14.

10. Ella Fitzgerald, *Live at Mister Kelly's*, Verve B0008923-2, 2007, 2-CD set.

11. John Tynan, "Portrait of Ira," *Down Beat*, July 23, 1959, 20.

12. Tad Hershorn, *Norman Granz: The Man Who Used Jazz for Justice* (Berkeley: University of California Press, 2011), 261.

13. Irving Kolodin, "Catfish Row and Wilshire," *Saturday Review*, June 13, 1959, 52.

14. Patricia Hill Collins, *Black Feminist Thought: Knowledge, Consciousness, and the Politics of Empowerment*, rev. ed. (New York: Routledge, 2014), 81.

15. Dolores Calvin, "Seein' Stars," *Arkansas State Press*, June 19, 1959, 11.

16. Fitzgerald, *Live at Mister Kelly's*.

17. Ray Charles, interview by the author, November 15, 2009.

18. "Ella Fitzgerald to Sing Sunday at Opera House," *Chicago Daily Tribune*, September 27, 1959, E8.

19. Bob McAleer, "Nat, Ella Still Tops," *Windsor Star* (Ont.), January 20, 1959, 20; advertisement in *Philadelphia Inquirer*, March 25, 1959, 25.

20. "Ella Fitzgerald to Appear at University," *Medford Mail Tribune* (Ore.), November 4, 1959.

21. "Behind the Walls," *Down Beat*, September 3, 1959, 10.

22. Gene Lees, "No. 3—Playboy," *Down Beat*, September 3, 1959, 17; Frank Arganbright, "Spellbound Fans Lap It Up," *Journal and Courier* (Lafayette, Ind.), August 22, 1959, 30.

23. Mimi Clar, "One-Woman Concert Given by Ella Fitzgerald," *Los Angeles Times*, March 15, 1959.

24. Ogden Dwight called the All-Star Jazz Telecast a "sorry circus," in "On Television," *Des Moines Register*, May 12, 1958, 16.

25. "1959 Set Torrid Record for 1960 Television Book," *Chicago Defender*, December 26, 1959, 18.

26. bell hooks, *Yearning: Race, Gender, and Cultural Politics* (Boston: South End Press, 1990), 3.

27. John P. Shanley, "TV Review: Ella and the Duke," *New York Times*, February 11, 1959, 78; William Ewald, "Bell Show Offers Half-Hour Special Stretched over Hour," *Republic* (Columbus, Ind.), February 11, 1959.

28. Hazel A. Washington, "This Is Hollywood," *Daily Defender* (Chicago, Ill.), March 9, 1959, A17.

29. June Bundy, "'Spring' Tasteful Musical Nostalgia," *Billboard*, April 20, 1959, 6.

30. Ella Fitzgerald, *Ella Fitzgerald Sings the George and Ira Gershwin Song Book*, Verve Records MG V-4024-8, 1959, 5-LP set.

31. Norman Granz, "A Statement on 'A Statement on Television,'" *Variety*, December 30, 1959, 35.

32. James Bacon, "Why Pat Boone Sings the Message of Civil Rights," *Press and Sun-Bulletin* (Binghamton, N.Y.), May 23, 1965, 59. Boone misremembered the date. Titles in "TV Key, Program Previews," *Decatur Daily Review* (Ill.), October 29, 1959, 20.

33. Will Friedwald, "When Ella Fitzgerald Sang Gershwin: A Chapter from the Great American Songbook," in Anna Harwell Celenza, ed., *The Cambridge Companion to Gershwin* (Cambridge, U.K.: Cambridge University Press, 2019), 259.

34. Milton Gabler, "Reminiscences," November 1959, transcript, p. 1923, Columbia Center for Oral History, Columbia University.

35. "The Swinging Riddle," pt. 1A of *Nelson Riddle* (documentary), BBC Radio 2, https://www.youtube.com/watch?v=J_2-otlmEws.

36. Ella Fitzgerald, "But Not for Me," Verve V-10180x45, 1959, 45 rpm.

37. "Ella Fitzgerald Doesn't Mind Being Called Commercial," *New Musical Express*, October 30, 1959.

38. Lee Jeske, "Ask Norman," *Jazziz*, November 1996, reprinted in Leslie Gourse, ed., *Ella Fitzgerald: Seven Decades of Commentary* (New York: Schirmer, 1998), 81.

39. Hershorn, *Norman Granz*, 260–61.

40. Edward Jablonski and Lawrence D. Stewart, *The Gershwin Years: George and Ira* (New York: Da Capo Press, 1973), 367.

41. John Rockwell, "Half a Century of Song with the Great 'Ella,'" *New York Times*, June 15, 1986, sec. 2, 1. The earliest publication of this quote has not been located.

42. Lawrence D. Stewart, liner notes to *Ella Fitzgerald Sings the George and Ira Gershwin Song Book*, Verve MG VS-6082-5, 1959, 5-LP set.

43. "Album Reviews," *Variety*, November 25, 1959, 54.

44. "Verve Issues Fitzgerald, Gershwin Set," *Billboard*, November 9, 1959, 4, 6. George Gershwin's signature was reproduced from canceled checks.

45. Jeske, "Ask Norman."

46. C. H. Garrigues, "An LP Tribute to Ella Fitzgerald," *San Francisco Examiner*, December 13, 1959, 154.

47. John S. Wilson, "Ella Meets the Gershwins with an Assist from Nelson Riddle," *High Fidelity*, January 1960, 63.

48. Don Heckman, "Record Reviews," *Jazz Review*, August 1960, 19.

49. Bruce Crowther and Mike Pinfold, *Singing Jazz: The Singers and Their Styles* (San Francisco: Miller Freeman, 1997), 69.

50. Hedda Hopper column, *Los Angeles Times*, December 10, 1959, 101.

Chapter 21: "It's Quite a Problem Trying to Please Everyone" (1960–1964)

1. Oscar Peterson, interview by John McDonough, March 20, 1997, courtesy of McDonough.

2. Tad Hershorn, *Norman Granz: The Man Who Used Jazz for Justice* (Berkeley: University of California Press, 2011), 292.

3. "Sinatra Tie with Verve in the Works," *Billboard*, September 19, 1960, 18.

4. Hershorn, *Norman Granz*, 292–93.

5. James Kaplan, *Sinatra: The Chairman* (New York: Anchor Books, 2015), 344–45.

6. Hershorn, *Norman Granz*, 361.

7.   Marc Myers, "Tad Hershorn: Norman Granz (Part 3)," *JazzWax*, October 2011, https://www.jazzwax.com/2011/10/tad-hershorn-norman-granz-pt-3.html.

8.   "Granz to Keep Watch over Ella," *Billboard*, January 30, 1961, 1.

9.   For Taylor's negative views on Granz's model of spontaneous one-take recording, see Ashley Kahn, *The House That Trane Built: The Story of Impulse Records* (New York: W. W. Norton, 2006), 14. See also Marc Myers, "Interview: Creed Taylor (Part 4)," *Jazzwax*, May 15, 2008, https://www.jazzwax.com/2008/05/interview-cre-3.html.

10. Creed Taylor, quoted in Marc Myers, liner notes to *Ella in Japan*, Verve B0015305-02, 2011, 2-CD set, 8.

11. Paul Smith, interview by the author, March 4, 2010.

12. Stephanie Brown, "Show Goes On, Despite Her Cold," *Minneapolis Star Tribune*, February 2, 1960, 30.

13. Will Jones, "Ella Just Can't Goof," *Minneapolis Star Tribune*, February 3, 1960, 34.

14. "1959 Grammy Winners," Recording Academy Grammy Awards, https://www.grammy.com/awards/2nd-annual-grammy-awards.

15. Rau quoted in "Ella in Berlin," BBC, April 2013, https://www.bbc.com/mediacentre/proginfo/2021/24/ella-in-berlin.

16. Phillip D. Atteberry, "Here's Why the Lady Is the Champ," *Mississippi Rag*, February 1996, 7.

17. Ibid.

18. Fritz Rau, *50 Jahre Backstage: Erinnerungen eines Konzertveranstalters* (Heidelberg: Palmya Verlag, 2006), 31.

19. Louie Robinson, "First Lady of Jazz," *Ebony*, November 1961, 136.

20. Joel Whitburn, *Top R&B Singles 1942–1988* (Menomonee Falls, Wis.: Record Research, 1988), 149; Jimmy Jungermann, "German News Notes: Southern Germany," *Billboard*, July 25, 1960, 8.

21. Howard Pollack, *Marc Blitzstein: His Life, His Work, His World* (New York: Oxford University Press, 2012), 365.

22. Will Friedwald, *Jazz Singing: America's Great Voices from Bessie Smith to Bebop and Beyond* (New York: Scribner's, 1990), 144.

23. Fitzgerald, *Ella in Berlin: Mack the Knife*, Verve MG V-4041, 1960, LP; Joel Whitburn, *Top Pop Albums 1955–2001* (Menomonee Falls, Wis.: Record Research, 2001), 292.

24. Robinson, "First Lady."

25. Phillip D. Atteberry, "Paul Smith Interview," *Cadence*, June 1994, 7.

26. The São Paulo date was April 28, 1960. An advertisement for Fitzgerald's performance at Teatro Record, May 4–8, 1960, in São Paulo Library was located by Michael Li. See clippings file in http://cartazes-internacionais-no-brasil.blogspot.com/2014/10/tv-record-1960.html.

27. Ella Fitzgerald, interview by Charles Collingwood, *Person to Person*, 1960, https://www.youtube.com/watch?v=jtPgNQ9AX14.

28. Ella Fitzgerald, *Ella Fitzgerald Sings Songs from Let No Man Write My Epitaph*, Verve MG V-4043, 1960, LP; John McAndrew, "Star Studded Shellac," *Record Research*,

April 1963, 12. Opinions varied from Barbara Gardner's pan in *Down Beat*, February 16, 1961, 40, to Max Jones, "'Epitaph' Album Represents a Different Ella," *Melody Maker*, December 3, 1960, 11.

29. Dr. Ian D. Clark, *Ella Fitzgerald in Australia: A History* (Self-published, 2014), 54.

30. "Norman Granz Discovers Global Concert Circuit as Ella Works 'Em in N.Z.," *Variety*, December 14, 1960, 52.

31. John F. Kennedy, *The Lost Inaugural Gala* (documentary), 2017. It was broadcast on June 3, 2017, and a CD made available through PBS.

32. Sammy Cahn, *I Should Care: The Sammy Cahn Story* (New York: Arbor House, 1974), 188.

33. Blake Green, "That Modest First Lady of Song," *San Francisco Chronicle*, December 17, 1976, 42; Mildred Schroeder, "Ella Is Singing the Calorie Blues," *San Francisco Examiner*, c. late fall 1961 (partially dated clip in Jim Blackman's private collection).

34. Phoebe Jacobs, interview by the author, March 27–28, 2011.

35. "Ella Is Shy About a Lot of Things—But Not Singing," *Stage and Television Today*, March 21, 1963, 5.

36. Ella Fitzgerald, *Ella Fitzgerald Sings the Harold Arlen Song Book*, Verve V-4046-2, 1961, 2-LP set; Murray Schumach, "Composer Tells of Movie Abuses," *New York Times*, August 10, 1961, 17.

37. Bill Matney, "Ella Sings the Arlen Song Book," *Michigan Chronicle*, June 17, 1961, A4.

38. George T. Simon, "Ella Fitzgerald Swinging Arlen," *New York Herald Tribune*, April 30, 1961, D22.

39. In album notes to *Ella Fitzgerald Sings the Harold Arlen Song Book*.

40. Billy May was in Charlie Barnett's band, and Barnett's mother owned the hotel. Billy May, interview by Steve Allen, 1971–74, transcript, Satchmo Collection, Louis Armstrong House Museum.

41. John McDonough, liner notes to *The Complete Ella Fitzgerald Song Books*, Verve 314519832-2, 1993, 16-CD set.

42. Walter Frisch, *Arlen and Harburg's Over the Rainbow* (New York: Oxford University Press, 2017), 56.

43. Ella Fitzgerald, *Clap Hands, Here Comes Charlie!*, Verve 4053, 1961, LP.

44. John Tynan, "Record Reviews: Vocal," *Down Beat*, March 1, 1962, 39.

45. Ella Fitzgerald and Nelson Riddle, *Ella Swings Brightly with Nelson*, Verve 4054, 1962, LP; and Ella Fitzgerald and Nelson Riddle, *Ella Swings Gently with Nelson*, Verve 4055, 1962, LP.

46. "Ella Fitzgerald for Europe Tour," *Disc*, December 17, 1960, 3; "Ella Schedules Biggest Overseas Tour to Date," *Down Beat*, January 19, 1961, 13.

47. "Foreign Television Reviews: An Evening with Ella Fitzgerald," *Variety*, April 19, 1961, 34.

48. Robin Douglas-Home, quoted in Sid Colin, *Ella: The Life and Times of Ella Fitzgerald* (London: Elm Tree Books, 1987), 122.

49. Hershorn, *Norman Granz*, 227.

50. "People Are Taking About," *Jet*, February 23, 1961, 42.

51. Louie Robinson, "First Lady of Jazz," *Ebony*, November 1961, 137–38.

52. Stuart Nicholson, *Ella Fitzgerald: The Complete Biography*, updated ed. (New York: Routledge, 2004), 223.

53. "Ella Bor Ved Vandet," *Berlingske Tidende*, August 27, 1961, translated for the author by Bruce Kirmsee.

54. George T. Simon, "11,000 Hear Ella Fitzgerald at Forest Hills Stadium," *New York Herald Tribune*, August 7, 1961, 11.

55. George Avakian, liner notes to Lambert, Hendricks, and Bavan, *Recorded Live at Basin Street East*, RCA Victor LPM-2635, 1963, LP.

56. Bob Rolontz, "Basin Street in Flurry over Ella," *Billboard*, April 24, 1961, 5.

57. Gros., "Basin Street East," *Variety*, April 19, 1961, 68.

58. June Bundy, "Applause, Laughs Aid Artists in Garnering Top Chart Positions," *Billboard*, October 30, 1961, 1.

59. Marc Myers, liner notes to *Ella in Japan*, Verve B0015305-02, 2011, 2-CD set.

60. Louella Parsons, "Big Turn Out for Ella Fitzgerald," *Modern Screen*, August 1961, 12.

61. John L. Scott, "Ella Fitzgerald Triumphs Again," *Los Angeles Times*, May 6, 1961, 23.

62. Ella Fitzgerald, *Ella in Hollywood*, Verve V6-4052, 1961, LP.

63. Scott Yanow, *The Jazz Singers: The Ultimate Guide* (New York: Backbeat Books, 2008), 78.

64. Atteberry, "Here's Why the Lady Is the Champ," 8.

65. Ella Fitzgerald, "Mr. Paganini," Verve Records VK 10237, 1961, 45 rpm.

66. Albert Anderson, "Ella Tops Diversified Fare," *Baltimore Afro-American*, March 10, 1962, 15.

67. Harry Weinger and Richard Seidel, liner notes to Ella Fitzgerald, *Twelve Nights in Hollywood*, Verve B0012920-02, 2009, 4-CD set.

68. Leonard Feather, "The Essentials of a Jazz Record Library," *HiFi/Stereo Review*, October 1962, 54.

69. See Lara Pellegrinelli, "Separated at 'Birth': Singing and the History of Jazz," in *Big Ears: Listening for Gender in Jazz Studies*, ed. Nichole T. Rustin and Sherrie Tucker (Durham, N.C.: Duke University Press, 2008). Pellegrinelli writes, "In the context of studies that address the issues of gender in jazz, singing presents its own unique challenges. Although the vast majority of women in jazz have been and continue to be vocalists, a role that can provide them with tremendous visibility and widespread recognition from audiences, surprisingly little has been done to investigate singing as a gendered domain" (p. 31). For a recent overview, see *The Routledge Companion to Jazz and Gender*, ed. James Reddan, Monika Herzig, and Michael Kahr (New York: Routledge, 2022).

70. Don Alpert, "The Ella Formula: I Sing It the Way I Feel It," *Los Angeles Times*, September 24, 1961, A5.

71. Richard Crawford, *The American Musical Landscape* (Berkeley: University of California Press, 1993), 89.

72. Joachim Berendt, *The New Jazz Book: A History and Guide*, trans. Dan Morgenstern (New York: Hill & Wang, 1962), 220.

73. Jean P. LeBlanc, "Is Jazz Sick?," *Esquire*, April 1962; reprinted in *Negro Digest*, June 1962, 38.

74. Fitzgerald stood on the front lines of this territorial dispute. In a review of *The Harold Arlen Song Book*, Martin Williams wrote, "Some say Miss Fitzgerald is not really a jazz singer. If she ain't singin' jazz, what is she doin'?" M.W., "The Month's Jazz," *American Record Guide*, September 1961, 60.

75. Francis Davis, "One Scats, the Other Doesn't. New Biographies of Ella Fitzgerald and Billie Holiday Examine Their Very Different Styles and Stories," *New York Times*, September 25, 1994, 14.

76. George T. Simon, "Hard and Soft Sell on Records," *New York Herald Tribune*, December 10, 1961, C8A.

77. Richard Hadlock, "Record Reviews: Vocal," *Down Beat*, July 19, 1962, 44.

78. Nat Hentoff, "Ella Fitzgerald: The Criterion of Innocence for Popular Singers," liner notes to *The Best of Ella Fitzgerald*, Decca DXB-156, 1959, 2-LP set.

79. Dom Cerulli, Burt Korall, and Mort Nasatir, eds., *The Jazz Word* (New York: Ballantine Books, 1960).

80. Nat Hentoff and Leonard Feather, "Is Ella Fitzgerald a Great Jazz Singer?," *HiFi/Stereo Review*, April 1962, 53–55.

81. Margot Hentoff, telephone conversation with the author, c. January 2017.

82. Hentoff and Feather, "Is Ella Fitzgerald a Great Jazz Singer?," 55.

83. Barbara Gardner, "Thoughts on Female 'Jazz Singers,'" *Down Beat's Music '63* (yearbook), 73.

84. Ibid.

85. "Lincoln Center Finally Takes Heed of Jazz," *Down Beat*, January 18, 1962, 15.

86. Leonard Lyons, "Best of Broadway," *Philadelphia Inquirer*, October 2, 1962, 29.

87. "False Alarm Brings a Few Lyons' Roars," *Down Beat*, November 22, 1962, 15–16.

88. "Whatever She Is, Ella Hits with French Jazz Buffs on 10th O'seas Tour," *Variety*, March 28, 1962, 42.

89. Elizabeth Vihlen McGregor, *Jazz and Postwar French Identity: Improvising the Nation* (Lanham, Md.: Lexington Books, 2016), 64.

90. "Ella Is Shy About a Lot of Things," 5.

91. Leonard Feather, "A Record Year," *Down Beat's Music '63* (yearbook), 27.

92. Ella Fitzgerald, "Desafinado," Verve VV 20, 1962, 45 rpm; George T. Simon, "On the Record: Singers," *Daily Journal* (Rapid City, S.D.), January 6, 1963, 30.

93. Ella Fitzgerald, *Rhythm Is My Business*, Verve Records V-4056, 1962, LP.

94. Army, "Night Club Reviews: Crescendo, L.A.," *Variety*, June 20, 1962, 59.

95. Fitzgerald to Norman Granz, telegram, 1962, quoted in Hershorn, *Norman Granz*, 301, 429n12.

96. Atteberry, "Paul Smith Interview," 7.

Chapter 22: Generation Gaps (1963–1965)

1. Ella Fitzgerald, interview by Fred Robbins, Hotel Americana, New York (radio), April 1963, Paley Center for Media, https://www.paleycenter.org/collection/item/?q=ella+fitzgerald&p=1&item=RB:22531. This interview may not have been aired.

2. Stephen Flynn, "Miami Beach's Winter Season Features Potpourri of Events," *Chicago Tribune*, January 13, 1963, C5.

3. Ren Grevatt, "Ella and the Room Both Good Show," *Billboard*, April 27, 1963, 12.

4. Fitzgerald interview by Robbins.

5. Don Alpert, "The Ella Formula: I Sing It the Way I Feel It," *Los Angeles Times*, September 24, 1961, A5.

6. "Dick Gregory Beaten; Rabbis Lead Negroes," *New York Amsterdam News*, May 11, 1963, 1.

7. "Ella Fitzgerald Sparks Crescendo Benefit Tues.," *Los Angeles Sentinel*, June 13, 1963, A14; "Ella Fitzgerald Cited for Civil Rights Efforts," *Atlanta Daily World*, July 7, 1963, 2.

8. "Hollywood Stars Set for March," *New York Amsterdam News*, August 17, 1963, 16.

9. Chester A. Higgins, "Black Stars DO Give a Damn," *Ebony*, September 30, 1971, 46.

10. Bob Hunter, "Do Top Entertainers Dodge Peace Parades, Integration Protests?" *Chicago Defender*, April 18, 1963, 24.

11. Barry Robinson, "Concert Thrills Fans of Ella Fitzgerald," *Asbury Park Evening Press*, July 22, 1963, 8.

12. Leonard Feather, "Ella Today (and Yesterday Too)," *Down Beat*, November 18, 1965, 23.

13. Ibid., 20.

14. Gilby, "Television Review: Tele Follow-Up Comment. The Chevy Show," *Variety*, January 13, 1960, 31.

15. Mike Connolly, "Notes from Hollywood," *Pasadena Independent*, November 11, 1964, 13.

16. Dave Hepburn, "In the Wings: Sullivan's Hour," *New York Amsterdam News*, June 29, 1963, 14.

17. Harold V. Cohen, "At Random," *Pittsburgh Post-Gazette*, February 5, 1964, 18; "Opinion Page," *Mason City Globe-Gazette*, February 11, 1964, 4.

18. Ella Fitzgerald, *Ella Fitzgerald Sings the Jerome Kern Song Book*, Verve V6-4060, 1964, LP; Ella Fitzgerald, *Ella Fitzgerald Sings the Johnny Mercer Song Book*, Verve V6-4067, 1965, LP.

19. Feather, "Ella Today," 20.

20. William Zinsser, *Easy to Remember: The Great American Songwriters and Their Songs* (Jaffrey, N.H.: David R. Godine, 2001), 107. Zinsser quotes Richard Rodgers describing Kern as "a giant with one foot in Europe and the other in America."

21. John S. Wilson, "Record Reviews," *Down Beat*, January 28, 1965, 24; Martin Williams, "Ella and Others," *Saturday Review*, November 28, 1964, 51.

22. Peter J. Levinson, *September in the Rain: The Life of Nelson Riddle* (Lanham, Md.: Taylor Trade, 2005), 195.

23. "Ella's 'Song Books' Win Her an ASCAP Award," *Variety*, May 26, 1965, 51.

24. Larry Stempel, *Showtime: A History of the Broadway Musical Theater* (New York: W. W. Norton, 2010), 249.

25. Ella Fitzgerald and Count Basie, *Ella and Basie!*, Verve V6-4061, 1963, LP.

26. Quincy Jones, *Q: The Autobiography of Quincy Jones* (New York: Harlem Moon, 2001), 130.

27. "Beatles Say Ella's Song's a Knockout!" *Disc*, May 9, 1964, 4.

28. Ella Fitzgerald, "Can't Buy Me Love," Verve VS-519, 1964, 45 rpm.

29. Ibid.; Beatles press conference and interview, Melbourne, June 14, 1964, http://www.beatlesinterviews.org/db1964.0614b.beatles.html.

30. John Lennon, interview by Fred Robbins, February 10, 1964, cited in John C. Winn, *Way Beyond Compare: The Beatles' Recorded Legacy*, vol. 1, *1957–1965* (New York: Crown, 2008); audiotape supplied by Michael Li.

31. Walter Winchell, "Blonde Beauty Comforting Ringo," *Eureka Humboldt Standard*, December 11, 1964, 4.

32. Ella Fitzgerald, "Ringo Beat," Verve VK 10340, 1964, 45 rpm.

33. "Singles Reviews," *Billboard*, December 12, 1964, 31.

34. Ella Fitzgerald, "A Hard Day's Night," Verve VK 10368, 1965, 45 rpm.

35. Walter Everett to the author, December 27, 2017.

36. Leonard Feather, "Ella Scans Song Scene from Top of the Hep," *Los Angeles Times*, October 24, 1965, B36.

37. Ella Fitzgerald, *Hello, Dolly!*, Verve V6-4064, 1964, LP.

38. Ella Fitzgerald, *Ella at Juan-les-Pins*, Verve V4065, 1965, LP.

39. UPI, "Ella Swings Out with Crickets," *Fresno Bee*, July 30, 1964, 15A.

40. John S. Wilson, "Belters, Crooners, Swingers," *New York Times*, August 8, 1965, X12; B.G., "Ella at Juan-les Pins," *Down Beat*, April 8, 1965.

41. "US Artists Still Tops in Europe," *Billboard*, April 24, 1965, 36; "Ella Fitzgerald in Warsaw," *New York Times*, April 4, 1965, 83.

42. "1962: The Year in Review," *Down Beat Music '63* (yearbook), 12.

43. Feather, "Ella Today," 23.

44. Ella Fitzgerald, *Ella in Hamburg*, Verve V6-4069, 1965, LP.

45. Werner Burkhardt, interview by Claus Lochbihler, *JazzZeitung*, March 2003, https://www.jazzzeitung.de/jazz/2003/03/dossier-burkhardt.shtml.

46. "Jazz Auds More Specialized: Granz," *Variety*, March 31, 1965, 55.

47. Chris Hutchins, "International News Reports: Music Capitals of the World," *Billboard*, May 1, 1965, 18.

48. Feather, "Ella Today," 22.

49. The interviewer was reporter Margaret Laing for the *Sunday Times*; excerpts were published in "Ad Lib," *Down Beat*, June 17, 1965, 16.

50. Jo Jones, as told to Albert Murray, *Rifftide: The Life and Opinions of Papa Jo Jones* (Minneapolis: University of Minnesota Press, 2011), 35–36.

51. Howard Klein, "Ella Fitzgerald Does Met Proud," *New York Times*, July 12, 1965, 21.

52. Feather, "Ella Today," 23.

53. Ibid., 22.

Chapter 23: A Jazz Oasis in a Changing Scene (1966–1967)

1. "Ella Fitzgerald Exits Verve; Will Trim Disk Output & Live Bookings," *Variety*, July 6, 1966, 38; Vincent Stephens, "Crooning on the Fault Lines: Theorizing Jazz and Pop Vocal Singing Discourse in the Rock Era, 1955–1978," *American Music* 26, no. 2 (2008): 160.

2. Bob Dawbarn, "Albums: Lining Up for the Chopper," *Melody Maker*, May 28, 1966, 8.

3. Ella Fitzgerald with Marty Paich and His Orchestra, *Whisper Not*, Verve V6 4071, 1966, LP.

4. Leonard Feather, "Ella Today (and Yesterday Too)," *Down Beat*, November 18, 1965, 20.

5. Marc Myers, *Why Jazz Happened* (Berkeley: University of California Press, 2013), 176ff.

6. Ray Brown, Jr., interview by the author, December 1, 2009.

7. "You can't lump Ella Fitzgerald with the different vocalists he [Duke] had," Granz observed. Norman Granz, liner notes to Ella Fitzgerald and Duke Ellington, *Ella and Duke at the Côte d'Azur*, Verve V6-4072-2, 1967, LP.

8. Dan Morgenstern, interview by the author, February 2021.

9. Ella Fitzgerald and Duke Ellington, *Ella at Duke's Place*, Verve V-4070, 1966, LP; "A New Umbrella for Duke and Ella," *Down Beat*, December 2, 1965, 10–11.

10. Keith Shadwick, liner notes to Fitzgerald and Ellington, *Ella at Duke's Place*, Verve 314-529-700-2, 1996, CD reissue.

11. Jimmy Jones, interview by Patricia Willard, December 1, 1977, Jazz Oral History Project, Institute of Jazz Studies, Rutgers University.

12. Hazel Garland, "Ella Teams Up with Duke in a Musical Masterpiece," *Pittsburgh Courier*, June 4, 1966, 7A; Don DeMicheal, "Record Reviews," *Down Beat*, April 21, 1966, 33.

13. Roger Lifeset, "Music on Campus," *Billboard*, July 9, 1966, 25.

14. Rick Bale, "When the Future Got Its Groove Back," *Stanford Magazine*, September–October 2015, 68.

15. Ralph J. Gleason, "Duke, Ella Make Glorious Music," *San Francisco Chronicle*, November 3, 1965, reprinted in Gleason, *Celebrating the Duke* (Boston: Atlantic Monthly Press, 1975), 217.

16. "Ella Fitzgerald Is in Hospital for Reset," *Fresno Bee*, November 2, 1965, 2.

17. Jim Blackman to the author, January 31, 2021.

18. *100 American Women of Accomplishment: Harper's Bazaar 100th Year, 1967* (New York: Harper's Bazaar, 1967), 15.

19. Advertisement, *Variety*, March 16, 1966, 80.

20. M.H., "Infallible Ella Walks Off with Duke's Concert," *Melody Maker*, February 5, 1966, 12; Lucien Malson, "Ella et Le Duke," *Le Monde*, February 1, 1966.

21. Catherine Tackley, "'Art or Debauchery?': The Reception of Ellington in the U.K.," in John Howland, ed., *Duke Ellington Studies* (Cambridge, U.K.: Cambridge University Press, 2017), 103.

22. "Jazz and Pop at the Festival Hall," *Stage*, February 17, 1966, 7.

23. Russ Wilson, "The Duke and Queen of Jazz," *Oakland Tribune*, May 1, 1966, 163.

24. William Buchanan, "Ella Fitzgerald Performance Brilliant at Newport Festival," *Boston Globe*, July 7, 1966, 47.

25. Dan Morgenstern, "Newport Report," *Down Beat*, August 11, 1966, 39–40.

26. Mike Hennessey, "Caught in the Act: International Jazz Festival," *Down Beat*, September 22, 1966, 33.

27. Jacques Muyal to the author, January 25, 2017.

28. "Granz Grooves 3 LPs, Gets Pic Too from Ella & Duke's Jazz on Riviera," *Variety*, September 28, 1966, 51.

29. Ella Fitzgerald and Duke Ellington, *Ella and Duke at the Côte d'Azur*, Verve V6-4072-2, 1967, 2-LP set; reissue, Verve 539 030-2, 1997, 2-CD set.

30. Norman Granz, liner notes, ibid. (1967).

31. Dorothy Johnson, interview by the author, November 11, 2022.

32. *Index of New York Marriage Certificates 1950–1968* lists the marriage of Frances Correy to Willie Gilmore on January 31, 1954, naming Ella as a witness. Chris McKay to the author, February 20, 2019.

33. Mike Hennessey, "Ella, Duke Make Antibes Swing," *Billboard*, August 13, 1966, 16.

34. Bent Henius, "Jeg Var Naer Blevet Danskers," *Berlingske Tidende*, January 22, 1967, 9, translated by Martin Lauge Christensen.

35. Hennessey, "Ella, Duke," 16.

36. Derek Jewell, *Duke: A Portrait of Duke Ellington* (New York: W. W. Norton, 1977), 164–65. For Granz's questioning of Jewell's account, see Tad Hershorn, *Norman Granz: The Man Who Used Jazz for Justice* (Berkeley: University of California Press, 2011), 316–18.

37. Jim Hughart, interview by the author, June 22, 2011.

38. Joyce Haber, "Ella the Worrybird Songbird," *Los Angeles Times*, September 4, 1966, 243.

39. Duke Ellington and Ella Fitzgerald, *Live at the Greek Theatre, Los Angeles*, Status DSTS1013, 1994, CD.

40. Cobey Black, "Ella Forever," *Honolulu Star-Bulletin*, March 7, 1967, 36.

41. Jimmy Jones, interview by Patricia Willard, December 21–23, 1977, Jazz Oral History Project, Institute of Jazz Studies, Rutgers University.

42. Ella Fitzgerald, interview in "ASCAP Presents the Billy Taylor Interviews," Performing Arts Research Collections, Recorded Sound, LDC 42656, New York Public Library.

43. Dr. M. Jelenski, "Applause for Ella," *Berliner Zeitung*, January 26, 1967; S.H., "Ella Fitzgerald at the Berlin Friedrichstadt-Palast," *Neues Deutschland*, January 29, 1967; both translated by Martin Lauge Christensen.

44. "Berlin," *Washington Afro American*, February 14, 1965, 14.

45. Terence Andrew, "In East Germany, US Jazz Is Corrupting, Verboten," *Sacramento Bee*, January 7, 1968.

46. Helen Pidd, "Ruth Hohmann: The First Lady of East German Jazz Sings Again," *Guardian*, December 2, 2011.

47. Patrick Scott, "Can JATP Turn Back the Clock?" *Toronto Daily Star*, April 1, 1967, 26.

48. Whitney Balliett, "Jazz Concerts: Heaven and Earth," *New Yorker*, April 8, 1967, 163–65.

49. John S. Wilson, "Ella, Duke, Hawk Sing, Swing, Wing," *New York Times*, March 27, 1967, 38.

50. Tape recording of the concert at Oakland Coliseum, June 30, 1967, by a private collector. For a review of the concert, see Ralph J. Gleason, "Jazz-Touring JATP Went Out Swinging," *San Francisco Examiner*, July 9, 1967, 37.

51. Robert Self, "'To Plan Our Liberation': Black Power and the Politics of Place in Oakland, California, 1965–1977," *Journal of Urban History* 26, no. 6 (September 2000): 760.

52. Various, *The Greatest Jazz Concert in the World*, Pablo 2625 704, 1975, 4-LP set.

53. John S. Wilson, "Old-Timers Reign at ASCAP Salute," *New York Times*, October 16, 1967, 56.

54. Hazel Garland, "Video Vignettes," *New Pittsburgh Courier*, November 25, 1967, 9.

55. John L. Wasserman, "Ella Wields That Old Charm," *San Francisco Chronicle*, September 5, 1967, 31.

56. Jack Rosenbaum, "Seconds, Anyone?" *San Francisco Sunday Examiner and Chronicle*, September 10, 1967, B1.

57. Herm, "The Best on Record," *Variety*, May 31, 1967, 34.

58. Frank Sinatra, *A Man and His Music + Ella + Jobim*, dir. Michael Pfleghar, 1967, https://tubitv.com/movies/468418/frank-sinatra-a-man-and-his-music-plus-ella-plus-jobim.

59. Jack Gould, "TV: Sinatra + Ella + Jobim = Joy," *New York Times*, November 14, 1967, 95.

60. Peter J. Levinson, *September in the Rain: The Life of Nelson Riddle* (Lanham, Md.: Taylor Trade, 2005), 158.

61. Norman Granz, interview by Elliot Meadow, February 27, 1987, James "Tad" Hershorn Collection on Norman Granz, Institute of Jazz Studies, Archival Collections, IJS.0081, Rutgers University.

62. Fitzgerald interview in "ASCAP Presents Billy Taylor Interviews."

63. "Ella Wants Her Own TV Show," *Los Angeles Sentinel*, November 16, 1967, B7.

64. John S. Wilson, "Ella Changes Her Tunes for a Swinging Generation," *New York Times*, November 12, 1967, 149.

65. Ibid.

66. Ray Brown, Jr., interview by the author, June 18, 2011.

67. John S. Wilson, "Philharmonic Hall Sold Out, Naturally, for Ella Fitzgerald," *New York Times*, November 23, 1967, 58.

68. Black, "Ella Forever."

69. Phoebe Jacobs, interview by the author, December 7, 2009.

70. Dorothy Johnson, interview by the author, November 14, 2022.

71. Black, "Ella Forever."

72. Gertrude Gipson, "Media Women Fun Ride," *Los Angeles Sentinel*, January 18, 1968, B8.

73. "Ella Stays in Style," *Ithaca Journal*, November 1, 1969, 32.

Chapter 24: Reinventing Herself (1968–1969)

1. "Ella Fitzgerald Visits Berlin (1968)," *Radio Video Music*, https://rvm.pm/ella -fitzgerald-visits-berlin-1968.

2. "I Can't Stop Loving You" had been covered by a wide range of musicians, including Duke Ellington and Count Basie.

3. Darlene Clark Hine and Kathleen Thompson, *A Shining Thread of Hope: The History of Black Women in America* (New York: Broadway Books, 1998), 303–4.

4. "Ella on Ella: A Personal Portrait," *Essence* (television program), NBC, April 26, 1986, Paley Center for Media, https://www.paleycenter.org/collection/item/?q= first&p=248&item=T:08316; quoted in Jim Haskins, *Ella Fitzgerald: A Life Through Jazz* (London: Hodder & Stoughton, 1991), 26.

5. E. Sandor, "Hope and Caution," *Problems of Communism* 19 (January–February 1970): 62.

6. "Hungarians Rave over 'First Lady of Song' Ella," *Jet*, April 11, 1968, 57.

7. Ella Fitzgerald, interview in "ASCAP Presents the Billy Taylor Interviews," Performing Arts Research Collections, Recorded Sound, LDC 42656, New York Public Library. Ray Brown, Oscar Peterson, and Ella visited Aretha's home sometime in the early 1950s, when JATP was in Detroit, and made music in Reverend C. F. Franklin's home. David Ritz, *Respect: The Life of Aretha Franklin* (Boston: Little, Brown, 2015), 41–42.

8. Taylor's advocacy of "America's classical music" was both rooted in and distinct from the Black radical cultural thought of the 1960s. See Tom Arnold-Forster, "Dr. Billy Taylor, 'America's Classical Music,' and the Role of the Jazz Ambassador," *Journal of American Studies* 51 (2017): 117–39.

9. Aaron Stern, "Ella Fitzgerald Strong as Ever," *Billboard*, May 11, 1968, 12.

10. Ella Fitzgerald, interview by William B. Williams, May 30, 1968, in "Make Believe Ballroom, the Ella Fitzgerald Live from the Rainbow Room (Radio)," Paley Center for Media, https://www.paleycenter.org/collection/item/?q=what &p=138&item=R87:0748.

11. Fitzgerald interview in "ASCAP Presents the Billy Taylor Interviews."

12. John S. Wilson, "Ella Fitzgerald Sings for Listeners Not Dancers," *New York Times*, May 10, 1968, 50.

13. Fitzgerald interview in "ASCAP Presents the Billy Taylor Interviews."

14. Bill Morrison, "Rude New York Crowd Upsets Ella Fitzgerald," *News and Observer* (Raleigh, N.C.), December 5, 1968, 34.

15. Hazel Garland, "Video Vignettes," *New Pittsburgh Courier*, November 30, 1968, 13.

16. "Ella Speaks Out," *San Francisco Sunday Examiner and Chronicle*, September 15, 1968, A2.

17. Dick Hallgren, "Ella Praises Co-op Venture," *San Francisco Chronicle*, September 21, 1968.

18. "Ella Fitzgerald to Be Honored at a Dinner Party on Sunday," *New York Times*, November 26, 1968, 51; Robert Windeler, "Tributes Pour on Ella Fitzgerald," *New York Times*, December 2, 1968, 63.

19. Dave Dexter, "Newman, Kansas City, Mo.," *Billboard*, December 10, 1938, 24.

20. Ella Fitzgerald, *Brighten the Corner*, Capitol ST 2685, 1967, LP.

21. William Buchanan, "A Jazz Legend," *Boston Globe*, May 28, 1967, 35.

22. Walter Trohan, "Report from Washington: A Few Timely Remarks About Racial Harmony," *Chicago Tribune*, April 24, 1968, 6.

23. Chris Wammen, "Folk elsker mig. Ella Fitzgerald," *Århus Stiftstidende*, June 7, 1970. The Danish word *hyggeligt* is translated here as "nice."

24. Ella Fitzgerald, *Ella Fitzgerald's Christmas*, Capitol ST 2805, 1967, LP.

25. Ella Fitzgerald, *Misty Blue*, Capitol ST 2888, 1968, LP.

26. "Dexter Plans Ella Program," *Billboard*, October 14, 1967, 4.

27. Karen Price, "Misty Blue," *Soul*, August 1968, 14.

28. Dave Dexter, Jr., *Playback: A Newsman–Record Producer's Hits and Misses from the Thirties to the Seventies* (New York: Billboard, 1976), 194–200.

29. Ibid., 196.

30. Jim Blackman, conversation with the author, August 14, 2021.

31. Ella Fitzgerald, *30 by Ella*, Capitol ST 2960, 1968, LP.

32. Dexter, Jr., *Playback*, 198, 200.

33. Jim Blackman to the author, February 14, 2018.

34. Ella Fitzgerald, *Sunshine of Your Love*, MPS 15250, 1969, LP.

35. Marc Myers, *Why Jazz Happened* (Berkeley: University of California Press, 2013), 212.

36. Ella Fitzgerald, *Ella*, Reprise RS 6354, 1969, LP.

37. Advertisement, *Billboard*, September 20, 1969, 15.

38. Robert Christgau, "Who Makes Singers Great?," *New York Times*, January 18, 1970, 112.

39. David Cook, "Elena Souliotis Gives an Appealing Portrait," *Tallahassee Democrat*, July 18, 1971, 47.

40. Geoffrey Mark Fidelman, *First Lady of Song: Ella Fitzgerald for the Record* (New York: Citadel Press, 1994), 196–97.

41. Ray Brown, Jr., to the author, February 2, 2018.

42. "Prague Welcomes Ella Fitzgerald," *New York Times*, June 28, 1969, 19.

43. Ella Fitzgerald, *Live at Montreux 1969*, Eagle Vision EREDV458, 2005, DVD.

44. Wez, "Ella Fitzgerald Copenhagen," *Berlingske Tidende*, May 3, 1968, 24, translated by Martin Lauge Christensen.

45. Bent Henius, "The Sublime Art," *Berlingske Tidende*, July 6, 1969, translated by Martin Lauge Christensen.

46. Anders Stefansen, interview by the author, July 12, 2013.

47. No recording of her appearance on *For Blacks Only* has survived; the quotes are from "Ella Fitzgerald Says: 'Regret' Not Being Home More with Son," *Jet*, May 24, 1969, 60–61. *Boards* is a theater expression for the stage.

48. Ray Brown, Jr., interview by the author, December 1, 2009.

49. Earl Calloway, "Ella Climaxes Ravinia in Symphony Pop Concert," *Chicago Defender*, August 13, 1969, 14.

50. Perdita Duncan, "Music in Review: Ella Fitzgerald," *New York Amsterdam News*, November 29, 1969, 14.

Chapter 25: Keeping On (1970–1972)

1. AP, "Ella's Vision to Return," *Muncie Evening Press* (Ind.), August 13, 1971, 20.

2. Mary Campbell, "Ella Fitzgerald: Match for Rock, Jazz, or Louie," *Daily Reporter* (Dover, Ohio), April 29, 1970, 14.

3. Armstrong asked for "You Won't Be Satisfied Until You Break My Heart."

4. Jose, "Waldorf-Astoria," *Variety*, April 8, 1970, 115.

5. Dan Morgenstern, "Newport '70: Back in Orbit," *Down Beat*, September 3, 1970, 42.

6. Harvey Siders, "Caught in the Act: Duke Ellington/Ella Fitzgerald," *Down Beat*, January 7, 1971, 30. As Siders notes, Ella interpolated "Happy Day" into "Raindrops Keep Fallin' on My Head" along with improvisational allusions to Claude Thornill's classic "Snowfall."

7. Donald E. Mullen, "Duke Goes to His Tearful 'Solitude,'" *Norfolk Journal and Guide*, June 1, 1974, 1.

8. The *Voice of America Jazz Hour* radio program hosted by Willis Conover broadcast the complete jazz portion of the funeral on May 27, 1974, and replayed it on May 2, 1975. The recording is preserved in Willis Conover Collection, Music USA #7428-B, University of North Texas.

9. Alan Handley and Art Fisher, dir., "The Andy Williams Show," in David Meeker, *Jazz on the Screen: a Jazz and Blues Filmography* (Washington, D.C.: Library of Congress, 2017), 85, https://www.loc.gov/item/ihas.200028017.

10. "Highlights This Week: Sat./Nov. 21," *The Gazette TV Times* (Montreal, Canada), November 21, 1970, 4; "Ella Fitzgerald and Flip Wilson on The Flip Wilson Show," https://www.youtube.com/watch?v=FoRDCvy9tz4.

11. "Ella Fitzgerald with Tom Jones—Sunny—Live 1970," https://www.dailymotion.com/video/xfy51v.

12. Chris Sheridan, *Count Basie: A Bio-Discography* (Westport, Conn.: Greenwood Press, 1986), 747–48.

13. Count Basie, interview by Albert Murray, 1970, published in *Good Morning Blues: The Autobiography of Count Basie* (New York: Random House, 1985), 295.

14. Fitzgerald to Phoebe Jacobs, April 21, 1970, Phoebe Jacobs Collection, Special Collections, Butler Library, Columbia University.

15. "Ella, Basie Whip Up Lots of B.O. Noise in Tour of West Germany," *Variety*, May 6, 1970, 85.

16. Excerpts on "Ella Fitzgerald, Germany 1970," https://www.youtube.com/watch ?v=Tmt4FNEgjDs&t=456s. Along with footage of Ella meeting the press backstage and a reference to her "serious eye operation," *Ella Fitzgerald in Deutschland 1970* also incorporated rare interviews with Norman Granz and members of her trio.

17. Ella Fitzgerald, *Ella Fitzgerald in Budapest*, Pablo 5308-2, 1999, CD.

18. Tad Hershorn, *Norman Granz: The Man Who Used Jazz for Justice* (Berkeley: University of California Press, 2011), 327.

19. Jim Blackman, interview by the author, August 7, 2022.

20. Jack O'Brian, "Mike Wallace Burns Ella Fitzgerald," *News* (Paterson, N.J.), May 14, 1968, 23.

21. Chris Wammen, "Folkelsker mig. Ella Fitzgerald," *Århus Stiftstidende*, June 7, 1970, 13, translated by Martin Lauge Christensen.

22. Ibid.

23. Phoebe Jacobs, interview by the author, December 7, 2009.

24. Fitzgerald to Jacobs, April 21, 1970, Phoebe Jacobs Collection.

25. Blake Green, "That Modest First Lady of Song," *San Francisco Chronicle*, December 17, 1976, 42.

26. Audrey Franklyn (publicist) to Barbaralee Diamonstein-Spielvogel, c. 1970, Barbaralee Diamonstein-Spielvogel Collection, Duke University Libraries.

27. Barbaralee Diamonstein, *Open Secrets: Ninety-Four Women in Touch with Our Time* (New York: Viking Press, 1972), 133–38.

28. *100 American Women of Accomplishment: Harper's Bazaar 100th Year, 1967* (New York: Harper's Bazaar, 1967), 15.

29. "Ella Cited by Harpers," *New Pittsburgh Courier*, July 29, 1967, 9.

30. Jack Meredith, "Showcase," *Windsor Star* (Ont.), February 13, 1971.

31. Ella Fitzgerald, *Things Ain't What They Used to Be (And You Better Believe It)*, Reprise SR 6432, 1971, LP.

32. Norman Granz, album notes to Fitzgerald, *Things Ain't What They Used To Be*.

33. Leonard Feather, "A Bit of Jazz, Bop, Blues, Rock," *Los Angeles Times*, May 30, 1971, N53.

34. "Strictly Ad Lib," *Down Beat*, September 16, 1971, 16.

35. John S. Wilson, "Two Jazz Techniques Ring Out in Park," *New York Times*, July 14, 1971, 21.

36. Magda Abu-Fadil, "Baalbeck: Marriage of History and Performing Arts," *HuffPost*, April 23, 2014 (updated December 6, 2017), https://www.huffpost.com/entry/baalbeck-marriage-of-hist_b_5198391.

37. Ella Fitzgerald, *Ella à Nice*, CBS 64812, 1972, LP.

38. Jacques Muyal, interview by the author, February 26, 2017.

39. Christina Robb, "Boston Benefit in Sight by Briefly Blinded Ella," *Boston Globe*, August 14, 1971, 3; "Ella Fitzgerald's Condition Is Listed as Satisfactory," *Nashua Telegraph* (N.H.), August 5, 1971, 18.

40. Arlie Small to Jim Blackman, December 7, 1971, James W. Blackman Media Collection, 1960 to the present, private collection.

41. Jim Blackman, interview by author, c. July 2010.

42. "Fabulous Las Vegas Magazine," November 27, 1971, Ella Fitzgerald Papers, series 7, box 51, Archives Center, National Museum of American History, Smithsonian Institution; Leonard Feather, "Return of Ella Fitzgerald," *Los Angeles Times*, November 6, 1971, 5.

43. Chuck Thurston, "Time's a Problem for Ella—DST Time That Is," *Detroit Free Press*, June 19, 1972, 18.

44. Louie Robinson, "Las Vegas: New Black Entertainment Capital of the World," *Ebony*, April 1972, 174–81.

45. Laura Deni, "Vegas Hotels Seek a Soulful Crowd for Black Artists," *Billboard*, January 29, 1972, 43.

46. John S. Wilson, "Fine Fettle Shown by Ella Fitzgerald," *New York Times*, May 15, 1972, 43.

47. Various, *Jazz at the Santa Monica Civic '72*, Pablo PACD 2625-701-2, 1991, 3-CD set.

48. Eliot Tiegel, "Granz Bows Twin Bill: Disks and Jam Session," *Billboard*, June 17, 1972, 17.

49. Ernest Dunbar, "Ella Still Sings Just This Side of the Angels," *New York Times*, November 24, 1974, D15.

50. Thomas Cleary, "Ellavolution: Ella Fitzgerald's Evolution as an Improviser," *BirdFeed* blog, November 23, 2021, https://blog.uvm.edu/tgcleary/2021/11/23/ellavolution-ella-fitzgeralds-evolution-as-an-improviser/.

51. Ray Brown, Sr., in *Ella Fitzgerald: Something to Live For* (documentary), American Masters Digital Archives (WNET), April 3, 1999, https://www.pbs.org/wnet/americanmasters/archive/interviews/494. Accessed April 11, 2021, but this interview is no longer available.

52. "Ella Submits Bulky Eye to Laser-Beam Surgery," *Baltimore Afro-American*, August 26, 1972, 10.

53. Bill Lane, "People, Places 'n' Situwayshuns," *Los Angeles Sentinel*, August 24, 1972, B2A.

54. Hazel Garland, "Video Vignettes," *Pittsburgh Courier*, December 16, 1972, 14.

55. Wayne Warga, "Ella Fitzgerald: A Superstar Who Remembers," *Boston Globe*, December 28, 1972, 30.

56. Oscar Szmuch, interview by the author, summer 2011.

57. Eneid Routte, headline unknown, *San Juan Star*, April 15, 1973, 5 (from clippings file).

58. Various, *All Star Swing Festival*, Delta Entertainment 82 328, 2005, DVD.

59. "Betty Carter," in Arthur Taylor, *Notes and Tones: Musician-to-Musician Interviews*, expanded ed. (New York: Da Capo Press, 1993), 270.

60. Advertisement, *Los Angeles Times*, December 24, 1972, 251.

61. Leonard Feather, "Ella at Home in 5 Decades," *Los Angeles Times*, December 28, 1972, D15.

Chapter 26: "You Can Always Learn" (1973–1978)

1. Eneid Routte, headline unknown, *San Juan Star*, April 15, 1973, 5 (from clippings file).
2. Alain Druout, "Vibes Legend Burton Bids Fond Farewell," *Down Beat*, June 2017, 13.
3. Eneid Routte, headline unknown, *San Juan Star*, April 15, 1973, 5.
4. Michelle Mercer, "The Voice That Shattered Glass," *All Things Considered*, NPR, September 3, 2019.
5. Larry Eckholt, "'I Broke Glass in TV Ad,' Ella Fitzgerald Asserts," *Des Moines Register*, September 26, 1974, 11.
6. "Ella Captures Friends, Rivals for Memorex," *Memorex Intercom Newsletter* (April 1976), 4.
7. "Ella Can't Live Down Memorex Tag," *Jet*, December 27, 1979, 55.
8. Michael Freedland, "No Labels for Ella," *London Times*, July 26, 1980, 12.
9. Ayden Wren Adler, "Classical Music for People Who Hate Classical Music: Arthur Fiedler and the Boston Pops, 1930–1950," Ph.D. diss., University of Rochester, Eastman School of Music, 2007, 389–91.
10. Freedland, "No Labels," 12.
11. *Evening at Pops: Ella Fitzgerald*, Paley Center for Media, https://www.paleycenter .org/collection/item/?q=&p=1&item=T:15679.
12. Robert A. McLean, "Ella Fitzgerald Goes Pow! at Pops," *Boston Globe*, May 25, 1973, 23.
13. Johanna Fiedler, *Papa, the Pops, and Me* (New York: Doubleday, 1994), 138–39.
14. Harry Ellis Dickson, *Arthur Fiedler and the Boston Pops* (Boston: Houghton Mifflin, 1981), 120–22.
15. Steve Allen, *Satchmo: The Story of Louis Armstrong*, BBC 2 (radio documentary), December 1974, Satchmo Collection, Louis Armstrong House Museum.
16. Philip Hart, *Orpheus in the New World: The Symphony Orchestra as an American Cultural Institution* (New York: W. W. Norton, 1973), 164.
17. Advertisement, *St. Louis Post-Dispatch*, October 21, 1973, 93.
18. Betty Dietz Krebs, "Ella Brought Along Her Incredible Ear," *Dayton Daily News*, September 24, 1973, 32.
19. The concert with the New Jersey Symphony Orchestra and Henry Lewis took place within the Waterloo Summer Festival series in Byram, New Jersey, as a fundraiser for Waterloo Village, a historical restoration site. "Ella Fitzgerald Featured at Benefit," *Central New Jersey Home News* (New Brunswick), June 24, 1973, 96.
20. Ibid.
21. Vernon E. Jordan, Jr., "To Be Equal: Orchestrated Discrimination," *Call and Post*, December 7, 1974, 2B.
22. Dizzy Gillespie and Al Fraser, *To Be, or Not . . . to Bop* (New York: Doubleday, 1979), 501.
23. Tad Hershorn, *Norman Granz: The Man Who Used Jazz for Justice* (Berkeley: University of California Press, 2011), 338.

24. Carmen McRae, *The Great American Songbook*, Atlantic SD2-904, 1972, LP.

25. Hershorn, *Norman Granz*, 347.

26. Ella Fitzgerald, interview by Leonard Feather, January 15, 1983, Ella Fitzgerald Project, Leonard Feather Collection, University of Idaho.

27. Ella Fitzgerald and Joe Pass, *Take Love Easy*, Pablo 2310 702, 1974, LP.

28. Geoffrey Mark, *Ella: A Biography of the Legendary Ella Fitzgerald* (New York: Ultimate Symbol, 2018), 219.

29. Max Jones, "Smoke Gets in Your Eyes," *Melody Maker*, April 13, 1974, 8.

30. Ella Fitzgerald, interview for Finnish TV network YLE, Helsinki, c. March 1974, https://www.youtube.com/watch?v=OnE4qQyle-M.

31. Jon Balleras, "Record Reviews," *Down Beat*, October 10, 1974, 22.

32. Ella Fitzgerald and various, *Fine and Mellow: Ella Fitzgerald Jams*, Pablo 2310 829, 1979, LP.

33. AP, "Ella Fitzgerald Receives Medal," *Paducah Sun* (Ky.), February 6, 1974, 22.

34. John S. Wilson, "Pop Music: A Medallion, Too, for Ella Fitzgerald," *New York Times*, January 21, 1974, 35.

35. Fitzgerald interview in Helsinki.

36. Ella Fitzgerald, *Live in Cologne 1974*, Jazzline N 77 027, 2016, CD.

37. "Ella Fitzgerald: The First Lady of Jazz, Germany 1974," https://www.dailymotion.com/video/x179jwe.

38. Josef Woodard, "Memories of Ella," *JazzTimes*, October 1996, 36.

39. Ella Fitzgerald, *Ella in London*, Pablo 2310 711, 1974, LP.

40. Jones, "Smoke Gets in Your Eyes."

41. Hollie I. West, "New Music for Ella," *Washington Post*, June 26, 1975, G10.

42. "Count Basie and Ella Fitzgerald," *Guardian*, October 4, 1975, 8.

43. Mary Campbell, AP review, "Sinatra, Fitzgerald, Basie Wowing 'Em on Broadway," *Green Bay Press-Gazette*, September 9, 1975, 12; Jack O'Brian, "Concert Finds Sinatra in Best Voice in Years," *Sarasota Journal*, September 22, 1975, singles out Miles's virtuoso drumming—Miles later recorded a tribute album to Chick Webb; "Sinatra-Fitzgerald-Basie Had Gross of $1.08-Million," *New York Times*, September 22, 1975, 43; "We Love You," *Variety*, September 24, 1975, 77.

44. Ella Fitzgerald, *Montreux '75*, Pablo 2310 751, 1975, LP.

45. Ella Fitzgerald and Oscar Peterson, *Ella and Oscar*, Pablo 2310 759, 1976, LP.

46. Ella Fitzgerald and Joe Pass, *Fitzgerald and Pass . . . Again*, Pablo 2310 772, 1976, LP.

47. Mark, *Ella*, n.p.

48. Stuart Nicholson, *Ella Fitzgerald: The Complete Biography*, updated ed. (New York: Routledge, 2004), 20.

49. "1976 Grammy Winners," *Recording Academy Grammy Awards*, https://www.grammy.com/awards/19th-annual-grammy-awards.

50. Joseph McLellan and Dorothy McCardle, "White Ties and Country Music," *Washington Post*, July 21, 1976, B3.

51. Blake Green, "That Modest First Lady of Song," *San Francisco Chronicle*, December 17, 1976, 42.

52. Jacqueline Trescou, "The Black Caucus Has Come of Age," *Washington Post*, Sep-

tember 27, 1976, B1; "Black Caucus Weekend Brings Out Stars, Goodwill, Big Plans," *Jet*, October 14, 1976, 29–30.

53. Hazziezah, "Ella Fitzgerald Headlines National Medical Fellowships Inc. Benefit," *New York Amsterdam News*, November 20, 1976, D14.

54. "Tribute to Fitzgerald," *Billboard*, October 30, 1976, 57.

55. Hazziezah, "Fitzgerald Headlines."

56. "Pablo Jazz at L.A. Shubert, *Billboard*, March 20, 1976, 33.

57. Mark Baszak, ed., *Such Sweet Thunder: Views on Black American Music* (Amherst: University of Massachusetts Fine Arts Center, 2003).

58. Shifra Stein, "Jazz Fans Turn Out for Count," *Kansas City Times*, October 1, 1977, 10.

59. J.B., "A Few Testy Words from Ella Fitzgerald," *Toronto Globe and Mail*, September 30, 1974, 14.

60. "Ella Fitzgerald & Mel Tormé perform scat at the 18th Grammy, Feb. 1976," https://www.dailymotion.com/video/x23t25p; "The Tonight Show Starring Johnny Carson," The Paley Center for Media, https://www.paleycenter.org/collection/item/?q=tonight+show+starring+johnny+carson&advanced=1&p=120&item=B:81896; "The Mike Douglas Show, S17.E54," https://www.imdb.com/title/tt4840960; "Dinah and the First Ladies," https://www.imdb.com/title/tt3342680.

61. Betty Dietz Krebs, "Ella Fitzgerald Melts the Heart," *Cincinnati Post*, September 24, 1973, 23; Ben Ratliff, "Tommy Flanagan, Elegant Jazz Pianist, Is Dead at 71," *New York Times*, November 19, 2001, F7.

62. Barbara Hunting, "Ella: Songstress Fills Hall with Mellow Melodies," *Tampa Tribune*, November 28, 1975, 69.

63. Michael Ullman, *Jazz Lives* (Washington, D.C.: New Republic Books, 1980), 120.

64. Jacques Lowe, "Tommy Flanagan," *JazzTimes*, January 1, 2001 (updated April 25, 2019), https://jazztimes.com/archives/tommy-flanagan.

65. Elizabeth George, "Ella Selects Songs to Fit Audience," *Greenville News* (S.C.), June 18, 1978, 38.

66. John S. Wilson, "Newport Jazz: 'Angel Eyes' Is Triumph for Ella Fitzgerald," *New York Times*, June 26, 1978, C14.

67. It was large enough to accommodate Basie and his band. "Give me that again," Leonard Feather said, when Ella told him the story in 1983. "You had the whole Basie band in here?" Fitzgerald interview by Feather, Ella Fitzgerald Project.

Chapter 27: "Push Me, Push Me" (1979–1985)

1. Bob Thomas, "When Ella Fitzgerald Takes On an Acting Role, People Sit Up and Take Notice of the Event," *Atlanta Constitution*, April 5, 1981, 4EB.

2. Ella Fitzgerald, interview by Leonard Feather, January 10, 1983, Ella Fitzgerald Papers, ser.10.4, Smithsonian Archives Center, National Museum of American History.

3. Proverbs 31:10–31. Eshet Chayil (original text), trans. Aya Baron, Jewish Women's Archive, https://jwa.org/nodc/23712.

4. John S. Wilson, "Pop Concert: Ella Fitzgerald Is Full of Surprises," *New York Times*, September 8, 1979, 12.

5. Hugh Downing, dir., *Previn & the Pittsburgh: Ella Fitzgerald*, PBS, April 3, 1979, The Paley Center for Media, https://www.paleycenter.org/collection/item/?q=bell&p=56&item=T:11503. See John N. Goudas, *Star Press* (Muncie, Ind.), March 31, 1979, 22. Hazel Garland, "Video Vignettes," *New Pittsburgh Courier*, April 14, 1979, 20, said her stories revealed "many things about herself that had never been reported" previously on television.

6. Bob Karlovits, "Ella, Joe, and André. Enough Electricity but No Sparks," *Pittsburgh Press*, October 17, 1984, 42. The performance was a benefit for Rehabilitation Institute of Pittsburgh. The album was Ella Fitzgerald and André Previn, *Nice Work If You Can Get It*, Pablo Today D2312140, 1983, LP.

7. "PBS," *Public Opinion* (Chambersburg, Penn.), February 13, 1984.

8. John McDonough, "Caught! An Evening with Ella Fitzgerald," *Down Beat*, February 1980, 56.

9. Ella Fitzgerald and Count Basie, *A Classy Pair*, Pablo Today 2312-132, 1982, LP; Ella Fitzgerald and Count Basie, *A Perfect Match*, Pablo Today 2312 110, 1980, LP.

10. Stanley Dance, "Ella Fitzgerald and Count Basie: A Perfect Match," *JazzTimes*, December 1980, 17.

11. Charles Hamm, *Putting Popular Music in Its Place* (Cambridge, U.K.: Cambridge University Press, 1995), 127.

12. "Five Receive Kennedy Awards," Associated Press, December 3, 1979, 20. The first group of honorees, in 1978, had included Marian Anderson, Fred Astaire, George Balanchine, Richard Rodgers, and Arthur Rubinstein, three from classical music and dance, and two from popular music. Anderson was the lone African American and the lone woman among them.

13. For Lee's introduction and the rest of the tribute, see "Kennedy Center Honors 1979 (Honorees: . . . Ella Fitzgerald)," Paley Center for Media, https://www.paleycenter.org/collection/item/?item=T81:0032. See also Barbara Gamarekian, "Kennedy Center Honors Five for Life Achievements in Arts," *New York Times*, December 3, 1979, C14.

14. "I think I was more excited when I saw Count Basie's band on the stage. And Peggy Lee came. She flew all the way there just to be on the program. She's been ill. I didn't know that she was ill when she came to the Kennedy thing." Fitzgerald interview by Feather, January 10, 1983, Fitzgerald Papers, Smithsonian.

15. Joseph Litsch, "A Night to Remember for Ella, Tennessee," *Atlanta Constitution*, February 12, 1980, 13.

16. Thomas, "When Ella Fitzgerald Takes On an Acting Role."

17. Watt, "Concert Reviews," *Variety*, April 22, 1981, 178.

18. Ella Fitzgerald, *Ella Fitzgerald in Concert*, BBC CN4000/S, 1982, LP.

19. Mike Hennessey, "Ella Fitzgerald/Count Basie Orchestra/Oscar Peterson Trio with Joe Pass," *Billboard*, October 30, 1982, 52.

20. Dave Gelly, "Ella & Oscar: Jazz," *Observer*, July 27, 1980, 31.

21. "Dinner Is Served: Ella Fitzgerald," https://stories.state.gov/dinner-is-served/dance/ella-fitzgerald.

22. Robert Palmer, "Ella Fitzgerald's Songs, Plus Terry and Sims," *New York Times*, July 3, 1981, C14.

23. Bob Karlovits, "Ella Puts Magic in the Music for Multitude of Fans," *Pittsburgh Press*, June 14, 1982, A10.

24. Leonard Feather, "Jimmy Rowles: Compleat Pianist," *Los Angeles Times*, June 6, 1982, L84.

25. Carol Sloane, interview by the author, April 9, 2014.

26. Jim Blackman, interview by the author, September 26, 2018.

27. Jim Haskins, *Ella Fitzgerald: A Life Through Jazz* (London: Hodder & Stoughton, 1991), 178.

28. Les Matthews, "Anniversary Luncheon: Mr. 1–2–5 Street," *New York Amsterdam News*, April 26, 1980, 39.

29. June Norton, in *Ella Fitzgerald: Something to Live For* (documentary), American Masters Digital Archive (WNET), March 4, 1999, https://www.pbs.org/wnet/americanmasters/archive/interview/june-norton.

30. "Judy Bayron" is listed among the bandmembers in "Sweethearts of Rhythm Play Sweet Music—Look Sweeter," *Pittsburgh Courier*, December 28, 1940, 21.

31. Judy Cammarota, in *Ella Fitzgerald: Something to Live For* (documentary), American Masters Digital Archive (WNET). March 31, 1999, https://www.pbs.org/wnet/americanmasters/archive/interview/judy-cammarota. Carol Sloane, interview by the author, April 25, 2017.

32. Jim Blackman, conversation with the author, September 21, 2018.

33. André Previn, interview by the author, January 30, 2017.

34. Jim Blackman, interview by the author, July 16, 2018.

35. "Resolution, California Legislature, 1983 April 5," Ella Fitzgerald Papers, AC.0584, ser. 6, box 49, Smithsonian Archives Center, National Museum of American History.

36. Ray Brown, Jr., interview by the author, December 1, 2009.

37. Jim Blackman, conversation with the author, c. 2012; Oscar Peterson, interview by John McDonough, March 20, 1997, courtesy of McDonough.

38. Haskins, *Ella Fitzgerald*, 185–86; Jim Blackman, interview by the author, March 11, 2012.

39. Dorothy Johnson, interview by the author, August 23, 2012.

40. James H. Cleaver, "Child Abuse Suspected in Death of Two-Year-Old," *Los Angeles Sentinel*, March 4, 1982, A1. Karen Gilmore married Gary Fortzen on April 11, 1979. Information supplied by Christine McKay.

41. Ella Fitzgerald, *The Best Is Yet to Come*, Pablo 2312-138, 1982, LP.

42. Spencer Manning, "Exploring the History of Jazz at University of Idaho: Ella Fitzgerald at the Festival, 1982," Lionel Hampton Jazz Festival Collection, https://www.lib.uidaho.edu/digital/jazzfest/history.html#ella.

43. Clarence Waldron, "Jazz Great Ella Fitzgerald Performs In-Flight Concert," *Jet*, January 31, 1983, 62, 64.

44. Fitzgerald interview by Feather, January 10, 1983, Fitzgerald Papers, Smithsonian.

45. Michael Barrett, "Manhattan Transfer: How High the Moon," *New York Festival of Song*, https://nyfos.org/manhattan-transfer-high-moon. "The Story of the

Manhattan Transfer," https://manhattantransfer.net/about. Janis Siegel, interview by the author, June 2021.

46. Joel E. Siegel, "Ella, the 'Lady Be Good,'" *Washington Post*, June 4, 1983, D1.

47. Stephen Holden, "Jazz: Ella Fitzgerald Sings with Count Basie Group," *New York Times*, November 27, 1983, 77.

48. Tad Hershorn, *Norman Granz: The Man Who Used Jazz for Justice* (Berkeley: University of California Press, 2011), 366.

49. Virginia Wicks, interview by the author, March 2, 2010.

50. Ella Fitzgerald, *Ella Abraça Jobim: Ella Fitzgerald Sings the Antonio Carlos Jobim Song Book*, Pablo 2630-201, 1981, 2-LP set.

51. James Harper, "Ella Sings the Praises of Others," *Tampa Bay Times*, January 8, 1984.

52. Ella Fitzgerald, *The Best Is Yet to Come*, Pablo 2312-138, 1982, LP.

53. Jack Sohmer, "Record Reviews: Ella Fitzgerald," *Down Beat*, April 1983, 37.

54. Nelson Riddle, *Arranged by Nelson Riddle* (Van Nuys, Calif.: Alfred Music, 1985), 173.

55. Fitzgerald interview by Feather, January 10, 1983, Fitzgerald Papers, Smithsonian.

56. Ella Fitzgerald and Joe Pass, *Speak Love*, Pablo D2310888, 1983, LP.

57. Ella Fitzgerald and André Previn, *Nice Work If You Can Get It: Ella Fitzgerald and Andre Previn Do Gershwin*, Pablo D2312140, 1983, LP.

58. Michael Feinstein and Ian Jackman, *The Gershwins and Me: A Personal History in Twelve Songs* (New York: Simon & Schuster, 2012), 215.

59. Derrick Stewart-Baxter, "Record Reviews," *Jazz Journal International*, September 1984, 28.

60. Norman Granz, interview by John McDonough, March 6, 1989.

61. Jim Blackman, interview by the author, March 27, 2011.

62. Phoebe Jacobs, interview by the author, March 27, 2011.

63. Lisa Massoth and Howard Goodman, "Friends, Fans Mourn the Count," *Kansas City Times*, April 27, 1984, A6.

64. Michael Taylor, "UL Hails Ella Fitzgerald," *Los Angeles Sentinel*, March 29, 1984, A1.

65. Jube Shiver, "Ella Fitzgerald Receives Urban League Award," *Los Angeles Times*, March 22, 1984, F1.

66. Photo in *Springfield Leader and Press* (Mo.), April 14, 1985, 8.

67. "Ella in D.C. Hospital," *Daily News* (New York), August 13, 1985, 11.

68. Jon Pareles, "Fitzgerald and Peterson Perform at Wolf Trap," *New York Times*, August 25, 1986, C24.

69. Leonard Feather, "A Slimmer Ella in a Free Flight," *Los Angeles Times*, September 13, 1985, OC D1.

70. John S. Wilson, "Another Side of Ella Fitzgerald," *New York Times*, June 22, 1986, 44.

71. "Ella on Ella: A Personal Portrait," *Essence* (television program), NBC, April 26, 1986, Paley Center for Media, https://www.paleycenter.org/collection/item/?q=first&p=248&item=T:08316. See also "Essence TV Zooms In," *Essence*, May 1986, 50; Jennifer Baily Woodard and Teresa Mastin, "Black Womanhood: 'Essence' and Its Treatment of Stereotypical Images of Black Women," *Journal of Black Stud-*

ies 36, no. 2 (November 2005): 269; and Noliwe M. Rooks, *Ladies' Pages: African American Women's Magazines and the Culture That Made Them* (Newark, N.J.: Rutgers University Press, 2004), 147.

72. "'Ella on Ella: A Personal Portrait' on Essence TV," *Philadelphia Tribune*, April 25, 1986, 5C.

73. Charlotte Sutton, "Fairfax Symphony's Date with Ella," *Washington Post*, July 24, 1986, VAA1.

74. Gregg Field, interview by the author, February 28, 2014.

75. AP, "Ella Fitzgerald in Hospital," *Victoria Advocate* (Victoria, Tex.) September 4, 1986, 12.

76. Ella Fitzgerald, interview by Leonard Feather, April 23, 1987, Ella Fitzgerald Project, Leonard Feather Collection, University of Idaho.

77. Jim Blackman to the author, August 28 and 29, 2018.

Chapter 28: "Don't Ever Wish for the Phrase to End" (1986–1996)

1. Ken Franckling, "1987 JVC Jazz: Compelling Music, Many Milestones," UPI, June 27, 1987, https://www.upi.com/Archives/1987/06/27/1987-JVC-Jazz-Compelling-music-many-milestones/3013551764800/.

2. Ella Fitzgerald, interview by Leonard Feather, April 23, 1987, Ella Fitzgerald Project, Leonard Feather Collection, University of Idaho.

3. "Is It Ella, or a Fire?" *Sacramento Bee*, March 7, 1987, 2.

4. Jim Blackman, conversation with the author, March 11, 2012.

5. Ernie Santosuosso, "Ella Makes a Comeback at New York Jazz Festival," *Boston Globe*, June 26, 1987, 60. Her trio was Paul Smith, (piano), Keter Betts (double bass), and Jeff Hamilton (drums).

6. Lucinda Chodan, "Ella Sings Jazzfest to a Close," *Gazette* (Montreal), July 6, 1987, 17.

7. "Memorable Photos from the Ebony Files," *Ebony*, September 1987, 50.

8. "Boxscore of Top Concert Grosses," *Billboard*, March 4, 1989, 35; May 12, 1990, 42; April 27, 1991, 27; May 16, 1992, 12.

9. "Fitzgerald at Festival," *South Florida Sun-Sentinel*, June 27, 1988, 2A.

10. Steve Zipay, "An Evening with Ella Fitzgerald and Her Fellas," *Newsday*, February 13, 1989, 107.

11. Ella Fitzgerald, Nancy Wilson, and Al Jarreau Performing at the NAACP Image Awards, 1988, https://www.youtube.com/watch?v=2HyfTTp5Vrc.

12. Kathy Cavello, interview by the author, August 25, 2012.

13. "Ella & Ray: Get Your Kicks on Route 66," https://www.dailymotion.com/video/x18kdj7.

14. The show was broadcast on February 4, 1990. "1990 TV Broadcast, Sammy Davis Jr's 60th Anniversary Celebration," VHS (The Vista Group, 1990), *Internet Archive*, https://archive.org/details/TheVistaGroup-TVProgramSammyDavisJrs60thAnniversaryCelebration1990.

15. Jim Blackman, conversation with the author, September 1, 2018.

16. "1989 Grammy Winners: 32nd Annual Grammy Awards," https://www.grammy .com/awards/32nd-annual-grammy-awards.

17. "Ella Fitzgerald Suffering from Diabetes," UPI, September 19, 1987, 3.

18. James Standifer, interview with Ella Fitzgerald, March 25, 1989, Afro-American Music Collection, University of Michigan.

19. Jim Blackman, conversation with the author, September 1, 2018.

20. Andrew Massey to the author, August 13, 2013.

21. Ella Fitzgerald, *Ella in Rome: The Birthday Concert*, Verve 835-454-2, 1988, CD.

22. Stuart Nicholson, *Ella Fitzgerald: The Complete Biography*, updated ed. (New York: Routledge, 2004), 269.

23. Ella Fitzgerald, *All That Jazz*, Pablo 2310-938, 1990, LP.

24. John McDonough, "Ella Fitzgerald: Songbird Lives," *Wall Street Journal*, May 31, 1990, A16.

25. Mike Wofford, interview by the author, February 28, 2014.

26. Ken Franckling, "Ella Fitzgerald: All That Jazz," *Miami Herald*, June 15, 1990, 17G.

27. Michael Ullman, "Recordings: Ella Fitzgerald, *All That Jazz*, Pablo," *Boston Globe*, May 10, 1990, A8.

28. "Artist: Ella Fitzgerald," *Recording Academy Grammy Awards*, https://www.grammy .com/artists/ella-fitzgerald/16685.

29. Stephen Holden, "A Pop Virtuoso Who Can Do It All," *New York Times*, December 3, 1989, H1.

30. Stuart Troup, "A Reunion of Jazz Giants," *Newsday*, April 25, 1990, A7.

31. Edith Kiggen, conversation with the author, December 8, 2009.

32. Tad Hershorn, telephone conversation with the author, March 28, 2010.

33. Steve Futterman, "It's All Hearts and Flowers at Ella Fitzgerald's Gala," *Chicago Tribune*, February 14, 1990.

34. Leonard Feather, "A Tribute to Ella . . . from the Heart," *Los Angeles Times*, February 14, 1990, F5.

35. Jim Blackman to the author, July 4, 2021.

36. Paul Easton, "Jazz FM Debuts as UK's First Specialty Radio Station," *Billboard*, March 24, 1990, 102.

37. "Fitzgerald on Aspel, 3 March 1990: Part 1," https://www.youtube.com/watch?v=DX _IYXt7Bg; Part 2, https://www.youtube.com/watch?v=DFDJ4PiXm2E&t=45s.

38. Caroline Phillips, "Red-Hot Grandma," *Evening Standard*, March 5, 1990, 140.

39. Clancy Sigal, "Ella and All That Jazz: Clancy Sigal Meets the Legend," *Observer* (London), February 25, 1990, 21.

40. Antony Thorncroft, "Ella Fitzgerald; Albert Hall," *Financial Times*, March 9, 1990, 19.

41. Hans Ruland, "Ella Fitzgerald," in Gunna Wendt, ed., *Die Jazz-Frauen* (Munich: Luchterhand Literaturverlag, 1992), 31–36, translated by Meredith Soeder.

42. "Ella Fitzgerald Given Top French Arts Award," *Los Angeles Times*, May 29, 1990, https://www.latimes.com/archives/la-xpm-1990-05-29-ca-351-story.html; "*Pour L'Amour d'Ella* by Ella Fitzgerald Sales and Awards," https://bestsellingalbums .org/album/13364. Ella Fitzgerald, *Pour l'amour d'Ella Fitzgerald*, Verve 839 237-2, 1989, 2-CD set.

43. "World: Ella Fitzgerald Hospitalized in Europe. Treated for Exhaustion," *Los Angeles Times*, July 10, 1990, P1.

44. Don Heckman, "Mature Craftsmanship from Ella Fitzgerald," *Los Angeles Times*, July 17, 1992, 220.

45. Jim Blackman, conversation with the author, September 21, 2018.

46. "Overture, the Raymond F. Kravis Center for the Performing Arts," *Palm Beach Daily News*, April 11, 1993, 41.

47. Tim Smith, "Time Goes By but Fitzgerald Still Has Style," *South Florida Sun-Sentinel*, December 5, 1992, 56.

48. "Presidential Medal of Freedom, given to Ella Fitzgerald," National Museum of American History, Smithsonian.

49. Gertrude Gipson, "Candid Comments: A Salute to Ella Fitzgerald," *Los Angeles Sentinel*, February 24, 1994; Gertrude Gipson, "Candid Comments: Vanessa Williams in Broadway Debut," *Los Angeles Sentinel*, March 10, 1994; Dennis Schatzman, "Singer Ella Fitzgerald Reveals Amputations, Diabetes Blamed," *Los Angeles Sentinel*, April 14, 1994, A4.

50. Gunther Schuller, *The Swing Era: The Development of Jazz, 1930–1945* (New York: Oxford University Press, 1989), 293.

51. Gunther Schuller, interview by the author, December 7, 2011.

52. Ella Fitzgerald, *75th Birthday Celebration: The Original Decca Recordings,* GRP GRD-2-619, 1993, 2-CD set.

53. Ella Fitzgerald, *Best of Ella Fitzgerald: First Lady of Song*, Verve P2-23382, 1994, 3-CD set.

54. Ella Fitzgerald, *The Complete Ella Fitzgerald Song Books*, Verve 314 519 832-2, 1994, 16-CD set.

55. Ella Fitzgerald, *The Best of the Song Books*, Verve 314 519 804-2, 1993, CD.

56. Alec Wilder, *American Popular Song: The Great Innovators, 1900–1950* (New York: Oxford University Press, 1972). This book was honored with a 50th Anniversary Edition, published in 2022, edited and revised by Robert Rawlins.

57. Benny Green, "The Ella Fitzgerald/Norman Granz Songbooks: Locus Classicus of American Song," *High Fidelity*, March 1980, 46–50.

58. Jim Blackman to the author, July 4, 2021.

59. Ozgun Akalin, "Society of Singers Night to Honor Frank Sinatra, 3 December 1990," *Frank Sinatra*, April 7, 2013, https://www.thefranksinatra.com/articles/society-of-singers-night-frank-sinatra.

60. Phoebe Jacobs, interview by the author, March 27, 2011.

61. Claudia Booker, interview by the author, November 17, 2017.

62. "Physician Clifford Booker Dies; Specialized in Pediatric AIDS," *Washington Post*, October 26, 1995, B6.

63. Fitzgerald interview by Feather, April 23, 1987, Ella Fitzgerald Project.

64. Sigal, "Ella and All That Jazz," 21.

65. Phoebe Jacobs, conversation with the author, April 13, 2011.

66. Charles J. Gan, "Bridgewater's 'Dear Ella' a Tribute to a Jazz Legend," *New Pittsburgh Courier*, March 21, 1998, 6.

67. Tad Hershorn, *Norman Granz: The Man Who Used Jazz for Justice* (Berkeley: University of California Press, 2011), 375.

68. Virginia Wicks, interview by the author, December 5, 2009.

69. Bea Wain, "Remembrances of Ella," *SOS Newsletter*, c. 1996–97.

70. Lillian Randolph, interview by the author, 2011.

71. Bea Wain, interview by the author, May 25, 2010.

72. Hershorn, *Norman Granz*, 375.

73. Virginia Wicks, interview by the author, December 5, 2009.

74. Leonard Feather, "Ella Reaps Her Just Rewards," *Los Angeles Times*, June 14, 1987.

SELECTED BIBLIOGRAPHY

This bibliography is very selective and abbreviated in light of the length of Fitzgerald's career, her fame, and the vast press coverage she received over time. Today many more items are available through digital newspaper banks, and still more will certainly come. My list includes some archival collections, a list of interviews with Ella Fitzgerald in chronological order, articles about her published through 1996, an inclusive category for books, articles, liner notes, and assorted media, and four references for discographies.

Archival Sources and Digital Repositories

Apollo Theater Oral History Project, Columbia Center for Oral History, Columbia University.

Arthur Fiedler Collection, Howard Gotlieb Archival Research Center, Boston University.

Dizzy Gillespie Collection, Smithsonian Archives Center, National Museum of American History.

Duke Ellington Collection, Smithsonian Archives Center, National Museum of American History.

Ella Fitzgerald Charitable Foundation, https://www.ellafitzgerald.com/foundation/#.

Ella Fitzgerald Collection, 1935–1997, Institute of Jazz Studies, MC 104, Rutgers University.

Ella Fitzgerald Collection, 1956–1992, Library of Congress. Musical arrangements, including scores and parts.

Ella Fitzgerald Collection of Sheet Music, 1897–1991, Performing Arts Special Collections, University of California, Los Angeles. Photographs and sheet music.

Ella Fitzgerald Papers, Smithsonian Archives Center, National Museum of American History.

Ella Fitzgerald Project, Leonard Feather Collection, University of Idaho.

Entertainment Industry Magazine Archive, ProQuest Digital Platform. Fourteen key industry U.S. and U.K. trade and consumer magazines.

Helen Curl Harris Papers, 1936–1980, Special Collections, Emory University.

Historical Black Newspapers, ProQuest Digital Platform. Ten key newspapers.

Historical Newspapers, ProQuest Digital Platform.

James Haskins Collection, Howard Gotlieb Archival Research Center, Boston University.

James "Tad" Hershorn Collection on Norman Granz, Institute of Jazz Studies Archival Collections, IJS.0081, Rutgers University.

James W. Blackman Media Collection, privately held. 1960 to the present.

Jazz Digital Archive, Retrospective Index to Music Periodicals (RIPM). One hundred nineteen American jazz periodicals.

Jazz Oral History Project, Institute of Jazz Studies, Rutgers University. Files and memorabilia.

Jazzinstitut, Darmstadt, Germany. Bibliography and digitized articles.

John S. Wilson Collection, Institute of Jazz Studies, Rutgers University.

Louis Armstrong House Museum. Interviews, radio tapes, and photographs.

Michel Macaire Archives, privately held. Focus on European dates and reviews.

Milt Gabler Collection, Smithsonian Archives Center, National Museum of American History.

Nelson Riddle Collection, University of Arizona.

Paley Center for Media, New York.

Performing Arts Research Collections, New York Public Library.

Phoebe Jacobs Collection, Special Collections, Butler Library, Columbia University.

Schomburg Center for Research in Black Culture, New York Public Library. Photographs, clippings, memorabilia.

Smithsonian Jazz Oral History Program, National Museum of American History.

Willis Conover Collection, University of North Texas.

Selected Interviews with Ella Fitzgerald, 1937–1992, in Chronological Order

Ottley, Roi. "Popularity Runs in Cycles, Says Savoy Exponent of Swing." *New York Amsterdam News*, February 13, 1937, 10.

Johnson, Lillian. "Ella Fitzgerald's Hardest Job Was to Get Folks to Listen!" *Baltimore Afro-American*, October 9, 1937, 10.

———. "Ella Fitzgerald Hasn't Let Success Spoil Her. Swing Music's Biggest Star Hasn't a Boyfriend, Likes Men Short and Hats Dizzy." *Baltimore Afro-American*, October 9, 1937, 5.

Unsigned. "Rivals? Why Ethel Gave Ella Her Biggest Thrill!" *Baltimore Afro-American*, October 16, 1937, 10.

Unsigned. "'Swing Here to Stay,' Bandleader Webb and Ella Fitzgerald, Vocalist, Agree." *Harvard Crimson*, February 23, 1938.

Wilson, Earl. "A Tisket, a Tasket, the Wrong Colored Basket." *New York Post*, August 15, 1938.

Nunn, William G. "Will Keep My Orchestra Ella Tells Courier." *Pittsburgh Courier*, May 11, 1940, 21.

Hazen, David W. "Singer Lacks Time for Play: Ella Fitzgerald Pinochle Love." *Oregonian*, July 17, 1940, 6.

"Top Jazz Singer Tells How She Got That Way." *PM*, October 24, 1947, 16.

"Ella Fitzgerald, First Lady of Song." *Our World*, December 1949, 2.

"Ella Fitzgerald Is Radio and Film 'Must' to All But Powers." *Chicago Defender*, May 20, 1950, 21.

"Any Style Will Do." *Newsweek*, June 7, 1954, 82.

Hentoff, Nat. "Ella Tells of Trouble in Mind Concerning Discs, Television." *Down Beat*, February 23, 1955, 2.

Conover, Willis. "Ella Fitzgerald, April 18, 1956," broadcast May 16, 1956, on *Voice of America*. Library of Congress no. 89740651.

Tynan, John. "Ella: It Took a Hit Album to Make Miss F. a Class Nitery Attraction." *Down Beat*, November 28, 1956, 13.

Fields, Sidney. "Songbird Is Missing a Note." *New York Mirror*, June 21, 1957.

Okon, May. "She Still Gets Stage Fright." *New York Daily News*, September 8, 1957, Sunday News section, 4.

Burman, Maurice. "ELLA." *Melody Maker*, May 10, 1958, 5.

Gleason, Ralph J. "Ella's Just Trying to Be Herself—And They Love It." *San Francisco Sunday Chronicle*, November 8, 1958, 15D.

Alpert, Don. "The Ella Formula: I Sing It the Way I Feel It." *Los Angeles Times*, September 24, 1961, A5.

Robinson, Louie. "First Lady of Jazz." *Ebony*, November 1961, 136.

Pitts, George E. "Ella Has Yearning to Be TV Actress." *Pittsburgh Courier*, June 2, 1962, 14.

Unsigned. "Ella Is Shy About a Lot of Things—But Not Singing." *Stage and Television Today*, March 21, 1963, 5.

Robbins, Fred. Interview of Ella Fitzgerald, Hotel Americana, New York. Radio, April 1963. Paley Center for Media, RB:22531.

Simon, George T. "Nat Cole, Frank Sinatra Top Ella Fitzgerald's List." *Herald Tribune* (N.Y.) News Service. As printed in *Salina Journal* (Kan.), May 8, 1963, 18.

Feather, Leonard. "Ella Today (and Yesterday Too)." *Down Beat*, November 18, 1965, 23.

Henius, Bent. "Jeg Var Naer Blevet Danskers." *Berlingske Tidende*, January 22, 1967, 9.

Black, Cobey. "Ella Forever." *Honolulu Star-Bulletin*, March 7, 1967, 36.

Wilson, John S. "Ella Changes Her Tunes for a Swinging Generation." *New York Times*, November 12, 1967, 149.

"ASCAP Presents the Billy Taylor Interviews: Ella Fitzgerald." Performing Arts Research Collections, Recorded Sound, LDC 42656, New York Public Library.

Wammen, Chris. "Folk elsker mig. Ella Fitzgerald." *Århus Stiftstidende*, June 7, 1970, 13.

Allen, Steve. Seven-part interview of Ella Fitzgerald, 1971–74. Satchmo Collection, Louis Armstrong House Museum.

Diamonstein, Barbaralee. *Open Secrets: Ninety-Four Women in Touch with Our Time.* New York: Viking Press, 1972.

Dunbar, Ernest. "Ella Still Sings Just This Side of the Angels." *New York Times,* November 24, 1974, sec. 2, 1.

George, Elizabeth. "Ella Selects Songs to Fit Audience." *Greenville News* (S.C.), June 18, 1978, 38.

Feather, Leonard. Interview of Ella Fitzgerald, January 10, 1983. Ella Fitzgerald Papers, ser.10.4. Smithsonian Archives Center, National Museum of American History.

———. Interview of Ella Fitzgerald, January 15, 1983. Ella Fitzgerald Project, Leonard Feather Collection, University of Idaho.

———. "Ella." *Los Angeles Times,* January 30, 1983, K1.

"Ella on Ella: A Personal Portrait." *Essence.* Television Program, NBC, April 26, 1986. Paley Center for Media, https://www.paleycenter.org/collection/item/?q=first&p=248&item=T:08316.

Rockwell, John. "Half a Century of Song with the Great 'Ella.'" *New York Times,* June 15, 1986, sec. 2, 1.

Feather, Leonard. Interview of Ella Fitzgerald, April 23, 1987. Ella Fitzgerald Project, Leonard Feather Collection, University of Idaho.

Smith, Joe, ed. *Off the Record: An Oral History of Popular Music.* New York: Warner Books, 1988.

Feather, Leonard. "L.A. Honors the First Lady of Song." *Los Angeles Times,* April 23, 1989.

Sigal, Clancy. "Ella and All That Jazz: Clancy Sigal Meets the Legend." *Observer* (London), February 25, 1990.

Lees, Gene. "Ella by Starlight." *Gene Lees' Jazzletter* 11, no. 2 (January 1992): 1–5; adapted in Gene Lees, *Singers and the Song II.* New York: Oxford University Press, 1998.

Ruland, Hans. "Ella Fitzgerald." In *Die Jazz-Frauen,* edited by Gunna Wendt. Munich: Luchterhand Literaturverlag, 1992.

Selected Articles and Interviews, 1937–1996, in Chronological Order, Excluding Reviews and Obituaries

Bourne, St. Clair. "'Blues'—'Swing': Death of Bessie Smith Marks Close of 'Blues Era.'" *New York Amsterdam News,* October 16, 1937, 18.

Kolodin, Irving. "The Dance Band Business: A Study in Black and White." *Harper's Magazine,* June 1941.

Rowe, Billy. "Billy Rowe's Notebook." *Pittsburgh Courier,* January 19, 1946, 13.

Key, Alyce. "Keynotes." *Los Angeles Sentinel,* April 4, 1946.

Simon, George T. "Ella, Now Making Records That Are Stellar." *Metronome,* May 1946, 30.

"Ella Fitzgerald. Her Vocal Versatility Continues to Amaze Musicians." *Ebony*, May 1949, 49–51.

"Apollo's Girl." *Time*, April 3, 1950, 71.

Simon, George T. "Ella Fitzgerald: The Greats' Great." *Metronome*, April 1950, 14.

Coss, Bill. "Ella!" *Metronome*, October 1953, 13.

Hentoff, Nat, and Leonard Feather. "Is Ella Fitzgerald a Great Jazz Singer?" *HiFi/Stereo Review*, April 1962.

Gardner, Barbara. "Thoughts on Female 'Jazz Singers.'" *Down Beat's Music '63* (yearbook).

Green, Benny. "The Ella Fitzgerald/Norman Granz Songbooks: Locus Classicus of American Song." *High Fidelity Musical America* 30 (March 1980): 46–50.

Siegel, Joel E. "Ella, the 'Lady Be Good.'" *Washington Post*, June 4, 1983, D1.

Harrington, Richard. "In the Key of Ella." *Washington Post*, May 6, 1988, B1.

McDonough, John. "Ella Fitzgerald: Songbird Lives," *Wall Street Journal*, May 31, 1990, A16.

———. "Ella at Seventy-Five: What Becomes a Legend Most: Ella Fitzgerald." *Down Beat*, June 1993, 22–25.

Bernstein, Nina. "Ward of the State. The Gap in Ella's Life." *New York Times*, June 23, 1996.

Jeske. "Ask Norman." *Jazziz*, November 1996, 59–60.

Jefferson, Margo. "Ella in Wonderland." *New York Times*, December 29, 1996, 41.

Selected Books, Articles, Liner Notes, and Video Documentaries

Ake, David. *Jazz Cultures*. Berkeley: University of California Press, 2002.

Ake, David, Charles Hiroshi Garrett, and Daniel Goldmark, eds. *Jazz/Not Jazz: The Music and Its Boundaries*. Berkeley: University of California Press, 2012.

Alexander, Van, and Stephen Fratallone. *From Harlem to Hollywood: My Life in Music*. Albany, Ga.: BearManor Media, 2009.

Alpern, Sara, Joyce Antler, Elisabeth Israels Perry, and Ingrid Winther Scobie, eds. *The Challenge of Feminist Biography: Writing the Lives of Modern American Women*. Urbana: University of Illinois Press, 1992.

Barlow, William. *Voice Over: The Making of Black Radio*. Philadelphia: Temple University Press, 1999.

Baszak, Mark, ed. *Such Sweet Thunder: Views on Black American Music*. Amherst: University of Massachusetts Press, 2003.

Basie, Count, and Albert Murray. *Good Morning Blues: The Autobiography of Count Basie as Told to Albert Murray*. London: Paladin, 1987.

Bauer, William R. *Open the Door: The Life and Music of Betty Carter*. Ann Arbor: University of Michigan Press, 2002.

Berendt, Joachim-Ernst. *The Jazz Book: From New Orleans to Rock and Free Jazz*. Translated from German by Dan Morgenstern and Helmut and Barbara Bredigkeit. New York: Lawrence Hill & Co., 1975.

Bogle, Donald. *Prime Time Blues. African Americans on Network Television.* New York: Farrar, Straus & Giroux, 2001.

———. *Heat Wave: The Life and Career of Ethel Waters.* New York: HarperCollins, 2011.

Burger, Morroe, Edward Berger, and James Patrick. *Benny Carter: A Life in American Music.* Metuchen, N.J.: Scarecrow Press, 1982.

Burnim, Mellonee V., and Portia K. Maultsby, eds. *Issues in African American Music: Power, Gender, Race, Representation.* New York: Routledge, 2016.

Cartwright, Katharine. "'Guess These People Wonder What I'm Singing': Quotation and Reference in Ella Fitzgerald's 'St. Louis Blues.'" In *Ramblin' on My Mind: New Perspectives on the Blues*, edited by David Evans, 281–327. Champaign: University of Illinois Press, 2008.

Cohen, Harvey G. *Duke Ellington's America.* Chicago: University of Chicago Press, 2010.

Cohodas, Nadine. *Queen: The Life and Music of Dinah Washington.* New York: Billboard Books, 2006.

Collins, Patricia H. *Black Feminist Thought: Knowledge, Consciousness, and the Politics of Empowerment*, 2nd ed. New York: Routledge, 2000.

Cott, Nancy F., ed. *No Small Courage: A History of Women in the United States.* New York: Oxford University Press, 2000.

Crawford, Richard. *America's Musical Life: A History.* New York: W. W. Norton, 2001.

Crease, Stephanie Stein. *Rhythm Man: Chick Webb and the Beat That Changed America.* New York: Oxford University Press, 2023.

Da Silva, Catherine M. "The Influence of Dizzy Gillespie's Bebop Style on Ella Fitzgerald's 'Flying Home,' 'Lady Be Good,' and 'How High the Moon' Solos." D.M.A. diss., Five Towns College, 2013.

Dahl, Linda. *Stormy Weather: The Music and Lives of a Century of Jazz Women.* New York: Limelight, 1989.

Dance, Stanley. *The World of Swing.* New York: Da Capo Press, 1979.

David, Norman. *The Ella Fitzgerald Companion.* Westport, Conn.: Praeger, 2004.

Davis, Angela Y. *Blues Legacies and Black Feminism: Gertrude "Ma" Rainey, Bessie Smith, and Billie Holiday.* New York: Pantheon Books, 1998.

DeVeaux, Scott. *The Birth of Bebop: A Social and Musical History.* Berkeley: University of California Press, 1997.

Elson, Arthur. *Woman's Work in Music.* Boston: L.C. Page, 1904.

Ennis, Philip H. *The Seventh Stream: The Emergence of Rock 'n' Roll in American Popular Music.* Middletown, Conn.: Wesleyan University Press, 1992.

Erenberg, Lewis. *Swingin' the Dream: Big Band Jazz and the Rebirth of American Culture.* Chicago: University of Chicago Press, 1999.

Feather, Leonard. *Inside Jazz* (originally titled *Inside Bebop*). New York: Da Capo Press, 1977.

———. *From Satchmo to Miles.* New York: Hachette Books, 1987.

Fidelman, Geoffrey Mark. *First Lady of Song: Ella Fitzgerald for the Record.* New York: Citadel Press, 1994. Revised as Geoffrey Mark, *Ella: A Biography of the Legendary Ella Fitzgerald.* New York: Ultimate Symbol, 2018.

Firestone, Ross. *Swing, Swing, Swing: The Life and Times of Benny Goodman*. New York: W. W. Norton, 1993.

Flamming, Douglas. *Bound for Freedom: Black Los Angeles in Jim Crow America*. Berkeley: University of California Press, 2006.

Floyd, Samuel A. *The Power of Black Music: Interpreting Its History from Africa to the United States*. New York: Oxford University Press, 1995.

Fox, Ted. *In the Groove: The Men Behind the Music*. New York: St. Martin's Press, 1988.

Friedwald, Will. *Jazz Singing: America's Great Voices from Bessie Smith to Bebop and Beyond*. New York: Scribner's, 1990.

———. *A Biographical Guide to the Great Jazz and Pop Singers*. New York: Pantheon Books, 2010.

Fritts, Ron, and Ken Vail. *Ella Fitzgerald: The Chick Webb Years & Beyond 1935–1948*. Lanham, Md.: Scarecrow Press, 2003.

Gabbard, Krin, ed. *Jazz Among the Discourses*. Durham, N.C.: Duke University Press, 1995.

Garland, Phyl. *The Sound of Soul: The Story of Black Music*. Chicago: Henry Regnery, 1969.

Garofalo, Reebee. "Black Popular Music: Crossing Over or Going Under?" In *Rock and Popular Music: Politics, Policies, Institutions*, edited by Tony Bennett et al. New York: Routledge, 1993.

Gates, Henry Louis, Jr. *The Signifying Monkey: A Theory of Afro-American Literary Criticism*. New York: Oxford University Press, 1988.

Gaunt, Kyra D. *The Games Black Girls Play: Learning the Ropes from Double-Dutch to Hip-Hop*. New York: New York University Press, 2006.

Gennari, John. *Blowin' Hot and Cool: Jazz and Its Critics*. Chicago: University of Chicago Press, 2006.

George, Nelson. *The Death of Rhythm and Blues*. New York: Pantheon Books, 1988.

Gibson, Maya C. "Alternate Takes: Billie Holiday at the Intersection of Black Cultural Studies and Historical Musicology." Ph.D. diss., University of Wisconsin, 2008.

Giddings, Paula. *When and Where I Enter: The Impact of Black Women on Race and Sex in America*. New York: Bantam Books, 1985.

Giddins, Gary. *Bing Crosby: A Pocketful of Dreams—The Early Years 1903–1940*. New York: Little, Brown, 2001.

———. *Bing Crosby, Swinging on a Star: The War Years 1940–1946*. New York: Little, Brown, 2018.

Giddins, Gary, and Scott DeVeaux. *Jazz*. New York: W. W. Norton, 2009.

Gitler, Ira. *Swing to Bop: An Oral History of the Transition in Jazz in the 1940s*. New York: Oxford University Press, 1987.

Gourse, Leslie, ed. *The Ella Fitzgerald Companion: Seven Decades of Commentary*. London: Omnibus Press, 1998.

Green, Benny. *Such Sweet Thunder: Benny Green on Jazz*. New York: Scribner, 2001.

Griffin, Farah Jasmine. *If You Can't Be Free, Be a Mystery: In Search of Billie Holiday*. New York: Free Press, 2001.

———. "When Malindy Sings: A Meditation on Black Women's Vocality." In *Uptown*

Conversation: The New Jazz Studies, edited by Robert G. O'Meally, Brent Hayes Edwards, and Farah Jasmine Griffin. New York: Columbia University Press, 2004.

Hajdu, David. *Lush Life: A Biography of Billy Strayhorn*. New York: North Point Press, 1996.

Hammond, John Henry, and Irving Townsend. *John Hammond on Record: An Autobiography*. 77. Rpt. New York: Penguin, 1981.

Handy, D. Antoinette. *Black Women in American Bands and Orchestras*, 2nd ed. Metuchen, N.J.: Scarecrow Press, 1998.

Harris, Paisley. "Gatekeeping and Remaking: The Politics of Respectability in African American Women's History and Black Feminism." *Journal of Women's History* 15, no. 1 (Spring 2003): 212–20.

Haskins, Jim. *Ella Fitzgerald: A Life Through Jazz*. London: Hodder & Stoughton, 1991.

Hasse, John Edward. *Beyond Category: The Life and Genius of Duke Ellington*. New York: Simon & Schuster, 1993.

Havers, Richard. *Verve: The Sound of America*. New York: Thames & Hudson, 2013.

Hayes, Eileen, and Linda Williams, eds. *Black Women and Music: More than the Blues*. Urbana: University of Illinois Press, 2007.

Hentoff, Nat. *At the Jazz Band Ball: Sixty Years on the Jazz Scene*. Berkeley: University of California Press, 2010.

Hershorn, Tad. *Norman Granz: The Man Who Used Jazz for Justice*. Berkeley: University of California Press, 2011.

Higginbotham, Evelyn Brooks. "African-American Women's History and the Metalanguage of Race." *Signs* 17, no. 2 (Winter 1992): 251–74.

Hine, Darlene Clark, ed. *Black Women in America,* 2nd ed. 3 vols. New York: Oxford University Press, 2005.

Hine, Darlene Clark, and Kathleen Thompson. *A Shining Thread of Hope: The History of Black Women in America*. New York: Broadway Books, 1998.

hooks, bell. *Black Looks: Race and Representation*. Boston: South End Press, 1992.

———. *Outlaw Culture: Resisting Representations*. New York: Routledge, 1994.

———. *Yearning: Race, Gender, and Cultural Politics*. Boston: South End Press, 1990.

Hubbard, Karen, and Terry Monaghan. "Negotiating Compromise on a Burnished Wood Floor: Social Dancing at the Savoy." In *Ballroom, Boogie, Shimmy Sham, Shake: A Social and Popular Dance Reader*, edited by Julie Malnig. Urbana: University of Illinois Press, 2009.

Jingermann, Jimmy. *Ella Fitzgerald, Ein Porträt*. Wetzlar: Pegasus Verlag, 1960.

Kaplan, James. *Frank Sinatra: The Voice*. New York: Anchor Books, 2011.

Kaufman, Jeff, dir. *The Savoy King: Chick Webb and the Music That Changed America*. Documentary, 2012.

Kernodle, Tammy L. "Black Women Working Together: Jazz, Gender, and the Politics of Validation." *Black Music Research Journal* 34, no. 1 (2014): 27–55.

———. *Soul on Soul: The Life and Music of Mary Lou Williams*. Boston: Northeastern University Press, 2004.

Lees, Gene. *Oscar Peterson: The Will to Swing*, updated ed. New York: Cooper Square Press, 2000.

Levinson, Peter J. *September in the Rain: The Life of Nelson Riddle*. Lanham, Md.: Taylor Trade, 2005.

MacDonald, J. Fred. *Blacks and White TV: African Americans in Television Since 1948*, 2nd ed. Chicago: Nelson-Hall, 1992.

McDonough, John. "The History of the Songbooks." Liner notes to Ella Fitzgerald, *The Complete Ella Fitzgerald Song Books*. Verve 314519832-2, 1993, 16-CD box set.

———. Liner notes to Chick Webb and Ella Fitzgerald, *The Complete Chick Webb and Ella Fitzgerald Decca Sessions (1934–1941)*. Mosaic Records MD8-252, 2013, 8-CD box set.

McGee, Kristin A. *Some Liked It Hot: Jazz Women in Film and Television, 1928–1959*. Middletown, Conn.: Wesleyan University Press, 2009.

Miller, Norma, and Evette Jensen. *Swingin' at the Savoy: The Memoir of a Jazz Dancer*. Philadelphia: Temple University Press, 1996.

Monson, Ingrid. *Freedom Sounds: Civil Rights Call Out to Jazz and Africa*. New York: Oxford University Press, 2007.

Morgenstern, Dan. *Living with Jazz: A Reader*. Edited by Sheldon Meyer. New York: Pantheon Books, 2004.

———. "Louis Armstrong and the Development and Diffusion of Jazz." In *Louis Armstrong: A Cultural Legacy*, edited by Marc H. Miller. New York: Queens Museum of Art in conjunction with the University of Washington Press, 1994.

Morgenstern, Dan, James Gavin, Milt Gabler, and Bud Katzel. Liner notes to Ella Fitzgerald, *The 75th Birthday Celebration: The Original Decca Recordings*. GRP GRD-2-619, 1993, 2-CD set.

Myers, Marc. *Why Jazz Happened*. Berkeley: University of California Press, 2013.

Nicholson, Stuart. *Ella Fitzgerald: A Biography of the First Lady of Jazz*. New York: Scribner's, 1994.

———. *Ella Fitzgerald: The Complete Biography*, updated ed. New York: Routledge, 2004.

O'Neal, Hank. *The Ghosts of Harlem: Sessions with Jazz Legends*. Nashville, Tenn.: Vanderbilt University Press, 1997.

O'Meally, Robert. *Lady Day: The Many Faces of Billie Holiday*. New York: Arcade, 1991.

———, ed. *The Jazz Cadence of American Culture*. New York: Columbia University Press, 1998.

Pellegrinelli, Lara. "Separated at 'Birth': Singing and the History of Jazz." In *Big Ears: Listening for Gender in Jazz Studies*, edited by Nichole T. Rustin and Sherrie Tucker. Durham, N.C.: Duke University Press, 2008.

———. "The Song Is Who? Locating Singers on the Jazz Scene." Ph.D. diss., Harvard University, 2005.

Perchard, Tom. "Writing Jazz Biography: Race, Research and Narrative Representation." *Popular Music History* 2, no. 2 (2007): 119–45.

Placksin, Sally. *American Women in Jazz, 1900 to the Present: Their Words, Lives, and Music*. New York: Wideview Books, 1982.

Pleasants, Henry. *The Great American Popular Singers*. New York: Simon & Schuster, 1974.

Poiger, Uta G. *Jazz, Rock, and Rebels: Cold War Politics and American Culture in a Divided America*. Berkeley: University of California Press, 2000.

Porter, Eric. *What Is This Thing Called Jazz? African American Musicians as Artists, Critics, and Activists*. Berkeley: University of California Press, 2002.

Price, Emmett G., Tammy L. Kernodle, and Horace Maxille, eds. *Encyclopedia of African American Music*. Santa Barbara, Calif.: Greenwood Press, 2010.

Radano, Ronald M. *Lying Up a Nation: Race and Black Music*. Chicago: University of Chicago Press, 2003.

Ramsey, Guthrie P., Jr. *Race Music: Black Cultures from Bebop to Hip-Hop*. Berkeley: University of California Press, 2003.

Riccardi, Ricky. *What a Wonderful World: The Magic of Louis Armstrong's Later Years*. New York: Vintage, 2012.

Rustin, Nichole T., and Sherrie Tucker, eds. *Big Ears: Listening for Gender in Jazz Studies*. Durham, N.C.: Duke University Press, 2008.

Sanjek, Russell. *American Popular Music and Its Business: The First Four Hundred Years, Volume 3, From 1900 to 1984*. New York: Oxford University Press, 1988.

Schroeder, David. *From the Minds of Jazz Musicians: Conversations with the Creative and Inspired*. New York: Routledge, 2018.

Schuller, Gunther. *The Swing Era: The Development of Jazz, 1930–1945*. New York: Oxford University Press, 1989.

Shaw, Arnold. *Honkers and Shouters: The Golden Years of Rhythm and Blues*. New York: Macmillan Collier Books, 1978.

Simon, George T. *Simon Says: The Sights and Sounds of the Swing Era, 1935–1955*. New Rochelle, N.Y.: Arlington House, 1971.

Soeder, Meredith. "Jazz in a Transatlantic World: Legitimizing American Jazz in Germany, 1920–1957." Ph.D. diss., Carnegie Mellon University, 2017.

Southern, Eileen. *The Music of Black Americans: A History*, 3rd ed. New York: W. W. Norton, 1997.

Stephen, Alexander, ed. *The Americanization of Europe: Culture, Diplomacy, and Anti-Americanism After 1945*. New York: Berghahn Books, 2006.

Stephens, Vincent. "Crooning on the Fault Lines: Theorizing Jazz and Pop Vocal Singing Discourse in the Rock Era, 1955–1978." *American Music* 26, no. 2 (2008): 156–95.

Stowe, David W. *Swing Changes: Big-Band Jazz in New Deal America*. Cambridge, Mass.: Harvard University Press, 1994.

Taylor, Arthur. *Notes and Tones: Musician-to-Musician Interviews*, expanded ed. New York: Da Capo Press, 1993.

Tucker, Sherrie. *Swing Shift: "All-Girl" Bands of the 1940s*. Durham, N.C.: Duke University Press, 2000.

———. "Women in Jazz." *Grove Music Online*, 2003.

Ulanov, Barry. *A History of Jazz in America*. New York: Viking Press, 1952.

Wells, Christi Jay. *Between Beats: The Jazz Tradition and Black Vernacular Dance*. New York: Oxford University Press, 2021.

Wells, Christopher J. "'A Dreadful Bit of Silliness': Feminine Frivolity and Ella Fitzgerald's Early Critical Reception." *Women and Music: A Journal of Gender and Culture* 21 (2017): 43–65.

Whitburn, Joel. *Pop Memories 1890–1954.* Menomonee Falls, Wis.: Record Research, 1986.

———. *Top R&B / Hip-Hop Singles 1942–2004.* Menomonee Falls, Wis.: Record Research, 2006.

Williams, Martin. Liner notes to *Smithsonian Collection of Classical Jazz.* Smithsonian Institution, 1973.

Woodhead, Leslie, dir., and Reggie Nadelson, prod. *Ella Fitzgerald: Just One of Those Things.* Video documentary. Eagle Rock, 2019.

Yanow, Scott. *The Jazz Singers: The Ultimate Guide.* New York: Backbeat Books, 2008.

Zwerin, Charlotte, dir. *Ella Fitzgerald: Something to Live For.* Documentary. PBS/American Masters, 1999.

Discographies

Discogs, www.discogs.com.

Johnson, J. Wilfred. *Ella Fitzgerald: An Annotated Discography; Including a Complete Discography of Chick Webb.* Jefferson, N.C.: McFarland & Co., 2001.

Lord, Tom. *The Jazz Discography.* TJD Online, https://www.lordisco.com.

Scasso, Michele. *Ella Fitzgerald Discography,* 2006. http://jazzdiscography.com/Artists/ella-discography/index/php.

INDEX

Page numbers in *italics* refer to illustrations.